A HIGHER SANSKRIT GRAMMAR

A HIGHER SANSKRIT GRAMMAR

FOR THE USE OF SCHOOLS AND COLLEGES

By

LATE MORESHWAR RAMCHANDRA KALE, B.A.,

GYAN

Published by

Gyan Publishing House
5, Ansari Road
Daryaganj, New Delhi-110002
Phone: 011-47034999, 9811692060
E-mail: books@gyanbooks.com

Distribution Network
gyanbooks.com
India, USA, Canada, UK, Australia, France

ISBN : 978-81-212-6667-3 (PB)
First Published, 1867

2nd Impression 2022

Printed at: Gyan Press, Delhi.

A HIGHER SANSKRIT GRAMMAR
Author: LATE MORESHWAR RAMCHANDRA KALE

A

HIGHER SANSKRIT GRAMMAR

FOR THE USE OF SCHOOLS AND COLLEGES,

BY

LATE MORESHWAR RAMCHANDRA KALE, B.A.,

Author of the 'Sahityasârasangraha,' &c. &c.

PREFACE

The present Grammar has been prepared with a view to meet the growing wants of the Indian University students. The University examiners have been, of late, evincing a desire to exact a more thorough knowledge of the obscurer and therefore more difficult parts of Sanskrit Grammar, than was required formerly. In fact, a student of the present day, with Sanskrit for his second language, must, if he wishes to pass his University Eaxminations with credit, acquire more than a general knowledge of the various departments of Sanskrit Grammar, while none of the grammars now accessible to the Indian student, with the exception of one or two, supply him with the necessary information on the various topics discussed in the original Sanskrit works. Dr. Bhándarkar's books, though ingeniously sketched and admirably executed, are admittedly meant to introduce a student to the vast field of Sanskrit Grammar. Dr. Kielhorn's Grammar aims more at brevity and perspicuity than at fullness of treatment with conciseness. Prof. Whitney's grammar is too elaborate, and therefore too high for the ordinary student. Prof. Monier Williams' grammar and others, though excellent in themselves, are expressly written for European students and are more suited to them than to the Indian students. I have, therefore, done my best to bring the present Grammar upto the requirements of the high standard.

Now, a few words on the scope and arrangement of the work and I will conclude. As remarked by Dr. (Now Sir) Bhandarkar* "Grammar was not an empiric study with Pánini and the other ancient grammarians of India." In fact in the hands of the ancient Grammarians of India, Sanskrit Grammar rose to the dignity of a science and must

*Introduction to the 3rd Ed. of the 2nd Book of Sanskrit.

be studied as such. To quote the words of the learned Doctor again "its study possesses an educational value of the same kind as that of Euclid and not much inferior to it in degree. For to make up a particular from the mind of the student has to go through a certain process of synthesis." To split up, therefore, a general rule of the ancient Indian grammarians into a number of the praticular cases it comprehends, as is done by some modern writers on sanskrit grammar, is not to build up but to destroy, not to simplify the difficulties of the student but to embarrass him. For a Grammar, then, to be practical and correct, in my humble opinion, it must be based on indigenous words understood and studied in their genuine scientific spirit. In writing the various chapters of this book (except the one on the 'Conjugation of Verbs') I have closely followed Panini as explained by Bhattoji Dikshit (the Káshiká of Vámana being also occasionally referred to). Many of the rules given are translations of the Sutras of Pánini, much matter being thus compressed into a small compass. The original Sutras where necessary, are given in foot-notes as help to memory. *Sandhis* and declensions are very fully treated. Compounds which play such an important part in Sanskrit literature, and which, yet, are very summarily disposed of in many grammars, have received special attention, almost everything in the Siddhanta Kaumudi being included. The formation of *feminine* bases which is not considered separately in other grammars has been treated of here in a separate chapter (VI). The seventh chapter deals with the Taddhita affixes (i. *e.* affixes forming secondary nominal bases) which, for the convenience of the student and the occassional referer, have been arranged here in an alphabetical order, each followed by a number of the derivatives formed by it. The question of gender which so much perplexes the foreigner has been dealt with in the eighth chapter, while the ninth treats of "Indeclinables." The first nine chapters thus form what may be called the first part of the book, in as much as they deal with all that relates to the noun (declinable and indeclinable) But a special feature of the pres nt Grammar is the chapter on the 'Conjugation of Verbs.' No part of Sanskrit Grammar is more difficult and perplexing and therefore more calculated, to tire out the patience of the young student, than the conjugation of Verbs.' It is, therefore, written with a special attention to the student's difficulties. The general rules given are amply illustrated by example. Almost all the roots which are likely to puzzle the student in conjugating them in a particular tense or mood have been fully conjugated. In the eleventh chapter, all the verbs which change their *pada* when preceded by particular prepositions are given in an alphabetical order with illustrations where necessary. Two more chapters, one on syntax and the other on prosody, have also been added. The chapter on syntax contains almost everything given in the first 20 chapters of Prof. Apte's 'Guide to Sanskrit Composition,' the same original having been followed by the both. The chapter on prosody is based on the Chhandomanjari and the Vrittaratnakara. The book closes with a list of verbs (added at the suggestion of my publishers) containing almost all the roots in Sanskrit and giving the 3rd pers. sing. in the important tenses and moods.

Thus it will be seen that I have spared no pains to make the book as useful and as complete as possible. Also such of the technical terms used in original Sanskrit Grammars as the student always meets with in Sanskarit commentaries, are given in their proper places with their explanations.

In writing this Grammar, I have occasionally used Monier Williams's, Dr. Kielhorn's and Whitney's grammars to all of whom I make ample acknowledgements. My special thanks are due to Dr. Bhándárkar whose two books of Sanskrit were my chief guide in writing out the chapter on the 'Conjugation of Verbs,' and to the late Prof Apte to whose excellent 'Guide to Sanskrit Composition,' I am indebted for some of the illustrations given in the Thirteenth chapter. I have also to thank my friend Mr. Uddhavácharya Ainápure for his occasional help and for the pains he took in preparing for this Grammar the list of Verbs added at the end and carrying it through the press.

This being the first attempt of the Author to bring into one volume the various departments of Sanskrit

Grammar as full and as concisely as possible, the Author hopes that the public will take an indulgent view of the work, and pardon him for any of the inaccuracies, mistakes of typography, &c., that might have crept in notwithstanding his best care. It is a sufficient excuse for these to say that the whole volume was written and carried through the press in less than a year. Before concluding I have also to thank Mr. Vinayaka Narayana, Proprietor of the firm of Messrs. Gopal Narayen & Co., my publishers of this Grammar, for the care with which he passed the sheets through the press.

Lastly I beg to say that I shall be very grateful for any corrections and suggestions that may be sent to me by my indulgent readers and critics and will try to profit by them if the book reaches a second edition.

Bombay,
30th April 1894.

M. R. KALE.

CONTENTS.

ABBREVIATIONS USED IN THE WORK.

Of the names of the works and Grammatical, &c.

Amara.—Amarakosh.
Bhatt. or Bhatti.—Bhatti-kávya.
Bh.—Bhartrihari. Ni. Sa.—Nitiśataka. Vai. Sa. Variágyaśataka.
Dev.-Devibhágavata Purána
Hit.—Hitopadeśa.
Kád.—Kádambari.
Kátyá.—Kátyáyana.
D. Káv—Dandin's Kávyádarsa
Kir.—Kirátárjuniya.
Mál.—Malavikagnimitra.
Mb. or Mah. Bhás.—Mahabhashya of Patanjali.
Mah. Bhár.—Mahabharata.
Meg.—Meghaduta.
Pán.—Panini's Sutras.
Rag.—Raghuvamśa of Kalidasa.
Ram.ch.—Ramacharita.
Sak.—Abhijnanaśakuntala of Kalidasa.
Sid. Kau.—Sidhantakaumudi, Bhattoji Dikshita's commentary on Pánini's sütras.
&c. &c. &c.

Sis.—Siśupálavadha.
Uttar.—Uttararāmacharita.
Vop. or Bop.—Vopadeva.
A. or Atm.—Atmanepada.
Abl.—Ablative.
Acc.—Accusative.
Adj.—Adjective.
Adv.—Adverb.
Avy.—Avyayibhava.
Bah.—Bahuvrihi.
Cau.—Causal.
Cf.—Compare.
Comp.— Compound.
Dat.—Dative.
Den.—Denominative.
Des.—Desiderative.
Freq.—Frequantative.
Indecl.—Indeclinable.
Inst.—Instrumental.
Loc.—Locative.
Nom.—Nominative.
P. or Par.—Parasmaipada.
Pass.—Passive.
Pot.P.-Potential participle.
P.P.-Past Passive participle.
Pres.p.—Present participle.
Pron.—Pronouns.
&c. &c. &c.

§ 2. The Devanâgarî alphabet consists of *forty-two* letters or varṇas, *nine* vowels or svaras, and *thirty-three* consonants or vyañjanas.*

(*a*) These express nearly every gradation of sound, and every letter stands for a particular and invariable sound.

Note :—This explains why there are no names, as in Greek, for the different letters of the alphabet.

---

* Thus given by Pâṇini :—

Vowels :—अइउण् । ऋऌक् । एओङ् । ऐऔच् ।

Consonants :—हयवरट् । लण् । ञमङणनम् । झभञ् । घढधष् । जबगडदश् । खफछठथचटतव् । कपय् । शषसर् । हल् ।

The alphabet, it will be seen, is divided into 14 sections by Pâṇini, which are called Śivasútráṇi, or the sútras revealed by Śiva. Each section ends with an indicatory letter called 'इत्' which is not to be counted among the letters of the alphabet. These "Its" serve an important purpose in Sanskrit grammar as they enable the grammarians to express several letters, or groups of letters, in a very convenient and condensed form. For any letter, with the following इत् added to it, is not only expressive of itself but of all letters that intervene between it and this इत्; *e. g.* अण् means अ, इ, उ, इक् means इ, उ, ऋ, ऌ, &c. Similarly अल् means technically the whole alphabet, अच् any vowel, and हल् any consonant; यण् a semivowel, हश् a soft consonant, खर् a hard consonant, जश् a soft unaspirate, झष् a soft aspirate &c. Each of these significant terms is technically called a 'प्रत्याहार'.

Since short vowels include the long and the protracted vowels (See § 3, *a.*) another इत् 'त' is generally employed to mark a

§ 3. The nine primary vowels consist of five simple vowels viz. अ, इ, उ, ऋ and ऌ, and four diphthongs viz. ए, ऐ, ओ and औ.

(*a*) A vowel may be ह्रस्व or short. दीर्घ or long, and प्लुत or protracted (also called prolated by some) according to the time required to pronounce it. * The vowels are thus divided into—

(1) Short vowels—अ a, इ i, उ u, ऋ ṛ, ऌ ḷ;

(2) Long vowels—आ â, ई î, ऊ ú, ॠ ṝ, ए e, ऐ ai, ओ o, औ au; and.

(3) Protracted vowels आ ३ â 3, ई ३ î 3, ऊ ३ û 3, ऋ ३ ṛ 3 ऌ ३ ḷ 3, ए ३ e 3, ऐ ३ ai 3, ओ ३ o 3, and औ ३ au 3.

N. B.—As the Pluta or protracted vowels are not commonly to be met with in classical Sanskrit, the vowels are usually given as thirteen, represented by the thirteen signs given above under (1) and (2).

(*b*) Each of these vowels may be again of two kinds, अनुनासिक or nasalised, and अननुनासिक or without a nasal sound.†

(*c*) Vowels are also further discriminated into उदात्त or acute, अनुदात्त or grave, and स्वरित or circumflex. उदात्त is

---

particular vowel : *e. g.* अ means अ, आ and आ ३, but अत् means अ (of six kinds) only; so ईत् means ई and nothing else.

* ऊकालोऽज्झ्रस्वदीर्घप्लुतः। Pân. I. 2. 27. The crowing of the cock in the morning represents in its three stages these three kinds of vowels. The time required to pronounce a short vowel is called a *mátrâ*. A long vowel has two mâtrás and a *Pluta* vowel three.

† मुखनासिकावचनोऽनुनासिकः Pân. I. 1. 8.

that which proceeds from the upper part of the vocal organs, अनुदात्त that which proceeds from their lower part, while स्वरित arises out of a mixture of these two.* But these are ignored in classical Sanskrit. They are marked only in Vedic works: the *Udátta* is left unmarked; the *Anudátta* is marked with a horizontal line underneath; and *Svarita* has a perpendicular stroke above it. *e. g.* क्व१ वोऽश्वाः, &c. Ṛg. V. 61. 2 रथानां न ये३ राः । &c. Ṛg. X. 78. 4. शतचक्रं यो३ ह्यः &c. Ṛg. X. 145. 4.

Thus there are eighteen different modifications of each of the vowels अ, इ, उ, ऋ, and twelve of ऌ, ए, ऐ, ओ and औ; for there is no long ḷ and the last four have not their corresponding short vowels.

§ 4. The consonants are divided into *spars'a* or mutes (those involving a complete closure or contact and not an approximate one of the organs of pronunciation), *Antastha* (or intermediate *i. e.* the Semivowels,) and *úshman* or sibilants.

These are represented by thirty-three syllabic signs arranged as below :—

(*a*) mutes
- (1) कवर्ग or the group कु—क् k, ख् kh, ग् g, घ् gh, ङ् ṅ.
- (2) चवर्ग or the group चु—च् ç, छ् çh, ज् j, झ् jh, ञ् ñ.
- (3) टवर्ग or the group टु—ट् ṭ, ठ् ṭh, ड् ḍ, ढ् ḍh, ण् ṇ.
- (4) तवर्ग or the group तु—त् t, थ् th, द् d, ध् dh, न्
- (5) पवर्ग or the group पु—प् p, फ् ph, ब् b, भ् bh, म् m.

---

* उच्चैरुदात्तः । नीचैरनुदात्तः । समाहारः स्वरितः । Pán. 1. 2. 29, 31.

These are also called the five classes designated as *Kavarga*, *Chavarga*, *Tavarga*, *Tavarga*, and *Pavarga* respectively.

(*b*) Semivowels———य् y, र् r, ल् l, व् v.
(*c*) Sibilants———श् ś ष् sh, स् s.
(*d*) Sonant Aspirate—ह् h.

Besides these we have two more characters occurring in the Veda, viz. ळ and ळ्ह (often substituted for ड and ढ; as ईळे for ईडे, मीळ्हुषे for मीढुषे &c.). In Maráthi ळ is generally substituted for the final ल् of Sanskrit words.

§ 5. The first two letters of the five classes and the sibilants are called *surds* or *hard consonants*. The rest are called *sonants* or *soft consonants*.

§ 6. In addition to the characters given above there are in Sanskrit two nasal sounds:—the one called *Anusvâra*, is denoted by ˙ *i. e.* a dot placed above the letter after which it is to be pronounced, *e. g.* कं; the other, called *Anunásika* is denoted by ँ *i. e.* a dot within a semi-circle placed above the letter after which it is to be pronounced *e. g.* सँ.

(*a*) And a sort of hard breathing is known as Visarga (generally called Visarjanîya by Sanskrit grammarians). It is denoted by the sign : *i. e.* two vertical dots placed after the letter after which it is to be pronounced. In pronunciation it is a harder aspirate than ह्. The Visarga is not an original character but only a substitute for a final स् s or र् r.

(*b*) Jihvámúlîya (जिह्वामूलीय) and Upadhmánîya (उपध्मानीय) are terms given to a sort of Semi-Visarga, when pronounced before क् ख्, and प् फ् respectively. It is written symbolically as ><. These may be regarded as the spirants of *Kavarga* and *Pavarga* respectively.

§ 7. Some consonants are pronounced with a slight aspiration and are designated as *Alpa-prâṇa*, while others which are pronounced with a stronger aspiration are called *Mahá-práṇa*. The first and third letters of each class, the nasals and the semi-vowels belong to the first class; the rest belong to the second class. For the sake of convenience the first and third letters of each class are sometimes called "unaspirates."

§ 8. In the following table is given a complete classification of these letters according to the organs with which they are pronounced.

(*a*) The organs of pronunciation are the five parts situated in the mouth, viz., the throat, the palate, the roof or upper part of the palate, the teeth and the lips.

Note.—In the following table the nether stroke (see § a 10 below) is omitted. It should be supposed to be present.

	The Five Classes.					Semi-vowels.	Sibilants.	Simple vowels St. Lg.	Diphthongs.	
	Unaspirate.	Aspirate.	Unaspirate.	Aspirate.	Nasals.					
Gutturals.	क	ख	ग	घ	ङ	ह*	>< Jiv.	अ. आ	ए }	ओ औ
Palatals.	च	छ	ज	झ	ञ	य	श	इ ई	ऐ }	
Linguals.	ट	ठ	ड	ढ	ण	र	ष	ऋ ॠ		
Dentals.	त	थ	द	ध	न	ल } व	स	ऌ		
Labials.	प	फ	ब	भ	म	} व	⌣ Upa.	उ. ऊ	..	ओ औ

* ह though not a semivowel is put here as it is a guttural.

This can be more easily remembered from its Sanskrit form which is as follows :—

अकुहविसर्जनीयानां कण्ठः ।	एदैतोः कण्ठतालु ।
इचुयशानां तालु ।	ओदौतोः कण्ठोष्ठम् ।
ऋटुरषाणां मूर्धा ।	वकारस्य दन्तोष्ठम् ।
ऌतुलसानां दन्ताः ।	जिह्वामूलीयस्य जिह्वामूलम् ।
उपूपध्मानीयानां ओष्ठौ ।	नासिकाऽनुस्वारस्य ।
ञमङणनानां नासिका च ।	

The linguals are called cerebrals in some European Grammars. ए and ऐ are both guttural and palatal; ओ and औ are guttural and labial; व is dental and labial. The nose is the organ of pronunciation of the Anusvára, while the root of the tongue is that of the Jihvâmûlîya.

§ 9. Those letters are called सवर्ण or homogeneous whose place of pronunciation in the mouth and the effort required to pronounce them is the same or equal.* Letters which are not सवर्ण or similar are called असवर्ण or heterogeneous.

§ 10. A *svara* or vowel is that which can be pronounced without the help of any other letter; a *vyañjana* or consonant is that which is pronounced with the help of a vowel. The consonants, therefore, are written with a slanting nether stroke to denote their imperfect character.

(*a*) Hence the consonants are given, in the system of Pâṇini, with an अ added to them for the sake of pronunciation.

(*b*) As already remarked, there are no separate names for

---

* तुल्यास्यप्रयत्नं सवर्णम् । Pâṇ. I. 1. 9.

the letters of the Sanskṛt alphabet, except the two mentioned before, *viz.* Anusvâra and Visarga, and Refa which is the name sometimes given to र्. The word कार is therefore used as an affix to denote a particular letter; *e. g.* अकार the letter 'अ', ककार the letter 'क', &c.

§ 11. A vowel by itself or a consonant, simple or conjunct, with a vowel added to it, is called an *Akshara* or a syllable.

§ 12. The forms which the vowel signs assume when added to consonants and the changes which some letters undergo when compounded are given below, under (*a*) and (*b*).

(*a*) अ added to a consonant is denoted by the removal of the nether stroke; as क् + अ = क ka. The remaining vowels when compounded with a consonant become ा, ि, ी, ु, ू, ृ, ॄ, ॢ, े, ै, ो, ौ, respectively; as क् + आ = का ká, क् + इ = कि ki; similarly की kí कु ku, कू kū, कृ kṛ, कॄ kṝ, कॢ kl. के ke, कै kai, को ko, कौ kau.

Exception:—ऋ when following upon र् remains unchanged, as र्ऋ.

(*b*) In compounding consonants they should be taken in the order in which they are pronounced; the last consonant takes a vowel, the preceding ones generally losing their nether and perpendicular strokes when combined *e. g. tsna* ought to be written as त्स्न, ṇṇa as ण्ण, &c. Some letters, however, change their form slightly and others entirely, when compounded with other consonants; *e. g.* ल्प lpa; त्र tra; श्च sça; ग्र gra, &c.; र् immediately preceding another consonant (or the vowel ऋ) is denoted by the sign र्‍ written above the following consonant as र्क rka. It is then necessarily called a रेफ refa.

(*c*) In the conjuncts क्ष (क् + ष) ksh, and ज्ञ (ज् + ञ) jña, the component elements are scarcely discernible.

(*d*) A few consonants are written in two ways; *e. g.* त्र, त्र tra; क्र, क्र, kra; स्थ, स्थ, stha; क्त, क्त, kta; स्त्र, स्त्र, stra.

(*e*) The following are the principal conjunct consonants :-

क्क k-ka, क्क्ण k-kṇa, क्क्य k-kya, क्ख k-kha, क्त k-ta, क्थ k-tha, क्त्य k-tya, क्त्र or क्त्र k-tra, क्त्व k-t-va, क्थ्न k-th-na, क्न k-na, क्न्य k-n-ya, क्म k-ma, क्य k-ya, क्र or क्र k-ra, क्ल k-la, क्व k-va, क्ष k-sha, क्ष्ण k-sh-ṇa, क्ष्म k-sh-ma, क्ष्य k-sh-ya, क्ष्व k-sh-va.

ख्न kh-na, ख्य kh-ya, ख्र kh-ra.

ग्ध g-dha, ग्न g-na, ग्य g-ya, ग्र g-ra, ग्र्य g-r-ya, ग्ल g-la, ग्व g-va, घ्न gh-na, घ्न्य gh-n-ya, घ्म gh-ma, घ्य gh-ya, घ्र gh-ra, घ्व gh-va, ङ्क ṅ-ka, ङ्क्त ṅ-k-ta, ङ्क्ष ṅ-k-sha, ङ्क्ष्व ṅ-k-sh-va, ङ्ख ṅ-kha, ङ्ख्य ṅ-kh-ya, ङ्ग ṅ-ga, ङ्घ ṅ-gha, ङ्घ्य ṅ-gh-ya, ङ्घ्र ṅ-gh-ra, ङ्ङ ṅ-ṅa, ङ्म ṅ-ma, ङ्य ṅ-ya.

च्च çça, च्छ çcha, च्छ्र ç-çh-ra, च्छ्व ç-çh-va, च्ञ ç-ña, च्म ç-ma, च्य ç-ya.

छ्य çh-ya, छ्र çh-ra.

ज्ज j-ja, ज्झ j-jha, ज्ञ j-ña, ज्ञ्य j-ñ-ya, ज्म j-ma, ज्य j-ya, ज्र j-ra, ज्व j-va.

ञ्च ñ-ça, ञ्छ ñ-çha, ञ्ज ñ-ja.

ट्क ṭ-ka, ट्ट ṭ-ṭa, ट्य ṭ-ya, ठ्य ṭh-ya, ठ्र ṭh-ra, ड्ग ḍ-ga, ड्घ ḍ-gha, ड्म ḍ-ma, ड्य ḍ-ya, ढ्य ḍh-ya; ढ्र ḍh-ra.

ण्ट ṇ-ṭa, ण्ठ ṇ-ṭha, ण्ड ṇ-ḍa, ण्ढ ṇ-ḍha, ण्ण ṇ-ṇa, ण्म ṇ-ma, ण्य ṇ-ya, ण्व ṇ-va.

त्क t-ka, त्क्र t-k-ra, त्त t-ta, त्त्य t-t-ya, त्त्र t-t-ra, त्त्व t-t-va, त्थ t-tha, त्न t-na, त्न्य t-n-ya, त्प t-pa, त्म t-ma, त्म्य t-m-ya, त्य

t-ya, त्र or त्र t-ra. त्र्य or त्र्य t-r-ya, त्व t-va, त्स t-sa, त्स्न t-s-na, त्स्न्य t-s-n-ya, त्स्य t-s-ya.

थ्न th-na, थ्य th-ya, थ्व th-va.

द्ग d-ga, द्घ d-gha, द्द d-da, द्य d-ya, द्ध d-dha, द्ध्य d-dh-ya, द्ध्व d-dh-va, द्न d-na, द्ब d-ba, द्ब्र d-bra, द्भ d-bha, द्भ्य d-bh-ya, द्म d-ma, द्र d-ra, द्र्य d-r-ya, द्व d-va, द्व्य d-v-ya, द्व्र d-v-ra.

ध्न dh-na, ध्न्य dh-n-ya, ध्म dh-ma, ध्य dh-ya, ध्र dh-ra, ध्र्य dh-rya, ध्व dh-va.

न्त n-ta, न्त्य n-t-ya, न्त्र n-t-ra, न्द n-da, न्द्र n-d-ra, न्ध n-dha. न्ध्य n-dh-ya, न्ध्र n-dh-ra, न्न n-na, न्प्र n-p-ra, न्म n-ma, न्य n-ya. न्र n-ra, न्स n-sa.

प्त p-ta, प्त्य t-p-ya, प्न p-na, प्प p-pa, प्म p-ma, प्य p-ya, प्र p-ra, प्ल p-la, प्व p-va, प्स p-sa, प्स्व p-s-va.

ब्ज b-ja, ब्द b-da, ब्ध b-dha, ब्न b-na, ब्ब b-ba, ब्भ b-bha, ब्य b-ya ब्र b-ra, ब्व b-va,

भ्न bh-na, भ्य bh-ya, भ्र bh-ra, भ्व bh-va.

म्न m-na, म्प m-pa, म्प्र m-p-ra, म्ब m-ba, म्भ m-bha, म्य m-ya, म्र m-ra, म्ल m-la, म्व m-va

य्य y-ya, य्र y-ra, य्व y-va.

र्क r-ka, र्ख r-kha, र्ग r-ga, &c.; र्क्ष r-k-sha, र्ग्य r-g-ya, र्घ्य r-gh-ya, र्त्य r-t-ya, &c.; र्क्ष्य r-k-sh-ya, र्त्त्य r-tt-ya, र्त्स्य r-t-s-ya. र्द्ध r-d-dh-a.

ल्क l-ka, ल्प l-pa, ल्म l-ma, ल्य l-ya, ल्ल l-la, ल्व l-va.

व्न v-na, व्य v-ya, व्र v-ra, व्व v-va.

श्च śça, श्च्य ś-çya. श्न ś-na, श्य ś-ya, श्र ś-ra, श्र्य ś-r--ya, श्ल ś-la, श्व ś-va, श्व्य śv-ya, श्श ś-śa.

ष्ट sh-ṭa, ष्ट्य sh-ṭya, ष्ट्र sh-ṭ-ra, ष्ट्र्य sh-ṭ-r-ya, ष्ट्व sh-ṭ-va, ष्ठ्र sh-ṭh-ra, ष्ठ्य sh-ṭh-ya, ष्ण sh-ṇa, ष्ण्य sh-ṇ-ya, ष्प sh-pa, ष्प्र sh-p-ra, ष्म sh-ma, ष्य sh-ya, ष्व sh-va.

स्क s-ka, स्ख s-kh-a, स्त s-ta, स्त्य s-t-ya, स्त्र or स्र s-t-ra, स्त्व s-t-va, स्थ s-tha, स्न s-na, स्न्य s-n-ya, स्प s-pa, स्फ s-pha, स्म s-ma, स्य s-ya, स्र s-ra, स्व s-va, स्स s-sa.

ह्ण h-ṇa, ह्न h-na, ह्म h-ma, र्ह r-ha, ह्र h-ra, ह्ल h-la, ह्व h-va.

Sometimes five consonants are found in conjunction : *e. g.* र्त्स्न्य r-t-s-n-ya, as in कार्त्स्न्य.

§ 13. As *sandhi* is of primary importance in Sanskṛt, *virâma* or pause can be indicated only at the end of a sentence. The signs of punctuation, therefore, are only two, । and ॥. The former is used to mark the close of a sentence or the first half of a s'loka or poetical stanza; the latter is employed to denote the close of a s'loka.

(*a*) The sign called *Avagraha* (and which represents half अ Ardhákára) is generally employed to mark the elision of short अ after ए or ओ ; *e. g.* तेऽपि (ते + अपि), कालोऽस्ति (कालो + अस्ति). The double mark ऽऽ is sometimes used to indicate the elision of आ after initial long आ ; तथा + आस्ते = तथाऽऽस्ते.

(*b*) The mark ० is sometimes used to show that something is omitted, and which is to be understood from the context ; *e. g.* अ० may stand for अर्जुन, ०प्रार्थी for कवियशःप्रार्थी, &c.

§ 14. Short vowels when followed by a conjunct consonant are said to be *prosodially long*

§ 15. The vowels अ, ए, ओ and the syllables अर् and अल् are called Guṇa; the vowels आ, ऐ, औ and the syllables आर् and आल् are called Vṛddhi*. The Guṇa and Vṛddhi vowels and syllables that are substituted for the simple vowels will appear from the following table :—

Simple V.	अ	इ & ई	उ & ऊ	ऋ & ॠ	ऌ
Guṇa.	अ	ए	ओ	अर्	अल्
Vṛddhi.	आ	ऐ	औ	आर्	आल्

* वृद्धिरादैच् । अदेङ्गुणः । उरण् रपरः Pâṇ. 1, 1. 2; 1, 51.

§ 16. The three semivowels य्, ल् and व् are sometimes nasalised and then they are written with the *anunâsika* sign over them, as यँ्, लँ्, वँ्.

§ 17. The numerical figures in Sanskṛt are :—

१, २, ३, ४, ५, ६, ७, ८, ९, ०.
1, 2, 3, 4, 5, 6, 7, 8, 9, 0.

These are combined to express larger figures precisely in the same way as in English; १२५ 125, ५४० 540, &c.

Chapter II.

RULES OF SANDHI.

§ 18. By *Sandhi* (from सम् together, and धा to join) is meant the coalescence of two letters coming in immediate contact with each other.*

(*a*) Saṁhitâ† or sandhi is necessary in the case of the internal structure of a *pada*, prepositions and roots joined together and a compound word (समास), while in that of a sentence *i. e.* in the case of the finals and initials of the different words in a sentence, it depends on the will of the writer.

I SVARASANDHI, OR THE COMBINATION OF FINAL AND INITIAL VOWELS.

§ 19. If a simple vowel, short or long, be followed by a

* परः सन्निकर्षः संहिता । Pân. 1. 4. 109. Saṁhitá is the extreme contiguity of letters.

† संहितैकपदे नित्या नित्या धातूपसर्गयोः । नित्या समासे वाक्ये तु सा विवक्षामपेक्षते. ॥ Sid. Kau. This couplet gives the rule for the observation of Sandhi.

similar vowel, short or long, the substitute for them both is the similar long vowel *e. g.* *दैत्य + अरिः = दैत्यारिः; अत्र + आसीत् = अत्रासीत्; यदा + अभवत् = यदाभवत्; विद्या + आतुरः = विद्यातुरः eager to gain knowledge; इति + इव = इतीव; अपि + ईक्षते = अपीक्षते; श्री + ईशः = श्रीशः; भानु + उदयः = भानूदयः; साधु + ऊचुः = साधूचुः; चमू + ऊर्जः = चमूर्जः the strength of the army; कर्तृ + ऋजुः = कर्तॄजुः, कृ + ऋकारः = कॄकारः; होतृ + ऌकारः = होतॄकारः the ḷkâra pronounced by the sacrificer (since there is no long ऌ long ॠ is substituted for both).

(*a*) If ऋ or ऌ be followed by a short ऋ or ऌ, short ऋ or ऌ is optionally substituted for both; † होतृ + ऋकारः = होतृकारः, and also होतृऋकारः (vide‡ 23. sec. *b.*); so three forms altogether होतॄकारः, होतृकारः and होतृऋकारः; होतृ + ऌकारः = होत्ऌकारः and also होतॄऌकारः.

§ 20. When अ or आ is followed by इ, उ, ऋ ऌ, short or long, the गुण letter corresponding to the latter takes the place of both‡ *e. g.* उप + इन्द्रः = उपेन्द्रः Vishnu; परम + ईश्वरः = परमेश्वरः the great lord; रमा + इच्छा = रमेच्छा the wish of Ramâ; यथा + ईप्सितं = यथेप्सितम् according to wish or desire; हित + उपदेशः = हितोपदेशः friendly instruction; कृष्ण + ऊरुः = कृष्णोरुः Kṛshṇa's thigh; गङ्गा + उदकं = गङ्गोदकम्, महा + ऊरुः = महोरुः, कृष्ण + ऋद्धिः = कृष्णर्द्धिः Kṛshṇa's prosperity; महा + ऋषिः = महर्षिः a great sage; तव + ऌकारः = तवल्कारः The *ḷkára* pronounced by you.

(*a*) If a consonant be followed by homogeneous consonants, except the nasals, the semivowels, and ह्, the first of them is

---

* अकः सवर्णे दीर्घः । Pâṇ. VI. 1. 101.

† ऋति सवर्णे ऋ वा । ऌति सवर्णे ऌ वा । Várttikas on the above.

‡ आद्गुणः । Pâṇ. VI. 1. 86.

optionally dropped;* कृष्ण+ऋद्धिः=कृष्णर्द्धिः by the general rule; then कृष्णर्+द्+ध्+इः=कृष्णर्धिः by this rule, the द् being dropped; and also a third form कृष्णर्द्द्धिः (vide § 22, sec. *d.* below).

(*b*) A consonant of the first five classes except ञ् coming after a semivowel is optionally doubled; so तवल्कारः also becomes तवल्क्कारः, तवल्लकारः and तवल्ल्क्कारः, 4 forms altogether.

Exceptions :—Vṛddhi substitute takes place in the following cases †

(*a*) When a word ending in अ is followed by ऊह, and प्र by ऊह, ऊढ and ऊढि; *e. g.* प्रष्ठ+ऊहः=प्रष्ठौहः, chief guess (or this may be the acc. pl. of प्रष्ठवाह् a young bull trained to the yoke); प्र+ऊहः=प्रौहः principal reasoning. Similarly प्रौढः full grown; प्रौढिः; but प्रोढवान् (as ऊढवान् is not mentioned in the Sûtra).

(*b*) अक्ष+ऊहिनी=अक्षौहिणी a complete army.‡ (The change of न् to ण् will be explained further on).

(*c*) When स्व is followed by ईर and ईरिन् both derived from ईर् to go; *e. g.* स्व+ईरः=स्वैरः, one acting wilfully; selfwilled; स्व+ईरिणी=स्वैरिणी; so स्वैरं, स्वैरी (स्वेन ईरितुं शीलमस्य इति).

---

* झरो झरि सवर्णे ; Pân. VIII. 4. 65.

† एत्येधत्यूठ्सु । Pâṇ. VI. 1. 89. The first part of the sûtra (*viz.* एत्येधति) forms a counter-exception to § 21. *a* (which see); प्रादूहोढोढ्येषैष्येषु; 'अक्षादूहिन्यामुपसंख्यानम्' 'स्वादीरेरिणोः' ऋते च तृतीयासमासे' 'प्रवत्सतरकम्बलवसनार्णदशानामृणे,' Vártikas on the above Sútra.

‡ Properly an army consisting of 21870 chariots, as many elephants, 65610 horse and 109350 foot. अक्षौहिण्याः प्रसंख्याता रथानां द्विजसत्तमाः । संख्या गणिततत्त्वज्ञैः सहस्राण्येकविंशतिः ॥ शतान्युपरि चैवाष्टौ तथा भूयश्च सप्ततिः । गजानां तु परीमाणमेतदेव विनिर्दिशेत् ॥ ज्ञेयं शत सहस्रं तु सहस्राणि नवैव तु । नराणामपि पञ्चाशच्छतानि त्रीणि चानघाः ॥ पञ्चषष्टिः सहस्राणि तथाश्वानां शतानि च । दशोत्तराणि षट् प्राहुर्यथावदिह संख्यया ॥ Mahâ-Bhâr. Ad. P. II. 23-26.

(*d*) When अ is followed by ऋत: and there is an inst. Tat.; as सुख+ऋत=सुखार्त: blessed with happiness (सुखेन ऋतः), but परमर्त: very adorable (परमश्चासौ ऋतश्च).

(*e*) When the word ऋण comes after प्र, वत्सतर, कम्बल, वसन and ऋण; प्र+ऋणं=प्रार्णम्, principal debts, so वत्सतरार्णं debt for a calf; ऋणार्णम् (a debt contracted to liquidate a previous debt); दशार्ण: (Name of a country; lit. the country with ten fortresses), also दशार्णा नदी (lit. the river into which ten other rivers flow).

(*f*) When* a preposition ending in अ is followed by a root having an initial ऋ; as उप+ऋच्छति=उपार्च्छति; प्रार्छति; but if the root be a denominative, the Vṛiddhi is optional; प्र+ऋष. भीयति=प्रर्षभीयति or प्रार्षभीयति acts like a bull: but उप+ॠकारीयति =उपर्कारीयति, as the ॠ is long; also प्र-ऌकारीयति=प्रा-प्रल्कारीयति very much wishes for ऌ ḷkára; for ऌ is grammatically considered to be similar to ऋ

§ 21. When अ or आ is followed by ए or ऐ and ओ or औ ऐ and औ are respectively substituted for both†; कृष्ण+एकत्वं= कृष्णैकत्वम्; देव+ऐश्वर्यं=देवैश्वर्यम् the majesty of god; सा+एव=सैव she alone; भव+ओषधं=भवौषधम् medicine against birth and re-birth; विद्या+औत्सुक्यं=विद्यौत्सुक्यम longing for knowledge.

Exceptions :—

(*a*) ‡ If a preposition ending in अ be followed by a root beginning with ए or ओ, ए or ओ is substituted; प्र+एजते=प्रेजते quakes very much; उप+ओषति=उपोषति burns something near; but if the root be a denominative, *vṛddhi* is optional; उप+एड-कीयति=उपेडकीयति or उपैडकीयति; प्र+ओघीयति=प्रोघीयति or प्रौघीयति.

---

* उपसर्गादृति धातौ । Pân. VI. 1. 91. वा सुप्यापिशलेः । Pân. VI. 1. 92.
† वृद्धिरेचि Pâṇ. VI. 1. 88. ‡ एङि पररूपम् । Pâṇ. VI. 1. 94.

Counter-exception:—If a form of the root इ to go, or एध् to grow, with an initial ए, comes after अ, and एष or एष्य derived from इष् of the 4th, 6th or 9th conj., after प्र, *vṛidhi* takes place; उप+एति=उपैति; उप+एधते=उपैधते; (but उप+इतः=उपेतः; अवेहि know; from अव+एहि which is equal to अव+आ+इहि, and not अवैहि; मा भवान् प्र+इदिधत्=प्रेदिधत्); प्र+एषः=प्रैषः sending or directing; प्र+एष्यः=प्रैष्यः a servant. But प्रेषः, प्रेष्यः (from ईष्)

(*b*) *When अ is followed by एव in an indefinite sense, ए is substituted for both: क्व+एव=क्वेव भोक्ष्यसे where will you dine to-day? (The place being not definitely known); but तवैव (why, I shall dine at *your* house).

(*c*) † अ followed by ओम् and आ (prep.) is dropped *e. g.* शिवाय+ओं नमः=शिवायों नमः; शिव+एहि (आ+इहि) =शिवेहि.

(*d*) ‡The *vṛddhi* is optional when the ending अ of a word is followed by ओतु a cat, or ओष्ठ the lower lip, in a compound स्थूल+ओतुः=स्थूलोतुः or स्थूलौतुः; बिम्बोष्ठः, बिम्बौष्ठः.

(*e*) §The final vowel or the final consonant with the preceding vowel is dropped in the case of the following words when followed by certain words in a compound†:—शक the country of the Śakas+अन्धु a well=शकन्धुः, कर्क name of a country+अन्धुः=कर्कन्धुः; कुल+अटा=कुलटा one who moves from one mansion to another, a woman of bad character; सीमन्+अन्तः=

---

* एवे चानियोगे Vártik. † ओमाङोश्च Pâṇ. VI. 1. 95.

‡ 'ओत्वोष्ठयोः समासे वा ।' § शकन्ध्वादिषु पररूपं वाच्यम् Várt.

† And also in the case of an onomatopœic wording in अत् followed by इति *e. g.* पटत्+इति=पटिति; but not in the case of a monosyllabic word श्रद्+इति=श्रदिति; and when the word is repeated, only the त् is optionally dropped, as पटत्पटत्+इति=पटत्पटेति or पटत्पटदिति.

of bad character; सीमन्+अन्तः=सीमन्तः (the white line left by the parting of the hair on each side of the head); but सीमान्तः when the meaning of the word is 'The last line or limit of a boundary.' मनस्+ईषा=मनीषा wish; so लाङ्गलीषा the pole of a plough; हलीषा; पतन्+अञ्जलिः=पतञ्जलिः name of the celebrated author of the Mahábhásya (a vast commentary on the sûtras of Páṇini); lit. fit to be adored with joined hands; or according to tradition 'who fell down from the hands of a certain sage as he was offering water to the sun at the time of Sandhyâ adoration.' सार+अङ्गः=सारङ्गः an antelope with a spotted skin or a kind of bird; but साराङ्गः one with a beautiful skin. This is an *Âkṛtigaṇa* i. e. words of similar formation and requiring grammatical explanation but not actually found in the *gaṇa* may be classed under it; e. g. मार्त+अण्डः=मार्तण्डः (derived from मृताण्ड) lit. born of a dead egg, the sun.

§ 22. When इ, उ, ऋ and ऌ, short or long, are followed by a dissimilar vowel, य्, व्, र्, and ल् are respectively substituted for them*; e. g. इति+आह=इत्याह; सुधी+उपास्यः=सुध्युपास्यः adored by the wise; मधु+अरिः=मध्वरिः the enemy of मधु i. e. Vishṇu, धातृ+अंशः=धात्रंशः a portion of the creator; ऌ+आकृतिः=लाकृतिः a figure like that of ऌ &c.

Ob.—Several of the above words may have more than one form when combined; e. g. सुधी+उपास्यः=सुध्य्+उपास्यः by the general rule:—

N. B. The following rules and the two (*a*), (*b*) given under § 20, though they properly from the subject of the next section, are given here to avoid confusion. Ordinary students may pass over these except sec. (*b*) of the present art.

---

* इको यणचि Páṇ. VI. 1. 77.

(*a*) A consonant except ह, preceded by a vowel, is optionally doubled, if no vowel follows*; सुध्य्+उपास्यः=सुद्ध्युपास्यः and सुध्ध्य्+उपास्यः—

(*b*) When a consonant, except a nasal or a semivowel, is followed by a soft unaspirate or aspirate (3rd or 4th letter of a class) it is changed to the soft unaspirate (3rd letter) of its class†; सुध्ध्य्+उपास्यः=सुद्ध्युपास्य

(*c*) Semivowels, when preceded by a letter of the first five classes except ञ are optionally doubled§; thus सुध्य्+उपास्यः= सुध्य्+उपास्यःand सुध्य्य्+उपास्यः;सुद्ध्य्+उपास्यः=सुद्ध्य्+उपास्यः and सुद्ध्य्य्+उपास्यः। Thus there are four forms ultimately, *viz.* सुध्युपास्यः, सुद्ध्युपास्यः and सुद्ध्य्युपास्यः।

Similarly मधु+अरिः=मध्वरिः. मध्व्वरिः, मद्ध्वरिः, and मद्ध्व्वरिः धातृ+अंशः=धात्रंशः and धात्त्रंशः In लृ+आकृतिः of course there is no possibility of any other form.

(*d*) A consonant except ह, coming after र् or ह preceded by a vowel is optionally doubled‡; *e. g.* हरि+अनुभवः=हर्य्+अनुभवः= हर्यनुभवः by the general rule; and optionally हर्य्य्+अनुभवः= हर्य्यनुभवः (Hari's experience) by this rule; so न हि+अस्ति=न ह्यस्ति and न ह्य्यस्ति।

§ 23. (*a*) इ, उ, ऋ or ऌ, short or long, at the end of a word followed by a dissimilar vowel except in a compound, are optionally not combined, and when so they are shortened if long × *e. g.* चक्री+अत्र=चक्र्यत्र, Vishṇu here, and चक्रि अत्र; but वापी+अश्वः=वाप्यश्वः a horse in a well, गौरी+औ (a term.) गौर्यौ.

---

* अनचि च। Páṇ VIII. 4. 47.

† झलां जश् झशि। Páṇ. 4. 53. § यणो मयो द्वे वाच्ये Vârt.

‡ अचो रहाभ्यां द्वे। Páṇ. VIII. 4. 46.

× इकोऽसवर्णे शाकल्यस्य ह्रस्वश्च।

(*b*) अ, इ, उ and ऌ, short or long, at the end of a word followed by a short ऋ, are also optionally not combined, and when not combined are shortened if long*; *e. g.* ब्रह्मा + ऋषिः = ब्रह्मर्षिः A Brâhmaṇa saint, and ब्रह्म ऋषिः; सप्तर्षीणाम् of the seven sages, and सप्तऋषीणाम् (a comp. expression).

§ 24. ए, ओ, ऐ and औ, when followed by a vowel, are changed to अय्, अव्, आय्, and आव् respectively†; *e. g.* हरे + ए = हरये for Hari; विष्णो + ए = विष्णवे for Vishṇu; नै + अकः = नायकः A leader; पौ + अकः = पावकः the purifier *i. e.* fire.

(*a*) य् or व् at the end of a word and preceded by अ or आ is optionally dropped when followed by a vowel or a soft consonant§; *e. g.* हरे + एहि = हरयेहि or हर एहि; विष्णो + इह = विष्णविह or विष्ण इह; श्रियै + उद्यतः = श्रियायुद्यतः or श्रिया उद्यतः intent on getting money; गुरौ + उत्कः = गुरावुत्कः or गुरा उत्कः longing to see the preceptor.

Note—Two vowels brought together by the disappearance of an intervening consonant or visarga do not coalesce.

(*b*) ओ and औ, when followed by a termination beginning with य्, become अव् and आव् respectively ‡; *e. g.* गो + यं = गव्यम् produced from a cow as milk, ghee &c. नौ + यं = नाव्यम् accessible by a boat, navigable.

N. B. This rule holds good, in the case of roots, only when the ओ or औ is brought in by virtue of a termination; × *e. g.* लू + यं = लो + यं = लव्यम् fit to be lopped off. अवश्यलु + यं = अवश्यलौ + यं = अवश्यलाव्यम् which ought necessarily to be cut off.

(c) The ओ of the word गो is also changed to अव् when followed

* ऋत्यकः Pâṇ VII. 1. 127,

† एचोऽयवायावः Pâṇ. VI 1. 78. § लोपः शाकल्यस्य । Pâṇ. VIII 3.19

‡ वान्तो यि प्रत्यये । × धातोस्तन्निमित्तस्यैव । Pâṇ. VI. 1. 79. 80.

by the word यूति (in the Veda and) in ordinary language when it means a particular measure of length*; e. g. गव्यूतिः four miles.

(*d*) The ए of the roots क्षि and जि is changed to अय् when followed by the य of the potential participle indicating capability† e. g. क्षि+य=क्षे+य=क्षय्यं what can be reduced; so जय्यं what can be conquered; but क्षेतुं जेतुं योग्यं क्षेयं (what is fit to be removed but may not be so) पापं, जेयं (what ought to be curbed but which it may not be always possible to curb as) मनः

§ 25. When ए or ओ at the end of a word is followed by अ the latter merges into the former § and the sign ऽ is sometimes written in its place; e. g. हरे+अव=हरेऽव protect, Oh Hari; विष्णो+अव=विष्णोऽव.

(*a*) ‡If the word गो, ending in ओ, be followed by अ, the अ is optionally retained, and if by a vowel, अव is optionally substituted for ओ; गो+अग्रम्=गोग्रम्, गोअग्रम् and गवाग्रम् a multitude of cows or chief among cows; but if it be followed by इन्द्र and अक्ष it necessarily changes its ओ to अव; गो+इन्द्रः=गवेन्द्रः an excellent bull; गवाक्षः a lattice-window, similarly.

§ 26. No *sandhi* is possible in the case of ×—

1 What are called the *Pragṛhya* exceptions; *viz.*—

(*a*) When a dual from (whether of a noun, pronoun or verb) ends in ई, ऊ, or ए÷; e. g. हरी एतौ; विष्णू इमौ; गङ्गे अमू; पचेते इमौ.

---

* गोर्यूतौ छंदस्युपसंख्यानम् । अध्वपरिमाणे च । Vârtikas.

† क्षय्यजय्यौ शक्यार्थे । Páṇ. VI. 1. 81.

§ एङः पदान्तादति । Páṇ. VI. 1. 109. ‡ सर्वत्र विभाषा गोः । अवङ् स्फोटायनस्य । इन्द्रे च । Páṇ. VI. 1. 122-24.

× प्लुतप्रगृह्या अचि नित्यम् Páṇ. VI. 1. 125.

÷ ईदूदेद्द्विवचनं प्रगृह्यम् ।

(*b*) When ई or ऊ follows the म् of the pronoun अदस्* *e. g.*, अमी ईशाः these lords; अमू आसाते the two sit down.

Ob. The ए of the Vedic forms अस्मे and युष्मे also does not blend with a following vowel (शे । Pân. 1. 1. 13.); *e. g.* अस्मे इन्द्राबृहस्पती &c. Rg. IV. 49. 4. Similarly a Vaidic word having the sense of the loc. (but not ending in the termination of the loc.) remains unaffected by a following vowel; सोमो गौरी अधिश्रितः &c. Ṛg. X. 12. 3. where गौरी stands for गौर्याम् the loc. term, being dropped by सुपां सुलुक् Pân. VII. 1. 30.

(*c*) § Particles consisting of a single vowel, except आ meaning 'a little, or a limit' exclusive or inclusive or used as a preposition, when followed by a vowel, *e. g.* इ इन्द्र Oh Indra, उ उमेश, आ एवं नु मन्यसे ah, you think so; but आ + उष्णम् = ओष्णम् (a little warm) &c.

(*d*) When an indeclinable ends in ओ; *e. g.* अहो ईशाः, the final ओ of a noun the vocative case optionally combines when followed by इति; *e. g.* विष्णो इति = विष्णविति, and विष्णो इति; also विष्ण इति (*see* § 24 *a.*).

N. B. All these vowels which do not blend with others, and sometimes the words in which they occur are technically called प्रगृह्य

II. and *pluta* vowels; *e. g.* एहि कृष्ण ३ अत्र गौश्चरति Come Kṛshṇa; here is the cow grazing.

A vowel becomes *pluta* under the following circumstances:–‡

(1) The last vowel of a sentence uttered in reply to a salutation from a male person other than a S'ûdra when the

---

* अदसो मात् । Pâṇ. I. 1. 11. 12.

§ निपात एकाजनाङ् । ओत् । संबुद्धौ शाकल्यस्येतावनार्षे । Pân. I. 14–16.

‡ वाक्यस्य टेः प्लुत उदात्तः । प्रत्यभिवादेऽशूद्रे । Pâṇ. VIII. 2. 82–83. स्त्रियां न । भोराजन्यविशां वेति वाच्यम् । Vârtikas on the latter sutra. दूराद्धूते च । हैहेप्रयोगे हैहयोः । Pâṇ. VIII. 2 84–85.

name or the family is actually mentioned; *e. g.* भो आयुष्मानेधि देवदत्त ३ live long, O Devadatta, which is said in reply to "अभिवादये देवदत्तोहम्" I, Devadatta, bow to you; but the last इ in "भो आयुष्मती भव गार्गि" or in आयुष्मानेधि is not *pluta*; for in the 1st we have the name of a female and in the 2nd no name at all.

But if the sentence end in the word भोः or in the name of a *Kshatriya* or *Vaishya* the last vowel becomes optionally *pluta e. g.* आयुष्मान् एधि भोः or भो ३ः आयुष्मानेधीन्द्रवर्मन् or वर्म ३ न् आयुष्मानेधीन्द्रपालित or त ३ ।

(2) The final vowel of a sentence addressed from a distance to a person; and that of the particles हे and है used in such a sentence; *e. g.* सक्तून् पिब देवदत्त ३; हे राम; राम; हे ३ ।

§ 27 The particle उ, preceded by a letter of the first five classes except ञ् and followed by any vowel, is optionally changed to व्*; किमु उक्तं किम्वुक्तम् and किमु उक्तं (by § 26 *c.*).

II. HALSANDHI, OR THE COALESCENCE OF FINAL CONSONANTS WITH VOWELS AND CONSONANTS.

§ 28 When स् or a consonant of the dental class comes in contact with:—

(*a*) †श or a consonant of the palatal class, the corresponding letter of the latter class is substituted for the former, and श for स् ; हरिस् + शेते = हरिश्शेते Hari sleeps; रामः + चिनोति = रामश्चिनोति Râma collects; सत् + चित् = सच्चित् Reality and knowledge; शार्ङ्गिन् + जय = शार्ङ्गिञ्जय Be you victorious, Oh Kṛshṇa.

Exception:-(1) Dentals coming after श् are not changed into the corresponding palatals; *e. g.* विश्नः that which spreads lustre; प्रश्नः.

---

* मय उञो वो वा । Pâṇ. VIII. 3-33.

† स्तोःश्चुना श्चुः । शात् ।-ष्टु नाष्टुः । Pâṇ. VIII. 4, 40, 44, 41.

(*b*) ष् or a consonant of the lingual class, ष् is substituted for स् and the corresponding letter of the latter class for the former; रामस् + षष्ठः = रामष्षष्ठः Râma who is sixth. रामस् + टीकते= रामष्टीकते Rama goes; तत् + टीका = तट्टीका A commentary on that; चक्रिन् + ढौकसे = चक्रिण्ढौकसे Oh Kṛshṇa, thou goest; पेष् + ता = पेष्टा one who pounds.

Exception—*(1) If a letter of the lingual class coming at the end of a word be followed by स् or a letter of the dental class, the स् as well as the dentals except the न् of नाम्, नवति and नगरी remain unaffected; षट् + सन्तः = षट्सन्तः six good men; (see also § 39.); षट् + ते: = षट्ते these six; but ईट्टे (since the ट् of ईड् is not at the end of a word) he praises. So षण्णवति Ninety-six, षण्णगर्यः six towns; but सर्पिस् + तमम् = सर्पिष्टमम् abundance of ghee; as the exception excludes स्.

§ 29. If a letter of the group त् be followed by ष् it does not substitute its corresponding lingual†; सन् + षष्ठः = सन्षष्ठः sixth good man.

§ 30. If a consonant, except र् or ह्, coming at the end of a word, be followed by a nasal, the nasal of its class is optionally substituted for it‡; एतद् + मुरारिः = एतन्मुरारिः and एतद्मुरारिः (see § 22 sec. *b*.) this Murâri; षट् + मासाः = षण्मासाः and षड्मासाः six months.

N. B. If the nasal belong to a termination the change is necessary; तन्मात्रम् that alone; चिन्मात्रं mere knowledge. वाक् + मय = वाङ्मय। The word ककुद्मत् (see Rag. IV. 22) is irregularly formed.

§ 31. A letter of the dental class, followed by ल् is changed

---

* न पदान्ताट्टोरनाम् । Pâṇ. VIII. 4. 42. अनाम्नवतिनगरीणामिति वाच्यम् । Vârt.

† तोः षि. Pâṇ. VIII. 4. 43.

‡ यरोऽनुनासिकेऽनुनासिको वा । Pâṇ. VIII. 4. 45.

to ल्, the nasalised ल् taking the place of न्*; तद्+लयः=तल्लयः the destruction of that; विद्वान्+लिखति=विद्वाँल्लिखति a learned man writes.

§ 32. The स् of स्था and स्तम्भ् is changed into थ् when after the preposition उद्†; उद्+स्थानम्=उद्+थ्थानम्=उद्थानम् and उद्थ्थानम् (see. § 20. *a*), and then उत्थानम्, उत्थ्थानम् rising up; similarly उत्तम्भनम् and उत्थ्तम्भनम् upholding.

§ 33. ह् coming after any of the first four letters of a class is optionally changed to the soft aspirate (4th letter) of that class‡; वाक्+हरिः=वाग्हरिः (see *b.* under § 22), and by this वाग्घरिः (वाचां हरिः) the possessor of speech, Bṛhaspati.

§ 34. Any consonant, except a nasal or a semi-vowel, is changed to the first of its class, when followed by a hard consonant, and to the first or third when followed by nothing; वाक्, वाग.

§ 35. श preceded by a word ending in any of the first four letters of a class and followed by a vowel, a semi-vowel, a nasal or ह्, is optionally changed to छ्;÷ *e. g.* तद्+शिवः=तद्+शिवः; and तद्+छिवः, and then तत्+शिवः, and तत्+छिवः by the above, and finally तच्शिवः and तच्छिवः that Siva (see. *a.* § 28.). Similarly तच्श्लोकेन, तच्छ्लोकेन; but वाक्श्चोतति speech falters (as श is not followed by any of the letters mentioned in the rule).

§ 36. ×म् at the end of a word is changed into an Anuswâra

---

* तोर्लि । Páṇ. VIII. 4. 60.

† उदः स्थास्तम्भोः पूर्वस्य । Páṇ. VIII. 4. 61.

‡ झयो होऽन्यतरस्याम् । Páṇ. VIII. 4. 62.

÷ शश्छोऽटि । खरि च । Páṇ. VI. I. 4. 63. 55.

× मोऽनुस्वारः । नश्चापदान्तस्य झलि । Páṇ. VII. 3, 23, 24 and Pâṇ VIII. 3, 27, I. 3. 10. (see sec. *b*).

when followed by a consonant; *e. g.* हरिम्+वन्दे=हरिं वन्दे I salute Hari. But गम्+य+ते=गम्यते as म् is not at the end of a word. The word सम्राट् is an exception (see Pán. VIII. 3. 25)·

(*a*) म् and न्, not at the end of a *pada,* are turned into an Anuswára when followed by a consonant except a nasal or a semivowel or ह; आक्रम्+स्यते=आक्रंस्यते he will overcome; यशान्सि=यशांसि (nom. pl. of यशस् fame); but मन्यते he thinks, as न् is followed here by य which is a semi-vowel; ग्रामान्+गच्छति=ग्रामान्गच्छति as न् is at the end of a *pada* (grammatical form).

(*b*) This change is optional in the case of म् when ह followed by म् comes after it; *e. g.* किम्+ह्मलयति=किंह्मलयति and किम्ह्मलयति what does he shake?; but if this ह be followed by न्, and if by य़, व़, ल़, the nasalised य़, व़, ल़, are optionally substituted for म् *e. g.* किं+ह्नुते=किंह्नुते or किन्ह्नुते what does he conceal? किम्+ह्यः=किंह्यः and किँय्ह्यः what! yesterday! so किंह्वलयति, किंव्ह्वलयति; किंह्लादयति and किल्ँह्लादयति; but अहम्+आगतः=अहमागतः।

§ 37. An Anuswára followed by any consonant except श्, ष, स् or ह् is changed to the nasal of the class to which the following letter belongs, necessarily when in the middle, and optionally when at the end of a word*; *e. g.* अन्क्+इतः=अं+क्+इतः (by the preceding rule and then) अङ्कितः marked (by this); so अन्च्+इतः=अञ्चितः honoured; कुण्ठितः obstructed; शान्तः calmed; गुम्फितः woven; त्वम्+ करोषि=त्वं करोषि or त्वङ्करोषि thou doest; similarly संयन्ता or सय्ँयन्ता a restrainer; संवत्सरः or सव्ँवत्सरः a year; यं लोकम् or यल्ँलोकम् to which people.

§ 38. If ङ् and ण् be followed by a sibilant, क् and ट् respectively are suffixed to them optionally; and hard unaspirates are optionally changed into hard aspirates when followed by a

---

* अनुस्वारस्य ययि परसवर्णः। वा पदान्तस्य Pâṇ. VIII. 4. 48–52.

sibilant ||; प्राङ्+षष्ठः=प्राङ्षष्ठः, प्राङ्क्षष्ठः; प्राङ्ख्षष्ठः; the sixth man gone before; सुगण्+षष्ठः=सुगण्षष्ठः, सुगण्ट्षष्ठः, सुगण्ठ्षष्ठः, the sixth good counter.

§ 39. If ड् or न् at the end of a word be followed by स्, ध् (changed to त्) is optionally inserted between them; * e. g. षड्+सन्तः=षड्सन्तः or षड्+ध्+सन्तः=षड्त्सन्तः six good men; so सन् +सः=सन्सः or सन्त्सः that good man.

(a) ङ्, ण् and न् at the end of a word and preceded by a short vowel double themselves when followed by a vowel †; e. g. प्रत्यङ्+आत्मा=प्रत्यङ्ङात्मा the individual soul; so सुगण्णीशः the best reckoner; सन्नच्युतः good Achyuta.

§ 40. Ob. If the ending न् of a word be followed by श्, त् is optionally inserted between them ‡ e. g. सन्+शंभुः=सन्शंभुः and सन्छंभु Śambhu existing for all times; and सन्त्शंभुः=सन्त्शंभुः and सन्तछंभुः (by § 35); then by § 28 (a) न् being changed to ञ् (and त् to च्) सञ्शंभुः, सञ्च्शंभुः and सञ्च्छंभुः and finally by dropping च् optionally (by § 20 a.) सञ्शंभुः, सञ्च्शंभुः and सञ्छंभु सञ्च्छंभुः.

§ 41. न् coming after र्, ष्, or ऋ short or long, in the same word is changed to ण् even though a vowel, a semi-vowel except ल्, a nasal, or a letter of the guttural or labial class or ह् comes between र्, ष् or ऋ and न्;÷ e. g. रामेन=रामेण; पूष्+ना पूष्णा by the sun, पितॄणाम् &c.; but राम+नाम=राम नाम (as these are two separate words). This change does not take place when न is at the end of a word × रामान्.

|| ङ्णोः कुक्टुक् शरि । Páṇ. VIII. 3. 28.

* ङः सि धुट् । नश्च । Páṇ. VIII. 3. 22. 32.

† ङमो ह्रस्वादचि ङमुण्नित्यम् । Páṇ. VIII. 3. 32.

‡ शि तुक् । Páṇ. VIII. 3. 31.

÷ रषाभ्यां नो णः समानपदे । अट्कुप्वाङ्नुम्व्यवायेऽपि Páṇ. VIII. 4. 1. 2.

× पदान्तस्य न । Páṇ. VIII. 4. 37.

§ 42. स् belonging to a substitue (आदेश) or a termination (प्रत्यय) and not at the end of a grammatical form is changed to ष् when preceded by any vowel except अ or आ, a semivowel, a letter of the guttural class or ह्*; *e. g.* रामे+सु=रामेषु; but रामस्य as स् is preceded by अ, सुपीः सुपिसौ &c., as सु belongs to the word सुपिस्. This change takes place even if an *anuswára* substituted for न्, a *visarga* or श् ष् or स् intervene†; *e. g.* धनून्+सि=धनूंषि nom. pl. of धनुस् neu. a bow. पिपठोष्+सु= पिपठीष्षु.

§ 43. The म् of सम् is changed to an Anuswâra and Visarga when followed by a form of the root कृ, the Anuswâra again is optionally changed to an Anunâsika; *e. g.* सम्+कर्ता=संस्कर्ता and सँस्कर्ता ; स् is affixed to the ending of the words सम्, पुम् and कान्‡; so संस्स्कर्ता and सँस्स्कर्ता.

N. B. The word संस्कर्ता is capable of having 108 different forms as several *sútras* are brought to bear upon it; but they are not given here as being tedious and of no material value.

Sections *a, b, c,* and *d* may be omitted by beginners.

(*a*) ×The म् of पुम् is optionally nasalised and has स् added to it as above, when it is followed by a hard consonant except a sibilant, preceding a vowel, a semivowel, a nasal or ह; पुम्+ कोकिलः=पुम्+स्+कोकिलः=पुंस्कोकिलः, पुँस्कोकिलः a male *kokila* bird; so पुंस्पुत्रः and पुँस्पुत्रः the son, a grown up man; but पुंक्षीरम् milk for a man; पुंदासः a man-servant. Exception पुंख्यानम् the account of a man

(*b*) न् at the end of a word (except प्रशाम्) followed by च्, छ्, ट्, ठ्, or त्, थ् which is itself followed by a vowel, a semi-

---

* अपदान्तस्य मूर्धन्यः । इण्कोः । आदेशप्रत्यययोः । Pâṇ. VIII. 3. 55 57, 59.

† नुम्विसर्जनीयशर्व्यवायेऽपि । Pâṇ. VIII. 3. 58.

‡ संपुंकानां सो वक्तव्यः । Vârt.

× पुमः खय्यम्परे Pâṇ. VIII, 3. 6. ख्यात्रादेशे न । Vârt.

vowel, a nasal or ह्, undergoes the same changes*; *e. g.* शार्ङ्गिन्+छिन्द्धि=शार्ङ्गिन्+स्+छिन्द्धि=शार्ङ्गिन्+श्+छिन्द्धि (by § 28, sec. *a*) शार्ङ्गिंश्छिन्द्धि and शार्ङ्गिँश्छिन्द्धि Oh Krisna, cut off; similarly चक्रिन्+त्रायस्व=चक्रिंस्त्रायस्व and चक्रिँस्त्रायस्व; save, Oh Krshna; but हन्ति as the न् is not at the end of a word. सन्त्सरु, a fine handle of a sword. प्रशान्तनोति a good man spreads.

(*c*) The न् of नॄन् when followed by प् undergoes this change optionally; नॄन्+पाहि=नॄन्पाहि, नॄंःपाहि, and नॄँःपाहि.

(*d*) The न् of कान् followed by कान् also undergoes this change optionally; कान्+कान्=कांस्कान्, काँस्कान् to whom? स् or ष् is substituted for the visarga when the following sets are combined: कः+कः=कस्कः; similarly कौतस्कुतः wherefrom, भ्रातुष्पुत्रः, सद्यस्कालः the present time; सर्पिष्कुण्डिका a ghee-pot; धनुष्कपालम् a bowstaff; यजुष्पात्रम् a sacrificial vessel; अयस्कान्त a magnet; तमस्काण्डः great darkness; अयस्काण्डः; भास्करः; अहस्करः the sun.

§ 44. च् is necessarily inserted between छ् and the preceding vowel, short or long; and optionally when a long vowel at the end of a word, except that of the particle मा and the preposition आ, precedes it †; *e. g.* शिव+छाया=शिवच्छाया Śiva's shadow; so स्वच्छाया; चेच्छिद्यते what is cut again and again; लक्ष्मी+छाया=लक्ष्मीछाया or लक्ष्मीच्छाया; मा+छिदत्=माच्छिदत् may he not cut; आ+छादयति=आच्छादयति he covers.

VISARGASANDHI.

§45. स् at the end of a word followed by any letter or not, the

---

* तश्छव्यप्रशान् । Pâṇ. VIII. 3. 7.

† छे च । Pân. VI. 1. 73. Properly त् is inserted, but it is changed to च् by § 28. आङ्माङोश्च । दीर्घात् । पदान्ताद्वा । Pan. VI. I. 74–76.

ष् of सजुष् and र् followed by a hard consonant or by nothing, are changed to a *Visarga*; as रामः पठति Ráma reads. पितर्=पितः Oh father. भ्रातुः कन्यका a brother's daughter.

§ 46. Visarga, followed by च्, छ्, ट्, ठ् and त्, थ्, themselves not followed by a sibilant, is changed to स्* e. g., विष्णुस्त्राता Vishṇu, the protector : हरिश्चरति, Hari walks: रामष्टीकते Râma goes; (Vide § 28); but कः त्सरुः (as the त् is followed by स्); and optionally when followed by श्, ष् or स् †; रामः स्थाता or रामस्स्थाता Râma who would stand; हरिः शेते or हरिश्शेते &c.

(*a*) Visarga, not belonging to an indeclinable is changed to स् when preceded by अ, and to ष् , when preceded by इ or उ, short or long, and followed by the terminations पाश, कल्प, क and काम्य ‡; e. g. पयस्पाशम् Bad milk: यशस्कल्पम् little short of fame; यशस्कम् with fame; यशस्काम्यति he desires fame; but प्रातःकल्पम् almost dawn (where प्रातः is an indec.); सर्पिष्पाशम् bad ghee, सर्पिष्कल्पम्, सर्पिष्कम्, सर्पिष्काम्यति. If the visarga, however, is a substitute for a final र्, it is not changed to स् before काम्य§; गीः काम्यति speech desires.

(*b*) ×The Visarga of नमः and पुरः when prefixed as indeclinables to verbs beginning with क् or ख् and प् or फ् is optionally changed to स् in the case of the former and necessarily in that of the latter e. g. नमस्करोति or नमः करोति, पुरस्करोति puts in the front; but पुरः प्रवेश्याः towns fit to be entered (as पुर् is a noun).

---

*विसर्जनीयस्य सः शर्परे विसर्जनीयः Pán. VIII. 3. 34–35.

† वा शरि । Pán. V. 3. 36.

‡ सोऽपदादौ । Pán. VIII. 3. 38. पाशकल्पककाम्येष्विति वाच्यम् । अनव्ययस्येति वाच्यम् । Vártikas. इणः षः Pân. VIII. 3. 39.

§ काम्ये रोरेवेति वाच्यम् । Várt.

× नमस्पुरसोर्गत्योः । Pân. VIII. 3. 40.

(c) *Visarga, preceded by इ or उ and not belonging to a termination, is changed to ष् except in the case of मुहुः; often, if followed by a hard consonant of the guttural of the labial class : निः+प्रत्यूहं=निष्प्रत्यूहम् without obstacle. आविष्कृतम् disclosed; दुष्कृतम् a bad action; but मुहुः कृतम्; अग्निः करोति as the Visarga is substituted for स् a term. so मातुः कृपा and not मातुष्कृपा. भ्रातुष्पुत्रः is an exception.

(d) †तिरस् optionally retains its स् when followed by क्, ख्, प्, or फ्; तिरः करोति or तिरस्करोति hides or scorns.

द्विः, त्रिः and चतुः; all of them adverbs showing frequency, change their Visarga to ष् optionally under the same circumstances‡; द्विष्करोति or द्विःकरोति does twice; but चतुष्कपालम् having four parts (where चतुः is not an adverb).

(e) § The ending इः or उः of a word changes its visarga to ष् optionally under the same circumstances when the presence of the following word is necessary for the completion of the sense; सर्पिष्करोति or सर्पिःकरोति turns into ghee; धनुष्करोति or धनुःकरोति makes a bow; but तिष्ठतु सर्पिः पिब त्वमुदकम्, as there is no connection here between the words सर्पिः and पिब.

And necessarily when at the end of the first member of a compound; as सर्पिष्कुण्डिका a pot for clarified butter; but परमसर्पिः कुण्डिका a big ghee-pot (as the word सर्पिः is an *uttara pada*).

(*f*) Visarga coming after the अ of a word other than an indeclinable and forming the first member of a compound is changed to स् when followed by a derivative of the roots कृ, कम्, and by कंस, कुंभ, पाश, कुशा and कर्णी × *e. g.* अयस्कारः an iron-smith; अयस्कामः one who desires iron; अयस्कंसम् an iron pot; अयस्पात्रम्: अयस्कुशा a bridle; अयस्कर्णी a kind of iron pot:

---

* इदुदुपधस्य चाप्रत्ययस्य Pân. VIII, 3. 41.

†तिरसोऽन्यतरस्याम् । Pân. VIII. 3. 42.

‡ द्विस्त्रिश्चतुरिति कृत्वोर्थे । Pân. VIII. 3. 43.

§ इसुसोः सामर्थ्ये । नित्यं समासेऽनुत्तरपदस्थस्य । Pân. VIII. 3. 44-45.

अतः कृकमिकंसकुम्भपात्रकुशाकर्णीष्वनव्ययस्य । Pân. VIII. 3. 46.

but गीःकारः Bṛhaspati; स्वःकामः one desiring heaven (where स्वर् is an indec.); यशः करोति (as there is no comp.); and परमयशःकारः producing great fame (as the word यशस् is not the first member of the com.).

(*g*) *The words अधः and शिरः change their visarga to स् when followed by पद् under the same circumstances as those mentioned above; अधस्पदम्, शिरस्पदम् but अधःपदं when there is no comp.; परमशिरः पदम् (as शिर is the latter member उत्तरपद).

§ 47. Visarga (substituted for स् and not र्) preceded by short अ and followed by short अ or a soft consonant is changed to उ; शिवः + अर्च्यः = शिव + उ + अर्च्यः = शिवो + अर्च्यः = शिवोर्च्यः Śiva is adorable; (see § 25); देवः + वन्द्यः = देवो वन्द्यः God should be saluted; but तिष्ठतु पय अं ३ ग्निदत्त (where the अ after पयः is *pluta*); प्रातः + अत्र = प्रातरत्र (for here the visarga is substituted for र्); so प्रातर्गच्छ &c.

§ 48. Visarga preceded by आ is dropped necessarily when followed by a soft consonant, and optionally when followed by a vowel; it is also optionally dropped when preceded by अ and followed by a vowel except अ; when it is not dropped it is changed to य् in both these cases; देवाः + नम्याः = देवा नम्याः; देवा + इह = देवा इह, देवायिह ।

§ 49. (*a*) Visarga, preceded by any vowel except अ or आ and followed by a vowel or soft consonant, is changed to र् : हरिः + जयति = हरिर्जयति Hari conquers; so भानुरुदेति the sun rises; गौरागच्छति a cow or bull comes.

Exception :—The Visarga of the particles भोः, भगोः and अघोः obeys § 48; *e. g.* भो + अच्युत = भो अच्युत or भोयच्युत Oh Achyuta; भगो नमस्ते Bhago ! a bow to thee; अघो याहि Oh you go.

(*b*) The न् of अहन्, not followed by a declensional termination, is always changed to र् but if followed by पति ‡ and other words such as गिर्, धुर् &c. the change is optional and if by रूप

---

* अधःशिरसी पदे । Pân. VIII. 3. 47.

‡ अहरादीनां पत्यादिषु वा रेफः । Vârt.

and रात्रि, visarga is substituted for it; अहः, अहरहः day by day; अहःपतिः or अहर्पतिः the lord of the day, the sun; गीर्पतिः or गीष्पतिः Bṛhaspati; धूर्पतिः or धूष्पतिः a leader; but अहोभ्याम् Inst. dual; अहोरूपम् the form of the day गतमहो रात्रिरेषा; अहोरात्रः day and night; अहोरथन्तरम् a protection of Śaman to be chanted by day.

(c) *र् or ढ् followed by र् or ढ् respectively is droppped, and the preceding अ, इ or उ if short is made long; पुनर् + रमते = पुना रमते sports again; हरिः + रम्य = हरिर् + रम्यः = हरी रम्यः Hari is graceful; but वृढ् + ढः = वृढः (form वृह् + त) p. p. of वृह् to grow.

§ 50. †(a) The स् of the nom. sing. of तद् and एतद् *mas.* is dropped before a consonant when they do not end in क or are not used in a negative Tatpurusha; *e. g.* स शंभुः; एष विष्णुः; but एषको रुद्रः this Rudra; असःशिवः that is not Śiva (a neg. Tat.); एषोऽत्र

(b) ‡ Sometimes in poetry the स् of सः and एषः is considered as not existing when followed by a vowel other than अ, so that the two vowels may combine in order to meet the exigencies of the metre; *e. g.* सेमामविड्ढि प्रभृतिं य ईशिषे &c. Ṛg. II. 24. I.

सैष दाशरथी रामः सैष राजा युधिष्ठिरः ।
सैष कर्णो महात्यागी सैष भीमो महाबलः ॥

Chapter III.

SUBANTA OR DECLENSION

§ 51. In the present chapter *Declension* or the inflection of nouns, substantive and adjective, is considered.

§ 52. The crude form of a noun (any declinable word) not yet inflected is technically called a Prâtipadika (प्रातिपदिक).

---

* रोरि । ढ्लोपे पूर्वस्य दीर्घोऽणः Pân. VIII. 3. 14. VI. 3. 111.

† एतत्तदोः सुलोपोऽकोरनञ्समासे हलि । ‡ सोचि लोपे चेत्पादपूरणम् । Pân. VI. 1. 132, 134.

§ 53. A noun has three genders: masculine gender (mas.), a feminine gender (fem.), and the neuter (neu.). The question about the determination of the gender of nouns will be considered in a separate chapter.

§ 54. There are three numbers:—Singular (sing.), dual (du.) and plural (pl.). The singular number denotes one, the dual two and the plural three or more.*

§ 55. There are eight cases in each number:—Nominative (Nom. or N.), Vocative (Voc. or V.), Accusative (Acc. or A.) Instrumental (Ins. or I.), Dative (Dat. or D.), Ablative (Abl. or Ab.), Genitive (Gen. or G.), and Locative (Loc or L.). These express nearly all relations between words in a sentence.

N. B. These genders, numbers and cases will, for the sake of convenience, be denoted by their abbreviations enclosed into brackets after each.

§ 56. Sup (सुप्†) is the technical term for a case termination in Sanskṛit. Declension consists in adding the case termination to the crude form or base.

---

* द्व्येकयोर्द्विवचनैकवचने । बहुषु बहुवचनम् । Pan. I. 4. 22. 21.

† The general terminations as given by Paṇini are—स्वौजसमौट्छष्टाभ्याम्भिस्ङेभ्याम्भ्यस्ङसिभ्याम्भ्यस्ङसोसाम्ङ्योस्सुप् । IV. 1. 2. *i. e.* Nom. सु ओ जस्; Acc. अम् औट् शस्; Ins. टा भ्याम् भिस्; Dat. ङे. भ्याम् भ्यस्; Ab ङसि भ्याम् भ्यस्; Gen. ङस् ओस् आम्, Loc. ङि ओस् सुप्. Some of these terminations, as in common with Paṇini's system of nomenclature, have certain *Its* (servile letters) added or prefixed to them; *e.g.* उ in सु, ऩ् in जस् &c. It will be easily seen that the term सुप् is obtained by taking the first letter and the last *It* in the sûtra.

§ 57. **The following are the normal case-terminations :—**

	Mas. and Fem.				*Neu.*		
	Sing.	Dual	Plural.		Sing.	Dual	Plural.
N. V.	स्	औ	अस्	N. A.	म्	ई	इ
A.	अम्	„	„	V.		„	„
I.	आ	भ्याम्	भिस्	The rest like the mas.			
D.	ए	„	भ्यस्				
Ab.	अस्	„	„				
G.	„	ओस्	आम्				
L.	इ	„	सु				

§ 58. The Vocative is considered to be a different aspect of the nom. and is identical with it in the dual and plural, It is, therefore, supposed to have no separate terminations of its own. In the sing. it sometimes coincides with the original stem, sometimes with the nom., at others, it differs from both.

DECLENSION OF NOUNS AND ADJECTIVES.

§ 59. Declension is for the sake of convenience divided into two classes:—

I. BASES ENDING IN VOWELS.

II. BASES ENDING IN CONSONANTS.

§ 60. The declension of adjectives does not, in general, differ from that of substantives. It will not, therefore, be given here separately; the points of difference only will be noted.

SECTION I.

1. BASES ENDING IN VOWELS.

Note:—The variations and modifications, which the general terminations given above undergo when applied to several of the vowel bases are so numerous, that it has been thought advisable not to notice them here, as being tedious, but simply to give the forms and leave the students to find them out for themselves. Every word declined here should be considered a model and words alike in form should be declined similarly to it.

Nouns ending in अ Mas. and Neu.

§ 61. राम *m*. Râma. ज्ञान *n*. knowledge.

	Sing.	Dual.	Plural.
N.	रामः	रामौ	रामाः
V.	राम	,,	,,
A.	रामम्	,,	रामान्
I.	*रामेण	रामाभ्याम्	रामैः
D.	रामाय	,,	रामेभ्यः
Ab.	रामात्	,,	,,
G.	रामस्य	रामयोः	रामाणाम्
L.	रामे	रामयोः	रामेषु

	Sing.	Dual.	Plural
N.	ज्ञानम्	ज्ञाने	ज्ञानानि
V.	ज्ञान	,,	,,
A.	ज्ञानम्	,,	,,

The rest like राम.

§ 62. Decline all nouns ending in अ mas. and neu. similarly.

(*a*) The Loc. sing. of words ending in अह्न (substituted for अहन् a day, at the end of a Tat. comp.) is optionally formed like that of nouns ending in न्; *e. g.* त्र्यह्न has त्र्यह्ने, त्र्यह्नि or त्र्यहनि. So व्यह्ने, व्यह्नि or व्यहनि &c. See p. 73.

Nouns ending in आ *Mas* and *Fem*.

§ 63. गोपा *mas*. a cow-herd.

(*a*) Mas. nouns ending in आ take the general terminations. The final आ is dropped before a vowel termination beginning with the Acc. plu.

---

* The न of इन is changed to ण by § 41. Ins. sing. of जन is जनेन.

N. V.	गोपाः	गोपौ	गोपाः
A.	गोपाम्	"	गोपः
I.	गोपा	गोपाभ्याम्	गोपाभिः
D.	गोपे	"	गोपाभ्यः
Ab.	गोपः	"	"
G.	"	गोपोः	गोपाम्
L.	गोपि	"	गोपासु

§ 64. Decline similarly विश्वपा the protector of the world, शंखध्मा a conch-shell-blower, सोमपा one who quaffs the some-juice, धूम्रपा one who inhales smoke, बलदा strength-giver or Indra, and other comp. nouns derived from roots ending in आ.

(*a*) If the latter member be not a root the final आ is not dropped; *e. g.* हाहा name of a Gandharva, Acc. plu. हाहान्; D. Ab. G. and L. sing. हाहै, हाहाः, हाहाः and हाहे respectively. The rest like गोपा.

§ 65. रमा *fem.* the goddess of wealth.

N.	रमा	रमे	रमाः
V.	रमे	"	"
A.	रमाम्	"	"
I.	रमया	रमाभ्याम्	रमाभिः
D.	रमायै	"	रमाभ्यः
Ab.	रमायाः	"	"
G	"	रमयोः	रमाणाम्
L.	रमायाम्	"	रमासु

§ 66. Decline all other *fem.* nouns ending in आ similarly.

§ 67. Irregular bases:—The Voc. sing. of अम्बा, अल्ला and अक्का, all meaning 'a mother' is अम्ब, अल्ल and अक्क respectively.

§ 68. Several adjectives ending in अ follow the declension of pronouns, for which see the chap. on pronouns.

Nouns ending in इ and उ mas. fem. and neu.

§ 69. हरि &c.—

हरि *mas.* Hari.

	Sing.	Dual.	Plural.
N.	हरिः	हरी	हरयः
V.	हरे	,,	,,
A.	हरिम्	,,	हरीन्
I.	हरिणा	हरिभ्याम्	हरिभिः
D.	हरये	,,	हरिभ्यः
Ab.	हरेः	,,	,,
G.	,,	हर्योः	हरीणाम्
L.	हरौ	,,	हरिषु

मति *fem.* intellec

	Sing.	Dual.	Plural.
N.	मतिः	मती	मतयः
V.	मते	,,	,,
A.	मतिम्	,,	मतीः
I.	मत्या	मतिभ्याम्	मतिभिः
D.	मतये or मत्यै	,,	मतिभ्यः
Ab.	मतेः or मत्याः	,,	,,
G.	मतेः or मत्याः	मत्योः	मतीनाम्
L.	मतौ or मत्याम्	,,	मतिषु

गुरु *mas.* preceptor.

N.	गुरुः	गुरू	गुरवः

V.	गुरो	गुरू	गुरवः
A.	गुरुम्	गुरू	गुरून्
I.	गुरुणा	गुरुभ्याम्	गुरुभिः
D.	गुरवे	,,	गुरुभ्यः
Ab.	गुरोः	,,	,,
G.	,,	गुर्वोः	गुरूणाम्
L.	गुरौ	,,	गुरुषु

धेनु *fem.* a cow.

N.	धेनुः	धेनू	धेनवः
V.	धेनो	,,	,,
A.	धेनुम्	,,	धेनूः
I.	धेन्वा	धेनुभ्याम्	धेनुभिः
D.	धेनवे, धेन्वै	,,	धेनुभ्यः
Ab.	धेनोः, धेन्वाः	,,	,,
G.	,, ,,	धेन्वोः	धेनूनाम्
L.	धेनौ, धेन्वाम्	,,	धेनुषु

वारि *neu.* water.

N.	वारि	वारिणी*	वारीणि
V.	वारे or वारि	,,	,,
A.	वारि	,,	,,
I.	वारिणा	वारिभ्याम्	वारिभिः
D.	वारिणे	,,	वारिभ्यः
Ab.	वारिणः	,,	,,
G.	वारिणः	वारिणोः	वारीणाम्
L.	वारिणि	,,	वारिषु

* इकोऽचि विभक्तौ । Pán. VII. 1. 73. Neu. nouns ending in इ, उ, ऋ or ऌ take the augment न् before vowel case terminations.

मधु *neu.* honey.

N.	मधु	मधुनी	मधूनि
V.	मधो or मधु	„	„
A.	मधु	„	„
I.	मधुना	मधुभ्याम्	मधुभिः
D.	मधुने	„	मधुभ्यः
Ab.	मधुनः	„	„
G.	„	मधुनोः	मधूनाम्
L.	मधुनि	„	मधुषु

§ 70. Adjectives ending in इ and उ when used with neuter nouns are optionully declined like mas. nouns in इ and उ in the Da. Ab. Gen. and Loc. singulars and Gen. Loc. duals; *e. g.* शुचि neu. white, pure; गुरु neu. heavy :—

शुचि *neu.*

N.	शुचि	शुचिनी	शुचीनि
V.	शुचि or शुचे	„	„
Ac.	शुचि	„	„
I.	शुचिना	शुचिभ्याम्	शुचिभिः
D.	शुचये or शुचिने	„	शुचिभ्यः
Ab.	शुचेः or शुचिनः	„	„
G.	„ „	शुच्योः or शुचिनोः	शुचीनाम्
L.	शुचौ or शुचिनि	„ „	शुचिषु

गुरु *neu.*

N.	गुरु	गुरुणी	गुरूणि
V.	गुरु or गुरो	„	„

Ac.	गुरु	गुरुणी	गुरूणि
I.	गुरुणा	गुरुभ्याम्	गुरुभिः
D.	गुरवे or गुरुणे	"	गुरुभ्यः
Ab.	गुरोः or गुरुणः	"	"
L.	" "	गुर्वोः, गुरुणोः	गुरूणाम्
L.	गुरौ or गुरुणि	" "	गुरुषु

§ 71. Decline all other nouns and adjectives ending in इ or उ mas. fem. and neu. similarly.

§ 72. Irregular bases :—

सखि *mas.* friend.

N.	सखा	सखायौ	सखायः
V.	सखे	"	"
A.	सखायम्	"	सखीन्
I.	सख्या	सखिभ्याम्	सखिभिः
D.	सख्ये	"	सखिभ्यः
Ab.	सख्युः	"	"
G.	"	सख्योः	सखीनाम्
L.	सख्यौ	"	सखिषु

Obs. (*a*) The words सुसखि a good friend (शोभनः सखा), अतिसखि a close friend (अतिशयितः सखा), परमसखि a great friend, or one having a great friend (परमः सखा यस्य, परमः सखा वा), are declined like सखि in the N. V. and A. and like हरि in other cases; but अतिसखि (सखीमतिक्रान्तः one who has abandoned a female companion) is declined like हरि. *N. B.* सखी fem. is declined like नदी.

पति *mas.* a master.

N.	पतिः	पती	पतयः
V.	पते	"	"
A.	पतिम्	"	पतीन्

I.	पत्या	पतिभ्याम्	पतिभिः
D.	पत्ये	,,	पतिभ्यः
Ab	पत्युः	,,	,,
G	,,	पत्योः	पतीनाम्
L.	पत्यौ	,,	पतिषु

§ 73 Compound nouns ending with पति such as भूपति &c. are declined like हरि regularly. प्रियत्रि (प्रियाः त्रयः यस्य यस्या वा) is declined like हरि mas. & मति fem.; the Gen. plu. is optionally like that of त्रि; परमत्रीणाम्, or ०त्रयाणाम्.

§ 74 *Obs.* (*a*) औडुलोमि a descendant of Uduloman (उडुलोम्नः अपत्यं पुमान्) is declined like हरि in the sing, and dual and like राम in the plural, the original word उडुलोम being substituted;* N. औडुलोमि. औडुलोमी, उडुलोमाः &c.

(*b*) Words of similar derivation (see Pân.. II. 4. 62. 63. 65. 66 and IV. 1. 105) also substitute their originals in the plural, *e. g.* गर्गस्य अपत्यं गार्ग्यः N. गार्ग्यः गार्ग्यौ गर्गाः &c.

Words ending in ई and ऊ mas. and fem.

§ 75. नदी *f.* a river; वधू *f.* a woman, a bride.

नदी *fem.*

N.	नदी	नद्यौ	नद्यः
V.	नदि	,,	,,
A.	नदीम्	,,	नदीः
I.	नद्या	नदीभ्याम्	नदीभिः
D.	नद्यै	,,	नदीभ्यः
Ab.	नद्याः	,,	,,

* From उडुलोमन् name of a sage, + इञ् (इ) added अपत्यार्थे by 'बाह्वादिभ्यश्च' Pân. IV. 1. 96, the final न् being dropped (Pân. VI. 4. 144).

G.	नद्याः	नद्योः	नदीनाम्
L.	नद्याम्	,,	नदीषु

Decline all other fem. nouns in ई similarly.

(*a*) The words अवी a woman in her monthly course, लक्ष्मी wealth, तरी a boat, स्तरी smoke, and तन्त्री a lute, do not drop the स् of the nom.* *e. g.* अवीः; लक्ष्मीः &c.

वधू *f*

N.	वधूः	वध्वौ	वध्वः
V.	वधु	,,	,,
A.	वधूम्	,,	वधूः
I.	वध्वा	वधूभ्याम्	वधूभिः
D.	वध्वै	,,	वधूभ्यः
Ab.	वध्वाः	,,	,,
G.	,,	वध्वोः	वधूनाम्
L.	वध्वाम्	,,	वधूषु

Decline श्वश्रू a mother-in-law, चमू an army, कर्कन्धू the jujube tree, कफेलू a phlegmatic woman, यवागू rice-gruel, चम्पू a class of compositions, and other feminine nouns in ऊ similary. अतिचमू mas. and fem. is declined like चमू except in the Acc. plu. mas. which is अतिचमून्.

§ 76. Mas. nouns ending in ई :—

वातं प्रमिमीते असौ वातप्रमीः 'an antelope as fleet as the wind; fr. वात + प्रमा + ई Uṇâdi IV. 1.—

N. V.	वातप्रमीः	वातप्रम्यौ	वातप्रम्यः
A.	वातप्रमीम्	,,	वातप्रमीन्
L.	वातप्रम्या	वातप्रमीभ्याम्	वातप्रमीभिः
D.	वतप्रम्ये	,,	वातप्रमीभ्यः
A. b.	वातप्रम्यः	,,	,,

* अवीतन्त्रीतरीलक्ष्मीधीह्रीश्रीणामुणादिषु । सप्तस्त्रीलिङ्गशब्दानां न सुलोपः कदाचन ॥

G	वातप्रम्यः	वातप्रम्योः	वातप्रम्याम्
L.	वातप्रम्ये	„	वातप्रमीषु

Decline (यान्ति अनेन इति) ययी a way or horse, (पाति लोकं इति) पपी the sun, &c. similarly.

Obs. Decline (बह्वयः श्रेयस्यः यस्य) बहुश्रेयसी mas. one having many good wives, and (लक्ष्मीम् अतिक्रान्तः) अतिलक्ष्मी mas. like नदी except in the Acc. plu. which is बहुश्रेयसीन् and अतिलक्ष्मीन् respectively. अतिलक्ष्मी fem. should be declined like लक्ष्मी.

The word वातप्रमी, derived with the affix क्विप्, is declined like प्रधी which see.

§ 77. Root nouns in ई or ऊ *M. F. N.*

Rule of *Sandhi*—(*a*) The ending इ or उ, short or long, of nouns derived from roots with the affix क्विप् (o) and of भ्रू, is changed to इय् or उव् before the vowel terminations*; the fem. nouns of this description are optionally declined like नदी in the Da. Ab. Gen. and Loc. singulars and the Gen. plu.

(*b*) But if the ending इ or उ of a many-voweled noun having a root at the end be not preceded by a radical conjunct consonant or the root noun has a preposition termed गति (*e. g.* as added to the root) or a word governed by the root preceding it, it is changed to य् or व्, except in the case of सुधी and nouns ending in भू†.

धी *fem.*				भू *fem.*			
N.	धीः	धियौ	धियः	N.	भूः	भुवौ	भुवः
V.	„	„	„	V.	„	„	„
A.	धियम्	„	„	V.	भुवम्	„	„

* अचि श्नुधातुभ्रुवां य्वोरियङुवङौ । Pân. VI. 4. 77.

† एरनेकाचोऽसंयोगपूर्वस्य । ओः सुपि Pân. VI. 4. 82. 83. गतिकारकेतरपूर्वपदस्य यण् नेष्यते । Vâr. न भूसुधियोः । Pân. VI. 4. 85.

I.	धिया	धीभ्याम्	धीभिः	I.	भुवा	भूभ्याम्	भूभिः
D.	धिये-यै	,,	धीभ्यः	D.	भुवे-वै	,,	भूभ्यः
Ab.	धियः-याः,	,,	,,	Ab.	भुवः-वाः	,,	,,
G.	,, ,,	धियोः	धियाम् / धीनाम्	G.	,, ,,	भुवोः	भुवाम् / भूनाम्
L.	धियि-याम्	,,	धीषु	L.	भुवि-वाम्	,,	भूषु

Decline similarly ह्री, श्री, सुश्री, सुधी, शुद्धधी, दुर्धी, भी, वृश्चिकभी, &c. Decline similarly सू, जू, सुभ्रू, भ्रू, सुभ्रू &c.

प्रधी *mas.* (प्रकृष्टं ध्यायति.)

N. V.	प्रधीः	प्रध्यौ	प्रध्यः
A.	प्रध्यम्	प्रध्यौ	प्रध्यः
I.	प्रध्या	प्रधीभ्याम्	प्रधीभिः
D.	प्रध्ये	,,	प्रधीभ्यः
Ab.	प्रध्यः	,,	,,
G.	,,	प्रध्योः	प्रध्याम्
L.	प्रध्यि	,,	प्रधीषु

Decline similarly वेगी (वेगं इच्छति), जलपी, उन्नी, ग्रामणी, सेनानी, &c. mas. and fem.; the Loc. sing. of nouns ending in नी is made up by adding आम्* e. g. उन्न्याम्, ग्रामण्याम्, सेनान्याम्, &c.

खलपू *mas.* (खलं पुनाति.)

N. V.	खलपूः	खलप्वौ	खलप्वः
A.	खलप्वम्	,,	,,
I.	खलप्वा	खलपूभ्याम्	खलपूभिः
D.	खलप्वे	,,	खलपूभ्यः
Ab.	खलप्वः	,,	,,
G.	,,	खलप्वोः	खलप्वाम्

* See * on page 45.

L खलप्वि खलप्वोः खलपुषु

Decline similarly लू (लुनाति), दृम्भू (the thunderbolt of Indra or the god of death), करभू, पुनर्भू, वर्षाभू, &c. mas. and mas. and fem.

प्रधि* *neu.* like वारि.			
N. A. प्रधि	प्रधिनी	प्रधीनि	
V. प्रधि-धे	„	„	

I. प्रध्या-धिना &c. optionally like the mas. before the vowel terminations.

खलपु† *neu.* like मधु.			
N. A. खलपु	खलपुनी	खलपूनि	
V. खलपो-पु	„	„	

I. खलप्वा-पुना &c. optionally like the mas. before the vowel terminations.

प्रधी *fem. mas.*

(प्रकृष्टा धीः fem. प्रकृष्टा धीर्यस्याः यस्य वा fem. mas.)

Voc. sing., Da. Ab. Gen. and Loc. sings. Gen. plu. like नदी; the rest like प्रधी mas.; *e. g.*

N.	प्रधीः	प्रध्यौ	प्रध्यः
V.	प्रधि	„	„
A.	प्रध्यम्	„	„
I.	प्रध्या	प्रधीभ्याम्	प्रधीभिः
D.	प्रध्यै	„	प्रधीभ्यः
Ab.	प्रध्याः	„	„
G.	„	प्रध्योः	प्रधीनाम्
L.	प्रध्याम्	„	प्रधीषु

Decline similarly कुमारी (कुमारीम् इच्छतीति कुमारीव आचरतीति वा) except in the Nom. sing. which is कुमारी.

---

* ङेराम्नद्याम्नीभ्यः । Pân. VII. 3. 116. आम् is subsituted for the loc. sing. in the case of words ending in नदी, आ and the word नी.

† ह्रस्वो नपुंसके प्रातिपदिकस्य । Pân. I. 2. 47. A *prátipadika* ending in a long vowel has a short vowel substituted for it when becoming neu.

सुधी (सुष्टु ध्यायति) *m.* and *f.* also according to Kaiyata.

N. V.	सुधीः	सुधियौ	सुधियः
A.	सुधियम्	,,	,,
I.	सुधिया	सुधिभ्याम्	सुधिभिः
D.	सुधिये	,,	सुधिभ्यः
Ab.	सुधियः	,,	,,
G.	,,	सुधियोः	सुधियाम्
L.	सुधियि	,,	सुधीषु

Decline similarly सुश्री, शुद्धधी, परमधी, नी &c. mas. and fem. The L. sing. of नी is नियाम्.

स्वभू *mas.* (स्वेन भवति) self-existent.

N. V.	स्वभूः	स्वभुवौ	स्वभुवः
A.	स्वभुवम्	,,	,,
I.	स्वभुवा	स्वभूभ्याम्	स्वभूभिः
D.	स्वभुवे	,,	स्वभूभ्यः
Ab.	स्वभुवः	,,	,,
G.	,,	स्वभुवोः	स्वभुवाम्
L.	स्वभुवि	,,	स्वभूषु

Decline similarly स्वयंभू, परमलू, (परमश्चासौ लूश्च) दृग्भू, काराभू &c. mas. and mas. and fem.

सुधि *neu.* like वारि.

N. A.	सुधि	सुधिनी	सुधीनि
V.	सुधि-धे	,,	,,

I. सुधिया-सुधिना &c. optionally like the mas before the vowel terminations. G. Dual सुधियोः-नोः.

N. A.	स्वभु	स्वभुनी	स्वभूनि
V.	स्वभु-भो	,,	,,

I. सुभुवा-ना &c. optionally like the mas. before the vowel termination.

वर्षाभू *fem.*

N.	वर्षाभूः	वर्षाभ्वौ	वर्षाभ्वः
V.	वर्षाभु	"	"
A.	वर्षाभ्वम्	"	वर्षाभ्वः
I.	वर्षाभ्वा	वर्षाभूभ्याम्	वर्षाभूभिः
D.	वर्षाभ्वै	"	वर्षाभूभ्यः
Ab.	वर्षाभ्वाः	"	"
G.	"	वर्षाभ्वोः	वर्षाभूणाम्
L.	वर्षाभ्वाम्	"	वर्षाभूषु

Decline similarly प्रसू, वीरसू, पुनर्भू a widow remarried; &c.

§ 78. *Obs.* (सखायमिच्छतीति) सखी; (सह खेन वर्तते इति सखः, तमिच्छतीति) सखी; (सुतमिच्छतीति) सुती; (सुखमिच्छतीति) सुखी, (लूनमिच्छतीति) लूनी, (क्षाममिच्छतीति) क्षामी; (प्रस्तीममिच्छतीति) प्रस्तीमी &c:—

सखी (सखायमिच्छतीति).

N.	सखा	सखायौ	सखायः
V.	सखीः	"	"
A.	सखायम्	"	सख्यः
I.	सख्या	सखीभ्याम्	सखीभिः
D.	सख्ये	"	सखीभ्यः
Ab.	सख्युः	"	"
G.	"	सख्योः	सख्याम्
L.	सख्यि	"	सखीषु

सखी (सखयमिच्छतीति)

N. V.	सखीः	सख्यौ	सख्यः
A.	सख्यम्	"	"

The rest like the other सखी. Decline similary सखी, सुती, लूनी, क्षामी, प्रस्तीमी &c.

Words like शुष्की, पक्की should be declined like सुधी.

§ 79. **स्त्री** *fem*, a woman.*

N.	स्त्री	स्त्रियौ	स्त्रियः	D. स्त्रियै	स्त्रीभ्याम्	स्त्रीभ्यः
V.	स्त्रि	,,	,,	Ab. स्त्रियाः	,,	,,
A.	स्त्रियम्-स्त्रीम्	,,	,, स्त्रीः	G. स्त्रियाः	स्त्रियोः	स्त्रीणाम्
I.	स्त्रिया	स्त्रीभ्याम्	स्त्रीभिः	L. स्त्रियाम्	,,	स्त्रीषु

Obs. अतिस्त्रि *m. n. f.*

mas.

N.	अतिस्त्रिः	अतिस्त्रियौ	अतिस्त्रियः
V	अतिस्त्रि	,,	,,
H.	अतिस्त्रियम्-अतिस्त्रिम्	,,	अतिस्त्रियः-अतिस्त्रीन्
I.	अतिस्त्रिणा	अतिस्त्रिभ्याम्	अतिस्त्रिभिः
D.	अतिस्त्रये	,,	अतिस्त्रिभ्यः
Ab.	अतिस्त्रेः	,,	,,
G.	,,	अतिस्त्रियोः	अतिस्त्रीणाम्
L.	अतिस्त्रौ	,,	अतिस्त्रिषु

fem.

Acc. plu. अतिस्त्रियः अतिस्त्रीः; the I. D. Ab. G. and L. singulars, अतिस्त्रिया, अतिस्त्रियै—त्रये, अतिस्त्रियाः—त्रेः--अतिस्त्रियाः—त्रेः; अतिस्त्रियाम्—स्त्रौ respectively; the rest like the mas.

neu

Like शुचि except in the Gen. and Loc. duals forms which are अतिस्त्रियोः—णोः.

§ 80. Mas. words ending in ऊ not derived from roots; *e. g.* हूहू name of a *Gandharva*.

N. V.	हूहूः	हूह्वौ	हूह्वः
A.	हूहूम्	,,	हूहून्
I.	हूह्वा	हूहूभ्याम्	हूहूभिः
D.	हूह्वे	,,	हूहूभ्यः
Ab.	हूह्वः	,,	,,

* स्त्रियाः । वाम्शसोः । Pân. VI. 4. 79. 80.

G.	हूह्वः	हूह्वोः	हूह्वाम्
L.	हूह्वि	,,	हूहूषु

Decline similarly दृम्भू (दृम्भति इति one who strings together).

Nouns ending in ऋ *mas. fem.* and *neu.*

§ 81. Nouns derived from roots with the affix तृ (तृच् and तृन् Pán. III. 1. 133. and 2. 135), such as कर्तृ a maker, &c. and the words स्वसृ *f*, नप्तृ, नेष्टृ, क्षत्तृ, होतृ, पोतृ, and प्रशास्तृ as also उद्गातृ change their ऋ to आ in the Nom. sing. and to आर् in the first five inflections. The ऋ is lengthened in the Acc. and Gen. pl. and changed to उर् before the Ab. and Gen. sing; the Voc. sing. ends in अर्.

धातृ *mas.* the creator.

N.	धाता	धातारौ	धातारः
V.	धातः (र्)	,,	,,
A.	धातारम्	,,	धातॄन्
I.	धात्रा	धातृभ्याम्	धातृभिः
D.	धात्रे	,,	धातृभ्यः
Ab.	धातुः	,,	,,
G.	,,	धात्रोः	धातॄणाम्
L.	धातरि	धात्रोः	धातृषु

Decline similarly कर्तृ, नेतृ, नप्तृ, शास्तृ, उद्गातृ &c

धातृ *neu*

A.	धातृ	धातृणी	धातॄणि
V.	धातः-तृ	,,	,,
A.	धातृ	,,	,,
I.	धात्रा-तृणा	धातृभ्याम्	धातृभिः
D.	धात्रे-तृणे	,,	धातृभ्यः

* अप्तृन्तृच्स्वसृनप्तृनेष्टृत्वष्टृक्षत्तृहोतृपोतृप्रशास्तॄणाम् । Pán. VI. 4. 11. उद्गातृशब्दस्य भवत्येव समर्थसूत्रे ' उद्गातारः ' इति भाष्यप्रयोगात् । Sid. Kau.

Ab.	धातुः-तृणः	धातृभ्याम्	धातृभ्यः
G.	,,	धात्रोः-तृणोः	धातॄणाम्
L.	धातरि	,,	धातृषु

Decline similarly कर्तृ, नेतृ, ज्ञातृ, &c.

स्वसृ and other fem. nouns should be declined like धातृ except in the Acc. plu. which is स्वसॄः. See below.

§ 82. Nouns expressive of relationship like पितृ *m.* a father, मातृ *f.* a mother, देवृ *m.* a husband's brother, &c. with the exception of नप्तृ a grandson, भर्तृ a husband and स्वसृ a sister, as also the words शंस्तृ one who praises (Un. II. 92), नृ a man (Un. II. 98) and सव्येष्टृ a charioteer, do not change their ऋ to आर् in the N. dual and plural and Acc. sing. and dual; *e. g.*

N.	पिता	पितरौ	पितरः
V.	पितः(र्)	,,	,,
A.	पितरम्	,,	पितॄन्

The rest like धातृ.

Decline similarly भ्रातृ, जामातृ, देवृ, शंस्तृ, सव्येष्टृ and... नृ. The Gen. plu. of नृ is नृणाम् or नॄणाम्*

N.	माता	मातरौ	मातरः
V.	मातः(र्)	,,	,,
A.	मातरम्	,,	मातॄः

The rest like स्वसृ

Decline similarly यातृ a husband's brother's wife, दुहितृ a daughter, and ननान्दृ or ननन्दृ a husband's sister.

§ 83. The word क्रोष्टु a jackal, is declined like a word ending in ऋ necessary in the first five inflections and optionally before the vowel terminations beginning with the Inst. sing. except that of the Gen. plu.‡ *e. g.*

---

* नृ च । Pân. VI. 4. 9. नृ इत्येतस्य नामि वा दीर्घः स्यात् । Sid. Kau.

† नञि च नन्देः । Un. II 97 न नन्दति ननान्दा । इह वृद्धिर्नानुवर्तते इत्येके । 'ननन्दा तु स्वसा पत्युर्ननन्दा नन्दिनी च सा' इति शब्दार्णवः । Sid. Kau

‡ तृज्वत्क्रोष्टुः विभाषा तृतीयादिष्वचि । Pân. VII. I. 95. 97.

N.	क्रोष्टा	क्रोष्टारौ	क्रोष्टारः
V.	क्रोष्टो	,,	,,
A.	क्रोष्टारम्	,,	क्रोष्टून्
I.	क्रोष्ट्रा-ष्टुना	क्रोष्टुभ्याम्	क्रोष्टुभिः
D.	क्रोष्ट्रे-ष्टवे	,,	क्रोष्टुभ्यः
Ab.	क्रोष्टुः-क्रोष्टोः	,,	,,
G.	,,	क्रोष्ट्रोः-ष्ट्वोः	क्रोष्टूनाम्
L.	क्रोष्टरि-ष्टौ	,,	क्रोष्टुषु

(*a*) क्रोष्टु becomes क्रोष्टृ in the *fem.* also (by स्त्रियां च Pân. VIII. 1. 96.) which with the *fem.* term. ई becomes क्रोष्ट्री and is declined like नदी.

Obs.—The word प्रियक्रोष्टु *neu.* is declined like मधु and optionally like क्रोष्टु *mas.* before the vowel terminations from the I. sing.; *e. g.* D. sing. प्रियक्रोष्ट्रे-ष्टवे-ष्टुने.

Words ending in ॠ and ऌ.

§ 84. There are no words ending in ॠ or ऌ; therefore, the imitative sounds of the roots कॄ and तॄ and गम्ऌ and शक्ऌ are taken to show what the forms of such words will be, if there be need to use such words.

कॄ *m.*

N. V.	कीः, कॄः	किरौ, क्रौ	किरः, क्रः
A.	किरम्, कॄम्	,,	किरः, कॄन्
I.	किरा, क्रा	कीर्भ्याम्, कॄभ्याम्,	कीर्भिः, कॄभिः
D.	किरे, क्रे	,,	कीर्भ्यः, कॄभ्यः
Ab.	किरः, क्रुः	,,	,,
G.	,,	किरोः, क्रोः	किराम्, क्राम्
L.	किरि, क्रि	,,	कीर्षु, कॄषु

Decline तॄ similarly.

गम्लृ *m.*

N.	गमा	गमलौ	गमलः
V.	गमल्	,,	,,
A.	गमलम्	,,	गमॄन्
I.	गम्ला	गम्लृभ्याम्	गम्लृभिः
D.	गम्ले	,,	गम्लृभ्यः
Ab.	मसुल्	,,	,,
G.	,,	गम्लोः	गमॄणाम्
L.	गमलि	,,	गम्लृषु

Decline शक्लृ similarly.

Words ending in ए and ऐ.

§ 85. Here simply the terminations should be added and *Sandhi* rules observed.

से (सह इना कामेन वर्ततेऽसौ)

N.	सेः	सयौ	सयः
V.	से*	,,	,,
A.	सयम्	,,	,,
I.	सया	सेभ्याम्	सेभिः
D.	सये	,,	सेभ्यः
Ab.	सेः	,,	,,
G.	,,	सयोः	सयाम्
L.	सयि	,,	सेषु

रै *m. f.* wealth.

N. V.	राः	रायौ	रायः
A.	रायम्	,,	,,
I.	राया	राभ्याम्	राभिः
D.	राये	,,	राभ्यः
Ab.	रायः	,,	,,
G.	,,	रायोः	रायाम्
L.	रायि	,,	रासु

*The Kau. does not specially mention this form. Just as it stops after giving the Nom. forms in the case of words like रै, गो, स्मृतो &c., so does it do in the case of से also, implying thereby that the Voc. forms of से are also like the Nom. ones. But the Sutra एङ्ह्रस्वात्संबुद्धेः Páṇ. VI. 1. 69 (एङन्तात् ह्रस्वान्ताच्च अङ्गात् हल् लुप्यते सम्बुद्धेः चेत्) (Kau.) seems to apply in the present case and by dropping the final स् we get the form से.

Decline similarly स्मृते (स्मृतः तत्) one who has thought of *Káma*.

The neu. प्ररै (प्रकृष्टा रै यस्य) changed to प्ररि (by एच इग्घ्रस्वादेशे Pán. I. 1. 48. and I. 2. 47.) should be declined like वारि except before the consonantal terminations, when it should be declined like रै *m. f.*

N. A.	प्ररि	प्ररिणी	प्ररीणि
I.	प्ररिणा	प्रराभ्याम्	प्रराभिः &c.

Words ending in ओ and औ.

§ 86. Vṛiddhi (औ) is substituted for the ओ of words ending in ओ in the first five inflections except the Acc. sing.; आ is substituted for ओ in the Acc. sing. and plural.* Nouns ending in औ are regularly declined.

गो *mas. fem.* a bull or a cow.

N. & V	गौः	गावौ	गावः
A.	गाम्	,,	गाः
I.	गवा	गोभ्याम्	गोभिः
D.	गवे	,,	गोभ्यः
Ab.	गोः	,,	,,
G.	,,	गवोः	गवाम्
L.	गवि	,,	गोषु

Decline similarly स्मृतो (स्मृतः उः शंकरः येन) and द्यो *f.* the sky. The neu. प्रद्यो (प्रकृष्टा द्यौः यस्मिन् तत्) changed to प्रद्यु should be declined like मधु.

ग्लौ *mas.* the moon.

N. & V.	ग्लौः	ग्लावौ	ग्लावः
A.	ग्लावम्	,,	,,
I.	ग्लावा	ग्लौभ्याम्	ग्लौभिः
D.	ग्लावे	,,	ग्लौभ्यः
Ab.	ग्लावः	,,	,,
G.	,,	ग्लावोः	ग्लावाम्
L.	ग्लावि	,,	ग्लौषु

Decline similarly नौ *f.* a boat, a ship. The neu. सुनौ (सुष्ठु नौः यस्मिन्) changed to सुनु should be declined like मधु.

---

* गोतो णित् । औतोऽम्शसोः । Pán. VII. 1. 90. VI. 1. 93.

SECTION II.

BASES ENDING IN CONSONANTS.

§ 87. Bases ending in any of the first four letters of a class, and in ण्, र्, ल्, श्, ष्, स् and ह्. The declension of these bases consists, for the most part, in adding the general case terminations and observing the rules of *sandhi*.

§ 88. Bases ending र्, ल्, and ण्.

§ 89. (*a*) After final ल् the सु of the loc. is changed to षु.

(*b*) ट्(optionally changeable to ट्) may be optionally inserted between ण् and सु.

कमल् *mas. fem. neu.* naming the goddess of wealth or a lotus (कमलं कमलां वा आचक्षाणाः—णा-णं-वा)—

Mas. and *Fem.*

N. & V.	कमल्*	कमलौ	कमलः
A.	कमलम्	,,	,,
I.	कमला	कमल्भ्याम्	कमल्भिः
D.	कमले	,,	कमल्भ्यः
Ab.	कमलः	,,	
G.	,,	कमलोः	कमलाम्
L.	कमलि	,,	कमल्षु

Decline similarly सुगण्, सुगाण्, *m.f.* one who counts well, द्वार् *f.* a door and other words ending in र् or ल्. The loc. plu. of सुगण् is सुगण्सु-ण्ट्सु,-ण्ट्सु. The Nom. sing. of द्वार् is द्वाः.

Neu.

N. N. & A.	कमल्	कमली	कमलि

The rest like the mas.

---

* See § 91. *a*.

Decline similarly सुगण्, वार् and other words ending in ण्, र् or न्. e. g.

N. A.	वाः	वारी	वारि
I.	वारा	वार्भ्याम्	वार्भिः
L.	वारि	वारोः	वार्षु

§ 90. Bases ending in क्, ख्, ग्, घ्, ट्, ठ्, ड्, ढ्, त्, थ्, द्, ध्, and प्, फ्, ब्, भ्.

§ 91. (a) As a general rule the स् of the nom. singular is dropped. If there be a conjunct consonant at the end of a word the first consonant only is retained.

(b) The final letter is changed to the first or third of its class when followed by nothing, to the third when followed by a soft consonant and first when followed by a hard consonant and remains unchanged before a vowel termination.

(c) न् is prefixed to the इ of the N. & Acc. plural in the case of neuter nouns ending in a consonant except a nasal or a semi-vowel; but not in the case of a noun derived from the frequentative base.

§ 92. Paradigms :—

समिध् *f.* a holy stick.

N. & V.	समित्	समिधौ	समिधः	Ab.	समिधः	समिद्भ्याम्	समिद्भ्यः
A.	समिधम्	,,	,,	G.	,,	समिधोः	समिधाम्
In.	समिधा	समिद्भ्याम्	समिद्भिः	L.	समिधि	,,	समित्सु
D.	समिधे	,,	समिद्भ्यः				

Neu. सुसमिध् (शोभनाः समिधः यस्मिन्)

N. V. A. सुसमित् सुसमिधी सुसमिन्धि

The rest like समिध् *f.*

Decline similarly सर्वशक्, चित्रलिख्, भूभृत्, मरुत्, सरित्, हरित्, विश्वजित्, अग्निमथ्, तमोनुद्, दृषद्, शरद्, वेभिद्, चोरिच्छिद्, सुबुध्, क्षुध्, गुप्, ककुभ् &c.; *e. g.*

	Nom. sing.	Nom. dual.	I. dual.	Loc. plu.
सर्वशक्	सर्वशक्-ग्	सर्वशकौ	सर्वशग्भ्याम्	सर्वशक्षु
चित्रलिख्	चित्रलिक्-ग्	चित्रलिखौ	चित्रलिग्भ्याम्	चित्रलिक्षु
भूभृत्	भूभृत्-द्	भूभृतौ	भूभृद्भ्याम्	भूभृत्सु
अग्निमथ्	अग्निमत्-द्	अग्निमथौ	अग्निमद्भ्याम्	अग्निमत्सु
तमोनुद्	तमोनुत्-द्	तमोनुदौ	तमोनुद्भ्याम्	तमोनुत्सु
गुप्	गुप्-ब्	गुपौ	गुब्भ्याम्	गुप्सु

Neu.

N. V. A.			N. V. A.		
सर्वशक्	सर्वशकी	सर्वशङ्कि	अग्निमत्	अग्निमथी	अग्निमन्थि
हरित्	हरिती	हरिन्ति	तमोनुद्	तमोनुदी	तमोनुन्दि
सुयुत्	सुयुधी	सुयुन्धि	बेभित्	बेभिदी	बेभिदि

The rest like the mas. So चेच्छिदि N. V. A. pl. &c.

§ 93. Bases ending in च्, छ्, ज्, or झ् and श्, ष्, ह्.

§ 94. (*a*) च् or ज् is changed to क् when followed by a hard consonant or by nothing, and to ग् when followed by a soft consonant.*

(*b*) The ending श् or छ् of root-nouns and the final of व्रश्च्, भ्रस्ज्, सृज्, मृज्, यज्, राज्, and भ्राज् are changed to ष् when followed by any consonant except a nasal or a semi-vowel or by nothing†; the ष् is changed to ट् or ड् when at the end of a word, and to ड् when followed by a soft consonant. The ज् of परिव्राज् is similarly changed to ट् or ड्.

(*c*) But the श् of the root-nouns दिश्, दृश्, स्पृश् and मृश् is changed to क् as also the ष् of दधृष् 'a bold or impudent man' and the क्ष् of such words as विपक्ष् &c The श् of नश् is optionally changed to ट् or क्, as also the क्ष् of तक्ष् and गोरक्ष्. The ज् of ऋत्विज् is changed to क्.

---

* चोः कुः । Pán. VIII. 2. 30. † व्रश्चभ्रस्जसृजमृजयजराजभ्राजच्छशां षः । Pân. VIII. 2. 36.

(*d*) त् may optionally be inserted between ड् and the loc. pl. term. सु.

(*e*) Before vowel terminations final छ् may optionally be changed to श्.

§ 95. (*a*) ह् is changed to ढ् when at the end of a *pada* or when followed by a consonant except a nasal or a semi-vowel. (*b*) In the case of roots beginning with द् it is changed to घ् under the same circumstances; (*c*) when forming part of the roots द्रुह्, मुह्, स्नुह् and स्निह्, it is optionally changed to घ् *i. e.* to ढ् or घ्; (*d*) and in the case of the root नह् it is changed to ध् under the above-mentioned circumstances.*

(*e*) The ह् of उष्णिह् *f.* a kind of metre is changed to क् when followed by a hard consonant or by nothing, and to ग् before a soft consonant (Pán. III. 2. 59).

§ 96. When a mono-syllabic root (or root-noun) begins with ब्, ग् or द् and ends with घ्, ढ्, ध्, भ् or ह्, the ब्, ग् or द् is respectively changed to भ्, घ् or ध् before स् or ध्व् or when followed by nothing or when the final soft aspirate is changed to an unaspirate letter†.

§ 97. Paradigms—वाच् *f.* speech, राज् shining, मुह् becoming faint &c.

वाच्				राज्		
N. V.	वाक्	वाचौ	वाचः	N. V.	राट्-ड्	राजौ	राजः
A.	वाचम्	,,	,,	A.	राजम्	,,	,,
I.	वाचा	वाग्भ्याम्	वाग्भिः	I.	राजा	राड्भ्याम्	राड्भिः
D.	वाचे	,,	वाग्भ्यः	D.	राजे	,,	राड्भ्यः
Ab.	वाचः	,,	,,	A.	राजः	,,	,,

* हो ढः । दादेर्धातोर्घः । वा द्रुहमुहष्णुहष्णिहाम् । नहो धः । Pán. VIII. 2. 31–34.

† एकाचो बशो भष् झषन्तस्य स्ध्वोः । Pán. VIII. 2. 37.

G.	वाचः	वाचोः	वाचाम्	G.	राजः	राजोः	राजाम्
L.	वाचि	„	वाक्षु	L.	राजि	राजोः	राट्सु-ट्त्सु

Decline similarly पयोमुच्, ऋत्विज्, भिषज्, रुज्, स्रज्, सुयुज्, विभ्राज्,* दिश्, दृश् and words ending in दृश्, स्पृश्, दधृष्, उष्णिह्, विपक्ष्, विचक्ष्, दिधक्ष्, विविक्ष्, and words ending in च् and ज्.

Decline similarly सुवृश्च्, सर्वप्राश्, भृज्ज्, विश्वसृज्, सम्राज्, परिव्राज्, परिमृज्, देवेज्, विभ्राज् the sun, त्विष्, प्राश्, त्विष्, द्विष्, मुष्, प्रावृष्, लिह्; प्रच्छ्, and root nouns in छ्, श्, ष् and ह्.

E. g.

	N. Sing.	N. dual	I. dual.	Loc. plu.
पयोमुच्	पयोमुक्†	पयोमुचौ	पयोमुग्भ्याम्	पयोमुक्षु
भिषज्	भिषक्	भिषजौ	भिषग्भ्याम्	भिषक्षु
स्रज्	स्रक्	स्रजौ	स्रग्भ्याम्	स्रक्षु
दृश्	दृक्	दृशौ	दृग्भ्याम्	दृक्षु
दधृष्	दधृक्	दधृषौ	दधृग्भ्याम्	दधृक्षु
उष्णिह्	उष्णिक्	उष्णिहौ	उष्णिग्भ्याम्	उष्णिक्षु
विविक्ष्	विविक्	विविक्षौ	विविग्भ्याम्	विविक्षु
	&c.	&c.	&c.	
सुवृश्च्	सुवृट्-ड्	सुवृश्चौ	सुवृड्भ्याम्	सुवृट्सु-ट्त्सु
सर्वप्राच्छ्-श्	सर्वप्राट्	सर्वप्राच्छौ-शौ	सर्वप्राड्भ्याम्	सर्वप्राट्सु-ट्त्सु
भृज्ज्	भृट्	भृज्जौ	भृड्भ्याम्	भृट्सु
विश्वसृज्	विश्वसृट्	विश्वसृजौ	विश्वसृड्भ्याम्	विश्वसृट्सु

---

* भ्राज् derived from भ्राजृ mentioned along with एजृ &c. यस्तु एजृभ्रेजृभ्राजृदीप्ताविति तस्य कुत्वमेव । Sid. Kau. The other विभ्राज् is derived from टुभ्राजृ दीप्तौ mentioned in the फणादि group.

† Hereafter only the first letter will be given, the third letter should always be supposed to be understood.

N. Sing.	N. dual.		I. dual.	Loc. plu.
देवेज्	देवेट्	देवेजौ	देवेड्भ्याम्	देवेट्सु-ट्त्सु
विश्	विट्	विशौ	विड्भ्याम्	विट्सु ,,
त्विष्	त्विट्	त्विषौ	त्विड्भ्याम्	त्विट्सु ,,
प्रच्छ्	प्रट्	प्रच्छौ	प्रड्भ्याम्	प्रट्सु ,,
लिह्	लिट्	लिहौ	लिड्भ्याम्	लिट्सु ,,

Irregular base :—युज् N. V. युङ् युञ्जौ युञ्जः A. युञ्जम् युञ्जौ युजः the rest like सुयुज्.

मुह् *mas.*

N.	मुक्-ट्	मुहौ	मुहः
A.	मुहम्	,,	,,
I.	मुहा	मुग्भ्याम्, मुड्भ्याम्	मुग्भिः, मुड्भिः
D.	मुहे	,,	मुग्भ्यः, मुड्भ्यः
Ab.	मुहः	,,	,,
G.	,,	मुहोः	मुहाम्
L.	मुहि	,,	मुक्षु or मुट्सु or ट्त्सु

Decline similarly स्निह्; स्नुह्, नश्; तक्ष्, गोरक्ष् and द्रुह् &c.—

	N. sing.	N. dual.	Instr. dual.	Loc. plu.
स्निह्	स्निक्-ट्	स्निहौ	स्निग्भ्याम्-ड्भ्याम्	स्निक्षु-ट्सु or ट्त्सु
स्नुह्	स्नुक्-ड्	स्नुहौ	स्नुग्भ्याम्-स्नुड्भ्याम्	स्नुक्षु-ट्सु or ,,
नश्	नक्-ट्	नशौ	नग्भ्याम्-ड्भ्याम्	नक्षु-ट्सु or ,,
तक्ष्	तक्-ट्	तक्षौ	तग्भ्याम्-ड्भ्याम्	तक्षु-ट्सु or ,,
गोरक्ष्	गोरक्-ट्	गोरक्षौ	गोरग्भ्याम्-ड्भ्याम्	गोरक्षु-ट्सु or ,,
द्रुह्	ध्रुक्-ट्	द्रुहौ	ध्रुग्भ्याम्-ड्भ्याम्	ध्रुक्षु-ट्सु or ,,
दुह्	धुक्	दुहौ	धुग्भ्याम्	धुक्षु
गुह्	घुट्	गुहौ	घुड्भ्याम्	घुट्सु or ट्त्सु
बुध्	भुत्	बुधौ	भुद्भ्याम्	भुत्सु

Neu.

The neu. forms of these have no peculiarities other than those mentioned above; *e. g.*

N. V. A.

घृतस्पृक्	घृतस्पृशी	घृतस्पृंशि	स्रुक्-ट्	स्रुही	स्रुंहि
सत्यवाक्	सत्यवाची	सत्यवाञ्चि	भुज्	भुजी	भुञ्जि
लिट्	लिही	लिंहि	दधृक्	दधृषी	दधृंषि
विश्वसृट्	विश्वसृजी	विश्वसृञ्जि	प्राट्	प्राच्छी or प्राशी	प्राञ्छि or प्राञ्शि

The remaining forms like those of the *mas.* or *fem.*

IRREGULAR BASES.

§ 98. (1) The स् of तुरासाह् 'Indra' is changed to ष् before the consonantal terminations;* *e. g.*

N. V. तुराषाट् तुरासाहौ तुरासाहः I. तुरासाहा तुराषाड्भ्याम् तुराषाड्भिः
A. तुरासाहम् „ „ L. तुरासाहि तुरासाहोः तुराषाट्सु-ट्त्सु

§ 99. विश्व becomes विश्वा when followed by राट्† (that particular form of the root-noun राज्)—

N. V.	विश्वाराट्	विश्वराजौ	विश्वराजः
A.	विश्वराजम्	„	„
I.	विश्वराजा	विश्वाराड्भ्याम्	विश्वाराड्भिः
L.	विश्वराजि	विश्वराजोः	विश्वाराट्सु-ट्त्सु

§ 100. The वा of root-nouns ending in वाह् is changed to ऊ before the vowel terminations beginning with the Acc. plu.‡; *e. g.* विश्ववाह् *m* the sustainer of the universe, a lord :—

---

* Pân. VIII. 3. 56.

† विश्वस्य वसुराटोः । Pâṇ. VI. 3. 128.

‡ वाह ऊठ् । सम्प्रसारणाच्च । Pân. VI. 4. 132. VI. 1. 108. आ and ऊ combine into औ by Pân. VI. 1. 89. See § 20.

N. V.	विश्ववाट्-ड्	विश्ववाहौ	विश्ववाह
A.	विश्ववाहम्	,,	विश्वौह
I.	विश्वौहा	विश्ववाड्भ्याम्	विश्ववाड्भि
D.	विश्वौहे	,,	विश्ववाड्भ्य
Ab.	विश्वौह	,,	,,
G.	,,	विश्वौहो:	विश्वौहाम्
L.	विश्वौहि	,,	विश्ववाट्सु

Decline similarly हव्यवाह्, भारवाह्, भूवाह्, श्वेतवाह् &c. The Acc. plu., Inst. sing. &c. of भूवाह्, are भूहः, भूहा &c.

§ 101. The ह् of उपानह् *f.* 'a shoe' is changed to त् before स् and to द् before the भ् of the termination; *e. g.* Nom. उपानत्. उपानहौ, उपानहः, Ins. sing. and dual उपानहा, उपानद्भ्याम्; Loc. उपानहि, उपानहोः, उपानत्सु.

§ 102 अनडुह् *m.* an ox.

N.	अनड्वान्	अनड्वाहौ	अनड्वाहः
V.	अनड्वन्	,,	,,
A.	अनड्वाहम्	,,	अनडुहः
I.	अनडुहा	अनडुद्भ्याम्	अनडुद्भिः
D.	अनडुहे	,,	अनडुद्भ्यः
Ab.	अनडुहः	,,	,,
G.	,,	अनडुहोः	अनडुहाम्
L.	अनडुहि	,,	अनडुत्सु:

स्वनडुह् *neu.* (शोभनः अनड्वान् यस्मिन्)

N. V. A.	स्वनडुत्	स्वनडुही	स्वनड्वांहि

The rest like अनडुह् *mas.*

§ 103. The words अवयाज् 'a kind of priest' and पुरोडाश 'sacrificial food' change their final to स् before consonantal terminations the preceding आ becoming अ:—

अवयाज्.

N. V.	अवयाः	अवयाजौ	अवयाजः
A.	अवयाजम्	,,	,,
I.	अवयाजा	अवयोभ्याम्	अवयोभिः
L.	अवयाजि	अवयाजोः	अवयस्सु

पुरोडाश्.

N. V.	पुरोडाः	पुरोडाशौ	पुरोडाशः
A.	पुरोडाशम्	,,	,,
I.	पुरोडाशा	पुरोडोभ्याम्	पुरोडोभिः
L.	पुरोडाशि	पुरोडाशोः	पुरोडस्सु

Bases derived from the root अञ्च् 'to go' to worship.

§ 104. Nouns derived form the root अञ्च् ' to go ' by means of such affixes as क्विन्, क्विप् &c. such as प्राञ्च् (प्रा-अञ्च्) eastern, प्रत्यञ्च् (प्रति-अञ्च्) western, सम्यङ् (सह-अञ्च्) a companion, तिर्यञ्च् (तिरस्-अञ्च्) going away, सम्यञ्च् (सम्-अञ्च्) going with or well, विष्वञ्च् (विष्वञ्च्-अञ्च्) following, देवद्र्यञ्च् (देव-अञ्च्)adoring a deity, सर्वद्र्यञ्च् (सर्व-अञ्च्) going everywhere, उदञ्च् northen,, अन्वञ्च् following, उदद्र्यञ्च्, अदमुयञ्च्, अमुमुयञ्च् going to that (all these derived from अदस्+अञ्च्), गोअञ्च् &c.

(*a*) In the Nom sing. अञ्च् becomes अङ्. The nasal of अञ्च् is dropped before all terminations beginning with the Acc. plu. and the preceding semi-vowel is changed to its corresponding long vowel before the vowel terminations after which अ is dropped. When अञ्च् is not preceded by a semi-vowel, its अ is changed to ई if not preceded by a long vowel; otherwise it remains unchanged. तिर्यञ्च् becomes तिरश्च् under similar circumstances. In other respects these words are declined like words ending in च्.

प्राञ्च् *mas.*

N. V.	प्राङ्	प्राञ्चौ	प्राञ्चः
A.	प्राञ्चम्	प्राञ्चौ	प्राचः
I.	प्राचा	प्राग्भ्याम्	प्राग्भिः
D.	प्राचे	„	प्राग्भ्यः
Ab.	प्राचः	„	„
G.	„	प्राचोः	प्राचाम्
L.	प्राचि	„	प्राक्षु

प्रत्यञ्च् *mas*

N. V.	प्रत्यङ्	प्रत्यञ्चौ	प्रत्यञ्चः
A.	प्रत्यञ्चम्	„	प्रतीचः
I.	प्रतीचा	प्रत्यग्भ्याम्	प्रत्यग्भिः
D.	प्रतीचे	„	प्रत्यग्भ्यः
Ab.	प्रतीचः	„	„
G.	„	प्रतीचोः	प्रतीचाम्
L.	प्रतीचि	„	प्रत्यक्षु

तिर्यञ्च् *mas.*

N. V.	तिर्यङ्	तिर्यञ्चौ	तिर्यञ्चः
A.	तिर्यञ्चम्	„	तिरश्चः
I.	तिरश्चा	तिर्यग्भ्याम्	तिर्यग्भिः
L.	तिरश्चि	तिरश्चोः	तिर्यक्षु

The forms of the rest should be similarly made up; *e. g.*

N. sing.	N. plu.	A. plu.	Inst. duel.	Loc. plu.
सध्र्यङ्	सध्र्यञ्चः	सध्रीचः	सध्र्यग्भ्याम्	सध्र्यक्षु
सम्यङ्	सम्यञ्चः	समीचः	सम्यग्भ्याम्	सम्यक्षु
विष्वङ्	विष्वञ्चः	विषूचः	विष्वग्भ्याम्	विष्वक्षु
देवद्र्यङ्	देवद्र्यञ्चः	देवद्रीचः	देवद्र्यग्भ्याम्	देवद्र्यक्षु

उदङ्	उदञ्चः	उदीचः	उदग्भ्याम्	उदक्षु
अन्वङ्	अन्वञ्चः	अनूचः	अन्वग्भ्याम्	अन्वक्षु
अदद्र्यङ्	अदद्र्यञ्चः	अदद्रीचः	अदद्र्यग्भ्याम्	अदद्र्यक्षु
अदमुयङ्	अदमुयञ्चः	अदमुईचः	अदमुयग्भ्याम्	अदमुयक्षु
गवाङ्	गवाञ्चः	गोचः	गवाग्भ्याम्	गवाक्षु
गोअङ्	गोअञ्चः	,,	गोअग्भ्याम्	गोअक्षु
गोङ्	गोञ्चः	,,	गोग्भ्याम्	गोक्षु

Neu.

The neu. forms should be similarly made up.

N. V. A.	प्राक्	प्राची	प्राञ्चि
	प्रत्यक्	प्रतीची	प्रत्यञ्चि
	तिर्यक्	तिरश्ची	तिर्यञ्चि
	सध्र्यक्	सध्रीची	सध्र्यञ्चि
	सम्यक्	समीची	सम्यञ्चि
	विष्वक्	विषूची	विष्वञ्चि
	देवद्र्यक्	देवद्रीची	देवद्र्यञ्चि
	उदक्	उदीची	उदञ्चि
	अन्वक्	अनूची	अन्वञ्चि
	अदद्र्यक्	अदद्रीची	अदद्र्यञ्चि
	अदमुयक्	अदमुईची	अदमुयञ्चि
	गवाक्	गोची	गवाञ्चि
	गोअक्	,,	गोअञ्चि
	गोक्	,,	गोञ्चि

The rest like the mas.

(*b*) When अञ्च् means 'to worship' or 'honour' the nasal of अञ्च् is not dropped and these words are regularly declined. * They drop their final च् only before the consonantal terminations; *e. g.*

---

* नाञ्चेः पूजायाम् । Pán. VI. 4. 30.

N. V.	प्राङ्	प्राञ्चौ	प्राञ्चः
A.	प्राञ्चम्	"	"
I.	प्राञ्चा	प्राङ्भ्याम्	प्राङ्भिः
D.	प्राञ्चे	"	प्राङ्भ्यः
&c. &c.			
L.	प्राञ्चि	प्राञ्चोः	प्राङ्षु or प्राङ्क्षु

तिर्यञ्च् *m.*

N. V.	तिर्यङ्	तिर्यञ्चौ	तिर्यञ्चः
A.	तिर्यञ्चम्	"	"
I.	तिर्यञ्चा	तिर्यङ्भ्याम्	तिर्यङ्भिः
&c. &c.			
L.	तिर्यञ्चि	तिर्यञ्चोः	तिर्यङ्षु or तिर्यङ्क्षु

The rest should be similarly declined.

Neu.

N. V. A.	तिर्यङ्	तिर्यञ्ची	तिर्यञ्चि

Irregular Bases.

§ 105. कुञ्च् a heron &c. (derived from क्रुञ्च् कौटिल्याल्पीभावयोः), खञ्ज् a lame man, and सुवल्ग् beautifully bounding become क्रुङ्, खन् and सुवल् before consonantal terminations; *e. g.*

N. sing.	N. dual	I. dual.	Loc. plu.
क्रुङ्	क्रुञ्चौ	क्रुङ्भ्याम्	क्रुङ्क्षु or षु
खन्	खञ्जौ	खन्भ्याम्	खन्सु
सुवल्	सुवल्गौ	सुवल्भ्याम्	सुवल्सु

The remaining froms should be similarly made up.

Neu.

N. V. A.	क्रुङ्	क्रुञ्ची	क्रुञ्चि
	खन्	खञ्जी	खञ्जि

The rest like the mas.

§ 106. ऊर्ज् *m.* *n.* strength, is regularly declined; *e. g.* *m.* ऊर्क्-ग् ऊर्जौ ऊर्जः N.; ऊर्जा ऊर्भ्याम् ऊर्भिः I.; ऊर्जि ऊर्जोः ऊर्क्षु L.

Neu.

N. V. A. ऊर्क् ऊर्जी ऊर्ञ्जि; *the rest like the *mas.*
with बहु— बहूर्क् बहूर्जी बहुर्जि or बहूर्ञ्जि †

§ 107. Nouns ending in म्. There are a few nouns derived from the roots ending in म्. They have no other peculiarity than this, that they change their म् to न् before consonantal terminations, *e. g.* प्रशाम् *m. f.* one who is tranquil.

N.	प्रशान्	प्रशामौ	प्रशामः
A.	प्रशामम्	"	"
I.	प्रशामा	प्रशान्भ्याम्	प्रशान्भिः
L.	प्रशामि	प्रशामोः	प्रशान्सु or प्रशांसु

Neu.

N. V. A.	प्रशाम्	प्रशामी	प्रशामि

The rest like the *mas.*

Bases ending in स् :—

§ 108. The penultimate अ of nouns ending in स् is lengthened in the Nom. sing. if it does not belong to root nouns.‡

चन्द्रमस् *m.* the moon.

N.	चन्द्रमाः	चन्द्रमसौ	चन्द्रमसः
V.	चन्द्रमः	"	"
A.	चन्द्रमसम्	चन्द्रमसौ	चन्द्रमसः

* नरजानां संयोगः । Sid. Kau. †बहूर्जि नुम्प्रतिषेधः । अन्त्यात्पूर्वो वा नुम् । Vârt.

‡ अत्वसन्तस्य चाधातोः । Pân. VI. 4. 14. The penultimate vowel of nouns ending in मत् or वत् and in अस् not belonging to a root is lengthened when followed by सु (स्) not belonging to the Vocative

I.	चन्द्रमसा	चन्द्रमोभ्याम्	चन्द्रमोभिः
D.	चन्द्रमसे	„	चन्द्रमोभ्यः
Ab.	चन्द्रमसः	„	„
G.	„	चन्द्रमसोः	चन्द्रमसाम्
L.	चन्द्रमसि	„	चन्द्रमःसु-स्सु

Decline similarly वेधस् god Brahmā, सुमनस् good-minded, दुर्मनस् ill-minded, उन्मनस् anxious-hearted &c.

मनस् *neu.* the mind.

N. V. A.	मनः	मनसी	मनांसि

The rest like चन्द्रमस्.

Decline similarly पयस्, milk, वयस् age, अवस् protection, fame &c. श्रेयस् good, सरस्, वचस्, &c.

(*a*) Nouns in इस्, उस् or ओस् such as उदर्चिस् flaring upwards अचक्षुस् blind, दीर्घायुस् long-living, दोस् an arm &c. are similarly declined; *e. g.*

	N. sing.	N. dual.	I. sing.	I. dual.	Loc. plu.
उदर्चिस्	उदर्चिः	उदर्चिषौ	उदर्चिषा	उदर्चिर्भ्याम्	उदर्चिष्षु-ःषु
अचक्षुस्	अचक्षुः	अचक्षुषौ	अचक्षुषा	अचक्षुर्भ्याम्	अचक्षुष्षु-ःषु
दीर्घायुस्	दीर्घायुः	दीर्घायुषौ	दीर्घायुषा	दीर्घायुर्भ्याम्	दीर्घायुष्षु-ःषु
दोस्	दोः	दोषौ	दोषा	दोर्भ्याम्	दोष्षु-ःषु

Neu.

N. V. A.	उदर्चिः	उदर्चिषी	उदर्चींषि
	अचक्षुः	अचक्षुषी	अचक्षूंषि
	दोः	दोषी	दोंषि

Decline similarly ज्योतिस् lustre, हविस् an oblation, चक्षुस् the eye, धनुस् a bow, &c.

सुवस् (सुष्ठु वस्ते) one who wears a garment well.

Mas.			*Neu.*		
N. सुवः	सुवसौ	सुवसः	N. V. A. सुवः	सुवसी	सुवंसि
The rest like चन्द्रमस्.			The rest like मनस्.		

Decline similarly पिण्डग्रस्, पिण्डग्लस् &c.

§ 109. The Nom. sing. of अनेहस् time, पुरुदंसस् name of Indra, and उशनस् name of Śukrâchârya is अनेहा, पुरुदंसा and उशना respectively; the Voc. sing. of उशनस् is उशनन, उशन. and उशनः; the other forms are regular.

§ 110. To feminine nouns ending in स् simply add the terminations.

भास् *f.* splendour.

N.	भाः	भासौ	भासः
I.	भासा	भाभ्याम्	भाभिः
L.	भासि	भासोः	भास्सु:

§ 111. *Obs.* The शा of उक्थशास् uttering hymns, becomes श before the consonantal terminations, except that of the Nom. sing., *e. g.* Nom. उक्थशाः sing. उक्थशासौ dual.; Instr. sing. उक्थशासा; dual उक्थशोभ्याम्; Loc. plu. उक्थशःसु-स्सु.

Irregular bases.

§ 112. स्रस् that falls, ध्वस् a destroyer, सुहिंस् one who kills well, जिघांस् desirous of killing. The first two change their स् to त् before consonantal terminations while the last two change their स् to न् under the same circumstances, the preceding nasal being dropped.

Mas.

	N. V. sing.	N. V. dual.	I. sing.	I. dual.	Loc. plu.
स्रस्	स्रत्	स्रसौ	स्रसा	स्रद्भ्याम्	स्रत्सु
ध्वस्	ध्वत्	ध्वसौ	ध्वसा	ध्वद्भ्याम्	ध्वत्सु
सुहिंस्	सुहिन्	सुहिंसौ	सुहिंसा	सुहिन्भ्याम्	सुहिन्सु-न्त्सु
जिघांस्	जिघान्	जिघांसौ	जिघांसा	जिघान्भ्याम्	जिघान्सु-न्त्सु

The remaining forms should be similarly made up by adding the terminations.

Neu.

N. V. A.	स्रत ध्वत सुहिन्	स्रसी ध्वसी सुहिंसी	स्रंसि ध्वंसि सुहिंसि

The remaining forms like those of the *mas*.

§ 113.

पुम्स् *m.* a man.

N.	पुमान्	पुमांसौ	पुमांसः
V.	पुमन्	"	"
A.	पुमांसम्	पुमांसौ	पुंसः
I.	पुंसा	पुम्भ्याम्	पुंभिः
D.	पुंसे	पुम्भ्याम्	पुम्भ्यः
Ab.	पुंसः	"	"
G.	पुंसः	पुंसोः	पुंसाम्
L.	पुंसि	"	पुंसु

Neu.

सुपुम्स् (शोभनः पुमांसः यस्मिन्).

N. V. A.	सुपुम्	सुपुंसी	सुपुमांसि

The rest like the *mas*.

§ 114. The penultimate इ or उ of the words पिपठिष् wishing to read, सजुष् *m. f.* a companion, चिकीर्ष् wishing to do, सुपिस् one stepping well, आशिष् *f.* a blessing, सुतुस्, cutting well, and also of गिर्, speech, धुर् a yoke, पुर् a town all *fem.* is lengthened before consonantal terminations; their final is changed to *visarga* in the Nom. Sing. *e. g.* पिपठिष्—

N. V.	पिपठीः	पिपठिषौ	पिपठिषः
A.	पिपठिषम्	पिपठिषौ	पिपठिषः
I.	पिपठिषा	पिपठीर्भ्याम्	पिपठीर्भिः
D.	पिपठिषे	पिपठीर्भ्याम्	पिपठीर्भ्यः
L.	पिपठिषि	पिपठिषोः	*पिपठीष्षु-ःषु

* नुम्विसर्जनीयशर्व्यवायेपि । Pán. VIII. 3. 58. The स् belonging to a term. coming after इ or उ, short or long, and after a guttural letter, is changed to ष् even when either a nasal, or a visarga or श्, ष् or स् intervenes.

The remaining forms should be similarly made up by adding the terminations. सजुष् and the following words should be similarly declined.

	N. sing.	N. dual.	I. sing.	I. dual.	Loc. Plu.
सजुष् *f*	सजूः	सजुषौ	सजुषा	सजूर्भ्याम्	सजूष्षु-ःषु
चिकीर्ष्	चिकीः	चिकीर्षौ	चिकीर्षा	चिकीर्भ्याम्	चिकीर्षु
सुपिस्	सुपीः	सुपिसौ	सुपिसा	सुपीर्भ्याम्	सुपीष्षु-ःषु
आशिष्	आशीः	आशिषौ	आशिषा	आशीर्भ्याम्	आशीष्षु-ःषु
सुतुस्	सुतूः	सुतुसौ	सुतुसा	सुतूर्भ्याम्	सुतूष्षु-ःषु
गिर् *f*	गीः	गिरौ	गिरा	गीर्भ्याम्	गीर्षु
धुर् *f*	धूः	धुरौ	धुरा	धूर्भ्याम्	धूर्षु
पुर् *f*	पूः	पुरौ	पुरा	पूर्भ्याम्	पूर्षु

Neu.

N. V. A.	पिपठीः	पिपाटिषी	पिपठीषि
	चिकीः	चिकीर्षी	चिकीर्षि
	सुपीः	सुपिसी	सुपिंसि
	सुतूः	सुतुसी	सुतुंसि

The remaining forms like those of the mas. or fem.

Nouns ending in अत्, मत्, and वत् :—

§ 115. अ is lenthened in the Nom. sing.*, and न् is inserted between अ and the final त् in the first five inflections. The final त् is dropped in the Nom. sing.; the अ of महत् is lengthened before this न् except in the Voc. sing.

धीमत् *mas.* talented.

N.	धीमान्	धीमन्तौ	धीमन्तः
V.	धीमन्	,,	,,
A.	धीमन्तम्	धीमन्तौ	धीमतः

* See ft. note p. 66

I.	धीमता	धीमद्भ्याम्	धीमद्भिः
D.	धीमते	"	धीमद्भ्यः
Ab.	धीमतः	"	"
G.	धीमतः	धीमतोः	धीमताम्
L.	धीमति	"	धीमत्सु

Neu.

N. V. A. धीमत् धीमती धीमन्ति

The rest like the mas.

Decline similarly गोमत् having cows, विद्यावत्, श्रीमत् बुद्धिमत् भगवत् मघवत् m. Indra, भवत् *pron.*, यावत्, तावत्, एतावत्, कियत्, इयत्

महत् *mas.* great.

N.	महान्	महान्तौ	महान्तः
V.	महन्	"	"
A.	महान्तम्	महान्तौ	महतः

The rest like धीमत्.

Neu.

N. V. A. महत् महती महान्ति The rest like the mas.

§ 116. Participial bases ending in अत् :—

(*a*) The declension of these does not differ from that of nouns in मत् except in the Nom. sing. mas. in which the अ of अत् is not lengthened. In the case of the dual of the Nom. Voc. and the Acc. neu. न् is inserted before the final त् necessarily in the case of the present participles of the roots of the 1st. 4th, and 10th classes, and of causal, desiderative and nominal verbs, optionally in the case of those of the 6th class, of roots ending in आ of the 2nd class, and of those of the Fut. in स्यत् or ष्यत्, and not at all in the case of the remaining participles of the present tense.

भवत् being.			अदत् eating.		
mas.			*mas.*		
N. V. भवन्	भवन्तौ	भवन्तः	N. V. अदन्	अदन्तौ	अदन्तः
A. भवन्तम्	„	भवतः	A. अदन्तम्	„	अदतः
The rest like धीमत्			The rest like धीमत्.		

Decline all other participles of the Present and Fu. Par. in the *mas.* similarly.

N. V. A. *Neu.*

भवत्—भवद्	भवन्ती	भवन्ति	The rest like the *mas.*
अदत्—अदद्	अदती	अदन्ति	
यात्—याद्	याती-न्ती	यान्ति	
दास्यत्—दास्यद्	दास्यती-न्ती	दास्यन्ति	
तुदत्—तुदद्	तुदती-न्ती	तुदन्ति	

Decline पचत्, दीव्यत्, चोरयत्, चिकीर्षत्, बुबोधिषत्, पुत्रीयत् &c., like भवत्; करिष्यत् &c. like तुदत्; सुन्वत्, तन्वत्, रुन्धत्, क्रीणत्, &c., like अदत्.

N. B. The *fem.* of these ends in ई being the same as Nom. dual of the Neu. and has no declensional peculiarities.

Decline बृहत् *m. n.* great, पृषत् *m.* a deer; *n.* a drop of water and जगत् the world, like अदत् *mas.* & *neu.*

(*b*) न् is not inserted at all in the case of the participle of the Pre. of roots of the third class and of the Parasm. frequentative and the participles शासत्, जक्षत्, चकासत्, दरिद्रत्, जाग्रत्, दीध्यत् and वेव्यत्; in the case of the Nom. Voc. and Acc. plu. neu., however, it is optionally inserted :—

mas.

ददत् giving.			जाग्रत् awaking.		
N. V. ददत्	ददतौ	ददतः	जाग्रत्	जाग्रतौ	जाग्रतः
A. ददतम्	„	„	जाग्रतम्	„	„
&c.			&c.		

neu.

N. V. A. ददत् ददती ददन्ति-ति जाग्रत् जाग्रती जाग्रन्ति-ति
The rest like भवत्.

Nouns ending in अन् and इन्.

§ 117. न् is dropped in the Nom. sing. and before all consonantal terminations. In the case of *mas.* nouns the preceding अ is lengthened in the first five inflections and इ in the Nom. sing. only. The अ and इ are lengthened in the plu. of the Nom. Voc. and Acc. of neuter nouns. The अ is dropped before the vowel terminations beginning with that of the Acc. plu. except when it is preceded by a conjunct consonant having म् or व् for its latter member; it is optionally dropped in the Loc. sing. of mas. and neuter nouns and optionally in the Nom. Voc. and Acc. dual of the latter.

In the Voc. sing. the न् of *neu.* nouns is optionally retained.

Nouns ending in अन्.

ब्रह्मन् *mas.* the creator.

N.	ब्रह्मा	ब्रह्माणौ	ब्रह्माणः
V.	ब्रह्मन्	,,	,,
A.	ब्रह्माणम्	ब्रह्माणौ	ब्रह्मणः
I.	ब्रह्मणा	ब्रह्मभ्याम्	ब्रह्मभिः
D.	ब्रह्मणे	ब्रह्मभ्याम्	ब्रह्मभ्यः
Ab.	ब्रह्मणः	,,	,,
G.	,,	ब्रह्मणोः	ब्रह्मणाम्
L.	ब्रह्मणि	,,	ब्रह्मसु

Decline similarly आत्मन् the self, यज्वन् a sacrificer, सुशर्मन्, कृष्णवर्मन् &c.

राजन् *mas.* a king.

N.	राजा	राजानौ	राजानः
V.	राजन्	,,	,,
A.	राजानम्	,,	,,

I.	राज्ञा	राजभ्याम्	राजभिः
D.	राज्ञे	,,	राजभ्यः
Ab.	राज्ञः	,,	,,
G.	,,	राज्ञोः	राज्ञाम्
L.	राज्ञि-राजनि	,,	राजसु

Decline similarly सीमन् *fem.* a boundary, तक्षन् a carpenter, मज्जन् *m.* marrow, गरिमन् greatness, महिमन्, लघिमन्, अणिमन् &c., सुनामन् auspicious-named, दुर्नामन्, प्रतिदिवन् a day or the sun (दि of the word is lengthened when the अ is dropped), &c.

E. g.

	Nom. sing.	Acc. plu.	Loc. sing.
सीमन्	सीमा	सीम्नः	सीम्नि-मनि
तक्षन्	तक्षा	तक्ष्णः	तक्ष्णि-क्षणि
मज्जन्	मज्जा	मज्ज्ञः	मज्ज्ञि-ज्जनि
गरिमन्	गरिमा	गरिम्णः	गरिम्णि-मणि
महिमन्	महिमा	महिम्नः	महिम्नि-मनि
लघिमन्	लघिमा	लघिम्नः	लघिम्नि-मनि
अणिमन्	अणिमा	अणिम्नः	अणिम्नि-मनि
सुनामन्	सुनामा	सुनाम्नः	सुनाम्नि-मनि
प्रतिदिवन्	प्रतिदिवा	प्रतिदीव्नः	प्रतिदीव्नि-दिवनि

neu.

N. V.	ब्रह्म	ब्रह्मणी	ब्रह्माणि
V.	ब्रह्म-न्	,,	,,

The rest like the mas.

Decline similarly चर्मन् a hide, वर्मन् an armour, भर्मन् a house, old &c., शर्मन् happiness, नर्मन् sport, jest, जन्मन्, पर्वन् a joint-&c.

नामन् *neu.*

N.	नाम	नामनी-नाम्नी	नामानि
V.	नाम-न्	,,	,,
A.	नाम	,,	,,
I.	नाम्ना	नामभ्याम्	नामभिः
D.	नाम्ने	नामभ्याम्	नामभ्यः
Ab.	नाम्नः	,,	,,
G.	,,	नाम्नोः	नाम्नाम्
L.	नाम्नि-मनि	,,	नामसु

Decline similarly व्योमन् the sky, क्लोमन् the bladder, प्रेमन् love, सामन् a hymn, धामन् lustre, a house, &c.

Irregular Bases.

§ 118. पूषन्, अर्यमन् and nouns ending in हन् lengthen their अ in the Nom. sing. only; the न् of हन् is changed to ण् after ह्; *e. g.*

पूषन् *mas.*, the sun.

N.	पूषा	पूषणौ	पूषणः
V.	पूषन्	,,	,,
A.	पूषणम्	,,	पूष्णः
I.	पूष्णा	पूषभ्याम्	पूषभिः
D.	पूष्णे	,,	पूषभ्यः
Ab.	पूष्णः	,,	,,
G.	,,	पूष्णोः	पूष्णाम्
L.	पूष्णि-षणि	,,	पूषसु

वृत्रहन् *mas.*, 'name of Indra'.

N.	वृत्रहा	वृत्रहणौ	वृत्रहणः
V.	वृत्रहन्	,,	,,
A.	वृत्रहणम्	,,	वृत्रघ्नः
I.	वृत्रघ्ना	वृत्रहभ्याम्	वृत्रहभिः

D.	वृत्रघ्ने	वृत्रहभ्याम्	वृत्रहभ्यः
Ab.	वृत्रघ्नः	,,	,,
G.	वृत्रघ्नः	वृत्रघ्नोः	वृत्रघ्नाम्
L.	वृत्रघ्नि-वृत्रहणि	,,	वृत्रहसु

अर्यमन् *m.* name of a deity.

N.	अर्यमा	अर्यमणौ	अर्यमणः
V.	अर्यमन्	,,	,,
A.	अर्यमणम्	अर्यमणौ	अर्यम्णः
	&c.	&c.	&c.

Neu.

बहुपूषन्, बह्वर्यमन् बहुवृत्रहन् :—

N. V. A.	बहुपूषन्	बहुपुष्णी-षणी	बहुपूषाणि
	बह्वर्यमन्	बह्वर्यम्णी-मणी	बह्वर्यमाणि
	बहुवृत्रहन्	बहुवृत्रघ्नी-हणी	बहुवृत्रहाणि

§ 119. The व of श्वन् *mas.* 'a dog,' युवन् *mas.* 'a young man,' and मघवन् *mas.* 'name of Indra' is changed to उ before the vowel terminations beginning with that of the Acc. plu.*

श्वन्.

N.	श्वा	श्वानौ	श्वानः
V.	श्वन्	,,	,,
A.	श्वानम्	,,	शुनः
I.	शुना	श्वभ्याम्	श्वभिः
D.	शुने	श्वभ्याम्	श्वभ्यः
Ab.	शुनः	,,	,,
G.	,,	शुनोः	शुनाम्
L.	शुनि	,,	श्वसु

* श्वयुवमघोनामतद्धिते । Pán. VI. 4. 133.

मघवन् *m.*

N.	मघवा	मघवानौ	मघवानः
V.	मघवन्	„	„
A.	मघवानम्	„	मघोनः
I.	मघोना	मघवभ्याम्	मघवभिः
&c.	&c.		
L.	मघोनि	मघोनोः	मघवसु

युवन्.

N.	युवा	युवानौ	युवानः
V.	युवन्	„	„
A.	युवानम्	„	यूनः
I.	यूना	युवभ्याम्	युवभिः
&c.	&c.		
L.	यूनि	यूनोः	युवसु

Neu.

बहुश्वन्, बहुयुवन्.

N. V. A.	बहुश्व*	बहुशुनी	बहुश्वानि
	बहुयुव*	बहुयुनी	बहुयुवानि

The rest like the mas.

§ 120. अहन् *n.* meaning 'a day' changes its final to र् (and finally to *visarge*) when followed by consonantal terminations or by nothing; in other cases it is declined like नामन्.

N. V. A.	अहः	अह्नी, अहनी	अहानि
I.	अह्ना	अहोभ्याम्	अहोभिः
D.	अह्ने	„	अहोभ्यः
Ab.	अह्नः	„	„

* Also the optional forms in न् in the Voc. sing.

G.	अह्नः	अह्नोः	अह्नाम्
L.	अह्नि-हनि	„	अहस्सु-ःसु

Obs :—दीर्घाहन् when *mas.* is declined like चन्द्रमस् when it takes the consonantal terminations and like राजन् when it takes the vowel terminations; when *neu.* it is declined like अहन्.

N.	दीर्घाहाः	दीर्घाहाणौ*	दीर्घाहाणः
V.	दीर्घाहः	„	„
A.	दीर्घाहाणम्	„	दीर्घाह्नः
I.	दीर्घाह्ना	दीर्घाहोभ्याम्	दीर्घाहोभिः
D.	दीर्घाह्ने	„	दीर्घाहोभ्यः
Ab.	दीर्घाह्नः	„	„
G.	दीर्घाह्नः	दीर्घाह्नोः	दीर्घाह्नाम्
L.	दीर्घाह्नि	„	दीर्घाहस्सु

Neu.

N. V. A. दीर्घाहः दीर्घाहणी-दीर्घाह्नी दीर्घाहाणि

The rest like the *mas.*

§ 121. अर्वन् *m.* a horse, except when preceded by the negative particle अन् (forming a neg. Tat.) is declined like a word ending in त् in all cases except the Nom. and Voc. singulars; *e. g.* N. अर्वा अर्वन्तौ अर्वन्तः; V. अर्वन् अर्वन्तौ, अर्वन्तः; A. अर्वन्तम्, अर्वन्तौ, अर्वतः &c. But अनर्वन् (न विद्यतेऽर्वास्य) is regularly declined like यज्वन्; अनर्वा अनर्वाणौ &c.

स्वर्वन् *neu.* is declined as स्वर्वत् स्वर्वती स्वर्वन्ति Nom. Voc. Acc.; the rest like अर्वन् *mas.*

§ 122. Words ending in इन्—

---

* The न् may be optionally retained (दीर्घाहानौ &c.) by Pán. VIII. 4. 11.

करिन् *mas.* an elephant

N.	करी	करिणौ	करिणः
V.	करिन्	"	"
A.	करिणम्	"	"
I.	करिणा	करिभ्याम्	करिभिः
D.	करिणे	"	करिभ्यः
Ab.	करिणः	"	"
G.	"	करिणोः	करीणाम्
L.	करिणि	"	करिषु

Decline similarly शशिन् the moon, दण्डिन् one having a stick, धनिन् a wealthy man, हस्तिन् an elephant, स्रग्विन् one having a garland, आततायिन् and all other words in इन्.

दण्डिन् *neu.*

N. A.	दण्डि	दण्डिनी	दण्डीनि
V.	दण्डि-न्	"	"

The rest like the *mas.* Decline similarly स्रग्विन् *n.*, वाग्मिन् *n.*, eloquent, भाविन् *n.* &c.

Irregular Bases.

§ 123. The first five forms of पथिन् a road, मथिन् a churning handle, and ऋभुक्षिन् name of Indra are irregular.* They drop their इन् before vowel terminations beginning with the Acc. plu.

पथिन् .

N. V.	पन्थाः	पन्थानौ	पन्थानः
A.	पन्थानम्	"	पथः
I.	पथा	पथिभ्याम्	पथिभिः
D.	पथे	"	पथिभ्यः

---

* पथिमथ्यृभुक्षामात् । इतोऽत्सर्वनामस्थाने । थोन्थः । भस्य टेर्लोपः । Pân. VII. 1. 85-88.

Ab.	पथः	पथिभ्याम्	पथिभ्यः
G.	पथः	पथोः	पथाम्
L.	पथि	"	पथिषु

Decline similarly मथिन् and ऋभुक्षिन्; the latter word, however, does not insert the न् in the first five inflections; *e. g.* Nom. मन्थाः मन्थानौ मन्थानः, ऋभुक्षाः-क्षाणौ-क्षाणः; Acc. मन्थानम् मन्थानौ-मथः; ऋभुक्षाणम्-ऋभुक्षाणौ-ऋभुक्षः

Bases ending in वस् or इवस्—

§ 124. These are the perfect participles derived from roots with the affix वस् to which the intermediate इ is prefixed in some cases. They have a न् prefixed to their final स् in the first five inflections, the penultimate अ being lengthened before it. In the Nom. sing. *m.* the स् is dropped and the Voc. sing. ends in वन्. उ is substituted for व, before which the preceding short इ, if any, is dropped, before the vowel terminations beginning with those of the Acc. plu. and before the ई of the Nom. Voc. and Acc. dual of the neuter nouns. The final म् of a root is changed to न् before वस् reappears before this उ; final स् is changed to द् before the consonantal terminations and in the Nom. Voc. and Acc. sing of the neuter.

विद्वस् *m.* a learned man.

N.	विद्वान्	विद्वांसौ	विद्वांसः
V.	विद्वन्	"	"
A.	विद्वांसम्	"	विदुषः
I.	विदुषा	विद्वद्भ्याम्	विद्वद्भिः
D.	विदुषे	"	विद्वद्भ्यः
Ab.	विदुषः	"	"
G.	"	विदुषोः	विदुषाम्
L.	विदुषि	"	विद्वत्सु

Neu.

N. V. A.	विद्वत्	विदुषी	विद्वांसि

The rest like the *mas.*

Decline similarly जग्मिवस् or जगन्वस् one who has gone, तस्थिवस् one who has stood, निनीवस् one who has carried, मीढ्वस् bountiful, शुश्रुवस् one who has heard, सेदिवस् one who has sat, दाश्वस् honouring or serving the gods, &c. *m.* and. *n.*; *e. g.*

Nom. sing.	Nom. dual.	I. sing.	I. dual
जग्मिवान्	जग्मिवांसौ	जग्मुषा	जग्मिवद्भ्याम्
जगन्वान्	जगन्वांसौ	„	जगन्वद्भ्याम्
तस्थिवान्	तस्थिवांसौ	तस्थुषा	तस्थिवद्भ्याम्
निनीवान्	निनीवांसौ	निन्युषा	निनीवद्भ्याम्
मीढ्वान्	मीढ्वांसौ	मीढुषा	मीढ्वद्भ्याम्
शुश्रुवान्	शुश्रुवांसौ	शुश्रुवुषा	शुश्रुवद्भ्याम्
सेदिवान्	सेदिवांसौ	सेदुषा	सेदिवद्भ्याम्
दाश्वान्	दाश्वांसौ	दाशुषा	दाश्वद्भ्याम्

Bases in यस् or ईयस्

§ 125. Comparatives in यस् are declined like bases in वस् in the first five inflections and the Voc. sing. and like nouns in अस् in other respects; *e. g.*

श्रेयस् (comparative of प्रशस्य) more praiseworthy.

N.	श्रेयान्	श्रेयांसौ	श्रेयांसः
V.	श्रेयन्	„	„
A.	श्रेयांसम्	„	श्रेयसः
I.	श्रेयसा	श्रेयोभ्याम्	श्रेयोभिः

The rest like चन्द्रमस्. Decline all comparatives in ईयस् such as गरीयस्, लघीयस्, द्राघीयस्, &c. similarly.

Neu.

N. V. A.	श्रेयः	श्रेयसी	श्रेयांसि

The rest like मनस्. Decline *n.* nouns in ईयस् similarly.

WORDS OF IRREGULAR DECLENSION.

§ 126. अस्थि *n.* a bone, दधि *n.* curds, सक्थि *n.* a thigh and अक्षि *n.* an eye, become अस्थन्, दधन्, सक्थन्, and अक्षन् respectively before the vowel terminations beginning with the I. sing.* and then they follow the declension of nouns in न्; in other respects they are declined like वारि.

अस्थि.

N.	अस्थि	अस्थिनी	अस्थीनि
V.	अस्थे-स्थि	"	"
A.	अस्थि	"	"
I.	अस्थ्ना	अस्थिभ्याम्	अस्थिभिः
D.	अस्थ्ने	अस्थिभ्याम्	अस्थिभ्यः
Ab.	अस्थ्नः	"	"
G.	"	अस्थ्नोः	अस्थ्नाम्
L.	अस्थ्नि-स्थनि	"	अस्थिषु

दधि and the rest should be similarly declined.

§ 127. अप् *f.* water, is declined in the plural; it lengthens its अ in the N. and changes its प् to द् before consonantal terminations. आपः-अपः-अद्भिः-अद्भ्यः-अद्भ्यः-अपाम्-अप्सु.

§ 128. The words जरा *f.* old age, अजर *m.* one not getting old and निर्जर a god, optionally assume the forms जरस्, अजरस्; and निर्जरस् before the vowel terminations:—

जरा.

N.	जरा	जरे, जरसौ	जराः, जरसः
V.	जरे	"	"
A.	जराम्, जरसम्	"	"
I.	जरया, जरसा	जराभ्याम्	जराभिः
D.	जरायै, जरसे	"	जराभ्यः
Ab.	जरायाः, जरसः	"	"

* अस्थिदधिसक्थ्यक्ष्णामनङुदात्तः । VII. 1. 75.

G.	जरायाः, जरसः	जरयोः, जरसोः	जराणाम्, जरसाम्
L.	जरायाम्, जरसि	,,	जरासु

Decline निर्जर &c. like राम and चन्द्रमस् :—

N.	निर्जरः	निर्जरौ-निर्जरसौ	निर्जराः-निर्जरसः
A.	निर्जरम्-निर्जरसम्	,,	निर्जरान्-निर्जरसः
I.	निर्जरेण-निर्जरसा &c.	निर्जराभ्याम् &c.	निर्जरैः-निर्जरसैः &c.
G.	निर्जरस्य-निर्जरसः	निर्जरयोः-निर्जरसोः	निर्जराणाम्-निर्जरसाम्
L.	निर्जरे-निर्जरसि	,, ,,	निर्जरेषु

अजर *m.* like निर्जर.

अजर *n.*

N	अजरम्	अजरे-अजरसी	अजराणि, अजरांसि
V.	अजर	,,	,,
A.	अजरम्	,,	,,

The rest like the *ma*

§ 129. The words पाद, दन्त, नासिका, मास, हृदय, निशा, असृज्, यूष, दोस्, यकृत्, शकृत्, उदक, आस्य*; मांस, पृतना, and सानु † optionally assume the forms पद्, दत्, नस्, मास्, हृद्, निश्, असन्, यूषन्, दोषन्, यकन्, शकन्, उदन्, आसन्, मांस्, पृत्, and स्नु before all terminations beginning with the Acc. plu.

दोस् *m.* an arm.

N. V.	दोः	दोषौ	दोषः
A.	दोः	,,	दोषः-दोष्णः
I.	दोषा-ष्णा	दोर्भ्याम्-षभ्याम्	दोर्भिः-षभिः
D.	दोषे-ष्णे	,,	दोर्भ्यः-षभ्यः
Ab.	दोषः-ष्णः	,,	,,
G.	,,	दोषोः-ष्णोः	दोषाम्-ष्णाम्
L.	दोषि-ष्णि-षणि	,,	दोःषु-ष्षु-षसु

* पद्दन्नोमास्हृन्निशसन्यूषन्दोषन्यकञ्छकन्नुदन्नासञ्छस्प्रभृतिषु VI. 1. 63.

† मांसपृतनासानूनां मांस्पृत्स्नवो वाच्याः ।

Neu.

N. V. A.	दोः	दोषी	दोंषि

The rest like *mas.*

निशा *f.* night.

N.	निशा	निशे	निशाः
V.	निशे	"	"
A.	निशाम्	"	निशाः-शः
I.	निशया-शा	निशाभ्याम्, निज्भ्याम्-ड्भ्याम्	निशाभिः, निज्भिः-ड्भिः
D.	निशायै-शे	"	निशाभ्यः, निज्भ्यः-ड्भ्यः
Ab.	निशायाः-शः	"	"
G.	"	निशयोः-शोः	निशानाम्-शाम्
L.	निशायां-शि	"	निशासु, निच्छु, निट्सु-ट्त्सु

सानु *Neu.* a summit, a table-land.

N.	सानु	सानुनी	सानूनि
V.	सानु-नो	"	"
A.	सानु	"	सानूनि-स्नूनि
I.	सानुना-स्नुना	सानुभ्याम्-स्नुभ्याम्	सानुभिः-स्नुभिः
D.	सानुने-स्नुने	सानुभ्याम्-स्नुभ्याम्	सानुभ्यः-स्नुभ्यः
Ab.	सानुनः-स्नुनः	"	"
G.	"	सानुनोः-स्नुनोः	सानूनाम्-स्नूनाम्
L.	सानुनि, स्नुनि	"	सानुषु-स्नुषु

सानु is also *m.* declined like गुरु with the optional forms from the Acc. pl. which is सानून्, स्नून्.

The remaining words should be similarly declined according to the declensions which their various endings follow :—

पाद *m.* a foot.

N.	पादः	पादौ	पादाः
V.	पाद	"	"
A.	पादम्	"	पादान्-पदः
I.	पादेन-पदा	पादाभ्याम्-पद्भ्याम्	पादैः-पद्भिः
L.	पादे-पदि	पादयोः-पदोः	पादेषु-पत्सु

दन्त *m.* a tooth.

N.	दन्तः	दन्तौ	दन्ताः
A.	दन्तम्	,,	दन्तान्-दतः
I.	दन्तेन-दता	दन्ताभ्याम्-दद्भ्याम्	दन्तैः-दद्भिः
L.	दन्ते-दति	दन्तयोः-दतोः	दन्तेषु-दत्सु

नासिका *f.* the nose.

N.	नासिका	नासिके	नासिकाः
A	नासिकाम्	,,	नासिकाः-नसः
I.	नासिकया-नसा	नासिकाभ्याम्-नोभ्याम्	नासिकाभिः-नोभिः
D.	नासिकायै-नसे	,,	नासिकाभ्यः-नोभ्यः
L.	नासिकायाम्-नासि	नासिकयोः-नसोः	नासिकासु-नःसु-नस्सु

मास *m.* month.

N.	मासः	मासौ	मासाः
A.	मासम्	,,	मासान्, मासः
I.	मासेन-मासा	मासाभ्याम्-माभ्याम्	मासैः-माभिः
L.	मासे-मासि	मासयोः-मासोः	मासेषु,माःसु-मास्सु.

हृदय *n.* heart.

N.	हृदयम्	हृदये	हृदयानि
A.	,,	,,	हृदयानि-हृन्दि
I.	हृदयेन-हृदा	हृदयाभ्याम्-हृद्भ्याम्	हृदयैः-हृद्भिः
L.	हृदये-हृदि	हृदययोः-हृदोः	हृदयेषु-हृत्सु

असृज् *n.* blood.

N.	असृक्-ग्	असृजी	असृञ्जि
A.	असृक्-ग्	असृजी	असृञ्जि-असानि
I.	असृजा-अस्ना	असृग्भ्याम्-असभ्याम्	असृग्भिः-असभिः
D.	असृजे-अस्ने	,,	असृग्भ्यः-असभ्यः
L.	असृजि अस्नि-असनि }	असृजोः-अस्नोः	असृक्षु-असस्सु

यूष *m.* soup.

N.	यूषः	यूषौ	यूषाः
A.	यूषम्	,,	यूषान्-यूष्णः
I.	यूषेण-यूष्णा	यूषाभ्याम्-यूषभ्याम्	यूषैः-यूषभिः
L.	यूषे, यूष्णि-यूषणि	यूषयोः-यूष्णोः	यूषेषु-यूषसु

यकृत् *n.* the liver.

N.	यकृत्-द्	यकृती	यकृन्ति
A.	,,	,,	यकृन्ति, यकानि
I.	यकृता-यक्ना	यकृद्भ्याम्-यकभ्याम्	यकृद्भिः-यकभिः
L.	यकृति, यक्नि-यकनि	यकृतोः-यक्नोः	यकृत्सु-यकसु

शकृत् *n.* dung.

N.	शकृत्	शकृती	शकृन्ति
A.	शकृत्	शकृती	शकृन्ति-शकानि
I.	शकृता, शक्ना	शकृद्भ्याम्, शकभ्याम्	शकृद्भिः, शकभिः
L.	शकृति, शक्नि-शकनि	शकृतोः, शक्नोः	शकृत्सु, शकसु

उदक *n.* water.

N.	उदकम्	उदके	उदकानि
A.	उदकम्	उदके	उदकानि-उदानि
I.	उदकेन-उद्ना	उदकाभ्याम्-उदभ्याम्	उदकैः, उदभिः
L.	उदके, उद्नि-उदनि	उदकयोः, उद्नोः	उदकेषु, उदसु

आस्य *n.* mouth.

N.	आस्यम्	आस्ये	आस्यानि
A.	,,	,,	,, -आसानि
I.	आस्येन, आस्ना	आस्याभ्याम्-आसभ्याम्	आस्यैः, आसभिः
L.	आस्ये, आस्नि-आसनि	आस्ययोः, आस्नोः	आस्येषु, आससु

मांस *n.* flesh.

N.	मांसम्	मांसे	मांसानि
A.	,,	,,	,, -मांसि

I.	मांसेन, मांसा	मांसाभ्याम्, मान्भ्याम्	मांसैः, मान्भिः
L.	मांसे, मांसि	मांसयोः, मांसोः	मांसेषु,मान्सु-मान्त्सु

पृतना *f.* an army.

N.	पृतना	पृतने	पृतनाः
A.	पृतनाम्	”	” –पृतः
I.	पृतनया, पृता	पृतनाभ्याम्, पृद्भ्याम्	पृतनाभिः-पृद्भिः
D.	पृतनायै-पृते	”	पृतनाभ्यः-पृद्भ्यः
L.	पृतनायाम्, पृति	पृतनयोः, पृतोः	पृतनासु, पृत्सु

§ 130. The following suffixes are sometimes added to nominal bases to express the meanings of cases.

(*a*) The suffix तस् added to the base of a noun gives it the sense of the Ab.*; as प्रमादतः, from carelessness'. वस्तुतः from the real state of the thing, in reality, ज्ञानतः 'from knowledge,' बहुतः &c.

(*b*) The suffix त्र is used to denote the meaning of the Loc.* case, and is generally added to pronominal adjectives; as तत्र 'in that place, there'; सर्वत्र 'in every place, everywhere, &c.

§ 131. A few nouns such as भूर् 'the lowest world,' स्वर् 'heaven,' संवत् 'a year of an era', अस्तम् 'setting,' शम् 'ease,' नमस् 'a bow', स्वस्ति 'hail, farewell' &c. are indeclinables.

Chapter IV.

PRONOUNS AND THEIR DECLENSION.

§ 132. The following 35 words are termed 'Pronouns' in Sanskrit:—सर्व, विश्व, उभ, उभय, डतर, डतम (*i. e.* the word formed by the addition of the terminations अतर and अतम to the

---

* पञ्चम्यास्तसिल् । सप्तम्यास्त्रल् Pân. V. 3. 7. 10. By 'इतराभ्योऽपि दृश्यन्ते । Pân. V. 3. 14. तस्, त्रल् &c. may stand for all cases except the Nom. (though they may be used for the Nom. also).

pronouns किम्, यद्, and तद् which become क, य and त respectively before these; e. g. कतर, कतम, यतर, यतम, and ततर, ततम) अन्य, अन्यतर, इतर, त्वत्, त्व, नेम, सम, सिम, पूर्व, पर, अवर, दक्षिण, उत्तर, अपर, अधर, स्व, अन्तर; त्यद्, तद् एतद्, इदम्, अदस्, एक, द्वि, युष्मद्, अस्मद्, भवत् and किम्.

1—Personal Pronouns.

§ 133. The pronouns अस्मद् 'I,' युष्मद् 'thou', and भवत् 'your honour:'—

N. B.—The declension of the first two of these pronouns is the same in all the three genders.

अस्मद्* *m. f. n.*

N.	अहम्	आवाम्	वयम्
A.	माम्, मा	आवाम, नौ	अस्मान्, नः
I.	मया	आवाभ्याम्	अस्माभिः
D.	मह्यम्, मे	आवाभ्याम्, नौ	अस्मभ्यम्, नः
Ab.	मत्	आवाभ्याम्	अस्मत्
G.	मम, मे	आवयोः, नौ	अस्माकम्, नः
L.	मयि	आवयोः	अस्मासु

युष्मद् *m. f. n.*

N.	त्वम्	युवाम्	यूयम्
A.	त्वाम्, त्वा	युवाम्, वाम्	युष्मान्, वः
I.	त्वया	युवाभ्याम्	युष्माभिः
D.	तुभ्यम्, ते	युवाभ्याम्, वाम्	युष्मभ्यम्, वः
Ab.	त्वत्	युवाभ्याम्	युष्मत्
G.	तव, ते	युवयोः, वाम्	युष्माकम्, वः
L.	त्वयि	युवयोः	युष्मासु

* युष्मदस्मदोः षष्ठीचतुर्थीद्वितीयास्थयोर्वांनावौ । बहुवचनस्य वस्नसौ । तेमयावेकवचनस्य । त्वामौ द्वितीयायाः । Pân. VIII. 1. 20-23.

भवत् to be declined like भगवत्; भवान् भवन्तौ भवन्तः N. भवन्तम् भवन्तौ भवतः A. &c. अत्रभवत्, तत्रभवत् (see Syntax 'Pronouns') are similarly declined.

§ 134. (*a*) The optional shorter forms of the pronouns अस्मद् and युष्मद् are never used at the beginning of a sentence or of a foot of a metre;* nor can they be used immediately before the particles च, वा, ह or हा, अह and एव†; as मम गृहं my house, and not मे गृहम्; वेदैरशेषैः संवेद्योऽस्मान् कृष्णः सर्वदावतु (Sid. Kau.), 'may Kṛshna, revered throughout or capable of being known properly from all the Vedas, always protect us; and not नः कृष्णः &c.; तवैव कृत्यमेतत् 'this is surely your deed,' and not ते एव &c. But if these particles do not connect these forms they may be used with them‡; as हरो हरिश्च मे स्वामी (Sid. Kau.) Hara and Hari are my lords, &c.

Obs.—(*b*) The shorter forms may be used in a sentence having one verb; शालीनां ते ओदनं दास्यामि; but ओदनं पच तव भविष्यति as there are two verbs ‡.

(*c*) These shorter forms are not also used immediately after the Vocative case except when a qualifying adjective follows it; + देवास्मान् (and not नः) पाहि सर्वदा (Sid. Kau.) 'Oh God! do thou protect us always'; but हरे दयालो नः पाहि (Sid. Kau.) 'Oh merciful Hari, protect us.'

---

*पदात्। अनुदात्तं सर्वमपादादौ। Pán. VIII. 1. 17. 18. The following couplets illustrate the use of these short forms:—श्रीशस्त्वावतु मापीह दत्तात्ते मेऽपि शर्म सः। स्वामी ते मेऽपि स हरिः पातु वामपि नौ विभुः॥ सुखं वां नौ ददात्वीशः पतिर्वामपि नौ हरिः। सोऽव्याद्वो नः शिवं वो नो दयात्सेव्योऽत्र वः स नः॥ Sid. Kau. † न चवाहाहैवयुक्ते। Pán. VIII. 1. 24.

‡ युक्तग्रहणात्साक्षाद्योगेऽयं निषेधः। परम्परासम्बन्धे तु आदेशः स्यादेव। Sid. Kau.

‡ समानवाक्ये निघातयुष्मदस्मदादेशा वक्तव्याः। Vârt.

+ Pán. VIII. 1. 72. 73.

(d) The shorter forms may or may not be used when there is no अन्वादेश (the subsequent mention of a thing already mentioned); धाता ते भक्तोऽस्ति, धाता तव भक्तोऽस्ति, इति वा ।; but must be used when there is *anvades'a**; तस्मै ते नमः 'bow to thee (already described) only.'

2—Demonstrative Pronouns.

§ 135. The pronouns तद् 'that or he, she, it,' एतद् 'this,' इदम् 'this' and अदस् 'that'. The Nom. sing of the first two is respectively सः and एषः *mas.* and सा and एषा *fem.* In other cases they become त and एत and are declined like nouns in अ except in the Nom. pl., D. Ab. sings., G. pl. and L. sing. the terminations of which are ई, स्मै, स्मात्, इषाम् and स्मिन् *mas.* and स्यै, स्यास्, स्यास्, साम् and स्याम् *fem.* respectively. All pronouns ending in अ are similarly declined.

तद् *mas.*

N.	सः	तौ	ते
A.	तम्	तौ	तान्
I.	तेन	ताभ्याम्	तैः
D.	तस्मै	„	तेभ्यः
Ab.	तस्मात्	„	„
G.	तस्य	तयोः	तेषाम्
L.	तस्मिन्	„	तेषु

Fem.

N.	सा	ते	ताः
A.	ताम्	„	„
I.	तया	ताभ्याम्	ताभिः
D.	तस्यै	„	ताभ्यः
Ab.	तस्याः	„	„
G.	„	तयोः	तासाम्
L.	तस्याम्	„	तासु

* एते वांनावादय आदेशा अनन्वादेशे वा वक्तव्याः । Vārt.

Decline त्यद् which means the same thing as तद्, similarly. *e. g.* त्यः त्यौ त्ये Nom.; त्यं त्यौ त्यान् Acc. &c.

तद् *neu.*

N. and A.	तद्	ते	तानि

The following cases like the *mas.*

एतद् *mas.*

N.	एषः	एतौ	एते
A.	एतम्-एनम्*	एतौ-एनौ	एतान्-एनान्
I.	एतेन-एनेन	एताभ्याम्	एतैः
D.	एतस्मै	"	एतेभ्यः
Ab.	एतस्मात्	"	"
G.	एतस्य	एतयोः-एनयोः	एतेषाम्
L.	एतस्मिन्	"	एतेषु

Fem.

N.	एषा	एते	एताः
A.	एताम्-एनाम्	एते-एने	एताः-एनाः
I.	एतया-एनया	एताभ्याम्	एताभिः
D.	एतस्यै	"	एताभ्यः
Ab.	एतस्याः	"	"
G.	एतस्याः	एतयोः एनयोः	एतासाम्
L.	एतस्याम्	"	एतासु

Neu.

N.	एतत्	एते	एतानि
A.	एतत्-एनत्	एते-एने	एतानि-एनानि

The rest like the *mas.*

---

* द्वितीयाटौस्स्वेनः । Pán. II. 4. 34. एन is optionally substituted for इदम् and एतद् in the Acc., Inst. Sing. and Gen. and Loc. Duals when there is अन्वादेश (see § 137).

Notes:—The *visarga* of सः and एषः is dropped when followed by any letter except अ in which case the usual Sandhi takes place; स गच्छतु, एष आयाति; but एषोऽगच्छत् &c. Vide § 50.

इदम् *mas.*

N.	अयम्	इमौ	इमे
A.	इमम्-एनम्	इमौ-एनौ	इमान्-एनान्
I.	अनेन-एनेन	आभ्याम्	एभिः
D.	अस्मै	,,	एभ्यः
Ab.	अस्मात्	,,	,,
G.	अस्य	अनयोः-एनयोः	एषाम्
L.	अस्मिन्	,,	एषु

Fem.

N.	इयम्	इमे	इमाः
A.	इमाम्-एनाम्	इमे-एने	इमाः-एनाः
I.	अनया-एनया	आभ्याम्	आभिः
D.	अस्यै	,,	आभ्यः
Ab.	अस्याः	,,	,,
G.	,,	अनयोः-एनयोः	आसाम्
L.	अस्याम्	,,	आसु

Neu.

N.	इदम्	इमे	इमानि
A.	इदम्-एनत्	इमे-एने	इमानि-एनानि

The rest like the *mas.*

अदस् *mas.*

N.	असौ	अमू	अमी
A.	अमुम्	,,	अमून्
I.	अमुना	अमूभ्याम्	अमीभिः
D.	अमुष्मै	,,	अमीभ्यः
Ab.	अमुष्मात्	,,	अमीभ्यः
G.	अमुष्य	अमुयोः	अमीषाम्
L.	अमुष्मिन्	,,	अमीषु

Fem.

N.	असौ	अमू	अमूः
A.	अमूम्	„	„
I.	अमुया	अमूभ्याम्	अमूभिः
D.	अमुष्यै	„	अमूभ्यः
Ab.	अमुष्याः	„	„
G.	„	अमुयोः	अमूषाम्
L.	अमुष्याम्	„	अमूषु

Neu.

N. & A.	अदः	अमू	अमूनि

The rest like the *mas.*

§ 136. The following couplet (Kârikâ) gives a rule for the correct use of these pronouns :—

इदमस्तु सन्निकृष्टं समीपतरवर्ति चैतदो रूपम् ।
अदसस्तु विप्रकृष्टं तदिति परोक्षे विजानीयात् ॥

इदम् is used with reference to a person or thing near at hand, and एतद् to one nearer still; अदस् is used of a person or thing at a distance, while तद् is used of one that is absent.

§ 137. The optional forms of इदम् and एतद् in the Acc., Inst. Sing. and Gen. & Loc. Duals are to be used when there is *anvádes'a** *i. e.* their proper forms have already been used in a previous clause; *e. g.* अनेन व्याकरणमधीतं एनं छन्दोध्यापय 'he has studied grammar, teach him prosody,' अनयोः पवित्रं कुलं, एनयोः प्रभूतं स्वम्, 'The family of them both is pure, and their wealth ample.'

3—The Relative Pronouns.

§ 138. The pronouns यद् 'who, which'; *mas. fem.* and *neu.*; *mas.* base य, *fem.* base या.

---

* किंचित्कार्यं विधातुमुपात्तस्य कार्यान्तरं विधातुं पुनरुपादानमन्वादेशः । Sid. Kau.

यद् *mas*

N.	यः	यौ	ये
A.	यम्	यौ	यान्
I.	येन	याभ्याम्	यैः
D.	यस्मै	,,	येभ्यः
Ab.	यस्मात्	,,	,,
G.	यस्य	ययोः	येषाम्
L.	यस्मिन्	,,	येषु

Fem.

N.	या	ये	याः
A.	याम्	,,	,,
I.	यया	याभ्याम्	याभिः
D.	यस्यै	,,	याभ्यः
Ab.	यस्याः	,,	,,
G.	,,	ययोः	यासाम्
L.	यस्याम्	,,	यासु

Neu.

N. & A.	यत्	ये	यानि

The rest like the *mas.*

4—The Interrogative Pronouns.

§ 139. The pronoun किम् *mas. fem.* & *neu.*; *m.* base क; *fem.* base का.

Mas.

N.	कः	कौ	के
A.	कम्	,,	कान्
I.	केन	काभ्याम्	कैः
D.	कस्मै	,,	केभ्यः
Ab.	कस्मात्	,,	,,
G.	कस्य	कयोः	केषाम्
L.	कस्मिन्	,,	केषु

Fem.

N.	का	के	काः
A.	काम्	,,	,,

I.	कया	काभ्याम्	काभिः
D.	कस्यै	,,	काभ्यः
Ab.	कस्याः	,,	,,
G.	कस्याः	कयोः	कासाम्
L.	कस्याम्	,,	कासु

Neu.

N. & A. किम्	के	कानि

The remaining cases like the *mas.*

5—Reflexive Pronouns.

§ 140. The sense of the reflexive pronoun is, in Sanskṛt, expressed by the word आत्मन् 'self' which is invariably used in the masculine gender and singular number, and by the reflexive adverb स्वयम् *e. g.* यसं ददृशुरात्मानं सर्वाः स्वप्नेषु वामनैः "they all (the wives of Das'aratha) saw in dreams that they were guarded by dwarfs;" so स or सा कृतापराधमिव आत्मानमवगच्छति । राजा स्वयं समरभूमिं जगाम, &c.

6—Indefinite Pronouns.

§ 141. Indefinite pronouns are formed by the additiop of चित् or चन or अपि and sometimes of स्वित् to the various cases of the pronoun किम् in all the genders; *e. g.* कश्चित्, कश्चन a certain one, कोपि, केनापि, कयाचन, कयापि; कास्वित, &c.

§ 142. The terminations given above are also added to interrogative adverbs in the sense of indefiniteness; as कदाचित at some time, कदाचन, कतिचित् some, क्वचित् somewhere, &c.

7—Correlative Pronouns.

§ 143. Correlatives are formed by the affixes वत् added to यद्, तद् and एतद्, and यत् added to इदम् and किम् in the sense of 'as much as;' and दृश or दृश् in the sense of 'similar to'; तद्, एतद् and यद् become ता, एता and या respectively before these, and इदम् and किम् इ and कि before यत् and ई and की before दृश or दृश्; *e. g.* तावत् (तत्परिमाणमस्य), इयत् (इदं परिमाणमस्य), तादृश like that, ईदृश, like this, कियद् how much, &c.

§ 144. The affix अति is added to तद्, यद् and किम् to show number or measure *e. g.* तति 'so many', यति 'as many,' and कति 'how many'. These are declined in the plural only, and take no termination in the Nom. and Acc.; *e. g.* Nom. and Acc. कति Inst. कतिभिः the rest like हरि.

8—Reciprocal Pronouns.

§ 145. Reciprocity is expressed by the repetition of the pronominal adjectives अन्य, इतर and पर; *e. g.* अन्योन्य, इतरेतर, and परस्पर. These are generally used in the sing. and also adverbially *e. g.* परस्परेण स्पृहणीयशोभं &c. (Rag. VII. 14); परस्परं विवदन्ते &c. They are more commonly used as the first members of compounds; as अन्योन्यशोभाजननाद् बभूव &c. (Ku. I, 44; इतरेतरयोगाः (Śis. X. 24.) &c.

9--Possessive Pronouns.

§ 146. Possessive pronouns are formed by means of the secondary affix ईय added to तद्, एतद्, अस्मत्, and युष्मत्; and अ and ईन added to अस्मत्, and युष्मत्, changed respectively to मामक् and तावक् in the sing. and आस्माक् and यौष्माक् in the plu. before these; *e. g.*

अस्मत्

Mas.

Sing.	Plural.
मदीय 'my, mine'	अस्मदीय 'our, ours'
मामक ,,	आस्माक ,,
मामकीन ,,	आस्माकीन ,,

Fem.

Sing.	Plural.
मदीया my, mine'	अस्मदीया 'our, ours'
मामिका ,,	आस्माकी ,,
मामकीना ,,	आस्माकीना ,,

युष्मद्

mas.		*fem.*	
Sing.	Plural.	Sing.	Plural.
त्वदीय 'thy, thine.'	युष्मदीय 'your, yours.'	त्वदीया 'thy, thine.'	युष्मदीया 'your, yours.'
तावक ,,	यौष्माक ,,	तावकी ,,	यौष्माकी ,,
तावकीन ,,	यौष्माकीण ,,	तावकीना ,,	यौष्माकीणा ,,

तद्		एतद्	
mas.	*fem.*	*mas.*	*fem.*
तदीय	तदीया	एतदीय	एतदीया

N. B. These are declined like nouns ending in अ, आ or ई regularly. स्व is a possessive pronoun by itself.

10—Pronominal Adjectives.

§ 147. अन्य 'another,' अन्यतर 'either of two,' इतर 'other,' एकतम 'one of many,' कतर 'who or which of two,' कतम 'who or which of many,' यतर 'who or which of two,' यतम 'who or which of many,' ततर 'that one (of two),' ततम 'that one (of many),' are declined in all the three genders like यद् *e. g.*

		mas.	
N.	कतरः	कतरौ	कतरे
&c		*fem.*	
N.	कतरा	कतरे	कतराः
&c.		*neu.*	
N. & A.	कतरत्	कतरे	कतराणि
&c.			

N. B. अन्यतम is not a pronoun, as it is not mentioned in the group सर्वादि (तत्रान्यतमशब्दस्य गणे पाठाभावान्न संज्ञा Sid. Kau.). It is, therefore, declined like nouns ending in अ.

§ 148. Decline सर्व, विश्व, सम and सिम all having the same meaning, उभ (declined in the dual only) and उभय (which has no dual according to Kaiyata and other grammarians) both meaning 'both,' इतर and एकतर 'one of two,' like यद् except in the Nom. and Acc. sing. of the *neu.* which is formed by adding म्; *e. g.*

सर्व *mas.* 'all.'

N.	सर्वः	सर्वौ	सर्वे
A.	सर्वम्	सर्वौ	सर्वान्
I.	सर्वेण	सर्वाभ्याम्	सर्वैः
D.	सर्वस्मै	„	सर्वेभ्यः
Ab	सर्वस्मात्	„	„
G	सर्वस्य	सर्वयोः	सर्वेषाम्
L.	सर्वस्मिन्	„	सर्वेषु

Fem.

N.	सर्वा	सर्वे	सर्वाः
A.	सर्वाम्	„	„
I.	सर्वया	सर्वाभ्याम्	सर्वाभिः
D.	सर्वस्यै	„	सर्वाभ्यः
Ab	सर्वस्याः	„	„
G.	„	सर्वयोः	सर्वासाम्
L.	सर्वस्याम्	„	सर्वासु

Neu.

N. & A.	सर्वम्	सर्वे	सर्वाणि

The rest like the *mas.*

(*a*)—सम when it means 'equal' is not a pronoun and is declined like nouns in अ; *e. g.* समः समौ समाः Nom., समाय D. sing., समानाम् G. plu. as in the Sutra of Páṇ. यथासंख्यमनुदेशः समानाम् । 1. 3. 10.

§ 149. *Obs* :—त्व and त्व (the 10th and 11th सर्वादिs) the one उदात्त (udátta), the other अनुदात्त (anudâtta), both synonyms of अन्य are declined like सर्व. The former is of the form त्वत् according to some and then it is declined regularly by adding the terminations; *e. g.* त्वत् त्वतौ त्वतः Nom. &c.

§ 150. स्व when it does not mean "a class" or "wealth" is a pronoun and is declined like सर्व* *m. f. n.*; but it forms its

* स्वमज्ञातिधनाख्यायाम् । Pan. I. 1. 35.

Nom plu. and Ab. and Loc. sing. optionally like राम when *mas.*; as स्वे or स्वाः 'one's own' Nom plu.; but स्वाः 'people of one's class' only (declined like राम).

§ 151. अन्तर is a pronoun (and therefore declined like सर्व *m. n. f.*) when it means "exterior, outer; or what is to be worn out-side, as a garment"* except when followed by पुर; it is optionally declined like nouns ending in अ in the Nom. pl. and Ab. and Loc. sing. of the *mas. e. g.* अन्तरे अन्तरा वा गृहाः; अन्तरे-अन्तरा वा शाटकाः (garments). But अन्तरायां पुरि.

§ 152. नेम meaning 'half' is a pronoun, but it is optionally declined like राम in the Nom. plu. *mas.*; in other respects it is declined like सर्व.

§ 153. पूर्व 'prior, eastern', अवर 'posterior, western', दक्षिण 'southern,' उत्तर 'superior, northern, subsequent', अपर 'other,' and अधर 'inferior, lower,' when they denote relation in space, time or person with reference to a particular thing or point of time &c. and are not a name, are pronouns† and are then declined like सर्व; but they are optionally declined like राम in the Nom. plu. and Ab. and Loc. sing. when *mas*; *e. g.* Nom. पूर्वः पूर्वौ पूर्वे or पूर्वाः Ab. पूर्वात्-पूर्वस्मात् पूर्वाभ्याम् पूर्वेभ्यः; Loc. पूर्वे-पूर्वस्मिन्; &c.; but दाक्षिणाः गायकाः (skilful musicians) only, and not दाक्षिणे, for दक्षिण does not show any relation here; so उत्तराः कुरवः and not उत्तरे, as उत्तराः is a name here.

§ 154. एक when a numeral is declined in the sing. and द्वि in the dual only; द्वि, is considered as द्व, and they are both declined like सर्व in all the three genders; *e. g.*

	एक		द्वि.	
	Mas.	*fem.*	*mas*	*fem. &c. neu.*
N.	एकः	एका	द्वौ	द्वे
V.	एक	एके	,,	,,

* अन्तरं बहिर्योगोपसंख्यानयोः । Pán. I. 1. 36. अन्तरं बहिर्योगेति गणसूत्रेऽपुरीति वक्तव्यम् । Vârt.

† पूर्वपरावरदक्षिणोत्तरापराधराणि व्यवस्थायामसंज्ञायाम् । Pán. I. 11. 34.

A.	एकम्	एकाम्	द्वौ	द्वे
I.	एकेन	एकया	द्वाभ्याम्	The rest like
D.	एकस्मै	एकस्यै	„	the mas.
Ab.	एकस्मात्	एकस्याः	„	
G.	एकस्य	„	द्वयोः	
L.	एकस्मिन्	एकस्याम्	„	

एक *neu.* एकम् N. A. The rest like the *mas.*

एक when it does not mean 'one' is declined in the dual and plural also.

§ 155. The various meanings of एक are:—

एकोल्पार्थे प्रधाने च प्रथमे केवले तथा।
साधारणे समानेति संख्यायां च प्रयुज्यते ॥

अल्प or little, प्रधान or chief, pre-eminent, प्रथम or foremost केवल or sole, only, साधारण or common (as अविमृश्यकारित्वं हि आपद एको हेतुः), समान or the same (as अयं एकान्वयो मम), and संख्या or number (one).

§ 156. प्रथम, चरम, अल्प, अर्ध, कतिपय, and words ending in the termination तय optionally form their Nom. plu. like that of pronouns; *e. g.* प्रथमे-प्रथमाः, कतिपये-कतिपयाः, द्वितये-द्वितयाः &c.

11—Pronominal Adverbs.

§ 157. The pronominal adverbs that are most commonly met with are derived from the pronouns तद्, एतद्, यद्, इदम्, किम्, and सर्व and the pronominal adjectives पूर्व, पर &c. by means of such affixes as तस्, त्र, *ह, क &c. added in the sense of the Ab. or the Loc., दा, †दानीम्, र्हि &c. showing time, तात्‡ showing point of time, place or direction, आ, आत्, आहि &c. expressing direction, था, थ+ &c. expreseing way or manner &c.; *e. g.*

* See § 130.

† सर्वैकान्यकियत्तदः काले दा। इदमोर्हिल्। अधुना दानीं च। तदो दा च। अनद्यतनेर्हिलन्यतरस्याम्। Pán. V. 3. 15–19. 21.

‡ दिक्शब्देभ्यः सप्तमीपञ्चमीप्रथमाभ्यो दिग्देशकालेष्वस्तातिः। Pàn. V. 3. 27.

+ उत्तराधरदक्षिणादातिः। दक्षिणादाच् आहि च दूरे। Pán. V. 3. 34. 36. 3. प्रकारवचने थाल्। इदमस्थमुः किमश्च। Pán. V. 23–25.

तद्.........................तदा, then; तदानीम्, at that time; तर्हि then, therefore; तथा, so, तत्र, there; ततः, thence, thereupon, therefore, &c.

इदम्.........................इदानीम्, now; इत्थम्, thus; अत्र, here; अतः, therefore; इतः, from this, hence; अधुना, now; इह, here.

एतद्.........................एतर्हि, now; इत्थम् thus; अतः hence, therefore; अत्र here.

यद्.........................यर्हि, when; यदा when; यथा as; यत्र where; यतः, whence,, since, because.

किम्.........................कर्हि, when; कदा, when; कथम्, how; कुत्र, where; क्व, where; कुतः, where, whence; कुह, whence, how.

सर्व.........................सर्वदा, always; सदा, always; सर्वतः, everywhere, on all sides; सर्वत्र everywhere, in all places.

पर.........................परतः further on, beyond, &c.

पूर्व.........................पुरः, पुरस्तात् before, in front, &c.

अधर.........................अधः, अधस्तात् or अधरस्तात्, अधरतः, अधरात् down, below.

अवर.........................अवः, अवस्तात् or अवरस्तात्, अवरतः, behind, below, downwards.

अपर.........................पश्चात्, from behind, afterwards, westward, &c.

दक्षिण.........................दक्षिणा, दक्षिणात्, दक्षिणाहि to or in the south, on the right side.

उत्तर.........................उत्तरा उत्तरात्, उत्तराहि to or in the north, &c.

§ 158. When a pronominal word is used as the subordinate member of a compound, or is at the end of an Inst. Tat., or of a sentence having the sense of the Inst. Tat., or at the end of a Dwandwa, it is not declined like a pronoun*; *e.g.* अतिक्रान्तः

---

* संज्ञोपसर्जनीभूतास्तु न सर्वादयः । Vârt. तृतीयासमासे । द्वंद्वे च ॥ Pân. I. 1. 30. 31.

सर्वे अतिसर्वः, तस्मै अतिसर्वाय and not सर्वस्मै; so अतिकतरं कुलम्; मासपूर्वाय or मासेन पूर्वाय and not मासपूर्वस्मै; वर्णाश्रमेतराणाम् &c.; in the case of a Dwandwa comp., however, it is optionally declined like a pronoun in the Nom. plu.,* as वर्णाश्रमेतरे or वर्णाश्रमेतराः।

CHAPTER V.

NUMERALS AND THEIR DECLENSION.

§ 159. *Cardinals* *and* *Ordinals*

		Cardinals	Ordinals *mas.*	*fem.*
1	१	एक	प्रथम, अग्रिम, आदिम *mas. neu.*	प्रथमा *fem.*
2	२	द्वि	द्वितीय,	० या
3	३	त्रि	तृतीय,	० या
4	४	चतुर्	चतुर्थ,	० र्थी
5	५	पञ्चन्	पञ्चम,	० मी
6	६	षष्	षष्ठ,	० ष्ठी
7	७	सप्तन्	सप्तम,	० मी
8	८	अष्टन्	अष्टम,	० मी
9	९	नवन्	नवम,	० मी
10	१०	दशन् †	दशम,	० मी
11	११	एकादशन्	एकादश,	० शी
12	१२	द्वादशन्	द्वादश,	० शी
13	१३	त्रयोदशन्	त्रयोदश,	० शी
14	१४	चतुर्दशन्	चतुर्दश,	० शी
15	१५	पञ्चदशन्	पञ्चदश	० शी
16	१६	षोडशन् ‡	षोडश	० शी

* विभाषा जसि। Pân. 1. 1 32.

† The word पङ्क्ति also denotes ten. *Cf.* Rag. IX. 74.

‡ षष् becomes षो necessarily when followed by दत् (substituted for दन्त) and दशन्, optionally when followed by धा, after which द् is changed to ड् and ध् to ढ्; *e. g.* षोढा (vide § 169. *b.*)

17	१७	सप्तदशन्	सप्तदश, ०शी
18	१८	अष्टादशन्	अष्टादश, ०शी
19	१९	नवदशन् or	नवदश, ०शी;
		एकोनविंशति or	एकोनविंश, ०शी, ०विंशतितम, ०मी or
		ऊनविंशति or	ऊनविंश, ०शी, ०विंशतितम, ०मी or
		एकान्नविंशति	एकान्नविंश, ०शी, ०शतितम, ०मी
20	२०	विंशति *f.*	विंश, ०शी or विंशतितम ०मी
21	२१	एकविंशति	एकविंश, ०शी or तितम, ०मी
22	२२	द्वाविंशति	द्वाविंश, ०शी, or ०तितम, ०मी
23	२३	त्रयोविंशति	त्रयोविंश, ०शी, or ०तितम, ०मी
24	२४	चतुर्विंशति	चतुर्विंश, ०शी ,, ,, ,,
25	२५	पञ्चविंशति	पञ्चविंश, ०शी ,, ,, ,,
26	२६	षड्विंशति	षड्विंश, ०शी ,, ,, ,,
27	२७	सप्तविंशति	सप्तविंश, ०शी ,, ,, ,,
28	२८	अष्टाविंशति	अष्टाविंश, ०शी ,, ,, ,,
29	२९	नवविंशति or	नवविंश, ०शी, or नवविंशतितम, ०मी
		एकोनत्रिंशत् or	एकोनत्रिंश, ०शी, ०त्रिंशत्तम, ०मी
		ऊनत्रिंशत् or	ऊनत्रिंश, ०शी, or ऊनत्रिंशत्तम, ०मी
		एकान्नत्रिंशत्	एकान्नत्रिंश, ०शी, ०त्रिंशत्तम, ०मी
30	३०	त्रिंशत् *f*	त्रिंश, ०शी or त्रिंशत्तम ०मी
31	३१	एकत्रिंशत्	एकत्रिंश, ०शी or एकत्रिंशत्तम, ०मी
32	३२	द्वात्रिंशत्	
33	३३	त्रयस्त्रिंशत्	
34	३४	चतुस्त्रिंशत्	
35	३५	पञ्चत्रिंशत्	
36	३६	षट्त्रिंशत्	
37	३७	सप्तत्रिंशत्	
38	३८	अष्टात्रिंशत्	
39	३९	नवत्रिंशत्	
		एकोनचत्वारिंशत् &c.	
40	४०	चत्वारिंशत् *f.*	चत्वारिंश, ०शी or चत्वारिंशत्तम, ०मी
41	४१	एकचत्वारिंशत्	

42	४२	द्वाचत्वारिंशत् or द्विचत्वारिंशत्	
43	४३	त्रयश्चत्वारिंशत् or त्रिचत्वारिंशत्	
44	४४	चतुश्चत्वारिंशत्	
45	४५	पञ्चचत्वारिंशत्	
46	४६	षट्चत्वारिंशत्	
47	४७	सप्तचत्वारिंशत्	
48	४८	अष्टचत्वारिंशत् or अष्टाचत्वारिंशत्	
49	४९	नवचत्वारिंशत् or एकोनपञ्चाशत् &c.	
50	५०	पञ्चाशत् *f*	पञ्चाश, ०शी or पञ्चाशत्तम, ०मी
51	५१	एकपञ्चाशत्	
52	५२	द्वापञ्चाशत् or द्विपञ्चाशत्	
53	५३	त्रयःपञ्चाशत् or त्रिपञ्चाशत्	
54	५४	चतुःपञ्चाशत्	
55	५५	पञ्चपञ्चाशत्	
56	५६	षट्पञ्चाशत्	
57	५७	सप्तपञ्चाशत्	
58	५८	अष्टापञ्चाशत् or अष्टपञ्चाशत्	
59	५९	नवपञ्चाशत् एकोनषष्टि &c	
60	६०	षष्टि *fem.*	षष्टितम, ०मी
61	६१	एकषष्टि	एकषष्ट, ०ष्टी or एकषष्टितम, ०मी
62	६२	द्वाषष्टि or द्विषष्टि	
63	६३	त्रयःषष्टि or त्रिषष्टि	
64	६४	चतुष्षष्टि	
65	६५	पञ्चषष्टि	
66	६६	षट्षष्टि	
67	६७	सप्तषष्टि	

68	६८	अष्टाषष्टि or अष्टषष्टि	
69	६९	नवषष्टि or एकोनसप्तति &c.	
70	७०	सप्तति *fem.*	सप्ततितम, ०मी
71	७१	एकसप्तति	एकसप्तत, ०ती or एकसप्ततितम, ०मी
72	७२	द्वासप्तति or द्विसप्तति	
73	७३	त्रयस्सप्तति or त्रिसप्तति	
74	७४	चतुस्सप्तति	
75	७५	पञ्चसप्तति	
76	७६	षट्सप्तति	
77	७७	सप्तसप्तति	
78	७८	अष्टासप्तति or अष्टसप्तति	
79	७९	नवसप्तति or एकोनाशीति &c.	
80	८०	अशीति *fem.*	अशीतितम, ०मी
81	८१	एकाशीति	एकाशीत ०ती, or एकाशीतितम ०मी
82	८२	द्व्यशीति	
83	८३	त्र्यशीति	
84	८४	चतुरशीति	
85	८५	पञ्चाशीति	
86	८६	षडशीति	
87	८७	सप्ताशीति	
88	८८	अष्टाशीति	
89	८९	नवाशीति or एकोननवति &c.	
90	९०	नवति *fem.*	नवतितम, ०मी
91	९१	एकनवति	एकनवत, or ०ती or एकनवतितम ०मी
92	९२	द्वानवति or द्विनवति	
93	९३	त्रयोनवति or त्रिनवति	

94	९४	चतुर्नवति	
95	९५	पञ्चनवति	
96	९६	षण्णवति	
97	९७	सप्तनवति	
98	९८	अष्टानवति or अष्टनवति	
99	९९	नवनवति एकोनशतम् &c.	
100	१००	शत *neu.*	शततम *mas. neu.* ०मी *f.*
200	२००	द्विशत *neu* or द्वे शते	
300	३००	त्रिशत *neu.* or त्रीणि शतानि	
1000	१०००	सहस्र *neu.* or दशशत *neu.*	सहस्रतम ०मी or दशशती

10,000 अयुत *neu.* 100,000 लक्ष *neu.* or लक्षा *fem.*, प्रयुत *neu.*, कोटि *fem.*, अर्बुद *neu.*, अब्ज *neu.*, खर्व *mas. neu.* निखर्व *mas. neu.* महापद्म *mas.*, शंकु *mas.*, जलधि *mas.*, अन्त्य *neu.* मध्य *neu.*, and परार्ध *neu.* Each of these is ten times as great as the preceding.*

§ 160. The cardinal numbers between विंशति and त्रिंशत्, त्रिंशत् and चत्वारिंशत्, it will be seen, are made up by prefixing एक, द्वि, &c. up to नवन् to the lower. The ninth intermediate number may also be made up by prefixing एकोन, ऊन or एकान्न to the higher. In these compounds द्वि, त्रि and अष्टन् are changed to द्वा, त्रयः, and अष्टा necessarily before विंशति and त्रिंशत्, and optionally before the rest except अशीति before which they remain unchanged. †

---

* एकदशशतसहस्रायुतलक्षप्रयुतकोटयः क्रमशः ।
अर्बुदमब्जं खर्वनिखर्वमहापद्मशंकवस्तस्मात् ॥
जलधिश्चान्त्यं मध्यं परार्धमिति दशगुणोत्तराः संज्ञाः ।
संख्यायाः स्थानानां व्यवहारार्थं कृताः पूर्वैः ॥

† द्व्यष्टनः संख्यायामबहुव्रीह्यशीत्योः । त्रेस्त्रयः । विभाषा चत्वारिंशत्प्रभृतौ सर्वेषाम् । Pân. VI. 3. 47–49

§ 161. The cardinal numbers between 100 and 200, 200 and 300, &c. are generally expressed by means of अधिक added to the number showing the excess and then optionally prefixing the whole to 100, 200, &c, *e. g.* एकाधिकं शतं or एकाधिकशतं 101, द्वादशाधिकं शतं or द्वादशाधिकशतं 112, पञ्चाशदधिकं शतं 150. &c. After 1000 this अधिक may be repeated with every multiple of ten or hundred; *e. g.* द्वि-द्वानवत्यधिकाष्टशताधिकसहस्रम् 1892, एकोनचत्वारिंशदधिकषट्शताधिकसप्तसप्ततिसहस्राधिकं लक्षम् 177639, &c. Similarly उत्तर may also be used insted of अधिक *e. g.* चतुःपञ्चाशदुत्तरं सप्तशतम् 754. Or these may also be, at times, expressed by the copulative particle च as सप्त च शतानि विंशतिश्च 720.

§ 162. The Tad. affix अ* may be used, instead of अधिक, in the case of the cardinal numbers ending in दशम्, the numeral विंशति and those ending in शत् *i. e.* in the case of the numerals 111-159, 211-259, 311-359, &c. and qualifying the numerals शत and सहस्र before which the final अन्, अति and अत् are dropped *e. g.* एकादशं शतम् 111, विंशं शतं 120, पञ्चाशं शतं 150, सप्तदशं द्विशतं 217, त्रिंशं त्रिशतं 330 and so on.

§ 163. The ordinals from एक, द्वि, त्रि, चतुर् and षष् † are irregularly formed. The ordinal from other numerals up to दशन् inclusive are formed by dropping the final न् and adding म and after दशन् up to नवदशन् by simply dropping the न्. The ordinals from विंशति ‡ above are formed by adding तम or by dropping the ति of विंशति and the final consonant of the rest; the compound numerals, in this latter case, change the final vowel to अ, while the simple ones ending in a vowel *i. e.* षष्टि

---

*तदस्मिन्नधिकमिति दशान्ताड्डः । शदन्तविंशतेश्च । Pân. V. 2. 45. 46. शतसहस्रयोरेवेष्यते । Vârt.

† षट्कतिकतिपयचतुरां थुक् । Pân. V. 2. 51; so कतिथः, चतुर्थः &c.; 'चतुरश्छयतावाद्यक्षरलोपश्च' Vârt. तुरीय, तुर्य, । द्वेस्तीयः । त्रेः सम्प्रसारणं च । Pân. V. 2. 54, 55.

‡ विंशत्यादिभ्यस्तमडन्यतरस्याम् ।षष्ट्यादेश्चासंख्यादेः ।Pân. V.3.56,58.

सप्तति, अशीति and नवति form their ordinals in the first way only; as एकषष्टः or एकषष्टितमः, but षष्टितम only. शत has invariably शततम.

DECLENSION OF THE NUMERALS (CARDINALS AND ORDINALS)

§ 164. एक (एका *fem.*), द्वि (द्वा *fem.*), त्रि (तिसृ* *fem.*), and चतुर् (चतसृ *fem.*), are all adjectives and takes the gender, number and case of the nouns they qualify.

§ 165. एक is declined in the sing. (though it may have the dual and plural also), and द्वि in the dual alone. For further particulars see § 154. त्रि and चतुर् are declined in the plu. alone. *E. g.*

	त्रि *mas.*	त्रि *fem.*		चतुर *mas.*	चतुर *fem.*
N.	त्रयः	तिस्रः	N.	चत्वारः	चतस्रः
A.	त्रीन्	"	A.	चतुरः	"
I.	त्रिभिः	तिसृभिः	I.	चतुर्भिः	चतसृभिः
D. Ab.	त्रिभ्यः	तिसृभ्यः	D. Ab.	चतुर्भ्यः	चतसृभ्यः
G.	त्रयाणाम्	तिसृणाम्	G.	चतुर्णाम्	चतसृणाम
L.	त्रिषु	तिसृषु	L.	चतुर्षु	चतसृषु

neu.

त्रि		चतुर्	
N. V. A.	त्रीणि	N. V. A.	चत्वारि

The rest like the *mas.* The rest like the *mas.*

§ 166. पञ्चन्—नवदशन्. These are also adjectives agreeing in case with the nouns to which they are applied. They are declined in the pl. and are uniform in all the three genders.

	पञ्चन्	षष्	अष्टन्
N. V. A.	पञ्च	षट्-ड्	अष्ट
I.	पञ्चभिः	षड्भिः	अष्टभिः-अष्टाभिः
Dat. & Ab.	पञ्चभ्यः	षड्भ्यः	अष्टभ्यः-अष्टाभ्यः

* त्रिचतुरोः स्त्रियां तिसृचतसृ । Pàn. VII. 2. 99.

G.	पञ्चानाम्	षण्णाम्	अष्टानाम्
L.	पञ्चसु	षट्सु	अष्टसु-अष्टासु

सप्तन्, नवन् and the following cardinals up to नवदशन् ought to be declined like पञ्चन्.

§ 167. ऊनविंशति, विंशति and other cardinal numbers up to नवनवति are all *feminine* substantives, the numerals शत, सहस्र, &c. are all *neuter*, with the exception of लक्ष which is *neu.* and *fem.* कोटि which is *fem.* and शंकु and जलधि both of which are *mas.* and have no declensional peculiarities. They are declined in the sing. and so used with a plural noun; *e. g.* पंचविंशतिर्ब्राह्मणाः 25 Brâhmaṇas; एकादशाधिकशतेन or एकादशोत्तरेण शतेन नरैः or स्त्रीभिः by 111 men or women; एकोनसहस्रेण रूपकैः with Rs. 999 &c. They may be made to have duals and plurals by being used as fixed standards of counting; *e. g.* ब्राह्मणानां विंशतयः many twenties of Brâhmaṇas; द्वे शते नारीणाम् two hundreds of women &c.

§ 168. The ordinals are declined regularly except:—

प्रथम (see § 156) and द्वितीय and तृतीय which are optionally declined like pronouns in the Dat. Ab. Gen. and Loc. sing; *e. g.* द्वितीयस्मै-द्वितीयाय, &c. द्वितीयायाः-द्वितीयस्याः &c.

NUMERAL ADVERBS.

§ 169. (*a*) सकृत् once, द्विः twice, त्रिः thrice, चतुः four times; from पञ्चन् onwards adverbs of frequency are formed by adding कृत्वः before which final न् is dropped *e. g.* पञ्चकृत्वः five times, सप्तकृत्वः seven times, &c.

(*b*) एकधा* or ऐकध्यम् in one way or part, द्विधा or द्वेधा or द्वैधं in two ways or parts; त्रिधा or त्रेधा or त्रैधम् in three ways, &c.; चतुर्धा in four ways, षोढा or षड्धा in six ways, सप्तधा, अष्टधा, &c.

*संख्याया विधार्थे धा। अधिकरणविचाले च। एकाद्धो ध्यमुञन्यतरस्याम्। द्वित्र्योश्च धमुञ्। एधाच्च Pân. V. 3. 42–46.

(c) एकशः one by one; द्विशः two and two, by twos; so त्रिशः शतशः &c.

§ 170. Other derivatives from the numerals:—

(a) by the Taddhita affix क which is added to numerals ending in शत् and ति e. g. पञ्चकः bought for five (rupees &c.) चत्वारिंशत्कः bought for forty; वैंशतिकः bought for twenty (coins, &c.)

(b) *by means of the Tad. affix तय in the sense of "consisting of parts" or "collection"; e. g. चतुष्टय (चतुष्टयी *fem.*) consisting of four parts or a collection of four; so पञ्चतय (*fem.* यी); तय is optionally changed to अय after द्वि and त्रि e. g. द्वय or द्वितय (-यी *fem.*) twofold, consisting of two parts, or a pair; त्रय or त्रितय (-यी *fem.*) threefold or consisting of three parts, a collection of three, a triad.

(c) by means of क and अत् e. g. षट्क a collection of six, पञ्चत् collection of five, दशत् a collection of ten, a decade, &c.

Chapter VI

DEGREE OF COMPARISON.

§ 171. तर and तम are the most common terminations of the comparative and the superlative degrees respectively.† They are added to that crude form of words which they assume, before the Inst. dual termination; e. g. अयमेतयोरतिशयेन लघुः लघुतरः, अयमेषामतिशयेन लघुतमः; similarly युवन्,—युवतर, युवतम;

---

* See Chap. IX. Intro. rules.

† अतिशायने तमबिष्ठनौ। द्विवचनविभज्योपपदे तरबीयसुनौ। तिङश्च। तरप्तमपौ घः Pân. V. 3. 55. 57. 56; I. 1. 22. When *atis'aya* or excess of the one thing over many is to be shown तम and इष्ठ are the affixes used; and when out of two things one is to be separated as possessing some quality in excess तर and ईयस् are affixed. तर and तम may also added to verbs.

विद्वस्-विद्वत्तर, विद्वत्तम; प्राच्-प्राक्तर, प्राक्तम; धनिन्-धनितर, धनितम; धर्मभुध्-धर्मभुत्तर, धर्मभुत्तम; गुरु-गुरुतर, गुरुतम, &c; आति-आतितर अतितम; उत्-उत्तर, उत्तम, &c.

§ 172. Before these the final ई and ऊ of a *prátipadika* are optionally shortened, *e g.* श्रीतरा or श्रितरा, श्रीतमा or श्रितमा; घेमूतरा (more lame) or घेमुतरा, घेमूतमा, घेमुतमा, &c.

§ 173. तर and तम when attached to verbs, and indeclinables forming adverbs, assume the forms of तराम् and तमाम्*; पचतितराम्, पचतितमाम्; उच्चैस्तराम्; उच्चैस्तमाम्; नितराम् नितमाम्; or सुतराम् &c.; but उच्चैस्तर: adj. (higher).

§ 174. ईयस् is another termination of the comparative degree and इष्ठ of the superlative. These are added to adjectives of quality only †. Before these the last vowel of a word with the following consonant if any is dropped; *e. g.* लघु-लघीयस्, लघिष्ठ; पटु, पटीयस्, पटिष्ठ; महत् महीयस. महिष्ठ; &c. but पाचकतर, पाचकतम only.

§ 175. The possessive affixes at the end of words and the affix तृ are dropped before ईयस् and इष्ठ‡ and then these terminations are applied subject to the above rule; *e. g.* मतिमत् talented मतीयस्, मतिष्ठ; मेधाविन्-मेधीयस्, मेधिष्ठ; धनिन्-धनीयस्-धनिष्ठ, कर्तृ-करीयस्, करिष्ठ (अतिशयेन कर्ता); स्तोतृ-स्तवीयस्, स्तविष्ठ; so स्रजीयस्, स्रजिष्ठ from स्रग्विन् one having a garland &c.

§ 176. § र is substituted for the ऋ (short) of a base preceded by a consonant before ईयस्, इष्ठ and the Tad. aff. इमन् *e. g.*

---

* किमेत्तिङव्ययघादाम्वद्रव्यप्रकर्षे । Pân. V. 4. 11. आम् is added to तर and तम after किम्, or a word ending in ए or a *subanta* or *tiñantá* (तिङन्त) except when they form adjectives.

† अजादी (*i. e.* ईयस् and इष्ठ) गुणवचनादेव । Pân. V. 3. 58.

‡ विन्मतोर्लुक् । तुरिष्ठेमेयःसु । Pân. VI. 4, 154.

§ र ऋतो हलादेर्लघोः । Pân. VI. 4. 1J1.

कृश 'thin'	comp. क्रशीयस्	superl. क्रशिष्ठ
दृढ 'strong, firm'	,, द्रढीयस्	,, द्रढिष्ठ
परिवृढ 'head, chief'	,, परिव्रढीयस्	,, परिव्रढिष्ठ
पृथु 'broad'	,, प्रथीयस्	,, प्रथिष्ठ
भृश 'much'	,, भ्रशीयस्	,, भ्रशिष्ठ
मृदु 'soft'	,, म्रदीयस्	,, म्रदिष्ठ

§ 177. The following is an alphabetical list of the irregular comparatives and superlatives that are commonly met with:—

Positive	Comparative	Superlative
अन्तिक 'near'*	नेदियस्	नेदिष्ठ
अल्प 'little'†	अल्पीयस्	अल्पिष्ठ
	कनीयस्	कनिष्ठ
उरु 'wide'‡	वरीयस्	वरिष्ठ
क्षिप्र 'quick'§	क्षेपीयस्	क्षेपिष्ठ
क्षुद्र 'mean,' 'small'	क्षोदीयस्	क्षोदिष्ठ
गुरु 'heavy'	गरीयस्	गरिष्ठ
तृप्र 'restless or anxious' 'satisfied'	त्रपीयस्	त्रपिष्ठ
दीर्घ 'long'	द्राघीयस्	द्राघिष्ठ
दूर 'distant'	दवीयस्	दविष्ठ
प्रशस्य 'praiseworthy' ×	श्रेयस् or ज्यायस्	श्रेष्ठ or ज्येष्ठ
प्रिय 'dear'	प्रेयस्	प्रेष्ठ

* अन्तिकबाढयोर्नेदसाधौ । Pán. V. 3. 36.

† युवाल्पयोः कनन्यतरस्याम् । Pân. 3. 64.

‡ प्रियस्थिरस्फिरोरुबहुलगुरुवृद्धतृप्रदीर्घवृन्दारकाणां प्रस्थस्फवर्बंहिगर्वर्षित्रप्द्राघिवृन्दाः । Pân. VI. 4. 157. प्र, स्थ, स्फ, वर् &c. are substituted for प्रिय, स्थिर, स्फिर, &c. respectively.

§ स्थूलदूरयुवह्रस्वक्षिप्रक्षुद्राणां यणादिपरं पूर्वस्य च गुणः । Pân. VI 4. 156. The words स्थूल &c. drop iheir final portion beginning with यण् (य्, र्, ल् or व्) and the preceding vowel takes guṇa.

× प्रशस्यस्य श्रः । ज्य च । वृद्धस्य च Pán. V. 3. 60–62.
बहोर्लोपो भू च बहोः । इष्ठस्य यिट् च । Pân. VI. 4. 158–159.

बहु 'much'*	भूयस्	भूयिष्ठ
बहुल ,,	बंहीयस्	बंहिष्ठ
बाढ 'firm, well'	साधीयस्	साधिष्ठ
युवन् 'young'	यवीयस्, कनीयस्	यविष्ठ, कनिष्ठ
विपुल 'much'	ज्यायस्	ज्येष्ठ
वृद्ध 'old'	वर्षीयस्, ज्यायस्	वर्षिष्ठ, ज्येष्ठ
वृन्दारक 'great lovely'	वृन्दीयस्	वृन्दिष्ठ
स्थिर 'steady'	स्थेयस्	स्थेष्ठ
स्थूल 'big, large'	स्थवीयस्	स्थविष्ठ
स्फिर 'much'	स्फेयस्	स्फेष्ठ
ह्रस्व 'short'	ह्रसीयस्	ह्रसिष्ठ

§ 178. **Sometimes the terminations तर and तम are added to the comp. and super. in ईयस् and इष्ठ to intensify the meaning; as पापीयस्तर, पापीयस्तम; श्रेष्ठतर, श्रेष्ठतम.**

Chapter VII.

COMPOUNDS.

§ 179. Vṛitti (वृत्ति) is the general term for any complex formation in Sanskṛit requiring explanation or resolution. These Vṛittis are five in number; *viz.* कृद्वृत्ति or the formation of words from roots by primary affixes; तद्धितवृत्ति or the formation of derivative bases from nouns by secondary affixes; धातुवृत्ति or the formation of derivative verbs from primitive roots; समासवृत्ति or the formation of a compound word by the composition of several words; and एकशेषवृत्ति or the composition of words in which one of several nouns generally alike in form is retained. The first three will be treated in their proper places. We will treat of the last two in this Chapter.

---

* See note × p. 112.

§ 180. In Sanskrit simple words, whether substantives, adjectives, verbs or indeclinables, have the power of entering into combination with one another and forming what are called '*Samâsas**', compound words or, in short, compounds.

(*a*) A compound thus formed may further be compounded with another simple or compound word, and this again may become the member of a new compound.

§ 181. In a compound, as a general rule, words are simply joined together, without any relation between the component parts being actually expressed; the whole compound word has the power to express the various relations that exist between the several parts. The last word only takes the case termination required by its grammatical position in a sentence, the remaining words (those ending in a consonant) generally assuming their crude forms before the consonantal case terminations; *e. g.* विद्वस्+जनः=विद्वज्जनः (see below), राजन्+पुरुषः=राजपुरुषः, &c.

§ 182. Final vowels or consonants (modified as mentioned above) of preceding members of compounds combine with the initial letters of the succeeding members according to the usual rules of Sandhi.

§ 183. In a few cases, the intermediate members retain their case endings in which case the compounds are called '*Aluk*' (अलुक्); *e. g.* देवानांप्रियः a fool, युधिष्ठिरः name of the eldest Pándava &c.

§ 184. The expounding of a *Samása* (*i. e.* giving its *Vigrahavákya*) consists in the expression of the various relations existing between the objects or ideas denoted by the various members of a *Samása* by means of the proper cases or subordinate sentences.

(*a*) When the *Vigrahavákya* cannot be given, or cannot be given by using the words actually compounded, the compound is called *nityasamása* (अविग्रहो नित्यसमासः अस्वपदविग्रहो वा । Sid. Kau.).

---

* From अस् with सम् to throw together.

§ 185. Compounds are divided into four principal classes:*— (1) *Dwandwa* or Copulative, (2) *Tatpurusha* or Determinative, (3) *Bahuvrîhi* or Attributive, and (4) *Avyayîbhâva* or Adverbial.

N. B. These names themselves mean nothing *i. e.* they do not denote any of the characteristics of the different compounds. They are simply proper names distinguishing the various classes from one another (to which they vaguely refer if they do so at all).

DWANDWA OR THE COPULATIVE COMPOUNDS.

§ 186. A Dwandwa compound consists of two or more nouns which, if not compounded, would be connected by the copulative particle च (and); † as रामकृष्णौ which is equal to रामः च कृष्णः च; पाणिपादं which is the same as पाणी च पादौ च. There are three species of the Dwandwa; *viz.* इतरेतरद्वन्द्व, समाहारद्वन्द्व and एकशेष. ‡

---

* This is true only generally speaking. For there is a fifth class of compounds, *viz,* सह सुपा-compounds not governed by any of the rules given under the four classes but explained on the general principle that any *subanta pada* may be compounded with any other *subanta pada.* According to some there are six kinds of compounds, *viz.* सुपां सुपा तिङा नाम्ना धातुनाथ तिङा तिङा। सुबन्तेनेति विज्ञेयः समासः षड्विधो बुधैः ॥ *e. g.* सुपां सुपा राजपुरुषः। तिङा पर्यभूषत्। नाम्ना कुम्भकारः। धातुना कटप्रूः, अजस्रम्। तिङा तिङा पिबतखादता, खादतमोदता। तिङा सुपा कृन्तविचक्षणेति यस्यां क्रियायां सा कृन्तविचक्षणा। एहीडादयोन्यपदार्थे इति मयूरव्यंसकादौ पाठात्समासः। Sid. Kau.

† चार्थे द्वन्द्वः। Pân. II. 2. 22.

‡ The *Ekaśesha* is not strictly speaking a subdivision of Dwandwa. It is a separate Vṛitti by itself (Vide § 179). Sanskṛit grammarians do not regard it as a Dwandwa, though it may be so regarded for the sake of convenience. 'It is not a *Dwandwa,*' remarks Bhattoji Dîkshita, 'as it does not contain more than one *subanta* (अनेकसुबन्ताभावाद्द्वन्द्वः).' It should be further remembered that since it is not a *samâsa,* its final vowel does not become *udâtta,* as in the case of a Dwandwa compound.

§ 187. When the several members of a Dwandwa compound are viewed separately, it is called *Itaretara* Dwandwa, *e. g.* धवखदिरौ छिन्धि, 'cut down the Dhava and the Khadira trees' In this species each member is of equal importance *i. e.* has its own independent meaning. It takes the dual or the plural according as the objects denoted by it are two or more in number; the gender of the final noun is the gender of the whole;* as कुक्कुटश्च a cock मयूरी a pea-hen च कुक्कुटमयूर्यौ इमे (*fem.* dual of इदम्); but मयूरी च कुक्कुटश्च मयूरकुक्कुटौ इमौ; रामश्च लक्ष्मणश्च भरतश्च शत्रुघ्नश्च रामलक्ष्मणभरतशत्रुघ्ना: &c.

Exceptions—अश्वश्च वडवा च अश्ववडवौ (*mas.* dual) a horse and a mare; अहश्च रात्रिश्च अहोरात्रः (*mas.* sing. day and night).

§ 188. Samâhâra Dwandwa is that species of Dwandwa which implies an aggregate or the things enumerated in which constitute a complex idea. It is always singular and *neuter.* Thus आहारनिद्राभयम् does not merely mean 'food, sleep and fear' but all that characterises animal life. In this species the meaning of the different members is subordinate to the collective sense of the whole compound.

§ 189. †A Dwandwa compound of words denoting limbs of the body of an animal, players on musical instruments, parts of an army, inanimate objects (things or द्रव्य and not qualities) names of rivers differing in gender, as also of countries (and not villages), and insects, and animals between which there is natural antipathy, is always of this nature; पाणी च पादौ च पाणिपादम् hands and feet; रथिकाश्च अश्वारोहाश्च रथिकाश्वारोहम् chariot-warriors and horse-men मार्दङ्गिकाश्च पाणविकाश्च मार्दङ्गिकपाणविकम् players on

* परवल्लिङ्गं द्वंद्वतत्पुरुषयोः। Pân. II. 4. 26.

† द्वंद्वश्च प्राणितूर्यसेनाङ्गानाम्। Pân. II. 4. 2; जातिरप्राणिनाम् Pân. II. 4. 6.; विशिष्टलिङ्गो नदीदेशोऽग्रामाः। Pân. II. 4. 7., क्षुद्रजन्तवः Pân. II. 4. 8. येषां च विरोधः शाश्वतिकः Pân. II. 4. 9.

mridanga and *panava* (kinds of tabors); धानाश्च fried barley or rice शष्कुल्यश्च a kind of sweetmeat धानाशष्कुलि; but रूपं च रसश्च रूपरसौ form and flavour, as these denote qualities; गंगा च शोणश्च गंगाशोणम् the rivers Ganges and Sona; but गंगायमुने as these do not differ in gender; कुरवश्च कुरुक्षेत्रं च कुरुकुरुक्षेत्रम् names of countries; but जाम्बवशालूकिन्यौ (two villages of that name); मद्राश्च केकयाश्च मद्रकेकयाः (two names of the same gender); यूका a louse च लिक्षा a nit च यूकालिक्षम्; अहिश्च नकुलश्च अहिनकुलम् a snake and an ichneumon, &c.

§ 190. Names of trees, deer, grass, corn, condiments, beasts. birds, the pairs of words—अश्व and वडव, पूर्व and अपर, उत्तर and अधर—and words of opposite import not qualifying things (द्रव्यs), are optionally compounded into a Samâhâra Dwandwa;* instances in order—प्लक्षाश्च न्यग्रोधाश्च प्लक्षन्यग्रोधम्-धाः ; similarly रुरुपृषतम्-ताः (kinds of deer), कुशकाशम्-शाः kinds of grass, व्रीहियवम्-वाः kinds of corn, दधिघृतं-ते, गोमहिषम्-षाः, शुकबकं-काः, अश्ववडवं-वौ, पूर्वापरं-रे, अधरोत्तरं-रे; but शीतोष्णे जले.

§ 191. The names of fruits, parts of an army. herbs. deer. birds, insects, corn and grass, form a Samâhâra-Dwandwa, only when they are taken in the plural;† as बदराणि च आमलकानि च बदरामलकम्, but बदरं च आमलकं च बदरामलके; रथिकश्च अश्वारोहश्च रथिकाश्वारोहौ, &c.

§ 192. The following compounds are always what they are laid down to be (though they do not conform to the proper rules); *viz.*

(*a*) Samâhâra Dwandwas:—गावश्च अश्वाश्च गवाश्वम्; पुत्राश्च

---

* विभाषा वृक्षमृगतृणधान्यव्यञ्जनपशुशकुन्यश्ववडवपूर्वापराधोत्तराणाम्। विप्रतिषिद्धं चानधिकरणवाचि। Pân. II. 4. 12, 13.

† फलसेनावनस्पतिमृगशकुनिक्षुद्रजन्तुधान्यतृणानां बहुप्रकृतिरेव द्वंद्व एकवदिति वाच्यम्। Vârtika.

पौत्राश्व; पुत्रपौत्रम; so स्त्रीकुमारम्, उष्ट्रखरम् camels and asses, उष्ट्रशशम् camels and rabbits, मांससोणितम्, दर्शशरम् holy grass and reeds, तृणोलपम् grass and soft grass or shrubs, दासीदासम् &c.

(*b*) Itaretara Dwandwas:—दधिपयसी curds and milk, इध्माबर्हिषी holy sticks and grass, सर्पिर्मधुनी, मधुसर्पिषी honey and ghee, शुक्लकृष्णौ, अध्ययनतपसी, आद्यवसाने, उलूखलमुसले, ऋक्सामे (ऋक्+सामन्) Rik and the Sâman verses; वाङ्मनसे (वाक्+मनस्) speech and mind (the न् of सामन् dropped and अ added to मनस् irregularly by Pán. V. 4. 77)

§ 193. When words ending in ऋ and implying relationship by blood or literary avocation are compounded together, the last but one word changes its ऋ to आ. The same happens when the word पुत्र follows a word ending in ऋ under the same circumstances; * होता च पोता च होतापोतारौ two priests so called, होता च पोता च नेष्टा च उद्गाता च होतृपोतृनेष्टोद्गातारः, (but if two words be taken at a time the ऋ may, at every step, be changed into आ; as होता च पोता च होतापोतारौ तौ च उद्गाता च होतापोतोद्गारः &c.); पिता च पुत्रश्च पितापुत्रौ, माता च पिता च मातापितरौ, also मातरपितरौ (Pán. VI. 3. 32.), and पितरौ (vide § 197 *a*).

§ 194. (*a*) When the names of deities well known to be in constant association with each other are compounded, आ is substituted for the final vowel of the preceding word, except in the case of the word वायु ×; *e. g.* मित्रावरुणौ, सूर्याचन्द्रमसौ, अग्नामरुतौ, &c. but अग्निवायू or वाय्वग्नी.

(*b*) The word अग्नि followed by the word सोम or वरुण lengthens its इ; as अग्नीषोमौ, अग्नीवरुणौ.

---

* आनङ् ऋतो द्वन्द्वे । Pân. VI. 3. 25. द्वयोर्द्वयोर्द्वंद्वं कृत्वा पुनर्द्वंद्वे तु होतापोतोद्गातारः । Sid. Kau.

× देवताद्वंद्वे च । Pán. VI. 3. 26. वायुशब्दप्रयोगे प्रतिषेधः । Vârt. ईदग्नेः सोमवरुणयोः । Pán. VI. 3. 27.

§ 195. When a Samâhâra-Dwandwa ends in a consonant of the palatal class or द्, ष्, or ह्, अ is added to it : वाक् च त्वक् च वाक्त्वचम् speech and skin, त्वक्स्रजम् a bark and a garland, शमीदृषदम्, वाक्त्विषम्, छत्रोपानहम् an umbrella and shoes, &c, But प्रावृट्शरदौ (as it is not a Sám. Dwa.).

§ 196. The following compounds are instances of irregular Dwandwas:—

(*a*) द्यौश्च पृथिवी च द्यावापृथिव्यौ or दिवस्पृथिव्यौ † heaven and earth; so द्यावाभूमी, द्यावाक्षमे; उषस् + सूर्य = उषासासूर्यौ the goddess of dawn and the sun.

(*b*) जाया + पति = दम्पती,‡ जम्पती and जायापती husband and wife.

(*c*) ¶ स्त्री च पुमांश्च स्त्रीपुंसौ, धेनुश्च अनड्वांश्च धेन्वनडुहौ, अक्षिणी च भ्रुवौ च अक्षिभ्रुवम्, दाराश्च गावश्च दारगवम्, ऊरू च अष्ठीवन्तौ च ऊर्वष्ठीवम् (thighs and knees.), पादौ च अष्ठीवन्तौ च पदष्ठीवम्; नक्तं च दिवा च नक्तंदिवम्, रात्रौ च दिवा च रात्रिन्दिवम्, अहनि च दिवा च अहर्दिवम्, all meaning 'day and night'.

§ 197. When several words of the same form (or dissimilar in form but of the same import ×) are compounded together, only one of them is retained with the necessary number-

---

* द्वंद्वाच्चुदषहान्तात्समाहारे । Pán. V. 4. 106.

† दिवो द्यावा । दिवसश्च पृथिव्याम् । Pán. VI. 3. 29, 30.

‡ दम्पती is considered by some to be a word of regular formation. दम् in the Vedic literature means 'a house' and पति 'a master'. Hence the full word दम्पती would mean 'the mistress of the house.'

¶ [A final अ is added in the case of these compounds according to a Sûtra of Pàn. (अचतुर V. 4. 77.) quoted further on under § 284.

× विरूपाणामपि समानार्थानाम् । Vârt. वक्रदण्डश्च कुटिलदण्डश्च वक्रदण्डौ or कुटिलदण्डौ ।

e. g. रामश्च रामश्च रामौ, रामश्च रामश्च रामश्च रामाः। This is called एकशेषद्वन्द्वः. In the case of the *mas.* and *fem.* genders the one of the *mas.* gender is retained;* as हंसी च हंसश्च हंसौ; similarly ब्राह्मणौ, शूद्रौ, अजौ, &c.

(*a*) This principle is further extended to some words dissimilar in form, as in the following examples:—भ्राता च स्वसा च भ्रातरौ, पुत्रश्च दुहिता च पुत्रौ†; माता च पिता च पितरौ (see also §193.), श्वश्रूश्च श्वशुरश्च श्वशुरौ ‡ (also श्वश्रूश्वशुरौ); स च सा च तौ स च देवदत्तश्च तौ, स च यश्च यौ or तौ×. In the case of words of the *mas. fem.* and *neu.* gender that of the *neu.* gender is retained; as तच्च देवदत्तश्च ते; तच्च देवदत्तश्च यज्ञदत्ता च तानि।

§ 198. The following rules should be observed in arranging the various members of a Dwandwa Compound:—

(*a*) △ A word ending in इ or उ should be placed first, and when there are more than one of such words one of these should be placed first, the rest being arranged according to the will of the speaker or writer; हरिहरौ, हरिहरगुरवः, हरिगुरुहराः, &c.

(*b*) †† Words beginning with a vowel and ending in अ ought to precede others; as अश्वरथेन्द्राः or इन्द्राश्वरथाः. This rule should have preference even over the above rule in case both would be simultaneously applicable; इन्द्राग्नी.

(*c*) || A word that has fewer syllables should be placed

---

* पुमान् स्त्रिया। Pân. 1. 2. 67.

† भ्रातृपुत्रौ स्वसृदुहितृभ्याम्। पिता मात्रा। Pân. 2. 68, 70.

‡ श्वशुरः श्वश्र्वा। त्यदादीनि सर्वैर्नित्यम्। Pân. 1. 2. 71. 72.

× पूर्वशेषोपि दृश्यते इति भाष्यम्। Sid. Kau. on Pân. 1. 2. 72.

△ द्वन्द्वे घि। Pân. II. 2. 32. अनेकप्राप्तावेकत्र नियमोऽनियमः शेषे। Vârt.

†† अजाद्यदन्तम्। Pân. II. 2. 33.

|| अल्पाच्तरम्। Pân. II. 2. 34. लघ्वक्षरं पूर्वम्। ऋतुनक्षत्राणां समानाक्षराणामानुपूर्व्येण। अभ्यर्हितं च। Vârt.

first and in case there are more words than one having an equal number of syllables, the one that has more short syllables should be placed first; *e. g.* शिवकेशवौ, ग्रीष्मवसन्तौ, कुशकाशम्, &c.; the names of seasons and stars, under this latter circumstance, should be arranged according to their astronomical order; as हेमन्तशिशिरवसन्ताः, कृत्तिकारोहिण्यौ, &c. Also a word of more important significance should precede others; as तापसपर्वतौ.

(*d*) * Names of the four castes of men should be arranged according to their order, beginning from the highest and so should be the names of brothers beginning from the eldest; *e. g.* ब्राह्मणक्षत्रियविट्शूद्राः; युधिष्ठिरार्जुनौ.

§ 199. In the case of words of the राजदन्तादि class that which ought to be placed first is placed last; while in the case of words of the धर्मादि group (a sub-division of राजदन्तादि) the rule is observed optionally †; शूद्रार्यम् a Śudra and an Arya, धर्मश्च अर्थश्च धर्मार्थौ or अर्थधर्मौ; so अर्थशब्दौ or शब्दार्थौ, अर्थकामौ or कामार्थौ, &c.

II. TATPURUSHA OR THE DETERMINATIVE COMPOUNDS.

§ 200. When a compound consists of two members and the first determines the sense of the other, that is called *Tatpurusha.*

§ 201. According to the grammatical nature of the first or attributive member the Tatpurusha is divided into six varieties:–

(1) *Tatpurusha* proper or the Inflectional, (2) *Nañ* or the Negative Tatpurusha, (3) *Karmadhâraya* or the Appositional including 'Dwigu'. (4.5) *Prâdi* and *Gati* or the Prepositional compounds, and (6) *Upapada.* These are either nouns, adjectives or abverbs.

§ 202. The final vowel of a feminine noun ending in any of

* वर्णानामानुपूर्व्येण । भ्रातुर्ज्यायसः । Vartikas on the above Sútra.

† राजदन्तादिषु परम् । Pân. II. 2. 31. धर्मादिष्वनियमः । Vârt.

the affixes आ, ई or ऊ and forming the second member of a compound used adjectively is shortened; the ओ of गो is changed to उ under the same circumstances*; *e. g.* प्राप्त + जीविका = प्राप्तजीविकः (Tat.), अतिमालः (Tat.); पञ्चगुः something bought for five cows; बह्व्यो नाड्यो यस्मिन् बहुनाडिः many-veined देहः (Bah.); चित्रा गावो यस्य चित्रगुः having variegated cows, &c. but कल्याणपञ्चमीकः as the ई is not final.

(*a*) If the final ई or ऊ be not a fem. termination, it remains unchanged; सुष्ठु धीः सा सुधीः, बहुतन्त्रीर्धमनी.

1 Tatpurusha.

§ 203. The first variety consists of such Tatpurusha compounds as have the attributive member in any one of the oblique cases when dissolved. There are six sub-varieties of this corresponding to the six oblique cases

§ 204. (*a*) A noun in the Accusative case is compounded with श्रित, अतीत, पतित, गत, अत्यस्त, प्राप्त. आपन्न, गमी, बुभुक्षु, and others †; as कृष्णं श्रितः कृष्णश्रितः one who has resorted to Krishṇa (as his refuge); दुःखमतीतः दुःखातीतः one who has overcome pain; सुखं आपन्नः सुखापन्नः one who has obtained happiness, ग्रामं गमी ग्रामगमी going to a village, a passenger; अन्नं बुभुक्षुः अन्नबुभुक्षुः &c.

N. B. प्राप्त and आपन्न may also be placed first; as प्राप्तो जीविकां प्राप्तजीविकः or जीविकाप्राप्तः one who has obtained livelihood; similarly आपन्नजीविकः or जीविकापन्नः; प्राप्तजीविका स्त्री, &c.

(*b*) A word expressive of the duration of an action or state is compounded with another expressive of the action or state, in the

---

* गोस्त्रियोरुपसर्जनस्य । Pán. I. 2. 48.

† द्वितीया श्रितातीतपतितगतात्यस्तप्राप्तापन्नैः । Pân. II. 1. 24. गम्यादीनामुपसंख्यानम् । Vârtika.

Accusative case; *e. g.* मुहूर्तं सुखं मुहूर्तसुखम् 'happiness lasting fo a moment'; संवत्सरं वासः संवत्सरवासः 'residence for a year' &c.

(*c*) The word खट्वा forms an Accusative Tatpurusha with a p. p. participle when censure is implied or contempt is to be shown†; as खट्वाम् आरूढः खट्वारूढः 'a silly fool'. *cf.* Bhatti. V. 10

(*d*) Sometimes a preposition or a word denoting a period of time may take the place of the Accusative‡; as सामिकृतं 'half done,' मासप्रमितः (प्रतिपच्चन्द्रः) 'what marks the commencement of a month as the new moon.'

§ 205. A noun in the Instrumental may be compounded—

(*a*) × with another expressive of an effect produced by what is denoted by the noun in the Instrumental case, and with अर्थ, as शङ्कुलया खण्डः शङ्कुलाखण्डः severed by means of a knife; धान्येन अर्थः धान्यार्थः wealth obtained by means of grain.

(*b*) ÷ with verbal derivatives when the Instrumental has thes ense of the agent or the instrument or means of the action; as हरिणा त्रातः हरित्रातः saved by Hari; नखैर्भिन्नः नखभिन्नः torn with the nails &c.

(*c*) with the words†† पूर्व, सदृश, सम, ऊन and words having the sense of ऊन, कलह, निपुण, मिश्र, श्लक्ष्ण and अवर; as मासेन पूर्वः मासपूर्वः; मात्रा सदृशः मातृसदृशः like his mother; पितृसमः equal to his

---

* अत्यन्तसंयोगे च । Pán. II. 1. 29.

† खट्वाक्षेपे । Pán. II. 1. 26.

‡ सामि । कालाः । Pân. II. 1. 27, 28.

× तृतीया तत्कृतार्थेन गुणवचनेन । Pán. II. 1. 30.

÷ कर्तृकरणे कृता बहुलम् । Pân. II. 1. 32.

†† पूर्वसदृशसमोनार्थकलहनिपुणमिश्रश्लक्ष्णैः । Pán. II. 1. 31.

father; माषेण ऊनं माषोनं; so माषविकल (less by one *másha*, a particular weight); वाचा कलहः वाक्कलहः a quarrel (in words); आचारनिपुणः; गुडमिश्रः, आचारश्लक्ष्णः 'thin by the discharge of religious duties' मासेन अवरः मासावरः 'younger by a month.'

(*d*)* With another noun signifying an article of food or something eatable, the noun in the Instrumental case denoting some kind of condiment used to season it or another article of food mixed with it; as दध्ना ओदनः दध्योदनः rice mixed with curds; गुडेन धानाः गुडधानाः fried rice mixed with treacle.

(*e*) Sometimes स्वयं may take the place of the Instrumental as स्वयंकृतः done by one's self.

§ 206. Instances of the *Aluk* of the Instrumental† (*i. e.* in which the noun in the Inst. does not drop its case term.)—अञ्जसा कृतम् अञ्जसाकृतम् 'done honestly'; ओजसाकृतम् 'done with might'; पुंसानुजः 'one having an elder brother'; जनुषान्धः 'blind from birth'; मनसागुप्ता, मनसाज्ञायी, when proper names, otherwise मनोगुप्ता, मनोज्ञायी, &c. आत्मन् followed by an ordinal number retains its case ending; as आत्मना पञ्चमः आत्मनापञ्चमः ।

§ 207. A noun in the Dative is compounded ×—

(*a*) with another expressive of the material of which the thing expressed by the noun in the Dative case is made; as यूपाय दारु यूपदारु, 'wood for a sacrificial post.'

(*b*) and with the words अर्थ, बलि, हित, सुख and रक्षित. The compound with अर्थ is a *nityasamása* and takes the gender and number of the noun it qualifies; द्विजाय अयं द्विजार्थः सूपः

---

* अन्नेन व्यञ्जनम् । भक्ष्येण मिश्रीकरणम् । Pān. II. 1. 34. 35.

† ओजःसहोम्भस्तमसस्तृतीयायाः। Pán. VI. 3. 3. अञ्जस उपसंख्यानम् । Vart. × चतुर्थी तदर्थार्थबलिहितसुखरक्षितैः । Pán. II. 1. 36.

broth for a Brâhmana; द्विजाय इयं द्विजार्था यवागूः (water-gruel) द्विजाय इदं द्विजार्थं पयः; भूतेभ्यो बलिः भूतबलिः an offering to the *bhûtas*(certain created beings); गवे हितं गोहितम् good for a cow; गवे सुखं गोसुखम्; गवे रक्षितं गोरक्षितम्.

§ 208. Instances of the *Aluk* of the Dat. परस्मैपदम्, परस्मैभाषा; आत्मनेपदम्, आत्मनेभाषा.

§ 209. A noun in the Ablative case is compounded*—

(*a*) with words expressive of fear or rather with the words भय, भीत, भीति and भीः; as चौराद् भयं चौरभयम् fear from a thief; वृकाद् भीतः वृकभीतः afraid of a wolf, &c.

(*b*) in a few cases with the words अपेत, अपोढ, मुक्त, पतित, and अपत्रस्त;† as सुखादपेतः सुखापेतः deprived of happiness; कल्पनाया अपोढः कल्पनापोढः 'transcending thought' or 'a fool;' चक्रमुक्तः, स्वर्गपतितः 'fallen from heaven, as a sinner'; तरङ्गापत्रस्तः 'afraid of waves'.

(*c*) in the case of the words स्तोक a little, अन्तिक near, दूर after, and words having the sense of these; and कृच्छ्र a difficulty, there is an *Aluk* of the Ablative;‡ as स्तोकाद् मुक्तः स्तोकान्मुक्तः; अल्पान्मुक्तः; अन्तिकादागतः; अभ्याशादागतः; दूरादागतः; विप्रकृष्टादागतः; कृच्छ्रादागतः ।

§ 210. A noun in the Genitive may, as a general rule, be compounded with any other noun; राज्ञः पुरुषः राजपुरुषः the king's man (an officer or a servant).

§ 211. †† (*a*) It is not compounded with verbal derivatives

* पञ्चमी भयेन। Pân. II. 1. 37. भयभीतभीतिभीभिरिति वाच्यम्। Vartika.

† अपेतापोढमुक्तपतितापत्रस्तैरल्पशः। Pân. II. 1. 38.

‡ स्तोकान्तिकदूरार्थकृच्छ्राणि क्तेन। Pân. II. 1. 39

†† तृजकाभ्यां कर्तरि। Pân. II. 2. 15.

ending in तृ and अक and denoting the agent of the action; अपां स्रष्टा and not अप्स्रष्टा; घटस्य कर्ता, ओदनस्य पाचकः &c.; but इक्षूणां भक्षणम् इक्षुभक्षिका as the अक here does not denote the agent.

Exception*:—But a compound is allowed in the case of the words याजक one who employs as sacrificing priests, पूजक, परिचारक, परिषेचक a waiter at meals, स्नापक a servant who bathes his master or brings bathing water for him, अध्यापक, उत्सादक one who destroys, होतृ, भर्तृ, when it does not mean 'a holder,' and others not very important; ब्राह्मणयाजकः, देवपूजकः, राजपरिचारकः &c.; अग्निहोता, भूभर्ता, &c. but वज्रस्य भर्ता 'the thunder-bolt-bearer'.

(*b*) † A specific Genitive (*i. e.* from which a singling out is made) is not compounded with any other words; as नृणां द्विजः श्रेष्ठः

(*c*) ‡ A noun in the Genitive is not compounded with ordinal numbers, words denoting qualities, words implying satisfaction present participles, past participles meaning 'honoured or approved of' or showing the place of the act, verbal indeclinables and verbal nouns ending in तव्य; *e. g.* सतां षष्ठः, ब्राह्मणस्य शुक्लाः (दन्ताः); काकस्य कार्ष्ण्यम्; फलानां सुहितः 'satisfied with fruits'. (an Inst. Tat. is, of course, allowed in these cases); द्विजस्य कुर्वन् कुर्वाणो वा किंकरः, सतां मतः esteemed by the good; राज्ञां पूजितः, इदमेषां आसितं (place of sitting) गतं भुक्तं वा; ब्राह्मणस्य कृत्वा, नरस्य कर्तव्यम् &c.

---

* याजकादिभिश्च । Pân. II. 2. 9

† न निर्धारणे । Pân. II. 2. 10.

‡ पूरणगुणसुहितार्थसदव्ययतव्यसमानाधिकरणेन । क्तेन च पूजायाम् अधिकरणवाचिना च । Pân. II. 2. 11-13. The prohibition with respect to a word expressive of a quality (गुण) is not obligatory, remarks Dîkshita; as Pân. himself uses such compounds as संज्ञाप्रमाणत्व &c. Hence compounds like अर्थगौरवम्, बुद्धिमान्द्यम्, &c. are justified (अनित्योयं गुणेन निषेधः तदशिष्यं संज्ञाप्रमाणत्वादित्यादिनिर्देशात् । तेनार्थगौरवं बुद्धिमान्द्यमित्यादि सिद्धम् ।).

N. B. Compounds like राजपूजितः, राजमतः, &c. ought to be considered as Instrumental Tatpurushas.

Exceptions.

(1) If the word denoting a quality ends in तर it does combine with a noun in the Genitive, and the तर is dropped; सर्वेषां श्वेततरः सर्वश्वेतः whiter than all others; similarly सर्वेषां महत्तरः सर्वमहान् &c.

(2)*The words द्वितीय, तृतीय, चतुर्थ and तुर्य are componuded with nouns signifying the whole of which they are parts, and are optionally placed first; द्वितीयं भिक्षायाः द्वितीयभिक्षा, भिक्षाद्वितीयम् half of the quantity of alms; but द्वितीयं भिक्षायाः (begging alms a second time) भिक्षुकस्य.

Note.—Compounds like द्वितीयभिक्षा, पूर्वकायः (see further on) &c. are not strictly Gen. Tat. as the case of the first word determines the name, but mere Tat.; some call these Nom. Tat. (प्रथामतत्पुरुष).

(*a*) †A noun in the Genitive, used as an object in a sentence, when the agent and object of the action denoted by the nouns formed by krit affixes are both used, is not compounded, as आश्चर्यो गवां दोहोऽगोपेन 'the milking of cows by one, not a cowherd, is a wonder.'

§ 212. ‡ पूर्व, अपर, अधर उत्तर and अर्ध n. are compounded with nouns in the Genitive expressive of the whole and are placed first; *e. g.* पूर्वं कायस्य पूर्वकायः the forepart of the body; अपरकायः अधरकायः &c. अर्धं पिप्पल्याः अर्धपिप्पली; but ग्रामार्धः as (अर्ध is *mas.* here).

N B. In order that the above rule should hold the noun expressive of the whole must denote a single object; hence पूर्वः

---

* द्वितीयतृतीयचतुर्थतुर्याण्यन्यतरस्याम् । Pân. II. 2. 3.

† कर्मणि च । Pân. II. 2. 14.

‡ पूर्वापराधरोत्तरमेकदेशिनैकाधिकरणे । अर्धं नपुंसकम् । Pân. II. 2. 1, 2.

the first छात्राणां, among pupils, अर्धं पिप्पलीनाम् half of a number of *pippalis* &c. and not पूर्वछात्रः &c.

§ 213. A word expressive of a part is compounded with another signifying a period of time and is placed first; मध्यं अह्नः मध्याह्नः mid-day; सायाह्नः, मध्यरात्रं &c.

§ 214.* A word expressive of a period of time that has passed since a certain occurrence is compounded with another expressive of the occurrence; as मासो जातस्य यस्य स मासजातः 'one since whose birth a month has elapsed'; so द्व्यहजातः, संवत्सरमृतः &c.

§ 215 † Instances of the *Aluk* of the Gen. The noun in the Genitive may retain its case ending—

(*a*) when reproach is to be implied; as चौरस्यकुलम्, but ब्राह्मणकुलम्. Also when देवानां is followed by प्रिय and the whole means a fool; otherwise देवप्रियः.

(*b*) when the words वाच्, दिश् and पश्यत् are followed by युक्ति, दण्ड and हर respectively; as वाचोयुक्तिः 'skilful speech;' दिशोदण्डः 'a particular appearance of stars in the shape of a staff in the sky;' पश्यतोहरः 'one who robs another in his very presence while he is looking on,' hence 'a goldsmith, a rogue.'

(*c*) in the following cases:—दिवोदासः 'a king of Kâshi,' दिवस्पतिः 'Indra,' वाचस्पतिः lord of speech, Brihaspati; शुनःशेपः, शुनःपुच्छः and शुनोलाङ्गूलः 'sons of Ajigarta.'

(*d*) and optionally when followed by पुत्र and censure is implied; दास्याः पुत्रः or दासीपुत्रः a bastard, a knave; but ब्राह्मणीपुत्रः

---

* कालाः परिमाणिना । Pân. II. 2. 5.

† षष्ठ्या आक्रोशे । Pân VI. 3. 21. देवानांप्रिय इति च मूर्खे । वाग्दिक्पश्यद्भ्यो युक्तिदण्डहरेषु । शेपपुच्छलाङ्गूलेषु शुनः । दिवश्च दासे । Vartikas. 'पुत्रेऽन्यतरस्याम्' Pan. VI. 3. 22.

(*c*)* When a word ending in ऋ is compounded with another and there is the relation by blood or some kind of learning, the *aluk* is necessary; and optional when it is followed by स्वसृ and पति. The initial स् of स्वसृ is optionally changed to ष् when preceded by मातृ or पितृ and when there is *aluk*, and necessarily when there is no *aluk* in a compound; *e. g.* होतुःपुत्रः, होतुरन्तेवासी, a pupil of the *hotri*; मातुःस्वसा, or मातुःष्वसा and मातृष्वसा; so पितुःस्वसा, &c. (but मातुः स्वसा, पितुः स्वसा when uncompounded); स्वसृपतिः or स्वसुःपतिः; but होतृधनम्.

§ 216. A noun in the Locative is compounded—

(*a*) †with शौण्ड, धूर्त, कितव a rogue, प्रवीण, संवीत adorned, invested with, अन्तर, अधि, पटु, पण्डित, कुशल, चपल, निपुण, सिद्ध, शुष्क, पक्व, and बन्ध; as अक्षेषु शौण्डः अक्षशौण्डः skilled in dice; ईश्वरे अधि ईश्वराधीनः dependent on God (when compounded the affix ख *i. e.* ईन is compulsory; so the compounded form is always with अधीन); आतपशुष्कः dried in the sun; स्थालीपक्वः cooked in a pot; चक्रबन्धः a kind of poetic composition; &c.

(*b*) ‡ with words meaning a 'crow' when contempt is implied; तीर्थे ध्वाङ्क्ष इव तीर्थध्वाङ्क्षः said in contempt of one who is very greedy; so तीर्थकाकः; similarly नगरकाकः—वायसः &c. &c.

There are a few Loc. Tat. compounds given in the list पात्रेसमितादि having a similar sense; *e. g.* कूपे मण्डूक इव कूपमण्डूकः a well-abiding frog *i. e.* one who knows nothing of the world

---

* ऋतो विद्यायोनिसम्बन्धेभ्यः । विभाषा स्वसृपत्योः Pân. VI. 3. 23. 24; मातुःपितुर्भ्यामन्यतरस्याम् । मातृपितृभ्यां स्वसा । Pân. VIII. 3. 84, 85.

† सप्तमी शौण्डैः । सिद्धशुष्कपक्वबन्धैश्च । Pân. II. 1. 40, 41.

‡ ध्वाङ्क्षेण क्षेपे । पात्रेसमितादयश्च । Pân. II. 1. 42, 48. चकारोऽवधारणार्थः । तेनैषां समासान्तरे घटकतया प्रवेशो न । Sid. Kau.

outside the pale of his own village; so कुंभ-उदपान-मण्डूकः; उदुम्बरकृमिः–मशकः *lit.* an insect in the fruit of the *Udumbara* tree; metaphorically it means the same as कूपमण्डूकः, कूपकच्छप: &c. In some cases there is an *aluk* of the Loc.; as गेहेशूरः 'a boasting coward', गेहेव्याडः 'a braggadocio'; गेहेनर्दी 'a house-hero', 'a carpet knight', पात्रेकुशलः 'clever in eating only' *i. e.* 'a good-for-nothing fellow'; पात्रेसमिताः; गोष्ठेशूरः; गोष्ठेविजयीः; गेहेधृष्टः, &c.

Note:—Words of this class do not enter into further combination with other words.

(*c*) * with another, when they both imply a name (संज्ञा); there is an *aluk* of the Loc. term. when the noun ends in a consonant or अ; as अरण्येतिलकाः *lit.* 'wild sesamum yielding no oil, hence anything not answering to one's expectations;' similarly वनेकसेरुकाः; त्वचिसारः 'a bamboo' (also त्वक्सारः, vide Si. IV. 61.). These compounds are *nitya* (obligatory) as remarked by Bhaṭṭoji (वाक्येन संज्ञानवगमान्नित्यसमासोयम्).

(*d*) with potential p. participles in य implying an obligation; मासेदेयं (ऋणम्); पूर्वाह्णेगेयं (साम); the *aluk* by § 217 (*b*) below.

(*e*) † with p. p. participles when it expresses a part of the day or night; तत्र may take the place of the Loc.; as पूर्वाह्णे कृतं पूर्वाह्णकृतम्; अपररात्रकृतम्: तत्रभुक्तम् &c; but अह्नि दृष्टं; and with the p. p. participles when reproach is implied, with an *aluk* of the Loc; as 'अवतप्तेनकुलस्थितं तवैतत्' 'this thy action is similar to that of a mungoose on the hot ground.' अवतप्तेनकुलस्थितं is used to express the inconstancy of a person.

---

* संज्ञायाम्। हलदन्तात्सप्तम्याः संज्ञायाम्। गवियुधिभ्यां स्थिरः। Pân I. I. 44. VI. 3 9. VIII. 3. 9. 5.

† क्तेनाहोरात्रावयवाः। तत्र। क्षेपे। Pân. II. 2. 45–47.

§ 217. Additional instances of the *aluk* of the Loc.

(*a*) *Aluk* is necessary in the case of the words—(1) गो and युध् followed by स्थिर; as गविष्ठिरः, stationary in the sky, युधिष्ठिरः firm in battle; (2) हृद् and दिव् followed by स्पृश्; हृदिस्पृक्, दिविस्पृक् (हृदयं दिवं च स्पृशतीति); (3) अन्त and मध्य followed by गुरु; मध्येगुरुः, अन्तेगुरुः and (4) words expressive of parts of the body except मूर्धन् and मस्तक and not followed by काम; कण्ठेकालः, उरसिलोमा (having the hair on the breast: Bah.), but मूर्ध-मस्तकशिखः, मुखे कामो अस्य मुखकामः.

(*b*) * When a noun in the Loc. is compounded with a verbal derivative and the whole is a name, *aluk* takes place in most cases; *e. g.* स्तम्बेरमः (स्तम्बे a kind of grass रमते असौ) an elephant; कर्णेजपः one who whispers into the ear, a spy; खेचरः a heavenly being; पंकेरुहं a lotus; कुशेशयम्, जलेशयः a fish; but कुरुचराः, सरसिजं or सरोजम् &c.

(*c*) There is optional *aluk* of the Loc. of a word expressive of time when compounded with काल and words ending in the affixed तर, तम and तन; पूर्वाह्ण-ह्णे-काले; पूर्वाह्ण-ह्णे-तरे &c. पूर्वाह्ण-ह्णे तने.

(*d*) † When the compound is not a name, *aluk* is necessary when ज comes after प्रावृट्, शरद्, काल and दिव्; and optional when it comes after वर्ष, क्षर, शर and वर; as प्रावृषि-शरदि-काले-दिवि जः; वर्षेजः or वर्षजः produced in the rainy season, &c.

Exceptions‡:—No *aluk* takes place in the case of verbal derivatives ending in इन् and the words सिद्ध, बद्ध, and स्थ in the ordinary language; as स्थण्डिलशायी 'an ascetic,' साङ्काश्यसिद्धः, चक्रबद्धः; समस्थः; but कृष्णोऽस्याखरेष्ठः &c.

---

* तत्पुरुषे कृति बहुलम्। Pán. VI. 3. 14.

† प्रावृट्शरत्कालदिवां जे। विभाषा वर्षक्षरशरवरात्। Pán VI. 3. 15.16.

‡ नेन्सिद्धबध्नातिषु च। स्थे च भाषायाम्। Pán. VI. 3. 19. 20.

(e) *When a noun in the Loc case ending in अ or a consonant and not denoting time is compounded with शय, वास and वासिन् and with बन्ध *aluk* is optional; खे-खशयः, ग्रामे-मवासः, ग्रामे-मवासी, हस्ते-स्तबन्धः, but भूमिशयः, गुप्तिबन्धः &c.

2. Nañ or the Negative Tatpurusha.

§ 218. (a) The negative particle न changed to अ before a consonant and अन् before a vowel, may be compounded with any noun to form the Negative-Tatpurusha†; as न ब्राह्मणः अब्राह्मणः, one not a Brâhmaṇa; न अश्वः अनश्वः, असत्, non-existent, or not good, &c.

§ 219. The न is not changed to अ or अन् in the following cases‡—नभ्राट् 'that which does not shine,' 'a cloud;' नपात् (pre. p.) 'one who does not protect;' नवेदाः 'one who does not know;' नासत्याः [न सत्याः असत्याः न असत्याः नासत्याः ×] the two Aświns, the physicians of the gods. नमुचिः [न मुञ्चतीतिः] name of a demon slain by Indra; नकुलः [न कुलमस्य, for the mungoose is supposed to belong to no particular species of animals]; नखं [न खमस्य that which leaves no cavity, or does not go to heaven being burnt down with the dead body]; नपुंसकं [न स्त्री पुमान्]; नक्षत्रं [न क्षरतीति] that which does not move from its proper place, hence a star; नक्रः [न क्रामतीति that which does not go far off from water]; नाकः [न कं अकं न अकं अस्मिन्]; नग when it

---

* बन्धे च विभाषा । शयवासवासिष्वकालात् । Pán. VI. 3. 13. 18.

† नञ् । Pán. II.2.6. न लोपो नञः । तस्मान्नुडचि। Pán. VI. 3,73.74

‡ नभ्राण्नपान्नवेदानासत्यानमुचिनकुलनखनपुंसकनक्षत्रनक्रनाकेषु प्रकृत्या । Pán. VI. 3. 75. नगोऽप्राणिष्वन्यतरस्याम् । Pân. VI. 3. 77.

× अत्र बहुवचनमविवक्षितं (is not the point) तेन 'नासत्यावाश्विना दस्रौ' इति सिद्धम् । Tatvabodhinî.

does not qualify an animal retains its न optionally as नगः or अगः 'a mountain or a tree;' but अगः वृषलः 'a Sudra that cannot move.'

N. B. It should be noted that some of these are Bahuvrihi compounds.

---

3. KARMADHA'RAYA OR THE APPOSITIONAD COMPOUNDS.

§ 220. Panini defines a 'Karmadhâraya' as समानाधिकरण तत्पुरुषः* or Tatpurusha both the members of which are in the same case relation *i. e.* have the same case when dissolved.

N. B. The difference between the Tatpurusha proper and Karmadhâraya is this:—In the case of the former the attributive member has one of the oblique cases when dissolved, while in the case of the latter it is in apposition to the other member. It may thus be a noun or an adjective qualifying the other member.

§ 221. (*a*) † A word expressive of the standard of comparison (उपमान) may be compounded in a Karmadhâraya with another denoting the common quality or ground of comparison; as घन इव श्यामः घनश्यामः dark like a cloud. Such compounds are called उपमानपूर्वपदकर्मधारयs.

(*b*) ‡ Similarly a noun denoting the person or thing compared (उपमेय) may be compounded with words indicative of excellence, such as व्याघ्र§, सिंह, चन्द्र, कमल, &c. no mention of

---

* तत्पुरुषः समानाधिकरणः कर्मधारयः । Pân. I. 2. 42.

† उपमानानि सामान्यवचनैः । Pân. II. 1. 55.

‡ उपमितं व्याघ्रादिभिः सामान्याप्रयोगे । Pân. II. 1. 56.

§ All these words are included under what is called the group of व्याघ्र. The more important of these words are व्याघ्र, सिंह, ऋक्ष, ऋषभ, चन्दन, वृक, वृष, वराह, हस्तिन्, रुरु, पृषत, पुण्डरीक, &c.; चन्द्र, पद्म, कमल, किसलय, &c.; *cf.* स्युरुत्तरपदे व्याघ्रपुंगवर्षभकुञ्जराः । सिंहशार्दूलनागाद्याः पुंसि श्रेष्ठार्थगोचराः ॥ Amara III. 1. 59.

the common attribute (of similarity) being made; as पुरुषो व्याघ्र एव पुरुषव्याघ्रः a man like a tiger (*i. e.* as bold as a tiger); मुखं चन्द्र इव मुखचन्द्रः a moon-like face *i. e.* as delightful as the moon; मुखं कमलमिव मुखकमलम् &c.; these are called उपमानोत्तरपदकर्मधारय.

Note. 1.—The difference between the two is this:—In the former the common quality of comparison is actually expressed; while in the latter it is left to be understood; in fact if it be expressed there can be no compound; as पुरुषः व्याघ्र इव शूरः।

Note. 2.—The above Karmadhárayas may be dissolved as मुखमेव चन्द्रः मुखचन्द्रः, मुखमेव कमलं मुखकमलम्, &c. Dissolved in either way there will be no difference in the formation of the compounds; but there will be difference both in the meaning and in the metaphor. In one case prominence will be given to चन्द्र or the moon and the figure will be '*upamá* (a simile),' while in the other to मुख or the face in which case the figure will be '*Rûpaka**.' Compounds like पाद एवपद्मं पादपद्मम्, विद्या एव धनं विद्याधनं, &c. are termed अवधारणापूर्वपदकर्मधारयs.

§ 222. An adjective may be compounded with the noun it qualifies in most cases † as नीलं च तदुत्पलं च नीलोत्पलं, a blue lotus &c.; कृष्णश्चासौ सर्पश्च कृष्णसर्पः where the comp. is necessary; but जामदग्न्यो रामः। Such compounds are called विशेषणपूर्वपदकर्मधारयs.

As a general rule in such compounds the qualifying word is placed first; but there are several exceptions which are given below.

---

* So when the common attribute is applicable in its expressed (वाच्य) sense to the उपमेय as in मुखपद्मं सहास्यं dissolve the comp, as मुखं पद्ममिव and when to the उपमान as in मुखपद्मं विकसितं dissolve as मुखमेव पद्मम्.

† विशेषणं विशेष्येण बहुलम्। Pân. II. 1. 57.

(*a*) *The qualified word is placed first and is always of the *mas.* gender if it denotes a class or species, when compounded with certain adjectives; *e. g.* इभयुवतिः 'a young female elephant', अग्निस्तोकः 'a small fire', उदश्वित्कतिपयम् 'butter-milk mixed with a little water', गोगृष्टिः 'a cow that has brought forth a calf for the first time', गोधेनुः 'a milch-cow (नवप्रसूतिका)'; गोवशा 'a barren cow', गोवेहत् (गर्भघातिनी गौः), गोबष्कयणी 'a cow whose calf is one year old,' कठश्रोत्रियः 'an *agnihotrin* Brâhmaṇa of the Kaṭha branch of the Yajurveda,' कठाध्यापकः 'a teacher of the Kaṭha branch,' † गो-मतल्लिका-मचर्चिका-प्रकाण्ड (also *mas.* according to some) —उद्धः (गवोद्ध)-तल्लज 'an excellent cow'. The last mentioned five words, all of which denote excellence, retain their own gender invariably; as ब्राह्मणमतल्लिका 'an eminent Brâhmaṇa' &c.; but कुमारी मतल्लिका, as no class is meant here.

(*b*) ‡ The words कडार, खञ्ज, खोड lame, काण, कुण्ठ blunt, dull, खलति bald-headed, गौर, वृद्ध, भिक्षुक पिंग, पिंगल, तनु, जरठ hard, stiff, बधिर, कुब्ज and बर्बर, may optionally precede the words in apposition to them; as जैमिनिकडारः or कडारजैमिनिः Jaimini who is turned tawny on account of his having practised penance in the sun.' &c.

(*c*) §Words expressive of the persons or things condemned

---

* पोटायुवतिस्तोककतिपयगृष्टिधेनुवशावेहद्बष्कयणीप्रवक्तृश्रोत्रियाध्यापकधूर्तैर्जातिः । पुंवत्कर्मधारयजातीयदेशीयेषु । Pán. II. 1. 65. VI. 3. 42.

† प्रशंसावचनैश्च । Pán. II. 1. 66. (मतल्लिकादयो नियतलिङ्गा न तु विशेष्यनिघ्नाः । Sid. Kau). मतल्लिकामचर्चिकाप्रकाण्डमुद्धतल्लजौ । प्रशस्तवाचकान्यमूनि । Amara.

‡ कडाराः कर्मधारये । Pán. II. 2. 38.

§ कुत्सितानि कुत्सनैः । पापाणके कुत्सितैः । Pán. II. 1. 53 54. किं क्षेपे । Pán. II 1. 64.

or reproached are placed first; as वैयाकरणखसूचिः 'a bad grammarian,' 'one who has forgotten his grammar and therefore can make no use of his knowledge;' (पृष्टः सन् प्रश्नं विस्मारयितुं खं सूचयति अभ्यासवैधुर्यात्स एकमुच्यते । Tatv.); so मीमांसकादुर्दुरूढः 'a *mimâmsaka* who is a sceptic' or 'an unbeliever'; except in the case of the words पाप, अणक and किम्; as पापनापितः 'a bad barber,' अणककुलालः 'a mean, silly potter,' कुत्सितः राजा किंराजः, किंसखा (कुत्सितः सखा), &c.

(*d*)* Words in apposition to वृन्दारक, नाग and कुञ्जर are also placed first; *e. g.* नृपवृन्दारकः 'an eminent king,' तापसकुञ्जरः, पुरुषनागः, &c.

(*e*) † कतर and कतम are compounded only when they ask a question with reference to a class (जाति family), and are placed first; *e. g.* कतर-कतम-कठः 'which Brâhmaṇa of the Kaṭha branch?' कतर-कतम-कलापः 'which Brâhmaṇa of the Kalápa branch?' But कतरः पुत्रः 'which son'?

(*f*) ‡ The word कुमार (and also कुमारी changed to कुमार) is placed first when compounded with one of the words श्रमणा, प्रव्रजिता कुलटा, गर्भिणी, तापसी, दासी, अध्यापक, पण्डित, पटु, मृदु, कुशल, चपल and निपुण; as कुमारश्रमणा 'a female mendicant,' कुमारप्रव्रजिता 'a young female ascetic'; कुमारमृदुः-द्वी 'a delicate boy or girl, कुमारगर्भिणी, कुमाराध्यापकः, &c.

(*g*)§ The words एक, सर्व, जरत, पुराण, नव and केवलः and the

---

* वृन्दारकनागकुञ्जरैः पूज्यमानम् । Pân. II. 1. 62.

† कतरकतमौ जातिपरिप्रश्ने Pân. II. 1. 63.

‡ कुमारः श्रमणादिभिः । Pân. II. 1. 70.

§ पूर्वकालैकसर्वजरत्पुराणनवकेवलाः समानाधिकरणेन । Pân. II. 1 49. पूर्वापरप्रथमचरमजघन्यसमानमध्यमध्यमवीराश्च । Pân. II. 1. 58. अपरस्यार्धे पश्चभावो वक्तव्यः । Vârt.

words पूर्व, अपर, चमर, जघन्य 'hindmost,' समान, मध्य, मध्यम and वीर are always placed first in a Karmadharaya compound. अपर when followed by अर्ध is changed to पश्च: as एकनाथ: 'sole master or lord', सर्वशाला:, जरन्नैयायिक:, 'an old logician,' पुराणमीमांसका:, 'old *mimamsa* philosophers,' नवपाठका:, पूर्ववैयाकरणा:, 'the old grammarians,' अपराध्यापक: अपरश्चासौ अर्धश्च पश्चार्ध: 'the hinder part or side of the body;' चरमराज: the last king, समानाधिकरणम् 'being in the same category or predicament'; वीरैक: 'a sole warrior *i. e.* an eminent warrior', &c. The form एकवीर (found used by great writers) also may be defended.*

(*h*) † The words सत्, महत्, परम, उत्तम and उत्कृष्ट are compounded with another noun when they are used as terms of praise or excellence; सद्वैद्य: 'an excellent physician' महावैयाकरण:. &c. but उत्कृष्टो गौ: where उत्कृष्ट means 'uplifted, or 'drawn out of '

§ 223. ‡ Names of quarters and numerals form a Karm. compound with any *subanta* (a declinable word) but only when the whole compound is an appellation; *e. g.* सप्तर्षय: 'Name of a constellation of stars,' 'Ursa Major;' पञ्चजना:†† &c., पूर्वेषुकामशमी

---

* कथमेक वीर इति। पूर्वकालैकेति बाधित्वा परत्वादनेन समासे वीरैके इति हि स्यात्। बहुल ग्रहणाद्भविष्यति। How do you justify the form एकवीर ? For the Sútra पूर्वापर &c. being a subsequent one ought to have preference over the preceding Sûtra पूर्वकालैक &c. and we should have वीरैक: We reply.—The form may be justified by supposing that the rule operates in most cases only बहुलग्रहणात् and not in a few).

† सन्महत्परमोत्तमोत्कृष्टाः पूज्यमानै:। Pân. II. 1. 61

‡ दिक्संख्ये संज्ञायाम्। Pân. II. 1. 61.

†† These are gods, men, Gandharvas, serpents, and Pitṛis, according to some; and Brâmaṇas, Kshatriyas, Vaishyas, S'ûdras and Nishâdhas or barbarians, according to others. (Vide Shankarâchârya on Brah. Su. I. 4. 11.-13.)

'Name of a town in the east;' उत्तरा वृक्षाः 'Northern trees; पञ्च ब्राह्मणाः &c. The compound is forbidden in other cases.

(*a*) *But words denoting a cardinal point or numerals may be compounded with any other noun when a *Taddhita* termination is to be affixed to the compound so formed (or it conveys in addition to its sense as a Karm. a derivative meaning such as is usually denoted by a Tad. aff.) or when the compound itself becomes the first member of another compound or when the compound forms a proper name; पूर्वा शाला पूर्वशाला; पूर्वस्यां शालायां भवः पौर्वशालः 'being in the eastern hall' from पूर्वशाला+अ (*i. e.* Tad. aff. ञ added by दिक्पूर्वपदादसंज्ञायां ञः। Pân. IV. 2, 107); so षष्+मातृ=षण्मातृ 'six mothers'+Tad. अ=षाण्मातुरः the son of six mothers; पूर्वा शाला प्रिया यस्य स पूर्वशालाप्रियः where पूर्वशाला is a पूर्वपद and not used independently; उत्तरध्रुवः, दक्षिणध्रुवः &c. which are names.

§ 224. The particle कु forms a Karm. compound with any other word, कुपुरुषः (कुत्सितः पुरुषः) a bad man; कुपुत्रः &c.

(*a*) † कु is changed to (1) कत् when followed by a noun with an initial vowel in a Tat. by त्रि and the nouns रथ and वद and by तृण 'denoting a species;' कुत्सितोऽश्वः कदश्वः 'bad horse;' so कदन्नं 'coarse food;' but कूष्ट्रः 'having bad camels' (a Bah. comp.) राजा; कुत्सिताः त्रयः कत्त्रयः 'three inferior things;' कद्रथः 'a bad chariot,' कद्वदः 'speaking ill, a bad speaker;' कत्तृणम् 'a kind of fragrant grass.'

(2) To का when followed by पथिन् and अक्ष and when meaning 'a little;' and optionally when prefixed to पुरुष; कापथम्, काक्षः 'a sidelong look or a frown of displeasure;' see Bh.V. 54 (अक्षशब्देन

---

* तद्धितार्थोत्तरपदसमाहारे च। Pân. II. 1. 51.

† कोः कत्तत्पुरुषेऽचि। ('त्रौ च' Vârt:) रथवदयोश्च। तृणे च जातौ। कापथ्यक्षयोः। ईषदर्थे। विभाषा पुरुषे। कवं चोष्णे। Pân. VI. 3. 101-107.

तत्पुरुषः अक्षिशब्देन बहुव्रीहिर्वा Sid- Kau.). ईषज्जलं काजलं 'a little water,' ईषत्पुरुषः कापुरुषः, but कुत्सितःपुरुषः कुपुरुषःor कपुरुषः.

(3) And to का or कव when follwed by उष्ण; कोष्णं, कवोष्णं and कदुष्णं by (1), all meaning 'luke-warm'.

§ 225. Two adjectives may also be compounded into what is called the विशेषणोभयपदकर्मधारयः as शुक्लकृष्णः, कृष्णसारंगः.

(*a*), * Two participles expressive of two consecutive actions of the same individual may be compounded together, the one expressive of the previous action being placed first; आदौ स्नातः पश्चादनुलिप्तः स्नातानुलिप्तः 'first bathed and then anointed'; similarly पीतोद्गीर्णम् 'first drunk and afterwards vomited out', पीतप्रतिबद्धः, गृहीतप्रतिमुक्तः (Rag. II. 1. IV. 43), &c.

(*b*). In the case of the two sets of words given above (§ 222.*g.*) forming compounds with one another those beginning with पूर्व are placed first. In the case of एक compounded with वीर it may precede or follow it; as वीरैकः or एकवीरः; the former, however, is preferable. In the case of the first set of words *viz.* एक......केवल the one succeeding precedes the one preceding when compounded together; as पुराणजरत्, केवलपुराणम्, &c.

(*c*) † A past participle is compounded with another with the negative particle prefixed to it; 'कृताकृतम्,' what is done and not done, *i. e.* 'partially done'.

(*d*). ‡ The word युवन् (*m. f.*) enters into a Karm. comp. with the words खलति, पलित, वलिन having wrinkles, and जरती, and is placed first; *i. e.* युवा + खलतिः युवखलतिः 'a young

---

* See Pán. II. 1. 49. (पूर्वकाल-पूर्वत्वस्य ससंबन्धिकत्वात्पूर्वकालोऽपरकालेन समस्यते । Tatv. quoted above)

† क्तेन नञ्विशिष्टेनानञ् । Pán. II. 1. 60.

‡ युवाखलतिपलितवलिनजरतीभिः । Pán. II. 67.

bald-headed man';–ती 'a young bald-headed woman'; युवजरती 'a young woman looking old'; युवपलित: 'a young man whose hair is grey', &c.

§ 226. * The word ईषत 'little' is compounded with any other word except a verbal derivative, and even with a verbal derivative when it expresses a quality; as ईषात्पिङ्गल: 'a little brown', ईषद्रक्तम् 'reddish.' &c.

§ 227. † Words ending in the terminations तव्य. अनीय, य and तुल्य and words having a similar meaning, may be compounded with any *subanta* not importing a particular kind; *e. g.* भोज्योष्णम् 'any hot eatable,' तुल्यश्वेत: 'of a similar white colour,' सदृशश्वेत:, &c.; but भोज्य: ओदन: as the latter word refers to a kind of food here.

§ 228. ‡ The following are the more important of the compounds given by Pân. as irregular under the class मयूरव्यंसकादि—मयूरश्चासौ व्यंसकश्च मयूरव्यंसक: 'a cunning peacock', so छात्रव्यंसक: उदक् च अवाक् च उच्चावचम्, so उच्चनीचम् 'high and low', 'great and small', निश्चितं च प्रचितं च निष्प्रचम्, नास्ति किंचन यस्य अकिंचन:, नास्ति कुतो भयं यस्य स अकुतोभय:, अन्यो राजा राजान्तरम्, अन्यो ग्राम: ग्रामान्तरम्, चिदेव चिन्मात्रं (these are *nitya-samâsas*). अश्नीत पिबत इत्येवं सततं यत्राभिधीयते सा अश्नीतपिबता that in which are constantly uttered the words 'eat and drink', so पचतभृज्जता, खादतमोदता; अहं अहं इति यस्यां क्रियायामभिधीयते सा अहमहमिका, that in which are uttered the words 'I alone; I alone;' hence hard competition, &c. अहं पूर्वं अहं पूर्वमिति यस्यां क्रियायामभिधीयते सा अहंपूर्विका; so आहोपुरुषिका 'great self-conceit or pride' (Bhaṭṭi. V. 27); 'vaunting', (Br.I. 84) &c. Also कान्दिशीक 'put to flight,' यदृच्छा 'accident,' &c.

---

* ईषदकृता। Pân. II. 2. 7. ईषद्गुणवचनेनेति वाच्यम्। Vârt

† कृत्यतुल्याख्या अजात्या। Pân. II. 1. 68.

‡ मयूरव्यंसकादयश्च। Pân. II. 1. 72.

§ 229. In some Karmadhâraya compounds the last member of the first word which is itself a compound word is dropped*; *e. g.* शाकप्रियः पार्थिवः शाकपार्थिवः 'a king who likes vegetables;, देवपूजको ब्राह्मणः देवब्राह्मणः &c. These compounds, though they should be properly called "*Uttamapadalopi*" are popularly designated "*Madhyamapadalopi*". Any compound requiring a similar explanation is classed under this group (शाकपार्थिवादि) which is an आकृतिगण.

DWIGU OR NUMERAL APPOSITIONAL COMPOUNDS.

§ 230. † When the first member of a Karmadhâraya compound is a numeral it is called 'Dwigu'.

§ 231. A Dwigu compound is possible (*a*) under the circumstances mentioned in § 223 (*a*) *i. e.*–

(1) when a Taddhita affix is to be added to the compound so formed; षण्णां मातृणामपत्यं षाण्मातुरः 'the son of six mothers, Kârtikeya' (vide Ku. IX); पञ्चकपालः &c; or (2) when the compound itself becomes the first member of another compound, as पञ्चगावः धनं यस्य असौ पञ्चगवधनः, पञ्च ॰प्रियः &c.

(*b*) And when the compound denotes an aggregate; in this case it is singular; ‡ as त्रयाणां भुवनानां समाहारः त्रिभुवनम् the three worlds (taken collectively); as पञ्चपात्रम्, पञ्चगवम्, &c.

---

* शाकपार्थिवादीनां सिद्धये उत्तरपदलोपस्योपसंख्यानम्। Vârt on Pân. II. 1. 60.

† संख्यापूर्वो द्विगुः । Pân. II. 1. 52.

‡ द्विगुरेकवचनम् । Pân. II. 4. 1

PREPOSITIONAL COMPOUNDS.

4. *Pradi.*

§ 232. Those Tatpurusha compounds whose first member is a preposition are termed Prâdi by Sanskrit grammarians*; some of these prepositions combine with a following noun in the Nom., with a noun in the Acc. &c.; *e. g.* प्रगतः आचार्यः प्राचार्यः 'an eminent teacher', संगतः अध्वानं समध्वः 'taken to a path-way' (vide Bhatti. III. 45). प्रकृष्टो वातः प्रवातः 'strong or excessive wind,' &c.; अतिक्रान्तो मालां अतिमालः 'excelling a garland' (in fragrance or beauty), अतिक्रान्तो रथं रथिनं वा अतिरथः 'a chariot-warrior who has no rival or equal'; so अतिमात्र 'exceeding measure,' अतिसर्व &c. अवकृष्टः कोकिलया अवकोकिलः 'attracted by the cuckoo;' परिग्लानः अध्ययनात पर्यध्ययनः 'tired of studying;' निष्क्रान्तः कौशाम्ब्याः निष्कौशाम्बिः 'gone out of Kauśámbi;' so निर्लङ्कुः &c. A compound with prepositions which govern cases (कर्मप्रवचनीय) is forbidden; वृक्षं प्रति.

5 *Gati.*

§ 233. Compounds of the following words with verbal indeclinables are called Gati.

(*a*) † The particles ऊरी, उररी, वौषट्, वषट्, स्वाहा, स्वधा, प्राडुः, आविस् and श्रत् and the word कारिका meaning an action; as ऊरीकृत्य, उररीकृत्य 'having accepted; वषट्कृत्य 'having uttered the word *Vashat*;' प्रादुर्भय, कारिकाकृत्य 'having done the act.'

(*b*) ‡ Onomatopoetic words not followed by इति, as खाटकृत्य; but खाडेति कृत्वा (निरष्टीवत्).

---

* कुगतिप्रादयः। Pan. II. 2. 18. प्रादयो गताद्यर्थे प्रथमया। अत्यादयः क्रान्ताद्यर्थे द्वितीयया। अवादयः क्रुष्टाद्यर्थे तृतीयया। पर्यादयो ग्लानाद्यर्थे चतुर्थ्या। निरादय क्रान्ताद्यर्थे पञ्चम्या। कर्मप्रवचनीयानां प्रतिषेधः। Vàrtikas.

† ऊर्यादिच्विडाचश्च । Pân. I. 4. 61. कारिकाशब्दस्योपसंख्यानम्। Vártikas.

‡ अनुकरणं चानितिपरम् । Pán. I. 4. 62.

(*c*) *The words सत् and असत् showing respect and disrespect respectively, the prepositions अलं in the sense of 'adorning,' पुरः, अदः अंतः, कणे, मनः, अस्तं, अच्छ, and तिरः; as अलंकृत्य 'having adorned', but अलं कृत्वा doing enough (पर्याप्तमित्यर्थः Sid. Kau.); पुरस्कृत्य 'placing in the front'; अदःकृत्य (अदःकृतम्) अन्तर्हत्य (मध्ये हत्वा Sid. Kau.); कणेहत्य, as कणेहत्य पयः पिबति 'he drinks milk to his heart's content'; अच्छोद्य 'having gone up to and spoken' (अभिमुखं गत्वा उक्त्वा च इत्यर्थः Sid. Kau.); तिरोभूय, मनोहत्य (till disgust is produced); अस्तंगत्य, अच्छगत्य 'going towards.'

(*d*) †The words हस्ते, पाणौ and प्राध्वं; as हस्तेकृत्य, पाणौकृत्य, 'having married'; प्राध्वंकृत्य 'having forced to yield.'

(*e*) ‡The particles उपाजे, अन्वाजे, साक्षात्, मिथ्या, अमा, प्रादुः, आविः and नमस्, the words मनसि, उरसि, (except when there is the sense of juxtaposition or extreme contact), मध्ये, and the word पदे form compounds with verbal indeclinables optionally; उपाजेकृत्य, उपाजे कृत्वा, अन्वाजेकृत्य अन्वाजे कृत्वा 'giving strength to the weak' [दुर्बलस्य बलमाधाय इत्यर्थः Sid. Kau.]; साक्षात्कृत्य-त्वा, लवणंकृत्य-त्वा, उरसिकृत्य-त्वा (having accepted) मनसिकृत्य कृत्वा; but उरसि कृत्वा पाणिं शेते; मध्येकृत्य-त्वा, पदेकृत्य, पदे कृत्वा, &c.

(*f*) These compounds are also formed with nouns derived from roots for their second members; *e. g.* अस्तमयः 'setting of the sun,' पुरस्कारः 'reception, showing respect,' तिरस्कारः, सत्कारः, अलंकृतिः, &c.

§ 234. The च्वि formations (see Chap. XI.) are also classed as prepositional Tatpurusha compounds; as शुक्लीकृत्य having turned white what was not so before.

---

* Pân. I. 4. 63–71.

† Pân. I. 4. 77–78.

‡ Pân. I. 4. 73–76. (अनत्याधान उरसिमनसी ।).

6. UPAPADA COMPOUNDS.

§ 235. When the second member of a Tat. Comp. is a root-noun derived from a root which takes a particular Kṛit affix by virtue of the presence of the first member, it is called an Upapada Tat.; as कुम्भं करोतीति कुम्भकारः 'a potter;' so साम गायतीति सामगः 'one who chants a verse of the Sâman Veda;' मांसं कामयती मांसकामा 'desirous of meat'; similarly अश्वक्रीती (अश्वेन क्रीता) 'bought for a horse', कच्छपी 'a female tortoise,' &c. The noun prefixed to the last member, such as कुम्भ, is called an *upapada*.*

N. B. The latter member of such compounds must neither be the conjugated form of a root nor a separate verbal derivative *i. e.* formed independently of the last member; *e. g.* पयोधर is not an Upapada Tat., as the word धर can be independently formed; it is a Gen. Tat. धरतीति धरः पयसां धरः पयोधरः 'a cloud' or 'the female breast.'

§ 236. Sometimes the second member of an Upapada Tat. my be a *Namulanta* or the verbal indeclinable in अम्; as स्वादुंकारं भुंक्ते 'he eats having sweetened the food;' अग्रेभोजं 'having dined first;' sometimes this compound is optional. मूलकोपदंशं or मूलकेन उपदंशं भुङ्क्ते 'he eats the condiment with a raddish,' &c.

§ 237. Some *upapadas* such as उच्चैः, नीचैः, तिर्यक्, सुखतः, &c. also optionally form compounds with the verbal indeclinable in त्वा (changeable to य); as उच्चैःकृत्य (or उच्चैः कृत्वा), तिर्यक्कृत्य, सुखतोभूय, नानाकृत्य, एकधाभूय, &c. For further particulars vide the Chapter on verbal derivatives.

---

* तत्रोपपदं सप्तमीस्थम्। Pân. III. 1. 92. सप्तम्यन्ते पदे कर्मणीत्यादौ वाच्यत्वेन स्थितं कुम्भादि तद्वाचकं पदमुपपदसंज्ञं स्यात्। Sid. Kau.

GENERAL RULES APPLICABLE TO THE TATPURUSHA COMPOUNDS.

§ 238. *The word अङ्गुलि at the end of a Tatpurusha compound changes its final to अ when preceded by a numeral or an indeclinable, as द्वे अङ्गुली प्रमाणमस्य द्व्यङ्गुलं दारु 'a piece of wood measuring two fingers,' निर्गतमङ्गुलिभ्यो निरङ्गुलम् &c.

§ 239. The following words, when at the end of a Tatpurusha, drop the final vowel, together with the following consonant if there be any, and add अ under the circumstances mentioned:—

(*a*) † रात्रि when preceded by a numeral, an indeclinable, a word expressive of a part of the whole, such as पूर्व, अपर, &c., or by the words सर्व, संख्यात and पुण्य: as द्वयोः रात्र्योः समाहारः द्विरात्रम् an aggregate of two nights (Dwi.); आतिक्रान्तो रात्रिमतिरात्रः that has passed a night, the dead of night; पूर्वं रात्रेः पूर्वरात्रः the first part of the night, सर्वा रात्रिः सर्वरात्रः, संख्याता रात्रिः संख्यातरात्रः, पुण्यरात्रः an auspicious night.

The same happens when रात्रि is preceded by अहन् in a Dwandwa; as अहश्च रात्रिश्च अहोरात्रः.

(*b*) ‡ राजन्, अहन् and सखि; as परमः राजा परमराजः a great king, मद्राणां राजा मद्रराजः, उत्तमं अहः उत्तमाहः an excellent day, एकं च तदहः एकाहः; द्वयोरह्नोः समाहारः द्व्यहः, so त्र्यहः, सप्ताहः, &c. पुण्यं अहः पुण्याहं a holy day, सुदिनाहम्, (vide § 245. *b.*), कृष्णस्य सखा कृष्णसखः &c.

(*c*) Exceptions§—अहन् when preceded by an indeclinable, or a

---

* तत्पुरुषस्याङ्गुलेः संख्याव्ययादेः । Pân. V. 4. 86.

† अहः सर्वैकदेशसंख्यातपुण्याच्च रात्रेः । Pân. V. 4. 87.

‡ राजाहः सखिभ्यष्टच् । Pân. V. 4. 91.

§ अह्नोऽह्न एतेभ्यः । Pân. V. 4, 88.

word denoting a part of the whole, or by सर्व or by a numeral with a *Taddhita* affix added to the whole compound, becomes अह्न; as अतिक्रान्तमहः exceeding a day (in duration) अत्यह्नः, पूर्वाह्णः forenoon, सर्वाह्णः the whole day, संख्याताह्नः, द्वयोरह्नोः भवः द्व्यह्नः (-ह्ना *fem.*), द्व्यह्नप्रियः &c.; with संख्यात the change is optional; as संख्याताह्नः, or ह्नः.

N. B. The* न् of the substitute is changed to ण् when preceded by र् belonging to the first member ending in अ; as सर्वाह्णः; but परागतं अहः पराह्नः (as परा ends in आ).

(*d*) † तक्षन् when preceded by ग्राम or कौट, and श्वन् by अति or an inanimate object with which it is compounded; *e. g.* ग्रामस्य तक्षा ग्रामतक्षः 'a village carpenter *i. e.* one not very skilful;' कुट्यां भवः कौटः (स्वतन्त्रः) स चासौ तक्षा च कौटतक्षः 'an independent carpenter'; अतिश्वः [वराहः] 'fleeter than a dog'; अतिश्वी (worse than a dog's life) सेवा; आकर्षः श्वा इव आकर्षश्वः 'a dog like *i. e.* bad or unlucky throw of dice;' but वानरश्वा 'a monkey like a dog'.

(*e*) ‡ सक्थि when preceded by उत्तर, मृग or पूर्व or by a word denoting an inanimate object with which it is compounded; उत्तरसक्थम् 'the upper part of the thigh', मृगसक्थम् 'the thigh of a deer,' पूर्वसक्थम्, फलकमिव सक्थि फलकसक्थम् 'a thigh like a board'.

(*f*) A numeral when compounded in a Tat. निर्गतानि त्रिंशतः निस्त्रिंशानि वर्षाणि (चैत्रस्य) more than thirty; निर्गतः त्रिंशतोऽङ्गुलिभ्यः निस्त्रिंशः खड्गः a sword more than thirty fingers in length.

§ 240. The following words have an अ added to them when at the end of a Tatpurusha compound:—

(*a*) गो except when a Tad. aff. is added and then dropped§; *e. g.*

---

* अह्नोऽदन्तात् । Pán. VIII. 4. 7.

† ग्रामकौटाभ्यां च तक्ष्णः । अतेः शुनः । उपमानादप्राणिषु । Pán. V. 4. 96–97.

‡ उत्तरमृगपूर्वाच्च सक्थ्नः । Pân. V. 4. 98.

§ गोरतद्धितलुकि । Pân. V. 4. 92.

परमगवः an excellent bull, पञ्चगव-(a collection of five cows) धनः, but द्विगुः exchanged or bartered for two cows.

(*b*) * उरस् meaning 'chief or eminent'. अश्वानां उर इव अश्वोरसम् 'the chief of horses *i. e.* an excellent horse.'

(*c*) † The words अनस् अश्मन्, अयस् and सरस् when they denote a class or form names; उपानसम् (उपगतं अनः) 'a cart-load,' महानसः 'a kitchen'; अमृताश्मः 'a kind of stone like the moonstone' [in this case the final अन् is dropped]; कालायसम् 'black iron', मण्डुकसरसम् 'a lake full of frogs'; जलसरसम् 'a lake of that name.'

(*d*) ‡ नौ at the end of a Dwigu, except when the Tad. affix is dropped), as द्वाभ्यां नौभ्यामागतः द्विनावरूप्यः (when the aff. is not dropped), द्विनावम् 'a collection of two boats', so त्रिनावम् &c; but पञ्चभिः नौभिः क्रीतः पञ्चनौः, also when it is preceded by अर्ध; as नावः अर्धम् अर्धनावम् the *neuter* is irregular (लोकात् Sid. Kau.).

(*e*) § खारी (a measure of corn) under similar circumstances takes the अ optionally, the final ई being dropped before it: द्विखारम्-रिः अर्धखारम्-रि.

(*f*) + अञ्जलि, preceded by द्वि or त्रि in a Dwigu, optionally takes अ, except when the Tad. aff. is dropped, before which the final इ is dropped; द्व्यञ्जलं-लि 'two handfuls'; but द्वाभ्यामञ्जलिभ्यां क्रीतः द्व्यञ्जलिः ।

§ 241. †† The न् of ब्रह्मन् is optionally dropped when preced-

---

* अग्राख्यायामुरसः । Pân. V. 4. 93.

† अनोश्मायःसरसां जातिसंज्ञयोः । Pân. V. 4. 94.

‡ नावो द्विगोः । अर्धाच्च Pân. V. 4. 99. 100

§ खार्याः प्राचाम् । Pân. V. 4. 101.

+ द्वित्रिभ्यामञ्जलेः । Pân V. 4. 102.

†† ब्रह्मणो जानपदाख्यायाम् । कुमहद्भ्यामन्यतरस्याम् । Pân. V. 4. 104. 105.

ed by कु and महत्; कुब्रह्मा-ह्मः a bad Brâhmaṇa, महाब्रह्मा-ह्मः. The न् is dropped necessarily when the compound implies the country in which the Brâhmaṇa dwells; e. g. सुराष्ट्रब्रह्मा a Bráhmaṇa dwelling in Surâshtra.

§ 242. *The word महत् is changed to महा when it forms the first member of a Karmadhâraya or a Bahuvrîhi compound, or when the termination जातीय follows; as महादेवः the great god, महाबाहुः a great arm (Tat.) or one having a great arm (Bah.); महाजातीयः; but महतः सेवा महत्सेवा (Gen. Tat.).

Exception:—When it is followed by घास, कर and विशिष्ट the change takes place necessarily; महतो महत्या वा करः महाकरः; similarly महाघासः, महाविशिष्टः.

§ 243. † अष्टन् becomes अष्टा when followed by कपाल and गो and the compound so formed conveys the sense of 'an oblation' and 'yoked to' respectively; अष्टाकपालः 'prepared or offered in eight pans' (पुरोडाशः); अष्टागवं (शकटम्) 'a carriage with eight bullocks yoked to it'.

§ 244. ‡All the rules given above for the change of the finals of the Tat. compounds do not hold good in the case of the Neg. Tat.; e. g. न राजा अराजा one not a king; न सखा: असखा, &c.

(a) But in the case of the word पथिन् the final इन् is optionally dropped and अ added; अपथं or अपंथाः 'absence of a road'. पथिन् when so modified in a Tat. is neu.; § (but अपथः देशः).

---

* आन्महतः समानाधिकरणजातीययोः । Pân. VI. 3. 46. and the Vârtikas on it.

† अष्टनः कपाले हविषि । गवि च युक्ते । Vártikas.

‡ नञस्तत्पुरुषात् । पथो विभाषा । Pán. V. 4. 71. 72.

§ अपथं नपुंसकम् । Pán. II. 4. 3..

GENDERS OF TATPURUSHA COMPOUNDS.

§ 245. *As a general rule a Tatpurusha compound follows the gender of the final noun.

Exceptions †:—

(*a*) Compounds with प्राप्त and आपन्न for their first member and the Prâdi compounds follow the gender of the words they qualify; प्राप्तजीविकः नरः, प्राप्तजीविका स्त्री, निष्कोशाम्बिः पुरुषः &c.

(*b*) A Tatpurusha ending in रात्र, अह्न and अह is *masculine*, except when रात्र is preceded by a numeral and अह by पुण्य and सुदिन; *e. g.* पूर्वरात्रः, मध्याह्नः, सप्ताहः, नवरात्रम्, गणरात्रम्, पुण्याहम्, सुदिनाहम्; also that ending in पथ (substituted for पथिन्, vide § 280) preceded by a numeral or an indeclinable; as त्रयाणां पन्थाः त्रिपथम्, विरूपः पन्थाः विपथम्, a bad or a wrong way; but सुपन्थाः, अतिपन्थाः as they do not end in पथ; (see § 285)

(*c*) ‡A collective Dwigu is *neu.*; but that ending in अ is generally *feminine*, and that ending in आ is optionally so in which case it takes the termination ई; पञ्चगवं a collection of five cows; त्रयाणां लोकानां समाहारः त्रिलोकी; but पञ्चपात्रम्, त्रिभुवनम्, चतुर्युगम् &c.; पञ्चानां खट्वानां समाहारः पञ्चखट्वी, पञ्चखट्वम्. The न् of final अन् is dropped and the Dwigu is optionally *feminine* पञ्चतक्षी-क्षम्, (fr. पञ्च + तक्षन् a carpener).

---

* परवल्लिङ्गं द्वन्द्वतत्पुरुषयोः । Pân. II. 4. 26

† द्विगुप्राप्तापन्नालंपूर्वगतिसमासेषु । Vârt रात्राह्नाहाः पुंसि । Pân. II. 4. 29. संख्यापूर्वं रात्रं क्लीबम् । Sid. Kau. पुण्यसुदिनाभ्यामह्नः क्लीबतेष्टा । पथः संख्याऽव्ययादेः । Vârtikas.

‡ स नपुंसकम् । Pân. II. 4. 17. आकारान्तोत्तरपदो द्विगुः स्त्रियामिष्टः । आबन्तो वा । अनो नलोपश्च वा द्विगुः स्त्रियाम् । पात्राद्यन्तस्य न । Vârtikas on *ibid*.

(*d*) * A Tatpurusha ending in उपज्ञा and उपक्रम is of the *neuter* gender, when the idea of प्राथम्य 'being the first' of what is known or commenced (introduced) is meant to be expressed; पाणिनेरुपज्ञा पाणिन्युपज्ञं ग्रन्थः the work (grammar) first taught or composed by Pâṇini. नन्दोपक्रमं द्रोणः the *drona* (a measure of corn) first brought into use in the reign of King Nanda.

(*e*) § A Tatpurusha ending in छाया is *neuter* when the objects casting the shade are many इक्षूणां इक्षुच्छायम्.

(*f*) † A Tatpurusha having for its first member a synonym of राजन् (and not राजन् itself) or the words रक्षस्, पिशाच &c. and सभा for its latter member is *neuter*; as इनसभम्, ईश्वरसभम्, a king's council; but राजसभा; रक्षःसभम्, पिशाचसभम्; also that ending in सभा when it means 'a multitude'; as स्त्रीसभम् 'an assembly of women'; but धर्मसभा in the sense of धर्मशाला.

(*g*) × A Tatpurusha ending in सेना, सुरा, छाया, शाला and निशा is optionally *neuter*; ब्राह्मणसेना-नम्, यवसुरा-रम् malt liquor beer, कुड्यच्छाया-यम्, the shadow of a wall; गोशाला-लम्, श्वनिशा-शम् (the 14th day of the dark half of a month, so called because certain dogs observe a fast on this night, according to the Sâbarabhâshya).

N. B. These rules hold good in the case of Tat. alone; so दृढसेनो राजा (Bah.); असेना (Neg. Tat.), परमसेना (Karm.).

---

* उपज्ञोपक्रमं तदाद्याचिख्यासायाम्। Pân. II. 4. 21. उपज्ञा ज्ञानमाद्यं स्यात् ज्ञात्वारंभ उपक्रमः। Amara.

§ छाया बाहुल्ये। Pân. II. 4. 22.

† सभा राजाऽमनुष्यपूर्वा। Pân. II. 4. 23. पर्यायस्यैवेष्यते Vârt.- अशाला च। Pân. II. 4. 24. अमनुष्यशब्दो रूढ्या रक्षः पिशाचादीनाह। Sid. Kau.

विभाषा सेनासुराच्छायाशालानिशानाम्। Pân. II. 4. 25.

III. BAHUVRÎHI OR THE ATTRIBUTIVE COMPOUNDS.

§ 246. * A Bahuvrîhi compound consists of two or more nouns in apposition to each other the attributive member being placed first and denotes or refers to something else than what is expressed by its members. It generally attributes that which is expressed by its second member, determined or modified by what is denoted by its first member, to something denoted by neither of the two; *e. g*, महाबाहुः 'one whose arm is great;' पीताम्बरः 'one whose garment is yellow.' When dissolved it must have the pronoun यत् in any one of the oblique cases: as महान् बाहुः यस्य स महाबाहुः [नलः]; पीतं अम्बरं यस्य स पीताम्बरः [हरिः]. A Bahuvrîhi compound partakes of the nature of an adjective and assumes the gender of the substantive it qualifies.

Note—In English such compounds are by no means rare; *cf.* high-souled, good-natured, narrow-minded &c.

N. B. The difference between a Karm. and Bah. comp. is this:—In the former, one of the member alone is in apposition to the substantive it qualifies, while in the latter the whole compound is an adjective. In the former the sense is complete in the comp. itself; in the latter it is not so; *e. g.* घनश्यामः नलः, here one of the members *viz.* श्यामः is in apposition to नलः and therefore the comp. is a Karm. गंभिरनादः as a Karm. simply means गंभीरश्चासौ नादः 'a deep sound,' and the sense is complete; as a Bah. it is equivalent to गंभीरः नादः यस्य 'some one whose sound is deep'; here the sense is not complete unless it is known whose sound is meant.

§ 247. Bahuvrîhi compounds are divided into two classes, समानाधिकरणबहुव्रीहि and व्यधिकरणबहुव्रीहि. †

---

* अनेकमन्यपदार्थे । Pân. II. 2. 24. समस्यमानपदातिरिक्तस्य पदस्यार्थे इत्यर्थः । Tb.

† Strictly speaking this is not a division of the Bah. but an exception to the general rule. We have given it as a separate division to avoid confusion.

(*a*) That is a Samânâdhikarana Bah. in which both the members are in apposition to each other *i. e.* have the same case relation when dissolved. There are six kinds of this according as the पद् is in any one of the six oblique cases; *e. g.* प्राप्तं उदकं यं असौ प्राप्तोदको ग्रामः, ऊढः रथः येन असौ ऊढरथः अनड्वान्, उपहृतः पशुः यस्मै सः उपहृतपशुः रुद्रः, उद्धृतः ओदनः यस्याः सा उद्धृतौदना स्थाली, पीतं अम्बरं अस्य स पीताम्बरो हरिः, वीराः पुरुषाः यस्मिन् स वीरपुरुषो ग्रामः ।

§ 248. A Vyadhikarana Bah. is that whose members are not in apposition to each other *i. e.* are in different cases when dissolved. A Vyadhikarana Bah. is not allowed in any case except in the Genitive and the Locative.* as चक्रं पाणौ यस्य स चक्रपाणिः हरिः, चन्द्रस्य इव कान्तिर्यस्य स चन्द्रकान्तिः †; so पद्मगन्धः, शस्त्रपाणिः, &c. शशी शेखरे यस्य असौ शशिशेखरः &c.; but पञ्चभिर्भुक्तमस्य पञ्चभुक्तः is not allowed.

§ 249 *Obs.*—The Bah. compounds are also further divided into two kinds; तद्गुणसंविज्ञानबहुव्रीहिः and अतद्गुणसंविज्ञानबहुव्रीहिः. That in which the sense of the attributive member is also present is called *Tadguṇasamvijñâna.* पीताम्बरं हरिमाह्वय is an instance of the first; here such a हरि is meant as has the yellow silk garment actually on. चित्रगुं गोपं आनय is of the other;

---

* सप्तमीविशेषणे बहुव्रीहौ । Pân. II. 2. 35. In a Bah. the noun in the Loc. and an adjectival word are placed first; अत एव ज्ञापकात् व्यधिकरणपदो बहुव्रीहिः । Sid. Kau.

† This is allowed by the Vârt. 'सप्तम्युपमानपूर्वपदस्योत्तरपदलोपश्च वक्तव्यः । In a Bah. comp. the word following a noun in the Loc. or an *upamânapada* (a noun denoting a standard of comparison) is dropped; so this ought to be properly analysed as चन्द्रस्य कान्तिः चन्द्रकान्तिः चन्द्रकान्तिरिव कान्तिर्यस्य असौ चन्द्रकान्तिः । But later grammarians, such as Vâmana, Bhattoji &c., have rejected this Vârt. altogether as of no practical value.

here what is meant is herdsman only and not his variegated cows.

§ 250. *The negative particle अ or अन् and prepositions, may, sometimes, form Bah. compounds with substantives; the verbal derivatives used to express their sense may be optionally retained; अविद्यमानः पुत्रः यस्य स अपुत्रः, प्रपतितानि पर्णानि यस्य स प्रपर्णः a tree with its leaves dropped; निर्गता घृणा यस्य स निर्घृणः ruthless; उद्गता कन्धरा यस्य स उत्कन्धरः with the neck uplifted; विगतं जीवितं यस्य स विजीवितः dead &c. Also अविद्यमानपुत्रः, प्रपतितपर्णः &c.; अस्ति क्षीरं यस्याः सा अस्तिक्षीरा गौः a milk-cow (where अस्ति is an indeclinable meaning 'having').

§ 251. † The particle सह may be compounded with a noun in the Instrumental case in a Bahuvrîhi when there is equal participation in some action; in this case सह optionally becomes स; as पुत्रेण सह सहपुत्रः or सपुत्रः.

(*a*) सह remains unchanged when the compound involes a blessing but is necessarily changed to स when followed by गो a cow, वत्स a calf, or हल a plough, even when a blessing is pronounced; as स्वस्ति राज्ञे सहपुत्राय, सहामात्याय, &c.; सगवे, सवत्साय, सहलाय.

§ 252. ‡ A compound of an indeclinable or a numeral or of आसन्न, अदूर or अधिक with a numeral is a Bahuvrîhi. In the

---

* प्रादिभ्यो धातुजस्य वाच्यो वा चोत्तरपदलोपः। नञोऽस्त्यर्थानां वाच्यो वा चोत्तरपदलोपः। Vártikas on Pân. II. 2. 24.

† तेन सहेति तुल्ययोगे। Pân. II. 2. 28. वोपसर्जनस्य । प्रकृत्याशिषि। Pán. VI. 3. 82–83. अगोवत्सहलेष्विति वाच्यम्। Vârt. The restriction तुल्ययोगे is not universal as there are instances in which there is no equal participation; *e. g.* सकर्मक, सलोमक, सपक्षक &c.; hence the Vṛittikâra remarks–'प्रायिकं तुल्ययोगे इति विशेषणमन्यत्रापि समासो दृश्यते। Dîkshita also says तुल्ययोगवचनं प्रायिकम्।

‡ संख्ययाऽव्ययासन्नादूराधिकसंख्याः संख्येये। Pân. II. 2. 25.

formation of such compounds the final vowel except that of बहु and गण, or the final consonant with the preceding vowel of the latter numeral and the शति of विंशति* are dropped and अ added; दशानां समीपे ये सन्ति ते उपदशाः 'about ten' i. e. nine or eleven; द्वौ वा त्रयो वा द्वित्राः 'two or three'; द्वे वा त्रीणि वा द्वित्राणि; द्विः आवृत्ता दश द्विदशाः 'ten repeated twice i. e. twenty; so त्रिदशाः &c.; विंशतेः आसन्नाः आसन्नविंशाः 'nearly twenty', त्रिंशतः अदूराः अदूरत्रिंशाः 'not far from thirty', अधिकचत्वारिंशाः 'more than forty': but उपबहवः, उपगणाः.† चतुर् preceded by उप or त्रि does not drop any letter but simply has an अ added to it; त्रयो वा चत्वारो वा त्रिचतुराः, चतुर्णां समीपे ये सन्ति ते उपचतुराः.

§ 253. ‡Names of directions may form a Bahuvrîhi compound and signify the point of direction between them; दक्षिणस्याः पूर्वस्याश्च दिशोऽन्तरालं दक्षिणपूर्वा; so उत्तरपूर्वा, &c. But if the words so compounded are not the names of quarters, no compound is possible; as ऐन्द्र्याश्च कौबेर्याश्चान्तरालं दिक् the point between the East and the North, and not ऐन्द्रीकौबेरी as these are not the names of the Eastern and Northern quarters.

§ 254. The following words drop their final vowel or the final consonant with the preceding vowel and take अ when at the end of a Bah. compound:—

(a) §अक्षि and सक्थि 'both meaning parts of the body'; जलजवत् अक्षिणी यस्य स जलजाक्षः 'one whose eyes are like lotuses'; दीर्घे सक्थिनी यस्य स दीर्घसक्थः 'one having long thighs', 'spindlelegged'; कमले इव अक्षिणी यस्याः सा कमलाक्षी (स्त्री);

---

* बहुव्रीहौ संख्येये डजबहुगणात्। तिविंशतेर्डिति। Pân. V. 4. 75; VI. 4. 142. ड्युपाभ्यां चतुरोऽजिष्यते। Várt. under Pán. V. 4. 77. (see art. § 284).

† अत्र स्वरे विशेषः। Sid. Kau. (for the form is the same in both cases.)

‡ दिङ्नामान्यन्तराले। Pân. II. 2. 26.

§ बहुव्रीहौ सक्थ्यक्ष्णोः स्वाङ्गात्षच्। Pán. V. 4. 113.

but दीर्घसक्थि शकटम् 'a cart with long poles'; स्थूलाक्षा वेणुयष्टिः 'a bamboo stick with big eyelike holes'; (where अ is added by § 282 (*c*). and hence the *feminine* ends in आ; see *N. B.* For सक्थि see also (*e*) below.

N. B. The *fem.* of Bah. compounds ending in अक्ष is formed by adding आ when it qualifies an inanimate object.

(*b*) * अङ्गुलि, when the compound is an attribute of दारु; पञ्च अङ्गुलयो यस्य तत्पञ्चाङ्गुलं दारु (अङ्गुलिसदृशावयवं धान्यादिविक्षेपणकाष्ठम्); but पञ्चाङ्गुलिः हस्तः the hand having five fingers.

(*c*) † The words मूर्धन् preceded by द्वि or त्रि, लोमन् preceded by अन्तर् and बहिः, and नेतृ used in apposition to the name of a constellation of stars; द्वौ मूर्धानौ यस्य स द्विमूर्धः two-headed; त्रिमूर्धः but दशमूर्धा; अन्तर्लोमः; बहिर्लोमः, मृगो नेता यासां ताः मृगनेत्रा रात्रयः 'nights of which the *Mṛiga* constellation is the leader' *i.e.* 'whose position in the heavens marks their advance;' so पुष्यनेत्राः &c.

(*d*) ‡ *Feminine* words ending in a termination showing 'a complement of,' and the word प्रमाणी; *e. g.* कल्याणी पञ्चमी यासां रात्रीणां ताः कल्याणीपञ्चमा रात्रयः; 'nights whose complement is an auspicious fifth night.' स्त्री प्रमाणी यस्य असौ स्त्रीप्रमाणः 'one whose authority is a woman.'

(*e*) § हलि and सक्थि optionally become हल and सक्थ when preceded by अ, दुस् or सु; अहलः-लिः having no plough; असक्थः-

---

* अङ्गुलेर्दारुणि । Pàn. V. 4. 114.

† द्वित्रिभ्यां ष मूर्ध्नः । अन्तर्बहिर्भ्यां च लोम्नः । Pán. V. 4 115, 117. नेतुर्नक्षत्रे अब्वक्तव्यः । Vart.

‡ अप्पूरणीप्रमाण्योः । Pàn. V. 4. 116.

§ नञ्दुःसुभ्यो हलिसक्थ्योरन्यतरस्याम् । Pán. V. 4. 121. शक्त्योरिति पाठान्तरम् । Sid. Kau.

क्थिः 'one who has no thighs,' दुःसक्थः क्थिः 'one having deformed thighs'; सुसक्थः-क्थिः; &c. शक्थि is another reading for सक्थि in the sûtra; so अशक्तः-क्तिः; &c.

(*f*) *प्रजा and मेधा under similar circumstances drop their आ and take अस्; as अविद्यमाना प्रजा यस्य असौ अप्रजाः having no progeny, दुष्टा प्रजा यस्य स दुष्प्रजाः having bad progeny, शोभना मेधा यस्य स सुमेधाः of good intellect; similarly दुर्मेधाः, अमेधाः.

§ 255. (*a*) † धर्म when preceded by a single member in a Bahuvrîhi becomes धर्मन्; कल्याणं धर्मः यस्य स कल्याणधर्मा; similarly समानधर्मा (see Mâl. Mâd. Act. I Intro.); but परमः स्वः धर्मः यस्य स परमस्वधर्मा:; परस्वधर्मा may also be correct if परमस्व be regarded as one word compounded in a Karmadhâraya. संदिग्धसाध्यधर्मा, निवृत्तिधर्मा, अनुच्छित्तिधर्मा are to be similarly explained.

(*b*) धनुष् at the end of a Bah. becomes धन्वन्, as अधिज्यं धनुर्यस्य स अधिज्यधन्वा one whose bow is strung'; so शार्ङ्गधन्वा (शृङ्गस्य इदं शार्ङ्गं) ' one whose bow is made of horn'; *i. e.* the god Vishṇu. This change is optional when the whole compound is a name; शतधन्वा-नुः.

(*c*) Similarly जम्भ 'a tooth', 'food,' &c. becomes जम्भन् when preceded by सु, हरित, तृण or सोम; as शोभनः जम्भः अस्य सुजम्भा one having beautiful teeth; similarly हरितजम्भा *m.*; तृणं भक्ष्यं यस्य, तृणमिव दन्ता यस्येति वा तृणजम्भा, सोमजम्भा one whose food is the holy *soma* juice; but पतितजम्भः.

(*d*) The word ईर्म *n.* a wound, preceded by दक्षिण becomes ईर्मन् when the wound is inflicted by a hunter; दक्षिणे ईर्म यस्य दक्षिणेर्मा मृगः a stag wounded on the right side by a hunter. See Bhaṭṭi VI. 44.

---

* नित्यमसिच् प्रजामेधयोः । Pân. V. 4. 122.

† धर्मादनिच् केवलात् । Pân. V. 4. 124. धनुषश्च । वा संज्ञायाम् । जम्भा सुहरिततृणसोमेभ्यः । दक्षिणेर्मा लुब्धयोगे । Pân. V. 4. 132, 133, 125, 126.

§ 256. At the end of a Bah. compound—

(*a*) *जानु is changed to ज्ञु necessarily when preceded by प्र or सम् and optionally when preceded by ऊर्ध्व; प्रगते जानुनी यस्य स प्रज्ञुः 'one having the knees wide apart' *i. e.* 'bandylegged;' सज्ञुः 'one having well-turned or beautiful knees;' ऊर्ध्वजानुः—ज्ञुः 'long-shanked.'

(*b*) † जाया becomes जानि; युवती जाया यस्य स युवजानिः 'one whose wife is young;' भूजानिः *lit.* 'one whose wife is the earth, *i. e.* a king,' &c.

(*c*) ‡ गन्ध becomes गन्धि when preceded by उत्, पूति or सु; उद्गतः गन्धः यस्य स उद्गन्धिः 'whose smell is spread above,' पूतिगन्धिः 'having a repulsive smell,' सुगन्धिः. This change of गन्ध is possible only when the smell referred to is inseparably connected with (looks like a part and parcel of) the object denoted by the other member; as सुगन्धि पुष्पं सलिलं च (which receives its odour from the lotuses &c. growing in it;) सुगन्धिर्वायुः; but शोभना गन्धा अस्य सुगन्ध आपणिकः 'a perfumer dealing in sweet smells.' गन्ध is also changed to गन्धि § when it means 'a particle of,' 'a little of,' or when the compound involves comparison;

---

* प्रसंभ्यां जानुनोर्ज्ञुः । ऊर्ध्वाद्विभाषा । Pân. V. 4. 129. 130.

† जायाया निङ् । Pân. V. 4. 134. लोपो व्योर्वलि । Pân. VI. 1. 66. जाया at the end of a Bah. substitutes नि for its final आ. The preceding य् or व् is dropped before a consonant except य्.

‡ गन्धस्येदुत्पूतिसुसुरभिभ्यः । Pân. V. 4. 135. गन्धस्येत्वे तदेकान्तग्रहणम् । Vârt. There is a difference of opinion among critics as to the meaning of the Vârt. गन्धस्य &c. Some hold that the smell must be the natural property of a thing to necessitate the final इ. *Cf.* Jayamangala on Bhaṭṭi. आघ्रायिवान्गन्धवहः सुगन्धः &c. II. 10, and Mallinâtha on Rag. IV. 45. But the view of such eminent grammarians as Kaiyata, Bhaṭṭoji, Nagesha, &c. is as given above.

§ अल्पाख्यायाम् । उपमानाच्च । Pân. V. 4. 136–137.

सूपस्य गन्धः यस्मिन् तत् सूपगन्धि भोजनम्; so घृतगन्धि a dinner in which there is a scanty supply of ghee, &c.; पद्मस्य इव गन्धः यस्य तत् पद्मगन्धि 'that which has the smell of a lotus.'

(*d*) * नासिका becomes नस when it is preceded by a preposition or when the compound is used as a distinguishing name and it is preceded by any word except स्थूल; उद्गता नासिका यस्य स उन्नसः 'one having a prominent nose,' प्रणसः 'one having a good nose,' द्रुरिव नासिका यस्य द्रुणसः † 'one whose nose is like a tree,' 'large-nosed;' but स्थूलनासिकः. नस becomes नस् optionally when preceded by खुर or खर; as खुरणसः, or खुरणाः 'having a nose like a horse's hoof *i. e.* flat;' खरणसः-णाः 'sharp-nosed.' नासिका when preceded by वि becomes ग्र or ख्य; as विगता नासिका यस्य स विग्रः or विख्यः 'one having a deformed nose.'

§ 257. The following words lose their final vowel when at the end of a Bahuvrīhi:—

(*a*) ‡ The word पाद when it is preceded by a numeral or सु or when the compound involves comparison and it is not preceded by a word of the हस्त्यादि group (हस्तिन्, अज, कुसूल, अश्व, कपोत, जाल, गण्ड, दासी, गणिका and some others). द्वौ पादौ यस्य द्विपात् a biped; सुपात् fair-footed; (व्याघ्रस्य इव पादौ यस्य,) &c. but हस्तिपादः, कुसूलपादः, &c.

(*b*) पाद becomes पद् and the comp. takes ई in the *fem.* in the case of the words कुम्भपदी, and others (*i. e.* कुंभपदी, एकपदी, जालपदी, सूत्रपदी, शतपदी, त्रिपदी, द्विपदी, निपदी, दासीपदी, विष्णुपदी, सुपदी, &c.;) § but कुम्भपादः *mas.*

---

* अत्र नासिकायाः संज्ञायां नसं चास्थूलात्। उपसर्गाच्च। Pân. V. 4. 118. 119. वेर्ग्रो वक्तव्यः। ख्यश्च Vârtikas.

† पूर्वपदात्संज्ञायामगः। उपसर्गाद्बहुलम्। Pán. VIII. 4. 3. 28.

‡ पादस्य लोपोऽहस्त्यादिभ्यः। संख्यासु पूर्वस्य। Pán. V. 4. 138. 140.

§ कुम्भपदीषु च। Pán. V. 4. 139.

(c) * दन्त necessarily when it is preceded by a numeral or सु indicating age, or when the whole compound forms a feminine name; and optionally when it is preceded by श्याव, अरोक, a word ending in अग्र, शुद्ध, शुभ्र, वृष, or वराह; द्वौ दन्तौ यस्य स द्विदन् 'a child so small as to have two teeth only;' षड् दन्ता अस्य † षोडन्; शोभना दन्ता अस्य सुदन्, सुदती (i. e. youthful) fem; but द्विदन्तः करी, सुदन्तः (having beautiful teeth) पुरुषः, अयोदती, फलदती (both proper names,) &c. but समदन्ती having even rows of teeth; श्यावा (black) दन्ता यस्य स श्यावदन्-न्तः, अरोकदन्-दन्तः having black or thick-set teeth; कुमडलाग्रदन्-न्तः, having teeth like the points of buds; शुभ्रदन्-न्तः &c.

(d) ‡ ककुद 'when the compound denotes a particular stage of growth;' अजातं ककुदं यस्य सः अजातककुत् 'a bull that has not got his hump as yet' i. e. 'who is very young'; also when it is preceded by त्रि and the compound designates the mountain of that name; as त्रिककुत् 'name of a mountain with three peaks'; but त्रिककुदः 'having three humps'.

(e) § काकुद 'the palate' (काकुदं तालु Kás.) necessarily when preceded by उत् and वि and optionally when preceded by पूर्ण; as उत्काकुत्, विकाकुत्; पूर्णकाकुत्-कुदः.

§ 258. †† हृदय is changed to हृत् when preceded by सु or दुस् meaning 'a friend', or an 'enemy' respectively; शोभनं हृदयं यस्य स सुहृत् 'a friend', दुर्हृत् 'an enemy'; but सुहृदयः 'one who has got a good heart' i. e. 'one who is able to appreciate merits', &c.; दुर्हृदयः 'a man of wicked intentions.'

---

* वयसि दन्तस्य दतृ । स्त्रियां संज्ञायाम् । विभाषा श्यावारोकाभ्याम् । अग्रान्तशुद्धशुभ्रवृषवराहेभ्यश्च । Pán. V. 4. 141. 143-145.

† See Foot-note p. 102.

‡ ककुदस्यावस्थायां लोपः । त्रिककुत्पर्वते । Pán. V. 4. 146, 147.

§ उद्विभ्यां काकुदस्य पूर्णाद्विभाषा । Pán. V. 4. 148, 149.

†† सुहृद्दुर्हृदौ मित्रामित्रयोः Pán. V. 4. 150.

§ 259. * Two nouns alike in from in the Loc. and meaning 'something that can be seized,' or in the Instrumental, meaning 'weapons or things used as weapons,' may be compounded in a Bah. when the sense is 'the fight thus began' and the idea of an exchange of action is to be implied. In such compounds the final vowel of the first member is lengthened and that of the second is changed to इ. The compounds so formed are of the nature of Avyayíbhávas and are indeclinable. The final उ takes Guna substitute before the final इ; † e. g. केशेषु केशेषु गृहीत्वेदं युद्धं प्रवृत्तं केशाकेशि 'a battle in which the warriors fight seizing each other's hair'; दण्डैश्च दण्डैश्च प्रहृत्येदं युद्धं प्रवृत्तं दण्डादण्डि; similarly मुष्टीमुष्टि, हस्ताहस्ति, बाहूबाहवि, मुसलामुसलि, &c.; but if the instruments used by both the parties be not the same, no compound is possible; हलामुसलि will, therefore, be wrong.

Obs,—(*a*) The following words also change their final to इ; द्वौ दण्डौ यस्मिन्प्रहरणे तद् द्विदण्डि; similarly द्विमुसलि, उभा-उभया ञ्जलि, उभाहस्ति, उभयहस्ति, उभा-उभया-पाणि, ०बाहु &c.

§ 260. ‡ The following Bahuvríhis are laid down as irregular. शोभनं प्रातरस्य सुप्रातः *m.* 'one having an auspicious morning or a day having an aupicious dawn'; see Bhaṭṭi. II. 49. शोभनं श्वः अस्य सुश्वः 'having an auspicious morrow;' शोभनं दिवास्य सुदिवः 'one who has passed a happy day', शारेरिव कुक्षिरस्य शारिकुक्षः 'having a round belly;' चतस्रोऽश्रयोस्य चतुरस्र- 'four-cornered, quadrangular;' एण्या (of a female black deer) इव पादौ अस्य एणीपदः, अजपदः, प्रोष्ठस्य इव पादौ अस्य प्रोष्ठपदः having the feet like those of a bull'.

---

* तत्र तेनेदमिति सरूपे। Pân II. 2. 27. सप्तम्यन्ते ग्रहणविषये सरूपे पदे तृतीयान्ते च प्रहरणविषये इदं युद्धं प्रवृत्तमित्यर्थे समस्येते कर्मव्यतिहारे द्योत्ये स बहुव्रीहिः। Sid. Kau.

§ अन्येषामपि दृश्यते। इच् कर्मव्यतिहारे। Pân. VI. 3. 137. V. 4. 127. तिष्ठद्गुप्रभृतिष्विच्प्रत्ययस्य पाठादव्ययीभावत्वमव्ययत्वं च। Sid. Kau. ओर्गुणः। Pân. VI. 4. 146.

‡ सुप्रातसुश्वसुदिवशारिकुक्षचतुरश्रैणीपदाजपदप्रोष्ठपदाः। Pân. V. 4. 120.

§ 261. *The words उरस्, सर्पिस्, उपानह्, दधि, मधु, शालि-ली and पुंस्, अनडुह्, पयस्, नौ and लक्ष्मी when used in the singular, have a क added to them, when they form the latter member of a Bah. comp.; व्यूढं (expanded, well-developed) उरः यस्य व्यूढोरस्कः, प्रियसर्पिष्कः 'one fond of ghee', &c. एकः पुमान् यस्य असौ एकपुंस्कः 'having one man only', &c.; when पुंस् and the words following it are used in the dual and the plural they take क optionally. द्विपुमान् or द्विपुंस्कः &c.

(*a*) अर्थ takes the final क, necessarily when preceded by अन् and optionally in any other case; अनर्थकः 'useless'; but अपार्थ-र्थकं 'meaningless' वचः.

§ 262. † A *fem*. Bah. ending in इन् takes this क necessarily; as बहुदाण्डिका नगरी 'a city having many ascetics'; बहुवाग्मिका सभा 'an assembly having many eloquent speakers in it'; but बहुदण्डी or बहुदाण्डिको ग्रामः (vide § 263 below), as it is *mas*.

§ 263. ‡ And as a general rule, when the final word of a Bah. comp. does not undergo any additions or alterations mentioned in the foregoing rules, it optionally takes the affix क. महायशस्कः-महायशाः 'of mighty glory'; but उत्तरपूर्वा, व्याघ्रपात्, सुगन्धिः &c.

§ 264. But if the last word of a Bah. compound be a *fem*. noun ending in ई or ऊ not capable of being changed into इय् or उव् before the vowel case termination, or if it ends in ऋ, क is necessarily affixed; ईश्वरः कर्ता यस्य तद् ईश्वरकर्तृकं जगत्, बहुनदीको देशः, रूपवती वधूः यस्य स रूपवद्वधूकः, &c.; but सुधीः स्त्री is an exception; बहुस्त्रीकः, सस्त्रीकः &c.

---

* उरःप्रभृतिभ्यः कप् । Pân. V. 4. 151. इह पुमान्, अनड्वान्, पयः, नौः लक्ष्मीरिति एकवचनान्तानि पठ्यन्ते । द्विवचनान्तेभ्यस्तु 'शेषाद्विभाषा' इति विकल्पेन कप् । Sid. Kau. × अर्थान्नञः । Vârtika.

† इनः स्त्रियाम् । Pân. V. 4. 152.

‡ शेषाद्विभाषा । Pân. V. 4. 154.

§ 265. The final आ is optionally shortened before क*; as बहुमालः-मालाकः-मालकः, &c.

§ 266. † No क is affixed

(*a*) when the whole compound is used as a name or when it ends in ईयस्, as विश्वे देवाः यस्य विश्वदेवः 'whose deities are the Viswadevas'; बहवः श्रेयांसः यस्य बहुश्रेयान्. A Bah. ending in ईयस् *f.* (*i. e.* ईयसी ‡) does not shorten its final vowel; *e. g.* बह्व्यः श्रेयस्यो यस्य बहुश्रेयसीः 'one having many excellent wives.' But अतिश्रेयसिः as a Tatpurusha.

(*b*) to the word भ्रातृ preceded by a term of praise; प्रशस्तो भ्राता यस्य स प्रशस्तभ्राता; but मूर्खभ्रातृकः one whose brother is a fool.

(*c*) to the words नाडि and तन्त्री both referring to the body of an animal; बहुनाडिः कायः 'the body having many arteries'; बहुतन्त्रीर्ग्रीवा 'the many-veined neck'; but बहुनाडीकः स्तम्भः 'a pillar with many ornamental lines'; बहुतन्त्रीका (many-stringed) वीणा.

(*d*) to the final of the compound निष्प्रवाणिः (निर्गता प्रवाणी 'a weaver's shuttle' यस्य) पटः 'a new, unbleached garment.'

(*e*) to compounds formed according to rules §§ 251, 252, and 253, as सपुत्रः, उपबहवः, दक्षिणपूर्वा, &c.

§ 267. In the formation of a समानाधिकरणबहुव्रीहि, if the first member be a *fem.* noun derived from the *mas.* the affix आ or ई, the *mas.* is restored if followed by another *fem.* noun §; चित्रा गावः यस्य स चित्रगुः, जरती गौः यस्य स जरद्गुः, रूपवती भार्या यस्य स रूपवद्भार्यः; but गंगा भार्या यस्य स गंगाभार्यः; वामोरूभार्यः; कल्याणी प्रधानं यस्य स कल्याणीप्रधानः ।

---

* आपोऽन्यतरस्याम् । Pân. VII. 4. 15.

† न संज्ञायाम् । ईयसश्च । वन्दिते भ्रातुः । नाडीतन्त्र्योः स्वाङ्गे । निष्प्रवाणिश्च । Pân. V. 4. 155–57, 159–60.

‡ ईयसो बहुव्रीहेर्नेति वाच्यम् ।

§ स्त्रियाः पुंवद्भाषितपुंस्कादनूङ् समानाधिकरणे स्त्रियामपूरणीप्रियादिषु । Pân VI. 3. 34.

Exception:—(*a*) This change in the first member does not take place, when it is followed by an ordinal (*fem.*) or any of the words प्रिया, मनोज्ञा, कल्याणी, सुभगा, भक्ति, सचिवा, स्वसा, कान्ता, क्षान्ता, समा, चपला, दुहिता, वामा, अबला and तनया; as कल्याणी प्रिया, यस्य स कल्याणीप्रियः 'one to whom a virtuous woman is dear.' दृढा भक्तिर्यस्य स दृढाभक्तिः, but दृढं भक्तिर्यस्य दृढभक्तिः.*

(*b*) If the first member be a proper name, an ordinal number, name of a limb of the body of an animal ending ई, name of a class, or a word having a penultimate क in a few cases, it does not undergo this change; दत्ता (a proper name) भार्या यस्य स दत्ताभार्यः, पञ्चमीभार्यः, सुकेशीभार्यः, शूद्राभार्यः, रसिकाभार्यः, पाचिकाभार्यः, &c.; but अकेशा भार्या यस्य स अकेशभार्यः as the first word does not end in ई; पाका भार्या यस्य स पाकभार्यः &c.

IV. AVYAYÎBHA'VA OR THE ADVERBIAL COMPOUNDS.

§ 268. An Avyayîbhâva comp. consists of two members the first of which is, in most cases, an indeclinable (a preposition or an adverb) and the second a noun, the whole being treated like the Nom. sing. of *neu.* nouns. the comp. so formed is indeclinable; *e. g.* अधिहरि 'in Hari'; अन्तर्गिरि 'in a mountain,' &c.

§ 269. In forming the Avyayîbhâva compounds the following rules should be observed:—

(*a*) The final long vowel is shortened, and the ending ए or ऐ is changed to इ and ओ to उ; गोपायति गाः पातीति वा गोपाः। तस्मिन्निति अधिगोपम्, अनुविष्णु after Vishnu, उपगु near a cow, &c.

(*b*) †The final न् of *mas.* and *fem.* nouns in अन् is dropped; and optionally that of *neuter* nouns ending in अन्; उपराजम्; उपचर्मम्-र्म.

---

* स्त्रीत्वविवक्षायां तु दृढाभक्तिः। Sid. Kau. लिङ्गविशेषविवक्षायां तु दृढाभक्तिरित्यादि-सिद्धये प्रियादिषु भक्तिशब्दपाठः। Tb.

† अनश्च। नपुंसकादन्यतरस्याम्। Pân. V. 4 108, 109.

(*c*) *अ is optionally substituted for the final of नदी. पौर्णमासी, आग्रहायणी and गिरि; उपनदम्-दि, उपपौर्णमासम्-सि, उपाग्रहायणम्-णि 'near to the full-moon day of Mârgas'îrsha'; उपगिरम्-रि.

(*d*) † It is also optionally added to all nouns ending in any of the first four letters of a class; उपसमिधम्-मित्.

(*e*) अ is attached to the final of the following nouns when compounded in an Avyaya.‡;—शरद्, विपाश्, अनस्, मनस्, उपानह्, अनडुह्, दिव्. हिमवत्, दिश्, दृश्, विश्, चेतस्, चतुर्. तद्, यद्, कियत्, जरस् (substituted for जरा) &c; शरदः समीपम् उपशरदम्, प्रतिविपाशम्, 'towards the Vipâśa,' दिशोर्मध्ये अपदिशम् between two divisions of the compass. उपजरसम् towards old age, अध्यात्मम् on the soul, &c.; and to अक्षि when preceded by प्रति, पर changed to परो, सम् and अनु, the इ of अक्षि being dropped; अक्ष्णः प्रति प्रत्यक्षम् before one's eyes; अक्ष्ण परं परोक्षम् out of sight; समक्षम्, and अन्वक्षम् afterwards, forthwith.

§ 270. The indeclinables forming Avyayîbhâva compounds have various senses §; *e. g.* (1) the meaning of case; as गोपि इति अधिगोपम् 'in the protector of the cowherd;' so हराविति अधिहरि, अध्यात्मम् &c.; (2) सामीप्य or 'vicinity; as कृष्णस्य समीपमुपकृष्णम् near Krishṇa; so उपगवम् &c., (3) समृद्धि or 'prosperity' as मद्राणां समृद्धिः सुमद्रम्, 'in a country wherein the Madras are in a prosperous condition,' (4) व्यृद्धि (वि+ऋद्धिः) or 'bad condition;' as यवनानां व्यृद्धिः दुर्यवनम् 'when the Yavanas are in a bad condition;' (4) अभाव or absence; as मक्षिकाणामभावः निर्मक्षिकम् 'where flies are

---

* नदीपौर्णमास्याग्रहायणीभ्यः । गिरेश्च सेनकस्य । Pân. V. 4. 110,112.

† झयः । Pân. V. 4. 111.

‡ अव्ययीभावे शरत्प्रभृतिभ्यः । Pân. V. 4. 107.

§ अव्ययं विभक्तिसमीपसमृद्धिव्यृद्ध्यर्थाभावात्ययासम्प्रतिशब्दप्रादुर्भावपश्चाद्यथानुपूर्व्ययौगपद्यसादृश्यसंपत्तिसाकल्यान्तवचनेषु । Pân. II. 1. 6.

utterly absent ' *i. e.* ' perfect loneliness ', or ' quiet'; so निर्जनम् &c. (6) अत्यय or ' the close or the transgression of ' as हिमस्य अत्ययः अतिहिमम् , ' after the wintry season, ' so अतिवसन्तम् , अतियौवनम्, अतिमात्रम् ' transgressing the proper limits ', &c; (7) असम्प्राति or ' unfitness of time ;' as निद्रा संप्रति न युज्यते इति अतिनिद्रम् ' past sleeping time ;' as अतिनिद्रम् उत्तिष्ठति पुरुषः; (8) प्रादुर्भाव or ' manifestation ' as हरिशब्दस्य प्रकाशः इतिहरि in which the name Hari is manifested (loudly uttered); (9) पश्चात् or ' after '; as विष्णोः पश्चात् अनुविष्णु; (10) योग्यता* or ' fitness ' as रूपस्य योग्यमनुरूपम् in a corresponding manner; so अनुगुणम् agreeably or comfortably to, favourably; &c. (11) वीप्सा or ' repetition ' as अर्थम् अर्थं प्रति प्रत्यर्थम् ' in every case ;' अहन्यहनीति प्रत्यहम्-ह, ' every day ;' so प्रतिपर्वतम्, &c. (12) अनतिवृत्ति or the ' non-violation of '; as शक्तिमनतिक्रम्य यथाशक्ति ' not going beyond ' *i. e.* ' according to one's power '; so यथाविधि† &c. (13) सादृश्य or ' similarity ': as हरेः सादृश्यं सहरि ' like Hari. ' (14) आनुपूर्व्य or ' succession in order, priority ', as ज्येष्ठस्य आनुपूर्व्येण अनुज्येष्ठम् ' according to seniority ', so अनुक्रमम् ' according to the proper order, ' &c. (15) यौगपद्य or ' simultaneousness ', as चक्रेण युगपत् सचक्रम् ' along with the wheel '. (16) सम्पत्ति or ' power, influence ;' as क्षत्राणां सम्पत्तिः सक्षत्रम् ' with the Kshatriyas in a satisfactory condition, ' or ' very influential ' or ' powerful. ' (17) साकल्य or ' entirety, fulness '; as तृणमपि अपरित्यज्य सतृणम् ' in a manner not leaving out even grass ' अत्ति; and (18) अन्त or ' end '; as अन्तेअग्निग्रन्थपर्यन्तमधीते साग्नि ' including the work on fire (which is studied last of all); so समाप्यम्, &c.

§ 271. (*a*) ‡ यावत् showing a definite measure may be com-

---

* 10–13. are the senses of यथा; योग्यतावीप्सापदार्थानतिवृत्तिसादृश्यानि यथार्थाः । Sid. Kau.

† यथाऽसादृश्ये Pân. II. 1. 7. यथा is not compounded when it indicates similarity; यथा हरिस्तथा हरः &c.

‡ यावदवधारणे । Pân. II. 1. 8.

pounded with any word; *e. g.* यावन्तः श्लोकाः तावन्तः अच्युतप्रणामाः यावच्छ्लोकम् अच्युतप्रणामाः 'bowing down to Achyuta as many times as there are Ślokas;' so यावान् अवकाशः तावान् अभ्यासः यावदवकाशम् अभ्यासः &c.

§ 272. * प्रति meaning 'very little' is compounded with a noun and is placed last; शाकस्य लेशः शाकप्रति 'very little vegetable'. But वृक्षं वृक्षं प्रति विद्योतते विद्युत् where प्रति means 'towards'.

§ 273. † The words अक्ष, and शलाका and a numeral, are compounded with परि and placed first to express 'loss in a game'; अक्षेण विपरीतं वृत्तं अक्षपरि, 'so as to be a loser by an unlucky throw of dice'; शलाकापरि 'an unlucky throw or movement of one of the pieces at a game played with Śalákás'; एकपरि 'loss of one throw of dice', &c.

§ 274. (*a*) ‡ The prepositions अप, परि and बहिः and words derived from the root अञ्च् (प्राक्, प्रत्यच्, उदच्, अवाच्, तिर्यच्, &c.), are optionally compounded with a noun in the Ablative; अपविष्णु or अपविष्णोः 'away from Vishṇu'; परिविष्णु or परिविष्णोः; बहिर्वनम् or बहिर्वनात्; प्राग्वनम् or प्राग्वनात् 'to the east of the forest' &c.

(*b*) § आ showing limit, inclusive and exclusive, is optionally compounded with a noun in the Ablative; and so are अनु, अभि, and प्रति all meaning 'towards' with a noun in the Accusative; आमुक्ति or आमुक्तेः 'until final liberation' संसारः, आबालं or आबालेभ्यः up to the child; हरिभक्तिः; अभ्यग्नि or अग्निमभि towards the fire शलभाः पतन्ति; प्रत्यग्नि or अग्निं प्रति; अनुवनम् or वनमनु.

---

* सुप्प्रतिना मात्रार्थे । Pán. II. 1. 9.

† अक्षशलाकासंख्याः परिणा । Pán. II. 1. 10. द्यूतव्यवहारे पराजये एवायं समासः । Sid. Kau.

‡ विभाषा । अपपरिबहिरञ्चवः पञ्चम्या । Pán. II. 1. 11-12.

§ आङ्मर्यादाभिविध्योः । लक्षणेनाभिप्रती आभिमुख्ये । अनुर्यत्समया । यस्य चायामः । Pán. II. 1. 13-16.

(*c*) अनु meaning 'towards' or 'alongside of,' 'lengthwise,' is also similarly compounded; अनुवनम (वनस्य समीपं अशनिर्गतः 'the thunderbolt passed) towards the forest'; गङ्गाया अनु अनुगङ्गम् वाराणसी 'Varâṇasi is alongside the Ganges.' (गंगादैर्घ्यसदृशदैर्घ्यो-पलक्षिता इत्यर्थः S. K.)

§ 275. *The words पार and मध्य optionally form Avya. compounds with any nominal base, and are placed first, the final अ being changed to ए when thus compounded; *e. g.* पारे-मध्ये-गंगात् from the middle of the Gangetic stream; optionally of course, the Gen. Tat.; also गङ्गापारात्, गङ्गामध्यात्. In this case the Ab. termination is irregularly retained. If the final noun has the sense of the Loc. the final vowel may be changed to अम्; as पारे-मध्ये-गङ्गम्; *cf.* पारेसमुद्रम् Bhaṭṭi. V. 4.

§ 276. (*a*) † A numeral may optionally be compounded with a noun, showing relation by blood or by some kind of learning, to form an Avya. comp.; द्वौ मुनी वंश्यौ द्विमुनि, व्याकरणस्य त्रिमुनि; *e. g.* त्रिमुनि व्याकरणम्, 'Sans. Grammar of which the three sages, Páṇini, Kátyáyana and Patanjalî, are the authors in succession.'

(*b*) ‡ and with names of rivers, this comp. also shows an aggregate; सप्तगंगम्, द्वियमुनम्.

§ 277. †† Any noun may be compounded with the name of a river, into an Avya. comp. to form a name; उन्मत्तगंगम्, a place where the Ganges is very boisterous.' so लोहितगंगम्, &c.

§ 278. The indeclinables समया, निकषा, आरात्, अभितः, परितः, पश्चात्, do not combine with any noun; समया ग्रामं, निकषा लङ्काम् &c.

§ 279. The following Avya. compounds are anomalous ¶ :—

---

* पारेमध्ये षष्ठ्या वा । Pân. II. 1. 18.

† संख्या वंश्येन । Pân. II. 1. 19. वंशो द्विधा विद्यया जन्मना च । Sid. Kau.

‡ नदीभिश्च । Pân. II. 1. 20 समाहारे चायमिष्यते । Vârt.

†† अन्यपदार्थे च संज्ञायाम् । Pân. II. 1. 21.

¶ तिष्ठद्गुप्रभृतीनि च । Pân. II. 1. 17.

तिष्ठन्ति गावः यस्मिन् काले स तिष्ठद्गु दोहनकालः 'the time when cows stand for being milked;' see Bhaṭṭi. IV. 14. So वहद्गु 'the time when cows conceive or bulls bear the plough; आयत्याः गावः अस्मिन् काले आयतीगवम् 'the evening time,' 'the time when the cows come home'; खलेयवम्, 'the time when the barley is on the thrashing ground;' similarly खलेबुसम्; लूनयवम् 'when barley is reaped,' लूयमानयवम्, संहृतयवम्, &c. समभूमि 'when the ground is even;' समपदाति 'when the foot-soldiers are in right lines,; सुषमम्, विषमम्, अपसमम् at the end of the year; आयतीसमम्, पापसमम् in an evil year; पुण्यसमम्, प्राह्णम्, प्ररथम् 'when the chariots move forth,' प्रमृगम् 'when the deer comes,' विमृगम्, प्रदक्षिणम्, संप्रति and असंप्रति.

N. B.—According to all followers of Pâṇ. compounds of this group are precluded from being further compounded though poets do not seem to respect the prohibition except in so far as to place such words at the end of these comps.; *cf.* प्रदक्षिण-क्रियार्हायाम्। Rag. I. 76; also IV. 25, VII. 24, &c.

GENERAL RULES APPLICABLE TO ALL COMPOUNDS.

§ 280. * The words ऋच्, पुर्, अप्, धुर् when is does not mean 'the yoke of a carriage', and पथ्, † at the end of any compound take the suffix अ; अर्धर्चः-र्चम् 'half a Ṛik;' विष्णुपुरं ‡ 'the town of Vishṇu;' विमलाप सरः 'a lake with pure water;' राज्यधुरा 'the yoke of a kingdom', *i. e.* 'the heavy responsibilities of governing it' &c. रम्यपथो देशः 'a country with pleasant roads', &c.

(*a*) But in the case of ऋच् preceded by अन् or बहु the अ is added only when the compound denotes a student of the Rig Veda§; अनृचः one who does not study the Ṛig Veda;' बह्वृचः 'one that has studied the Ṛig Vada;' but अनृक् साम, 'the Sâma Veda that contains no ṛiks;' बह्वृक् सूक्तम् 'a hymn consisting of many ṛiks.'

---

* ऋक्पूरब्धूःपथामानक्षे। Pâṇ. V. 4. 14.

† Substituted for पथिन्। ‡ क्लीबत्वं लोकात्। Sid. Kau.

§ अनृचबह्वृचावध्येतर्येव। Sid. Kau.

(*b*) धुर् when it refers to अक्ष 'a car' does not take this अ; अक्षधूः the yoke of a carriage; दृढधूः अक्षः

§ 281. * The अ of the word अप् is changed to ई when preceded by द्वि, अन्तर्, or a preposition; and to ऊ when preceded by अनु and the compound is the name of a country; as द्विर्गता आपो यस्मिन् इति द्वीपम् 'peninsula; अन्तर्गता आपो अवेति अन्तरीपम् 'an island.' प्रतीपम् 'in oppsition to the force of waters;' समीपम्; अनूपः † (अनुगताः आपोऽत्र) 'name of a place or country.' The change of अ to ई is optional if the preposition end in अ; प्रकृष्टा आपः ‡ यस्मिन् प्रेपम्-प्रापम्; परेपम्-परापम् 'a pond or a tank, a passage for water.'

§ 282. †† The following words take the suffix अ before which the final vowel, with the following consonant, if any, is dropped.

(*a*) सामन् and लोमन् when preceded by प्रति, अनु or अव; प्रतिसामं, साम अनुगतः अनुसामः friendly; अवरं साम अवसामम् a bad hymn; प्रतिलोमम् 'in inverse order, inversely'; अनुलोमम 'in natural order, successively, directly.'

(*b*) भूमि preceded by कृष्ण, उदच्, पाण्डु or a numeral; कृष्णा भूमिः यस्य स कृष्णभूमः; similarly उदीची भूमिः यस्य स उदग्भूमः, पाण्डुभूमिः यस्य स पाण्डुभूमः; द्वे भूमी यस्य स द्विभूमः [प्रासादः] 'having two floors'

(*c*) The words नदी and गोदावरी preceded by a numeral; पञ्चनदम्, सप्तगोदावरम्.

(*d*) अक्षि when used in a metaphorical sense, and not meaning

---

* द्व्यन्तरुपसर्गेभ्योऽप ईत्। ऊदनोर्देशे। Pán. VI. 3. 97–98.

† नानाद्रुमलतावीरुन्निर्झरप्रान्तशीतलैः। वनैर्व्याप्तमनूपं तत् सस्यैर्व्रीहियवादिभिः॥

‡ अवर्णान्ताद्वा। Vártika.

†† अच् प्रत्यन्ववपूर्वात्सामलोम्नः। Pán. V. 4. 75. कृष्णोदक्पाण्डुसंख्यापूर्वाया भूमेरजिष्यते। संख्याया नदीगोदावरीभ्यां च। Vártikas. अक्ष्णोऽदर्शनात्। Pán. V. 4. 76. उपसर्गादध्वनः। Pán. V. 4. 85.

the eye'; as गवामक्षिव गवाक्षः *lit.* resembling the eye of a bull hence 'a round window.'

(*e*) अध्वन् when preceded by a preposition; प्रगतोऽध्वानं a carriage that has reached a road, प्रकृष्टो (distant) अध्वा journey वा प्राध्वः।

(*f*) * also नाभि in compounds like पद्मनाभः।

§ 283. † अ is added to the finals of the following—

(*a*) वर्चस् preceded by ब्रह्मन् or हस्तिन्; ब्रह्मवर्चसम् 'the devine Majesty of Bramhan or the glory of a Brâhmana'; 'pre-eminence or sanctity arising from sacred knowledge'; हस्तिवर्चसम् 'the splendour or magnificence of an elephant'.

(*b*) तमस् preceded by अव, सम् and अन्ध; *e. g.* अवततं तमः अवतमसम् 'slight darkness,' संततं तमः संतमसम् 'great or continnous darkness; अन्धं तमः अन्धतमसम् 'pitchy darkness.'

(*c*) रहस् preceded by अनु, अव or तप्त; अनुगतं रहः अनुरहसम् 'secret, solitary'; अवततं रहः अवरहसं 'a little secret,' or 'desolate'; तप्तं रहः तप्तरहसम् 'a hot secluded place.'

(*d*) उरस् in the Loc. and preceded by प्रति; उरसि प्रति प्रत्युरसम् 'against the breast.'

(*e*) गो preceded by अनु, when length is implie; अनुगव यानम 'a vehicle measuring as much as a bull in lengt

---

* अजिति योगविभागादन्यत्रापि। Sid. Kau.; this is obtained by separating the portion अच् from the Sûtra 'अच् प्रत्यन्वव०.' But this is no sanction for forming new compounds ending in नाभ. It is only a device used by grammarians to explain such words as नलिननाभ &c.

† ब्रह्महस्तिभ्यां वर्चसः। अवसमन्धेभ्यस्तमसः। अन्ववतप्ताद्रहसः। प्रतेरुरसः सप्तमीस्थात्। अनुगवमायामे। Pán. V. 4, 78, 79; 81-83.

§ 284. * अ is always added in the case of the following twentyfive compounds which are:—अविद्यमानानि चत्वारि अस्य अचतुरः destitute of four; so विचतुरः and सुचतुरः all three Bah. compounds; then eleven Dw. compounds for which see § 192 (*b*) the last two; and § 196 (*c*); रजोऽपि अपरित्यज्य सरजसम् Avya. (सरजः as a Bah.); निश्चितं श्रेयो निःश्रेयसम्, 'sure, never failing bliss;' पुरुषस्य आयुः पुरुषायुषम् 'the period of human life', both Tat.; द्वयोरायुषोः समाहारः द्व्यायुषम् 'the period of two lives;' similarly, त्र्यायुषम्, both Dwigus; ऋग्यजुषम् Dw.; जातश्चासौ उक्षा च जातोक्षः 'a young bull'; महोक्षः 'a grown up bull,' वृद्धोक्षः 'an old bull'; all Karms.; शुनः समीपम् उपशुनम् 'near the dog', Avya. गोष्ठे श्वा गोष्ठश्वः, 'a dog in a cowpen that barks at others'; hence figuratively 'a person who idly stays at home and slanders others'. Tat.

§ 285. † The finals of compounds having for their first member सु or अति in the sense of 'praise' and किं in the sense of 'censure', remain unchanged; सुराजा 'a good king' अतिराजा 'a pre-eminent king': अतिगौः 'an excellent bull' अतिश्वा &c. but परमराजः; गामतिक्रान्तः अतिगवः; कुत्सितो राजा किंराजा 'a bad king', किंसखा 'a bad friend'; but किंराजः, किंसखः in other cases. This prohibition does not apply to Bah. compounds सुसक्थः; स्वक्षः.

OTHER CHANGES IN CONNECTION WITH COMPOUNDS.

§ 286. ‡ The word पाद is changed to पद when followed by आजि, आति, ग and उपहत; and to पद् necessarily when followed by हिम, काषिन्, and हति, and optionally when followed by घोष,

* अचतुरविचतुरसुचतुरस्त्रीपुंसधेन्वनडुहर्क्सामवाङ्मनसाक्षिभ्रुवदारगवोर्वष्ठीवपदष्ठीवनक्तंदिवरात्रिंदिवाहर्दिवसरजसनिःश्रेयसपुरुषायुषद्व्यायुषत्र्यायुषर्ग्यजुषजातोक्षमहोक्षवृद्धोक्षोपशुनगोष्ठश्वाः । Pàn. V. 4. 77.

† न पूजनात् । Pán. V. 4. 69. स्वतिभ्यामेव । Várt. किमः क्षेपे । Pán. V. 4. 70.

‡ पादस्य पदाज्यातिगोपहतेषु । Pán. VI 3. 52. हिमकाषिहतिषु च । षा घोषमिश्रशब्देषु । Pàn. VI. 3. 54, 56

मिश्र, शब्द and निष्क; as पादाभ्यामजतीति पदाजिः, पद्भ्यामततीति पदातिः पद्भ्यां गच्छतीति पदगः all meaning one walking on foot, a pedestrian; a foot-soldier', &c.; पदोपहतः 'beaten down by the feet'; पद्धिमम् 'coldness of the feet;' पादौ कषितुं शीलमस्य पत्काषी 'one accustomed to tax his legs, a footman'; पदा हतिः पद्धतिः a beaten-track, a way, a road; पद्घोषः or पादघोषः, पन्मिश्रः or पादमिश्रः; पच्छब्दः or पादशब्दः पन्निष्कः or पादनिष्कः 'quarter of a Nishka' (a gold coin).

§ 287. * हृदय becomes हृद् necessarily when followed by लेख (formed with the affix अण्), and लास and the Tad. affixes य (यद्) and अ (अण्), and optionally when followed by शोक and रोग and the Tad. य (ष्यञ्); हृदयं लिखतीति हृल्लेखः 'heart-ache'; (घञि तु हृदयलेखः Sid. Kau.), हृल्लासः 'disquietude,' 'hiccough'; हृदयस्य प्रियं हृद्यं 'agreeable to the heart'; हृदयस्येदं हार्दं, हृच्छोकः or हृदयशोकः 'the pang of the heart;' हृदयरोगः, हृद्रोगः.

§ 288. (a) उदक† becomes उद necessarily (1) when it forms a proper name, also when it is final; or (2) when followed by the words पेषं, वास, वाहन, and धि; उदमेघः 'a particular cloud filled with water; उदधिः, क्षीरोदः the sea of milk; लवणोदः &c.; उदपेषं पिनष्टि, उदवासः standing in water; उदवाहनः, उदधिः 'a vessel for holding water' घटः, समुद्रे तु पूर्वेण सिद्धम् Sid. Kau.;

(b) and optionally when followed by a word beginning with a simple consonant and denoting 'a vessel to be filled up with water', and by मन्थ, ओदन, सक्तु, बिन्दु, वज्र, भार, हार, वीवध 'a yoke with a pan at each end for carrying loads' (कावड Marâthi) and गाह; उदककुम्भः or उदकुम्भः; but उदकस्थाली (as स्थाली begins with a conjunct consonant), उदकपर्वतः; उदमन्थः or उदकमन्थः barley-water; उदोदनः or उदकौदनः rice boiled with water,

---

* हृदयस्य हृल्लेखयदण्लासेषु । वा शोकष्यञ्रोगेषु । Pân. VI. 3. 50. 51.

† उदकस्योदः संज्ञायाम् । उत्तरपदस्य चेति वक्तव्यम् । Vârt. पेषंवासवाहनधिषु च । एकहलादौ पूरयितव्येऽन्यतरस्याम् । मन्थौदनसक्तुबिन्दुवज्रभारहारवीवधगाहेषु च । Pân. VI. 3. 57–60.

water-meal; उदवीवधः or उदकवीवधः, 'a yoke for carrying water;' उदगाहः or उदकगाहः 'plunging or bathing in water' &c.

§ 289. (*a*) * When the first member of a compound ends in ई or ऊ not capable of changing into इय् or उव् and not belonging to a *fem.* termination or an indeclinable, the ई or ऊ is optionally shortened; ग्रामणीपुत्रः or ग्रामणिपुत्रः the son of a leader of a village; &c.; but गौरीपतिः, श्रीमदः, भ्रूभङ्गः, शुक्लीभावः &c.

(*b*) But the word भ्रू followed by कुंस and कुटि is an exception; भ्रू+कुंस=भ्रू-भ्रुकुंसः (भ्रुवा कुंसो भाषणं, शोभा वा यस्य स स्त्रीवेषधारी नर्तकः Sid. Kau.) an actor; भ्रू-भ्रुकुटिः the knit eyebrow; according to some, भ्रू optionally becomes भ्र when followed by कुंस or कुटिः as भ्रकुंसः and भ्रकुटिः (see ft. note).

§ 290. *Obs.*—† The *fem.* affix आ or ई at the end of a word forming the first member of a compound is shortened in most cases when the whole is a name or in the Veda; रेवतिपुत्रः, भरणिपुत्रः, कुमारिदारा, प्रदर्विदा, अजक्षीरम् (as अजक्षीरेण जुहोति), शिलप्रस्थम्, &c.; but नान्दीकरः, नान्दीघोषः, फाल्गुनीपौर्णमासी, जगतीछन्दः, लोमकागृहम्, &c. The आ or ई is optionally shortened when followed by त्व; अजत्वं, अजात्वम्, रोहिणि-णी-त्वम्.

§ 291. *Obs.*—‡ The words इष्टका, इषीका and माला shorten their final when followed by चित, तूल and भारिन् respectively; इष्टकाचितम् made of bricks; पक्वेष्टकचितम्; इषीकतूलम् 'the point of a reed,' मुञ्जेषीकतूलम्, मालभारि having or wearing garlands; उत्पलमालभारि, (*cf.* Mâl. Mâd. IX. 2.) &c.

---

* इको ह्रस्वोऽङ्यो गालवस्य। Pân. VI. 3. 61. इयङुवङ्भाविनामव्ययानां च नेति वाच्यम्। अभ्रुकुंसादीनामिति वक्तव्यम् Vârtikas. अकारोऽनेन विधीयते इति व्याख्यान्तरम्। Sid. Kau.

† ङ्यापोः संज्ञाछन्दसोर्बहुलम्। त्वे च। Pân. VI. 3. 63. 64.

‡ इष्टकेषीकामालानां चिततूलभारिषु। Pân. VI. 3. 65.

§. 292. *Obs.*—* A nasal is inserted in the case of the following words:—सत्य, अगद and अस्तु followed by कार; धेनु by भव्या; लोक by पृणि; अनभ्याश by इत्य; भ्राष्ट्र and अग्नि by इन्ध, तिमि by गिल or गिलगिल; and उष्ण and भद्र by करण; as सत्यङ्कारः, 'making true, earnest money,' &c; *cf.* Kir. XI. 50. अगदङ्कारः 'a physician,' अस्तुङ्कारः, 'efficacious,' 'admittance' (अभ्युपगमः Tat. B.); धेनुम्भव्या (भविष्यती धनुः Tat. B.); लोकम्पृणः 'pervading or filling the world,' अनभ्याशमित्यः 'not to be approached, to be shunned from afar,' (दूरतः परिहर्तव्य इत्यर्थः Sid. Kau.); भ्राष्ट्रमिन्धः, 'one who fries or roasts in a frying-pan,' अग्निमिन्धः, 'one who kindles fire,' तिमिङ्गिलः 'a monstrous fish that swallows down Timi (a large fish said to be 100 Yojanas in length);' तिमिङ्गिलगिलः† 'a very large fish that swallows even a Timingila;' उष्णङ्करणम् heating; भद्रङ्करणम् conferring prosperity.

§ 293. रात्रि followed by a kṛit affix inserts a nasal optionally; रात्रिंचरः or रात्रिचरः, 'a night-rover,' 'a demon;' रात्रिमटः or रात्र्यटः &c.

§ 294. ‡ सह forming the first member of a compound, is changed to स—

(*a*) when the whole compound is a name, *e. g.* सपलाशम्; but सहयुध्वा a comrade in battle (Upapada comp.).

(*b*) when it means 'including a certain literary work,' or 'in addition to;' as समुहूर्तं (Avya. comp.) ज्योतिषमधीते 'he studies the science of astronomy, including that of finding out the auspicious times,' सद्रोणा खारी '*a khâri* with a drona in addition to it.'

---

* कारेसत्यागदस्य । Pân. VI. 3. 70. अस्तोश्चेति वक्तव्यम् । धेनोर्भव्यायाम् । लोकस्य पृणे । इत्येऽनभ्याशस्य । भ्राष्ट्राग्न्योरिन्धे । गिलेऽगिलस्य । गिलगिले च । उष्णभद्रयोः करणे । Vârtika.

† Vide Rag. XIII. 10. and Mallinâtha on it. 'अस्ति मत्स्यस्तिमिर्नाम शतयोजनमायतः । तिमिङ्गिलगिलोऽप्यस्ति तद्गिलोऽप्यस्ति राघवः ।'

‡ सहस्य सः संज्ञायाम् । ग्रन्थान्ताधिके च । द्वितीये चानुपाख्ये । Pân. VI. 3. 78–80.

(*c*) and when the object denoted by the latter member is not visibly seen, but is to be inferred: as सराक्षसीका (Bah-comp.) निशा 'a night in which presence of demoness is to be inferred'

§ 295. *समान becomes स—

(*a*) when followed by the words ज्योतिस्, जनपद, रात्रि, नाभि, नामन्, गोत्र, रूप, स्थान, वर्ण, वयस्, वचन, and बन्धु; समानं ज्योतिः अस्य सज्योतिः a kind of mourning which lasts from the rising of the sun or a particular collection of stars to its setting. (समानं ज्योतिरस्येति बहुव्रीहिः। यस्मिन् ज्योतिषि आदित्ये नक्षत्रे वा संजातं तदस्तमयपर्यन्तमनुवर्तमानमाशौचं सज्योतिरित्युच्यते। Tat. Bod.); सजनपदः belonging to the same country; सरात्रिः, सनाभिः 'connected by the same navel, sprung from the same ancestor,' &c.

(*b*) when followed by the word ब्रह्मचारिन् † 'a student of the Veda who lelongs to the same *S'âkhâ* or branch as another;' समानः ब्रह्मचारी सब्रह्मचारी.

(*c*) when followed by तीर्थ with the Tad. affix य added to it; as समानतीर्थे वासी सतीर्थ्यः 'a disciple of the same preceptor;' and optionally when followed by उदर under the same circumstances; समानोदरे शयितः सोदर्यः or समानोदर्यः 'born of the same womb,' 'a brother by whole blood.'

(*d*) when followed by दृक्, दृश and दृक्ष; सदृक्, सदृशः, सदृक्षः।

(*e*) ‡ and in the case of compounds like सपक्ष, साधर्म्य, सजातीय, &c.

---

* ज्योतिर्जनपदरात्रिनाभिनामगोत्ररूपस्थानवर्णवयोवचनबन्धुषु । चरणे ब्रह्मचारिणि। तीर्थे ये। विभाषोदरे। दृग्दृशवतुषु Pân. VI. 3. 85–89. दृक्षे चेति वक्तव्यम्। Várt.

† चरणः शाखा, ब्रह्म वेदः । तदध्ययनार्थं व्रतमपि ब्रह्म तच्चरतीति ब्रह्मचारी। Sk:

‡ समानस्य छन्दस्यमूर्धप्रभृत्युदर्केषु। Pân. VI. 3. 84. The proper meaning of this sûtra is that the word समान is changed to स in the Veda when followed by any other word than मूर्धन्, प्रभृति,

§ 296. स् is changed to ष् when the following words are compounded*;

(*a*) अङ्गुलि and सङ्ग; अङ्गुलिषङ्गः ।

(*b*) भीरु and स्थान *n*.; भीरुष्ठानम्.

(*c*) ज्योतिस् or आयुस् and स्तोम; ज्योतिष्टोमः, आयुष्टोमः a sacrifice performed for obtaining long life.

(*d*) and in the case of the words सुषामा and others; शोभनं साम यस्य सुषामा; so निःषामा, सुषेधः; सुषन्धिः, सुष्टु, दुष्टु &c.

§ 297. † अन्य in any other case than the Inst. and the Gen. is changed to अन्यत्, when followed by आशिस्, आशा, आस्था, आस्थित, उत्सुक, ऊति and राग; अन्या आशीः अन्यदाशीः 'another blessing'; अन्या आशा अन्यदाशा 'another desire'; अन्यदास्था, 'devotion or attachment to another'; अन्यदास्थितः 'resorting to another'; अन्यदुत्सुकः; 'eager for another'; अन्या ऊतिः अन्यदूतिः, अन्यः रागः अन्यद्रागः; but अन्यस्य अन्येन वा आशीः

---

and उदक; अनुभ्राता सगर्भ्यः (समानो गर्भः सगर्भः तत्र भवः); अनुसखा सयूथ्यः सनुत्यः &c.; but समानमुर्धा, समानप्रभृतयः, समानोदर्काः । But as compounds like सपक्ष &c., cannot be properly explained by any of the sûtras following this, grammarians like Vâmana think that the portion समानस्य ought to be separated from this sûtra and considered as a separate sûtra by itself; Bhaṭṭoji Dîkshita conform to this opinion of Vâmana, but following Haradatta suggests that the स in compounds like सपक्ष may also be taken to be a substitute for सह meaning like or similar to,' the compounds being considered as Bahuvrîhis; समानस्येति योगो विभज्यते । तेन सपक्षः, साधर्म्यं सजातीयमित्यादि सिद्धमिति काशिका । अथवा सहशब्दः सदृशवचनोऽप्यस्ति । सदृशः सख्या ससखीति यथा । तेनायमस्वपदविग्रहो बहुव्रीहिः । समानः पक्षोऽस्येत्यादि । Sid. Kau.

* समासेऽङ्गुलेः सङ्गः । भीरोः स्थानम् । ज्योतिरायुषस्तोमः सुषामादिषु च । Pân. VIII. 3. 80–81, 83. 98.

† अषष्ठ्यतृतीयास्थस्यान्यस्य दुगाशिराशास्थाऽऽस्थितोत्सुकोतिकारकरागच्छेषु । अर्थे विभाषा । Pân. VI. 3. 99. 100.

अन्याशीः; also when followed by कारक and the Tad. affix य in which cases the restriction is removed; अन्यस्य कारकः अन्यत्कारकः, अन्यस्यायम् अन्यदीयः; and optionally when followed by अर्थः. अन्यदर्थः or अन्यार्थः a different meaning &c.

§ 298. * A certain number of compounds and other words of irregular formation are classed under the head of पृषोदर. Any word whose formation cannot be properly explained is included into this group. These are to be taken as found in the language. The principal of these are:—पृषतः उदरं पृषोदरम् 'wind, air'; हन्ति गच्छतीति हसतीति वा हंसः† (either from हन् or हस्); हिनस्तीति सिंहः (fr. हिंस् conj. 7 to kill). गूढश्चासौ आत्मा गूढात्मा the soul that is concealed from the external senses; वारिणां वाहकाः बलाहकाः 'clouds' जीवनस्य मूतः (a bag) जीमूतः 'a cloud'; शवानः (dead bodies) शेरते अत्र श्मशानं or शवानां शयनं (Kâs.); ऊर्ध्वं च तत् खं च ऊर्ध्वखं तत् लातीति उलूखलम्, 'a wooden mortar'; पिशितमाचामतीति पिशाचः, ब्रुवन्तोऽस्यां सीदन्तीति बृसी 'the seat of ascetics or holy sages discussing philosophical subjects'; मयते असौ, मह्यां रौतीति वा, मयूरः 'a peacock.'

(a) ‡ तीर becomes तार optionally when compounded with the names of directions; as दक्षिणतीरम् or दक्षिणतारम्; उत्तरतीरम्-तारम् &c.

(b) Obs.—§ दुर् becomes दू in the following cases-दुःखेन दाश्यते दूडाशः 'difficult to be given or hurt'; दुःखेन नाश्यते दूणाशः 'not easy to be destroyed:' दुःखेन दभ्यते दूडभः 'difficult to be injured or impelled:' दुःखेन ध्यायतीति दूढ्यः &c.

§ 299. The vowel of the first member is lengthened in the following cases¶:—

* पृषोदरादीनि यथोपदिष्टम् । Pân. VI. 3. 109.

† भवेद्वर्णागमाद्धंसः सिंहो वर्णविपर्ययात् ।
गूढोत्मा वर्णविकृतेर्वर्णनाशात्पृषोदरम् ॥ Sid. Kau.

‡ दिक्शब्देभ्यस्तीरस्य तारभावो वा । Vártika.

§ दुरो दाशनाशदभध्येषूत्वमुत्तरपदादेः ष्टुत्वं च । Vârtika.

¶ नहिवृतिवृषिव्यधिरुचिसहितनिषु क्वौ । वले । मतौ बह्वचोऽनजिरादीनाम् । शरादीनां च । उपसर्गस्य घञ्यमनुष्ये बहुलम् । इकः काशे । अष्टनः संज्ञायाम् । नरे संज्ञायाम् । मित्रे चर्षौ । Pân. VI. 3. 116; 118-120. 122. 123. 125, 129, 130.

(*a*) When the nouns derived from the roots नह्, वृत्, वृष्, व्यध्, रुच्, सह, and तन् with the aff. क्विप् (o) follow prepositions termed *Gati* or nouns which they govern; उपानह्, नीवृत् an inhabited country, a realm, प्रावृट् the rainy season, मर्माविद् piercing the vitals; so मृगाविद् a hunter (*cf.* Bhaṭṭi II. 7). नीरुक्, अभीरुक्, ऋतीषट् overpowering an assailant परीतत्. But परिहणनम् as नह् is not followed by *Kuip*.

(*b*) When followed by the aff. वल, and the whole is a name; कृषीवलः a husbandman.

(*c*) Words containing more than two vowels when followed by मत (वत्) except in the case of अजिर, खदिर, पुलिन, हंस, कारण्डव and चक्रवाक and the whole is a name; अमरावती and इरावती which are names; but अजिरवती; व्रीहिमती, वलयवती which is not a name. Also in the case of शर, वंश, धूम, अहि, कपि, मुनि, शुचि, and हनु; शरावती &c.

(*d*) When a verbal derivative with the aff. अ (घञ्) follows a preposition, in most cases, when the comp. does not signify a human being; परिपाकः-परीपाकः; but निषादः one of a mountain-tribe. Similarly प्रति-ती-वंशः; प्रति-ती-कारः &c.

(*e*) When काश follows a preposition ending in इ; वीकाशः, नीकाशः; but प्रकाशः

(*f*) When अष्टन् is the first, and नर the second member of a compound, and the whole is a name; अष्टापदम् gold, अष्टापदः a spider; but अष्टपुत्रः, विश्वानरः an epithet of Savitṛi.

(*g*) When मित्र is the latter member and the whole is the name of a ṛishi; विश्वामित्रः, but विश्वमित्रो माणवकः ।

§ 300. *स् is inserted in the case of the following compounds:—

---

* अपरस्पराः क्रियासातत्ये । आश्चर्यमनित्ये । वर्चस्केऽवस्करः । अपस्करो रथाङ्गम् । विष्किरः शकुनिर्विकिरो वा । प्रतिष्कशश्च कशेः । मस्करमस्करिणौ वेणुपरिव्राजकयोः । कारस्करो वृक्षः । पारस्करप्रभृतीनि च संज्ञायाम् । Pâṇ. VI. 1. 144, 147, 148–152, 154, 156, 157. तद्बृहतोः करपत्योश्चोरदेवतयोः सुट् तलोपश्च । Vârt. प्रायस्य चित्तिचित्तयोः । Vârt.

(a) अपर followed by पर when continuity of an action is implied; अपरस्पराः सार्था गच्छन्ति । सततमविच्छेदेन गच्छन्तीत्यर्थः; but अपरपरा गच्छन्ति । अपरे च परे च सकृदेव गच्छन्तीत्यर्थः । and in the case of आ+चर्य when wonder is meant; आश्चर्यं यदि स भुञ्जीत । But आचर्यं कर्म शोभनम् ।

(b) अवकीर्यते इति अवस्करः when it means वर्चस्कं (कुत्सितं वर्चः वर्चस्कमन्नमलम् । Sid. Kau.) otherwise अवकरः; अपस्करः when it means रथाङ्गम् 'part of a carriage'; विष्किरः (or विकिरः) 'a bird'. प्रतिष्कशः (सहायः पुरोयायी वा Sid. Kau.), but प्रतिगतः कशां प्रतिकशः 'one who boldly faces the whip, a disobedient servant' &c. मस्करः 'a bamboo', but मकरः 'a shark', मस्करिन् 'an ascetic' but मकरिन् 'the sea'; कारस्करः when it means 'a particular kind of tree,' otherwise कारकरः ।

(c) in the case of the words of the पारस्करादि group, such as पारस्करः, किष्कुः, किष्किन्धा, &c. when they are names.

(d) and when the words तद् and बृहत् are follow d by कर and पति and the meaning is 'a thief', and 'a deity' respectively, and द् and त् being dropped before स्; तस्करः, बृहस्पतिः. Also प्रायश्चित्तम्, प्रायश्चित्तिः, वनस्पतिः &c.

§ 301. *When the words पुरग, मिश्रक, सिध्रक, सारिक and कोटर are followed by वन in a compound they lengthen their ending vowel, and the न of वन is changed to ण (also after अग्र); पुरगावणम्, मिश्रकावणम्, सिध्रकावणम्, सारिकावणम्, कोटरावणम्; but असिपत्रवनम्; वनस्याग्रे अग्रेवणम्.

§ 302. *Obs*—† The न of वन is changed to ण necessarily when preceded by प्र, and optionally when compounded with names of herbs or plants containing two or three vowels प्रवणम्, कार्ष्यवणम्, &c. दूर्वावणम्-वनम्, शिरीषवणम्-वनम्; but देव-

---

* वनं पुरगामिश्रकासिध्रकासारिकाकोटराग्रेभ्यः । Pân. VIII. 4. 4.

† प्रनिरन्तः शरेक्षुप्लक्षाम्रकार्ष्यखदिरपीयूक्षाभ्योऽसंज्ञायामपि । विभाषौषधिवनस्पतिभ्यः । Pan. VIII. 4. 5–6.

वारुवनम्; (as the word contains more than three vowels); exceptions:—इरिकावनम्, मिरिकावनम्, and तिमिरावनम्.

§ 303. *The न of वाहन is changed to ण when preceded by a word denoting an object that can be borne; इक्षुवाहणम्; but इन्द्रवाहनम् (इन्द्रस्वामिकं वाहनमित्यर्थः Sid. Kau.).

§ 304. † The न of पान is changed to ण necessarily when the compound implies a country and optionally when it signifies merely the act of drinking; as सुरापाणाः (प्राच्याः); क्षीरपाणाः (उशीनराः); but क्षीरपाणम् or पानम्.

(a) न is also optionally changed to ण in the case of the following compounds:—गिरि-णदी-नदी, गिरि-णख-नख, गिरि-णद्ध-नद्ध, गिरिनितम्ब-णितम्ब, चक्र-णदी-नदी, चक्र-णितम्ब-नितम्ब, &c

Chapter VIII.

FORMATION OF FEMININE BASES.

§ 305. *Feminine* bases are derived from the *masculine* by the addition of the affixes आ (टाप्, डाप्, चाप्), ई (ङीप्, ङीष्, ङीन्), ऊ (ऊङ्) and ति.

§ 306. Before the affix ई—

(a) nouns ending in consonants assume that form which they take before the termination of Inst. sing.; प्रत्यञ्च्-प्रतीची, राजन्—राज्ञी, मघवन्—मघोनी, श्वन्—शुनी, अर्यमन्—अर्यम्णी, विद्वस्—विदुषी, &c. There are some exceptions, अर्वन्—अर्वणी &c.

* वाहनमाहितात् । Pân. VIII. 4. 8.

† पानं देशे । वा भावकरणयोः । Pân. VIII. 4, 9–10 गिरिनद्यादीनां वा । Vârt.

(*b*) the preceding अ or ई is dropped; as गोर—गौरी औ स—औत्सी, पार्वती. &c.

(*c*) if a *Prâtipadika** end in य, part of a Taddhita affix, that य is dropped गार्ग्य + ई = गार्गी. 'the daughter of Garga.' &c.

(*d*) the final य of the words सूर्य, तिष्य the constellation of stars called पुष्य, अगस्त्य and मत्स्य † is dropped; as सौरी, मत्सी, &c.

(*e*) in the case of the participles of the present and the future न् is inserted, as in the Nom. dual of the *neu.* (vide § 311. *a. b.*); for instances, see § 236.

§ 307. A *Prâtipadika* ending in अ and the words included in the Ajâdi group ‡ form their *feminine* in आ §; as भुञ्जान-भुञ्जाना; अज-अजा, एडका, अश्वा, चटका, मूषिका; बाला, वत्सा, होडा, मन्दा, विलाता, all meaning 'a young girl'; (of these the first five form an exception to § 313, and the second to § 308, *e*); आ is also added to फल when compounded with सत्, भस्त्रा, अजिन, पण and पिण्ड; to पुष्प when compounded with सत्, words ending in अच्, to काण्ड, प्रान्त, शत and एक; to शूद्र not preceded by महत्, when class is implied, and to मूल preceded by अ; संफला; भस्त्रफला, पणफला, &c all 'kinds of creeper'; सत्-पाक्-काण्ड-प्रान्त-शत-एक-पुष्पा, 'kinds of creeper' शूद्रा 'a woman of the शूद्र class;' अमूला.

(*a*) ¶ But if the *Prâtipadika* end in क (the member of the

---

* हलस्तद्धितस्य । Pán VI, 4. 150. For the meaning of the term *Prâtipadika* vide § 52.

† सूर्यतिष्यागस्त्यमत्स्यानां य उपधायाः । Pàn VI. 4. 149.

‡ The words included in the Ajâdi group are.—अज, एडक 'a ram', अश्व, चटक 'a sparrow', मूषक, बाल, वत्स, होड, पाक 'a young child,' मन्द, विलात, क्रुञ्च 'a heron,' उष्णिह्, देवविश् 'a deity,' ज्येष्ठ, मध्यम, कनिष्ठ and कोकिल.

§ अजाद्यतष्टाप् । Páṇ IV. 1. 4. 4. संभस्त्राजिनपणपिण्डेभ्यः फलात् सदच्काण्डप्रान्तशतैकेभ्यः पुष्पात् । शूद्रा चामहत्पूर्वा जातिः । मूलान्नञः । Vártikas.

¶ प्रत्ययस्थात्कात्पूर्वस्यात इदाप्यसुपः । Pán. VII. 3. 44. मामकनरकयोरुपसंख्यानम् । त्यक्त्यपोश्च । Vártikas.

termination) the preceding अ is changed to इ; सर्विका, कारिका, &c; the words मामक, नरक, and those ending in the Tad affix त्य with क suffixed to it, changed their अ to इ similarly; मामिका, नरान् कायति calls out to इति नरिका, दाक्षिणात्यिका, इहत्यिका a woman of this place.

Exceptions:—*The अ is not changed to इ when the क is added to the pronouns यद् and तद्, or when it is a part of the Tad. affix त्यका, or when there is a compound, or when there is a word included in the Kshipaka group † (क्षिपकगण); as यका, सका, अधित्यका, 'a tableland', उपत्यका 'the land at the foot of a mountain', बहुपरिव्राजका नगरी, क्षिपका, ध्रुवका, कन्यका, &c.

(*b*) ‡ अ is optionally changed to इ in the following cases.—

(1) तारका 'a star', तारिका 'able to protect,'; वर्णका 'a cloak, a garment,' वर्णिका (in other cases), वर्तका-वर्तिका शकुनौ प्राचाम् उदीचां तु वर्तिका; अष्टका 'kind of Shrâddha,' अष्टिका (in other cases).

(2) सूतिका-सूतका, a woman recently delivered; पुत्रिका or पुत्रका, वृन्दारका or वृन्दारिका, a goddess.

(3) when the क follows upon the *fem*, termination आ shortened to अ and is preceded by य or क; as आर्या+क=आर्यक+आ=आर्यिका or आर्यका; चटका+क=चटकक+आ=चटकिका or चटकका &c. but संकाश्ये भवा सांकाश्यिका, अश्विका, शुभंयातीति शुभंयाः; अज्ञाता शुभंयाः शुभंयिका.

---

* न यासयोः । Pân. VII. 3. 45. त्यकनश्च निषेधः । क्षिपकादीनां च । Vàrtikas.

† The following words are included in the क्षिपकगणः—क्षिपक 'an archer.' ध्रुवक, चरक 'a spy,' सेवक, करक 'a kind of bird, hail,' चटक; अवक 'a kind of plant,' हलक, अलका, कन्यका, and एडक.

‡ तारका ज्योतिषि । वर्णका तान्तवे । वर्तका शकुनौ प्राचाम् । सूतिकापुत्रिकावृन्दारकाणां वेति वक्तव्यम् । Vártika. उदीचामातः स्थाने यकपूर्वायाः Pàn. VII. 3. 46. यात्वन्तयकोस्तु नियम् । Vártika.

(c) This change of अ to इ is necessary when the क follows the य or क of a root सुनयिका, सुपाकिका, &c.

§ 308. (a) A* *prátipadika* ending in कर, except यत्कर, तत्कर, किंकर† and बहुकर; घ. सर, preceded by पुरः, अग्रतः अग्रे and पूर्व; and चर preceded by सेना, दाय and words expressive of place; the words नद, चोर, देव, माह, गर, प्लव, and नद, nominal bases ending in एय, nominal and verbal derivatives formed by the affix अ causing Vṛiddhi or Guṇa, such as औपगः, औत्सः, कुंभकारः, भारहारः, यादृशः, तादृशः, &c. and words ending in the Tad. affixes द्वयस, दघ्न, मात्र and इक (with some exceptions) and in the kṛit affix त्वर form their *feminine* in ई when they are not used adjectively; *e. g.* भोगकरी conducing to pleasures; एककरी &c.; पातिघ्नी, पित्तघ्नी, &c.; अग्रेसरी, &c.; सेनाचरी, कुरुचरी, a woman of the Kuru country; मत्स्यचरी, &c.; नदी, देवी, सूदी, &c.; सौपर्णेयी, वैनतेयी, &c.; ऐन्द्री, औत्सी, &c ; कुंभकारी, नगरकारी, &c.; उरुद्वयसी-दघ्नी-मात्री, measuring or reaching as far as the knee; &c. आक्षिकी, लावणिकी, &c.; यादृशी, तादृशी, इत्वरी, evanescent, an unchaste woman &c.; गत्वरी &c.; but किंकरा, बहुकुरुचरा नगरी.

(b) ‡Also words ending in the Tad. affixes न, स्न, ईक, य (causing Vṛiddhi) and the words तरुण and तलुन; स्त्रैणी, पौंस्नी *fit* for a man; शाक्तीकी, तरुणी, तलुनी, &c. also words ending in the kṛit. affix अन causing a nasal to be inserted before it; आढ्यंकरणी.

(c) § Words indicative of the stages of life except the last take the *fem.* ई; कुमारी, किशोरी, बर्करी, वधूटी, चिरण्टी (both meaning a 'a young woman'); but वृद्धा, स्थविरा &c. as these imply old age; कन्या is an exception.

---

* टिड्ढाणञ्द्वयसज्दघ्नञ्मात्रच्तयप्ठक्ठञ्कञ्क्वरपः । Pân. IV. 1. 15.

† Vide the Kâshikâ on Pân. III. 2. 21.

‡ नञ्स्नञीकक्ख्युंस्तरुणतलुनानामुपसंख्यानम् । Vart. यञश्च Pân. IV. 1. 16.

§ वयसि प्रथमे । Pân. IV. 1 20. वयस्यचरम इति वाच्यम् । Vart.

(*d*) *Obs*—*The words केवल, मामक, भागधेय पाप, अपर, समान, आर्यकृत, सुमङ्गल and भेषज form their *fem.* in ई when they are used as names (or in the Veda); केवली, मामकी, समानी, आर्यकृती &c ; but केवला, समाना, &c. when they are not names.

(*e*) The words नर्तक, खनक, रजक and रजक, those derived by adding the Kṛit affixes आक, and त्र (added to certain roots) and the words included in the गौरादिगण † form their *fem.* in ई; नर्तकी, रजकी &c. कुट्टाकी one who divides or cuts; लुंटाकी robbing or stealing, धात्री, &c.; गौरी, मनुषी, शृंगी, हरिणी, मातामही, पितामही &c.; सुंदर has सुंदरा and सुंदरी.

§ 309. ‡ Some *prâtipadikas* ending in the Tad. affix य insert आयन् before ई; गार्ग्यायणी (the grand-daughter of गर्ग), लौहित्यायनी, कात्यायनी, &c.

§ 310. The following eleven *prâtipadikas* form their *feminine* in ई under the circumstances mentioned §—जानपद when it qualifies वृत्ति or 'maintenance', कुण्ड when it means 'a vessel' or 'a man of a mixed class', गोण 'a full sack', स्थल 'natural site', भाज 'boiled,' नाग 'a huge elephant', and काल 'a particular colour, नील when it does not refer to a garment (or rather refers to an animal) or means 'indigo', कुश when it means 'something

---

* Vide Pân. V. 1. 30.

† षिद्गौरादिभ्यश्च । Pân. IV. 1. 41. The following are the more important of the words included in the गौरादि group:—गौर, मनुष्य, ऋष्य, पुट, द्रोण, हरिण, कण, आमलक, बदर, बिंब, पुष्कर, शिखण्ड, सुषम, आलिन्द, आढक, अश्वत्थ, उभय, भृङ्ग, मह, मठ, श्वन्, तक्षन्, अनडुह्, अनड्वाह, देह, देहली, रजन, आरट, नट, आस्तरण, आग्रहायण, मङ्गल, मन्थर, मण्डल, पिण्ड, हृद्, बृहत्, महत्, सोम, सौधर्म &c.

‡ सर्वत्र लोहितादिकतन्तेभ्यः । Pân. IV. I. 18.

§ जानपदकुण्डगोणस्थलभाजनागकालनीलकुशकामुककबराद्वृत्त्यमत्राऽवपनाकृत्रिमाश्राणास्थौल्यवर्णानाच्छादनायोविकारमैथुनेच्छाकेशवेशेषु । Pân. IV. 1. 42. अनाच्छादनेऽपि न सर्वत्र किंतु । नीलादोषधौ । प्राणिनि च । संज्ञायां वा । Vârt. शोणात्प्राचाम् । Pân. VI. 1. 43.

made of iron. कामुक 'desirous of enjoyment,' and कबर 'a knot of hair; as जानपदी [वृत्तिः], 'जानपदा नगरी'; कुण्डी अमत्रं [a vessel] कुण्डान्या, (one that burns). गोणी आवपनं चेत्, गोणा अन्या i. e. 'an empty sack;' स्थली अकृत्रिमा चेत्, स्थला अन्या i. e. ground artificially prepared; भाजी श्राणा (rice-gruel) चेत्, भाजा अन्या; नागी स्थूला चेत्, नागा अन्या, काली वर्णश्चेत्, काला अन्या; i. e. 'if it be a proper name;' नीली अवाच्छादनं [ओषधिविशेषो गौर्वा] चेत्, नीला अन्या नील्या रक्ता शाटी इत्यर्थ नीली or नीला (when a name), कुशी अयोविकारश्चेत् but कुशा 'a wooden peg'; कामुकी 'a woman desirous of enjoyment,' कामुका 'one anxious to meet her lover,' कबरी 'a braid of hair,' but कबरा variegated; शोण has शोणी–णा.

§ 311. * The *feminine* of nouns denoting 'a male' is formed by adding ई when the wife of that male is meant; गोपस्य स्त्री गोपी; शूद्री (sometimes शूद्राणी also) 'wife of a Sudra'.

(*a*) but not of nouns ending in पालक; as गोपालिका 'the wife of a cowherd' (but गोपाल has गोपाली); अश्वपालिका 'the wife of a horse-groom'.

(*b*) सूर्य has सूर्या 'the divine wife of Surya;' but सूरी i. e. कुन्ती who was a mortal.

§ 312. † The words इन्द्र, वरुण, भव, शर्व, रुद्र, मृड, and आचार्य. हिम and अरण्य both implying 'vastness; यव meaning 'bad or spoiled barley', यवन when the *feminine* denotes the alphabet of the Yavanas, मातुल and आचार्य form their *fem* in ई but insert आन् before this ई e. g. इन्द्राणी 'the wife of Indra;' वरुणानी 'the wife of Varuṇa', &c.; हिमानी 'a vast sheet of ice,' अरण्यानी 'an immense expanse of forests,' दुष्टो यवो यवानी, यवनानां लिपिर्यवनानी, but यवनी 'the wife of a Yavana or Yavana woman;' आचार्यानी ‡ (and not णी) 'the wife of an Achârya or a holy

---

* पुंयोगादाख्यायाम् । Pán. IV. 1. 48. पालकान्तान्न । Vártika. सूर्याद्देवतायां चाप् वाच्यः । Vârtika.

† इन्द्रवरुणभवशर्वरुद्रमृडहिमारण्ययवयवनमातुलाचार्याणामानुक् । Pàn. IV. 1. 49, हिमारण्ययोर्महत्त्वे । यवाद्दोषे । यवनाल्लिप्याम् । Vârtikas.

‡ आचार्यादणत्वं च । Vártika.

teacher'; but आचार्या 'a woman who teaches; a spititual preceptress'.

(*a*) * The words मातुल and उपाध्याय insert this आन् optionally; मातुलानी, मातुली; उपाध्यायानी, उपाध्यायी; 'the wife of a preceptor,' but उपाध्यायी or उपाध्याया 'a female preceptor', 'a woman who herself performs the work of an उपाध्याय'; in the case of अर्य and क्षत्रिय, आन् is optionally inserted before the ई, when no wife is meant · अर्या—अर्याणी, 'a mistress or a woman of the Vaiśya or trader class', क्षत्रिया, क्षत्रियाणी 'a woman of the Kshatriya or warrior class', अर्यी 'the wife of a Vaishya'; क्षत्रियी 'the wife of a Kshatriya.'

313. † Nouns ending in अ and not having य् for their penultimate except हय, गवय a wild ox, मुकय, मनुष्य and मत्स्य take ई when 'class' is implied *e. g.* वृषली 'A Śudra female' (also the wife of a वृषल, see § 311. above); similarly ब्राह्मणी, महाशूद्री, &c., हरिणी, मृगी, औपगवी 'a woman of the औपगव class of Brâhmaṇas,' कठी 'a woman of the कठ class of Brâhmaṇas', &c., हयी; गवयी, मुकयी, मनुषी, and मत्सी (vide § 306. *d.*); but देवदत्ता 'a woman of that name'; अश्वा as it is one of the words included in the Ajâdi group; (see § 307. and foot-note); शूद्रा 'a woman of the Śudra class (see § 307 above).'

(*a*) Words ending in पाक, कर्ण, पर्ण, पुष्प, फल, मूल and वाल form their fem. in ई when kind is implied; ओदनपाकी, शङ्कुकर्णी, शालपर्णी, शंखपुष्पी, दासीफली, दर्भमूली and गोवाली all names of particular herbs.

(*b*) Also words ending in ई and denoting mankind; दाक्षी 'a woman of the दाक्षि family,' औदमेयी (उदमेयस्यापत्यं), but तित्तिरिः.

---

* मातुलोपाध्याययोरानुक् वा । या तु स्वयमेवाध्यापिका तत्र वा ङीष् वाच्यः । अर्यक्षत्रियाभ्यां वा स्वार्थे । Vártikas.

† जातेरस्त्रीविषयादयोपधात । Pán IV. 1. 63. योपधप्रतिषेधे हयगवयमुकयमनुष्यमत्स्यानामप्रतिषेधः । Vàrtika. पाककर्णपर्णमूलवालोत्तरपदाच्च । इतो मनुष्यजातेः । Pân. IV. 1. 64. 65.

§ 314. * *Prátipadikas* expressive of colour, having त for their penultimate and ending in an Anudátta vowel, except असित black and पलित grey, and the word पिशङ्ग form their *feminine* in ई or आ; एता or एनी 'variegated' from एत: रोहिता, रोहिणी; पिशङ्गी-पिशङ्गा; but असिता, पलिता, श्वेता (as the त here is Udâtta).

(*a*) † But if the *Prátipadika* has no त for its penultimate, it simply takes ई; कल्माषी variegated, सारङ्गी; but कृष्णा कपिला (as the last vowels are not Anudâtta).

§ 315. The *Feminine* of नृ and नर is नारी and that of words included in the *Shârngaravâdi* (शार्ङ्गरवादिगण) group ‡ is formed by adding ई; as शार्ङ्गरवी, गौतमी, आतिथेयी, आशोकेयी, बैदी, पुत्री, &c.

§ 316. The *feminine* of words expressive of relationship is irregular; श्वशुर-श्वश्रू, पितृ-मातृ, &c.

§ 317. ¶ The *feminine* of पति is पत्नी meaning 'the sharer with her husband in the fruit of the sacrifices performed by him; but if it end a compound it may optionally remain unchanged except when preceded by समान, एक, वीर, पिण्ड, भ्रातृ, भद्र, and पुत्र &c. before which this change is necessary; गृहपति or गृहपत्नी, the mistress of the house; or दृढपति or दृढपत्नी; वृषलपति or वृषलपत्नी &c. but समानः पतिर्यस्याः सा सपत्नी a co-wife, एकपत्नी, वीरपत्नी.

N. B.—†† If there be no compound this change does not take

---

* वर्णादनुदात्तात्तोपधात्तो नः । Pân. IV. 1. 39. पिशङ्गादुपसंख्यानम् । असितपलितयोर्न । Vârtikas.

† अन्यतो ङीष् । Pân. IV. 1. 40.

‡ This group consists of the following words—शार्ङ्गरव, कापटव, ब्राह्मण, गौतम, आतिथेय, आशोकेय, वात्स्यायन, मौञ्जायन, शैब्य आश्मरथ्य, चाण्डाल, पुत्र and some others not very important.

¶ पत्युर्नो यज्ञसंयोगे । Pân. IV. 1. 33. पतिशब्दस्य नकारादेशः स्यात् यज्ञेन सम्बन्धे । वसिष्ठस्य पत्नी । तत्कर्तृकयज्ञस्य फलभोक्त्रीत्यर्थः । Sid. Kau.

†† विभाषा सपूर्वस्य । नित्यं सपत्न्यादिषु । Pân. IV. 1. 34. 35.

place; as, ग्रामस्य पतिः 'the mistress of a village', and not पत्नी, similarly गवां पतिः &c.

§ 318. * The words अन्तर्वत् and पतिवत् form their *feminine* in ई but have a न् prefixed to the ई, अन्तर्वत्नी 'a woman big with a child'. पतिवत्नी 'a woman whose husband is living'. But if the word पति means 'a lord or master of' ई only is added; as पतिमती पृथ्वी (the earth having a king).

§ 319. Adjectives ending in ई short or long, have no other form for the *feminine*; as शुचिः, सुधीः &c.

§ 320. † Adjectives ending in उ not preceded by a conjunct consonant, except खरु, take ई optionally; *e. g.* मृदु-मृदुः-द्वी. पटुः-ट्वी. बहुः-ह्वी; but खरुः 'a girl who chooses her husband' (पतिंवरा कन्या Sid. Kau.); पाण्डुः and not पाण्ड्वी as the उ is preceded by a conjunct consonant; आखुः as it is a noun.

§ 321. ‡ A *prátipadika* ending in उ not preceded by य and denoting mankind forms its *feminine* in ऊः *e. g.* कुरूः 'a woman of the Kuru country'; but अध्वर्युः 'the wife of an Adhvaryu'; also when it does not denote animal-kind §; as अलाबूः, कर्कन्धूः; except in the case of रज्जु and हनु; रज्जुः; हनुः.

(*a*) *Obs.* $ A *prátipadika* ending in बाहु and used as a proper name, and the word पङ्गु: also form their *feminine* in ऊः; as भद्रबाहूः 'a woman of that name'; but वृत्तबाहुः 'a woman having well-rounded arms'; पङ्गूः ।

---

* अन्तर्वत्पतिवतोर्नुक् । Pân. IV. 1. 32

† वोतो गुणवचनात् Pân. IV. 1. 44. खरुसंयोगोपधान्न । Vârtika.

‡ ऊङुतः Pân. IV. 1. 66. उकारान्तादयोपधान्मनुष्यजातिवाचिनः स्त्रियामूङ्स्यात् । Sid. Kau.

§ अप्राणिजातेश्चारज्ज्वादीनामुपसंख्यानम् । Pân. Vârtika.

$ बाह्वन्तात्संज्ञायाम् । Pân. IV. 1. 67. पङ्गोश्च । Pân. IV. 1. 68. संज्ञायाम् । Pân. IV. 1. 72.

(*b*) कद्रु and कमण्डलु: if used as proper names take ई; कद्रूः 'a woman of that name,' कमण्डलूः; but कमण्डलुः; कद्रुः in other cases.

§ 322. *If a compound has for its last member ऊरु and for its first, words signifying a standard of comparison, or one of the words संहित, शफ, लक्षण, वाम, सहित and सह, it forms its *feminine* in ऊ; रम्भोरूः रम्भे इव ऊरू यस्याः plantain-thighed; करभोरूः having thighs (beautifully tapering) like the fore-arm or the trunk of an elephant; संहितोरूः having well-turned thighs; शफौ खुरौ ताविव संश्लिष्टत्वादूरू यस्याः सा शफोरूः; [हितेन सह सहितौ ऊरू यस्याः सा] सहितोरूः; [सहेते इति सहौ ऊरू यस्याः सा] सहोरूः 'a woman whose thighs are capable of enduring great fatigue or pain'; or 'one having excellent thighs.'

§ 323. † The *fem.* of वृषाकपि, Vishṇu or Shiva, अग्नि, कुसित or कुसिद 'a usurer' is formed in ई before which the final vowel of these is changed to ऐ; वृषाकपायी, अग्नायी, कुसितायी or कुसिदायी.

§ 324. ‡ The *feminine* of मनु is optionally formed by adding ई before which the final उ is changed to औ or ऐ; मनावी, मनायी or मनुः।

§ 325. ¶ A *prâtipodika* ending in short ऋ or न् forms its *feminine* by the addition of ई; कर्तृ-कर्त्री, दण्डिन्-दण्डिनी, शुनी, राज्ञी, परिदिवन्-परिदिव्नी; &c.

N. B. Words like स्वसृ, ननान्दृ, तिसृ, दुहितृ, स्वसृ &c. being themselves *feminine* do not take this termination.

---

* ऊरूत्तरपदादौपम्ये । संहितशफलक्षणवामादेश्च । Pân. IV. 1. 69. 76. सहितसहाभ्यां चेति वक्तव्यम् । Vârtika.

† वृषाकप्यग्निकुसितकुसिदानामुदात्तः । Pán. IV 1. 37.

‡ मनोरौ वा । Pán. IV. 1. 38. मनुशब्दस्यौकारादेशः स्यादुदात्तैकारश्च Sid. Kau.

¶ ऋन्नेभ्यो ङीप् । Pân. IV. 1. 5.

(*a*)*युवन् forms its *feminine* by the addition of ति before which the final न् is dropped; युवतिः

§ 326. † If *prâtipadika* end in वन् it changes its न् to र् before ई; शकन्-शक्वरी the strong one; पीवन्- पीवरी, शर्वन्-शर्वरी the night, सुत्वानमतिक्रान्ता अतिसुत्वरी, अतिधीवरी, &c.

Exception.—‡ But if a base end in वन् applied to roots ending in a soft consonant; or if a compound has such a base for its latter member, the *fem.* is formed by adding आ only, before which the preceding अन् is dropped, *e. g.* अवावन्+आ-अवावा a Brâhmana woman (ब्राह्मणी) or a female thief; राजयुध्वा.

§ 327. § A Bahuvrîhi ending in अन् forms its *fem.* in आ optionally; as सु+पर्वन्=सुपर्वन्-र्वा, बहु+यज्वन्-ज्वा, &c. but if the word ending in अन् be such as drops its अ before the आ of the Inst. sing. it takes ई also optionally; *e. g.* बहु+राजन्—बहुराजन्—राजा-राज्ञी &c.

(*a*) × If a Bah. ends in वन्, the न् is optionally changed to र्; as बहुधीवन्-बहुधीवा or बहुधीवरी a town in which there are many fishermen.

§ 328. || If a Bah. end in ऊधस् it takes the suffix ई in the *fem.* before which न् is substituted for the final अस्; पीनं ऊधः यस्याः सा पीनोध्नी having a large udder: कुण्डोध्नी (see Rag. I. 84.); also when it is preceded by a numeral or an indeclinable;

---

* यूनस्तिः । † वनोरच । Pân. VI. 1. 77, 7.

‡ अनो बहुव्रीहेः । अन उपधालोपिनोऽन्यतरस्याम् Pân. IV 1. 12. 28.

§ वनो न हश इति वक्तव्यम् । Vârtika.

× बहुव्रीहौ वा । Várt. on Pân. IV. 1. 7

|| ऊधसोऽनङ् । Pân. V. 4. 131. बहुव्रीहेरूधसो ङीष् । संख्याव्ययादेर्ङीष् । दामहायनान्ताच्च Pân. IV. 1 25-27. वयोवाचकस्यैव हायनशब्दस्य ङीप्णत्वं चेष्यते । Vârtika.

as ह्युघ्नी, अत्युघ्नी having an udder exceedingly large; but ऊधः अतिकान्ता अत्यूधाः.

(*a*) Similarly a Bah. ending in दामन्, and हायन denoting age, and having a numeral for its first member takes ई in the *fem.*; द्विदाम्नी, द्विहायनी 'a girl two years old;, त्रिहायणी, &c; but द्विहायना शाला a building built two years since.

N. B.—the न of हायन is changed to ण after त्रि and चतुर only when it takes ई; चतुर्हायणी बाला; but त्रिहायना, चतुर्हायना शाला.

§ 329. * When a compound has for its second member a word denoting a limb of the body of an animal and having no conjunct consonant preceding its final vowel, the *fem.* is formed by the addition of आ or ई; अतिकेशा-शी; 'a women having abundant hair;' सुकेशा-शी, चंद्रमुखा-खी; but सुगुल्फा having beautiful ankles; सुस्तनी or सुस्तना (स्त्री वा प्रतिमा वा;) सुमुखा शाला 'an edifice with a beautiful front'.

(*a*) † If the word, denoting the limb, nowever, be one of the words क्रोड, नख खुर, उखा, शिखा, बाल, शफ, गुद, भुज, कर &c. or have more than two syllables, the *fem.* is formed in आ alone; कल्याणक्रोडा (अश्वानामुरः क्रोडा Sid. Kau.), पृथुजघना, having large hips; चटुलनयना, &c.

(*b*) ‡ Also when the first member is one of स, सह, or विद्यमान, the *fem.* is formed in आ necessarily; सकेशा, अकेशा, विद्यमाननासिका, सहनासिका &c.

§ 330. †† Of Bah. compounds having for their last member

---

* स्वाङ्गाच्चोपसर्जनादसंयोगोपधात् । Pân. IV 1. 54.

† न क्रोडादिबह्वचः । Pân. IV. 1. 56.

‡ सहनञ्विद्यमानपूर्वाच्च । Pân. IV. 1. 57.

†† नासिकोदरौष्ठजङ्घादन्तकर्णशृङ्गाच्च । Pân. IV. 1. 55. अङ्गगात्रकण्ठेभ्यो वक्तव्यम् । पुच्छाच्च । कबरमणिविषशरेभ्यो नित्यम् । उपमानात्पक्षाच्च पुच्छाच्च Vârtikas.

one of the words नासिका, उदर, ओष्ठ, जङ्घा, दन्त, कर्ण, शृङ्ग, अङ्ग, गात्र, कण्ठ and पुच्छ the *fem.* is fomed either in आ or ई; तुङ्गनासिका की; कृशोदरा-री 'a woman having a slender waist;' बिम्बोष्ठी-ष्ठा 'with a lip as red as the *bimba* fruit,' दीर्घे जङ्घे यस्याः सा दीर्घजङ्घा-ङ्घी 'one having long legs,' hence 'a she-camel;' स्वङ्गा ङ्गी (शोभन अङ्गं यस्याः सा) fair-bodied; सुपुच्छा-च्छी; &c.

(*a*) but if पुच्छ be preceded by कबर, मणि and विष, or if पुच्छ and पक्ष be used in a Bah. involving comparison, the *fem.* is formed in ई only; कबरपुच्छी, 'one having a variegated plumage' *i. e.* 'pea-hen'; उलूकपक्षी शाला 'a hall having its sides like the wings of an owl'; उलूकपुच्छी सेना 'an army with its rear arrayed in the shape of the tail of an owl'.

§ 331. * A Bah. ending in नख and मुख and used as proper names forms *fem.* in आ; शूर्पणखा, गौरमुखा; but ताम्रमुखी a girl having a ruddy face.

§ 332. † Names of the limbs of the body, preceded by words denoting a cardinal point in a compound, form their *fem.* in ई उदङ्मुखी, &c.

§ 333 A Bah. ‡ ending in पाद् (substituted for पाद) optionally forms its *fem.* in ई before which it is changed, to पद्; व्याघ्रस्य इव पादौ यस्याः सा व्याघ्रपाद्-पदी, द्विपाद्-पदी and in आ when पाद् means 'a foot of a Vedic verse'; द्विपदा ऋक्, एकपदा &c.

(*a*) But if पाद् be preceded by one of the words कुम्भ, शूल, तृण, हंस, काक, कृष्ण, सूकर, &c. the *fem.* is necessarily formed in ई. पाद् changing into पद् as before; कुम्भपदी 'a woman whose feet are as big as a pitcher.

---

* नखमुखात्संज्ञायाम्। Pân. IV. 1. 58.

† दिक्पूर्वपदान्ङीप्। Pân. IV. 1. 60.

‡ पादोऽन्यतरस्याम्। टाबृचि। Pân. IV.1. 8, 9.

(*b*) In other cases the *fem.* of *prâtipâdikas* ending in पाद् is formed by adding आ; हस्तिपादा, अजपादा, &c.

§ 334. * A Dwigu ending in अ forms its *fem.* in ई; as त्रिलोकी; but if the ending word be one of those included in the Ajâdi group (see foot-note on p. 108) its *fem.* is formed in आ; त्रिफला, त्र्यनीका (consisting of three battalions) सेना, &c.

§ 335. (*a*) A Dwigu ending in काण्ड † (a particular measure) and qualifying a word denoting 'a field' has its *fem.* formed by the addition of आ, but when a Taddhita affix has been first added to it and then dropped; as द्वे काण्डे प्रमाणं यस्याः असौ द्विकाण्ड + मात्रा = द्विकाण्डा क्षेत्रभक्तिः 'a piece of land 30 hands in extent'; but द्विकाण्डी रज्जुः 'a rope, 30 hands in length'; also when the ending word is one that does not denote a measure, except the words बिस्त 'a tola', आचित 'the load of a cart,' and कंबल्या (a weight equal to $3\frac{1}{3}$ tolas); पञ्चभिः अश्वैः क्रीता पञ्चाश्वा, द्वौ बिस्तौ पचतीति द्विबिस्ता स्थाली; so द्व्याचिता, द्विकंबल्या.

(*b*) ‡ When the word पुरुष expressive of measurement ends a Dwigu and the Taddhita affix is added and dropped as before, its *fem.* is formed both in आ and ई; द्वौ पुरुषौ प्रमाणं अस्याः द्विपुरुषा-षी परिखा 'a ditch two purushas (13 feet) in depth'

§ 336. Participles (those of the Pres. and Fut.) of Parasm. roots take ई in the *fem.*, न् being inserted before त् as in the Nom. or Acc. dual of the *Neu.* (see § 116) and so do adjectives ending in a consonant; पचन्ती; याती-न्ती, शासती, ददती, दीव्यन्ती, महती, &c.

---

* द्विगोः । अपरिमाणबिस्ताचितकम्बल्येभ्यो न तद्धितलुकि । Pân. IV. 1. 21. 22.

† काण्डान्तात्क्षेत्रे । Pân. IV. 1. 23.

‡ पुरुषात्प्रमाणेऽन्यतरस्याम् । Pân. IV. 1. 24.

Chapter IX.

SECONDARY NOMINAL BASES DERIVED BY THE ADDITION OF THE TADDHITA OR SECONDARY AFFIXES.

§ 337. The terminations used to form derivative bases, in Sanskṛit are distinguished into two classes; (1) *Kṛit* (कृत्) or Primary Affixes and (2) *Taddhita* (तद्धित) or Secondary affixes. Kṛit are those affixes that are added to verbs, and the Nominal Bases formed by their means are called PRIMARY NOMINAL BASES; while TADDHITA affixes are those that are added to substantives, primary or derived from roots, and the bases formed with them are called SECONDARY NOMINAL BASES (vide § 179).

§ 338. In this chapter we will treat of the more general secondary nominal bases formed by means of the Taddhita affixes, reserving for a future chapter the formation of the primary nominal bases derived by means of the Kṛit affixes from r

§ 339. The Taddhita affixes are added in various senses. They occasion various changes in the words to which they are added. The following general observations should be paid attention to.

(*a*) As a general rule the first vowel of a word takes its Vṛiddhi substitute before the terminations अ, य, इक, ईन, एय, स्य, &c.; as अश्वपति+अ=आश्वपति+अ.

(*b*) Before terminations beginning with a vowel or य (1) the final अ, आ, इ, and ई are rejected; (2) उ and ऊ take their Guṇa substitute; (3) ओ and औ obey the ordinary rules of sandhi; आश्वपति+अ=आश्वपत 'belonging to Asvapati,' &c. *m.* *n.*; मनु+अ=मानवः 'a descendant of Manu'; गो+य=गव्यं 'belonging to a cow', so नाव्यं fr. नौ &c.

(c) In the case of derivatives form compound words sometimes the initial vowel of the second word takes its Vṛiddhi substitute, and sometimes the Vṛiddhi is double; पूर्ववार्षिक 'belonging to the last year'; similarly सुपांचालक: &c. सौहार्द fr. सुहृद्, सौभाग्य from सुभग, &c. When these terminations are added to a Dwa. comp. both the words of which are the names of deities, Vṛiddhi is substituted for the initial vowel of both; आग्निमारुतं कर्म 'a sacrifice offered to Agni and the Marut deities,' &c.

(d) If the initial vowel of a word be preceded by the य् and व् of a preposition the य् or व् is first changed to इय् or उव् before Vṛiddhi substitute can take place; as व्याकरण+अ=वियाकरण+अ =वैयाकरण:; स्वश्व+अ=सुवश्व+अ=सौवश्व:; similarly सौवास्तिक from स्वस्ति; सौवर fr. स्वर, &c.

(e) Before consonantal Tad. affixes, a final न् is generally rejected; the final न् with the preceding vowel is sometimes dropped before vowel terminations and before such as begin with य; युवन्-युवत्वं, राजन्-राजकं, &c. आत्मन्-आत्म्य-आत्मीय. There are various exceptions to this latter part of the rule; *e. g.* राजन्य fr. राजन् &c.

N. B.—Other changes the student will easily note from the instances given.

§ 340. The following is a list of such of the Taddhita affixes as are commonly to be met with.

SECTION I.

MISCELLANEOUS AFFIXES.

अ—is added in the sense of:—(1) ' the son of'; as उपगो: अपत्यं पुमान् औपगव: 'the son of Upagu'; so वासुदेव: from वसुदेव; पर्वतस्य अपत्यं स्त्री पार्वती 'the daughter of the mountain,'

&c. (2) 'the descendant of'; as उत्सस्य गोत्रापत्यं पुमान् औत्सः 'a descendant of Utsa', उत्सस्य गोत्रापत्यं स्त्री औत्सी 'a female descendant of Utsa', (vide § 311, 313); (3) 'dyed with;' हरिद्रया रक्तं हारिद्रं वसनं 'a garment dyed with turmeric'; (4) 'made of;' देवदारोर्विकारः दैवदारवः 'made of the fir tree;' (5) 'belonging to,' &c ; देवस्य अयं दैवः 'belonging to a god;' शर्कराया इदं शार्करं 'of sand': ऊर्णाया इदं और्णं वस्त्रं 'a woolen garment,' ग्रैष्मः 'belonging to the sultry season'; नैशः 'nocturnal;' सांवत्सरः 'yearly' &c.; when added to हेमन्त the final त is dropped, हैमनः 'autumnal,' (vide *Sis*. VI. 65; *Kir*. XVII. 12). हैमन्तः means 'agreeable in the autumnal season;' (6) lord of'; पृथिव्या ईश्वरः पार्थिवः 'the lord of the earth'; पञ्चालानां स्वामी पाञ्चालः 'the king of the Panchâlas'; ऐक्ष्वाकः* 'the king of the Ikshvâku race', (7) 'a collection of'; काकानां समूहः काकं; बकानां समूहः बाकं 'a flock of cranes'; similarly मायूरं from मयूर 'a peacock,' कापोतं from कपोत 'a pigeon', भिक्षाणां समूहो भैक्षम्; गर्भिणीनां समूहो गार्भिणम् &c (8) 'knowing or studying'; व्याकरणं अधीते वेद वा वैयाकरणः 'one who studies grammar, grammarian', &c. (9) and to form abstract nouns; मुनेः भावः मौनं 'silence', युवन्-यौवनं 'youth;' सुहृद्-सौहार्दं 'friendship'; पृथोर्भावः पार्थवं 'greatness, width,' &c.

अक— forms derivatives with various significations:—(1) उष्ट्रे भवः औष्ट्रकः 'produced from or relating to a camel,' ग्रीष्मे भवः ग्रैष्मकः 'produced in the hot season,' (2) कुलालेन कृतं कौलालकं 'made by a potter,' ब्रह्मणा कृतं ब्राह्मकं 'made by Brahman;' (3) आरण्यकः 'a forester,' 'a wild

---

* For the declension of such words vide § 74. *a*., *b*.

man', (4) राज्ञां योग्यं राजन्यकं 'a place fit for kings to live in'; मानुष्यकं 'a country fit for men to live in' कुरुषु जातः कौरवकः (also कौरवः*) 'an inhabitant of Kuru'; युगन्धरेषु जातः यौगन्धरकः (also यौगन्धरः*) 'inhabiting Yugandhara'; (6) पथि जातं पन्थकं 'grown on a way'; (7) पन्थानं गच्छतीति पथिकः 'a traveller'; (8) पूर्वाह्णे भवः पूर्वाह्णिकः 'happening in the forenoon'; similarly अपराह्णिकः 'happening in the afternoon'; (9) is added to denote 'enmity' काकोलूकयोः वैरं काकोलूकिका † 'the antipathy between the crow and the owl'; similarly कुत्सकुशिकिका, &c.; (10) when added to words ending in the Tad. affixes signifying 'the child or the descendant', and to the words उक्षन्, उष्ट्र, उरभ्र 'a ram', राजन्, राजन्य, राजपुत्र, वत्स, मनुष्य and अज, it has the sense of 'a collection of'; उपगूनां समूहः औपगवकम् 'a number of the descendants of Upagu'; औक्षकं 'a herd of cattle'; राजकं 'a collection of kings', राजन्यकं 'an assemblage of kshatriyas'; वात्सकं 'a number of calves'; मानुष्यकं, अजकं &c.; (11) it is also added to क्रम, पद, शिक्षा, and मीमांसा in the sense of 'one who has studied them'; क्रमकः 'a student who goes through a regular course of study, or one who has studied the *krama* arrangement of a sacred text', मीमांसक 'a student of the *mîmâmsâ* philosophy', &c.

आमह—is added to the words पितृ and मातृ in the sense of 'the father of'; पितुः पिता पितामहः 'a paternal grandfather'; मातामहः 'a maternal grandfather'. (1) उल is added to मातृ in the sense of 'the brother of'; मातुर्भ्राता मातुलः

---

* विभाषा कुरुयुगन्धराभ्याम् । Pán. IV. 2. 30.

† Vide *supra.* § 306. *a.* These are generally *fem.* There are some exceptions, as देवासुरम् 'the enmity between the gods and the demons' &c.

'a maternal uncle'; (2) and व्य is added to पितृ and भ्रातृ in the sense of 'the brother and the son of' respectively; पितुः भ्राता पितृव्यः 'a paternal uncle'; भ्रातुः पुत्रः भ्रातृव्यः 'a nephew.'

आयन—and आयनि, are added to patronymics formed by means of Tad. affixes in the sense of 'the child of,' दाक्षायणः-णिः 'the son of Dákshi'; गार्ग्यायणः-णिः 'the son of गार्ग्य, a descendant of Garga'. आयन is also added to the word कापिशी 'name of a town' in the sense of 'produced in'—कापिशायनः, and optionally to द्रोण; द्रौणायनः or द्रौणिः son of Droṇa.

इ—has the meaning of 'a son or a descendant of'; दाक्षिः 'the son of Daksha'; वैयासकिः 'the son of Vyâsa,' &c. (In the case of the words व्यास, वरुड 'name of a low caste,' निषाद, चण्डाल and बिंब, the final अ is changed to अक् before this इ.)

इक [ठक्, ठञ्, ठन्]—has various senses:—(1) रेवत्याः अपत्यं पुमान् रैवतिकः* 'the son of Revati; (2) 'happening or given once a month, monthly, lasting for a month', &c. मासेन दीयते इति मासिकं वेतनं पुस्तकं वा; similarly वार्षिकं आयुः &c. (3) 'gathering together', सैनिकाः; (4) 'asking;' सुस्नातं पृच्छतीति सौस्नातिकः 'one who asks another whether he had an auspicious ablution'; so सुखशयनं पृच्छतीति सौखशायनिकः 'one who asks another whether he had comfortable sleep'. (see Rag. VI. 61 X. 14.); सौखसुप्तिकः &c; (5) 'using an instrument'; असिः प्रहरणमस्य आसिकः 'one who strikes with a sword,' a swordsman'; धानुष्कः 'an archer;' (6) 'mixed with,'

* In this sense it is added to a few words only.

&c.; दध्ना संस्कृतं दाधिकं 'mixed with curds', मारीचिकं fr. मरीचि 'black pepper'; (7) धर्मं चरतीति धार्मिकः 'pious, religious', similarly अधार्मिकः. (8) उडुपेन तरतीति औडुपिकः 'a boatman'; नाविकः &c. (9) हस्तिना चरतीति हास्तिकः 'one who rides an elephant'; शकटेन चरतीति शाकटिकः 'one who drives in a carriage'; (10) दध्ना भक्षयतीति दाधिकः 'one who eats with curds'; (11) 'living upon' वेतनेन जीवतीति वैतनिकः 'one who lives upon wages'; so वाहनिकः, औपदेशिकः &c. (12) 'carrying upon'; उत्संगेन हरतीति औत्संगिकः (13) अस्तीति बुद्धिः अस्य आस्तिकः 'a believer in God and sacred writings'; नास्तिकः &c. (14) it is added to लाक्षा, रोचना, शकल and कर्दम in the sense of 'dyed with', लाक्षया रक्तं लाक्षिकं 'dyed with lac'. रोचनिकः, शाकलिकः 'chequered or spotted', कार्दमिकः;-(15) वेद, न्याय, वृत्ति, लोकायत and words ending in सूत्र except कल्पसूत्र &c.; in the sense of 'one who studies them'; वेदमधीते वैदिकः 'a student of the Veda'; नैयायिकः 'one who studies Nyâya or logic'; वृत्तिमधीते वार्तिकः 'one who studies a commentary' &c.; लौकायतिकः 'an atheist, a student of the materialistic philosophy', सांग्रहसूत्रिकः; but काल्पसूत्रः; (16) to हस्तिन्, धेनु, केदार and कवच in the sense of 'a collection of'; हास्तिकं 'a herd of elephants', धैनुकं 'a herd of cows', कैदारिकं 'a collection of fields,' कावचिकं 'a collection of armours';-(17) to अध्यात्मन्, अधिदेव, अधिभूत, इहलोक, परलोक, &c. in the sense of 'relating to &c.;' आत्मानमधिकृत्य भवः आध्यात्मिक 'relating to the Supreme spirit', 'spiritual'; आधिदैविक 'relating to or coming from the governing deity', आधिभौतिकः 'proceeding from the elements', ऐहलौकिकः 'temporal', पारलौकिकः &c.-(18) to क्रय, विक्रय, क्रयविक्रय, and वस्न in the sense of 'living upon (in these cases no Vṛiddhi substitute takes place); क्रयेण जीवतीति क्रायिकः 'one who lives upon selling things, a trader', विक्रयिकः, वस्निकः,

'one who lives upon wages'.–(19) to words denoting musical instruments in the sense of 'playing upon'; &c. मृदंगवादनं शिल्पमस्य मार्दंगिकः 'one whose profession is to play on a tabor'; so वैणिकः fr. Viná; similarly वैणविकः, माड्डुकः or माड्डुकिकः, झार्झरिकः, &c.–(20) to पर्प and the remaining words* of that group in the sense of 'walking with the assistance of ;' पर्पिकः [पर्पेण चरति इति, येन पीठेन पङ्गवश्चरन्ति स पर्पः Sid. Kau.]; अश्वेन चरति आश्विकः, राथिकः &c. पथा चरति पथिकः 'a traveller'; this is also added to words denoting inanimate things. वारिपाथिकं दारु 'wood carried on by the force of water'; (21) to words included in the भस्त्रादि † group in the sense of 'bears or carries by means of' भस्त्रया हरतीति भस्त्रिकः, and to the word वि-वीवध; वि-वीवधेन हरति वि-वीवधिकः; also वैवधिकः—(22) to कुसीद and दशैकादशन् in the sense of 'lending on interest' कुसीदिकः 'a usurer;, दशैकादशिकः 'one who lends another ten rupees in order to get back eleven *i. e.* 'a usurer'; and (23) to आकर्ष; आकर्षेण चरति आकर्षिकः 'magnetic, attractive'.

इन्—(1) Added to पूर्व or words ending in पूर्व and to श्राद्ध it has the sense of 'done and eaten by' respectively; कृतपूर्वी कटं; श्राद्धमनेन भुक्तं श्राद्धी 'one who has eaten at a Śráddha'; (2) it is added to a few words, such as खल, कुडुम्ब, &c. in the sense of 'a collection of' with *fem.* term. ई added to it; खलानां समूहः खलिनी a multitude of thrashing floors or wicked men', कुडुम्बिनी 'a number

* These are अश्व, अश्वत्थ, रथ, जाल, न्यास, and पाद.

† भस्त्रा, भट, भरण, शीर्ष-में-भार, अंस-से-भार, &c.

of families'. डाकिनी 'a host of female goblins or imps,' शाकिनी, &c.

इमन् (इमनिच्)—forms abstract nouns when added to the words पृथु, मृदु, महत, तनु, पटु लघु, बहु, साधु, आशु, उरु, गुरु, बहुल, खण्ड, दण्ड, अकिंचन, षण्ढ, बाल, वत्स, होड, पाक, मन्द, स्वादु, ह्रस्व, दीर्घ, प्रिय, वृष, ऋजु, क्षिप्र, क्षुद्र, अणु, दृढ, वृढ, परिवृढ, कृश, भृश, वक्र, शीत, उष्ण, जड, बधिर, मधुर, पण्डित, मूर्ख, मूक, स्थिर, and words expressive of colour; before this term. these undergo the same changes as before the ईयस् of the comparative and are always *mas.*; as प्रथिमा 'greatness', म्रदिमा 'softness' तनिमा, 'thinness' पटिमा 'dexterity,' sharpness.' &c.; बालिमा, वत्सिमा, होडिमा, पाकिमा 'childhhood'; ह्रसिमा, क्षोदिमा, द्रढिमा, उष्णिमा, क्रशिमा, जडिमा, शुक्लिमा, &c.

इय (घ)—this is added to (1) क्षत्र in the sense of born of the race of; क्षत्रियः;-(2) राष्ट्र in the sense of 'relating to'; राष्ट्रियः;—(3) महेन्द्र in the sense of 'an oblation offered to'; महेन्द्रियः हविः;-(4) अग्र; अग्रियः 'foremost.'

ई (ईकक्)—is added to शक्ति and यष्टि in the sense of 'striking with'; शक्त्या प्रहरतीति शाक्तीकः; 'a spearman' (also शाक्तिकः); याष्टीकः 'one who strikes with a stick'.

ईन (ख, खञ्)—(1) added to कुल and words ending in कुल it means 'born of', कुले जातः कुलीनः or कौलीनः 'of a good family,' आढ्यकुलीनः—कौलीनः 'sprung from a noble and rich family'; it is added to—(2) the words पार and अवार separately or taken together in any order in the sense of 'going'; as पारं गामीति पारीणः 'going over to the other bank'; (when used at the end of a comp. it means, versed or adept in; vide Bhaṭṭi II.46). अवारीणः 'coming over to this side (of a river, &c.);' पारावारीणः 'one who goes to both sides or one who crosses the sea': अवारपारीण: 'crossing a river,' &c.-(3) the word ग्राम in the sense of 'rustic' as ग्रामीण:;-(4) the words आत्मन्, विश्वजन and words ending in भोग in the sense of 'beneficial to;' आत्मने हितः आत्मनीनः, विश्वजनीनः, मातृभोगीणः 'fit to be enjoyed by a mother'; पितृभोगीणः &c—(5) नव changed to नू; as नवीनः;-(6) अध्वन् in the sense of 'journeying' अध्वानं गच्छतीति अध्वनीनः 'a traveller';-(7) सर्वान्न and अनुपद in the senses of 'eating and fastended on' respectively; सर्वान्नीनः 'eating every kind of food'; *अनुपदं बद्धा अनुपदीना (उपानत्) 'a shoe or boot of the length of the foot;-(8) तिल and माष in the sense of 'a field of'; as तैलीनं 'a sesamum field', माषीणं, &c.; and to सप्तपद and हियंगु substituted for ह्यः+गोदोह; सप्तभिः पदैः अवाप्यते साप्तपदीनं 'formed by walking together seven steps or speaking seven words'; ह्योगोदोहस्य विकार हैयंगवीनं † 'fresh butter or ghee' (vide Rag. 1. 45. Bhatti. V.12).

ईय (छ छण्)—(1) is added in the sense of 'of or belonging to'; शालायाः अयं शालीयः fr. शाला; मालीयः fr. माला; पाणिनीयः 'belonging to the school of Pāṇini'; it is added to (2) स्वसृ and पितृस्वसृ and भ्रातृ in the senses of 'the son of' and 'relating to,' respectively; स्वस्रीयः 'a sister's son' पैतृस्वस्रीयः; भ्रात्रीय 'fraternal';-(3) अश्व in the sense of 'relating to or a number of' आश्वीयं (also आश्वं) 'relating to horses, a number of horses';-(4) when added to the words स्व, जन, पर देव, राजन्, वेणु and वेत्र, कु is

* Pān. V. 2. 23. and Sid. Kau.

† तत्तु हैयंगवीनं यद् ह्योगोदोहोद्भवं घृतम् । Amara.

inserted; स्वकीय 'one's own,' जनकीय 'of the people' परकीय, राजकीय, वैणुकीय, 'of a bamboo,' वैत्रकीय.

एण्य—प्रावृषेण्य 'produced in or relating to the rainy season,' fr. प्रावृष्.

एय (ढक्, ढकञ्, ढञ्,)—is chiefly added (1) to words ending in *fem.* affix in the sense of 'the child or offspring of'; वैनतेयः 'the son of Vinatâ i. e. Garuda'; भागिनेयः 'the son of a sister'; when added to कुलटा meaning 'a poor woman', इन is inserted optionally; कौलटेयः or कौलटिनेयः; when कुलटा means 'a harlot' or 'an adulteress' एर; is optionally substituted for एय; कौलटेयः or कौलटेरः 'the son of an adulteress'; it is optionally changed to एर when added to words denoting 'a female having some kind of defect', काणेयः-रः 'son of a one-eyed woman,' दासेयः-रः 'son of a female slave';—(2) to words of two syllables ending in इ but not formed by the affix इ (इञ्), to मण्डूक and words included in the शुभ्रादि group*; आत्रेयः 'son of Atri', माण्डूकेयः 'son of Mândûka', शौभ्रेयः 'son of Śubhra (Name of a sage), मैत्रेयः &c.;—(3) and to मातृस्वसृ, and पितृस्वसृ, the final ऋ being dropped before it; मातृस्वसेयः, पितृस्वसेयः, (4) added to नदी and कलि it has various senses; आग्नेयः 'son of Agni', 'relating to fire', 'having Agni for the presiding deity', &c.; it is affixed to-(5) नदी and other words in the sense of 'produced from, &c.'; नद्याः इदं नद्यां भवं वा नादेयं 'riverborn'; 'rock-salt'; माहेयं fr. मही 'produced from the earth', वाराणसेयः &c.; (6) व्रीहि and शालि in the sense of 'a field of' व्रैहेयं, शालेयं;—(7) कुल, कुक्षि, मीवा, and words included in

---

* शुभ्र, पुर, ब्रह्मकृत, रोहिणी, रुक्मिणी, धर्मिणी, विमातृ, विधवा, शुक, विश्र, शकुनि, शुक्र, बन्धकी, &c.

the कव्यादि group*, with different significations and with a क added to it; कौलेयकः 'a dog', pertaining to a noble family'; कौक्षेयकः a sword', ग्रैवेयकः 'a neck ornament', कुत्सिताः त्रयः कत्रयः तत्र जातः कात्रेयकः, ग्रामेयकः, 'village-born, rustic'; नागरेयकः, &c. (8) कोश in the sense of 'made of'; कौशेयं 'a silken garment';—(9) पुरुष in different senses; पौरुषेयः 'man-slaughter', 'human work', 'derived from or incidental to man, composed or propounded by man'; and (10) to पथिन्, अतिथि, वसति and स्वपति in the sense of 'useful in, good for'; पथि साधु पाथेयं 'what is useful on the way'. i. e. 'provisions for a journey'; अतिथिषु साधुः आतिथेयः 'attentive to guests, hospitable वसतौ साधुः वासतेयः 'hospitable':—वसति रात्रिः; स्वपतेः गतं स्वापतेयं (धनं) 'wealth, property'; vide Kir. XIV. 8.

क (कन्)—is affixed (1) to words expressive of countries in the sense of 'born or produced in'; मद्रकः 'born or produced in the Madra country';—(2) to पीत in the sense of 'dyed with'; पीतकः 'dyed yellow';—(3) in the sense of 'belonging to'; मत्कः, त्वत्कः, &c.—(4) 'bought for' पञ्चकः 'bought for five rupees';—(5) in the sense of 'acting' शीतकः 'one who is cold' i. e. 'slow in action,' 'a dilatory or lazy man;' उष्णकः 'an active man';—(6. 7. 8.) to express pity or diminution, or depreciation-पुत्रकः 'poor son', देवदत्तकः 'unhappy Devadatta'; ह्रस्वो वृक्षो वृक्षकः, 'a small or stunted tree'; अश्वकः a bad horse, a hack; शूद्रकः 'a wicked Śudra,' (9) and sometimes with no signification; अविकः i. e. अविः 'a ram' मणिकः 'a jewel', बालकः 'a young boy'; &c.

कट (कटच्)—is affixed (1) to words denoting names of beasts, in the sense of 'a collection of'; अविकटं 'a flock of sheep'

---

* काश्रि, पुष्कर, पुष्कल, कुम्भी, कुण्डिन, ग्राम. &c.

&c. (2) and in various senses to the prepositions सं, प्र, वि, नि and उत्; संकट 'narrow, impassable, crowded' &c.; प्रकट 'manifest'; विकट 'huge, fierce, large', &c.; निकट 'near, close to' &c.; उत्कट 'large, excessive, powerful' &c.

कटया—रथकटया 'a number of chariots'

कल्प, देश्य and देशीय (कल्पप्, देश्य, देशीयर्,) are added to express 'equality with, little inferiority to'; विदुषः ईषन्न्यून, विद्वत्कल्पः-देश्यः—देशीयः 'almost learned'; कुमारकल्पः 'nearly equal to Kumâra in valour'; कविकल्पः, मृतकल्प 'nearly dead', &c.; these are also added to verbs; पचतिकल्पं 'cooks tolerably well'.

चण (चणप्)
चुञ्चु (चुञ्चुप्) } are added in the sense of 'reputed or remarkable for'; as विद्यया वित्तः-विद्याचणः 'remarkable or known for one's knowledge'. अस्त्रचुञ्चुः-'renowned for his skill in the use of weapons' (vide Bhaṭṭi II. 32.)

तन (ट्यु, ट्युल्)-is added to adverbs of time in the senses of relating or belonging to,' सायं भवः सायंतनः, अद्यतनः, ह्यस्तनः प्राह्णेतनः, दिवातनः, दोषातनः, चिरंतनः, सनातनः,—to प्र; as प्रतनः old;—to the word नव changed to नु; नूतनः.

तर (ष्टरप्)-expresses diminution; गोणीतरा 'a small sack,' वत्सतरः 'a young calf', &c.

त्न—is similarly added to चिर, परुत् 'last year', परारि 'the year before the last', प्र and नव; चिरत्नं, परुत्नं, परारित्नं, प्रत्नं and नूत्नं.

ता (तल)—forms abstract nouns स्त्रीता, पुंस्ता, समता, &c.; added to ग्राम, जन, बन्धु, सहाय, and गज it has the sense of 'a collection of;' ग्रामता, जनता, बन्धुता, &c.

तिथ—बहुतिथ 'manifold'.

त्य-(त्यक्) is added in the sense of 'living in, belonging to,' &c. to the words दक्षिणा, पश्चात्, पुरस्, अमा, इह, क, ह्यस्, श्वस्, and indeclinables ending in तस्; दाक्षिणात्यः a southerner, पाश्चात्यः, पौरस्त्यः, an inhabitant of the east; अमात्यः, one who accompanies a king, a minister, इहत्यः क्वत्यः, ह्यस्त्यः, ततस्त्यः &c.; also to the preposition नि, नित्यः 'eternal'.

त्यक (त्यकन्) is added to उप and अधि; उपत्यका land at the foot of a mountain, अधित्यका 'a table-land.'

त्र—is affixed to गो only; गवां समूहो गोत्रा *f.* 'a herd of kine'.

त्व—forms abstract nouns; गोत्वं.

दघ्न, द्वयस and मात्र* (दघ्नच्, द्वयसच्, मात्रच्,) are added in the sense of 'measuring as much as'; जानु प्रमाणं अस्य जानुदघ्नं-द्वयसं-मात्रं उदकं 'water reaching as far as the knee', &c.

न and स्न†(नञ्, स्नञ्)—are added to स्त्री and पुंस respectively in different senses:—स्त्रैण 'womanly, *feminine*, suited to women, (*n*) womenhood' &c.; पौंस्न 'manly, heroic, fit for a man, (*n.*) manhood, virility'.

पाश—is added as a depreciatory termination; भिषक्पाशः 'a bad doctor, a quack'; वैयाकरणपाशः &c.; added to केश it has the sense of 'a collection of', as केशपाशः (पक्ष and हस्त are also added to केश in the same sense)

मय (मयट्)—§ is added in the sense of (1) 'made of'; मृदः विकारः मृन्मयं 'made of earth,' काष्ठमयं 'made of wood' &c.; and (2) in that of profusion or excess' घृतं प्रचुरं.

---

* प्रमाणे द्वयसज्दघ्नञ्मात्रचः । Pân. V. 2, 37.

† स्त्रीपुंसाभ्यां नञ्स्नञौ भवनात् । Pân. VI. 1, 87.

§ मयड् वा एतयोर्भाषायामभक्ष्याच्छादनयोः Pân. IV. 3. 143.

यस्मिन् घृतमयो यज्ञः 'a sacrifice consisting for the most part of clarified butter,' अन्नमयः &c. It is not added to words denoting 'an article of food or a covering'; *e. g.* मौद्गः सूपः.

य (यक्, यत्, यञ्, ण्य)—is added to nouns with different meanings:—(1) गवां समूहो गव्या *f.* 'a herd of cattle,' वातानां समूहो वात्या, so खल्या, रथ्या, (रथानां समूहः), पाश्या, धूम्या, 'a dense mass of smoke,' तृण्या, नड्या, &c. (2) सभायां साधुः सभ्यः a 'courtier'; (3) सतीर्थ्याः 'disciples of the same preceptor,' सोदर्यः, समानोदर्यः 'a brother of whole blood'; (4) forms abstract nouns राज्य, सैनापत्यं, पौरोहित्यं, सारथ्यं, आस्तिक्यं, &c.; it is added—(5) to the words राजन् and मनु in the sense of 'born of the race of.' राजन्यः 'a man of the Kshatriya class,' मनोर्जातः मनुष्यः (in this case ष् is inserted) 'a man;'–(6) to श्वशुर in the sense of 'the son of;' श्वाशुर्यः, (7) to कुल; कुल्य–'of noble descent;' (8) to वायु, ऋतु, पितृ, and उषस् in the sense of 'having any of these for one's presiding or tutelary deity,' &c. वायुः देवता अस्य वायव्यं अस्त्रं 'a missile having Váyu for its presiding deity,' ऋतव्यः 'worshipping the Seasons (as divinities),' पित्र्यः 'sacred to the manes, offered to the manes'; उषस्यः 'sacred to the Dawn;'–(9) to दण्ड and words included under the दण्डादि group in the sense of 'deserving or meriting'; दण्ड्यः 'deserving punishment,' वध्यं 'fit to be killed,'; अर्घ्यः 'deserving worship,' &c. In the derivatives given hereafter य should be considered as added in the sense attached to each word:—स्तेय 'theft' from स्तेनः, उरस्यः 'born of the breast' (also औरसः fr. उरस् +

अ) fr. उरस्; दन्त्यं 'wholesome to the teeth' (in this sense it is added to words denoting the limbs of the body; as कण्ठ्य 'good for the neck,' &c.); शुनं-शुन्यं 'fit for a dog' fr. श्वन्; नाभ्यं fit for being the central part of a wheel' fr. नाभि 'the nave of a wheel,' नस्य 'fit for the nose' from नासिका; रथ्य 'drawing a chariot, a horse, धुर्य 'harnessed to the yoke, a bull'; वयस्य 'of equal age, a friend'; तुल्य 'what is weighed in a balance and found equal', hence 'equal,' fr. तुला; न्याय्य (न्यायादनपेतं) just; पथ्यं (पथि साधु) 'wholesome;' हृद्यं (हृदि स्पृश्यते मनोज्ञत्वात्) 'agreeable to the heart', धन्यः (धनं लब्धा) obtaining wealth, धर्म्यं (धर्मादनपेतं लब्धा वा) 'consistent with *dharma*', or 'obtained justly'; जन्यं 'talk of the people,' वश्य 'capable of being controlled, obedient', &c. द्रव्य (द्रोर्विकारः) 'wooden or of a tree,; मूल्यं (मूलेनानाम्यं Pân. IV. 4. 49.) 'price'; &c यशस्यः (यशसा युतः) 'glorious, leading to glory'; (नाव्यं नावा तार्यं)' fit to be crossed over in a boat'; धुर्यः (धुरं वहतीति 'a horse or bullock yoked to the pole of a carriage'; गव्यं (गवे हितं) 'proper or fit for a cow, got from a cow'; &c.

र—(1) is added to कुटी, शमी and शुण्ड, as a diminutive term., ह्रस्वा कुटी-कुटीर *m. n.* 'a small hut,' शमीरः a smal S'ami tree', शुण्डारः 'the trunk of a young elephant'.

शकट and शाल-are affixed to वि in the sense of 'largeness,' विशंकट 'great, large'; विशाल 'extensive,' 'spacious,' &c.

§ 341. The मत्वर्थीय affixes or affixes expressive of possession have the following additional senses:—भूमन् or 'greatness,eminence,' निन्दा or 'depreciation,' प्रशंसा or 'praise,,· नित्ययोग or 'constant connection, अतिशायन or 'excess over,' सम्बन्ध or 'being in connection with,' and अस्तिविवक्षा or 'to express the meaning of 'Poession'* The instances in order are—यवमान्, ककुदावर्तिनी कन्या, रूपवान्, क्षीरिणो वृक्षाः, उदरिणी कन्या, दण्डी.

SECTION II.

AFFIXES SHOWING POSSESSION. (मत्वर्थीय).

अ (अच्)—is affixed to words included in the अर्शआदि group†; अर्शसः (अर्शांसि अस्य विद्यन्ते) 'suffering from piles;' जटा अस्यास्तीति जटः 'having matted hair'; उरसः 'having a prominent breast.'

आट and आल—are attached to वाच् in the sense of 'speaking much or speaking badly'; वाचाटः or वाचालः a prattler, a garrulous or talkative person.'

आलु-हृदयालुः one who possesses a 'heart' *i. e.* 'a kind-hearted man;' this is added to शीत, उष्ण, and तृप्र in the sense of 'not capable of enduring;' शीतं न सहते शीतालुः 'unable to endure cold'; similarly उष्णालुः, तृप्रालुः (तृप्रः पुरोडाशः तं न सहते । तृप्रं दुःखं इति माधवः S. K.).

इत—is affixed to तारका and other words ‡ in the sense of 'that

---

* भूमनिन्दाप्रशंसासु नित्ययोगेऽतिशायने ।
संबन्धेऽस्तिविवक्षायां भवन्ति मतुबादयः ॥ (Sid. Kau.)

† अर्शस्, उरस्, तुन्द, चतुर, पलित, जटा, घटा, अघ, कर्दम, अम्ल, लवण, and words expressive of the deformed limbs of the body and of colour.

‡ तदस्य संजातं तारकादिभ्य इतच् । Pân. V. 2. 36. The following are some of the words of the तारकादि group:—पुष्प, मञ्जरी, ऋजीष, क्षण, सूत्र, प्रचार, विचार, कुड्मल, मुकुल, कण्टक, मुसल, कुसुम, कुतूहल, स्तबक, किसलय, पल्लव, खण्ड, वेग, निद्रा, मुद्रा, बुभुक्षा, धेनुष्या, पिपासा, श्रद्धा, अभ्र, पुलक, अङ्गारक, द्रोह, दोह, सुख, दुःख, उत्कंठा, भर, व्याधि, वर्मन्, व्रण, गौरव, शास्त्र, तरङ्ग, तिलक, चन्द्रक, अन्धक, गर्व, मुकुर, हर्ष,

is obtained or possessed by'; तारका अस्य संजाताः तारकितं नभः 'the sky studded with stars'; फलानि अस्य संजातानि असौ फलितः वृक्षः; similarly पुष्पित, सुखित, दुःखित &c.

इन् and इक (इनि, ठन्)—are added to words ending in अ, and to the words of the व्रीह्यादि group*; दण्डः अस्यास्तीति दण्डिन् or दण्डिक 'one who has a staff.' धनिन्, सुखिन्, दुःखिन &c.; व्रीहिन्, व्रीहिक, मायिन्, मायिक, शालिन्, मालिन्, &c. when added to वात and अतिसार, क is prefixed to it; वातकिन्, 'suffering from gout, rheumatic; आतिसारकिन्, 'one suffering from diarrhœa'; it is added to पुष्कर† and other words when the place is meant; पुष्करिणी 'the place where lotuses grow'; hence 'a tank or a lake: similarly कुमुदिनी, पद्मिनी &c.; it is also added to अर्थ and words ending in अर्थ; अर्थिन् one having some object in view; धान्यार्थिन् &c.; and to वर्ण-वर्णिन् 'an ascetic.'

इन—is affixed to फल, बर्ह and मल; फलिनः 'bearing fruit, fruitful', बर्हिणः 'a peacock;' मलिन 'dusky'.

इल—is added to तुन्द, उदर, पिचण्ड, यव, व्रीहि and प्रज्ञा optionally.

हर्ष, रण, कुवलय, सीमन्त, ज्वर, गर, रोमाञ्च, पण्डा, कज्जल, कोरक, स्थपुट, फल, शृङ्गार, अंकुर, बकुल, शैवल, श्वभ्र, कलंक, कर्दम, कन्दल, मूर्च्छा, हस्तक, प्रतिबिंब, प्रत्यय and दीक्षा.

* अत इनिठनौ । Pân. V. 2. 215. The words belonging to this group are:—व्रीहि, माया, शाला, शिखा, माला, मेखला, केका, अष्टका, पताका, चर्मन्, कर्मन, वर्मन, दंष्ट्रा, संज्ञा, वडवा, कुमारी, नौ, वीणा, बलाका and words ending in शीर्ष

† पुष्कर, पद्म, उत्पल, तमाल, कुमुद, नड, कपित्थ, बिस, मृणाल, कर्दम, शाक, विगर्ह, कराप, शिरीष, प्रवाह, हिरण्य, कैरव, कल्लोल, तट, तरङ्ग, पङ्कज, सरोज, राजीव, नालिक, सरोरुह, पुटक, अरविन्द, अम्भोज, अब्ज, कमल and पयस्.

to पिच्छ, उरस्, ध्रुवक, वर्ण, उदक and पङ्क necessarily to सिकता, शर्करा and फेन optionally; तुन्दिल 'having a protuberant belly, corpulent'; उदरिल, पिचण्डिल, (have the same sense); प्रज्ञिल 'intelligent'; पिच्छिल 'slimy, slippery'; उरसिल 'having a broad chest'; पङ्किल 'muddy' सिकतिल 'sandy', शर्करिल, फेनिल, &c.

उर—दन्तुर 'having projecting teeth, hence also rugged' &c.

ऊल—is added to बल and वात in the sense of 'not enduring'; as बलूलः 'not able to face the army of the enemy', 'one who cannot withstand the strength of another'; वातूल 'one that cannot bear the wind'. When added to वात it has also the sense of 'a collection'. वातूलः 'a hurricane'.

ग्मिन्—This is added to the word वाच् in a good sense, as आट or आल is added in a bad sense; वाग्मिन् 'eloquent, an orator.'

मत (ड्मतुप्)—is added to कुमुद, नड and वेतस्; कुमुद्वत् 'a place abounding in lotuses'; नड्वत् 'abounding in the *nada* grass', वेतस्वत 'abounding in canes'.

मत (मतुप्)—is the general term expressing possession;* it is added in the sense of 'it has that or that is in it', *e.g.* गावोऽस्यास्मिन्वा सन्तीति गोमान् 'possessing cows', &c. It is specially added to the words रस, रूप, वर्ण, गन्ध, स्पर्श, स्नेह, शब्द and स्व; रसवान्, रूपवान्, &c.; स्ववान्

§ 342. (*a*) The म of the termination मत् is changed to व when affixed to words ending in म् or अ, short or long, or having either for their penultimate †; किंवत् from किम्, विद्यावत्,

* तदस्यास्त्यस्मिन्निति मतुप्। रसादिभ्यश्च। Pân. V. 2. 94. 95.

† मादुपधायाश्च मतोर्वोऽयवादिभ्यः। Pân. VIII. 2. 9.

लक्ष्मीवत्, यशस्वत्, भास्वत्, &c.;* राजन्+वत्=राजन्वत्, as राजन्वान् देशः 'a country having a good or just king'; (cf. Rag. VI. 22.)=राजवत्, as राजवान् देशः 'a country governed by a king'; उदक+वत्=उदन्वत् m. 'the sea'; उदकवत् as उदकवान् (घटः 'a jar') containing water.

Exceptions:—म is not changed to व in the case of the words यव, दल्मि, ऊर्मि, भूमि, कृमि, क्रुञ्चा, वशा; द्राक्षा, ध्राजि, ध्रजि, ध्वजि, नजि, हरित्, ककुद्, गरुत्, इक्षु, द्रु and मधु; as यवमान्, ऊर्मिमान्, &c.

(b) † मत् also becomes वत् when added to words ending in any of the first four letters of a class; विद्युत्वान्, तडित्वान् m, 'possessing lightning' i.e. 'a cloud', &c. The त् of विद्युत् &c. is not changed to द् as it is not at the end of a पद.

(c) and when the whole expresses a संज्ञा (a name); अहीवती; मुनीवती &c.

§ 343. When added to words denoting qualities मत् is dropped; ‡ e.g. शुक्लो गुणोऽस्यास्तीति शुक्लः पटः a white (i.e. possessed of the white colour) garment, so कृष्णः &c.

य (यप्)—is added to रूप in the sense of 'a stamped coin or beautiful'; हिम्य 'possessing snow, snowy', गुण्य 'possessing merits'.

युस्—is added to ऊर्णा, शुभं, अहं, and शं; ऊर्णायुः 'woolen', शुभंयुः 'possessing bliss, fortunate', अहंयुः 'proud'; शंयुः 'happy'.

र—is added to पाण्डु, मधु, सुषि, ऊष, नग, मुष्क, पांसु, ख, मुख,

---

* राजन्वान्सौराज्ये । Pân. VIII. 2. 14. राजवानन्यत्र । Sid. Kau.

† झयः । संज्ञायाम् । Pân. VIII. 2. 10. 11.

‡ गुणवचनेभ्यो मतुपो लुगिष्टः । Vârt.

and कुब्ज (कुब्जो हस्तिहनुः); पाण्डुर 'possessing paleness,' i. e. 'pale'; मधुर 'sweet,' &c.

ल (लच्)—अंसलः 'having muscular shoulders' i. e. 'strong', वत्सल 'compassionate,' फेनल 'foamy'; it is also added to words ending in आ and denoting a limb of the body of an animal; चूडालः 'having a crest'.

व—केशवः 'having beautiful and luxuriant hair,' also (केशिन्, केशिक, केशवत् in this sense); मणिवः 'a kind of serpent', हिरण्यवः 'one of the nine treasures of Kubera'; अर्णस + व=अर्णवः 'the sea'.

वल (वलच्)—दन्तावलः 'an elephant'; शिखावलः 'a peacock'; रजस्वला, कृषीवलः 'a husbandman,' आसुतीवलः 'a sacrificial priest' 'a distiller of spirit'; परिषद्वलः 'a king'; and ऊर्जस्वलः 'powerful'.

विन्—* is added to माया, मेधा, स्रज् and words ending in स्; मायाविन् 'a magician;' &c., मेधाविन् 'talented,' स्रग्विन् 'possessing a garland,' तेजस्विन् 'lustrous,' &c.; also to आमय the final अ being lengthened; आमयाविन् 'diseased'.

श—लोमशः 'hairy,' 'a monkey'; रोमशः; कपिशः 'tawny'.

N. B.—† These affixes are prohibited after Karmadháraya compounds.

---

* अस्मायामेधास्रजो विनिः। Pân. V. 2. 121. आमयस्योपसंख्यानं दीर्घश्च।
† न कर्मधारयान्मत्वर्थीयः।

SECTION III.

AFFIXES FORMING ADVERBS.

अक (अकच्)—is inserted before the final vowel of indeclinables without any change of meaning; उच्चैः-उच्चकैः; नीचैः-नीचकैः

एन—is added to nouns indicating 'a direction' in the sense of 'not far from'; पूर्वेण ग्रामं 'to the east of the village not far from it'; अपरेण ग्रामं, &c.

तस् (तसि)—has the sense of the Ablative; आदितः 'from the beginning,' मध्यतः, स्वरतः, वर्णतः &c.; sometimes this is added in the sense of the Gen.; as देवा अर्जुनतोऽभवन् 'the gods declared themselves on the side of Arjuna'; (तसिल्)-परितः 'on all sides'; अभितः 'on both sides'.

ना—विना 'without', नाना 'in various ways', &c.

वत—* is affixed in the sense of 'equally with' or 'like to' when the equality or likeness refers to an action; ब्राह्मणेन तुल्यं ब्राह्मणवदधीते; but पुत्रेण तुल्यः स्थूलः and not पुत्रवत स्थूलः; similarly क्षत्रियवत्; or (2) 'as in the case of that मथुरायामिव मथुरावत् स्रुघ्ने प्राकारः; चैत्रस्य इव चैत्रवत (मैत्रस्य गावः); (3) विधिमर्हति विधिवत् पूज्यते.

शस्—अल्पशः 'little by little'; बहुशः &c.

च्वि—is added to nouns or indeclinables to express that a person or thing, not being like what is denoted by the base to which it is added, becomes or is made like it.

---

* तेन तुल्यं क्रिया चेद्वतिः । तत्र तस्येव । तदर्हम् । Pân. V. 1. 115-117 कृभ्वस्तियोगे सम्पद्यकर्तरि च्विः । Pân. V. 4. 50. अभूततद्भाव इति वक्तव्यम् । Vârt.

Before this the ending अ or आ is changed to ई, but not that of indeclinables; इ or उ is lengthened and ऋ changed to री; final न् and the ending consonant of अरुस्, मनस्, चक्षुस्, चेतस्, रहस्, and रजस्, are dropped and then the preceding rules are applied to the penultimate vowel. After this the termination is dropped and the verbal or other forms of कृ, भू and अस् are added to the base regarded as a proposition; अकृष्णः कृष्णः सम्पद्यते तं करोति (कृष्ण + च्वि = कृष्णी + च्वि = कृष्णी- + करोति) कृष्णीकरोति; न ब्रह्मा अब्रह्मा अब्रह्मा ब्रह्मा सम्पद्यते ब्रह्मीभवति; similarly गङ्गीस्यात्; दोषाभूतमहः 'the day is changed into the night'; दिवाभूता रात्रिः 'the night has become like the day'; शुचीभवति. पटूस्यात्; मात्रीभवती; मात्रीकरोति; &c., 'अरूकरोति, उन्मनीस्यात्; उच्चक्षूकरोति; विचेतीकरोति, विरजीकरोति, &c.

आ—is affixed like च्वि to (1) दुःख when the meaning is 'troubling one who ought not to be troubled', दुःखाकरोति स्वामिनम्;—(2) सुख and प्रिय in the sense of pleasing one who ought to be pleased', &c; सुखाकरोति, प्रियाकरोति गुरुं (अनुकूलाचरणेन आनन्दयति Sid. Kau.);—(3) शूल; शूलाकरोति मांसम् *i. e.* 'roasts it';—(4) सत्यः सत्याकरोति भाण्डं वणिक् *i. e.* 'settles its price'; (5) and to onomatopœic words not followed by इति and containing more than one vowel, the words being reduplicated; पटत्,—पटपटाकरोति, 'utters the words पटत्, पटत्.'

सात्—is optionally affixed like च्वि but when the change meant is complete*; (कृत्स्नं शस्त्रं अग्निः सम्पद्यते) अग्निसाद्भवति 'is

---

* अस्य च्वौ । Pân. VII 4. 32. अवर्णस्य ईत्स्यात् च्वौ । Sid. Kau; अव्ययस्य च्वावीत्वं नेति वाच्यम् । Vârt. च्वौ च । Pân. VII. 4. 26. अरुर्मनश्चक्षुश्चेतोरहोरजसां लोपश्च । Pân. V. 4. 51.

completely changed to fire'; (also अग्नीभवति); भस्मसात् करोति 'completely reduces to ashes'; in the case of this affix the forms of पद् with सम् are also added; अग्निसात्सम्पद्यते अग्निसाद्भवति शस्त्रं, जलसात्सम्पद्यते जलीभवति लवणम्; सात् also conveys the sense of 'making over or delivering something to another' &c.; राजसात्सम्पद्यते, राजसात्करोति; सात् and त्रा are similarly added when something is to be given to another; विप्रत्राकरोति, विप्रत्रासम्पद्यते; विप्रसात्करोति &c.

*N. B.**—The derivatives formed by means of the affix सात् do not share the properties of prepositions; the verbal indecl., therefore, from अग्निसात्करोति is अग्निसात्कृत्वा and not—कृत्य.

ADVERBS OF TIME IRREGULARLY FORMED FROM NOUNS:—

समाने अहनि सद्यः 'the same day'; पूर्वस्मिन्वत्सरे परुत् 'last year'; पूर्वतरे वत्सरे परारि 'the year before the last'; अस्मिन्संवत्सरे ऐषमः 'this year'; परस्मिन्नहनि परेद्यवि 'the other day', अस्मिन्नहनि अद्य 'to-day'; पूर्वस्मिन्नहनि पूर्वेद्युः 'yesterday'; अन्यस्मिन्नहनि अन्येद्युः 'the other or following day'; उभयोरह्नोः उभय-ये-द्युः 'both the days'.

Chapter X.

Gender.

§ 344. No definite rules can be laid down for the determination of the gender of words in Sanskṛit. It can best be studied

* विभाषा साति कार्त्स्न्ये । Pân. V 4. 52.

from the dictionary or from usage. The following hints, however, may be useful to the student in the majority of cases.

1 MASCULINE WORDS.

§ 345. Verbal derivatives formed by the affixes अ and न, and इ added to the roots दा and धा; *e. g.* पाकः, त्यागः, करः, गरः any beverage or drink, poison, गोचरः range, scope, यज्ञः, विघ्नः, आधिः mental pain or anguish. निधिः a treasure, &c.

Exceptions:—याच्ञा *fem.* and भय, लिङ्ग, and भग all *neu.*

§ 346. Words ending in उ and those having क, ट्, ण्, थ्, न्, भ्, म्, य्, र्, or स्, for their penultimate; as प्रभुः, भानुः, इक्षुः, स्तबकः 'a bunch of flowers' &c; घटः, पाषाणः, शोथः 'a swelling, फेनः, दीपः, स्तम्भः, सोमः, समयः, क्षुरः a razor,' अङ्कुरः, वृषः, वायसः &c.

Exceptions:—Words ending in—

(*a*) उ–धेनु, रज्जु (except when it ends a compound, in which case it is both *mas.* and *fem.*) कुहु–हू 'the last day of a lunar month on which the moon is invisible,' सरयु 'name of a river,' तनु, करेणु and प्रियंगु 'a kind of creeper,' which are all *fem.*; श्मश्रु, जानु, वसु 'wealth,' अश्रु, जतु 'lac,' त्रपु 'tin or lead', तालु, दारु, मधु 'honey,' स्वादु 'relish', वस्तु and मस्तु 'sour cream', which are all *neuter*.

(*b*) क–चिबुक 'the chin', शालूक, प्रातिपदिक, अंशुक 'a garment,' उल्मुक 'a fire brand.'

(*c*) ट and ण–किरीट, मुकुट, ललाट, शृङ्गाट 'a place where four roads meet;' ऋण, लवण, पर्ण, उष्ण.

(*d*) थ and न–काष्ठ, पृष्ठ, रिक्थ property left at death,' उक्थ 'a hymn of the Sâmaveda,' 'a kind of sacrifice,' जघन, अजिन 'the hairy skin of a black antelope', तुहिन 'snow', कानन,

विपिन, वन, वृजिन 'sin,' वेतन, शासन, सोपान 'a flight of steps', मिथुन, श्मशान, रत्न, चिह्न.

(e) प, भ, म—पाप 'sin' रूप, शिल्प, पुष्प, शष्प 'tender grass', अन्तरीप 'an island', कुङ्कुम 'saffron', रुक्म gold, iron, सिध्म 'a leprous spot', युध्म 'a battle', इध्म, गुल्म (generally *mas.*), अध्यात्म knowledge of the soul.

(*f*) य and र—हृदय, इन्द्रिय, उत्तरीय 'an upper garment', द्वार, अग्र, तक्र, वक्त्र, वप्र 'lead', छिद्र, नीर, कृच्छ्र, रन्ध्र, श्वभ्र, अस्र, तिमिर, विचित्र, केयूर, उदर, शरीर, कन्दर 'dry ginger', पञ्जर 'a cage', जठर, अजिर 'courtyard,' वैर, चत्वर, पुष्कर, गह्वर, कुहर 'a cave', कुटीर 'a hut' (*m.* also), कुलीर 'a crab', काश्मीर 'name of a country,' अम्बर, शिशिर, तन्त्र a loom, the ritual &c.; यन्त्र, क्षत्र, क्षेत्र, मित्र, कलत्र, चित्र, सूत्र, नेत्र, गोत्र a family, अङ्गुलित्र a finger-armour, शस्त्र, शास्त्र, वस्त्र, पत्र, पात्र, शुक्र.

(*g*) ष and स—ऋजीष 'a frying pan,' अम्बरीष 'a frying pan,' पीयूष, पुरीष, किल्मिष 'sin, guilt,' कल्मषः 'sin, stain,' (sometimes *mas.*), बिस, बुस, 'chaff' साहस which (*b.g.*) are all *neuter*.

§ 347. The words द्रव, दैत्य मनुष्य, पर्वत, समुद्र, स्वर्ग, मेघ, किरण, दिवस, असि, शर, यज्ञ, आत्मा, नख (also *neu.*), केश, दन्त, कण्ठ, गल, स्तन, भुज, गुल्फ, and their synonyms, and words expressive of the measures of corn &c., such as कुडव, &c.

Exceptions—द्यो *fem.*, दिव् *fem.*, खारी *fem.*, मानिका *fem.* 'a kind of weight,, त्रिविष्टप *neu*; दिन *usu*; अहन् *neu*; and अभ्र *neu.*

§ 348. The words दाराः 'a wife', अक्षताः 'uninjured rice,' लाजाः 'fried rice,' असवः 'life (the vital airs in the body)' and गृहाः 'a house,' which are always used in the plural.

§ 349. The words नाडीव्रण 'sinus, a kind of ulcer', अपाङ्ग the corner of the eye, जनपद, मरुत, गरुत् 'a wing,' ऋत्विज्, ऋषि, राशि, ग्रन्थि, क्रमि, ध्वान, बलि, मौलि, रवि, कपि, मुनि, ध्वज, गज, मुञ्ज 'a kind of grass (of which the girdle of a Brâhmaṇa ought to be made), पुञ्ज, हस्त, कुन्त 'a spear' अन्त, व्रात 'a collection.' वात' दूत, धूर्त, सूत, चूत 'the mango tree', मुहूर्त, षण्ड 'a eunuch,' करण्ड. मुण्ड 'name of a demon,' पाखण्ड a heretic, शिखण्ड a lock of hair, a peacock's tail, वंश, अंश, पुरोडाश 'a kind of sacrificial offering,' ह्रद, कन्द, कुन्द name of Vishṇu, a kind of flower (also *neu.* in this sense, sometimes), विशेष, बुद्बुद, शब्द, अर्घ, पथिन्, मथिन् 'a churning handle,' ऋभुक्षिन् name of Indra, स्तम्ब, नितम्ब, पूग 'a multitude, the betel-nut tree,' पल्लव, कफ, रेफ, कटाह 'large frying pan' &c., मठ, मणि, तरङ्ग, तुरङ्ग, गन्ध, स्कन्ध, मृदङ्ग, सङ्ग, पुंख the butt-end of an arrow to which the feathers are attached, अतिथि कुक्षि and अञ्जलि.

II. FEMININE WORDS.

§ 350. Verbal derivatives formed by the terminations आनि, मि, नि, ति, ई and ऊ; as अवनिः, भूमिः, ग्लानिः, गतिः, लक्ष्मीः, चमूः, &c.

Exceptions:—वह्नि, अग्नि and घृणि, all *mas.*

§ 351. (*a*) All the numerals from 20–99, monosyllabic words in ई and such as are formed by the affix ता; विंशतिः; श्रीः; तनुता &c.

(*b*) The synonyms of भूमि, सरित, लता and वनिता and these words themselves.

Exceptions:—स्रोतस् *n.* and यादस् *n.* both meaning a 'river'.

§ 352. The words भा, स्रुच् 'a sacrificial ladle,' स्रज्, दिक्, उष्णिह् 'a Vedic metre,' उपानह्, प्रावृष्, विप्रुष् 'a drop,' रुष्, त्विष्, तृष्, नाडि, रुचि, वीचि, नालि 'a tubular vessel of the body, a hollow lotus stalk,' किंकि 'a kind of bird,' केलि, छवि, रात्रि, शष्कुलि 'the orifice of the ear, a kind of cake,' राजि, कुटि 'a cottage,' वर्ति, भ्रुकुटि, त्रुटि 'a moment,' वलि, पंक्ति, दर्वि-र्वी, वेदि-दी, खनि-नी 'a mine (of jewels &c.)' शानि-नी 'a kind of cucumber,' अश्रि-श्री 'the edge of a sword,' कृषि-षी, ओषधि-धी, कटि-टी, अङ्गुलि-ली, प्रतिपत्, आपद्, विपद् सम्पद्, शरत्, संसद्, परिषद्, उषस्, संविद् 'knowledge, consciousness', क्षुध्, समिध्, आशिष्, धुर्, पुर्, गिर्, द्वार्, त्वच्, यवागू 'water gruel,' नौ, स्फिच् 'buttocks,' चुल्लि, खारी, तारा, धारा, ज्योत्स्ना, शलाका, and काष्ठा 'a limit or boundary.'

§ 353. अप्, सुमनस् when it means 'a flower,' समा a year, सिकता, वर्षा and अप्सरस् which are always used in the plural.*

NEUTER WORDS.

§ 354. Words ending in the Kṛit affixes अन and त and the Taddhita affixes त्व, य, एय, अक, and ईय; गमनं, हसनं, गीतं, शुक्लत्वं, धावल्यं, स्तेयं (स्तेनस्य भावः), सख्यं, कापेयं (कपेर्भावः) 'the monkey species' आधिपत्यं, औष्ट्रं (उष्ट्रस्य भावः), द्वैहायनं 'a period of two years;' पैतापुत्रकं &c.

§ 355. Words ending in इस् and उस्; in मन्, and अस्, and having two vowels in them; in त्र and such as have ल for their penultimate; सर्पिस् 'liquid ghee,' ज्योतिष्, धनुष्, चर्मन्, वर्मन् 'an armour,' यशस्, मनस्, पत्र, छत्र, &c., तुल, कूल, स्थल, &c.

Exceptions:—

(a) छदिस् *fem.* 'the roof of a carriage or house' and सीमन् *fem.* 'a boundary.'

(b) भृत्र, अमित्र (न मित्रम्), छात्र 'pupil', पुत्र, मन्त्र, वृत्र 'name

---

* अप्सुमनस्समासिकतावर्षाणां बहुत्वं च । *cf.* however Sid. Kau. बहुत्वं प्रायिकम् । एकापि सिकता तैलदानेऽसमर्थेति अर्थवत्सूत्रे भाष्यप्रयोगात् । समां समां विजायते इत्यत्र समायां समायामिति भाष्याच्च । &c.

of a demon' and उष्ट्र all *mas.*; यात्रा, मात्रा, भस्त्रा 'a smith's bellows', दंष्ट्रा, वरत्रा, 'a leather strap', all *fem.*

(*c*) and तूल, उपल, ताल, कुसूल 'a granary or store house for corn', तरल 'the middle gem of a necklace', कम्बल, देवल 'a Brâhmana who attends on an idol', and वृषल, which are all *mas.*

§ 356. Words denoting fruits, and all numerals from शत upwards, except शङ्कु mas., लक्ष which is also *fem.* and कोटि *fem.*; आम्रं, आमलकं, &c. शतं, सहस्रं &c.

§ 357. The words मुख, नयन, लोह, धन, मांस, रुधिर, कार्मुक 'a bow', &c., विवर, जल, हल, धन, बल, अन्न, कुसुम, शुल्व 'copper', पत्तन, रण, and their synonyms.

Exception:—सीर, 'a plough', अर्थ 'wealth', ओदन 'cooked rice', आहव 'a battle', संग्राम 'a battle', all *mas.*, and आजि 'war' and अटवी 'a forest', both *fem.*

§ 358. वियत्, जगत्, पृषत् 'a drop of water' (generally used in the plural), शकृत्, यकृत् 'the liver', उदश्वित 'butter-milk', नवनीत, अनृत, अमृत, निमित्त, वित्त, चित्त, पित्त, व्रत, रजत 'silver', वृत्त, पलित 'the greyness of hair brought on by old age,' श्राद्ध, पीठ, कुण्ड, अङ्क, अङ्ग, दधि, सक्थि 'the thigh', अक्षि, आज्य, आस्पद, कण्व 'sin', बीज, धान्य, सस्य, रूप्य silver, a stamped coin, कुप्य 'a baser metal,' पण्य, धिष्ण्य, 'a place,' हव्य 'an offering offered to the gods' (opposed to the following), कव्य 'an oblation offered to deceased ancestors' (opposed to the preceding), काव्य, सत्य, अपत्य, मूल्य, शिल्प mechanical art, शिक्य 'a loop or sling made of strings', कुड्य 'a wall', मद्य, हर्म्य, तुर्य,, सैन्य, द्वंद्व, दुःख, बडिश a fish hook, पिच्छ, कुटुम्ब, वर 'saffron,' शर, 'water', and अक्ष 'an organ of sense'.

IV. WORDS MASCULINE AND FEMININE.

§ 359. गो, मणि, यष्टि, मुष्टि, पाटलि 'a trumpet sounder,' वस्ति 'the pelvis,' शाल्मलि, मसि 'ink, a kind of black powder,' मरीचि

मृत्यु, सिन्धु, कर्कन्धु, किष्कु 'a measure of one hand in length,' कण्डु, रेणु, रज्जु (when at the end of a comp.), दुंदुभि, नाभि, इषुधि, इषु, बाहु, अशनि, अरणि, भरणि, दृति 'a leather strap,' श्रोणि, योनि, and ऊर्मि.

V. WORDS MASCULINE AND NEUTER.

§ 360. घृत, भूत, मुस्त 'a kind of grass (also मुस्ता)', क्ष्वेलित 'play, joke, tremor,' ऐरावत, पुस्त 'a wooden or earthen doll', बुस्त 'roasted meat,, लोहित 'blood', शृङ्ग, अर्घ, निदाघ, उद्यम, शल्य, दृढ, व्रज 'the name of Gokula,' कुञ्ज, कुथ, कूर्च 'a peacock's feather, the beard,' &c., कवच, दर्प, अर्भ 'a kind of eye disease', अर्ध, दर्भ, पुच्छ, कबन्ध, औषध, आयुध, अन्त, दण्ड, मण्ड 'the scum of boiled rice,' खण्ड, शव, सैन्धव, पार्श्व, आकाश, कुश, काश, अङ्कुश, कुलिश, गृह, मेह, बर्ह 'a peacock's feather,' देह, पट्ट, पटह, अष्टापद, 'gold' अम्बुद, दैव, ककुद, मद्गु 'name of an aquatic bird' मधु, सीधु, शीधु, सानु, कमण्डलु, सक्तु 'the flour of barley first fried and then ground' (used in the pl.), शालूक 'the root of the water lily', कण्टक, अनीक, सरक, मोदक 'spirituous liquor,' also 'the act of drinking liquor (vide. Sis. XV. 80), मोदक, चषक 'a drinking cup', मस्तक, पुस्तक, तटाक, निष्क, शुष्क, वर्चस्क 'lustre, vigour' पिनाक, 'a bow, the bow of Siva,' भाण्डक, पिण्डक 'incense', &c., पुलाक 'a lump of boiled rice', वट, लोष्ट, कुट, पट कपट, कपाट, कर्पट 'a rage,' नट 'a kind of plant', कीट, कट, रण, तोरण, कार्षापण 'a particular coin,' स्वर्ण, सुवर्ण, व्रण, चरण, वृषण, विषाण, तृण, तीर्थ (*n.*) 'a holy place' 'a descent into water, the stairs of a landing place, &c. (*m.*) a respectable person' (generally used as an affix, as भारतीतीर्थ, &c.), प्रोथ 'the nose or nostrils of a horse यूथ, गूथ, मान, यान, अभिधान, नलिन, पुलिन, उद्यान, शयन, आसन, स्थान, चंदन, आलान 'the tie-post or the tie-chain of an elephant,' समान *m.* a friend, *n.* a letter having the same organ of utterance, भवन, वसन, संभावन, वितान a canopy, विमान, शूर्प, a winnowing basket, कुतप,* the eighth

* अह्नो मुहूर्ता विख्याता दश पञ्च च सर्वदा।
तत्राष्टमो मुहूर्तो यः स कालः कुतपः स्मृतः॥

muhûrta of the day, (mostly *mas.*), 'a musical instrument'; कुणप, 'a corpse,' द्वीप, विटप, उडुप a small boat or the moon; तल्प, a bed, जृम्भ 'yawning,' बिंब, संग्राम, दाडिम m. the pomegranate tree; *n.* its fruit, कुसुम, आश्रम, क्षम, क्षौम, होम, उद्दाम (*m.*) 'Varuṇa,' गोमय, कषाय astringent flavour or taste, मलय, अन्वय, अत्यय, किसलय, चक्र, वप्र, वज्र, सार, वार *n.* a vessel for holding liquor. a mass of water; पार, क्षीर, तोमर 'an iron club, a javelin,' भृङ्गार 'a kind of vessel' (*Mar.* झारी), मन्दार, उशीर 'a kind of fragrant grass' (*Mar.* वाळा), तिमिर *m. n.* darkness, blindness iron-rust; शिशिर, कन्दर, यूष, करीष, 'dry cowdung,' मिष, विष, वर्ष, चमस 'sacrificial vessel of a particular shape', अर्स, रस, निर्यास exudation of trees, उपवास, कार्पास 'anything made of cotton', वास, मास, कास, कंस 'a drinking cup,' मांस, द्रोण *n.* a wooden vessel or cup, आढक, बाण, काण्ड, वक्त्र, अरण्य, गाण्डीव 'the bow of Arjuna,' शील *m.* 'a large serpent,' मूल, मङ्गल, साल, कमल *m.* the sârasa bird, name of Brahmâ; तल, मुसल, कुण्डल, पलल *m.* 'a demon *n.* flesh', मृणाल, बाल, निगाल 'a horse's neck,' पलाल 'forage', बिडाल a cat, the eye-ball, खिल a piece of waste or uncultivated land, शूल, पद्म, उत्पल *m.* a kind of plant, शत, अयुत, प्रयुत, पत्र the blade of a sword, a knife, पात्र, पवित्र, सूत्र, and छत्र *m.* a mushroom; *m.* a parasol, an umbrella.

VI. WORDS FEMININE AND NEUTER.

‡ 361 स्थूण-णा 'the post or pillar of a house', अर्चिस्, light, and लक्षं-क्षा one hundred thousand (according to some *n.* also).

Chapter XI.

AVYAYAS OR INDECLINABLES.

§ 362. That in an *Avyaya* whose form remaining the same in

all the genders, numbers and cases, undergoes no change.* The *Avyayas* may be divided into simple and compound ones. The latter are treated of in the chapter on compounds (Avyayîbhâvas and a few Bahuvrîhis and Tatpurusha).

§ 363. The indeclinables comprise (I) Prepositions (II) Adverbs, (III) Particles, (IV) Conjunctions, and (V) Interjections.

§ 364. Besides these there are in Sanskṛit a few nouns having one inflection only which are treated as indeclinable (*nipâtas*); *e. g.* अन्यत् another (reason), अस्तम् setting, अस्ति that exists, ओम् the well-known sacred syllable *om*, चनस् satisfaction, food, चाटु coaxing, नमस् a bow, नास्ति non-existence भूर् the earth, भुवर् the sky, वदि the dark fortnight, शम् happiness, शुदि or सुदि the bright fortnight, संवत् a year, स्वाहा food offered to gods, स्वधा food offered to the manes, स्वर् heaven, स्वस्ति happiness &c.

I. PREPOSITIONS.

§ 365. A preposition, styled 'Upasarga or Gāti,' in Sanskṛit is an indeclinable word, having an independent meaning and prefixed to verbs and also to their derivatives. These prepositions modify, intensify and sometimes totally alter the senses of roots†:

---

* सदृशं त्रिषु लिङ्गेषु सर्वासु च विभक्तिषु ।
वचनेषु च सर्वेषु यन्न व्येति तदव्ययम् ॥
स्वरादिनिपातमव्ययम् । Pân. I. 1. 37.

† धात्वर्थं बाधते कश्चित्कश्चित्तमनुवर्तते ।
तमेव विशिनष्टयन्य उपसर्गगतिस्त्रिधा ॥
Cf. also *Sid. Kau.* उपसर्गेण धात्वर्थो बलादन्यत्र नीयते ।
प्रहाराहारसंहारविहारपरिहारवत् ॥

Some think that prepositions have no meaning of their own, but they simply bring to light when prefixed to roots their hidden senses. (*cf.* Śiś. X. 15).

g. प्रहृ 'to strike," आहृ 'to eat, to perform as a sacrifice,' संहृ 'to contract,' विहृ 'to sport,' परिहृ 'to avoid, &c.' Sometimes they are prefixed without any alteration in the sense.

§ 366. The following are the prepositions (*upasargas*) commonly prefixed to roots:—

अति—'beyond, over'; अतिक्रमः 'overstepping' or 'going beyond. अतिसर्जन 'a gift, &c.'

अधि—'over, above, &c ;' अधिगमः 'going up, acquisition,' अधिकार 'high office or power,' अधिक्षेपः 'censure,' &c.

अनु—'after, behind, along, &c.' अनुक्रमणं 'following,' अनुकृतिः 'imitation,' अनुग्रहः 'favour,' &c.

अप—'away from, away,' अपनयनं 'the act of taking away,' अपहृ 'to plunder, seize' &c , अपकारः 'harm, wrong' &c.

अपि (sometimes पि)—'near to,' 'over,' 'taking to,' &c.; अपिगम् 'to be resolved into or reduced to, *, अपिधानं or पिधानं 'a covering,' अप्ययः 'destruction,' &c.

This prep. is more commonly used as an independent adverb having a cumulative force in classical Sanskṛit.

अभि—'towards, near to,' &c; अभिगम् 'to go towards,' अभिजनः 'noble descent or family,' अभिमानः 'self-respect,' अभिभू 'to defeat,' &c.

अव—(sometimes वः see अपि and ft. note)—'away, down,' &c. अव—or वगाहू 'to plunge into,' अवतारः 'descent,' अवगीत 'reproached,' अवमन् to disrespect,' &c.

---

* *Cf.* कारणेन अपिगच्छत् कारणं, &c. Shârîra Bhâshya. According to the grammarian Bhâguri the prepositions अपि and अव may optionally lose their अ- वष्टि भागुरिरल्लोपमवाप्योरुपसर्गयोः। (Sid.Kau.)

आ—'up to, towards, all round, a little,' &c.; आच्छाद् 'to cover all round,' आकार: 'form or shape (within due bounds), आकाश: 'that which shines all round' *i. e.* 'the ether'; आकम्प 'to shake a little,' &c.

उत्—द्-'upon,' &c.; उद्गम् 'to go up,' उद्यम: 'industry,' उत्सर्ग: 'pouring out, hence a gift, a general rule,' &c.

उप—'near to, towards, by the side of,' &c.; उपया 'to go near to,' उपकृति *f.* 'an obligation,' उपरति *f.* 'death,' उपस्थानं 'praise, worship,' उपमिति *f.* 'comparison,' &c.

दुस्—र्-'bad, hard to be done,' &c.; दुराचार: 'bad conduct,' दुष्कर 'hard to be done,' दु:सह 'difficult to be borne,' &c.

नि—'in, into, great, opposed),' &c.; निकृ 'to insult,' निकेत 'a house,' निचय 'a heap, a great collection,' निपीत 'drunk in,' निदेश 'a command,' &c.

निस्—र्-'out of, away from, without,' &c.; नि:सृ 'to issue out,' निर्गम: 'a passage out,' निर्दोष: 'out of *i. e.* free from blame,' नि: शंक 'without doubt,' &.

परा-'away, back, opposed to,' &c.; पराकृ 'to reject, to despise,' पराक्रम 'to act bravely,' परागत 'gone away,' पराञ्च् 'turn back,' पराजय 'what is opposed to victory; defeat,' &c.

परि—'all round, about,' &c.; परिधा 'to place all round *i. e.* to put on or wear,' परिधि: 'a wall &c. that surrounds,' परिणाम: 'ripening, maturity,' परिगणना 'counting all round, *i. e.* a complete enumeration,' &c.

प्रति—'towards, back, in return, in opposition to,' &c.; प्रतिगम् 'to go towards,' प्रतिभाषण 'a speech in return, an answer,' प्रति-ती-कार: 'an act in opposition to *i. e.* a remedy' &c.

वि—'apart, separate from, reverse to,' &c.; विचल् 'to move apart,' वियुज् 'to be separated,' विक्री opp. of क्री 'to sell,' 'to buy' &c.; sometimes this has an intensive force.

सम्—'together with, excellent, full,' &c. संगम्, 'to be united,' संस्कारः 'perfection,' संस्कृति 'refinement,' संहारः 'destruction, contraction,' &c.

सु—'well, thoroughly,' &c. (in this sense it is opposed to दुस्); सुकृतं 'done well,' सुशासित 'thoroughly trained, well governed,' &c. It is also used in the sense of 'very, excessively; सुमहत् 'very great.'

§ 367. Two or more of these prepositions may also be combined and prefixed; *e. g.* अभिनिविश् 'to enter into with resolution,' समुपागम् 'to come in close contact with,' &c.

§ 368. When used in a compound the verb may be omitted after the prepositions अति, अधि, अनु, अप, अव, अभि, उप, परि and प्रति; अतिक्रान्तो मालां अतिमालः &c. Vide § 232.

§ 369. There are several other words, also styled *Gati* by Sanskrit grammarians, used prepositionally. These are prefixed to certain roots only. We give the more important of them below.

(*a*) अच्छ* 'towards' is prefixed to वद् and to roots implying motion; अच्छगम्य-गत्य 'going near,' अच्छपतत् 'flying towards,' अच्छोद्य 'having spoken to.'

(*b*) (1) अन्वाजे 'giving strength to the weak,' अलं in the sense of 'decorating,' ऊरी, उररी, ऊररी all implying 'assent, acceptance or promise,' खात् and similar imitative sounds, असत् and सत् in the sense of 'dishonouring or honouring;' प्राध्वं denoting 'fastening,' &c. are prefixed to कृ; अन्वाजेकरणम्, ऊरीकरणम्, असत्कारः, सत्कृत्य, खात्कृत्य, प्राध्वंकरणम्, &c.

---

* अच्छगत्यर्थवदेषु । Pân. 1. 4. 69.

(2) नमः, प्रादुः, मिथ्या, वशे, साक्षात् and some other words may be optionally prefixed to कृ or remain separate; नमस्कारः, वशेकृ or वशे कृ 'to bring under subjection,' साक्षात् कृ or साक्षात्कृ 'to make manifest,' &c.

(*c*) अन्तर् is prefixed to roots meaning 'to go,' धा, भू, and similar roots; अन्तरित्य 'having disappeared,' अन्तर्धानं 'disappearance,' अन्तर्भूत, &c.

(*d*) अस्तम् is prefixed to roots implying motion; अस्तमयः 'setting,' अस्तंगत 'set,' अस्तंनी 'to cause to set, to lead to destruction,' &c

(*e*) आविः, and प्रादुः are prefixed to कृ, अस् and भू and तिरस् to भू, धा and similar roots, and optionally to कृ, आविष्करणं, आविर्भवनं 'manifestation,' प्रादुर्-आविर्भूत manifested,' &c.; तिरोभूय 'vanishing out of sight,' तरोधानं 'disappearance,' &c.

(*f*) पुरः is prefixed to कृ, भू, गम् &c.; पुरस्कृत 'placed before, headed by,' पुरोगत 'gone in the front,' &c.

§ 370. Several nouns, substantive and adjective, may be prefixed to the roots कृ, भू, and अस् to form what are called in Sanskṛt 'chvi-derivatives' (vide chap. IX. Sec. III.) कृष्णकरणम् = कृष्णीकरणम्ः, घन = भूत = घनीभूतः. Such nouns are also termed '*Gati.*'

§ 371. Like prepositions may be further used the words to which the Taddhita affix सात् is affixed, अग्निसात्कृ 'to consign to flames;' भस्मसात्कृतः 'reduced to ashes,' राजसाद्भूता 'made over to the king.' &c. (vide p. 216.)

II. Adverbs.

§ 372. Adverbs are either primitive or derived from nouns, pronouns or numerals. As adverbs may also be further used the

Acc. sing. *neu.* of nouns and adjectives; and sometimes the sing. of other cases also; सत्यम् 'truthfully,' मृदु 'softly,' सुखम् 'happily,' लघु 'quickly,' निर्भरम्, अवश्यम्, अत्यन्तम्, बलवत् 'strongly,' भूयः, 'again' &c.; दुःखेन, 'painfully,' सुखेन, धर्मेण 'virtuously, justly,' दक्षिणेन, उत्तरेण, अशेषेण, चिरेण 'after a long time,' क्षणेन &c.; चिराय, चिररात्राय 'for a long time,' अर्थाय 'for the sake of,' बलात् 'forcibly,' हर्षात्, शोकात्, दूरात्, तस्मात्, कस्मात् &c.; चिरात् 'for a long time,' दूरात्, उत्तरात् &c.; स्थाने 'properly,' दूरे, प्रभाते, प्राह्णे, अग्रे, एकपदे 'at once,' सपदि, ऋते, समीपे, अभ्यासे 'near,' &c.

N. B Adverbs formed from pronouns and numerals are given in their proper places; while those formed from nouns are given in Chapter IX.

§ 373. In the following list are alphabetically arranged almost all the words used adverbially in Sanskṛit.—

अकस्मात् Suddenly, all at once.

अग्रतस् In front of, before.

अग्रे In front of, before, ahead, at first.

अचिरम्, अचिरात्, अचिरेण, अचिराय } Not long since, recently, quickly.

अजस्रम् Ever, constantly.

अज्ञानतस् Through ignorance.

अञ्जसा Rightly, correctly, properly.

अन्तर् In, into.

अतः From this, on this account &c.

अतीव Exceedingly; rising superior to, with the Acc. अतीवान्यान् भविष्यावः M. B.

अत्र Here.

अथ Then, afterwards.

अथ किम् Yes.

अद्धा Truly, certainly, indeed.

अद्य To-day, this day.

अद्यत्वे Now, now-a-days.

अध, अधस्, अधस्तात् } Below, down.

अपरम् Again, moreover.

अपरेद्युः On the following day

अधुना Now, at this time.

अनिशम् Incessantly, ceaselessly.

अन्तर्, अन्तरा, अन्तरेण, अन्तरे — Except, without, inside. Between, amidst.

अन्यच्च, अन्यत् — Again, moreover, besides.

अन्यत्र Elsewhere, in another place.

अन्यथा Otherwise, in a different manner.

अभितः Near, close by, in the proximity of.

अभीक्ष्णम् Frequently, repeatedly.

अम् Quickly, little.

अमा Together with, in company with.

अमुत्र There, in the next world, above.

अरम् Quickly.

अर्वाक् Before.

अलम् Enough, sufficient for. It is a prefix also.

अवस् without, on the outside.

असकृत् Repeatedly, often and often.

असंप्रति, असांप्रतम् — Improperly, unfitly.

अह्नाय Instantly, speedily.

आनुषक्, आनुषट् — Uninterruptedly, one after another.

आरात् Near, in the vicinity of, at a distance.

आर्यहलम् Forcibly [Pán. I. 1. 47].

आविस् Openly, before the eyes.

इतस् Hence.

इतस्ततस् Hither and thither, to and fro, here and there, &c.

इति In this manner, so.

इतरम् Again.

इतरेद्युस् On another day, the other day.

इतिह Thus, indeed, quite in conformity to tradition.

इत्थम् Thus, so, in this manner.

इदानीम् Just now, at this moment.

इद्धा Truly.

इह Here.

ईषत् Slightly, little.

उच्चैस् Loudly.

उत्तरम् Then.

उत्तरेद्युस् On the day following.

उपांशु Secretly, in private.

उभयतस् From both sides.

उभयद्युस्, उभयेद्युस् — On both days.

उषा Early in the morning, at dawn.

ऋतम्, ऋधक् — Truly, Truthfully.

ऋते without, except.

एकत्र together, in one place.

एकदा once, once upon a time.

एकधा in one way, singly, at the same time.

एकपदे all at once, suddenly.

एतर्हि Now, at present.

एव Just, quite.

एवम् Thus, so.

ओम् So be it.

कच्चित / कच्चन } I trust, hope, &c.

कथम् How, in what way.

कथञ्चन / कथञ्चित् } With great difficulty, With great effort.

कथन्नाम How indeed, how possibly.

कदा When, at what time.

कदाचित् One time, once upon a time.

न कदाचित् Never.

कम् used as an enclitic.

कर्हि When, at what time?

कर्हिचित् At any time.

किङ्किल What a pity.

किञ्च Moreover, further, again.

किञ्चन / किञ्चित् } To a certain degree, little, somewhat.

किन्तु But, yet, nevertheless, however.

किन्नु What indeed, whether.

किम् who, what, which?

किमुत How much more?

किमुह What, how?

किंवा Or.

किंस्वित् Whether, how.

किल Verily, indeed, assuredly.

किमु What then, how much more, &c.

कुतस् Whence, from where?

कुत्र Where, in which place?

कुत्रचित् Somewhere, anywhere.

कुवित् Much.

कुषत् In the best manner.

कूपत् In a good manner.

कृतम् Enough, no more of.

केवलम् only, merely, simply.

क्व Whither, where?

क्वचित् In some place.

न क्वचित् Nowhere.

खलु Certainly, surely, indeed.

चिरम् A long time. The singular of any of the oblique cases of this word may be used adverbially in the sense of 'long,' 'for a long time,' as चिरेण, चिराय, &c.

चिररात्राय For a period of many nights, long.

जातु Perhaps, sometimes.

जोषम् Silently.

ज्योक् Soon.

झटिति } Quickly, at once.
झगिति }

तद् Therefore.

ततस् Therefore, consequently.

तत्र Then, in that case, &c.

तदा Then, at that time, in that case.

तदानीम् Then, at that time.

तथा So, in that manner, as surely as.

तथाहि As for instance, to be more plain, &c.

तस्मात् From that, therefore.

तर्हि Then, at that time.

तावत् In the first place, &c.

तिरस् } Crookedly, across, indirectly, badly.
तिर्यक् }

तूष्णिम् } Silently, without speaking or noise.
तूष्णीकम् }

तेन By that, on that account.

दिवा By day.

दिष्ट्या Fortunately, luckily.

दुष्टु } Ill, wickedly.
दुस्समम् }

दूरम् To a distance, deeply, highly.

दोषा At night.

द्राक् } Quickly, forthwith, immediately.
द्राङ् }

ध्रुवम् Certainly.

नकिम् } Not so.
नाकिर् }

नक्तम् By night.

न Nor.

नवरम् But.

नह } Not so, not at all.
नहि }

नाना In various ways, distinctly, separately.

नाम By name; indeed, certainly, probably, perhaps.

निकषा Near, close by.

निकामम् Very much, exceedingly, to one's satisfaction, agreeably to desire.

नूनम् Certainly, assuredly, most probably.

नो Not.

परम् Then, over, out of.

परश्वः Day after to-morrow.

परितः Around, on all sides, all round.

परेद्यवि } The other day, to-morrow.
परेद्युः }

पर्याप्तम् To one's satisfaction, sufficiently; willingly.

पश्य Well, behold! see!

पश्चात् Behind, backwards, at last, afterwards.

पुनः Again.

पुनः पुनः Again and again, repeatedly.

पुरतस्
पुरः
पुरस्तात् } Before, in front.

पुरा In former times, of yore, at first.

पर्वतः In or to the east, before, in front of &c.

पूर्वेद्युः On the former day, yesterday.

पृथक् Severally, apart from.

प्रकामम्
प्रकामतः } Exceedingly, at will, with pleasure.

प्रगे In the morning.

प्रतान् Extensively.

प्रताम्
प्रशाम् } Being exhausted.

प्रतिदिनम् Every day.

प्रत्युत On the contrary, on the other hand, rather, &c.

प्रवाहिका
प्रवाहुकम् } On high, at the same time.

प्रसह्य Forcibly, violently, exceedingly, much.

प्राक् Before, at first, in or to the east.

प्रातर् In the morning.

प्राध्वम् Crookedly, in an opposite manner favourably.

प्रायः Mostly.

प्राह्णे In the noon.

प्रेत्य After death.

बलवत्
बलात् } Forcibly, powerfully, excessively.

बहिः Out, beside, except.

भाजक् Quickly.

भूयः Exceedingly, again and again.

भृशम् Greatly, exceedingly, repeatedly.

मंक्षु Quickly, immediately.

मनाक् A little, slightly, slowly, tardily.

माकिम्
माकिर् } Except.

माचिरम् Without delay, immediately.

मिथः
मिथो } To each other, secretly.

मिथ्या Wrongly, incorrectly, to no purpose, in vain.

मुधा To no purpose, in vain, unprofitably, wrongly.

मुहुर् Often, again and again.

मृषा Falsely, lyingly, in vain.

यत् Since.

यतः Since, for which reason, wherefore.

यत्र Where, in which place.

यथा As, namely.

यथाकथा Somehow.

यथाक्रमम् In due order.

यथातथा In the manner mentioned, just as required.

यदा When.

*यावत् As much as, as long as.

युक् Badly.

युगपत् at once, simultaneously.

युत् Badly.

वत् Like.

वाव Only.

विना Except.

विषु Exceedingly.

विहायसा High up in the sky.

वृथा In vain.

वै Verily, to be sure.

शनैः Gently.

शश्वत् Always.

शुकम् Quickly.

सकृत् Once.

संक्षु Hurriedly, quickly.

सजुष Along with.

सत् Well.

सततम् Always.

सदा Always.

सद्यः At once.

सनत्, सना, सनात् Perpetually, always.

सनुतर् Stealthily, under cover.

सपदि At once, the very moment.

समन्ततः All round.

समम् Equally.

समया Near.

समीपम्, समीपे Near, in one's presence.

समीचीनम् Well, proprely.

समुपजोषम् joyfully, gladly.

संप्रति Now.

सम्मुखम् Face to face, in front.

सम्यक् Well, in a good manner.

सर्वतः On all sides, perfectly.

सर्वत्र Everywnere.

सर्वदा Always.

सह Together with, along with.

सहसा All at once, suddenly.

साहितम् Together with, along with.

साकम् With.

साक्षात् In the presence of, in person, in s bodily form.

साचि crookedly, in a sidelong manner.

सार्धम् With.

सामि Half.

---

* When पुरा and यावत् are prefixed to a personal form of the Present Tense, it has the sense of the Future Tense.

साम्प्रतम् Now, at present, fitly, properly.

सायम् In the evening.

सुकम् Very much.

सुधा In vain, to no purpose.

सुष्ठु Well, in a good manner.

स्वयम् Oneself, spontaneously.

हि Because, indeed, surely.

हिरुक् Without, except.

हेतोः }
हेतौ } On account of, because of,

ह्यस् Yesterday.

III. PARTICLES.

§ 374. The particles are either used as expletives or intensives; some of these are किल, खलु, च, तु, नु, वै, हि, &c.

§ 375. The following particles are used with certain words:—

अद्—अद्भुतं 'a wonder'.

का—कापुरुषः 'a bad man,' कोष्णं 'luke-warm,' काजलं 'a little water'.

कु—कुकृत्यं 'a bad deed'.

चन }
चित् } किंचित्, कश्चित्, कश्चन, किंचन &c.

न—is generally changed to अ or अन् when prefixed to words beginning with a consonant or a vowel respectively. This particle has six different senses* (1) सादृश्य 'likeness' or 'resemblance'; as अब्राह्मणः 'one not a Brâhmana, but resembling a Brâhmana' (wearing the sacred thread, &c.) *i. e.* 'a Kshatriya or a Vaiśya' (2) अभाव 'absence or negation'; अज्ञानं 'the absence of knowledge'; (3) अन्यत्व 'difference from'; as अयं अपटः 'this is something different from a cloth' *i. e.* 'a jar' or so; (4) अल्पता 'little-

---

* These are given in the following couplet:—

तत्सादृश्यमभावश्च तदन्यत्वं तदल्पता ।
अप्राशस्त्यं विरोधश्च नञर्थाः षट् प्रकीर्तिताः ॥

ness' or 'smallness'; as अनुदरा कन्या 'a girl having a slender waist'; (5) अप्राशस्त्य 'badness, unfitness' ,&c.; अकार्य 'something unfit to be done', अकाल: 'an improper time, not a favourable opportunity,' and lastly (6) विरोध or 'opposition'; अनीति: 'non-morality'; immorality असुर: 'opposed to a god' *i. e.* 'a demon'.

स्म—is generally used as an expletive. Used with a form of the present tense of a verb, it gives in the sense of the past tense; as भवति स्म *i. e.* अभवत्. When used with the particle मा it has an intensive force; as मा स्म शोके मन: कृथा: &c.

वित्—is added to किं and other indeclinables and asks a question or implies a doubt; किंस्वित्, अहोस्वित्, &c.

स्वी—is used with कृ and its derivatives like a preposition in the sense of 'acceptance'; स्वीकार:, स्वीकृतम्, &c.

IV. CONJUNCTIONS.

§ 376. The following are the principal conjunctions in Sanskṛt:—

(*a*) Copulative अथ, अथो, उत, च, किंच, &c.

(*b*) Disjunctive वा, वा...वा, &c.

(*c*) Adversative अथवा, तु, किंतु, किंवा, &c.

(*d*) Conditional चेद्, यदि, यद्यपि, नेत्, नोचेद्, वेट् (used in sacrificial ceremonies), &c.

(*e*) Causal हि, तद्, तेन, &c.

(*f*) Interrogative आहो अहोस्वित्, उत, उताहो, किं, किम्नु, किमुत, किंस्वित्, ननु, नवा, नु, &c.

(*g*) Affirmatives and negatives अङ्ग, अथ किम्, आम्, अद्धा &c.

(*h*) Conjunctions of time यावत्–तावत्, यदा, तदा &c.

(*i*) अथ and इति are used to mark the beginning and the close of a work respectively.

V. INTERJECTIONS.

§ 377. "The interjection is not properly a part of speech, as it does not enter into the construction of sentences. It is sudden exclamation prompted by some strong feeling or emotion. There are various utterances suited to the different emotions of the mind":—*Prof. Bain.*

(*a*) These are—आ, इ, उ, ए, ऐ, ओ, अह, अहह, अहो, बत, ह, हा, हाहा, &c. expressive of wonder, grief or regret, &c.

(*b*) किम्, धिक् &c. expressive of contempt.

(*c*) हा, बत, &c. expressing sorrow, dejection, &c.

(*d*) हा, हाहा, हन्त showing grief.

(*e*) आ, हम्, हुम्, &c. expressive of anger, contempt, &c.

(*f*) हन्त, &c. expressing joy.

(*g*) There are some interjections used to call attention. Of these.

(1) some show respect; such as अङ्ग, अये, अहो, अहो, बत, उ, ए, ओ, प्याट्, भोः, हंहो, हे, है, हो, &c.

(2) and others, disrespect or contempt; as अङ्ग, अरे, अव, रे, रेरे, अरेरे &c.

(3) The exclamations श्रौषट्, वौषट् and वषट् are used when offering oblations to gods or manes; and

(4) स्वाहा and स्वधा when offering oblations to gods and manes respectively.

Chapter XII.

CONJUGATION OF VERBS.

§ 378. There are in Sanskrit—

(*a*) Two kinds of verbs, Primitive and Derivative.

(*b*) Six Tenses (कालाः) and four Moods (अर्थाः) which are as follow:—

TENSES	TECHNICAL NAME	MOODS	TECHNICAL NAME.
वर्तमानः or Present	लट्	आज्ञा or Imperative	लोट्
भूतः or Aorist	लुङ्	विधि or Potential	विधिलिङ्
अनद्यतनभूतः or Imperfect	लङ्	आशीः or Benedictive	आशीर्लिङ्
परोक्षभूतः or Perfect	लिट्	संकेत or Conditional	लृङ्
अनद्यतन-भविष्यन् or 1 st Future	लुट्		
भविष्यन् or 2 nd Future	लृट्.		

लेट् or the Subjunctive is used only in the Veda and is therefore termed 'The Vedie Subjunctive.'

Note:—The ten tenses and moods are technically called the ten *Lakaras* in Sanskrit grammars.

(*c*) Three Voices (प्रयोगाः), the Active Voice (कर्तरिप्र०) as रामः सत्यं भाषते, the Passive Voice (कर्मणिप्र०), as हरिणा फलं भक्ष्यते, and the Impersonal Construction (भावेप्र०) रामेण गम्यते.

---

* These technical names are given in the following Kàriká.

लट् वर्तमाने लेट् वेदे भूते लुङ्लङ्लिटस्तथा ।
विध्याशिषोस्तु लिङ्लोटौ लुट् लृट् लङ् च भविष्यति ॥

This terminology of Pâṇini, it will be seen, is artificial. Other grammarians use different names. The ten Lakaras of Pâṇini are according to their nomenclature, as follow.—भवति (वृत्तिः), अद्यतनी, ह्यस्तनी, परोक्षा, श्वस्तनी, भविष्यन्ती, पञ्चमी, सप्तमी, क्रियातिपत्ति and आशीः—

'*Apte's Guide*'.

(*d*) Two sets of personal terminations, the one called ‘ Parasmaipada,’ the other ‘ Atmanepada.’ Some roots take exclusively the Par. terminations and some the Âtm. ones; while there are others which take either. Several roots again, though Parasmaipadi, become Atmanepadi and *vice versa*, when preceded by certain prepositions or in particular senses. These will be considered in a separate chapter.

§ 379. Primitive verbs or roots are those which originally exist in the language, while derivative verbs are those which may be derived from a parent stock—a root or a noun.

§ 380. Every verb, in Sanskrit. whether primitive or derivative, may be conjugated in the ten tenses and moods given above.

(*a*) Transitive verbs are conjugated in the Active and Passive voices and intransitive verbs in the active and the Impersonal form.

§ 381. In each tense and mood there are three numbers, singular, dual and plural, with three persons in each.

§ 382. In four of the tenses and moods given above, *viz.* the Present, the Imperfect, the Imperative and the Potential, the verds undergo peculiar modifications (विकरण) and these are therfore called Conjugational (सार्वधातुक)* or special tenses and moods; and

* Strictly the term Sárvadhátuka (belonging to the form of the verbal base) is given by Pâṇini to the terminations of all the tenses and moods, except those of the Perfect and the Benedictive, and to the affixes distinguished by an indicatory ś (शित) *i. e.* the various conjugational signs of the 9 classes (except that of the eighth), and the terminations of the Present Participle Pars. and Atm. All other verbal affixes *i. e.* the conjugational signs of the 8th and 10th classes, the affixes added to form the causal base and a few denominatives, the affixes स्य, ता, स, and य added to the bases of the two futures, the Desiderative and the Aor., and the Passive and the Frequentative respectively, and those forming the Past Participle (Act. and Pass.), the infinitive and the verbal indeclinables, and some others are called Ârdhadhâtuka, the remaining Non-Conju-

gational (आर्धधातुक) or generel. In the former the characteristic marks and terminations of each are mostly added to a special base formed from the roots in various ways, while in the latter they are combined with the roots itself.

(*a*) The base (अङ्ग) of a root is that form which it assumes before the personal terminations.

§ 383. When a root is capable of taking either pada, the Parasmaipada (lit. word for another) should be used when the fruit or result of the action of the verb accrues to any other person or thing than the agent, and the Atmanepada (*lit.* word for self). when it refers to the agent. Thus देवदत्तः यजति will mean 'Devadatta sacrifices for another (his Yajamâna);' while देवदत्तः यजते will mean 'Devadatta sacrifices for himself.'

SECTION I.

ACTIVE VOICE.

I. CONJUGATIONAL

or

SPECIAL TENSES AND MOODS.

PRESENT, IMPERFECT, IMPERATIVE and POTENTIAL.

§ 384. With reference to the various moods the verbs are divided into ten conjugational classes by Sanskrit grammarians, each class being denominated after the root which begins it *viz.* (1) भ्वादि (2) अदादि, (3) जुहोत्यादि, (4) दिवादि, (5) स्वादि, (6) तुदादि, (7) रुधादि, (8) तनादि (9) क्र्यादि and (10) चुरादि.

§ 385. The roots contained in the first nine classes and a few of the tenth are primitive roots, while almost all roots of the tenth class, the Causals, Desideratives, Frequentatives, Denominatives, and the roots गुप्, धूप्, विच्छ्, पण्, पन्, ऋत्, and कम्, are comprised under the head of Derivative roots.

§ 386. These ten classes may again be conveniently divided into two groups, the first comprising the 1st, 4th, 6th and 10th classes, and the second the remaining. In the first the base ends in अ and remains unchanged throughout; while in the second it does not end in अ and is changeable.

I. GROUP 1.

ROOTS WITH UNCHANGEABLE BASES
(1st, 4th, 6th and 10th classes).

§ 387. Terminations:—

Present

	Par			Âtm.		
	S.	D.	P.	S.	D.	P.
1.	मि	वस्	मस्	इ	वहे	महे
2.	सि	थस्	थ	से	इथे	ध्वे
3.	ति	तस्	अन्ति	ते	इते	अन्ते

Imperfect.

	S.	D.	P.	S.	D.	P.
1.	अम्	व	म	इ	वहि	महि
2.	स्	तम्	त	थास्	इथाम्	ध्वम्
3.	त्	ताम्	अन्	त	इताम्	अन्त

Imperative.

	S.	D.	P.	S.	D.	P.
1.	आनि	आव	आम	ऐ	आवहै	आमहै
2.	—*	तम्	त	स्व	इथाम्	ध्वम्
3.	तु*	ताम्	अन्तु	ताम्	इताम्	अन्ताम्

* तात् is optionally added in the 2nd and 3rd person singulars when the Imperative has a Benedictive sense.

Potential.

	Par.			Âtm.		
	S.	D.	P.	S.	D.	P.
1.	ईयम	ईव	ईम	ईय	ईवहि	ईमहि
2.	ईः	ईतम्	ईत	ईथाः	ईयाथाम्	ईध्वम्
3.	ईत्	ईताम्	ईयुः	ईत	ईयाताम्	ईरन्

Note:—Terminations beginning with vowels may be called Vowel terminations; those beginning with consonants, consonantal terminations.

Formation of the base of the roots of the first group:—

§ 388. अ (शप्) is added on to the roots of the First or भ्वादि class* before the terminations. Before this अ the penultimate short and the final vowel of a root take their Guṇa substitute; *e. g.*

बुध्+ति=बुध्+अ + ति=बोध् + अ+ति=बोधति; जि+अ+ति = जे+अ+ति†=जयति, &c.

§ 389. य (श्यन्) is added on to the final of a root of the Fourth or दिवादि class before the terminations; the radical vowel remains unchanged; *e. g.* कुप्+ति=कुप्+य+ति=कुप्यति.

§ 390. अ is added on to the roots of the sixth or तुदादि class before which the penultimate vowel remains unchanged, and the final इ, उ, short or long, ऋ and ॠ are changed to इय्, उव्, रिव्

* कर्तरि शप् । दिवादिभ्यः श्यन् । तुदादिभ्यः शः । Pân. III. 1. 68, 69, 77. Of about 2200 roots occurring in the Sanskṛt language nearly half (about 1076) belong to the first class.

† Vide § 24.

and इर् respectively; e. g. क्षिप्+ति=क्षिप्+अ+ति=क्षिपति; ध्रु+ति=ध्रुव्+अ+ति=ध्रुवति; रि+अ+ति=रियति; मृ+अ+ते=म्रियते; गॄ+अ+ति=गिर्+अ+ति=गिरति, &c.

§ 391. Roots of the tenth or चुरादि class* add अय before the personal terminations. Before अय (1) the penultimate short vowel (except अ) takes the Guṇa substitute; and the final vowel and the penultimate अ not prosodially long, take their Vṛiddhi substitute; e. g. चुर्+ति=चुर्+अय+ति=चोर्+अय+ति=चोरयति; भू+अय+ति=भौ+अय+ति=भाव्+अय+ति=भावयति; तड् + अय + ति=ताड्+अय + ति=ताडयति; but दण्ड्+अय+ति=दण्डयति, &c.

§ 392. (a)† The preceding अ is lengthened before a conjugational termination beginning with a semivowel, a nasal or झ् or भ्; e. g. नयामि &c.

(b) The final अ is dropped before terminations beginning with अ; नय+अन्ति=नयन्ति, &c.

1st class.

नी P. A. 'to carry.'

Present.

	Par.			Atm.	
1. नयामि	नयावः	नयामः	नये	नयावहे	नयामहे
2. नयसि	नयथः	नयथ	नयसे	नयेथे	नयध्वे
3. नयति	नयतः	नयन्ति	नयते	नयेते	नयन्ते

*This class contains a few primitive verbs, almost all the roots belonging to it being derivative; besides, all Causals and some Nominal verbs may be regarded as belonging to this class.

† अतो दीर्घो यञि । Pâṇ. VII. 3. 101.

Imperfect.

§ 393. The augment अ is prefixed to roots in this tense. This अ is replaced by आ in the case of roots beginning with a vowel*; this आ forms Vriddhi with an initial vowel; *e. g.* अ+इख्+त=आ+इख्+अ+त्=ऐखत; similarly ईक्ष्-ऐक्षत; उक्ष्-औक्षत; ऊह्-औहत्; ऋच्छ्-आर्च्छत् &c.

(*a*) When a preposition (उपसर्ग) is prefixed to a root, the augment अ or आ comes between the prep. and the roo s; *e. g.* हृ with प्र, प्राहरत्.

बुध् P. 'to know.'			इक्ष् Â. 'to see.'		
1. अबोधम्	अबोधाव	अबोधाम	ऐक्षे	ऐक्षावहि	ऐक्षामहि
2. अबोधः	अबोधतम्	अबोधत	ऐक्षथाः	ऐक्षेथाम्	ऐक्षध्वम्
3. अबोधत्	अबोधताम्	अबोधन्	ऐक्षत	ऐक्षेताम्	ऐक्षन्त

नी.

1. अनयम्	अनयाव	अनयाम	अनये	अनयावहि	अनयामहि
2. अनयः	अनयतम्	अनयत	अनयथाः	अनयेथाम्	अनयध्वम
3. अनयत्	अनयताम्	अनयन्	अनयत	अनयेताम्	अनयन्त

Imperative.

भू P. 'to be.'			लभ् Â. 'to get.'		
1. भवानि	भवाव	भवाम	लभै	लभावहै	लभामहै
2. भव or भवतात्	भवतम्	भवत	लभस्व	लभेथाम्	लभध्वम्
3. भवतु or भवतात्	भवताम्	भवन्तु	लभताम्	लभेताम्	लभन्ताम्

*आडजादीनाम्। Pân. VI. 4. 102.

Potential.

स्मृ P. 'to remember.'			मुद् Â 'to rejoice.'		
1. स्मरेयम्	स्मरेव	स्मरेम	मोदेय	मोदेवहि	मोदेमहि
2. स्मरेः	स्मरेतम्	स्मरेत	मोदेथाः	मोदेयाथाम्	मोदेध्वम्
3. स्मरेत्	स्मरेताम्	स्मरेयुः	मोदेत	मोदेयाताम्	मोदेरन्

4th Class.

तुष् P. 'to be pleased.' युध् A 'to fight'

Present.

1. तुष्यामि	तुष्यावः	तुष्यामः	युध्ये	युध्यावहे	युध्यामहे
2. तुष्यसि	तुष्यथः	तुष्यथ	युध्यसे	युध्येथे	युध्यध्वे
3. तुष्यति	तुष्यतः	तुष्यन्ति	युध्यते	युध्येते	युध्यन्ते

Imperfect.

1. अतुष्यम्	अतुष्याव	अतुष्याम	अयुध्ये	अयुध्यावहि	अयुध्यामहि
2. अतुष्यः	अतुष्यतम्	अतुष्यत	अयुध्यथाः	अयुध्येथाम्	अयुध्यध्वम्
3. अतुष्यत्	अतुष्यताम्	अतुष्यन्	अयुध्यत	अयुध्येताम्	अयुध्यन्त

Imperative.

1. तुष्याणि	तुष्याव	तुष्याम	युध्यै	युध्यावहै	युध्यामहै
2. तुष्य*	तुष्यतम्	तुष्यत	युध्यस्व	युध्येथाम्	युध्यध्वम्
3. तुष्यतु*	तुष्यन्ताम्	तुष्यन्तु	युध्यताम्	युध्येताम्	युध्यन्ताम्

* Hereafter the optional form in तात् will not be given as the student can easily form them by adding तात् to the base if he has to express the sense of the Benedictive.

Potential.

1. तुष्येयम्	तुष्येव	तुष्येम	युध्येय	युध्येवहि	युध्येमहि
2. तुष्येः	तुष्येतम्	तुष्येत	युध्येथाः	युध्येयाथाम्	युध्येध्वम्
3. तुष्येत्	तुष्येताम्	तुष्येयुः	युध्येत	युध्येयाताम्	युध्येरन्

6th Class.

क्षिप् P. Â. 'to throw.'

P. *Present.* A.

1. क्षिपामि	क्षिपावः	क्षिपामः	क्षिपे	क्षिपावहे	क्षिपामहे
2. क्षिपसि	क्षिपथः	क्षिपथ	क्षिपसे	क्षिपेथे	क्षिपध्वे
3. क्षिपति	क्षिपतः	क्षिपन्ति	क्षिपते	क्षिपेते	क्षिपन्ते

Imperfect.

1. अक्षिपम्	अक्षिपाव	अक्षिपाम	अक्षिपे	अक्षिपावहि	अक्षिपामहि
2. अक्षिपः	अक्षिपतम्	अक्षिपत	अक्षिपथाः	अक्षिपेथाम्	अक्षिपध्वम्
3. अक्षिपत्	अक्षिपताम्	अक्षिपन्	अक्षिपत	अक्षिपेताम्	अक्षिपन्त

Imperative.

1. क्षिपाणि*	क्षिपाव	क्षिपाम	क्षिपै	क्षिपावहै	क्षिपामहै
2. क्षिप	क्षिपतम्	क्षिपत	क्षिपस्व	क्षिपेथाम्	क्षिपध्वम्
3. क्षिपतु	क्षिपताम्	क्षिपन्तु	क्षिपताम्	क्षिपेताम्	क्षिपन्ताम्

Potential.

1. क्षिपेयम्	क्षिपेव	क्षिपेम	क्षिपेय	क्षिपेवहि	क्षिपेमहि
2. क्षिपेः	क्षिपेतम्	क्षिपेत	क्षिपेथाः	क्षिपेयाथाम्	क्षिपेध्वम्
3. क्षिपेत्	क्षिपेताम्	क्षिपेयुः	क्षिपेत	क्षिपेयाताम्	क्षिपेरन्

* For the change of न् to ण् see § 41.

10th Class.

चुर् P. A. 'to steal.'

Present.

	P.			A.		
1.	चोरयामि	चोरयावः	चोरयामः	चोरये	चोरयावहे	चोरयामहे
2.	चोरयसि	चोरयथः	चोरयथ	चोरयसे	चोरयेथे	चोरयध्वे
3.	चोरयति	चोरयतः	चोरयन्ति	चोरयते	चोरयेते	चोरयन्ते

Imperfect.

Par.

1.	अचोरयम्	अचोरयाव	अचोरयाम
2.	अचोरयः	अचोरयतम्	अचोरयत
3.	अचोरयत	अचोरयताम्	अचोरयन्

Atm.

1.	अचोरये	अचोरयावहि	अचोरयामहि
2.	अचोरयथाः	अचोरयेथाम्	अचोरयध्वम्
3.	अचोरयत	अचोरयेताम्	अचोरयन्त

Imperative.

	P.			A.		
1.	चोरयाणि	चोरयाव	चोरयाम	चोरयै	चोरयावहै	चोरयामहै
2.	चोरय	चोरयतम्	चोरयत	चोरयस्व	चोरयेथाम्	चोरयध्वम्
3.	चोरयतु	चोरयताम्	चोरयन्तु	चोरयताम्	चोरयेताम्	चोरयन्ताम्

Potential.

	P.			A.		
1.	चोरयेयम्	चोरयेव	चोरयेम	चोरयेय	चोरयेवहि	चोरयेमहि
2.	चोरयेः	चोरयेतम्	चोरयेत	चोरयेथाः	चोरयेयाथाम्	चोरयेध्वम्
3.	चोरयेत्	चोरयेताम्	चोरयेयुः	चोरयेत	चोरयेयाताम्	चोरयेरन्

The forms of other roots should be similarly made up.

§ 394. * The ॠ (long) of a root, penultimate or final, when it does not take Guṇa or Vṛddhi, is changed to इर्, and to उर् if a labial or व् precedes; and the इ or उ is lengthened when इर् or उर् is followed by a consonant; *e. g.* जॄ 4. P. 'to become old,' जीर्यति, अजीर्यत्, &c.; कॄ 6. P. किरति, अकिरत्, &c; here कि does not become long as किर् is followed by अ; कॄत् 10. P. A. कीर्तयति-ते, अकीर्तयत्-त, &c.

§ 395. The penultimate इ, उ, ऋ or ऌ of a root, followed by र् or व् is lengthened when a consonant follows; † *e. g.* उर्द् 1. A. to measure, to play, ऊर्दते; similarly कुर्द्, खुर्द्, गुर्द् all A. and meaning to play, हुर्छ्, to act dishonestly, to be crooked, मुर्छ् to faint; स्फुर्छ् to spread, to forget; स्फुर्ज् to thunder, to shine; उर्व्, तुर्व्, थुर्व्, दुर्व्, धुर्व् all meaning to kill, गुर्द् to try, मुर्व्, &c., all Parasm. and belonging to the 1st class, lengthen their penultimate vowel; दिव् 4. P. दीव्यति; similarly सिव् has सीव्यति, ष्ठिव्, ष्ठीव्यति, &c.

ROOTS OF THE 1ST, 4TH, 6TH, AND 10TH CLASSES WHICH FORM THEIR BASES IRREGULARLY.

1st class (भ्वादयः).

गुप् 'to protect,' गोपायति ‡
धूप् 'to heat,' धूपायति.
विच्छ् 'to go,' विच्छायति.

पण् 'to praise.' पणायति; but पणते when it means 'to barter or transact business. to bet.'

* ॠत इद्धातोः । उरण् रपरः । Pân. VII. I. 100, I. 1. 51. हलि च Pân. VII. 2. 77.

† 'हलि च' । रेफवान्तस्य धातोरुपधाया इको दीर्घः स्यात् हलि । Sid. Kau.

‡ गुपूधूपविच्छिपणिपनिभ्य आयः । Pân. III. 28. These roots insert आय before अ. The vowel of गुप् takes Guṇa substitute before this आय.

गुह्* U. 'to conceal, to keep secret,' गूहति-ते.

कम् Â. 'to wish,' कामयते.

ष्ठिव् † P. 'to spit,' ष्ठीवति

चम with आ 'to sip,' आचामति.

भ्राश् ‡ and म्लाश् A. 'to shine;' भ्राशते, भ्राश्यते, म्लाशते, म्लाश्यते

भ्रम P. 'to roam,' भ्रमति, भ्रम्यति, भ्राम्यति.

क्रम् P. 'to walk,' क्रामति, क्राम्यति

लष् P. A. 'to desire,' लषति-ते, लष्यति ते.

धिन्व् § P. 'to please,' धिनोति.

कृण्व् P. 'to kill, to hurt,' कृणोति.

अक्ष् || P. 'to pervade.' अक्षति अक्ष्णोति.

तक्ष् P. 'to pare,' तक्षति, तक्ष्णोति.

ऋत 'to reproach,' 'to pity,' ऋतीयते.

गम् ¶ P. 'to go,' गच्छति.

यम P. 'to restrain' यच्छति

पा $ P. 'to drink,' पिबति.

घ्रा P. 'to smell,' जिघ्रति.

ध्मा P. 'to blow,' धमति.

स्था P. 'to stand,' तिष्ठति.

म्ना P. 'to think,' मनति.

दा P. 'to give,' यच्छति.

दृश् P. 'to see.' पश्यति.

ऋ P. 'to go' ऋच्छति

---

* ऊदुपधाया गोहः । Pan. VI. 4. 89. The penultimate उ of गुह् is lengthened in the Special Tenses and before a strong termination beginning with a vowel

† ष्ठिवुक्लमुचमां शिति । Pân. VII. 3. 75. आङि चम इति वक्तव्यम् Vârt. These roots lengthen their vowel in the Special Tenses.

‡ वा भ्राशम्लाशभ्रमुक्रमुक्लमुत्रसित्रुटिलषः । Pân. III. 1. 70. These roots take the य of the 4th class optionally in the Special Tenses.

§ धिन्विकृण्व्योर च । अतो लोपः । Pân. III. 1 87. VI. 4 48. The roots धिन्व् and कृण्व् substitute अ for their व् and then add the augment उ (before which the अ is dropped). These are then conjugated like roots of the 5th class.

|| अक्ष् and तक्ष् when it means to make thin, belong to the 5th class optionally.

¶ इषुगमियमां छः (छे च । see § 44.) Pân. VII. 3. 77.

$ पाघ्राध्मास्थाम्नादाण्दृश्यर्तिसर्तिशदसदां पिबजिघ्रधमतिष्ठमनयच्छपश्यर्च्छधौशीयसीदाः । Pân. VII. 3. 78.

सृ P. 'to run,' धावति.
शद् P. (*A.) 'to perish,' शीयते.
सद् P. to sit, to perish, &c. सीदति.
दंश् † P. to bite, दशति.
सञ्ज् P. to adhere, सजति.
स्वञ्ज् A. to embrace, स्वजते.
रञ्ज् P. A. to dye, रजति, रजते.
मृज् P. to be clean, मार्जति.
जभ् A. to yawn, जम्भते.
कृप् A. to be adequate, कल्पते.
लस्ज् A. to blush, लज्जते.
सस्ज् P. 'to be ready' सज्जति.

396. The following seven roots form their bases like the Desiderative in the senses indicated. These are:—कित् to administer medicine, to treat as a patient चिकित्सति-ते; गुप् to censure, जुगुप्सते; तिज् to bear, to forgive, तितिक्षते; बध् to abhor, to act loathsomely, बीभत्सते; दान् to make straight, दीदांसति-ते; मान् to reason, to think, मीमांसते; शान् to sharpen, शीशांसति-ते. But कित् to desire केतति; to dwell, केतयति; दान् to cut दानयति-ते. &c.

§ 397. There are a few roots which add a penultimate nasal in the Special Tenses and Moods necessarily; *e. g.* भिद् to cut भिन्दति, अह् to go अंहते, पिड् to roll into a ball पिण्डते, शुठ् to purify, to go शुंठति &c; and a few more which do so optionally; *e. g.* दृह् to be firm दर्हति-दृंहति; म्रुच् or म्लुच् to go म्रोचयति-म्रुंचति, म्लोचयति-म्लुंचति; लुच् to pluck लोचति, लुञ्चति all P.; गुज् A. to hum गोजते, गुञ्जते; गृज् P. to roar गर्जति, गृंजति and others less important.

4th Class (दिवादयः).

क्रम् P. 'to go' क्राम्यति.
जन् A. 'to be born' जायते.
शम् ‡ P. 'to be pacific' शाम्यति.
तम् P. 'to desire' ताम्यति.

---

* शदेः शितः । Pân. I. 3. 60. शद् is Atm. in the Special Tenses.

† दंशसञ्जस्वञ्जां शपि । रञ्जेश्च P. VI. 4. 25-26. These roots drop their nasal in the Special Tenses.

‡ शमामष्टानां दीर्घः श्यनि । Pân. VII. 3. 94. Of these भ्रम् is given under भ्वादि.

दम् P. 'to pacify' दाम्यति.
भ्रम् P. 'to be wearied' भ्राम्यति.
क्षम् P. 'to endure' क्षाम्यति.
क्लम 'to be weary' क्लाम्याति, क्लामति.
मद् P. 'to be intoxicated' माद्यति.
यस् P. 'to endeavour' यस्यति, यसति; but when followed by a preposition except सम् it belongs to the 4th class alone; संयस्यति; संयसति, but प्रयस्यति only.
शो* P. 'to sharpen' श्यति.
छो P. 'to cut' छ्यति.
सो P. 'to put an end to' स्यति.
दो P. 'to cut' द्यति.
भ्रंश्-स् P. 'to fall' भ्रश्यति, भ्रस्यति.
रंज् P. A. 'to colour' रज्यति-ते.
मिद् P. 'to be unctuous' मेद्यति.
व्यध् 'to strike, to pierce' विध्यति.

§ 398. The following roots belong to the 1st and the 4th classes:—भ्राश्, भ्लाश् (भ्रास्), काश् all meaning to shine, डी to fly, all A. भ्रम्, क्रम्, त्रस् to fear, लष्, क्षिव् to spit, हृष् to be pleased, श्लिष् to embrace, रुष् to be angry or vexed राध् (1) to turn out auspiciously, (4) to succeed, all Par., सह्, 1. A. 4. P. to bear, भ्र-भ्रं-श् (स्) to fall, रञ्ज् to be dyed, शप् to curse, बुध् 1. P. 4. A. to know, शुच् 1. P. to bewail, 4 P. A. to be afflicted, क्रम्, क्षम् 1 A., 4. P. and स्विद् 4. P. to perspire, 1 A. to be anointed.

6th Class (तुदादयः)

इष् P. 'to wish' इच्छति.
कृत् P. 'to cut' कृन्तति.
कृ P. with उप or प्रति, उपस्किरति or प्रतिस्किरति.
खिद् P. to suffer pain खिन्दति.
गृ P. to swallow गिरति, गिलति.
त्रुट् P. to cut त्रुट्यति, त्रुटति.
प्रच्छ् P. to ask पृच्छति.
भ्रस्ज् P. A. to fry भृज्जति–ते.
मस्ज् P. to bathe मज्जति.
व्रश्च् P. to cut वृश्चति.
व्यच् P. to deceive विचति.
विच्छ् P. to go विच्छायति.
सस्ज् P. to go सज्जति.
मुच् U. to release मुञ्चति–ते.
लिप् to anoint लिम्पति-ते.

---

* ओतः श्यनि। Pân. 3. 71. These four roots drop their ओ before य.

लुप् U. to break or cut लुम्पति-ते	सिच् U. to sprinkle सिञ्चति-ते
विद्* U. to obtain विन्दति-ते	पिश् P. to form पिंशति.

§ 399. (*a*) The following roots belong optionally to the 1st and 6th Classes:– कृष् 1. P. 6. U. to plough, to draw, घुट् 1. A. to return, 6. P. to strike against, घुण् 1.A. 6. P. to roll, to whirl; 1. A. to take, to receive, घूर्ण् 1. A. 6. P. to reel, whirl round, move to and fro, छुर् 1. P. to divide, 6. P. to envelope, त्रुप्, त्रुम्प् P. to kill सद् P. to sit down, मिष् P. 1. to sprinkle, 6. to open the eyes, लड् P. 1. to stir, to churn, 6 to cover, to adhere, मुच् 1. A. to cheat, 6 U. to release, to leave &c.

(*b*) The following roots belong to the 4th as well as to the 6th class:—क्षिप् 4 P. 6. U. to throw, लुप् 4. P. to confound, 6. U. to take away, लुभ P. 4. to covet, to be perplexed, 6 A. to perplex, सृज् 4 A. to let loose, to send forth, 4, 6. P to create.

10th Class (चुरादयः)

धू† P. to 'shake' धूनयति.	प्री P. 'to please' प्रीणयति.
अर्थ्—अर्थयति, अर्थापयति.‡	गण्—गणयति, गणापयति.‡
लज्ज्—लज्जयति, लज्जापयति.‡	वण्ट्—वण्टयति, वण्टापयति.‡

*This root belongs to the 2nd, 4th, 6th, and 7th classes, with different senses. All these are given in the following couplet.

सत्तायां विद्यते ज्ञाने वेत्ति विन्ते विचारणे ।
विन्दते विन्दति प्राप्तौ श्यन्लुक्श्नम्शेष्विदं क्रमात् ॥

† The following stanza from the 'Kavirahasya' gives the various classes to which this root belongs:—

धूनोति चम्पकवनानि धुनोत्यशोकं चूतं धुनाति धुवति स्फुटितातिमुक्तम् ।
वायुर्विधूनयति चम्पकपुष्परेणून् यत्कानने धवति चन्दनमञ्जरीश्च ॥

‡ These optional forms are according to शाकटायन and others

§ 400. The following roots of the 10th class preserve their vowel unchanged; अघ् to sin, कथ् to tell, क्षप् to send, to pass; गण् to count, गल् U. to filter, A. to throw, वर् to choose or seek, to get, ध्वन् to sound, मह् to honour, रच् to compose, रस् to taste, रह् to forsake शठ् to speak ill of, deceive, रट् to scream, पट् to weave, (but पाटयति when it means to tear &c.), स्तन् to thunder, गद् to sound, पत् to go, कल् to count, स्वर् to sound, पद् A. to go, अंस् to divide, वट् to separate, लज् to shine, कर्ण् to bore, छद् to conceal, चप् to cheat, वस् to dwell, श्रथ् or श्लथ् to be weak or lax, व्यय् to give, to spend, स्पृह् to desire, मृग् to seek, मृष् to bear, कृप् to pity, to be weak, कुण्, गुण् to converse with, ग्रह् A. to take (also ग्राहयति when cau. of ग्रह्) कुह् A. to astonish, to deceive, पुट् to bind or string together, स्फुट् to become manifest, सुख् to make happy, and others less common.

§ 401. Some roots of the 10th class exclusively take the Âtmanepada *i. e.* even when the fruit of the action expressed by them does not accrue to the agent. These are:—अर्थ् to request, to desire, कुह् to astonish, to deceive, चित् to be conscious of, to think, दंश् to bite, दंस् (or दस् according to some) to see, to bite. डप् or डिप् to accumulate, तन्त्र् to support a family, मन्त्र् to counsel secretly, मृग् to search, to hunt, to seek. स्पृश् to take, to string together, तर्ज् and भर्त्स् to reprove, वस्त् and गन्ध् to injure, to hurt, त्रिष्क् to kill (ह्रिष्क् according to some), निष्क् to measure, लल् to desire, कण् to contract, तुण् to fill, भ्रूण् to fear, शल् to praise, यक्ष to worship, स्यम् to guess, गुर् to strike, सम् to look at, to inspect, कुत्स् to reproach, त्रुट् (according to some कुट्) to cut, गल् to drop down, भल् to see, to expound, कूट् to abstain from giving, to muddle, कुट् to cut, वञ्च् to deceive, वृष् to have the power of generation, to be eminent,

सुख् to gratify, क्लिन्द् to bewail, ज्ञ to know, चित् to know, to be conscious of, मत् to stop, गु to censure, and कुस्म् to smile improperly.

§ 402. The following roots belong to the 1st and the 10th classes:—

युज्, पृच् to unite, to restrain, अर्च् to worship, ईर् to throw, ली to melt वृज् to abandon, to avoid, वृ to cover, जॄ, ज्रि to grow old, रिच् to separate, to join, शिष् to leave a residue, तप् to burn, तृप् to be pleased or satisfied, छृद् to kindle, चृप्, छृप् दृप् to kindle, दृंभ् to fear, श्रथ् to release, to kill, मी to go, ग्रन्थ् to string together, शीक्, चीक् to endure, अर्द् to kill, हिंस् to kill, अर्ह् to worship, सद् with आ to go, to assail, शुन्ध् to purify, to cleanse, छद् to cover, जुष् to satisfy, to guess, to kill, प्री to please, श्रन्थ्, ग्रन्थ् to compose, arrange, आप् to obtain, तन् to confide, to stretch, चन् to confide, to hurt, वद् to inform, वच् to speak, मान् to honour, worship, भू A. to obtain (भवति also according to some), गर्ह् to censure, मार्ग् to seek, कण्ठ् to grieve, to remember with regret, मृज् to clean, मृष् to endure, धृष् to brave, to overcome, जस् to hurt, to injure, दिव् 10 A. 1. P. to torment, to beg, घुष् to aver, and some others.

II. GROUP II.

ROOTS WITH CHANGEABLE BASES.

(2nd, 3rd, 5th, 7th, 8th, and 9th Classes.)

§ 403. Terminations:—

Parasmaipada.

The terminations of the Present, the Imperfect and the Imperative are the same as these of the first group, the termi-

nation of the 2nd per. sing. of the Imperative is हि. The terminations of the Potential are as follow:—

1. याम्	याव	याम
2. यास्	यातम्	यात
3. यात्	याताम्	युस्

Âtmanepada.

Present			*Imperfect*		
1. ए	वहे	महे	इ	वहि	महि
2. से	आथे	ध्वे	थास्	आथाम्	ध्वम्
3. ते	आते	अते	त	आताम्	अत

Imperative

1. ऐ	आवहै	आमहै
2. स्व	आथाम्	ध्वम्
3. ताम्	आताम्	अताम्

Potential

The same as those given for the first group.

§ 404. The base of the roots of the 2nd group of Conjugationl classes undergoes many modifications with regard to which the terminations are divided into sets, one set is called 'strong', the other 'weak.' The base taking the strong terminations may be calld 'The strong base;' and that taking the weak ones 'The weak base'.

(*a*) The strong terminations are:—

The singulars of all persons of the Present and the Imperfect, the third person singular and all numbers of the first person of the Imperative, in the Parasmaipada, and all numbers of the first person of the Imperative in the Atmanepada.

(*b*) The rest are weak.

§ 405. Before strong terminations the penultimate short and the final vowel of the base take their Guna substitute.

Fifth, Eighth and Ninth classes

§ 406. * नु and उ are added on to the roots of the 5th and 8th classes respectively before the terminations.

§ 407 The final उ of the base is optionally dropped before व् and म् if it be not preceded by a conjunct consonant. It is changed to उव् before a weak termination beginning with a vowel, if preceded by a conjunct consonant and to व् in other cases. The हि of the Imperative 2nd per. sing. is dropped after उ not preceded by a conjunct consonant.

§ 408. † In the ninth class ना is inserted between the root and the terminations ना becomes न् before the weak terminations beginning with a vovel, and नी before the weak terminations beginning with a consonant.

§ 409. (*a*) The penultimate nasal of a root is dropped before ना &c. as ग्रथ्नामि. ग्रथ्नीवः, ग्रथ्नीमः &c. from ग्रन्थ् 'to put together.

(*b*) In the case of roots ending in a consonant, the imperative second person singular termination is आन instead of हि; as मुषाण from मुष् 'to steal'.

Paradigms.

5th Class.

सु P. A. 'to press out juice,' &c.

	P.	Present.		A.	
1. सुनोमि	सुनुवः, सुन्वः	सुनुमः, सुन्मः	सुन्वे	सुनुवहे, सुन्वहे	सुनुमहे, सुन्महे
2. सुनोषि	सुनुथः	सुनुथ	सुनुषे	सुन्वाथे	सुनुध्वे
3. सुनोति	सुनुतः	सुन्वन्ति	सुनुते	सुन्वाते	सुन्वते

* स्वादिभ्यः श्नुः । तनादिकृञ्भ्यः उः । Pân. III. 1. 73, 79.

† क्र्यादिभ्यः श्ना । Pân. III. 1. 81.

Imperfect.

	P.			*A.*	
1. असुनवम्	असुनुव, असुन्व	असुनुम, असुन्म	असुन्वि	असुनुवहि, असुन्वहि	असुनुमहि, असुन्महि
2. असुनोः	असुनुतम्	असुनुत	असुनुथाः	असुन्वाथाम्	असुनुध्वम्
3. असुनोत्	असुनुताम्	असुन्वन्	असुनुत	असुन्वाताम्	असुन्वत

Imperative.

1. सुनवानि	सुनवाव	सुनवाम	सुनवै	सुनवावहै	सुनवामहै
2. सुनु	सुनुतम्	सुनुत	सुनुष्व	सुन्वाथाम्	सुनुध्वम्
3. सुनोतु	सुनुताम्	सुन्वन्तु	सुनुताम्	सुन्वाताम्	सुन्वताम्

Potential.

1. सुनुयाम्	सुनुयाव	सुनुयाम	सुन्वीय	सुन्वीवहि	सुन्वीमहि
2. सुनुयाः	सुनुयातम्	सुनुयात	सुन्वीथाः	सुन्वीयाथाम्	सुन्वीध्वम्
3. सुनुयात्	सुनुयाताम्	सुनुयुः	सुन्वीत	सुन्वीयाताम्	सुन्वीरन्

साध् P. 'to accomplish.' अश् A. 'to pervade.'

Present.

1. साध्नोमि	साध्नुवः	साध्नुमः	अश्नुवे	अश्नुवहे	अश्नुमहे
2. साध्नोषि	साध्नुथः	साध्नुथ	अश्नुषे	अश्नुवाथे	अश्नुध्वे
3. साध्नोति	साध्नुतः	साध्नुवन्ति	अश्नुते	अश्नुवाते	अश्नुवते

Imperfect.

1. असाध्नवम्	असाध्नुव	असाध्नुम	आश्नुवि	आश्नुवहि	आश्नुमहि
2. असाध्नोः	असाध्नुतम्	असाध्नुत	आश्नुथाः	आश्नुवाथाम्	आश्नुध्वम्
3. असाध्नोत्	असाध्नुताम्	असाध्नुवन्	आश्नुत	आश्नुवाताम्	आश्नुवत

Imperative.

1. साध्नवानि	साध्नवाव	साध्नवाम	अश्नवै	अश्नवावहै	अश्नवामहै
2. साध्नुहि	साध्नुतम्	साध्नुत	अश्नुष्व	अश्नुवाथाम्	अश्नुध्वम्
3. साध्नोतु	साध्नुताम्	साध्नुवन्तु	अश्नुताम्	अश्नुवाताम्	अश्नुवताम्

Potential.

1. साध्नुयाम्	साध्नुयाव	साध्नुयाम	अश्नुवीय	अश्नुवीवहि	अश्नुवीमहि
2. साध्नुयाः	साध्नुयातम्	साध्नुयात	अश्नुवीथाः	अश्नुवीयाथाम्	अश्नुवीध्वम्
3. साध्नुयात्	साध्नुयाताम्	साध्नुयुः	अश्नुवीत	अश्नुवीयाताम्	अश्नुवीरन्

8th Class.

तन् P. A. 'to stretch.'

P.		Present.		A.	
1. तनोमि	तनुवः, तन्वः	तनुमः, तन्मः	तन्वे	तनुवहे, तन्वहे	तनुमहे, तन्महे
2. तनोषि	तनुथः	तनुथ	तनुषे	तन्वाथे	तनुध्वे
3. तनोति	तनुतः	तन्वन्ति	तनुते	तन्वाते	तन्वते

Imperfect.

1. अतनवम्	अतनुव अतन्व	अतनुम अतन्म	अतन्वि	अतनुवहि अतन्वहि	अतनुमहि अतन्महि
2. अतनोः	अतनुतम्	अतनुत	अतनुथाः	अतन्वाथाम्	अतनुध्वम्
3. अतनोत्	अतनुताम्	अतन्वन्	अतनुत	अतन्वाताम्	अतन्वत

Imperative.

1. तनवानि	तनवाव	तनवाम	तनवै	तनवावहै	तनवामहै
2. तनु	तनुतम्	तनुत	तनुष्व	तन्वाथाम्	तनुध्वम्
3. तनोतु	तनुताम्	तन्वन्तु	तनुताम्	तन्वाताम्	तन्वताम्

Potential.

1. तनुयाम्	तनुयाव	तनुयाम	तन्वीय	तन्वीवहि	तन्वीमहि
2. तनुयाः	तनुयातम्	तनुयात	तन्वीथाः	तन्वीयाथाम्	तन्वीध्वम्
3. तनुयात्	तनुयाताम्	तनुयुः	तन्वीत	तन्वीयाताम्	तन्वीरन्

§ 410. **Irregular base:—कृ. P. A. 'to do' is changed to कर् before the strong, and कुर् before the weak terminations. The उ of the base is dropped before व and म.**

Present.

	P.			A.		
1.	करोमि	कुर्वः	कुर्मः	कुर्वे	कुर्वहे	कुर्महे
2.	करोषि	कुरुथः	कुरुथ	कुरुषे	कुर्वाथे	कुरुध्वे
3.	करोति	कुरुतः	कुर्वन्ति	कुरुते	कुर्वाते	कुर्वते

Imperfect.

1.	अकरवम्	अकुर्व	अकुर्म	अकुर्वि	अकुर्वहि	अकुर्महि
2.	अकरोः	अकुरुतम्	अकुरुत	अकुरुथाः	अकुर्वाथाम्	अकुरुध्वम्
3.	अकरोत्	अकुरुताम्	अकुर्वन्	अकुरुत	अकुर्वाताम्	अकुर्वत

Imperative.

1.	करवाणि	करवाव	करवाम	करवै	करवावहै	करवामहै
2.	कुरु	कुरुतम्	कुरुत	कुरुष्व	कुर्वाथाम्	कुरुध्वम्
3.	करोतु	कुरुताम्	कुर्वन्तु	कुरुताम्	कुर्वाताम्	कुर्वताम्

Potential.

1.	कुर्याम्	कुर्याव	कुर्याम	कुर्वीय	कुर्वीवहि	कुर्वीमहि
2.	कुर्याः	कुर्यातम्	कुर्यात	कुर्वीथाः	कुर्वीयाथाम्	कुर्वीध्वम्
3.	कुर्यात्	कुर्याताम्	कुर्युः	कुर्वीत	कुर्वीयाताम्	कुर्वीरन्

9th Class.

क्री. P. A. 'to buy.'

Present.

	P.			A.		
1.	क्रीणामि	क्रीणीवः	क्रीणीमः	क्रीणे	क्रीणीवहे	क्रीणीमहे
2.	क्रीणासि	क्रीणीथः	क्रीणीथ	क्रीणीषे	क्रीणाथे	क्रीणीध्वे
3.	क्रीणाति	क्रीणीतः	क्रीणन्ति	क्रीणीते	क्रीणाते	क्रीणते

Imperfect.

1.	अक्रीणाम्	अक्रीणीव	अक्रीणीम	अक्रीणि	अक्रीणीवहि	अक्रीणीमहि
2.	अक्रीणाः	अक्रीणीतम्	अक्रीणीत	अक्रीणीथाः	अक्रीणाथाम्	अक्रीणीध्वम्
3.	अक्रीणात्	अक्रीणीताम्	अक्रीणन्	अक्रीणीत	अक्रीणाताम्	अक्रीणत

Imperative.

1.	क्रीणानि	क्रीणावः	क्रीणाम	क्रीणै	क्रीणावहै	क्रीणामहै
2.	क्रीणीहि	क्रीणीतम्	क्रीणीत	क्रीणीष्व	क्रीणीथाम्	क्रीणीध्वम्
3.	क्रीणातु	क्रीणीताम्	क्रीणन्तु	क्रीणीताम्	क्रीणाताम	क्रीणताम्

Potential.

1.	क्रीणीयाम्	क्रीणीयाव	क्रीणीयाम	क्रीणीय	क्रीणीवहि	क्रीणीमहि
2.	क्रीणीयाः	क्रीणीयातम्	क्रीणीयात	क्रीणीथाः	क्रीणीयाथाम्	क्रीणीध्वम्
3.	क्रीणीयात्	क्रीणीयाताम्	क्रीणीयुः	क्रीणीत	क्रीणीयाताम्	क्रीणीरन्

स्तम्भू P. 'to obstruct,' or 'to stop.'

	Present.			*Imperfect.*		
1.	स्तभ्नामि	स्तभ्नीवः	स्तभ्नीमः	अस्तभ्नाम्	अस्तभ्नीव	अस्तभ्नीम
2.	स्तभ्नासि	स्तभ्नीथः	स्तभ्नीथ	अस्तभ्नाः	अस्तभ्नीतम्	अस्तभ्नीत
3.	स्तभ्नाति	स्तभ्नीतः	स्तभ्नन्ति	अस्तभ्नात्	अस्तभ्नीताम्	अस्तभ्नन्

	Imperative.			*Potential.*		
1.	स्तभ्नानि	स्तभ्नाव	स्तभ्नाम	स्तभ्नीयाम्	स्तभ्नीयाव	स्तभ्नीयाम
2.	स्तभान	स्तभ्नीतम्	स्तभ्नीत	स्तभ्नीयाः	स्तभ्नीयातम्	स्तभ्नीयात
3.	स्तभ्नातु	स्तभ्नीताम्	स्तभ्नन्तु	स्तभ्नीयात्	स्तभ्नीयाताम्	स्तभ्नीयुः

IRREGULAR SPECIAL BASES OF THE NINTH CLASS.

§ 411. In the case of the root क्षुभ् the न् of ना is not changed to ण्; as क्षुभ्नाति, क्षुभ्नीतः, क्षुभ्नन्ति, &c.

§ 412. The roots ज्ञा 'to know' and ज्या 'to become old'

assume the forms जा and जि respectively; as जानाति-नीते, जिनाति, &c.

§ 413. The र् of ग्रह् is changed to ऋ; as गृह्णाति; अगृह्णाम, अगृह्णीव, अगृह्णीम, &c. Imperf 1st. pers.

§ 414. The roots री, ली, व्ली, प्ली, धू, पू, लू, ऋ, कॄ, गॄ, जॄ, नॄ, पॄ, भॄ, मॄ, वॄ, शॄ and स्तॄ have their finals shortened necessarily, and क्षी, भ्री, and व्री optionally in the Special Tenses; as धुनाति-नीते, स्तृणाति-णीते, वृणाति-णीते, &c. क्षीणाति, क्षिणाति, &c.

§ 415 The roots स्कु 'to go by leaps, to raise,' स्तम्भ् 'to obstruct,' स्तुम्भ् 'to stop,' स्कम्भ् and स्कुम्भ् 'to obstruct' belong to the 5th and 9th classes; as स्कुनाति, स्कुनीते, स्कुनोति, स्कुनुते, &c.

Second, Third and Seventh Classes.

§ 416. Special rules of Sandhi of the finals of roots and the initial letters of terminations:—

(1) The ending उ of a root takes its Vṛiddhi substitute when followed by a consonantal strong termination; as नु + मि=नौमि.

(2) The final इ or उ. short or long, of a root is changed to इय् or उव् before a vowel weak termination.

(3) The ending ह् of roots is changed to ढ् when followed by any consonant, except a nasal or a semivowel, or by nothing; and that of roots beginning with द् to घ् under the same circumstances.

(4) The initial त् or थ् of a termination is changed to ध् after a soft aspirate (4th letter of a class).

(5) ढ् or घ् followed by स is changed to क्.

(6) न् and म् when followed by a consonant are changed to the nasal of the class to which the following consonant belongs, and to an *anusvâra* when followed by श्, ष्, स् or ह्.

(7) The ending इ of a root, short or long, not preceded by a conjunct consonant is changed to य् before vowel weak terminations, when the base consists of more than one syllable.

(8) The ending द् of a root is optionally changed to र् or Visarga in the Imperfect second pers. sing. and the ending स् to त् or द् before the termination त् and optionally before स्.

(9) When a conjunct consonant having स् or क् for its first member is at the end of a word or is followed by a consonant except a nasal or a semivowel, the स् or क् is dropped.

N. B.—The usual Sandhi rules *i. e.* those given in the 2nd and 3rd Chapters should be observed.

§ 417. (1) * The second person sing. termination of the Parasm. Imperative is धि when the base ends in any consonant except a nasal or a semivowel; also in the case of the root हु 3 P. ' to sacrifice. '

§ 418. The स् and त् of the Imperfect 2nd and 3rd per. sing. are dropped after a consonant.

Second (or अदादि) Class.

§ 419. In this class the terminations are directly added to the root.

§ 420. In the case of roots ending in आ, the terminations of the third person plural of the Imperfect is optionally उस्.

* हुझल्भ्यो हेर्धिः । Pân. VI. 4. 101.

Paradigms.

या P. ' to go. '

	Present.			*Imperfect.*	
1. यामि	यावः	यामः	अयाम्	अयाव	अयाम
2. यासि	याथः	याथ	अयाः	अयातम्	अयात
3. याति	यातः	यान्ति	अयात्	अयाताम्	अयान्, अयुः

	Imperative.			*Potential.*	
1. यानि	याव	याम	यायाम्	यायाव	यायाम
2. याहि	यातम्	यात	यायाः	यायातम्	यायात
3. यातु	याताम्	यान्तु	यायात्	यायाताम्	यायुः

Conjugate similarly ख्या P. ' to tell, ' दा P. ' to cut, ' पा P. 'to protect,' प्रा P. 'to fill,' प्सा P. ' to eat,' द्रा P. ' to fly, भा P. ' to shine,' मा ' to measure, रा ' to give,' ला ' to give or take, ' वा ' to blow, ' श्रा ' to cook ; add स्ना ' to bathe '.

§ 421. In order to exemplify the rules given under §§ 416–418 we will give the forms of the regular verbs वी, तु, जागृ, ईर्, चक्ष्, कश्, दुह्, लिह् and निञ्ज्.

वी P. ' to go '

	Present.			*Imperfect.*	
1. वेमि	वीवः	वीमः	अवयम्	अवीव	अवीम
2. वेषि	वीथः	वीथ	अवेः	अवीतम्	अवीत
3. वेति	वीतः	वियन्ति	अवेत्	अवीताम्	अवियन् (or अव्यन् according to some)

Imperative.			*Potential.*		
1. वयानि	वयाव	वयाम	वीयाम्	वीयाव	वीयाम
2. वीहि	वीतम्	वीत	वीयाः	वीयातम्	वीयात
3. वेतु	वीताम्	वियन्तु	वीयात्	वीयाताम्	वीयुः

नु P ' to praise '

Present.			*Imperfect.*		
1. नौमि	नुवः	नुमः	अनवम्	अनुव	अनुम
2. नौषि	नुथः	नुथ	अनौः	अनुतम्	अनुत
3. नौति	नुतः	नुवन्ति	अनौत्	अनुताम्	अनुवन्

Imperative.			*Potential.*		
1. नवानि	नवाव	नवाम	नुयाम्	नुयाव	नुयाम
2. नुहि	नुतम्	नुत	नुयाः	नुयातम्	नुयात
3. नौतु	नुताम्	नुवन्तु	नुयात्	नुयाताम्	नुयुः

Conjugate similarly कु P. ' to sound, ' क्षु P. ' to seize, ' क्ष्णु P. ' to sharpen,' द्यु P. ' to attack, युP. ' to join, ' स्नु P. ' to possess supremacy, ' and स्नु ' to drop out, to distil. '

जागृ P. ' to awake. '

Present.			*Imperfect.*		
1. जागर्मि	जागृवः	जागृमः	अजागरम्	अजागृव	अजागृम
2. जागर्षि	जागृथः	जागृथ	अजागः	अजागृतम्	अजागृत
3. जागर्ति	जागृतः	जाग्रति*	अजागः	अजागृताम्	अजागरुः

Imperative.			*Potential.*		
1. जागराणि	जागराव	जागराम	जागृयाम	जागृयाव	जागृयाम
2. जागृहि	जागृतम्	जागृत	जागृयाः	जागृयातम्	जागृयात
3. जागर्तु	जागृताम्	जाग्रतु	जागृयात्	जागृयाताम्	जागृयुः

---

* See चकास् p. 272.

ईर् A. 'to go.'

	Present.			*Imperfect.*		
1.	ईरे	ईर्वहे	ईर्महे	ऐरि	ऐर्वहि	ऐर्महि
2.	ईर्षे	ईराथे	ईर्ध्वे	ऐर्थाः	ऐराथाम्	ऐर्ध्वम्
3.	ईर्ते	ईराते	ईरते	ऐर्त	ऐराताम्	ऐरत

	Imperative.			*Potential.*		
1.	ईरै	ईरावहै	ईरामहै	ईरीय	ईरीवहि	ईरीमहि
2.	ईर्ष्व	ईराथाम्	ईर्ध्वम्	ईरीथाः	ईरीयाथाम्	ईरीध्वम्
3.	ईर्ताम्	ईराताम्	ईरताम्	ईरीत	ईरीयाताम्	ईरीरन्

चक्ष् A. 'to speak.'

	Present.			*Imperfect.*		
1.	चक्षे	चक्ष्वहे	चक्ष्महे	अचक्षि	अचक्ष्वहि	अचक्ष्महि
2.	चक्षे	चक्षाथे	चड्ढ्वे	अचष्ठाः	अचक्षाथाम्	अचड्ढ्वम्
3.	चष्टे	चक्षाते	चक्षते	अचष्ट	अचक्षाताम्	अचक्षत

	Imperfect.			*Potential.*		
1.	चक्षै	चक्षावहै	चक्षामहै	चक्षीय	चक्षीवहि	चक्षीमहि
2.	चक्ष्व	चक्षाथाम्	चड्ढ्वम्	चक्षीथाः	चक्षीयाथाम्	चक्षीध्वम्
3.	चष्टाम्	चक्षाताम्	चक्षताम्	चक्षीत	चक्षीयाताम्	चक्षीरन्

कश् A. 'to go.'

	Present.			*Imperfect.*		
1.	कशे	कश्वहे	कश्महे	अकशि	अकश्वहि	अकश्महि
2.	कक्षे	कशाथे	कड्ढ्वे	अकष्ठाः	अकशाथाम्	अकड्ढ्वम्
3.	कष्टे	कशाते	कशते	अकष्ट	अकशाताम्	अकशत

Imperative.			*Potential.*		
1. कशै	कशावहै	कशामहै	कशीय	कशीवहि	कशीमहि
2. कक्ष्व	कशाथाम्	कड्ढ्वम्	कशीथाः	कशीयाथाम्	कशीध्वम्
3. कष्टाम्	कशाताम्	कशताम्	कशीत	कशीयाताम्	कशीरन्

दुह् P. A. 'to milk.'

Present.

P.			*A.*		
1. दोह्मि	दुह्वः	दुह्मः	दुहे	दुह्वहे	दुह्महे
2. धोक्षि*	दुग्धः	दुग्ध	धुक्षे	दुहाथे	धुग्ध्वे
3. दोग्धि	दुग्धः	दुहन्ति	दुग्धे	दुहाते	दुहते

Imperfect.

1. अदोहम्	अदुह्व	अदुह्म	अदुहि	अदुह्वहि	अदुह्महि
2. अधोक्-ग्	अदुग्धम्	अदुग्ध	अदुग्धाः	अदुहाथाम्	अधुग्ध्वम्
3. अधोक्-ग्	अदुग्धाम्	अदुहन्	अदुग्ध	अदुहाताम्	अदुहत

Imperative.

1. दोहानि	दोहाव	दोहाम	दोहै	दोहावहै	दोहामहै
2. दुग्धि	दुग्धम्	दुग्ध	धुक्ष्व	दुहाथाम्	धुग्ध्वम्
3. दोग्धु	दुग्धाम्	दुहन्तु	दुग्धाम्	दुहाताम्	दुहताम्

Potential.

1. दुह्याम्	दुह्याव	दुह्याम	दुहीय	दुहीवहि	दुहीमहि
2. दुह्याः	दुह्यातम	दुह्यात	दुहीथाः	दुहीयाथाम्	दुहीध्वम्
3. दुह्यात्	दुह्याताम्	दुह्युः	दुहीत	दुहीयाताम्	दुहीरन्

दिह् to be similarly cojugated; इ and ए being substitnted for उ and ओ respectively.

* For the change of द् to ध्, vide § 95.

लिह् P. A. 'to lick.'

Present.

	P.			*A.*	
1. लेह्मि	लिह्वः	लिह्मः	लिहे	लिह्वहे	लिह्महे
2. लेक्षि	लीढः	लीढ	लिक्षे	लिहाथे	लीढ्वे
3. लेढि	लीढः	लिहन्ति	लीढे	लिहाते	लिहते

Imperfect.

1. अलेहम्	अलिह्व	अलिह्म	अलिहि	अलिह्वहि	अलिह्महि
2. अलेट्-ड्	अलीढम्	अलीढ	अलीढाः	अलिहाथाम्	अलीढ्वम्
3. अलेट्-ड्	अलीढाम्	अलिहन्	अलीढ	अलिहाताम्	अलिहत

Imperative.

1. लेहानि	लेहाव	लेहाम	लेहै	लेहावहै	लेहामहै
2. लीढि	लीढम्	लीढ	लिक्ष्व	लिहाथाम्	लीढ्वम्
3. लेढु	लीढाम्	लिहन्तु	लीढाम्	लिहाताम्	लिहताम्

Potential.

1. लिह्याम्	लिह्याव	लिह्याम	लिहीय	लिहीवहि	लिहीमहि
&c.	&c.	&c.	&c.	&c.	&c.

निञ्ज् A.* 'to Purify'

Present.			*Imperfect.*		
1. निञ्जे	निञ्ज्वहे	निञ्ज्महे	अनिञ्जि	अनिञ्ज्वहि	अनिञ्ज्महि
2. निङ्क्षे	निञ्जाथे	निङ्ग्ध्वे	अनिङ्क्थाः	अनिञ्जाथाम्	अनिङ्ग्ध्वम्
3. निङ्क्ते	निञ्जाते	निञ्जते	अनिङ्क्त	अनिञ्जाताम्	अनिञ्जत

Imperative.			*Potential.*		
1. निञ्जै	निञ्जावहै	निञ्जामहै	निञ्जीय	निञ्जीवहि	निञ्जीमहि
2. निङ्क्ष्व	निञ्जाथाम्	निङ्ग्ध्वम्	निञ्जीथाः	निञ्जीयाथाम्	निञ्जीध्वम्
3. निङ्क्ताम्	निञ्जाताम्	निञ्जताम्	निञ्जीत	निञ्जीयाताम्	निञ्जीरन्

---

* शिं-षिञ्ज्, पिञ्ज्, पृंज्, वृज्, वृञ्ज्, पृच् all A. should be similarly conjugated.

IRREGULAR BASES.

Many of the roots of the 2nd class are of irregular conjugation. We will treat of them in alphabetical order.

§ 422. अद् P. 'to eat' forms the 2 and 3 sing. Imperf. as आदः and आदत् respectively. In other respects it is regular.

Present.			*Imperfect.*		
1. अद्मि	अद्वः	अद्मः	1. आदम्	आद्व	आद्म
2. अत्सि	अत्थः	अत्थ	2. आदः	आत्तम्	आत्त
3. अत्तिः	अत्तः	अदन्ति	3. आदत्	आत्ताम्	आदन्

Imperative.			*Potential.*		
1. अदानि	अदाव	अदाम	1. अद्याम्	अद्याव	अद्याम
2. अद्धि	अत्तम्	अत्त	2. अद्याः	अद्यातम्	अद्यात
3. अत्तु	अत्ताम्	अदन्तु	3. अद्यात्	अद्याताम्	अद्युः

§ 423. अन् P. 'to breathe,' जक्ष् 'to eat,' रुद् P. 'to weep,' श्वस् P. 'to sigh' and स्वप् P. 'to sleep.,' insert the augment इ between their final and the terminations beginning with any consonant except य; in the case of 2 and 3 sing. Imperf. they insert ई or अ; *e. g.*

अन् 'P. to breathe.'

Present.			*Imperfect.*		
1. अनिमि	अनिवः	अनिमः	आनम्	आनिव	आनिम
2. अनिषि	अनिथः	अनिथ	आनीः—आनः	आनितम्	आनित
3. अनिति	अनितः	अनन्ति	आनीत्-आनत्	आनिताम्	आनन्

Imperative.			*Potential.*		
1. अनानि	अनाव	अनाम	अन्याम्	अन्याव	अन्याम
2. अनिहि	अनितम्	अनित	अन्याः	अन्यातम्	अन्यात
3. अनितु	अनिताम्	अनन्तु	अन्यात्	अन्याताम्	अन्युः

Conjugate स्वप्, श्वस् and रुद् similarly; as स्वपिति 3 sing. Pre., अस्वपीः-पः 2. sing. Imperf.; अस्वपीत्-पत् 3 sing. Imperf.; स्वपानि 1. sing. Imp. स्वपिहि 2 sing. Imp.; स्वप्याम् 1. sing. Pot.; &c. श्वसिति 3. sing. Pre: अश्वसीः-सः 2 sing. Imperf.; अश्वसीत्-सत् 3 sing. Imperf.; श्वसानि 1. sing. Imp. श्वसिहि 2. sing. Imp. श्वसितु 3. sing. Imp.; श्वस्याम् 1. sing. Pot., &c.; रोदिमि, रुदिवः रुदिमः 1 Pre.; अरोदम् 1. sing. Imperf. अरोदीः-दः 2 sing. Imperf. अरोदीत-दत् 3. sing. Imperf.; रोदानि 1. sing. Imp. रुदिहि 2. sing. Imp. रोदितु 3. sing. Imp.; रुद्याम् 1. sing. Pot. &c.

§ 424. अस् P. (A.* rare) 'to be'—drops its अ before weak terminations and स् before a termination beginning with स् and ध्. Before 2 and 3 Imperf. it takes the augment ई. It is irregular in many respects.

Present.

	P.			A.		
1.	अस्मि	स्वः	स्मः	हे	स्वहे	स्महे
2.	असि	स्थः	स्थ	से	साथे	ध्वे
3.	अस्ति	स्तः	सन्ति	स्ते	साते	सते

Imperfect.

1.	आसम्	आस्व	आस्म	आसि	आस्वहि	आस्महि
2.	आसीः	आस्तम्	आस्त	आस्थाः	आसाथाम्	आध्वम्
3.	आसीत्	आस्ताम्	आसन्	आस्त	आसाताम्	आसत

Imperative.

1.	असानि	असाव	असाम	असै	असावहै	असामहै
2.	एधि	स्तम्	स्त	स्व	साथाम्	ध्वम्
3.	अस्तु	स्ताम्	सन्तु	स्ताम्	साताम्	सताम्

---

* अस् is Atmanepadi in a few cases. *Cf.* Bhaṭṭikâvya II. 35 'अन्यो व्यतिस्ते तु ममापि धर्मः' &c. where it implies कर्मव्यतिहार or an exchange of duty.

Potential.

1. स्याम्	स्याव	स्याम	सीय	सीवहि	सीमहि
2. स्याः	स्यातम्	स्यात	सीथाः	सीयाथाम्	सीध्वम्
3. स्यात्	स्याताम्	स्युः	सीत	सीयाताम्	सीरन्

§ 425. आस् A. 'to sit—also drops its स् before ध्व—

Present.			*Imperfect.*		
1. आसे	आस्वहे	आस्महे	आसि	आस्वहि	आस्महि
2. आस्से	आसाथे	आध्वे	आस्थाः	आसाथाम्	आध्वम्
3. आस्ते	आसाते	आसते	आस्त	आसाताम्	आसत

Imperative.			*Potential.*		
1. आसै	आसावहै	आसामहै	आसीय	आसीवहि	आसीमहि
2. आस्स्व	आसाथाम्	आध्वम्	आसीथाः	आसीयाथाम्	आसीध्वम्
3. आस्ताम्	आसाताम्	आसताम्	आसीत	आसीयाताम्	आसीरन्

Conjugate वस् A. 'to dress' similarly.

§ 426. The इ of the root इ P.* 'to go' is changed to य् before a weak vowel termination: एति इतः यन्ति 3 pers. Pre.; आयम् ऐव ऐम 1st Pers. Imperf.; ऐः 2 sing. Imperf.; अयानि, इहि, एतु 1. 2. 3. sings. Imp. यन्तु 3. pl. Imp.

इ with अधि A. † 'to study' &c. is regularly conjugated; as

---

* ई P. 'to go' is conjugated regularly like वी—एति ईतः इयन्ति 3rd Pers. Pre.; ईहि 2 sing. Imp. इयन्तु 3. plural. Imp.

† इ with अधि P. 'to remember' should be conjugated like इ, अधियन्ति 3rd pl. Pre. Some think that it is to be conjugated like इ in the Non-conjugational tenses only. According to them the third pers. plu. will be अधीयन्ति. The line of Bhaṭṭi 'ससीतयो राघवयोरधीयन्' III. 18. &c. is quoted in support of this opinion. केचित्तु आर्धधातुकाधिकारोक्तस्यैवातिदेशमाहुः । तन्मते यण्न । Sid. Kau.

	Present.			*Imperfect.*	
1. अधीये	अधीवहे	अधीमहे	अध्यैयि	अध्यैवहि	अध्यैमहि
2. अधीषे	अधीयाथे	अधीध्वे	अध्यैथाः	अध्यैयाथाम्	अध्यैध्वम्
3. अधीते	अधीयाते	अधीयते	अध्यैत	अध्यैयाताम्	अध्यैयत

	Imperative.			*Potential.*	
1. अध्ययै	अध्ययावहै	अध्ययामहै	अधीयीय	अधीयीवहि	अधीयीमहि
2. अधीष्व	अधीयाथाम्	अधीध्वम्	अधीयीथाः	अधीयीयाथाम्	अधीयीध्वम्
3. अधीताम्	अधीयाताम्	अधीयताम्	अधीयीत	अधीयीयाताम्	अधीयीरन्

§ 427. ईड् A. 'to praise,' and ईश् A. 'to rule' have an इ added to them before terminations beginning with स् or ध्व except that of the Imperf. 2. plu.

ईड्. A.

	Present			*Imperfect.*	
1. ईडे	ईड्वहे	ईड्महे	ऐडि	ऐड्वहि	ऐड्महि
2. ईडिषे	ईडाथे	ईडिध्वे	ऐट्ठाः	ऐडाथाम्	ऐड्ढ्वम्
3. ईट्टे	ईडाते	ईडते	ऐट्ट	ऐडाताम्	ऐडत

	Imperative.			*Potential.*	
1. ईडै	ईडावहै	ईडामहै	ईडीय	ईडीवहि	ईडीमहि
2. ईडिष्व	ईडाथाम्	ईडिध्वम्	ईडीथाः	ईडीयाथाम्	ईडीध्वम्
3. ईट्टाम्	ईडाताम्	ईडताम्	ईडीत	ईडीयाताम्	ईडीरन्

ईश् to be similarly conjugated; ईशिषे ईशाथे ईशिध्वे 2 Pre.; ऐशि 1. sing. Imperf. ऐष्ठाः 2. sing. Imperf. ऐष्ट 3. sing. Imperf. ऐड्ढ्वम् 2 pl. Imperf.; ईशै 1. sing. Imp. ईशिध्वम् 2. pl. Imp. ईशीत 3. sing. Pot. &c.

§ 428. ऊर्णु P. A. 'to cover'—substitutes Vṛiddhi for its उ optionally before consonantal strong terminations except those of the 2nd and 3rd sing. Imperf.

Present.

	P.			A.		
1.	ऊर्णोमि-ऊर्णौमि	ऊर्णुवः	ऊर्णुमः	ऊर्णुवे	ऊर्णुवहे	ऊर्णुमहे
2.	ऊर्णोषि-ऊर्णौषि	ऊर्णुथः	ऊर्णुथ	उर्णुषे	ऊर्णुवाथे	ऊर्णुध्वे
3.	ऊर्णोति-ऊर्णौति	ऊर्णुतः	ऊर्णुवन्ति	ऊर्णुते	ऊर्णुवाते	ऊर्णुवते

Imperfect.

1.	और्णवम्	और्णुव	और्णुम	और्णुवि	और्णुवहि	और्णुमहि
2.	और्णोः	और्णुतम्	और्णुत	और्णुथाः	और्णुवाथाम्	और्णुध्वम्
3.	और्णोत्	और्णुताम्	और्णुवन्	और्णुत	और्णुवाताम्	और्णुवत

Imperative.

1.	ऊर्णवानि	ऊर्णवाव	ऊर्णवाम	ऊर्णवै	ऊर्णवावहै	ऊर्णवामहै
2.	ऊर्णुहि	ऊर्णुतम्	ऊर्णुत	ऊर्णुष्व	ऊर्णुवाथाम्	ऊर्णुध्वम्
3.	ऊर्णोतु-ऊर्णौतु	ऊर्णुताम्	ऊर्णुवन्तु	ऊर्णुताम्	ऊर्णुवाताम्	ऊर्णुवताम्

Potential

1.	ऊर्णुयाम्	ऊर्णुयाव	ऊर्णुयाम	ऊर्णुवीय	ऊर्णुवीवहि	ऊर्णुवीमहि
2.	ऊर्णुयाः	ऊर्णुयातम्	ऊर्णुयात	ऊर्णुवीथाः	ऊर्णुवीयाथाम्	ऊर्णुवीध्वम्
3.	ऊर्णुयात्	ऊर्णुयाताम्	ऊर्णुयुः	ऊर्णुवीत	ऊर्णुवीयाताम्	ऊर्णुवीरन्

§ 429 **चकास्**, P. 'to shine,'—**चकास्**, **जक्ष्**, **जागृ**, **दरिद्रा** and **शास्** drop the **न्** of the 3rd pers. plu. termination when added to them. In the Imperf. they take **उस्** as 3. pl. termination. Imp. 2 sing. of **चकास्** is **चकाद्धि-धि**.

Paradigms.

	Present			*Imperfect.*		
1.	चकास्मि	चकास्वः	चकास्मः	अचकासम्	अचकास्व	अचकास्म
2.	चकास्सि	चकास्थः	चकास्थ	अचकाः-अचकात्-द्	अचकास्तम्	अचकास्त
3.	चकास्ति	चकास्तः	चकासति	अचकात्-द्	अचकास्ताम्	अचकासुः

	Imperative			*Potential*		
1.	चकासानि	चकासाव	चकासाम	चकास्याम्	चकास्याव	चकास्याम
2.	चकाद्धि-धि	चकास्तम्	चकास्त	चकास्याः	चकास्यातम्	चकास्यात
3.	चकास्तु	चकास्ताम्	चकासतु	चकास्यात्	चकास्याताम्	चकास्युः

जक्ष् P.—see अन and चकास above:—

Paradigms

	Present			*Imperfect*		
1.	जक्षिमि	जक्षिव	जक्षिमः	अजक्षम्	अजक्षिव	अजक्षिम
2.	जक्षिषि	जक्षिथ	जक्षिथ	अजक्षीः-अजक्षः	अजक्षितम्	अजक्षित
3.	जक्षिति	जक्षितः	जक्षति	अजक्षीत्-अजक्षत्	अजक्षिताम्	अजक्षुः

	Imperative.			*Potential.*		
1.	जक्षाणि	जक्षाव	जक्षाम	जक्ष्याम्	जक्ष्याव	जक्ष्याम
2.	जक्षिहि	जक्षितम्	जक्षित	जक्ष्याः	जक्ष्यातम्	जक्ष्यात
3.	जक्षितु	जक्षिताम्	जक्षतु	जक्ष्यात्	जक्ष्याताम्	जक्ष्युः

§ 430. दरिद्रा P. 'to be poor'—drops its आ before weak terminations beginning with a vowel and changes it to इ before those with an initial consonant.

Paradigms.

	Present.			*Imperfect.*		
1.	दरिद्रामि	दरिद्रिवः	दरिद्रिमः	अदरिद्राम्	अदरिद्रिव	अदरिद्रिम
2.	दरिद्रासि	दरिद्रिथः	दरिद्रिथ	अदरिद्राः	अदरिद्रितम्	अदरिद्रित
3.	दरिद्राति	दरिद्रितः	दरिद्रति	अदरिद्रात्	अदरिद्रिताम्	अदरिद्रुः

	Imperative.			*Potential.*		
1.	दरिद्राणि	दरिद्राव	दरिद्राम	दरिद्रियाम्	दरिद्रियाव	दरिद्रियाम

2. दरिद्रिहि	दरिद्रितम्	दरिद्रित	दरिद्रियाः	दरिद्रियातम्	दरिद्रियात
3. दरिद्रातु	दरिद्रिताम्	दरिद्रतु	दरिद्रियात्	दरिद्रियाताम्	दरिद्रियुः

§ 431. द्विष् P. A. 'to hate'—takes उस् optionally in the Imperf. 3. pl. Par.

Present.

1. द्वेष्मि	द्विष्व	द्विष्मः	द्विषे	द्विष्वहे	द्विष्महे
2. द्वेक्षि	द्विष्ठः	द्विष्ठ	द्विक्षे	द्विषाथे	द्विड्ढ्वे
3. द्वेष्टि	द्विष्टः	द्विषन्ति	द्विष्टे	द्विषाते	द्विषते

Imperfect.

1. अद्वेषम्	अद्विष्व	अद्विष्म	अद्विषि	अद्विष्वहि	अद्विष्महि
2. अद्वेट्-ड्	अद्विष्टम्	अद्विष्ट	अद्विष्ठाः	अद्विषाथाम्	अद्विड्ढ्वम्
3. अद्वेट्-ड्	अद्विष्टाम्	अद्विषन्-अद्विषुः	अद्विष्ट	अद्विषाताम्	अद्विषत

Imperative.

1. द्वेषाणि	द्वेषाव	द्वेषाम	द्वेषै	द्वेषावहै	द्वेषामहै
2. द्विड्ढि	द्विष्टम्	द्विष्ट	द्विक्ष्व	द्विषाथाम्	द्विड्ढ्वम्
3. द्वेष्टु	द्विष्टाम्	द्विषन्तु	द्विष्टाम्	द्विषाताम्	द्विषताम्

Potential.

1. द्विष्याम्	द्विष्याव	द्विष्याम	द्विषीय	द्विषीवहि	द्विषीमहि
2. द्विष्याः	द्विष्यातम्	द्विष्यात	द्विषीथाः	द्विषीयाथाम्	द्विषीध्वम्
3. द्विष्यात्	द्विष्याताम्	द्विष्युः	द्विषीत	द्विषीयाताम्	द्विषीरन्

§ 432. ब्रू P. A. 'to speak'—takes the augment ई before consonantal strong terminations.

Present.

1. ब्रवीमि	ब्रूवः	ब्रूमः	ब्रुवे	ब्रूवहे	ब्रूमहे

2. ब्रवीषि-आत्थ	ब्रूथः-आहथुः	ब्रूथ	ब्रूषे	ब्रुवाथे	ब्रूध्वे
3. ब्रवीति-आह	ब्रूतः-आहतुः	ब्रुवन्ति-आहुः	ब्रूते	ब्रुवाते	ब्रुवते

Imperfect.

1. अब्रवम्	अब्रूव	अब्रूम	अब्रुवि	अब्रूवहि	अब्रूमहि
2. अब्रवीः	अब्रूतम्	अब्रूत	अब्रूथाः	अब्रुवाथाम्	अब्रूध्वम्
3. अब्रवीत्	अब्रूताम्	अब्रुवन्	अब्रूत	अब्रुवाताम्	अब्रुवत

Imperative.

1. ब्रवाणि	ब्रवाव	ब्रवाम	ब्रवै	ब्रवावहै	ब्रवामहै
2. ब्रूहि	ब्रूतम्	ब्रूत	ब्रूष्व	ब्रुवाथाम्	ब्रूध्वम्
3. ब्रवीतु	ब्रूताम्	ब्रुवन्तु	ब्रूताम्	ब्रुवाताम्	ब्रुवताम्

Potential

1. ब्रूयाम्	ब्रूयाव	ब्रूयाम	ब्रुवीय	ब्रुवीवहि	ब्रुवीमहि
2. ब्रूयाः	ब्रूयातम्	ब्रूयात	ब्रुवीथाः	ब्रुवीयाथाम्	ब्रुवीध्वम्
3. ब्रूयात्	ब्रूयाताम्	ब्रूयुः	ब्रुवीत	ब्रुवीयाताम्	ब्रुवीरन्

§ 433. मृज् P. 'to cleanse' substitutes Vṛddhi for its vowel necessarily before strong terminations and optionally before vowel weak terminations.

Present.			*Imperfect.*		
1. मार्ज्मि	मृज्वः	मृज्मः	अमार्जम्	अमृज्व	अमृज्म
2. मार्क्षि	मृष्ठः	मृष्ठ	अमार्ट्-ड्	अमृष्टम्	अमृष्ट
3. मार्ष्टि	मृष्टः	मार्जन्ति, मृजन्ति	अमार्ट्-ड्	अमृष्टाम्	अमार्जन्, अमृजन्

Imperative.			*Potential.*		
1. मार्जानि	मार्जाव	मार्जाम	मृज्याम्	मृज्याव	मृज्याम

2. मृड्ढि	मृष्टम्	मृष्ट	मृज्याः	मृज्यातम्	मृज्यात
3. मार्ष्टु	मृष्टाम्	मार्जन्तु-मृजन्तु	मृज्यात्	मृज्याताम्	मृज्युः

§ 434. वच् P. 'to speak'—is deficient in the 3 plu. Pre, according to some in the whole plural, and according to others in all the third person plurals.*

Present			*Imperfect.*		
1. वच्मि	वच्वः	वच्मः	अवचम्	अवच्व	अवच्म
2. वक्षि	वक्थः	वक्थ	अवक्-ग्	अवक्तम्	अवक्त
3. वक्ति	वक्तः	...*	अवक्-ग्	अवक्ताम्	अवचन्

Imperative.			*Potential.*		
1. वचानि	वचाव	वचाम	वच्याम्	वच्याव	वच्याम
2. वग्धि	वक्तम्	वक्त	वच्याः	वच्यातम्	वच्यात
3. वक्तु	वक्ताम्	वचन्तु	वच्यात्	वच्याताम्	वच्युः

§ 435. वश् P. 'to wish'—changes its व to उ before weak terminations.

Present.			*Imperfect.*		
1. वश्मि	उश्वः	उश्मः	अवशम्	औश्व	औश्म
2. वक्षि	उष्ठः	उष्ठ	अवट्-ड्	औष्टम्	औष्ट
3. वष्टि	उष्टः	उशन्ति	अवट्-ड्	औष्टाम्	औशन्

Imperative			*Potential.*		
1. वशानि	वशाव	वशाम	उश्याम्	उश्याव	उश्याम
2. उड्ढि	उष्टम्	उष्ट	उश्याः	उश्यातम्	उश्यात
3. वष्टु	उष्टाम्	उशन्तु	उश्यात्	उश्याताम्	उश्युः

---

* अयमन्तिपरो न प्रयुज्यते । बहुवचनपर इत्यन्ये । झिपर इत्यपरे । (Sid. Kau)

§ 436. **विद् 'to know' takes optionally the terminations of the Perfect in the Present Tense. Its Imperative forms are optionally made up by adding आम् to it and then appending the forms of the Imperative of कृ.**

Present.			*Imperfect.*		
1. वेद्मि-वेद	विद्वः-विद्व	विद्मः-विद्म	अवेदम्	अविद्व	अविद्म
2. वेत्सि-वेत्थ	वित्थः-विदथुः	वित्थ-विद	अवेः, अवेत्-द्	अवित्तम्	अवित्त
3. वेत्ति-वेद	वित्तः-विदतुः	विदन्ति-विदुः	अवेत्-द्	अवित्ताम्	अविदुः

Imperative.

1. वेदानि	वेदाव	वेदाम	विदाङ्करवाणि	विदाङ्करवाव	विदाङ्करवाम
2. विद्धि	वित्तम्	वित्त	विदाङ्कुरु	विदाङ्कुरुतम्	विदाङ्कुरुत
3. वेत्तु	वित्ताम्	विदन्तु	विदाङ्करोतु	विदाङ्कुरुताम्	विदाङ्कुर्वन्तु

Potential.

1. विद्याम्	विद्याव	विद्याम
2. विद्याः	विद्यातम्	विद्यात
3. विद्यात्	विद्याताम्	विद्युः

§ 437. शास्* P. 'to govern, to teach,' &c.—changes its vowel to इ before consonantal weak terminations. See चकास् also p. 272.

Present.			*Imperfect*		
1. शास्मि	शिष्वः	शिष्मः	अशासम्	अशिष्व	अशिष्म
2. शास्सि	शिष्ठः	शिष्ठ	अशाः, अशात्-द्	अशिष्टम्	अशिष्ट
3. शास्ति	शिष्टः	शासति	अशात्-द्	अशिष्टाम्	अशासु:

Imperative.			*Potential.*		
1. शासानि	शासाव	शासाम	शिष्याम	शिष्याव	शिष्याम

* शास् with आ A. should be conjugated like आस्

2. शाधि	शिष्टम्	शिष्ट	शिष्याः	शिष्यातम्	शिष्यात
3. शास्तु	शिष्टाम्	शासतु	शिष्यात्	शिष्याताम्	शिष्युः

§ 438. शी A. 'to lie down' guṇates its vowel before all terminations and prefixes र् to the termination of the third pers. pl. except that of the Potential.

Present.			*Imperfect.*		
1. शये	शेवहे	शेमहे	अशयि	अशेवहि	अशेमहि
2. शेषे	शयाथे	शेध्वे	अशेथाः	अशयाथाम्	अशेध्वम्
3. शेते	शयाते	शेरते	अशेत	अशयाताम्	अशेरत

Imperative.			*Potential.*		
1. शयै	शयावहै	शयामहै	शयीय	शयीवहि	शयीमहि
2. शेष्व	शयाथाम्	शेध्वम्	शयीथाः	शयीयाथाम्	शयीध्वम्
3. शेताम्	शयाताम्	शेरताम्	शयीत	शयीयाताम्	शयीरन्

§ 439. सू A. 'to give birth to'—does not change its vowel to Guṇa before strong terminations.

Present.			*Imperfect.*		
1. सुवे	सूवहे	सूमहे	असुवि	असूवहि	असूमहि
2. सूषे	सुवाथे	सूध्वे	असूथाः	असुवाथाम्	असूध्वम्
3. सूते	सुवाते	सुवते	असूत	असुवाताम्	असुवत

Imperative.			*Potential.*		
1. सुवै	सुवावहै	सुवामहै	सुवीय	सुवीवहि	सुवीमहि
2. सूष्व	सुवाथाम्	सूध्वम्	सुवीथाः	सुवीयाथाम्	सुवीध्वम्
3. सूताम्	सुवाताम्	सुवताम्	सुवीत	सुवीयाताम्	सुवीरन्

§ 440. स्तु P. A. 'to praise,' तु P. 'to grow' and रु 'to sound' have ई optionally prefixed to the consonantal terminations.

स्तु P. Â.

Present.

	Par.			Âtm.	
1. स्तौमि	स्तुवः	स्तुमः	स्तुवे	स्तुवहे	स्तुमहे
स्तवीमि	स्तुवीवः	स्तुवीमः		स्तुवीवहे	स्तुवीमहे
2. स्तौषि	स्तुथः	स्तुथ	स्तुषे	स्तुवाथे	स्तुध्वे
स्तवीषि	स्तुवीथः	स्तुवीथ	स्तुवीषे		स्तुवीध्वे
3. स्तौति	स्तुतः		स्तुते	स्तुवाते	स्तुवते
स्तवीति	स्तुवीतः	स्तुवन्ति	स्तुवीते		

Imperfect.

1. अस्तवम्	अस्तुव	अस्तुम	अस्तुवि	अस्तुवहि	अस्तुमहि
	अस्तुवीव	अस्तुवीम		अस्तुवीवहि	अस्तुवीमहि
2. अस्तौः	अस्तुतम्	अस्तुत	अस्तुथाः	अस्तुवाथाम्	अस्तुध्वम्
अस्तवीः	अस्तुवीतम्	अस्तुवीत	अस्तुवीथाः		अस्तुवीध्वम्
3. अस्तौत्	अस्तुताम्	अस्तुवन्	अस्तुत	अस्तुवाताम्	अस्तुवत
अस्तवीत	अस्तुवीताम्		अस्तुवीत		

Imperative.

1. स्तवानि	स्तवाव	स्तवाम	स्तवै	स्तवावहै	स्तवामहै
2. स्तुहि	स्तुतम्	स्तुत	स्तुष्व	स्तुवाथाम्	स्तुध्वम्
स्तुवीहि	स्तुवीतम्	स्तुवीत	स्तुवीष्व		स्तुवीध्वम्
3. स्तौतु	स्तुताम्	स्तुवन्तु	स्तुताम्	स्तुवाताम्	स्तुवताम्
स्तवीतु	स्तुवीताम्		स्तुवीताम्		

Potential.

1. स्तुयाम्	स्तुयाव	स्तुयाम	स्तुवीय	स्तुवीवहि	स्तुवीमहि
स्तुवीयाम	स्तुवीयाव	स्तवीयाम			

2. स्तुयाः	स्तुयातम्	स्तुयात	स्तुवीथाः	स्तवीयाथाम्	स्तुवीध्वम्
स्तुव	स्तुवीयातम्	स्तुवीयात			
3. स्तुयात्	स्तुयाताम्	स्तुयुः	स्तुवीत	स्तुवीयाताम्	स्तुवीरन्
स्तुवीयात्	स्तुवीयाताम्	स्तुवीयुः			

Conjugate similarly तु and रु.

§ 441. हन् P. A. 'to kill'—drops its न् before a weak termination, beginning with any consonant except a nasal or a semi-vowel, and its अ before a vowel termination, the ह् then changing to घ्. The Imp. 2 sing. is जहि.

हन् P. 'to kill, to go

Present.			*Imperfect.*		
1. हन्मि	हन्वः	हन्मः	अहनम्	अहन्व	अहन्म
2. हंसि	हथः	हथ	अहन्	अहतम्	अहत
3. हन्ति	हतः	घ्नन्ति	अहन्	अहताम्	अघ्नन्

Imperative.			*Potential.*		
1. हनानि	हनाव	हनाम	हन्याम्	हन्याव	हन्याम
2. जहि	हतम्	हत	हन्याः	हन्यातम्	हन्यात
3. हन्तु	हताम्	घ्नन्तु	हन्यात्	हन्याताम्	हन्युः

हन् * Âtm.

Present.			*Imperfect.*		
1. घ्ने	हन्वहे	हन्महे	अघ्नि	अहन्वहि	अहन्महि
2. हसे	घ्नाथे	हध्वे	अहथाः	अघ्नाथाम्	अहध्वम्
3. हते	घ्नाते	घ्नते	अहत	अघ्नाताम्	अघ्नत

* This root is used in the A. in certain cases

Imperative.			*Potential.*		
1. घ्नै	घ्नावहै	घ्नामहै	घ्नीय	घ्नीवहि	घ्नीमहि
2. घ्नस्व	घ्नाथाम्	घ्नध्वम्	घ्नीथाः	घ्नीयाथाम्	घ्नीध्वम्
3. घ्नताम्	घ्नाताम्	घ्नताम्	घ्नीत	घ्नीयाताम्	घ्नीरन्

§ 442 ह्नु A. 'to take away'

Present.			*Imperfect.*		
1. ह्नुवे	ह्नुवहे	ह्नुमहे	अह्नुवि	अह्नुवहि	अह्नुमहि
2. ह्नुषे	ह्नुवाथे	ह्नुध्वे	अह्नुथाः	अह्नुवाथाम्	अह्नुध्वम्
3. ह्नुते	ह्नुवाते	ह्नुवते	अह्नुत	अह्नुवाताम्	अह्नुवत

Imperative.			*Potential.*		
1. ह्नवै	ह्नवावहै	ह्नवामहै	ह्नुवीय	ह्नुवीवहि	ह्नुवीमहि
2. ह्नुष्व	ह्नुवाथाम्	ह्नुध्वम्	ह्नुवीथाः	ह्नुवीयाथाम्	ह्नुवीध्वम्
3. ह्नुताम्	ह्नुवाताम्	ह्नुवताम्	ह्नुवीत	ह्नुवीयाताम्	ह्नुवीरन्

THIRD OR जुहोत्यादि CLASS.

§ 443. (*a*) The base is formed by reduplication of the root.

(*b*) The third personal plural termination loses its न्.

(*c*) The Imperfect third person plural termination is उस् (P.), before which the final आ of roots is dropped and the final इ, उ and ऋ, short or long, are guṇated.

Rules of Reduplication:—

§ 444. The first vowel of a root together with the initial consonant, if any, is reduplicated *i. e.* doubled; as पत्=पपत्, उस—उउस्, &c. after reduplication.

Note—The first syllable of a reduplicated root is called 'the reduplicative syllable; *e.g.* the first प in पपत्, or first उ in उवख्.

§ 445. If a conjunct consonant begins a root, the first consonant only with the following vowel is reduplicated; *e.g.* प्रच्छ्-पप्रच्छ्.

(*a*) If the first member of a conjunct consonant, however, be a sibilant (श्, ष् or स्) and the second a hard consonant, the hard consonant is reduplicated: स्पर्ध्-पस्पर्ध्, श्च्युत-चुश्च्युत्; but स्वन्-सस्वन् &c.

§ 446. A radical aspirate (2nd or 4th letter of a class) is changed to its corresponding unaspirate in the reduplicative syllable; as छिद्-चिच्छिद्, धु-दुधु, भुज्-बुभुज्, &c.

§ 447. The guttural of the reduplicative syllable is changed to the corresponding palatal (subject to the above rule) and ह् to ज्; *e. g.* कम्-ककम्-चकम्, खन्-खखन्-कखन्=चखन्, हु-जुहु &c.

§ 448. A radical long vowel becomes short and ऋ is changed to अ in the reduplicative syllable; as धा-दधा, नी-निनी, कृ-चकृ &c.

§ 449. The penultimate ए or ऐ and ओ or औ become इ and उ respectively in the reduplicative syllable; सेव्-सिषेव्, ढौक्—डुढौक्, &c.

Paradigms.

कि P. 'to know.'

	Present.			*Imperfect.*		
1.	चिकेमि	चिकिवः	चिकिमः	अचिकयम्	अचिकिव	अचिकिम
2.	चिकेषि	चिकिथः	चिकिथ	अचिकेः	अचिकितम्	अचिकित
3.	चिकेति	चिकितः	चिक्यति	अचिकेत्	अचिकिताम्	अचिकयुः

	Imperative.			*Potential.*	
1. चिकयानि	चिकयाव	चिकयाम	चिकियाम्	चिकियाव	चिकियाम
2. चिकिहि	चिकितम्	चिकित	चिकियाः	चिकियातम्	चिकियात
3. चिकेतु	चिकिताम्	चिक्यतु	चिकियात्	चिकियाताम्	चिकियुः

हु P. 'to sacrifice.

	Present.			*Imperfect.*	
1. जुहोमि	जुहुवः	जुहुमः	अजुहवम	अजुहुव	अजुहुम
2. जुहोषि	जुहुथः	जुहुथ	अजुहोः	अजुहुतम्	अजुहुत
3. जुहोति	जुहुतः	जुह्वति	अजुहोत्	अजुहुताम्	अजुहवुः

	Imperative.			*Potential.*	
1. जुहवानि	जुहवाव	जुहवाम	जुहुयाम्	जुहुयाव	जुहुयाम
2. जुहुधि	जुहुतम	जुहुत	जुहुयाः	जुहुयातम्	जुहुयात
3. जुहोतु	जुहुताम्	जुह्वतु	जुहुयात्	जुहुयाताम्	जुहुयुः

ह्री P. 'to be ashamed.'

	Present			*Imperfect.*	
1. जिह्रेमि	जिह्रीवः	जिह्रीमः	अजिह्रयम्	अजिह्रीव	अजिह्रीम
2. जिह्रेषि	जिह्रीथः	जिह्रीत	अजिह्रेः	अजिह्रीतम्	अजिह्रीत
3. जिह्रेति	जिह्रीतः	जिह्रियति	अजिह्रेत्	अजिह्रीताम्	अजिह्रयुः

	Imperative.			*Potential.*	
1. जिह्रयाणि	जिह्रयाव	जिह्रयाम	जिह्रीयाम्	जिह्रीयाव	जिह्रीयाम
2. जिह्रीहि	जिह्रीतम्	जिह्रीत	जिह्रीयाः	जिह्रीयातम्	जिह्रीयात
3. जिह्रेतु	जिह्रीताम्	जिह्रियतु	जिह्रीयात्	जिह्रीयाताम्	जिह्रीयुः

IRREGULAR BASES:—

§ 450 The vowel of the roots मा, हा 'to go' भृ, पृ or पॄ 'to fill' and ऋ is changed to इ in the reduplicative syllable.

§ 451. The इ of the reduplicative syllable of निज्, विज् and

विष्, takes its Guna substitute before all terminations and the radical इ is not guṇated before vowel strong terminations.

§ 452. दा and धा drop their आ after reduplication before weak terminations; दध् becomes धत् before स्, थ्व, त and थ. The Par. Imperative 2 per. singulars are देहि and धेहि respectively.

§ 453. भी optionally shortens its vowel before consonantal weak terminations.

(*a*) मा and हा 'to go' assume the forms मिम् and जिह् before vowel terminations and मिमी and जिही before consonantal terminations.

§ 454. हा 'to abandon' assumes the forms जहि or जही before consonantal weak terminations except in the Pot. and जह् before vowel terminations and those of the Pot. The Imp. 2 sing. forms are जहाहि, जहिहि and जहीहि.

Paradigms.

ऋ Par. 'to go.'

Present.			*Imperfect.*		
1. इयर्मि	इयृवः	इयृमः	ऐयरम्	ऐयृव	ऐयृम
2. इयर्षि	इयृथः	इयृथ	ऐयः	ऐयृतम्	ऐयृत
3. इयर्ति	इयृतः	इयृति	ऐयः	ऐयृताम्	ऐयरु.

Imperative.			*Potential.*		
1. इयराणि	इयराव	इयराम	इयृयाम्	इयृयाव	इयृयाम
2. इयृहि	इयृतम्	इयृत	इयृयाः	इयृयातम्	इयृयात
3. इयर्तु	इयृताम्	इयृतु	इयृयात्	इयृयाताम	इयृयुः

धा P. Â. 'to place, to hold.'

Present.

1. दधामि	दध्वः	दध्मः	दधे	दध्वहे	दध्महे

2. दधासि	धत्थः	धत्थ	धत्से	दधाथे	धद्ध्वे
3. दधाति	धत्तः	दधति	धत्ते	दधाते	दधते

Imperfect.

1. अदधाम्	अदध्व	अदध्म	अदधि	अदध्वहि	अदध्महि
2. अदधाः	अधत्तम्	अधत्त	अधत्थाः	अदधाथाम्	अधद्ध्वम्
3. अदधात्	अधत्ताम्	अदधुः	अधत्त	अदधाताम्	अदधत

Imperative.

1. दधानि	दधाव	दधाम	दधै	दधावहै	दधामहै
2. धेहि	धत्तम्	धत्त	धत्स्व	दधाथाम्	धद्ध्वम्
3. दधातु	धत्ताम्	दधतु	धत्ताम्	दधाताम्	दधताम्

Potential.

1. दध्याम्	दध्याव	दध्याम	दधीय	दधीवहि	दधीमहि
2. दध्याः	दध्यातम्	दध्यात	दधीथाः	दधीयाथाम्	दधीध्वम्
3. दध्यात्	दध्याताम्	दध्युः	दधीत	दधीयाताम्	दधीरन्

दा is similarly conjugated. The forms of दा will be obtained by changing ध् to द् wherever it occurs.

निज् P. A. 'to cleanse.'

Present.

1. नेनेज्मि	नेनिज्वः	नेनिज्मः	नेनिजे	नेनिज्वहे	नेनिज्महे
2. नेनेक्षि	नेनिक्थः	नेनिक्थ	नेनिक्षे	नेनिजाथे	नेनिग्ध्वे
3. नेनेक्ति	नेनिक्तः	नेनिजति	नेनिक्ते	नेनिजाते	नेनिजते

Imperfect.

1. अनेनिजम्	अनेनिज्व	अनेनिज्म	अनेनिजि	अनेनिज्वहि	अनेनिज्महि
2. अनेनेक्-ग्	अनेनिक्तम्	अनेनिक्त	अनेनिक्थाः	अनेनिजाथाम्	अनेनिग्ध्वम्
3. अनेनेक्-ग्	अनेनिक्ताम्	अनेनिजुः	अनेनिक्त	अनेनिजाताम्	अनेनिजत

Imperative.

1.	नेनिजानि	नेनिजाव	नेनिजाम	नेनिजै	नेनिजावहै	नेनिजामहै
2.	नेनिग्धि	नेनिक्तम्	नेनिक्त	नेनिक्ष्व	नेनिजाथाम्	नेनिग्ध्वम्
3.	नेनेक्तु	नेनिक्ताम्	नेनिजतु	नेनिक्ताम्	नेनिजाताम्	नेनिजताम्

Potential.

1.	नेनिज्याम्	नेनिज्याव	नेनिज्याम	नेनिजीय	नेनिजीवहि	नेनिजीमहि
2.	नेनिज्याः	नेनिज्यातम्	नेनिज्यात	नेनिजीथाः	नेनिजीयाथाम्	नेनिजीध्वम्
3.	नेनिज्यात्	नेनिज्याताम्	नेनिज्युः	नेनिजीत	नेनिजीयाताम्	नेनिजीरन्

Conjugate विज् P. A. similarly.

पृ P. 'to fill, to protect.'

	Present.			*Imperfect.*		
1.	पिपर्मि	पिपृवः	पिपृमः	अपिपरम्	अपिपृव	अपिपृम
2.	पिपर्षि	पिपृथः	पिपृथ	अपिपः	अपिपृतम्	अपिपृत
3.	पिपर्ति	पिपृतः	पिप्रति	अपिपः	अपिपृताम्	अपिपरुः

	Imperative.			*Potential.*		
1.	पिपराणि	पिपराव	पिपराम	पिपृयाम्	पिपृयाव	पिपृयाम
2.	पिपृहि	पिपृतम्	पिपृत	पिपृयाः	पिपृयातम्	पिपृयात
3.	पिपर्तु	पिपृताम्	पिप्रतु	पिपृयात्	पिपृयाताम्	पिपृयुः

पॄ P. 'to protect, to fill.'

	Present.			*Imperfect.*		
1.	पिपर्मि	*पिपूर्वः	पिपूर्मः	अपिपरम्	अपिपूर्व	अपिपूर्म
2.	पिपर्षि	पिपूर्थः	पिपूर्थ	अपिपः	अपिपूर्तम्	अपिपूर्त
3.	पिपर्ति	पिपूर्तः	पिपुरति	अपिपः	अपिपूर्ताम्	अपिपरुः

---

* See § 394.

Imperative.			*Potential.*		
1. पिपराणि	पिपराव	पिपराम	पिपूर्याम्	पिपूर्याव	पिपूर्याम
2. पिपूर्हि	पिपूर्तम्	पिपूर्त	पिपूर्याः	पिपूर्यातम्	पिपूर्यात
3. पिपर्तु	पिपूर्ताम्	पिपुरतु	पिपूर्यात्	पिपूर्याताम्	पिपूर्युः

भी P. ' to fear. '

Present.			*Imperfect.*		
1. बिभेमि	बिभीवः	बिभीमः	अबिभयम्	अबिभीव	अबिभीम
	बिभिवः	बिभिमः		अबिभिव	अबिभिम
2. बिभेषि	बिभीथः	बिभीथ	अबिभेः	अबिभीतम्	अबिभीत
	बिभिथः	बिभिथ		अबिभितम्	अबिभित
3 बिभेति	बिभीतः	बिभ्यति	अबिभेत्	अबिभीताम्	अबिभयुः
	बिभितः			अबिभिताम्	

Imperative.			*Potential.*		
1. बिभयानि	बिभयाव	बिभयाम	बिभीयाम्	बिभीयाव	बिभीयाम
			बिभियाम्	बिभियाव	बिभियाम
2. बिभीहि	बिभीतम्	बिभीत	बिभीयाः	बिभीयातम्	बिभीयात
बिभिहि	बिभितम्	बिभित	बिभियाः	बिभियातम्	बिभियात
3. बिभेतु	बिभीताम्	बिभ्यतु	बिभीयात्	बिभीयाताम्	बिभीयुः
	बिभिताम्		बिभियात्	बिभियाताम्	बिभियुः

भृ. P. Â. ' to hold; to maintain.

Present.

1. बिभर्मि	बिभृवः	बिभृमः	बिभ्रे	बिभृवहे	बिभृमहे
2. बिभर्षि	बिभृथः	बिभृथ	बिभृषे	बिभ्राथे	बिभृध्वे
3. बिभर्ति	बिभृतः	बिभ्रति	बिभृते	बिभ्राते	बिभ्रते

Imperfect.

1. अबिभरम्	अबिभृव	अबिभृम	अबिभ्रि	अबिभृवहि	अबिभृमहि

2.	अबिभः	अबिभृतम्	अबिभृत	अबिभृथाः	अबिभ्राथाम्	अबिभृध्वम्
3.	अबिभः	अबिभृताम्	अबिभरुः	अबिभृत	अबिभ्राताम्	अबिभ्रत

Imperative.

1.	बिभराणि	बिभराव	बिभराम	बिभरै	बिभरावहै	बिभरामहै
2.	बिभृहि	बिभृतम्	बिभृत	बिभृष्व	बिभ्राथाम्	बिभृध्वम्
3.	बिभर्तु	बिभृताम्	बिभ्रतु	बिभृताम्	बिभ्राताम्	बिभ्रताम्

Potential.

1.	बिभृयाम्	बिभृयाव	बिभृयाम	बिभ्रीय	बिभ्रीवहि	बिभ्रीमहि
2.	बिभृयाः	बिभृयातम्	बिभृयात	बिभ्रीथाः	बिभ्रीयाथाम्	बिभ्रीध्वम्
3.	बिभृयात्	बिभृयाताम्	बिभृयुः	बिभ्रीत	बिभ्रीयाताम्	बिभ्रीरन्

मा Â. 'to measure, to sound.'

	Present.			*Imperfect.*		
1.	मिमे	मिमीवहे	मिमीमहे	अमिमि	अमिमीवहि	अमिमीमहि
2.	मिमीषे	मिमाथे	मिमीध्वे	अमिमीथाः	अमिमाथाम्	अमिमीध्वम्
3.	मिमीते	मिमाते	मिमते	अमिमीत	अमिमाताम्	अमिमत

	Imperative.			*Potential.*		
1.	मिमै	मिमावहै	मिमामहै	मिमीय	मिमीवहि	मिमीमहि
2.	मिमीष्व	मिमाथाम्	मिमीध्वम्	मिमीथाः	मिमीयाथाम्	मिमीध्वम्
3.	मिमीताम्	मिमाताम्	मिमताम्	मिमीत	मिमीयाताम्	मिमीरन्

विष् P. Â. 'to pervade.'

Present.

1.	वेवेष्मि	वेविष्वः	वेविष्मः	वेविषे	वेविष्वहे	वेविष्महे
2.	वेवेक्षि	वेविष्ठः	वेविष्ठ	वेविक्षे	वेविषाथे	वेविड्ढे
3.	वेवेष्टि	वेविष्टः	वेविषति	वेविष्टे	वेविषाते	वेविषते

Imperfect.

1. अवेविषम्	अवेविष्व	अवेविष्म	अवेविषि	अवेविष्वहि	अवेविष्महि
2. अवेवेट्-ड्	अवेविष्टम्	अवेविष्ट	अवेविष्ठाः	अवेविषाथाम्	अवेविड्ढ्वम्
3. अवेवेट्-ड्	अवेविष्टाम्	अवेविषुः	अवेविष्ट	अवेविषाताम्	अवेविषत

Imperative.

1. वेविषाणि	वेविषाव	वेविषाम	वेविषै	वेविषावहै	वेविषामहै
2. वेविड्ढि	वेविष्टम्	वेविष्ट	वेविक्ष्व	वेविषाथाम्	वेविड्ढ्वम्
3. वेवेष्टु	वेविष्टाम्	वेविषतु	वेविष्टाम्	वेविषाताम्	वेविषताम्

Potential.

1. वेविष्याम्	वेविष्याव	वेविष्याम	वेविषीय	वेविषीवहि	वेविषीमहि
2. वेविष्याः	वेविष्यातम्	वेविष्यात	वेविषीथाः	वेविषीयाथाम्	वेविषीध्वम्
3. वेविष्यात्	वेविष्याताम्	वेविष्युः	वेविषीत	वेविषीयाताम्	वेविषीरन्

हा P. 'to abandon'

Present.			*Imperfect.*		
1. जहामि	जहीवः जहिवः	जहीमः जहिमः	अजहाम्	अजहीव अजहिव	अजहीम अजहिम
2. जहासि	जहीथः जहिथः	जहीथ जहिथ	अजहाः	अजहीतम् अजहितम्	अजहीत अजहित
3. जहाति	जहीतः जहितः	जहति	अजहात्	अजहीताम् अजहिताम्	अजहुः

Imperative.			*Potential.*		
1. जहानि	जहाव	जहाम	जह्याम्	जह्याव	जह्याम
2. जहाहि जहीहि जहिहि	जहीतम् जहितम्	जहीत जहित	जह्याः	जह्यातम्	जह्यात
3. जहातु	जहीताम् जहिताम्	जहतु	जह्यात्	जह्याताम्	जह्युः

Seventh or रुधादि Class.

§ 455. In this class the base is formed by inserting न between the radical vowel and the final consonant before the strong and न् before the weak terminations.

§ 456. (*a*) The original nasal of a root is dropped.

(*b*) In the case of the root तृह्, न is changed to ने before consonantal strong terminations.

Paradigms.

अञ्ज् P. 'to anoint,' &c.

	Present.			*Imperfect.*	
1. अनज्मि	अञ्ज्वः	अञ्ज्मः	आनजम्	आञ्ज्व	आञ्ज्म
2. अनक्षि	अङ्क्थः	अङ्क्थ	आनक्-ग्	आङ्क्तम्	आङ्क्त
3. अनक्ति	अङ्क्तः	अञ्जन्ति	आनक्-ग्	आङ्क्ताम्	आञ्जन्

	Imperative.			*Potential.*	
1. अनजानि	अनजाव	अनजाम	अञ्ज्याम्	अञ्ज्याव	अञ्ज्याम
2. अङ्ग्धि	अङ्क्तम्	अङ्क्त	अञ्ज्याः	अञ्ज्यातम्	अञ्ज्यात
3. अनक्तु	अङ्क्ताम्	अञ्जन्तु	अञ्ज्यात्	अञ्ज्याताम्	अञ्ज्युः

इन्ध् Â. 'to anoint,' &c.

	Present.			*Imperfect.*	
1. इन्धे	इन्ध्वहे	इन्ध्महे	ऐन्धि	ऐन्ध्वहि	ऐन्ध्महि
2. इन्त्से	इन्धाथे	इन्द्ध्वे	ऐन्द्धाः	ऐन्धाथाम्	ऐन्द्ध्वम्
3. इन्द्धे*	इन्धाते	इन्धते	ऐन्द्ध	ऐन्धाताम्	ऐन्धत

	Imperative.			*Potential.*	
1. इनधै	इनधावहै	इनधामहै	इन्धीय	इन्धीवहि	इन्धीमहि
2. इन्त्स्व	इन्धाताम्	इन्द्ध्वम्	इन्धीथाः	इन्धीयाथाम्	इन्धीध्वम्
3. इन्द्धाम्	इन्धाताम्	इन्धताम्	इन्धीत	इन्धीयाताम्	इन्धीरन्

* Also इन्धे, ऐन्धाः, ऐन्ध्वम्, इन्ध्वम्, इन्धाम्, &c. See § 20 (*a*)

क्षुद् P. Â. ' to pound. '

Present.

1. क्षुणद्मि	क्षुन्द्वः	क्षुन्द्मः	क्षुन्दे	क्षुन्द्वहे	क्षुन्द्महे
2. क्षुणत्सि	क्षुन्त्थः	क्षुन्त्थ	क्षुन्त्से	क्षुन्दाथे	क्षुन्द्धे
3. क्षुणत्ति	क्षुन्त्तः	क्षुन्दन्ति	क्षुन्त्ते	क्षुन्दाते	क्षुन्दते

Imperfect.

1. अक्षुणदम्	अक्षुन्द्व	अक्षुन्द्म	अक्षुन्दि	अक्षुन्द्वहि	अक्षुन्द्महि
2. अक्षुणः अक्षुणत्-द्	अक्षुन्त्तम्	अक्षुन्त्त	अक्षुन्त्थाः	अक्षुन्दाथाम्	अक्षुन्द्ध्वम्
3. अक्षुणत्-द्	अक्षुन्त्ताम्	अक्षुन्दन्	अक्षुन्त्त	अक्षुन्दाताम्	अक्षुन्दत

Imperative.

1. क्षुणदानि	क्षुणदाव	क्षुणदाम	क्षुणदै	क्षुणदावहै	क्षुणदामहै
2. क्षुन्द्धि	क्षुन्त्तम्	क्षुन्त्त	क्षुन्त्स्व	क्षुन्दाथाम्	क्षुन्द्ध्वम्
3. क्षुणत्तु	क्षुन्त्ताम्	क्षुन्दन्तु	क्षुन्त्ताम्	क्षुन्दाताम	क्षुन्दताम्

Potential.

1. क्षुन्द्याम्	क्षुन्द्याव	क्षुन्द्याम	क्षुन्दीय	क्षुन्दीवहि	क्षुन्दीमहि
2. क्षुन्द्याः	क्षुन्द्यातम्	क्षुन्द्यात	क्षुन्दीथाः	क्षुन्दीयाथाम्	क्षुन्दीध्वम्
3. क्षुन्द्यात्	क्षुन्द्याताम्	क्षुन्द्युः	क्षुन्दीत	क्षुन्दीयाताम्	क्षुन्दीरन्

भिद् P. A. to break, उन्द् P. to be wet, खिद् A. to suffer pain, छिद् P. A. to cut, छृद् P. A. to shine, to play; कृत P, to spin, to surround; तृद् P. A. to kill, to disregard; and विद् P. A. to know, to consider, should be similarly conjugated. उनत्ति 3rd. sing. Pre. of उन्द्; कृणत्ति 3 sing. Pre. of कृत, &c.

तृह् P. ' to kill. '

Present. *Imperfect.*

1. तृणेह्मि	तृंह्वः	तृंह्मः	अतृणहम्	अतृंह्व	अतृंह्म

2. तृणेक्षि	तृण्ढः	तृण्ढ	अतृणेट्-ड्	अतृण्ढम्	अतृण्ढ
3. तृणेढि	तृण्ढः	तृंहन्ति	अतृणेट्-ड्	अतृण्ढाम्	अतृंहन्

Imperative. *Potential.*

1. तृणहानि	तृणहाव	तृणहाम	तृंह्याम्	तृंह्याव	तृंह्याम
2. तृण्ढि	तृण्ढम्	तृण्ढ	तृंह्याः	तृंह्यातम्	तृंह्यात
3. तृणेढु	तृण्ढाम्	तृंहन्तु	तृंह्यात्	तृंह्याताम्	तृंह्युः

पिष् P. ' to grind. '

Present. *Imperfect.*

1. पिनष्मि	पिंष्वः	पिंष्मः	अपिनषम्	अपिंष्व	अपिंष्म
2. पिनक्षि	पिंष्ठः	पिंष्ठ	अपिनट्-ड्	अपिंष्टम्	अपिंष्ट
3. पिनष्टि	पिंष्टः	पिंषन्ति	अपिनट्-ड्	अपिंष्टाम्	अपिंषन्

Imperative. *Potential.*

1. पिनषाणि	पिनषाव	पिनषाम	पिंष्याम्	पिंष्याव	पिंष्याम
2. पिण्ड्ढि	पिंष्टम्	पिंष्ट	पिंष्याः	पिंष्यातम्	पिंष्यात
3. पिनष्टु	पिंष्टाम्	पिंषन्तु	पिंष्यात्	पिंष्याताम्	पिंष्युः

शिष् ' to distinguish ' should be similarly conjugated.

युज्. P. Â. ' to join.

Present.

1. युनज्मि	युञ्ज्वः	युञ्ज्मः	युञ्जे	युञ्ज्वहे	युञ्ज्महे
2. युनक्षि	युङ्क्थः	युङ्क्थ	युङ्क्षे	युञ्जाथे	युङ्ग्ध्वे
3. युनक्ति	युङ्क्तः	युञ्जन्ति	युङ्क्ते	युञ्जाते	युञ्जते

Imperfect.

1 अयुनजम्	अयुञ्ज्व	अयुञ्ज्म	अयुञ्जि	अयुञ्ज्वहि	अयुञ्ज्महि
2 अयुनक्-ग्	अयुङ्क्तम्	अयुङ्क्त	अयुङ्क्थाः	अयुञ्जाथाम्	अयुङ्ग्ध्वम्
3 अयुनक्-ग्	अयुङ्क्ताम्	अयुञ्जन्	अयुङ्क्त	अयुञ्जाताम्	अयुञ्जत

Imperative.

1. युनजानि	युनजाव	युनजाम	युनजै	युनजावहै	युनजामहै
2. युङ्धि	युङ्क्तम्	युङ्क्त	युङ्क्ष्व	युञ्जाथाम्	युङ्ग्ध्वम्
3. युनक्तु	युङ्क्ताम्	युञ्जन्तु	युङ्क्ताम्	युञ्जाताम्	युञ्जताम्

Potential.

1. युञ्ज्याम्	युञ्ज्याव	युञ्ज्याम	युञ्जीय	युञ्जीवहि	युञ्जीमहि
2. युञ्ज्याः	युञ्ज्यातम्	युञ्ज्यात	युञ्जीथाः	युञ्जीयाथाम्	युञ्जीध्वम्
3. युञ्ज्यात्	युञ्ज्याताम्	युञ्ज्युः	युञ्जीत	युञ्जीयाताम्	युञ्जीरन्

Conjugate similarly भञ्ज् P. 'to break,' भुज् P. 'to enjoy,' A. 'to eat,' विज् P. 'to shake, to ramble,' and वृज् P. 'to avoid.'

रिच् P. Â. 'to evacuate.'

Present.

1. रिणच्मि	रिंच्वः	रिंच्मः	रिंचे	रिंच्वहे	रिंच्महे
2. रिणक्षि	रिंक्थः	रिंक्थ	रिंक्षे	रिंचाथे	रिंग्ध्वे
3. रिणक्ति	रिंक्तः	रिंचन्ति	रिंक्ते	रिंचाते	रिंचते

Imperfect.

1. अरिणचम्	अरिंच्व	अरिंच्म	अरिंचि	अरिंच्वहि	अरिंच्महि
2. अरिणक्-ग्	अरिंक्तम्	अरिंक्त	अरिंक्थाः	अरिंचाथाम्	अरिंग्ध्वम्
3. अरिणक्-ग्	अरिंक्ताम्	अरिंचन्	अरिंक्त	अरिंचाताम्	अरिंचत

Imperative.

1. रिणचानि	रिणचाव	रिणचाम	रिणचै	रिणचावहै	रिणचामहै
2. रिंग्धि	रिंक्तम्	रिंक्त	रिंक्ष्व	रिंचाथाम्	रिंग्ध्वम्
3. रिणक्तु	रिंक्ताम्	रिंचन्तु	रिंक्ताम्	रिंचाताम्	रिंचताम्

Potential.

1. रिंच्याम्	रिंच्याव	रिंच्याम	रिंचीय	रिंचीवहि	रिंचीमहि

2. रिच्याः	रिंच्यातम्	रिंच्यात	रिंचीथाः	रिंचीयाथाम्	रिंचीध्वम्
3. रिंच्यात्	रिंच्याताम्	रिंच्युः	रिंचीत	रिंचीयाताम्	रिंचीरन्

Conjugate similarly विच् P. A. 'to separate,' तञ्च् P. 'to contract' and पृच 'to touch.'

रुध् P. Â. 'to obstruct.'

Present.

1. रुणध्मि	रुन्ध्वः	रुन्ध्मः	रुन्धे	रुन्ध्वहे	रुन्ध्महे
2. रुणत्सि	रुन्द्धः*	रुन्द्ध	रुन्त्से	रुन्धाथे	रुन्द्ध्वे
3. रुणद्धि	रुन्द्धः	रुन्धन्ति	रुन्द्धे	रुन्धाते	रुन्धते

Imperfect.

1. अरुणधम्	अरुन्ध्व	अरुन्ध्म	अरुन्धि	अरुन्ध्वहि	अरुन्ध्महि
2. अरुणत्-द् अरुणः	अरुन्द्धम्	अरुन्द्ध	अरुन्द्धाः	अरुन्धाथाम्	अरुन्द्ध्वम्
3. अरुणत्-द्	अरुन्द्धाम्	अरुन्धन्	अरुन्द्ध	अरुन्धाताम्	अरुन्धत

Imperative.

1. रुणधानि	रुणधाव	रुणधाम	रुणधै	रुणधावहै	रुणधामहै
2. रुन्द्धि	रुन्द्धम्	रुन्द्ध	रुन्त्स्व	रुन्धाथाम्	रुन्द्ध्वम्
3. रुणद्धु	रुन्द्धाम्	रुन्धन्तु	रुन्द्धाम्	रुन्धाताम्	रुन्द्धताम्

Potential.

1. रुन्ध्याम्	रुन्ध्याव	रुन्ध्याम	रुन्धीय	रुन्धीवहि	रुन्धीमहि
2. रुन्ध्याः	रुन्ध्यातम्	रुन्ध्यात	रुन्धीथाः	रुन्धीयाथाम्	रुन्धीध्वम्
3. रुन्ध्यात्	रुन्ध्याताम्	रुन्ध्युः	रुन्धीत	रुन्धीयाताम्	रुन्धीरन्

* Or रुन्धः &c.; see note * p. 290.

हिंस् P. 'to kill.'

	Present.			*Imperfect.*	
1. हिनस्मि	हिंस्वः	हिंस्मः	अहिनसम्	अहिंस्व	अहिंस्म
2. हिनस्सि	हिंस्थः	हिंस्थ	अहिनः-त-द्	अहिंस्तम्	अहिंस्त
3. हिनस्ति	हिंस्तः	हिंसन्ति	अहिनत्-द्	अहिंस्ताम्	अहिंसन्

	Imperative.			*Potential.*	
1. हिनसानि	हिनसाव	हिनसाम	हिंस्याम्	हिंस्याव	हिंस्याम
2. हिन्धि	हिंस्तम्	हिंस्त	हिंस्याः	हिंस्यातम्	हिंस्यात
3. हिनस्तु	हिंस्ताम्	हिंसन्तु	हिंस्यात्	हिंस्याताम्	हिंस्युः

II. GENERAL
OR
NON-CONJUGATIONAL TENSES AND MOODS.

§ 457. In the General Tenses and Moods and in the formation of verbal derivatives generally, the augment इ is prefixed (necessarily or optionally) to terminations beginning with any consonant except य in the case of certain roots. Such roots as take the augment इ necessarily are called *Set* (स+इट् i. e. with इ); such as take it optionally are called Wet (वा+इट्), and those that do not, are called Anit (अन्+इट् i. e. without इ).

§ 458. (a) Roots of more than one syllable, derived roots and roots of the 10th class are always *Set*.

(b) Of all monosyllabic roots ending in a vowel those given in the following couplet (Kârikâ) are Set and the rest Anit.

"ऊदॄदन्तैर्यौतिरुक्ष्णुशीस्नुनुक्षुश्विडीङ्श्रिभिः ।
वृङ्वृञ्भ्यां च विनैकाचोऽजन्तेषु निहताः स्मृताः ॥

i. e. roots ending in long ऊ and long ॠ, the roots यु, रु, क्ष्णु,

शी, स्नु, नु, क्षु, श्वि, डी, श्रि, वृ IX. cl. A. and वृ V. cl. P. A. are Set (excepting these, all monosyllabic roots ending in a vowel are Anit).

(c) Of monosyllabic roots ending in a consonant the following 102 are *Anit*; and the remaining *Set*.

* शक्ल पच् मुचि रिच् वच् विच् । सिच् प्रच्छि त्यज् निजिर्भजः ।
मज्ज् भुज् भ्रस्ज् मस्जि यज् युज् रुज् । रञ्ज् विजिर् स्वञ्जिसञ्ज्सृजः ॥

अद् क्षुद् खिद् छिद् तुदि नुदः । पद्य भिद् विद्यतिर्विनद् ।
शद्सदी स्विद्यतिः स्कन्दि । हदी क्रुध् क्षुधिबुध्यती ॥

बन्धिर्युधिरुधी राधि । व्यध्शुधः साधिसिध्यती ।
मन्यहन्नाप् क्षिप् छुपि तप् । तिपस्तृप्यतिदृप्यती ॥

लिप् लुप् वप् शप् स्वप् सृपि यम् । रभ् लभ् गम् नम् यमो रमिः ।
क्रुशिर्दंशिदिशी दृश् मृश् । रिश् रुश् लिश् विश् स्पृशः कृषिः ॥

त्विष् तुष् द्विष् दुष् पुष्य पिष् विष् । शिष् शुष् श्लिष्यतयो घसिः ।
वसतिर्दहदिहिदुहो नह् मिह् रुह् लिह् वहिस्तथा ॥
अनुदात्ता हलन्तेषु धातवो द्व्यधिकं शतम् ॥

(d) The following roots are Wet:—

स्वरतिः सूयते सूते पञ्चमे नवमे च धुञ् ।
तनक्तिर्वृश्चतिश्चान्तावनक्तिश्च तनक्तिना ॥ १ ॥

---

* The following couplet gives the endings of these roots and their number in each:—

कचछजा दधनपा भमशाः षसहाः क्रमात् ।
केचंकोणेणोटीः खंडो गेधंञोष्टखंर्जाः स्मृताः ॥

The first line gives the ending consonants and thus enables the students to know at once which root is Set and which is Anit; *e. g.* कुट् may be at once known to be a set root as ट् does not occur in the first line. The second line gives the number of roots ending in a particular consonant. Thus roots ending in क् are क् *i. e.* one (क् being the first consonant) in number; roots ending in च् are च् *i. e.* 6, (च् being the 6th consonant); roots ending in छ् are क् *i. e.* one, in number; and so on.

मार्ष्टि मार्जति जान्तेषु दान्तौ क्लियाति स्यन्दति ।
रध्यतिः सेधतिर्धान्तौ पान्ताः पञ्चैव कल्पते ॥ २ ॥
गोपायतिस्तृप्यतिश्च त्रपते दृप्यतिस्तथा ।
मान्तौ क्षाम्यति क्षमतेऽश्नुते क्लिश्नाति नश्यति ॥ ३ ॥
शान्तास्त्रयोथाक्षतिश्च निष्कुष्णातिश्च तक्षति ।
त्वक्षतिश्च षकारान्ता अथ हान्ताश्च गाहते ॥ ४ ॥
पदद्वये गूहतिश्च ऋकारोपान्त्यगर्हते ।
तृहतितृंहतिर्द्रुह्यतयो बृहति मुह्यति ॥ ५ ॥
स्तुहति स्निह्यति स्नुहत्येते वेट्का हि धातवः ।
अजन्तानां तु थल्येव वेट् स्यादन्यत्र सर्वदा* ॥ ६ ॥

§ 459. Roots ending ए, ऐ, and ओ are to be treated as roots ending in आ. Also the roots मि 5. A. 'to throw', मी 9 P. A. 'to kill,' and दी 4. A. 'to perish,' before a termination causing Guṇa or Vṛddhi; ली 9 P. 4 A. 'to adhere or cling to' changes its vowel to आ optionally under the same circumstances.

§ 460. Roots of the tenth class preserve their अय् (i. e. अय with the final अ dropped) with all the changes that the root undergoes before it in the general tenses.

§ 461. The roots गुप्, धूप्, विच्छ्, पण्, पन्, कम्, and ऋत् preserve their conjugational bases optionally.

§ 462. अस् and ब्रू substitute for themselves भू and वच् respectively.

§ 463. Neither Guṇa nor Vṛddhi is substituted for the vowel of a few roots of the 6th class even before a strong termination except the अ of the 1st and 3rd person sing. of the Perfect, the अय of the causal and the इ of the 3rd pers. sing. of the Passive

* These couplets as well as those bearing on the 2nd variety of the Aorist are composed by Mr. Chintámana Âtmárám Kelker, the present learned S'astri at the Poona Training College.

Aorist. These are कुट्, पुट्, कुच्, गुज्, छुर्, स्फुट्, त्रुट्, लुट्, स्फुर्, गुर्, नू, धू, कृ, and a few more not often to be met with.

§ 464. The root भ्रस्ज् assumes the forms भज्ज् and भर्ज् in the Non-conjugational Tenses.

§ 465. The penultimate ऋ of सृज् and दृश् is changed to र before a consonantal strong termination in the General Tenses.

§ 466. The intermediate इ is weak in the case of the root विज् 6. A. 7 P.; and optionally so in the case of ऊर्णु.

§ 467. The roots दीधी 2 A. 'to shine' and वेवी 2 A. 'to go' do not take Guṇa or Vṛddhi before any termination. They also drop their final vowel before the intermediate इ and य्. दरिद्रा also drops its आ before a non-conjugational termination except in the Desiderative and the Aorist where it retains it optionally.

THE TWO FUTURES AND CONDITIONAL.

(1) *First Future* (लुट्)

Also called Periphrastic Future.

§ 468. Terminations:—

	Parasm.			Âtm.		
1.	तास्मि*	तास्वः	तास्मः	1. ताहे	तास्वहे	तास्महे
2.	तासि	तास्थः	तास्थ	2. तासे	तासाथे	ताध्वे
3.	ता	तारौ	तारः	3. ता	तारौ	तारः

§ 469. To these terminations the augment इ is prefixed in the

---

* The forms of the First Future may be derived by adding to the Nom. sing. of the noun of agency derived with the affix तृ the forms of the Present Tense of the root अस् 'to be' in the 1st and 2nd persons. The forms of the Nom. are the forms of the 3rd pers.

case of Set roots, optionally in the case of Wet roots, and not fixed at all in that of Anit roots.

§ 470. All these terminations are strong. The final vowel and the penultimate short of a root therefore take their Guṇa substitute before these.

§ 471. Anit roots with a penultimate ऋ change it to र optionally before a strong termination beginning with any consonant except a nasal or a semi-vowel; सृप्—सर्प्तास्मि, स्रप्तास्मि &c.

दा P. Â. 'to give &c.,'

1.	दातास्मि	दातास्वः	दातास्मः	1.	दाताहे	दातास्वहे	दातास्महे
2.	दातासि	दातास्थः	दातास्थ	2.	दातासे	दातासाथे	दाताध्वे
3.	दाता	दातारौ	दातारः	3.	दाता	दातारौ	दातारः

नी P. A. 'carry'—नेतास्मि, नेतास्वः, नेतास्मः &c., नेताहे, नेतास्वहे, नेतास्महे, &c.

पत् P.—पतितास्मि, पतितास्वः, पतितास्मः &c.
ईक्ष A.—ईक्षिताहे, ईक्षितास्वहे, ईक्षितास्महे &c.

IRREGULAR BASES.

§ 472. The roots इष्, सह् 1 A., लुभ्, रिष् and रुष् admit इ optionally in the First Future; e. g. 1 sing. एषितास्मि, एष्टास्मि, सहिताहे, सोढाहे; लोभितास्मि, लोब्धास्मि; रेषितास्मि, रेष्टास्मि; रोषितास्मि, रोष्टास्मि.

§ 473. क्लृप् is optionally Parasm. in the First Future and when so it rejects इः कल्पिताहे, कल्प्ताहे; कल्प्तास्मि 1 sing. &c.

§ 474. The augment इ as added to ग्रह् is long in all Non-conjugational Tenses, except in the Perfect; ग्रहीतास्मि 1 sing.

§ 475. The intermediate इ is optionally lengthened in the case of वृ and roots ending in ॠ, except in the Perfect, the

Benedictive Atm. and the Aorist Par.; वरितास्मि, वरीतास्मि, 1 sing. कृ–करितास्मि, करीतास्मि 1 sing.

§ 476. न् is inserted before the ending consonant of the root मस्ज् before which स् is dropped, and after the vowel of नश्, when they are followed by any consonant except a nasal or a semi-vowel; मङ्क्ता &c.; नंष्टा, नशिता. The स् of मस्ज् is changed to ज् when not dropped.

§ 477 वी is substituted for अज् 1 P. 'to go' necessarily before any non-conjugational termination, and optionally before such as begin with any consonant except य्; वेता, अजिता; वेष्यति, अजिष्यति &c.

(2) *Second Future* (लृट्) and (3) *Conditional* (लृङ्).

§ 478. Terminations of the Second Future:—

Parasm.			*Âtmane.*		
1. स्यामि*	स्यावः	स्यामः	1. स्ये	स्यावहे	स्यामहे
2. स्यसि	स्यथः	स्यथ	2. स्यसे	स्येथे	स्यध्वे
3. स्यति	स्यतः	स्यन्ति	3. स्यते	स्येते	स्यन्ते

§ 479. Terminations of the Conditional:—

1. स्यम्†	स्याव	स्याम	1. स्ये	स्यावहि	स्यामहि
2. स्यः	स्यतम्	स्यत	2. स्यथाः	स्येथाम्	स्यध्वम्
3. स्यत्	स्यताम्	स्यन्	3. स्यत	स्येताम्	स्यन्त

§ 480. त् is substituted for the ending स् of a root when followed by any non-conjugational termination beginning with स्.

---

* These terminations, it will be seen, are obtained by adding those of the Present to स्य with its अ lengthened before initial म and व, and dropped before a vowel.

† These are obtained similarly by adding the terminations of the Imperfect to स्य the usual rules of Sandhi being observed.

§ 481. इ is to be prefixed, or not, or optionally to the terminations given above, according as the root is Set or Anit or Wet. Before the terminations the final vowel and the penultimate short take their Guṇa substitute.

§ 482. In the Conditional the augment अ is prefixed to the root as in the Imperfect.

Paradigms.

Second Future

शक् 5 P.			लभ् P.1 Â.		
1. शक्ष्यामि	शक्ष्यावः	शक्ष्यामः	1. लप्स्ये	लप्स्यावहे	लप्स्यामहे
2. शक्ष्यसि	शक्ष्यथः	शक्ष्यथ	2. लप्स्यसे	लप्स्येथे	लप्स्यध्वे
3. शक्ष्यति	शक्ष्यतः	शक्ष्यन्ति	3. लप्स्यते	लप्स्येते	लप्स्यन्ते

Conditional.

1. अशक्ष्यम्	अशक्ष्याव	अशक्ष्याम	1. अलप्स्ये	अलेप्स्यावहि	अलप्स्यामहि
2. अशक्ष्यः	अशक्ष्यतम्	अशक्ष्यत	2. अलप्स्यथाः	अलप्स्येथाम्	अलप्स्यध्वम्
3. अशक्ष्यत्	अशक्ष्यताम्	अशक्ष्यन्	3. अलप्स्यत	अलप्स्येताम्	अलप्स्यन्त

ग्रह्--ग्रहीष्यामि-ष्ये; अग्रहीष्यम-ष्ये &c.

IRREGULAR BASES.

§ 483. गम् P. हन् and Anit roots ending in ऋ admit इ in the Second Future and the Conditional; गम् P. (also that substituted for इ 'to go' and with अधि 'to remember') also admits it in the Desiderative; गमिष्यामि, हनिष्यामि, करिष्यामि, &c. Sec. Fu. 1. sing. अगमिष्यम्, अकरिष्यम्, अहनिष्यम्, &c. Con. 1. sing.

§ 484. The roots कृप्, वृत्, वृध्, शृध् and स्यन्द् optionally take Parasmaipada terminations in the Second Future, Conditional and the Desiderative. They reject the augment इ when Parasmaipadi; कल्पिष्ये; कल्प्स्ये, कल्प्स्यामि; वर्तिष्ये, वर्त्स्यामि; वर्धिष्ये,

वर्त्स्यामि; शर्धिष्ये, शर्त्स्यामि; स्यन्दिष्ये, स्यन्त्स्ये, स्यन्त्स्यामि 1 sing. 2nd Fut.; अकल्पिष्ये, अकल्प्स्ये, अकल्प्स्यम्; अवर्तिष्ये, अवर्त्स्यम्; अवर्धिष्ये, अवर्त्स्यम्; अशर्धिष्ये, अशर्त्स्यम्, अस्यन्दिष्ये, अस्यन्त्स्ये, अस्यन्त्स्यम् 1. sing. Cond.

§ 485. The roots कृत्, चृत्, छृद्, तृद् and नृत् take इ optionally when followed by an *ârdhadhâtuka* (Non-conjugational termination) beginning with स् except in the Aorist; कृत्–कर्तिष्यामि, कर्त्स्यामि; अकर्तिष्यम्, अकर्त्स्यम् Cond. &c.

§ 486. In the case of इ with अधि, गा is optionally substituted for इ in the Conditional and the Aorist. ई is substituted for the final vowel of the verbs दा 3 P. A. 1 P. धा, दो, दे, धे, मा, स्था, गा (substituted for इ 2. P and इ with अधि,) पा, हा, and सो before a consonantal weak termination. All terminations added to गा substituted for इ are weak.

Paradigms.

1. अध्यैष्ये	अध्यैष्यावहि	अध्यैष्यामहि
2. अध्यैष्यथाः	अध्यैष्येथाम्	अध्यैष्यध्वम्
3. अध्यैष्यत	अध्यैष्येताम्	अध्यैष्यन्त
1. अध्यगीष्ये	अध्यगीष्यावहि	अध्यगीष्यामहि
2. अध्यगीष्यथाः	अध्यगीष्येथाम्	अध्यगीष्यद्ध्वम्
3. अध्यगीष्यत	अध्यगीष्येताम्	अध्यगीष्यन्त

§ 487. We give below the first pers. sing. of some of the roots of more difficult conjugation. The student should find out the various rules by which he should arrive at them.

Roots.	1st Future.	2nd Future.	Conditional.
भू	भवितास्मि	भविष्यामि	अभविष्यम्
स्तॄ	स्तरितास्मि	स्तरिष्यामि-ष्ये	अस्तरिष्यम्-ष्ये
	स्तरीतास्मि	स्तरीष्यामि-ष्ये	अस्तरीष्यम्-ष्ये

Roots.	First Future.	Sec. Future.	Conditional.
यु 2. P.	यवितास्मि	यविष्यामि	अयविष्यम्
शी	शयिताहे	शयिष्ये	अशयिष्ये
स्नु	स्नवितास्मि	स्नविष्यामि	अस्नविष्यम्
श्वि	श्वयितास्मि	श्वयिष्यामि	अश्वयिष्यम्
श्रि	श्रयितास्मि-हे	श्रयिष्यास्मि-ष्ये	अश्रयिष्यम्-ष्ये
पच्	पक्तास्मि	पक्ष्यामि	अपक्ष्यम्
मुच्	मोक्तास्मि	मोक्ष्यामि	अमोक्ष्यम्
सिच्	सेक्तास्मि	सेक्ष्यामि	असेक्ष्यम्
भञ्ज्	भंक्तास्मि	भङ्क्ष्यामि	अभङ्क्ष्यम्
भुज्	भोक्तास्मि	भोक्ष्यामि	अभोक्ष्यम्
भ्रस्ज्	भ्रष्टास्मि	भ्रक्ष्यामि	अभ्रक्ष्यम्
	भर्ष्टास्मि	भर्क्ष्यामि	अभर्क्ष्यम्
मस्ज्	मङ्क्तास्मि	मङ्क्ष्यामि	अमङ्क्ष्यम्
रञ्ज्	रङ्क्तास्मि	रङ्क्ष्यामि	अरङ्क्ष्यम्
सृज्	स्रष्टास्मि	स्रक्ष्यामि	अस्रक्ष्यम्
अद्	अत्तास्मि	अत्स्यामि	आत्स्यम्
पद्	पत्ताहे	पत्स्ये	अपत्स्ये
स्कन्द्	स्कन्तास्मि	स्कन्त्स्यामि	अस्कन्त्स्यम
बन्ध	बन्द्धास्मि	भन्त्स्यामि	अभन्त्स्यम्
व्यध्	व्यद्धास्मि	व्यत्स्यामि	अव्यत्स्यम्
मन्	मन्ताहे	मंस्ये	अमंस्ये
तृप्	तर्पितास्मि,	तर्पिष्यामि, तर्प्स्यामि,	अतर्पिष्यम्
	तर्प्तास्मि, त्रप्तास्मि	त्रप्स्यामि	अत्रप्स्यम्–अतर्प्स्यम्,
गम् with सम्	संगन्ताहे	संगंस्ये	समगंस्ये
दृश्	द्रष्टास्मि	द्रक्ष्यामि	अद्रक्ष्यम्
घस्	घस्तास्मि	घत्स्यामि	अघत्स्यम्

Roots	1st Future.	2nd Future.	Conditional.
वस् to dwell	वस्तामि	वत्स्यामि	अवत्स्यम्
दह्	दग्धास्मि	धक्ष्यामि	अधक्ष्यम्
नह्	नद्धास्मि	नत्स्यामि	अनत्स्यम्
वह्	वोढास्मि*	वक्ष्यामि	अवक्ष्यम्

Wet roots:—

अञ्ज्	अञ्जितास्मि	अञ्जिष्यामि	आञ्जिष्यम्
	अङ्क्तास्मि	अङ्क्ष्यामि	आङ्क्ष्यम्
अश्	अशिताहे	अशिष्ये	आशिष्ये
	अष्टाहे	अक्ष्ये	आक्ष्ये
क्लिद्	क्लेदितास्मि	क्लेदिष्यामि	अक्लेदिष्यम्
	क्लेत्तास्मि	क्लेत्स्यामि	अक्लेत्स्यम्
क्लिश्	क्लेशितास्मि	क्लेशिष्यामि	अक्लेशिष्यम्
	क्लेष्टास्मि	क्लेक्ष्यामि	अक्लेक्ष्यम्
क्षम्	क्षमिताहे	क्षमिष्ये	अक्षमिष्ये
	क्षन्ताहे	क्षंस्ये	अक्षंस्ये
गाह्	गाहिताहे	गाहिष्ये	अगाहिष्ये
	गाढाहे	घाक्ष्ये	अघाक्ष्ये
गुप्	गोपितास्मि	गोपिष्यामि	अगोपिष्यम्
	गोप्तास्मि	गोप्स्यामि	अगोप्स्यम्
	गोपायितास्मि	गोपायिष्यामि	अगोपायिष्यम्
गुह्	गूहितास्मि	गूहिष्यामि	अगूहिष्यम्
	गोढास्मि	घोक्ष्यामि	अघोक्ष्यम्
तक्ष्	तक्षितास्मि	तक्षिष्यामि	अतक्षिष्यम्
	तष्टास्मि	तक्ष्यामि	अतक्ष्यम्

* For the change of अ to ओ in this and in सोढाहे see ft.-note p. 317.

Roots	1st Future	2nd Future	Conditional.
त्रप्	त्रपिताहे, त्रप्ताहे	त्रपिष्ये, त्रप्स्ये	अत्रपिष्ये, अत्रप्स्ये
धू	धविताास्मि, धोतास्मि	धविष्यामि, धोष्यामि	अधविष्यम्, अधोष्यम्
तृह्	तर्हितास्मि, तर्ढास्मि	तर्हिष्यामि, तर्क्ष्यामि	अतर्हिष्यम्, अतर्क्ष्यम्
मुह्	मोहितास्मि, मोढा-ग्धा-स्मि	मोहिष्यामि, मोक्ष्यामि	अमोहिष्यम्, अमोक्ष्यम्
मृज्	मार्जितास्मि, मार्ष्टास्मि	मार्जिष्यामि, मार्क्ष्यामि	अमार्जिष्यम्, अमार्क्ष्यम्
रध्	रधितास्मि,* रद्धास्मि	रधिष्यामि, रत्स्यामि,	अरधिष्यम्, अरत्स्यम्
व्रश्च्	व्रश्चितास्मि, व्रष्टास्मि	व्रश्चिष्यामि, व्रक्ष्यामि	अव्रश्चिष्यम्, अव्रक्ष्यम्
स्निह्	स्नेहितास्मि, स्नेढास्मि स्नेग्धास्मि†	स्नेहिष्यामि, स्नेक्ष्यामि	अस्नेहिष्यम्, अस्नेक्ष्यम्
स्वृ	स्वरितास्मि, स्वर्तास्मि	स्वरिष्यामि‡	अस्वरिष्यम्
कु	कुतास्मि	कुष्यामि	अकुष्यम्
कुट्	कुटितास्मि	कुटिष्यामि	अकुटिष्यम्
धू 6 cl.	धुवितास्मि	धुविष्यामि	अधुविष्यम्
धूप्	धूपितास्मि, धूपायितास्मि	धूपिष्यामि धूपायिष्यामि	अधूपिष्यम् अधूपायिष्यम्
विच्छ्	विच्छितास्मि विच्छायितास्मि	विच्छिष्यामि विच्छायिष्यामि	अविच्छिष्यम् . अविच्छायिष्यम्
ऋत्	अर्तिताहे, ऋतीयिताहे	अर्तिष्ये, ऋतीयिष्ये	आर्तिष्ये, आर्तीयिष्ये
कम्	कमिताहे, कामयिताहे	कमिष्ये, कामयिष्ये	अकमिष्ये, अकामयिष्ये
जभ्	जम्भिताहे*	जम्भिष्ये	अजम्भिष्ये
मि-मी	मातास्मि-हे	मास्यामि, मास्ये	अमास्यम्, अमास्ये
दी	दाताहे	दास्ये	अदास्ये
ली	लेतास्मि, लातास्मि	लेष्यामि, लास्यामि	अलेष्यम्, अलास्यम्
चृत्	चर्तितास्मि	चर्तिष्यामि, चर्त्स्यामि	अचर्तिष्यम्, अचर्त्स्यम्

* See ft. note p. 320. † See ft. note p. 323. ‡ स्वृ is set in the 2nd Fut. and the Condi.

छृद्	छर्दितास्मि-हे	छर्दिष्यामि-ष्ये	अच्छर्दिष्यम्-ष्ये
		छर्त्स्यामि-र्त्स्ये	अच्छर्त्स्यम्-र्त्स्ये

तृद् P. A. & नृत् P. are similarly conjugated.

ऊर्णु	ऊर्णवितास्मि-हे	ऊर्णविष्यामि-ष्ये	और्णविष्यम्-ष्ये
	ऊर्णुवितास्मि-हे	ऊर्णुविष्यामि-ष्ये	और्णुविष्यम्-ष्ये
दरिद्रा	दरिद्रितास्मि	दरिद्रिष्यामि	अदरिद्रिष्यम्
दीधी	दीधिताहे	दीधिष्ये	अदीधिष्ये

वेवी is similarly conjugated.

---

(4) THE PERFECT (लिट्)

§ 488. There are two kinds of Perfect, Reduplicative and Periphrastic.

§ 489. The Reduplicative Perfect is formed of all monosyllabic roots beginning with consonants, as well as of those beginning with the vowels अ or आ, and इ, उ, and ऋ short.

Exceptions—दय्, अय्, कास्, आस्. These take the Periphrastic Perfect necessary.

§ 490. The Periphrastic Perfect is formed of all roots beginning with any vowel except अ or आ which is naturally or prosodially long, and of roots of more than one syllable (roots of the 10th class and other derivative roots included). Exceptions:—ऊर्णु and ऋच्छ् which take the Reduplicative Perfects.

§ 491. The roots उष्, विद्, जागृ, भी, ह्री, भृ, हु, and दरिद्रा take both the perfects.

THE REDUPLICATIVE PERFECT.

§ 492. The root is reduplicated according to the rules laid down in §§ 444—449.

§ 493.

Terminations.

Parasmaipada.			Âtmanepada.	
1. अ	व	म	ए	वहे

2. थ	अथुस्	अ	से	आथे	ध्वे
3. अ	अतुस्	उस्	ए	आते	इरे

§ 494. The Parasmaipada singular terminations are strong; the rest weak. Before the strong terminations the penultimate short vowel takes its Guna substitute. The final vowel and penultimate अ take Vṛddhi necessarily in the third and optionally in the first person singular. In the 2nd person singular the final vowel takes Guṇa and the penultimate अ remains unchanged.

§ 495. *Special rules about the admission of the intermediate इ before the terminations थ, म, थ, से, वहे, महे, ध्वे; see (§ 457).

(*a*) All roots, whether set or anit, except कृ, सृ, भृ, वृ, स्तु, द्रु, स्रु, and श्रु admit इ. But कृ with सम्, and वृ admit it before थ; as संचस्करिथ, ववरिथ.

(*b*) Anit roots ending in short ऋ, except ऋ, reject it before थ; as सस्मर्थ from स्मृ; but आरिथ from ऋ.

(*c*) Anit roots with a final vowel or with a penultimate अ admit it optionally before थ.

§ 496. When initial इ or उ of a root takes Guṇa or Vṛddhi substitute, the reduplicative इ or उ is changed to इय् or उव्; otherwise the two vowels combine to form long ई or ऊ; as इएष्+अ=इयेष, उओख्+अ=उवोख; ईषिव; &c.

§ 497. The final उ, short or long, is changed to उव् before a vowel weak termiation and इ to इए् or य as it is preceded by a conjunct consonant or not; as दुधु+इव=दुधुविव 1 dual; निनी+इव=निन्य्+इव=निन्यिव. शिश्रि+इव=शिश्रियिव, &c.

---

* कृसृभृवृस्तुद्रुस्रुश्रुवो लिटि । Pán. VII. 2 13.
अजन्तोऽकारवान्वायस्तास्यानिट् थलि वेडयम् ।
ऋदन्त ईदृङ् नित्यानिट् क्राद्यन्यो लिटि सेड् भवेत् ॥ (Sid. Kau.)

§ 498. Roots ending in आ take औ instead of अ in the 1st and 3rd per. sing. and drop their final आ before vowel weak terminations, and before such as take the augment इ; as ददौ, ददिव, ददिम 1st Per. ददाथ, ददिथ 2. Per. sing. of दा.

§ 499. Guṇa is substituted for the final vowel of roots ending in ऋ preceded by a conjunct consonant, and in long ॠ and of the roots ऋ, ऋच्छ् and जागृ; as सस्मरिव 1 dual of स्मृ, &c. शॄ, दॄ and पॄ optionally take the Guṇa substitute before the weak terminations, and shorten their vowel when they do not; as शशरिव, शश्रिव, 1 dual of शॄ, &c.

§ 500. Monosyllabic roots, having a short अ for their penultimate, change it to ए and drop the reduplicative syllable before the weak terminations and before थ when it takes इ, provided their initial letter undergoes no change in the reduplication, *e. g.* पत् 1st dual पपत्+इव=पेत्+इव=पेतिव, पेतिथ 2 sing, शेकिथ, शशक्थ 2. sing. of शक्, but ननन्दिथ 2nd dual of नन्द् as the अ here is prosodially long.

Exceptions:—Roots beginning with व and the roots शस् and दद्.

§ 501. न् is inserted after the reduplicative syllable in the case of roots beginning with अ and ending in a conjunct consonant and in that of अश् 'to pervade' and ऋच्छ् 'to go.' The reduplicative अ is changed to आ; अञ्ज्-अअञ्ज्+अ=अ+न्+अञ्ज्+अ=आनञ्ज्+अ=आनञ्ज; similarly आनर्द 1 sing. of अर्द्, आनशे of अश्, &c

§ 502. The change of a semi-vowel to its corresponding vowel is called Samprasâraṇa. Samprasâraṇa generally takes place before weak terminations in the case of the following roots—वच्, यज्, वप्, वह्, वस् 'to dwell,' वे ज्ये, ह्वे, श्वि, वद्, स्वप्, ज्या, वश्, व्यच्, प्रच्छ्, व्रश्च्, भ्रस्ज्, ग्रह् and व्यध्. In the case of the Perfect the roots प्रच्छ्, व्रश्च् and, भ्रस्ज् form an exception.

§ 503 Before the strong terminations of the Perfect Samprasârana takes place in the reduplicative syllable only. In this case the initial conjunct consonant of a root is reduplicated as it is ; *i. e.* स्वप्-स्वस्वप् &c.

(*a*) The vowel following the Samprasâraṇa is dropped.

§ 504. The roots that reject इ altogether in the Perfect—

कृ P. Â. 'to do'

1. चकार, चकर	चकृव	चकृम	चक्रे	चकृवहे	चकृमहे
2. चकर्थ	चक्रथुः	चक्र	चकृषे	चक्राथे	चकृढ्वे‡
3. चकार	चक्रतुः	चक्रुः	चक्रे	चक्राते	चक्रिरे

Conjugate similarly सृ, भृ, and वृ except in the 2nd per. sing. which is ववरिथ.

But कृ with सम्*

1. सञ्चस्कार, सञ्चस्कर	सञ्चस्करिव†	सञ्चस्करिम	सञ्चस्करे	सञ्चस्करिवहे	सञ्चस्करिमहे
2. सञ्चस्करिथ	सञ्चस्करथुः	सञ्चस्कर	सञ्चस्करिषे	सञ्चस्कराथे	सञ्चस्करिध्वे-ढ्वे‡
3. सञ्चस्कार	सञ्चस्करतुः	सञ्चस्करुः	सञ्चस्करे	सञ्चस्कराते	सञ्चस्करिरे

---

* संपरिभ्यां करोतौ भूषणे । समवाये च । उपात्प्रतियत्नवैकृतवाक्याध्याहारेषु च Pan. VI. 1. 137—139. स् is prefixed to the root कृ after the prepositions सम् and परि when it means to ornament or collect together ; and after the preposition उप in the above sense, as well as in the senses of 'imparting an additional quality to a thing without destroying the thing itself (सतो गुणान्तराधानं प्रतियत्नः Kâs. on Pan. II. 3. 53.) or preparing as food, or supplying what is implied.'

† The ऋ is changed to Guṇa as it is preceded by a conjunct consonant now (Vide § 499. Sid. Kau. on Pan VII. 1. 10–11.)

‡ The ध् of the terminations षीध्वम्, ध्वम्, and ध्वे of 2nd per. pl of the Benedictive, the Aorist and the Perfect, is changed to ढ् when preceded by any vowel except अ or आ or by य्, र्, ल्, व् or ह्. When the intermediate इ is added, this change is optional, if the इ be preceded by one of the consonants given above.

स्तु P. Â.

1. तुष्टाव-तुष्टव	तुष्टुव	तुष्टुम	तुष्टुवे	तुष्टुवहे	तुष्टुमहे
2. तुष्टोथ	तुष्टुवथुः	तुष्टुव	तुष्टुषे	तुष्टुवाथे	तुष्टुढ्वे
3. तुष्टाव	तुष्टुवतुः	तुष्टुवुः	तुष्टुवे	तुष्टुवाते	तुष्टुविरे

Conjugate similarly हु, सु, श्रु.

§ 505. Roots that admit इ—

(1) Set roots ending in a vowel.

वॄ 9. Â. 'to choose.'

1. ववार-ववर	ववरिव	ववरिम	1. ववरे	ववरिवहे	ववरिमहे
2. ववरिथ	ववरथुः	ववर	2. ववरिषे	ववराथे	ववरिध्वे-ढ्वे
3. ववार	ववरतुः	ववरुः	3. ववरे	ववराते	ववीरिरे

स्तॄ, गॄ, भॄ &c. are similarly conjugated; तस्तार-तस्तर, तस्तरिव &c.

शॄ 9 P. 'to tear,' &c.

1. शशार शशर	शशरिव शश्रिव	शशरिम शश्रिम
2. शशरिथ	शशरथुः शश्रथुः	शशर शश्र
3. शशार	शशरतुः शश्रतुः	शशरुः शश्रुः

Conjugate similarly दॄ and पॄ.

क्ष्णु 2 P. 'to sharpen.'

1. चुक्ष्णाव चुक्ष्णव	चुक्ष्णुविव	चुक्ष्णुविम
2. चुक्ष्णविथ	चुक्ष्णुवथुः	चुक्ष्णुव
3. चुक्ष्णाव	चुक्ष्णुवतुः	चुक्ष्णुवुः

स्नु is similarly conjugated.

रु 2 P. Â. 'to warble, to go,' &c.

1. रुराव रुरव	रुरुविव	रुरुविम	1. रुरुवे	रुरुविवहे	रुरुविमहे
2. रुरविथ	रुरुवथुः	रुरुव	2. रुरुविषे	रुरुवाथे	रुरुविध्वे-ढ्वे
3. रुराव	रुरुवतुः	रुरुवुः	3. रुरुवे	रुरुवाते	रुरुविरे

Conjugate similarly यु P. नु P.

शी 2 Â. 'to lie down.'

1 शिश्ये	शिश्यिवहे	शिश्यिमहे
2 शिश्यिषे	शिश्याथे	शिश्यिध्वे-ढ्वे
3 शिश्ये	शिश्याते	शिश्यिरे

श्रि P. Â. 'to resort to.'

1 शिश्राय शिश्रय	शिश्रियिव	शिश्रियिम	1 शिश्रिये	शिश्रियिवहे	शिश्रियिमहे
2 शिश्रयिथ	शिश्रियथुः	शिश्रिय	2 शिश्रियिषे	शिश्रियाथे	शिश्रियिध्वे-ढ्वे
3 शिश्राय	शिश्रियतुः	शिश्रियुः	3 शिश्रिये	शिश्रियाते	शिश्रियिरे

(2) Anit roots ending in a vowel :—

दा 1. P. Â. 'to give.'

1 ददौ	ददिव	ददिम	1 ददे	ददिवहे	ददिमहे
2 ददाथ-ददिथ	ददथुः	दद	2 ददिषे	ददाथे	ददिध्वे
3 ददौ	ददतुः	ददुः	3 ददे	ददाते	ददिरे

गै P. 'to sing.'

1 जगौ	जगिव	जगिम
2 जगाथ-जगिथ	जगथुः	जग
3 जगौ	जगतुः	जगुः

All other roots ending in आ, ए, ऐ, and ओ are similarly conjugated. ध्यै—3rd per. दध्यौ, दध्यतुः, दध्युः; दो 'to cut' 3rd per. ददौ, ददतुः, ददुः &c.

इ 2 P. 'to go.'

1 इयाय-इयय	ईयिव	ईयिम
2 इयेथ-इययिथ	ईयथुः	ईय
3 इयाय	ईयतुः	ईयुः

इ 1 P. 'to go' is regular; इयाय-य, इयिव इयिम &c. ई 1. 2. P. 4 A. 'to go' takes the peri. perf.

नी P. Â. 'to carry.'

Par.			Âtm.
1 निनाय-निनय	निन्यिव	निन्यिम	See शी 'to lie down above.'
2 निनयिथ-निनेथ	निन्यथुः	निन्य	
3 निनाय	निन्यतुः	निन्युः	

स्मृ P. 'to remember.'

1 सस्मार-सस्मर	सस्मरिव	सस्मरिम
2 सस्मर्थ	सस्मरथुः	सस्मर
3 सस्मार	सस्मरतुः	सस्मरुः

मि 5 P. Â. 'to throw.'

1 ममौ	मिम्यिव	मिम्यिम
2 ममाथ ममिथ	मिम्यथुः	मिम्य
3 ममौ	मिम्यतुः	मिम्युः

मी 9. P. Â. 'to destroy.'

1 मिम्ये	मिम्यिवहे	मिम्यिमहे
2 मिम्यिषे	मिम्याथे	मिम्यिध्वे-ढ्वे
3 मिम्ये	मिम्याते	मिम्यिरे

ली. 9 P. 4 Â. 'to adhere.' 1. P. 'to melt.'

Par.			Âtm.
1 लिलाय, लिलय, ललौ	लिल्यिव	लिल्यिम	
2 लिलेथ, लिलयिथ ललाथ, ललिथ	लिल्यथुः	लिल्य	
3 लिलाय, ललौ	लिल्यतुः	लिल्युः	Like शी.

(3) Anit roots ending in a consonant:—

शक् 5 P. 'to be able.'

1 शशाक-शशक	शेकिव	शेकिम
2 शेकिथ-शशक्थ	शेकथुः	शेक
3 शशाक	शेकतुः	शेकुः

पच् P. Â. 'to cook.'

1. पपाच-पपच	पेचिव	पेचिम	1. पेचे	पेचिवहे	पेचिमहे
2. पेचिथ, पपक्थ	पेचथुः	पेच	2. पेचिषे	पेचाथे	पेचिध्वे
3. पपाच	पेचतुः	पेचुः	3. पेचे	पेचाते	पेचिरे

मुच् 6 P. Â. 'to release.'

1. मुमोच	मुमुचिव	मुमुचिम	1. मुमुचे	मुमुचिवहे	मुमुचिमहे
2. मुमोचिथ	मुमुचथुः	मुमुच	2. मुमुचिषे	मुमुचाथे	मुमुचिध्वे
3. मुमोच	मुमुचतुः	मुमुचुः	3. मुमुचे	मुमुचाते	मुमुचिरे

रिच् 1 P. 'to separate.' Â. 'to purge.'

1. रिरेच	रिरिचिव	रिरिचिम	1. रिरिचे	रिरिचिवहे	रिरिचिमहे
2. रिरेचिथ	रिरिचथुः	रिरिच	2. रिरिचिषे	रिरिचाथे	रिरिचिध्वे
3. रिरेच	रिरिचतुः	रिरिचुः	3. रिरिचे	रिरिचाते	रिरिचिरे

Conjugate विच् 7. P. A., सिच् 6. P. A., निज् 3 P. A., विज् 3. P. A., भुज् 7. P. A., युज् 7. P. A., क्षुद् 7. P. A. and others having इ or उ for their penultimate, similarly; सिच्—सिषेच 1 sing. सिषिचिव dual; सिषेचिथ 2 sing. &c., क्षुद्—चुक्षोद 1 sing. चुक्षोदिथ 2 sing. &c.

प्रच्छ् 6 P. 'to ask.'

1 पप्रच्छ	पप्रच्छिव	पप्रच्छिम
2 पप्रच्छिथ-पप्रष्ठ	पप्रच्छथुः	पप्रच्छ
3 पप्रच्छ	पप्रच्छतुः	पप्रच्छुः

त्यज् 1 P. 'to abandon.'

1 तत्याज तत्यज	तत्यजिव	तत्यजिव
2 तत्यजिथ तत्यक्थ	तत्यजथुः	तत्यज
3 तत्याज	तत्यजतुः	तत्यजुः

भञ्ज् 7 P. 'to break or to destroy.'

1 बभञ्ज	बभञ्जिव	बभञ्जिम
2 बभञ्जिथ-बभङ्क्थ	बभञ्जथुः	बभञ्ज
3 बभञ्ज	बभञ्जतुः	बभञ्जुः

भ्रस्ज् 6. P. Â. 'to fry.'

1 बभर्ज	बभर्जिव	बभर्जिम	1 बभर्जे	बभर्जिवहे	बभर्जिमहे
बभ्रज्ज	बभ्रज्जिव	बभ्रज्जिम	बभ्रज्जे	बभ्रज्जिवहे	बभ्रज्जिमहे
2 बभर्जिथ बभर्ष्ठ-बभ्रष्ठ	बभर्जथुः	बभर्ज	2 बभर्जिषे	बभर्जाथे	बभर्जिध्वे
बभ्रज्जिथ	बभ्रज्जथुः	बभ्रज्ज	बभ्रज्जिषे	बभ्रज्जाथे	बभ्रज्जिध्वे
3 बभर्ज	बभर्जतुः	बभर्जुः	3 बभर्जे	बभर्जाते	बभर्जिरे
बभ्रज्ज	बभ्रज्जतुः	बभ्रज्जुः	बभ्रज्जे	बभ्रज्जाते	बभ्रज्जिरे

सृज् 4. Â. 6. P.

1 ससर्ज	ससृजिव	ससृजिम	1 ससृजे	ससृजिवहे	ससृजिमहे
2 ससर्जिथ सस्रष्ठ	ससृजथुः	ससृज	2 ससृजिषे	ससृजाथे	ससृजिध्वे
3 ससर्ज	ससृजतुः	ससृजुः	3 ससृजे	ससृजाते	ससृजिरे

दृश् 1. P. 'to see.'

should be conjugated like सृज्; ददर्शिथ, दद्रष्ठ 2 sing.

छिद् 7. P. Â. 'to cut.'

1 चिच्छेद	चिच्छिदिव	चिच्छिदिम	1 चिच्छिदे	चिच्छिदिवहे	चिच्छिदिमहे
2 चिच्छेदिथ	चिच्छिदथुः	चिच्छिद	2 चिच्छिदिषे	चिच्छिदाथे	चिच्छिदिध्वे
3 चिच्छेद	चिच्छिदतुः	चिच्छिदुः	3 चिच्छिदे	चिच्छिदाते	चिच्छिदिरे

पद् 4. A. 'to go. शद् 1. 6. P. 'to decay.'

1 पेदे	पेदिवहे	पेदिमहे	1 शशाद-शशद	शेदिव	शेदिम

2 पेदिषे	पेदाथे	पेदिध्वे	2 शेदिथ-शशत्थ	शेदथुः	शेद
3 पेदे	पेदाते	पेदिरे	3 शशाद	शेदतुः	शेदुः

Conjugate मन् A., सद् P., तप् P. शप् P., A., यभ् P., रभ् A., लभ् A., नम् P., यम् P., रम् A., दह् P., नह् P. similary; मन्-मेनिषे 2 sing.., सद्-सेदिथ-ससत्थ 2 sing., नम्-नेमिथ-ननन्थ 2 sing., दह् देहिथ-ददग्ध 2 sing., नह्-नेहिथ-ननद्ध, &c.

स्कन्द् 1 P. 'to drop ' बन्ध्. 9 P. 'to bind '

1 चस्कन्द	चस्कन्दिव	चस्कन्दिम	1 बबन्ध	बबन्धिव	बबन्धिम
2 चस्कन्दिथ चस्कन्त्थ	चस्कन्दथुः	चस्कन्द	2 बबन्धिथ बबन्द्ध	बबन्धथुः	बबन्ध
3 चस्कन्द	चस्कन्दतुः	चस्कन्दुः	3 बबन्ध	बबन्धतुः	बबन्धुः

राध् 4. 5. P. 'to grow, to accomplish.' स्पृश् 6. P. 'to touch.'

1 रराध	रराधिव	रराधिम	1 पस्पर्श	पस्पृशिव	पस्पृशिम
2 रराधिथ	रराधथुः	रराध	2 पस्पर्शिथ	पस्पृशथुः	पस्पृश
3 रराध	रराधतुः	रराधुः	3 पस्पर्श	पस्पृशतुः	पस्पृशुः

सृश् and छश् are similarly conjugated.

(4) Set roots ending in a consonant.

नन्द् 1 P. 'to be glad.' वन्द् 1 Â 'to salute.'

1 ननन्द	ननन्दिव	ननन्दिम	1 ववन्दे	ववन्दिवहे	ववन्दिमहे
2 ननन्दिथ	ननन्दथुः	ननन्द	2 ववन्दिषे	ववन्दाथे	ववन्दिध्वे
3 ननन्द	ननन्दतुः	ननन्दुः	3 ववन्दे	ववन्दाते	ववन्दिरे

नृत् 4. 1. P. 'to dance मुद् Â. 1. 'to rejoice.

1 ननर्त	ननृतिव	ननृतिम	1 मुमुदे	मुमुदिवहे	मुमुदिमहे
2 ननर्तिथ	ननृतथुः	ननृत	2 मुमुदिषे	मुमुदाथे	मुमुदिध्वे
3 ननर्त	ननृततुः	ननृतुः	3 मुमुदे	मुमुदाते	मुमुदिरे

अर्द् 1. P. 'to afflict.' ऋच्छ् 6. P. 'to go.'

1 आनर्द	आनर्दिव	आनर्दिम	1 आनर्च्छ	आनर्च्छिव	आनर्च्छिम

2 आनर्दिथ	आनर्दथुः	आनर्द	2 आनर्च्छिथ	आनर्च्छथुः	आनर्च्छ
3 आनर्द	आनर्दतुः	आनर्दुः	3 आनर्च्छ	आनर्च्छतुः	आनर्च्छुः

अर्च् 1. P. 'to worship.' ऋज् 1. A. to go, to acquire' &c.

1 आनर्च	आनर्चिव	आनर्चिम	1 आनृजे	आनृजिवहे	आनृजिमहे
2 आनर्चिथ	आनर्चथुः	आनर्च	2 आनृजिषे	आनृजाथे	आनृजिध्वे
3 आनर्च	आनर्चतुः	आनर्चुः	3 आनृजे	आनृजाते	आनृजिरे

वम् P. 'to vomit.' दद् Â. 'to give.'

1 ववाम-ववम	ववमिव	ववमिम	1 ददे	ददिवहे	ददिमहे
2 ववमिथ	ववमथुः	ववम	2 ददिषे	ददाथे	ददिध्वे
3 ववाम	ववमतुः	ववमुः	3 ददे	ददाते	ददिरे

कुट् 6. P. 'to be crooked.' 'to cheat.' स्फुर् 6. P. 'to flash forth.' 'to throb.'

1 चुकोट, चुकुट*	चुकुटिव	चुकुटिम	1 पुस्फोर	पुस्फुरिव	पुस्फुरिम
2 चुकुटिथ	चुकुटथुः	चुकुट	2 पुस्फुरिथ	पुस्फुरथुः	पुस्फुर
3 चुकोट	चुकुटथुः	चुकुटुः	3 पुस्फोर	पुस्फरतुः	पुस्फुरुः

§ 506. Roots taking सम्प्रसारण (regular and irregular)—

यज् 1. P. Â. 'to worship.'

1 इयाज-इयज	ईजिव,	ईजिम	1 ईजे	ईजिवहे	ईजिमहे
2 इयजिथ-इयष्ठ	ईजथुः	ईज	2 ईजिषे	ईजाथे	ईजिध्वे
3 इयाज	ईजतुः	ईजुः	3 ईजे	ईजाते	ईजिरे

वच् † 1. 2. P. 'to speak.' वस् 1. P. 'to dwell.'

1 उवाच, उवच,	ऊचिव	ऊचिम	1 उवास–उवस	ऊषिव	ऊषिम

* Roots of the कुटादि class (see § 463) retain their vowel unchanged optionally in the 1st pers. sing. of the Perf.; नू-नुनाव, नुनव 1st sing.

† वच् as a substitute for ब्रू may also be conjugated in At. e. g. ऊचे, ऊचिवहे, ऊचिमहे, 1 Per &c.

2 उवचिथ-उवक्थ	ऊचथुः	ऊच	2 उवसिथ-उवस्थ	ऊषथुः	ऊष
3 उवाच	ऊचतुः	ऊचुः	3 उवास	ऊषतुः	ऊषुः

वप् 1. P. Â. 'to sow seed.'

1 उवाप-उवप	ऊपिव	ऊपिम	1 ऊपे	ऊपिवहे	ऊपिमहे
2 उवपिथ-उवप्थ	ऊपथुः	ऊप	2 ऊपिषे	ऊपाथे	ऊपिध्वे
3 उवाप	ऊपतुः	ऊपुः	3 ऊपे	ऊपाते	ऊपिरे

वह् 1. P. Â. 'to carry.'

1 उवाह-उवह	ऊहिव	ऊहिम	1 ऊहे	ऊहिवहे	ऊहिमहे
2 उवहिथ, उवोढ*	ऊहथुः	ऊह	2 ऊहिषे	ऊहाथे	ऊहिध्वे-ढ्वे
3 उवाह	ऊहतुः	ऊहुः	3 ऊहे	ऊहाते	ऊहिरे

वद् 1. P. 'to speak.' (Â. in some senses).

1 उवाद-उवद	ऊदिव	ऊदिम	1 ऊदे	ऊदिवहे	ऊदिमहे
2 उवदिथ	ऊदथुः	ऊद	2 ऊदिषे	ऊदाथे	ऊदिध्वे
3 उवाद	ऊदतुः	ऊदुः	3 ऊदे	ऊदाते	ऊदिरे

स्वप् 2. P. 'to sleep.' ज्या 2 P. 'to grow old.'

1 सुष्वाप, सुष्वप	सुषुपिव	सुषुपिम	1 जिज्यौ	जिज्यिव	जिज्यिम
2 सुष्वपिथ सुष्वप्थ	सुषुपथुः	सुषुप	2 जिज्यिथ जिज्याथ	जिज्यथुः	जिज्य
3 सुष्वाप	सुषुपतुः	सुषुपुः	3 जिज्यौ	जिज्यतुः	जिज्युः

वश् 2. P. 'to desire.' व्यच् 6. P. 'to deceive,' 'to surround.'

1 उवाश-उवश	ऊशिव	ऊशिम	1 विव्याच विव्यच	विविचिव	विविचिम

---

*When the ढ् substituted for the ह् of the roots सह् and वह् is dropped, the preceding अ is changed to ओ and not to आ; उवह् + थ = उवह् + थ = उवढ् + ध, by § 416, 3, 4 = उवढ् + ढ = उवोढ.

2 उवशिथ	ऊशथुः	ऊश	2 विव्यचिथ	विविचथुः	विविच
3 उवाश	ऊशतुः	ऊशुः	3 विव्याच	विविचतुः	विविचुः

ग्रह् 9. P. Â. 'to take.'

1 जग्राह-जग्रह	जगृहिव	जगृहिम	1 जगृहे	जगृहिवहे	जगृहिमहे
2 जग्रहिथ	जगृहथुः	जगृह	2 जगृहिषे	जगृहाथे	जगृहिध्वे-ढ्वे
3 जग्राह	जगृहतुः	जगृहुः	3 जगृहे	जगृहाते	जगृहिरे

व्यध् 4. P. Â. 'to pierce.'

1 विव्याध-विव्यध	विविधिव	विविधिम
2 विव्यधिथ, विव्यद्ध	विविधथुः	विविध
3 विव्याध	विविधतुः	विविधुः

श्वि* 1. P. 'to swell.'

1 शिश्वाय, शिश्वय	शिश्वियिव	शिश्वियिम
शुशाव, शुशव	शुशुविव	शुशुविम
2 शिश्वयिथ, शुशविथ	शिश्वियथुः, शुशुवथुः	शिश्विय, शुशुव
3 शिश्वाय, शुशाव	शिश्वियतुः, शुशुवतुः	शिश्वियुः, शुशुवुः

वे† (Regular).

1 ववौ	वविव	वविम	1 ववे	वविवहे	वविमहे
2 ववाथ, वविथ	ववथुः	वव	2 वविषे	ववाथे	वविध्वे-ढ्वे
3 ववौ	ववतुः	ववुः	3 ववे	ववाते	वविरे

वे (Irregular).

1 उवाय	ऊयिव	ऊयिम	1 ऊये	ऊयिवहे	ऊयिमहे
उवय	ऊविव	ऊविम	ऊवे	ऊविवहे	ऊविमहे

* श्वि is to be optionally considered as शु in the Perfect.

† वे optionally assumes the form उवय् before the strong, and ऊय् or ऊव् before the weak terminations of the Perfect.

2 उवयिथ	ऊयथुः	ऊय	2 ऊयिषे	ऊयाथे	ऊयिध्वे-ढ्वे
	ऊवथुः	ऊव	ऊविषे	ऊवाथे	ऊविध्वे-ढ्वे
3 उवाय	ऊयतुः	ऊयुः	3 ऊये	ऊयाते	ऊयिरे
	ऊवतुः	ऊवुः	ऊवे	ऊवाते	ऊविरे

व्ये* P. Â.

1 विव्याय, विव्यय	विव्यिव	विव्यिम	1 विव्ये	विव्यिवहे	विव्यिमहे
2 विव्ययिथ	विव्यथुः	विव्य	2 विव्यिषे	विव्याथे	विव्यिध्वे-ढ्वे
3 विव्याय	विव्यतुः	विव्युः	3 विव्ये	विव्याते	विव्यिरे

ह्वे† P. Â. 'to call.'

1 जुहाव जुहव	जुहुविव	जुहुविम	1 जुहुवे	जुहुविवहे	जुहुविमहे
2 जुहविथ, जुहोथ	जुहुवथुः	जुहुव	2 जुहुविषे	जुहुवाथे	जुहुविध्वे-ढ्वे
3 जुहाव	जुहुवतुः	जुहुवुः	3 जुहुवे	जुहुवाते	जुहुविरे

§ 507. **Wet roots:—**

§ 508. The roots स्वृ, सू and धू admit इ necessarily before consonantal terminations except थ; स्वृ-सस्वरिव 1 dual, सस्वरिथ, सस्वर्थ 2 sing.; दुधविथ, दुधोथ 2 sing. of धू, &c.

तञ्च् 1. 7. P. 'to shrink, to contract.'   व्रश्च् 6 P. 'to cut.'

1 ततञ्च	ततञ्चिव	ततञ्चिम	1 वव्रश्च	वव्रश्चिव	वव्रश्चिम
	ततञ्च्व	ततञ्च्म		वव्रश्च्व	वव्रश्च्म
2 ततञ्चिथ	ततञ्चथुः	ततञ्च	2 वव्रश्चिथ	वव्रश्चथुः	वव्रश्च
ततङ्क्थ			वव्रष्ठ		
3 ततञ्च	ततञ्चतुः	ततञ्चुः	3 वव्रश्च	वव्रश्चतुः	वव्रश्चुः

तञ्ज् is similarly conjugated.

---

* व्ये becomes विव्यय् before strong terminations and विवी before the weak ones in the Perf. † ह्वे is to be considered as हु in the Perf.

मृज् 1. 2. P. 'to purify.'

1	ममार्ज	ममृजिव ममृज्व ममार्जिव	ममृजिम ममृज्म ममार्जिम
2	ममार्जिथ ममार्ष्ठ	ममृजथुः ममार्जथुः	ममृज ममार्ज
3	ममार्ज	ममृजतुः ममार्जतुः	ममृजुः ममार्जुः

अञ्ज् 7. P. 'to anoint.'

1	आनञ्ज	आनञ्जिव आनञ्ज्व	आनञ्जिम आनञ्ज्म
2	आनञ्जिथ आनङ्क्थ	आनञ्जथुः	आनञ्ज
3	आनञ्ज	आनञ्जतुः	आनञ्जुः

क्लिद् 4 P. 'to be wet.'

1	चिक्लेद	चिक्लेदिव चिक्लिद्व	चिक्लेदिम चिक्लिद्म
2	चिक्लेदिथ चिक्लेत्थ	चिक्लिदथुः	चिक्लिद
3	चिक्लेद	चिक्लिदतुः	चिक्लिदुः

स्यन्द् 1. Â 'to distil.'

1	सस्यन्दे	सस्यन्दिवहे सस्यन्द्वहे	सस्यन्दिमहे सस्यन्द्महे
2	सस्यन्दिषे सस्यन्त्से	सस्यन्दाथे	सस्यन्दिध्वे सस्यन्द्ध्वे
3	सस्यन्दे	सस्यन्दाते	सस्यन्दिरे

रध्* 4. P. 'to destroy.'

1	ररन्ध	ररन्धिव-रेध्व	ररन्धिम-रेध्म
2	ररन्धिथ-ररद्ध	ररन्धतुः	ररन्ध
3	ररन्ध	ररन्धतुः	ररन्धुः

सिध् 1. P.

1	सिषेध	सिषिधिव-ध्व	सिषिधिम-ध्म
2	सिषेधिथ, सिषद्ध	सिषिधथुः	सिषिध
3	सिषेध	सिषिधतुः	सिषिधुः

क्लृप् 1. P. 'to be able.'

1	चक्लृपे	चक्लृपिवहे चक्लृप्वहे	चक्लृपिमहे चक्लृप्महे
2	चक्लृपिषे चक्लृप्से	चक्लृपाथे	चक्लृपिध्वे चक्लृब्ध्वे
3	चक्लृपे	चक्लृपाते	चक्लृपिरे

तृप् 4. P. 'to be pleased.'

1	ततर्प	ततृपिव ततृप्व	ततृपिम ततृप्म
2	ततर्पिथ, तत्रप्थ,† ततर्प्थ	ततृपथुः	ततृप
3	ततर्प	ततृपतुः	ततृपुः

दृप् is similarly conjugated.

---

* रध् and जभ् insert a nasal when their final is followed by a vowel. रध्, however, does not do it in the Aorist or when it takes इ, except in the Perf. † See § 471.

त्रप् 1. Ā. 'to be ashamed.'

1	त्रेपे*	त्रेपिवहे	त्रेपिमहे
		त्रेप्वहे	त्रेप्महे
2	त्रेपिषे	त्रेपाथे	त्रेपिध्वे
	त्रेप्से		त्रेब्ध्वे
3	त्रेपे	त्रेपाते	त्रेपिरे

क्षम् 4. P. 'to forgive.'

1	चक्षाम	चक्षमिव	चक्षमिम
	चक्षम	चक्षण्व†	चक्षण्म
2	चक्षमिथ	चक्षमथुः	चक्षम
	चक्षन्थ		
3	चक्षाम	चक्षमतुः	चक्षमुः

क्षम् 1. A. 'to forgive.'

1	चक्षमे	चक्षमिवहे	चक्षमिमहे
		चक्षण्वहे	चक्षण्महे
2	चक्षमिषे	चक्षमाथे	चक्षमिध्वे
	चक्षंसे		चक्षन्ध्वे
3	चक्षमे	चक्षमाते	चक्षमिरे

अश् 5. Â. 'to pervade.'

1	आनशे	आनशिवहे	आनशिमहे
		आनश्वहे	आनश्महे
2	आनशिषे	आनशाथे	आनशिध्वे
	आनक्षे		आनड्ढ्वे
3	आनशे	आनशाते	आनशिरे

क्लिश् P. 'to be afflicted.'

1	चिक्लेश	चिक्लिशिव	चिक्लिशिम
		चिक्लिश्व	चिक्लिश्म
2	चिक्लेशिथ	चिक्लिशथुः	चिक्लिश
	चिक्लेष्ठ		
3	चिक्लेश	चिक्लिशतुः	चिक्लिशुः

नश् 4. P. 'to perish.'

1	ननाश	नेशिव	नेशिम
	ननश	नेश्व	नेश्म
2	नेशिथ	नेशथुः	नेश
	ननंष्ठ‡		
3	ननाश	नेशतुः	नेशुः

अक्ष् 1. P. 'to occupy.'

1	आनक्ष	आनक्षिव	आनक्षिम
		आनक्ष्व	आनक्ष्म
2	आनक्षिथ	आनक्षथुः	आनक्ष
	आनष्ठ		
3	आनक्ष	आनक्षतुः	आनक्षुः

कुष् with निर् 9. P. 'to tear, to expel.'

1	निश्चुकोष	निश्चुकुषिव	निश्चुकुषिम
		निश्चुकुष्व	निश्चुकुष्म
2	निश्चुकोषिथ	निश्चुकुषथुः	निश्चुकुष
	निश्चुकोष्ठ		
3	निश्चुकोष	निश्चुकुषतुः	निश्चुकुषुः

त्वक्ष् and तक्ष् 'to pare' should be similarly conjugated.

---

* See § 512.

† Roots ending in म् change to न् when followed by म् or व्.

‡ See. § 476.

गाह् 1. Â. 'to enter.'			गृह् 1. Â. 'to take.'		
1 जगाहे	जगाहिवहे जगाह्वहे	जगाहिमहे जगाह्महे	1 जगृहे	जगृहिवहे जगृह्वहे	जगृहिमहे जगृह्महे
2 जगाहिषे जघाक्षे	जगाहाथे	जगाहिध्वे-ढ्वे जघाढ्वे	2 जगृहिषे जघृक्षे	जगृहाथे	जगृहिध्वे-ढ्वे जघृढ्वे
3 जगाहे	जगाहाते	जगाहिरे	3 जगृहे	जगृहाते	जगृहिरे

गर्ह् 2 A. is Set and should be conjugated as such. गर्ह् 10. P. A. takes the Periphrastic Perf.

गुह् 1. P. Â. 'to conceal.'

1 जुगूह	जुगुहिव जुगुह्व	जुगुहिम जुगुह्म	1 जुगुहे	जुगुहिवहे जुगुह्वहे	जुगुहिमहे जुगुह्महे
2 जुगूहिथ जुगोढ	जुगुहथुः	जुगुह	2 जुगुहिषे जुघुक्षे	जुगुहाथे	जुगुहिध्वे-ढ्वे जुघूढ्वे*
3 जुगूह	जुगुहतुः	जुगुहुः	3 जुगुहे	जुगुहाते	जुगुहिरे

तृह् 6. P. 'to kill.'			तृंह् 6. P. 'to kill.'		
1 ततर्ह	ततृहिव ततृह्व	ततृहिम ततृह्म	1 ततृंह	ततृंहिव ततृंह्व	ततृंहिम ततृंह्म
2 ततर्हिथ ततर्ढ	ततृहथुः	ततृह	2 ततृंहिथः ततृंढ	ततृंहथु	ततृंह
3 ततर्ह	ततृहतुः	ततृहुः	3 ततृंह	ततृंहतुः	ततृंहुः

द्रुह् 4. P. 'to bear malice.'			स्तृह् 6. P. 'to hurt, to kill.'		
1 दुद्रोह	दुद्रुहिव दुद्रुह्व	दुद्रुहिम दुद्रुह्म	1 तस्तर्ह	तस्तृहिव तस्तृह्व	तस्तृहिम तस्तृह्म

* When ढ् or ह् is dropped, the preceding अ, इ or उ is lengthened.

2 दुद्रोहिथ, दुद्रोढ, दुद्रोग्ध*	दुद्रुहथुः	दुद्रुह	2 तस्तर्हिथ तस्तर्ढ	तस्तृहथुः	तस्तृह
3 दुद्रोह	दुद्रुहतुः	दुद्रुहुः	3 तस्तर्ह	तस्तृहतुः	तस्तृहुः

मुह् is similarly conjugated मुमुहिव मुमुह्व 1 dual, मुमोहिथ, मुमोढ, मुमोग्ध 2 sing. &c.

वृह् is similarly conjugated ववर्हिथ-ववर्ढ 2nd sing, ववृहिव, ववृह्व 1 dual

स्निह् 4. P. 'to love.'

1 सिष्णेह	सिष्णिहिव सिष्णिह्व	सिष्णिहिम सिष्णिह्म
2 सिष्णेहिथ सिष्णेढ, सिष्णेग्ध	सिष्णिहथुः	सिष्णिह
3 सिष्णेह	सिष्णिहतुः	सिष्णिहुः

स्नुह् is to be similarly conjugated.

IRREGULAR BASES.

§ 509. The roots श्रन्थ्, ग्रन्थ्, दम्भ्, and स्वञ्ज् drop their nasal optionally before the terminations of the Perfect. श्रन्थ्, ग्रन्थ्, दम्भ् obey § 500, even before the strong terminations when their nasal is dropped.

श्रन्थ्			ग्रन्थ्		
1 शश्रन्थ श्रेथ	शश्रन्थिव श्रेथिव	शश्रन्थिम श्रेथिम	1 जग्रन्थ ग्रेथ	जग्रन्थिव ग्रेथिव	जग्रन्थिम ग्रेथिम
2 शश्रन्थिथ श्रेथिथ	शश्रन्थथुः श्रेथथुः	शश्रन्थ श्रेथ	2 जग्रन्थिथ ग्रेथिथ	जग्रन्थथुः ग्रेथथुः	जग्रन्थ ग्रेथ
3 शश्रन्थ श्रेथ	शश्रन्थतुः श्रेथतुः	शश्रन्थुः श्रेथुः	3 जग्रन्थ ग्रेथ	जग्रन्थतुः ग्रेथतुः	जग्रन्थुः ग्रेथुः

* The final ह् of the roots द्रुह्, मुह्, स्निह्, and स्नुह् is changed to घ् or ढ् when followed by any consonant except a nasal or a semi vowel or by nothing.

दम्भ् P.			स्वञ्ज् Â.		
1 ददम्भ	ददम्भिव	ददम्भिम	1 सस्वञ्जे	सस्वञ्जिवहे	सस्वञ्जिमहे
देभ	देभिव	देभिम	सस्वजे	सस्वजिवहे	सस्वजिमहे
2 ददम्भिथ	ददम्भथुः	ददम्भ	2 सस्वञ्जिषे	सस्वञ्जाथे	सस्वञ्जिध्वे
देभिथ	देभथुः	देभ	सस्वजिषे	सस्वजाथे	सस्वजिध्वे
3 ददम्भ	ददम्भतुः	ददम्भुः	3 सस्वञ्जे	सस्वञ्जाते	सस्वञ्जिरे
देभ	देभतुः	देभुः	सस्वजे	सस्वजाते	सस्वजिरे

* 510. The अ of the roots गम्, हन्, जन्, खन् and घस्, is dropped before vowel weak terminations except those of the 2nd variety of the Aorist; the ह् of हन् is then changed to घ्; and जन् and घस् become ज्ञ् and क्ष् respectively.

गम्			हन्		
1 जगाम	जग्मिव	जग्मिम	1 जघान	जघ्निव	जघ्निम
जगम			जघन		
2 जगमिथ	जग्मथुः	जग्म	2 जघनिथ	जघ्नथुः	जघ्न
जगन्थ			जघन्थ		
3 जगाम	जग्मतुः	जग्मुः	3 जघान	जघ्नतुः	जघ्नुः

जन् Â.			घस्
1 जज्ञे	जज्ञिवहे	जज्ञिमहे	Conjugated in the
2 जज्ञिषे	जज्ञाथे	जज्ञिध्वे	Perf. as a substitute
3 जज्ञे	जज्ञाते	जज्ञिरे	of अद्, which see.

खन् P. Â.					
1 चखान, चखन	चख्निव	चख्निम	1 चख्ने	चख्निवहे	चख्निमहे
2 चखनिथ	चख्नथुः	चख्न	2 चख्निषे	चख्नाथे	चख्निध्वे
3 चखान	चख्नतुः	चख्नुः	3 चख्ने	चख्नाते	चख्निरे

§ 511. घस् is optionally substituted for अद् in the Perfect.

1 आद	आदिव	आदिम
जघास, जघस	जक्षिव	जक्षिम
2 आदिथ*	आदथुः	आद
जघसिथ	जक्षथुः	जक्ष
3 आद	आदतुः	आदुः
जघास	जक्षतुः	जक्षुः

§ 512 † The roots तॄ, फल्, भज्, त्रप् and राध् when it means 'to offend or to injure' necessarily, and जॄ, भ्रम्, त्रस्, फण्, 1. P. to go, राज्, भ्राज्, भ्राश्, स्यम् and स्वन् optionally obey § 500.

तॄ 1 P. 'to cross.' फल् 1 P. 'te bear fruit.'

1 ततार–ततर	तेरिव	तेरिम	1 पफाल, पफल	फेलिव	फेलिम
2 तेरिथ	तेरथुः	तेर	2 फेलिथ	फेलथुः	फेल
3 ततार	तेरतुः	तेरुः	3 पफाल	फेलतुः	फेलुः

भज् 1. P. Â. 'to serve.' &c.

1 बभाज, बभज	भेजिव	भेजिम	1 भेजे	भेजिवहे	भेजिमहे
2 भेजिथ, बभक्थ	भेजथुः	भेज	2 भेजिषे	भेजाथे	भेजिध्वे
3 बभाज	भेजतुः	भेजुः	3 भेजे	भेजाते	भेजिरे

राध् 5. P. with अप.

1 अप-रराध	अप-रेधिव	रेधिम
2 अप-रेधिथ	अप-रेधथुः	अप-रेध
3 अप-रराध	अप-रेधतुः	अप-रेधुः

जॄ 4. P. 'to be old.' भ्रम् 1. 4. P. 'to wander.'

1 जजार	जजरिव	जजरिम	1 बभ्राम	बभ्रमिव	बभ्रमिम
जजर	जेरिव	जेरिम	बभ्रम	भ्रेमिव	भ्रेमिम

* Vide § 515 † तॄफलभजत्रपश्च । राधो हिंसायाम् । वा जॄभ्रमुत्रसाम् । फण च सप्तानाम् । Pán VI. 4. 122–125.

2 जजरिथ	जजरथुः	जजर	2 बभ्रमिथ	बभ्रमथुः	बभ्रम
जेरिथ	जेरथुः	जेर	भ्रेमिथ	भ्रेमथुः	भ्रेम
3 जजार	जजरतुः	जजरुः	3 बभ्राम	बभ्रमतुः	बभ्रमुः
	जेरतुः	जेरुः		भ्रेमतुः	भ्रेमुः

भ्राज् 1. A. 'to shine.' **स्यम्** 1. P. 'to sound.'

1 बभ्राजे	बभ्राजिवहे	बभ्राजिमहे	1 सस्याम	सस्यमिव	सस्यमिम
भ्रेजे	भ्रेजिवहे	भ्रेजिमहे	सस्यम	स्येमिव	स्येमिम
2 बभ्राजिषे	बभ्राजाथे	बभ्राजिध्वे	2 सस्यमिथ	सस्यमथुः	सस्यम
भ्रेजिषे	भ्रेजाथे	भ्रेजिध्वे	स्येमिथ	स्येमथुः	स्येम
3 बभ्राजे	बभ्राजाते	बभ्राजिरे	3 सस्याम	सस्यमतुः	सस्यमुः
भ्रेजे	भ्रेजाते	भ्रेजिरे		स्येमतुः	स्येमुः

भ्लाज्, भ्राश्, राज् are to be similarly conjugated.

§ 513 भू forms its base irregularly as बभूव—

1 बभूव	बभूविव	बभूविम	1 बभूवे	बभूविवहे	बभूविमहे
2 बभूविथ	बभूवथुः	बभूव	2 बभूविषे	बभूवाथे	बभूविध्वे
3 बभूव	बभूवतुः	बभूवुः	3 बभूवे	बभूवाते	बभूविरे

§ 414. जि and हि are respectively changed to गि and घि; and चि optionally to कि, after the reduplicative syllable in the Perf. and the Desiderative.

जि   हि

1 जिगाय	जिग्यिव	जिग्यिम	1 जिघाय	जिघ्यिव	जिघ्यिम
जिगय			जिघय		
2 जिगेथ	जिग्यथुः	जिग्य	2 जिघेथ	जिघ्यथुः	जिघ्य
जिगयिथ			जिघयिथ		
3 जिगाय	जिग्यतुः	जिग्युः	3 जिघाय	जिघ्यतुः	जिघ्युः

चि.

1 चिकाय-चिकय	चिक्यिव	चिक्यिम
चिचाय-चिचय	चिच्यिव	चिच्यिम

2 चिकयिथ-चिकेथ	चिक्यथुः	चिक्य
चिचयिथ-चिचेथ	चिच्यथुः	चिच्य
3 चिकाय-चिचाय	चिक्यतुः-चिच्यतुः	चिक्युः-चिच्युः

§ 515. अद्, ऋ and व्ये admit इ necessarily before थ.

ऋ

1 आर	आरिव	आरिम	For अद् and व्ये see p. p. 325, 319;
2 आरिथ	आरथुः	आर	
3 आर	आरतुः	आरुः	

मस्ज्.*

1 ममज्ज	ममज्जिव	ममज्जिम
2 ममज्जिथ,ममङ्क्थ	ममज्जथुः	ममज्ज
3 ममज्ज	ममज्जतुः	ममज्जुः

†अज् 'to go.'

1 विवाय, विवय	विव्यिव, आजिव	विव्यिम, आजिम
2 विवयिथ, विवेथ आजिथ	विव्यथुः	विव्य
3 विवाय	विव्यतुः	विव्युः

§ 516. इ 'to go' lengthens its reduplicative इ before the weak terminations.

For the forms see p. 311.

§ 517. The base of इ with अधि 'to study' is अधिजगा.

1 अधिजगे	अधिजगिवहे	अधिजगिमहे
2 अधिजगिषे	अधिजगाथे	अधिजगिध्वे
3 अधिजगे	अधिजगाते	अधिजगिरे

§ 518. ऊर्णु forms its base as ऊर्णुनु. Its vowel is optionally not guṇated before a strong termination when it takes इ.

* See § 476. † See § 477.

Par.

1 ऊर्णुनाव, ऊर्णुनव	ऊर्णुनुविव	ऊर्णुनुविम
2 ऊर्णुनुविथ ऊर्णुनविथ	ऊर्णुनुवथुः	ऊर्णुनुव
3 ऊर्णुनाव	ऊर्णुनुवतुः	ऊर्णुनुवुः

Âtm.

1 ऊर्णुनुवे	ऊर्णुनुविवहे	ऊर्णुनुविमहे
2 ऊर्णुनुविषे	ऊर्णुनुवाथे	ऊर्णुनुविध्वे-ढ्वे
3 ऊर्णुनुवे	ऊर्णुनुवाते	ऊर्णुनुविरे

519. ख्या and क्शा are optionally substituted for चक्ष् in the Perfect, and necessarily in the other Non-conjugational tenses.

ख्या and क्शा take both the Padas.

Par.

1 आचख्यौ	आचख्यिव	आचख्यिम
आचक्शौ	आचक्शिव	आचक्शिम
2 आचख्याथ, आचख्यिथ	आचख्यथुः	आचख्य
आचक्शाथ, आचक्शिथ	आचक्शथुः	आचक्श
3 आचख्यौ	आचख्यतुः	आचख्युः
आचक्शौ	आचक्शतुः	आचक्शुः

Âtm.

1 आचचक्षे	आचचक्षिवहे	आचचक्षिमहे
आचख्ये	आचख्यिवहे	आचख्यिमहे
आचक्शे	आचक्शिवहे	आचक्शिमहे
2 आचचक्षिषे	आचचक्षाथे	आचचक्षिध्वे
आचख्यिषे	आचख्याथे	आचख्यिध्वे-ढ्वे
आचक्शिषे	आचक्शाथे	आचक्शिध्वे
3 आचचक्षे	आचचक्षाते	आचचक्षिरे
आचख्ये	आचख्याते	आचख्यिरे
आचक्शे	आचक्शाते	आचक्शिरे

§ 520. य् is prefixed to vowel weak terminations in the case of दी 4. A. 'to obey.'

1 दिदीये	दिदीयिवहे	दिदीयिमहे
2 दिदीयिषे	दिदीयाथे	दिदीयिध्वे-ढ्वे
3 दिदीये	दिदीयाते	दिदीयिरे

§ 521. दे 1. A. 'to protect' assumes as its base the form दिगि in the Perfect. दिग्ये, दिग्यिवहे, 1 sing. and dual. दिग्यिध्वे-ढ्वे 2 pl.

§ 522. द्युत् after reduplication assumes the form दियुत्; दियुते, 1 sing., दिद्युतिषे 2 sing.

§ 523. पी is substituted for प्यै 'to grow fat' in the Perfect and in the Frequentative; पिप्ये 1 sing., पिप्यिध्वे-ढ्वे 2 pl.

§ 524. The root व्यथ् takes Samprasâraṇa in the reduplicative syllable in the Perfect; विव्यथे 1 & 3 sing. विव्यथिषे 2 sing.

§ 525. For the forms of विज्, see § 466, विवेज 1 sing., विविजिथ विविजथुः विविज 2 per. &c.

PERIPHRASTIC PERFECT.

§ 526. The Periphrastic Perfect is formed by adding आम to the root and then adding the forms of the reduplicated Perfect of कृ, भू, or अस् as terminations; when the forms of कृ, are added, a Parasmaipadi root takes the Parasmaipadi forms and an Atmanepadi one takes the Atmanepadi forms.

§ 527. Before आम् the final vowel and the penultimate short except that of विद्, take their Guṇa substitute.

Paradigms.

ईड् 2. Â. 'to praise.'

1 ईडांचक्रे	ईडांचकृवहे	ईडांचकृमहे
ईडामास	ईडामासिव	ईडामासिम

	ईडांबभूव	ईडांबभूविव	ईडांबभूविम
2	ईडांचकृषे	ईडांचक्राथे	ईडांचकृढ्वे
	ईडामासिथ	ईडामासथुः	ईडामास
	ईडांबभूविथ	ईडांबभूवथुः	ईडांबभूव
3	ईडांचक्रे	ईडांचक्राते	ईडांचक्रिरे
	ईडामास	ईडामासतुः	ईडामासुः
	ईडांबभूव	ईडांबभूवतुः	ईडांबभूवुः

ईक्ष्, ईह्, ऊह्, &c. are similarly conjugated.

दय् 'to give.'

1	दयांचक्रे	दयामास	दयांबभूव
2	दयांचकृषे	दयामासिथ	दयांबभूविथ
3	दयांचक्रे	दयामास	दयांबभूव

अय्—is similarly conjugated.

आस्.

1	आसांचक्रे	आसांचकृवहे	आसांचकृमहे
2	आसांचकृषे	आसांचक्राथे	आसांचकृढ्वे
3	आसांचक्रे	आसांचक्राते	आसांचक्रिरे

also आसामास, आसांबभूव &c.

कास्—is similarly conjugated.

उष् 1. P. 'to burn.'

1	उवोष	ऊषिव	ऊषिम
	ओषांचकार, &c.	ओषांचकृव, &c.	ओषांचकृम, &c.
2	उवोषिथ	ऊषथुः	ऊष
	ओषांचकर्थ, &c.	ओषांचक्रथुः, &c.	ओषांचक्र, &c.
3	उवोष	ऊषतुः	ऊषुः
	ओषांचकार, &c.	ओषांचक्रतुः, &c.	ओषांचक्रुः, &c.

विद् 2. P. 'to know.'

1	विवेद	विविदिव	विविदिम
	विदामास, &c.	विदामासिव, &c.	विदामासिम, &c.

2 विवेदिथ	विविदथुः	विविद
विदामासिथ, &c.	विदामासथुः, &c.	विदामास, &c.
3 विवेद	विविदतुः	विविदुः
विदामास, &c.	विदामासतुः, &c.	विदामासुः, &c.

जागृ 2. P. ' to awake.'

1 जजागार, जजागर	जजागरिव	जजागरिम
जागरामास, &c.	जागरामासिव, &c.	जागरामासिम, &c.
2 जजागरिथ	जजागरथुः	जजागर
जागरामासिथ, &c.	जागरामासथुः, &c.	जागरामास, &c.
3 जजागार	जजागरतुः	जजागरुः
जागरामास, &c.	जागरामासतुः, &c.	जागरामासुः, &c.

गुप्—जुगोप, गोपायांचकार. &c. 1 sing. **जुगुपिव, जुगुप्व, गोपायांचकृव.** &c. dual; **जुगोपिथ, जुगोप्थ गोपायांचकर्थ,** &c. 2 sing.

धूप—दुधूप, or **धूपायांचकार,** &c. 1 sing.

विच्छ्—विविच्छ, or **विच्छायाञ्चकार,** &c. 1 sing.

पण—पेणे or **पणायांचकार** (**पणयांचक्रे** according to Bopadeva) &c. 1 sing.

पन—पेने or **पनायांचकार,** &c. 1 sing.

ऋत्—आनर्त or **ऋतीयांचक्रे** &c. 1 sing.

§ 528. When **आम्** is added to the roots **भी, ह्री भृ** and **हु** they are first reduplicated as in the third conjugation; *e. g.*–

भी 3. P. 'to fear.'

1 बिभाय, बिभय	बिभ्यिव	बिभ्यिम
बिभयांचकार-चकर, &c.	बिभयांचकृव, &c.	बिभयांचकृम, &c.
2 बिभयिथ, बिभेथ	बिभ्यथुः	बिभ्य
बिभयांचकर्थ, &c.	बिभयांचक्रथुः, &c.	बिभयांचक्र, &c.
3 बिभाय	बिभ्यतुः	बिभ्युः
बिभयांचकार, &c.	बिभयांचक्रतुः &c.	बिभयांचक्रुः &c.

ह्री 3 P. ' to be ashamed.'

1 जिह्राय, जिह्रय	जिह्रियिव	जिह्रियिम
जिह्रयांचकार-चकर, &c	जिह्रयांचकृव,	जिह्रयांचकृम, &c.
2 जिह्रयिथ-जिह्रेथ	जिह्रियथुः	जिह्रिय
जिह्रयांचकर्थ &c.	जिह्रयांचक्रथुः &c.	जिह्रयांचक्र, &c.
3 जिह्राय	जिह्रियतुः	जिह्रियुः
जिह्रयांचकार, &c.	जिह्रयांचक्रतुः, &c.	जिह्रयांचक्रुः, &c.

भृ—बभार, बभर, बिभरांचकार-बभूव-रामास 1 sing. हु-जुहाव, जुहव; जुहवांचकार-बभूव—वामास 1. sing. &c.

(5) THE AORIST लुङ्.

§ 529. There are seven Varieties or Forms of the Aorist. The augment अ is perfixed to the root as in the Imperfect

First Variety or Form.

§ 530. The terminations of the First Variety are the same as those of the Imperf., except that of third person plural which is उस्:—

1 अम्	व	म
2 स्	तम्	त
3 त्	ताम्	उस्

§ 531. The radical आ is dropped before उस्.

§ 532. इ, स्था, दा, धा, and roots assuming the forms of दा and धा (Vide § 459), पा 'to drink' and भू take this Variety.

§ 533. The roots घ्रा, धे, शो, सो, and छो belong to this Variety optionally. They optionally take the Sixth Form. धे takes the Third Form also.

Paradigms.

स्था P.			शो P.		
1 अस्थाम्	अस्थाव	अस्थाम	1 अशाम्	अशाव	अशाम

2. अस्थाः	अस्थातम्	अस्थात	2. अशाः	अशातम्	अशात
3. अस्थात्	अस्थाताम्	अस्थुः	3. अशात्	अशाताम्	अशुः

§ 534. भू takes अन् instead of उस् in the 3rd per. pl. and changes its vowel to ऊव् before the vowel terminations; *e. g.* अभूवम्, अभूव, अभूम 1st pers.; अभूत्, अभूताम्, अभूवन् 3rd per.

§ 535. गा is substituted for इ in the Aorist; अगाम, अगाव, अगाम 1st per.; इ with अधि 'to remember' अध्यगाम्, अध्यगाव, अध्यगाम, &c.

§ 536. This Variety is exclusively Parasmaipadi. दा, धा, and स्था take the fourth Variety in the Atm. भू when Atm. takes the fifth; and इ with अधि Atm. the fourth.

Second Variety or Form.

§ 537. In this Variety अ is added on to the root and then the terminations of the Imperf. of the first group of conjugational classes are added; *viz.*

Par.			*Âtm.*		
1. अम्	व	म	1. इ	वहि	महि
2. स्	तम्	त	2. थास्	इथाम्	ध्वम्
3. त्	ताम्	अन्	3. त	इताम्	अन्त

§ 538. The preceding अ is dropped before अम्, अन्, and अन्त and lengthened before व and म. The radical vowel except a final ऋ, short or long, and the ऋ of दृश्, does not undergo Guṇa or Vṛddhi substitute.

§ 539. This Variety is Parasmaipada with a few exceptions such as ऋ with सम्, ख्या, वच्; and अस् 'to throw' with a preposition. The roots लिप्, सिच्, and ह्वे take this form in the Par. and optionally in the Atm., in which they also take the Fourth Form.

§ 540. The penultimate nasal of a root is dropped; as भ्रंश्-अभ्रशत्, स्कन्द्-अस्कदत्, &c.

§ 541. **The roots असु, ख्या, पत्, वच्, शास्, श्वि and ह्वे become अस्थ्, ख्य, पप्त्, वोच्, शिष्, श्व, and ह्व, respectively;** *e. g.* **आस्थत्, अख्यत, अवोचत्, अशिषत्,** &c. 3rd sing.

§ 542. **The roots giving the following couplets (Kárikâs belong to this Variety necessarily:—**

ख्यातीयर्ती सर्सिर्तहे कान्तौ शक्नोतिशक्यती ।
उच् मुच् वक्तिः शिचिश्चान्ता लुब्यतिः पततिस्तथा ॥ १ ॥
दान्ताः क्लिद् क्ष्विद् मदि मिदो विदन्तिः शद्सदिस्विदः ।
ऋधिकुधी क्षुधिगृधी रधिः शुध्यतिसिध्यती ॥ २ ॥
आप्कुपौ गुप्यातिडिपी युप् रुप् लिम्पतिलुप्यती ।
लुम्पतिः सर्पतिः पान्ताः क्षुभ्यतिस्तुभ्यातिर्नभिः ॥ ३ ॥
लुभ्यतिश्च भकारान्ता मान्ताः क्राम्यातिक्षाम्यती ।
गमिस्तमिर्दमिभ्रमी शाम्यतिः श्राम्यतिः समिः ॥ ४ ॥
शान्ताः पञ्च कृशिनशी मृशिर्भ्रंशतिवृश्यर्ती ।
तुष्यातितृष्यतिदुषः पिनष्टिः पुष्यतिः प्लुषिः ॥ ५ ॥
रिष्यरुष् चेवोश्चिवुषो व्युषिः सह शिनष्टिना ।
शुष्याथिर्हृष्यतिः षान्ताः सान्ता अस्यतिकुस्यती ॥ ६ ॥
घसिजसी तसिदसौ वस्यतिर्बिस्यतिर्व्युसिः ।
मस्मुसी यस्वसिविसो बुस्यतिः शास्तिरिन्यपि ॥ ७ ॥
दुहमुह्यस्निहिस्नुहो लुङ्यङ्विकरणा भवेत् ।
नवाशीतिश्च धातूनां परस्मैपदिनामियम् ॥ ८ ॥
समियर्तिः ख्यातिवक्ती अस्यतिश्चोपसर्गयुक् ।
आत्मनेपदिनोऽपीमे ह्वयतिर्लिपिसिञ्चती ॥ ९ ॥
एते विभाषयाङ्वन्त आत्मनेपदिनो यदा ।

ख्या P. with सम् Â.

1 अख्यम्	अख्याव	अख्याम	1 अख्ये	अख्यावहि	अख्यामहि
2 अख्यः	अख्यतम्	अख्यत	2 अख्यथाः	अख्येथाम्	अख्यध्वम्
3 अख्यत्	अख्यताम्	अख्यन्	3 अख्यत	अख्येताम्	अख्यन्त

ऋ 3 P. ' to go Â. with सम

1 आरम्	आराव	आराम	1 समारे	समारावहि	समारामहि
2 आरः	आरतम्	आरत	2 समारथाः	समारेथाम्	समारध्वम्
3 आरत्	आरताम्	आरन्	3 समारत	समारेताम्	समारन्त

सृ I. ' to go '

1 असरम्	असराव	असराम
2 असरः	असरतम्	असरत
3 असरत्	असरताम्	असरन्

ह्वे 1 P. Â.

1 अह्वम्	अह्वाव	अह्वाम	1 अह्वे	अह्वावहि	अह्वामहि
2 अह्वः	अह्वतम्	अह्वत	2 अह्वथाः	अह्वेथाम्	अह्वध्वम्
3 अह्वत्	अह्वताम्	अह्वन्	3 अह्वत	अह्वेताम्	अह्वन्त

वच् 2. P. (also that substituted for ब्रू Par. and Âtm.)

1 अवोचम्	अवोचाव	अवोचाम	1 अवोचे	अवोचावहि	अवोचामहि
2 अवोचः	अवोचतम्	अवोचत	2 अवोचथाः	अवोचेथाम्	अवोचध्वम्
3 अवोचत्	अवोचताम्	अवोचन्	3 अवोचत	अवोचेताम्	अवोचन्त

सिच् 6 P. Â.

1 असिचम्	असिचाव	असिचाम	1 असिचे	असिचावहि	असिचामहि
2 असिचः	असिचतम्	असिचत	2 असिचथाः	असिचेथाम्	असिचध्वम्
3 असिचत्	असिचताम्	असिचन्	3 असिचत	असिचेताम्	असिचन्त

लिप्.

1 अलिपम्	अलिपाव	अलिपाम	1 अलिपे	अलिपावहि	अलिपामहि
2 अलिपः	अलिपतम्	अलिपत	2 अलिपथाः	अलिपेथाम्	अलिपध्वम्
3 अलिपत्	अलिपताम्	अलिपन्	3 अलिपत*	अलिपेताम्	अलिपन्त

* लिप्, सिच् and ह्वे (also take the fourth Variety in the Atm.) अलिप्त, असिक्त अह्वास्त.

अस् 4. P.			Â. with परि.		
1 आस्थम्	आस्थाव	आस्थाम	1 पर्यास्थे	पर्यास्थावहि	पर्यास्थामहि
2 आस्थः	आस्थतम्	आस्थत	2 पर्यास्थथाः	पर्यास्थेथाम्	पर्यास्थध्वम्
3 आस्थत्	आस्थताम्	आस्थन्	3 पर्यास्थत	पर्यास्थेताम्	पर्यास्थन्त

We give below the 3rd per. sing. of the rest.

Roots.

शक्* (5. 4. P. A.) अशकत्
उच् 4. P. 'to collect.'—औचत्
मुच्—अमुचत्
लुट् 4. P. 'to wallow.'—अलुटत्
पत्—अपप्तत्
क्लिद् 4. P. 'to be wet.'—अक्लिदत्
श्विद् 4. P. 'to be oily.'—अश्विदत्
मद्—अमदत्
मिद् 1. 1. A 4. P. 'to be unctuous, to melt—अमिदत्
विद् † 6. P. A—अविदत्
शद् 1 P. 'to perish, to decay' अशदत्
सद्—असदत्
स्विद्—अस्विदत्
ऋध्—4. 5. P. 'to prosper'–आर्धत्
क्रुध्—अक्रुधत्
क्षुध्—अक्षुधत्
गृध् 4. P. 'to covet'—अगृधत्
रध् 4. P. 'to hurt'—अरधत्

Roots.

शुध्—अशुधत्
सिध्—असिधत्
आप्—आपत्
कुप्—अकुपत्
गुप्–4. P. 'to be confused'–अगुपत्
डिप्—4. P. 'to throw'—अडिपत्
युप्—अयुपत्
रुप्—अरुपत्
लुप् ‡—4. 6. P. A.—अलुपत्
सृप्—असृपत्
क्षुभ्—अक्षुभत्
तुभ्—' to kill.—अतुभत्
नभ्—4. P. 'to kill—अनभत्
लुभ्—अलुभत्
क्रम्—अक्रमत्
क्षम्—अक्षमत्
गम्—अगमत्
तम्—अतमत्
दम्—अदमत्
भ्रम्=अभ्रमत्

---

* शक् 4. A. takes the Fourth, as well as the Fifth Variety, in the Atm. अशक्त, अशकिष्ट 3rd sing.

† विद् A. takes the Fourth or Fifth Variety. अवित्त, अवेदिष्ट 3rd sing.

‡ लुप् takes the Fourth Form in the Atm; अलुप्त.

शम्—अशमत्
श्रम्—अश्रमत्
सम् 1. P. 'to be confused or agitated.'—असमत्
कृश् 4. P. 'to be thin' अकृशत्
नश्—अनशत्
भृश् 4. P. 'to fall'—अभृशत्
भ्रंश्—अभ्रशत्
वृश् 4. P. 'to choose'—अवृशत्
तुष्—अतुषत्
तृष् 4. P. 'to be thirsty'—अतृषत्
दुष् 4. P. 'to be spoiled,' &c. [अदुषत्
पिष्—अपिषत्
पुष्—अपुषत्
प्लुष्—4. P. 'to burn'—अप्लुषत्
रिष् 4. P. 'to injure, to kill'—अरिषत्
रुष् 4. P. 'to be angry or vexed'—अरुषत्
विष्* 3. P. A. 'to spread through' -अविषत्
वुष—अवुषत्
व्युष् 4. P. 'to divide'—अव्युषत्
शिष्—अशिषत्
शुष् 4. P. 'to be dry'—अशुषत्
हृष्—अहृषत्
कुस् 4. P. 'to embrace'—अकुसत्,
घस्—1. P. 'to eat'—अघसत्
जस् 4. P. 'to release'—अजसत्
तस् 4. P. 'to fade away' अतसत्
दस् 4. P. 'to decay, to perish' अदसत्
बस् 4. P. 'to be straight'—अबसत्
बिस् 4. P. 'to go, to direct'—अबिसत्
व्युस् 4. P. 'to throw'—अव्युसत्
मस् 4. P. 'to weigh, to change form'—अमसत्
मुस् 4. P. 'to cut' अमुसत्
यस् 4. P. 'to strive' अयसत्
वस्—same as बस्
विस्—same as बिस्
बु(वु)स्—अबु(वु)सत्
शास्—अशिषत्
दुह्—अदुहत्
मुह्—अमुहत्
लिह्—अलिहत्
स्नुह्—अस्नुहत्

§ 543. The following roots belong to the 2nd Variety optionally; they optionally take the Fourth or Fifth Variety according as they are Anit or Set.

श्वयतिर्जार्यतिग्रुची ग्लुचिग्लुञ्चिम्रुचिम्लुचः ।
रिणक्तिश्च विनक्तिश्च चान्तास्त्वष्टौ च शुच्यतिः ॥ १ ॥
नेनेक्तिश्च युनक्तिश्च वेवेक्तिस्फोटती चुतिः ।
च्युतिज्रुती श्चोततिश्च श्च्युतिर्दान्ता रुदादयः ॥ २ ॥

---

* विष् Atm. takes the Seventh Variety, अविक्षत.

क्षुदिछिदी छृदितृदी बुन्दतिश्च भिनत्तिना ।
रुदिस्कन्दी बोधतिश्च रुणद्धिश्च तृपिर्दृपिः ॥ ३ ॥
स्तभ्नातिः स्तभ्नोतिदृशी घोषतिश्लिष्यती उह्दिः ।
तोहतिर्दोहतिबृही चत्वारिंशदियं लुङि ॥ ४ ॥
विभाषयाङ्किरणा परस्मैपदिनी यदा ।

Roots.	3rd sing.	Optional forms.	Roots.	3rd sing.	Optional forms
श्वि	अश्वत्	आशिश्वियत्*, अश्वयीत्	श्चुत्	अश्चुतत्	अश्चोतीत्
जॄ	अजरत्	अजारीत्	श्च्युत्	अश्च्युतत्	अश्च्योतीत्
ग्रुच्	अग्रुचत्	अग्रोचीत्	क्षुद्	अक्षुदत्	अक्षौत्सीत्, अक्षुत्त
ग्लुच्	अग्लुचत्	अग्लोचीत्	छिद्	आच्छिदत्	अच्छैत्सीत्, आच्छित्त
ग्लुञ्च्	अग्लुञ्चत्	अग्लुञ्चीत्	छृद्	अच्छृदत्	अच्छर्दीत्, अच्छर्दिष्ट
म्रुच्	अम्रुचत्	अम्रोचीत्	तृद्	अतृदत्	अतर्दीत्, अतर्दिष्ट
म्लुच्	अम्लुचत्	अम्लोचीत्	बुन्द्	अबुदत्	अबुन्दीत्, अबुन्दिष्ट
रिच्	अरिचत्	अरैक्षीत्, अरिक्त	भिद्	अभिदत्	अभैत्सीत्, अभित्त
विच्	अविचत्	अवैक्षीत्, अविक्त	रुद्	अरुदत्	अरोदीत्
शुच्	अशुचत्	अशोचीत्, अशोचिष्ट	स्कन्द्	अस्कदत्	अस्कान्त्सीत्
निज्	अनिजत्	अनैक्षीत्, अनिक्त	बुध्	अबुधत्	अबोधीत्, अबोधिष्ट
युज्	अयुजत्	अयौक्षीत् अयुक्त	रुध्	अरुधत्	अरौत्सीत्, अरुद्ध
विज्	अविजत्	अवैक्षीत्, अविक्त	तृप्	अतृपत्	अताप्सीत्, अत्राप्सीत्, अतर्पीत्
स्फुट्	अस्फुटत्	अस्फोटीत्	दृप्	अदृपत्	आदार्प्सीत्, अद्राप्सीत्, अदर्पीत्
चुत्	अचुतत्	अचोतीत्	स्तम्भ्	अस्तभत्	अस्तम्भीत्
च्युत्	अच्युतत्	अच्योतीत्			
जुत्	अजुतत्	अजोतीत्, अजोतिष्ट			

* श्वि takes the Third and Fifth Varieties besides the 2nd.

Roots. 3 sing.	Optional forms.	Roots. 3 sing.	Optional forms.
दृश्—अदर्शत्	अद्राक्षीत्	तुह्—अतुहत	अतोहीत्
श्लिष्-अश्लिषत्	अश्लिक्षत्	दुह्—अदुहत्	अदोहीत
घुष्—अघुषत्	अघोषीत्	बृह्—अबृहत	अबर्हीत्
उह्—औहत्	औहीत्		

§ 544. The following 25 roots, which are all Atmanepadi, are conjugated in the Parasmaipada when they belong to this Variety. In the Atmanepada they take the Fourth or Fifth Variety according as they are Anit or Set.

> रुचिर्घुटिरुटिलुटो लोठते द्युतिवृतश्वितः ।
> क्ष्वेदते मेदते स्यन्दिः स्वेदते च वृधिः शृधिः ॥ १ ॥
> कल्पते क्षुभतुभिनभः शोभते स्रंभते भ्रशिः ।
> भ्रंशिध्वंसी भ्रंसिस्रंसी रुचादिः पञ्चविंशतिः ॥ २ ॥
> आत्मनेपदिनो नित्यं लुङि त्वेषा विभाषया ।
> अङं परस्मैपदिनो भजन्त्यन्यत्र सिज्वती ॥ ३ ॥

Roots. 3 sing.	Optional forms.	Roots. 3 sing.	Optional forms.
रुच्—अरुचत्	अरोचिष्ट	वृध्—अवृधत्	अवर्धिष्ट
घुट्—अघुटत्	अघोटिष्ट	शृध्—अशृधत्	अशर्धिष्ट
रुट्—अरुटत्	अरोटिष्ट	क्लृप्—अक्लृपत	अकल्पिष्ट, अक्लृप्त
लुट्—अलुटत्	अलोटिष्ट	क्षुभ्—अक्षुभत्	अक्षोभिष्ट
लुठ्—अलुठत्	अलोठिष्ट	तुभ्—अतुभत्	अतोभिष्ट
द्युत्—अद्युतत्	अद्योतिष्ट	नभ्—अनभत्	अनभिष्ट
वृत्—अवृतत्	अवर्तिष्ट	शुभ्—अशुभत्	अशोभिष्ट
श्वित्—अश्वितत्	अश्वेतिष्ट	स्रंभ्—अस्रभत्	अस्रंभिष्ट
क्ष्विद्—अक्ष्विदत्	अक्ष्वेदिष्ट	भ्रश्—अभ्रशत्	अभ्रशिष्ट
मिद्—अमिदत्	अमेदिष्ट	भ्रंश्—अभ्रशत	अभ्रंशिष्ट
स्यन्द्—अस्यदत्	अस्यन्दिष्ट, अस्यंत्त	ध्वंस्—अध्वसत्	अध्वंसिष्ट
		भ्रंस्—अभ्रसत्	अभ्रंसिष्ट
स्विद्—अस्विदत	अस्वेदिष्ट	स्रंस्—अस्रसत्	अस्रंसिष्ट

THIRD VARIETY OR FORM.

§ 545. Terminations:—

The same as those of the 2nd Variety.

§ 546. Roots of the tenth class, causals, some derivatives, the root कम् and the roots श्रि, द्रु, and स्रु when expressing the agent, take this Variety necessarily, and the roots धे and श्वि do it optionally.

§ 547. (a) The root is first reduplicated and then the augment अ and the terminations are added as in the 2nd Variety.

(b) Final इ and उ are changed to इय् and उव् before अ and final ओ is dropped.

Paradigms.

श्रि P. Â. 'to go,' &c.

Par.

1 अशिश्रियम्	अशिश्रियाव	अशिश्रियाम
2 अशिश्रियः	अशिश्रियतम्	अशिश्रियत
3 अशिश्रियत्	अशिश्रियताम्	अशिश्रियन्

Âtm.

1 अशिश्रिये	अशिश्रियावहि	अशिश्रियामहि
2 अशिश्रियथाः	अशिश्रियेथाम्	अशिश्रियध्वम्
3 अशिश्रियत	अशिश्रियेताम्	अशिश्रियन्त

द्रु—अदुद्रुवत् 3 Sing.; स्रु—असुस्रुवत् 3 Sing; कम्—अचकमत. (अचीकमत also, when it takes आय्; see § 461 and § 548.) 3 sing. श्वि-अशिश्वियत् (see p. 338. foot-note); धे—अदधत्. (धे also takes 1st and 6th Varieties besides this).

§ 548. Roots of the tenth Class and Causals:—

(a) The अय of the base is dropped (the vowel changes taking place before it being retained) and a short vowel substituted for the long one (ए and ऐ being shortened to इ, and ओ and औ to उ).

The base so modified is then reduplicated according to the general rules; भावय (Cau. B. of भू) = भाव् = भव् = बभव् after reduplication; चेतय् (from चित्)=चेत् = चित् = चिचित् &c.

(*b*) इ is substituted for the अ of the reduplicative syllable if the syllable following it be short, and not prosodially long; the इ of the reduplicative syllable is lengthened if not followed by a long syll. or a conjunct consonant; thus बभव् = बिभव् = बीभव्; चिचित् = चीचित्; स्खल् = चस्खल् = चिस्खल्, the इ is not lengthened as it is followed by a conjunct consonant; स्पन्द् = पस्पन्द् only, as प is followed by a syllable prosodially long.

(*c*) Roots having a penultimate ऋ, short or long, optionally preserve it, the long ॠ being changed to the short one; वृत् causal base वर्तय=वर्त् after dropping अय and वृत् by this: वर्त्=ववर्त्; वृत्=ववृत् = विवृत् = वीवृत्; कॄत्–कीर्तय = कीर्त् and कृत् by this; कीर्त्—चिकीर्त्; कृत्—चीकृत्.

(*d*) To the base so prepared the augment अ is to be prefixed and the terminations added, P. & A., as in the 2nd Variety:—अबीभवत्-त from भू; अचीचितत् from चित्; अचिस्खलत्-त from स्खल्; अपस्पन्दत्-त from स्पन्द्; अववर्तत्-त, अवीवृतत्-त from वृत्; अचिकीर्तत्-त, अचीकृतत्-त fr. कॄत्; अपपर्थत्-त, अपीपृथत्-त from पृथ्, &c.

N. B. The Atm. form in त when not given should be supposed to be understood.

§ 549. Bases with initial vowels:—

(*a*) If a root begins with a vowel and ends in a single consonant, the consonant is reduplicated and इ added to it in the reduplicative syllable: अट् = अट्ट् = आटिट् = आटिटत्-त; आप् = आपिपत्-त; ऊह् = औजिहत्-त; &c.

(*b*) If it ends in a conjunct consonant with न्, द् or र् for its first member, the second member of the conjunct is reduplioated: उन्द्=रन्द्द्=उन्दिद् and finally औन्दिदत्-त 3 sing., similarly आट्टिटत्-त from अट्ट् (considered as अट्ट्, otherwise आटिट्टत्), आर्जिहत्-त from अर्ह्; आर्जिजत्-त from अर्ज्, &c.

(c) The roots ऊन्, अङ्क्, अङ्ग्, अन्ध्, अंस्, अर्थ् Atm. and some others, substitute अ for इ in the reduplicative syllable; 3 sing. औननत्, आञ्चकत्, आञ्जगत्, आन्दधत्, आंससत्, आर्तथत, &c.

§ 550. Roots ending in उ, short or long, substitute उ (changeable to ऊ like ई) for इ in the reduplicative syllable, provided it be not (immediately) followed by a labial consonant or a semivowel or ज्, followed by अ or आ; नु-अनूनवत्-त, कू-अचूकवत्-त, दू-अदूदवत, युु-अदुयवत्-त, &c. But पू-अपीपवत्-त, भू-अबीभवत्-त, जु 'to hasten' अजीजवत, मु 'to bind'—अमीमवत्, यु 'to bind' अयीयवत्, रु-अरीरवत्-त; लू-अलीलवत, &c.

(a) The roots स्रु, श्रु द्रु, प्रु 'to go' प्लु 'to swim' and च्यु optionally retain the इ: असिस्रवत् or असुस्रवत्, आशिश्रवत् or अशुश्रवत्, अदिद्रवत् or अदुद्रवत, अपिप्रवत or अपुप्रवत्, अपिप्लवत् or अपुप्लवत्, अचिच्यवत् or अचुच्यवत्-त.

§ 551. The roots भ्राज्, भास्, भाष्, दीप्, जीव्, मील्, पीड्, कण् 'to moan' चण् 'to sound,' 'to go,' रण् 'to sound,' भण्, वण् to sound,' श्रण् 'to give' लुप् 6. P. A. 'to cut,' हेठ् 'to harass,' ह्वे, लुट्, लुठ् and लुप् 4. P; shorten their penultimate optionally; 1. sing.:—अबिभ्रजम् or अबभ्राजम्, अबीभसम् or अबभासम्, अबीभषम् or अबभाषम्. अदीदिपम् or अदिदीपम्, अजीजिवम् or अजिजीवम्, अमीमिलम् or अमिमीलम्, अपीपिडम् or अपिपीडम्, अचीकणम् or अचकाणम्, अचीचणम् or अचचाणम्, अरीरणम् or अरराणम्, अबीभणम् or अबभाणम्, अबीवणम् or अववाणम्, अशिश्रणम् or अशश्राणम्, अलूलुपम् or अलुलोपम्, अजीहिठम् or अजिहेठम्, अजूहवम् or अजुहावम् (see § 553 below), अलूलुटम् or अलुलोटम्, अलूलुठम् or अलुलोठम्; &c.

§ 552. The अ of the reduplicative syllable of स्मृ, दृ, त्वर्, प्रथ्, म्रद् 'to pound, to wish,' स्तृ, and स्पश्, is not changed to इ; वेष्ट् 1. A.

'to surround' and चेष्ट् optionally change their इ to अ; 1 sing असस्मरम्, अददरम्, अतत्वरम्, अपप्रथम्, अमम्रदम्, अतस्तरम्, अपस्पशम्; वेष्ट्—अविवेष्टम्, अववेष्टम्; चेष्ट्—अचिचेटम्, अचचेटम्.

§ 553. The roots ह्वे and स्वप् cau. take Samprasârana; श्वि does it optionally; ह्वे-हु-हावय्—हाव् or हव्, then जुहव्, जुहाव् by 550; then अजुहावम्, अजूहवम्; स्वप्—स्वापय्—स्वाप्—सुप्—सुषुप्—सूषुप्; असूषुपम्; श्वि—अशूशवम्, अशिश्वयम् 1st sing.

§ 554. The roots given under § 400 preserve their vowel unchanged; *i. e.* do not substitute इ in the reduplicative syllable, &c. कथ्—अचकथत्, वर्—अववरत्, शठ्—अशशठत्, रह्—अररहत्, पत्—अपपतत्, स्पृह्—अपस्पृहत्, सूच्—असुसूचत्.

§ 555. The roots शास्, एज्, काश्, क्रीड्, क्षीव्, खाद्, खेल्, ढौक्, ताय्, दाश्, देव्, नाथ्, प्रोथ्, बाध्, याच्, योध्, राध्, राज्, लाघ्, लेप्, लोक्, लोच्, वेप्, वेल्, श्लाघ्, श्लोक्, सेक्, सेव्, हेष्, and others less important, do not shorten their penultimate; 3 sing. अशशासत्, ऐजिजत्, अचकाशत्, अचिक्रीडत्, अचिक्षीवत्, अचखादत्, अचिखेलत्, &c.

§ 556. Roots which form their Causal Aorist irregularly:—

इ with अधि 'to study,—अध्यापिपत्, अध्यजीगपत्, (इ with अधि 'to remember' अध्यजीगमत्).

ईर्ष्य् 'to envy'—ऐर्षिष्यत्-त, ऐर्ष्ययत्-त

ऊर्णु—और्णुनवत्

गण्—अजगणत्, अजीगणत्

घ्रा—अजिघ्रपत्, अजिघ्रिपत्

चकास्—अचीचकासत्, अचचकासत्

द्युत्—अदुद्युतत्-त

पा 'to drink' अपीप्यत् (पा 'to protect' forms its Causal Aorist regularly as अपीपलत्).

स्था—अतिष्ठिपत्-त.
स्फुर्—अपुस्फुरत्-त.

Paradigms.

कृ 'to do.'

	Par.			Âtm.		
1	अचीकरम्	अचीकराव	अचीकराम	अचीकरे	अचीकरावहि	अचीकरामहि
2	अचीकरः	अचीकरतम्	अचीकरत	अचीकरथाः	अचीकरेथाम्	अचीकरध्वम्
3	अचीकरत्	अचीकरताम्	अचीकरन्	अचीकरत	अचीकरेताम्	अचीकरन्त

त्रप्.

1	अतित्रपम्	अतित्रपाव	अतित्रपाम	अतित्रपे	अतित्रपावहि	अतित्रपामहि
2	अतित्रपः	अतित्रपतम्	अतित्रपत	अतित्रपथाः	अतित्रपेथाम्	अतित्रपध्वम्
3	अतित्रपत्	अतित्रपताम्	अतित्रपन्	अतित्रपत	अतित्रपेताम्	अतित्रपन्त

चुर्.

1	अचूचुरम्	अचूचुराव	अचूचुराम	अचूचुरे	अचूचुरावहि	अचूचुरामहि
2	अचूचुरः	अचूचुरतम्	अचूचुरत	अचूचुरथाः	अचूचुरेथाम्	अचूचुरध्वम्
3	अचूचुरत्	अचूचुरताम्	अचूचुरन्	अचूचुरत	अचूचुरेताम्	अचूचुरन्त

SIXTH VARIETY OR FORM.

(Only Parasmaipadi)

N. B.—The Sixth and the Seventh Varieties are given here before the Fourth and Fifth as it is more convenient to do so.

§ 557. Terminations of the Sixth Form:—

1	सिषम्	सिष्व	सिष्म
2	सीः	सिष्टम्	सिष्ट
3	सीत्	सिष्टाम्	सिषुः

§ 558. Roots ending in आ (including those that change their final to आ), the roots यम्, रम् P. (*i. e.* with वि, आ, परि) and नम्

take this Variety. यम् with उप or उद्, A. and रम् A. take the fourth Variety.

§ 559. The roots ending in आ which are restricted to the First, Second and Third Varieties do not take this Variety.

PARADIGMS.

यम्.

1 अयंसिषम्	अयंसिष्व	अयंसिष्म
2 अयंसीः	अयंसिष्टम्	अयंसिष्ट
3 अयंसीत्	अयंसिष्टाम्	अयंसिषुः

विरम्—व्यरंसिषम्, व्यरंसिष्व, व्यरंसिष्म &c.: नम्—अनंसिषम्, अनंसिष्व, अनंसिष्म, &c ; शो—अशासिषम्, &c ; छो—अच्छासिषम्, &c.; मि or मी—अमासिषम्, अमासिष्व, अमासिष्म, &c.; ली—अलासिषम् अलासिष्व, अलासिष्म, &c.

SEVENTH VARIETY OR FORM.

(Parasm. and Atm.)

§ 560. Terminations:—

Par.			Âtm.		
1 सम्	साव	साम	1 सि	सावहि	सामहि
2 सः	सतम्	सत	2 सथाः	साथाम्	सध्वम्
3 सत्	सताम्	सन्	3 सत	साताम्	सन्त

§ 561. Anit roots ending in श्, ष्, स् and ह् and having इ, उ, ऋ or ऌ for their penultimate take this Form. दृश् is an exception; it therefore takes the Fourth Variety.

§ 562. मृश्, स्पृश् and कृष्, 1 P. 6 P. A. optionally belong to this Variety.

§ 563. The roots दुह्, दिह्, लिह्, and गुह् when Atmanepadi drop the initial स or सा of the terminations of the 1st dual, 3rd sing. and 2nd sing. and pl. optionally.

PARADIGMS.

दिश् P. A.

1 अदिक्षम्	अदिक्षाव	अदिक्षाम	1 अदिक्षि	अदिक्षावहि	अदिक्षामहि
2 अदिक्षः	अदिक्षतम्	अदिक्षत	2 अदिक्षथाः	अदिक्षाथाम्	अदिक्षध्वम्
3 अदिक्षत्	अदिक्षताम्	अदिक्षन्	3 अदिक्षत	अदिक्षाताम्	अदिक्षन्त

दिह् P. A.

1 अधिक्षम्	अधिक्षाव	अधिक्षाम	1 अधिक्षि	अधिक्षावहि अदिह्वहि	अधिक्षामहि
2 अधिक्षः	अधिक्षतम्	अधिक्षत	2 अधिक्षथाः अदिग्धाः	अधिक्षाथाम्	अधिक्षध्वम् अधिग्ध्वम्
3 अधिक्षत्	अधिक्षताम्	अधिक्षन्	3 अधिक्षत अदिग्ध	अधिक्षाताम्	अधिक्षन्त

दुह् is to be similarly conjugated.

लिह्

1 अलिक्षम्	अलिक्षाव	अलिक्षाम	1 अलिक्षि	अलिक्षावहि अलिह्वहि	अलिक्षामहि
2 अलिक्षः	अलिक्षतम्	अलिक्षत	2 अलिक्षथाः अलीढाः	अलिक्षाथाम्	अलिक्षध्वम् अलीढ्वम्
3 अलिक्षत्	अलिक्षताम्	अलिक्षन्	3 अलिक्षत अलीढ	अलिक्षाताम्	अलिक्षन्त

गुह्* P. A.

1 अघुक्षम्	अघुक्षाव	अघुक्षाम	1 अघुक्षि	अघुक्षावहि अगुह्वहि	अघुक्षामहि
2 अघुक्षः	अघुक्षतम्	अघुक्षत	2 अघुक्षथाः अगूढाः	अघुक्षाथाम्	अघुक्षध्वम् अघूढ्वम्

* गुह् being a Wet root optionally takes the Fifth Variety. अगूहिषम्, अगूहिषि, &c.

3 अघुक्षत्	अघुक्षताम्	अघुक्षन्	3 अघुक्षत अगूढ	अघुक्षताम्	अघुक्षन्त

Roots. 1 sing.	Roots 1 sing.
रिश्—अरिक्षम्	त्विष्—अत्विक्षम्, अत्विक्षि
रुश्—अरुक्षम्	द्विष्—अद्विक्षम्, अद्विक्षि
लिश्—अलिक्षम्, अलिक्षि	विष्—अविक्षम्
विश्—अविक्षम्	श्लिष्—अश्लिक्षम्
कुश्—अकुक्षम्	गृह्—अघृक्षि—अगर्हिषि
क्लिश्*—अक्लिक्षम्, अक्लेशिषम्	मिह्—अमिक्षम्
स्पृश्—अस्पृक्षम्, अस्पार्क्षम् अस्प्राक्षम्	तृह्—अतृक्षम्
मृश्—अमृक्षम्, अमार्क्षम्, अम्राक्षम्	स्तृह्—अस्तृक्षम्, अस्तर्हिषम्
कुष् with निर्—निरकुक्षम्, निरकोषिषम्	बृह्—अभृक्षम्, अबर्हिषम्
कृष्—अकृक्षम्, अकृक्षि, अकार्क्षम्, अक्राक्षम्, अकृक्षि	वृह्—अवृक्षम्, अवर्हिषम्
	रुह्—अरुक्षम्

FOURTH VARIETY OR FORM.

§ 564. Terminations:—

Parasm.			Âtm.		
1 सम्	स्व	स्म	1 सि	स्वहि	स्महि
2 सीः	स्तम्	स्त	2 स्थाः	साथाम्	ध्वम्
3 सीत्	स्ताम्	सुः	3 स्त	साताम्	सत

§ 565. (*a*) Anit roots not belonging to any of the preceding Varieties take this Form. Anit roots that optionally take any of the preceding Varieties and Wet roots optionally belong to this Varity.

---

* Wet roots which belong to this Variety, as Anit, optionally take the 5th as Set.

Exceptions:—

(1) स्तु and सु, when Parasmaipadi, belong to the Fifth Variety.

(2) Roots ending in ऋ preceded by a conjunct consonant may take Fourth or Fifth Form in the Atmanepada.

(3) भञ्ज् and धू Par. take the Fifth Form only. धू A. may take the Fourth or the Fifth Form.

(4) Of Set roots वृ and those ending in ॠ (long) when Atm. belong to either (4th or 5th Variety). स्तु, and क्रम् when A. belong to the Fourth.

§ 566 (*a*) In the Parasmaipada the radical vowel takes its Vṛddhi substitute; नी-अनैषीत्; कृ-अकार्षीत्; भञ्ज्-अभांक्षीत्, &c.

(*b*) In the Atmanepada, Guṇa is substituted for final इ or उ, short or long; final ऋ and the penultimate vowel remain unchanged; final ॠ is changed to ईर् or ऊर् in accordance with § 394; चि-अचेष्ट, नी-अनेष्ट, च्यु-अच्योष्ट, सू-असोष्ट, कृ see below, भिद्-अभित्त, स्तॄ-अस्तीर्ष्ट, वॄ-अवूर्ष्ट.

(*c*) The Penultimate ऋ of Anit roots is optionally changed to र; कृष्-अकार्क्षीत् or अक्राक्षीत्.

§ 567. After a short vowel, and after a consonant except a nasal or semi-vowel, the स् of terminations beginning with स्त and स्थ is dropped; हृ-अहृत 3 sing.; कृ-अकृथाः 2 sing.; क्षिप्-अक्षिप्थाः अक्षिप्त; कृष्-अकृष्ट 3rd sing. &c.

Paradigms.

पच्

1	अपाक्षम्	अपाक्ष्व	अपाक्ष्म	अपक्षि	अपक्ष्वहि	अपक्ष्महि
2	अपाक्षीः	अपाक्तम्	अपाक्त	अपक्थाः	अपक्षाथाम्	अपग्ध्वम्
3	अपाक्षीत्	अपाक्ताम्	अपाक्षुः	अपक्त	अपक्षाताम्	अपक्षत

Conjugate similarly other Anit roots ending in consonants; क्षिप-अक्षैप्सम् P. 1. sing.; अक्षिप्सि Atm. 1. sing.; युज-अयौक्षम्,

अयुक्षि 1. sing. P. & A.; सृज्-अस्राक्षम्* 1 sing. अस्राष्टम् 2nd dual, दृश्-अद्राक्षम्; with सम् A. समदृक्षि 1 sing.; प्रच्छ्-अप्राक्षम् 1 sing.; अप्राक्षीः अप्राष्टम् अप्राष्ट 2 per. &c; रुध्-अरौत्सम् 1 sing.; अरौत्सीः 2 sing.; अरौद्धम् 2 per. dual., &c; A. अरुत्सि 1st sing.; अरुद्ध, अरुत्साताम् 3rd sing. and dual; दह्—अधाक्षम् 1 sing.; अदाग्धम् 2nd dual.

जि P. with वि Âtm.

1 अजैषम्	अजैष्व	अजैष्म	व्यजेषि	व्यजेष्वहि	व्यजेष्महि
2 अजैषीः	अजैष्टम्	अजैष्ट	व्यजेष्ठाः	व्यजेषाथाम्	व्यजेढ्वम्
3 अजैषीत्	अजैष्टाम्	अजैषुः	व्यजेष्ट	व्यजेषाताम्	व्यजेषत

Conjugate similarly चि, नी, ली, † &c.; श्रु, यु, 9. P. A. &c.; चि—अचैषम्, अचेषि 1 sing.; ली 9. P. 4. A. अलैषम् 1 sing.; अलेषि, अलासि, 1 sing.; श्रु-अश्रौषम्, &c.

कृ P. Â.

1 अकार्षम्	अकार्ष्व	अकार्ष्म	अकृषि	अकृष्वहि	अकृष्महि
2 अकार्षीः	अकार्ष्टम्	अकार्ष्ट	अकृथाः	अकृषाथाम्	अकृढ्वम्
3 अकार्षीत्	अकार्ष्टाम्	अकार्षुः	अकृत	अकृषाताम्	अकृषत

स्तृ P. A. is similarly conjugated. Conjugate ह्र A. similarly.

वृ Â.   स्तॄ Â.

1 अवूर्षि	अवूर्ष्वहि	अवूर्ष्महि	1 अस्तीर्षि	अस्तीर्ष्वहि	अस्तीर्ष्महि
2 अवूर्ष्ठाः	अवूर्षाथाम्	अवूर्ढ्वम्	2 अस्तीर्ष्ठाः	अस्तीर्षाथाम्	अस्तीर्ढ्वम्
3 अवूर्ष्ट	अवूर्षाताम्	अवूर्षत	3 अस्तीर्ष्ट	अस्तीर्षाताम्	अस्तीर्षत

धू A.   कृष्‡ P.

1 अधोषि	अधोष्वहि	अधोष्महि	1 अकार्क्षम्	अकार्क्ष्व	अकार्क्ष्म
			अक्राक्षम्	अक्राक्ष्व	अक्राक्ष्म

* Vide § 465.

† Also take the 6th Variety when it substitutes आ for its final.

‡ कृश्, स्पृश् and मृश् also take the 7th Variety; तृप् and दृप् take the 2nd and 5th besides this.

2 अधोष्ठाः	अधोषाथाम्	अधोढ्वम्	2 अकार्क्षीः	अकार्ष्टम्	अकार्ष्ट
			अक्राक्षीः	अक्राष्टम्	अक्राष्ट
3 अधोष्ट	अधोषाताम्	अधोषत	3 अकार्क्षीत्	अकार्ष्टाम्	अकार्क्षुः
			अक्राक्षीत्	अक्राष्टाम्	अक्राक्षुः

मृज् Âtm. अकृक्षि, &c.

1 अमार्क्षम्	अमार्क्ष्व	अमार्क्ष्म	Conjugate similarly तृप्, दृप्, स्पृश्, &c.
2 अमार्क्षीः	अमार्ष्टम्	अमार्ष्ट	तृप्–अतार्प्सीत्, अत्राप्सीत्; &c.
3 अमार्क्षीत्	अमार्ष्टाम्	अमार्क्षुः	स्पृश्–अस्पार्क्षीत्, अस्प्राक्षीत्; &c.
			मृश्–अमार्क्षीत्, अम्राक्षीत्; &c.

*** वस् 1 P.**

1 अवात्सम्	अवात्स्व	अवात्स्म
2 अवात्सीः	अवात्तम्	अवात्त
3 अवात्सीत्	अवात्ताम्	अवात्सुः

वह् P. Â.

1 अवाक्षम्	अवाक्ष्व	अवाक्ष्म	अवक्षि	अवक्ष्वहि	अवक्ष्महि
2 अवाक्षीः	अवोढम्	अवोढ	अवोढाः	अवक्षाथाम्	अवोढ्वम्
3 अवाक्षीत्	अवोढाम्	अवाक्षुः	अवोढ	अवक्षाताम्	अवक्षत

† गाह् A. | **क्रम् with प्र.**

1 अघाक्षि	अघाक्ष्वहि	अघाक्ष्महि	1 प्राक्रंसि	प्राक्रंस्वहि	प्राक्रंस्महि
2 अगाढाः	अघाक्षाथाम्	अघाढ्वम्	2 प्राक्रंस्थाः	प्राक्रंसाथाम्	प्राक्रन्ध्वम्
3 अगाढ	अघाक्षाताम्	अघाक्षत	3 प्राक्रंस्त	प्राक्रंसाताम्	प्राक्रंसत

क्षम् to be similarly conjugatd
अक्षंसि 1 sing. &c.

---

* वस्–Vide § 480. अवास् + स्ताम् = अवात् + स्ताम् = अवात्ताम् 3rd dual. वस् A. takes the 5th Variety since it is Set.

† Also takes the 5th Variety.

Irregular Aorist or the Fourth Form.

§ 568. दा, धा, and roots assuming the forms of दा and धा (Vide § 459) and स्था substitute इ for their final vowel in the Atm. This इ does not take its Guṇa substitute. In the Parasm. these roots take the first Variety (vide § 532).

§ 569. हन् (with आ A.) drops its nasal before the terminations.

It takes the Fifth Form optionally both in the Parasm. and Atm. in which case वध् is substituted for it.

§ 570. गम्, and यम् with उप 'to marry,' optionally drop their nasal, when they take the Atm. terminations. यम् when it means 'to give out' (as the faults of others) necessarily drops its nasal.

§ 571. The third person sing. of पद् is अपादि. बुध 4. A. takes the termination इ optionally in the 3rd sing. before which the penultimate उ takes Guṇa.

Paradigms.

हन् Â (with आ)

1 आहसि	आहस्वहि	आहस्महि
2 आहथाः	आहसाथाम्	आहध्वम्
3 आहत	आहसाताम्	आहसत

यम् with उद् & आ.

1 उदायसि	उदायस्वहि	उदायस्महि
2 उदायथाः	उदायसाथाम्	उदायध्वम्
3 उदायत	उदायसाताम्	उदायसत

गम् with सम्.

1 समगंसि	समगंस्वहि	समगंस्महि
2 समगंस्थाः	समगंसाथाम्	समगन्ध्वम्
3 समगंस्त	समगंसाताम्	समगंसत

1 समगसि	समगस्वहि	समगस्महि
2 समगथाः	समगसाथाम्	समगध्वम्
3 समगत	समगसाताम्	समगसत

यम् with उप to be similarly conjugated; उपायंसि, उपायसि 1 sing.; उपायंस्वहि, उपायस्वहि 1 dual; उपायंस्थाः, उपायथाः 2 sing. &c.

बुध्.

1 अभुत्सि	अभुत्स्वहि	अभुत्स्महि
2 अबुद्धाः	अभुत्साथाम्	अभुध्वम्
3 अबुद्ध, अबोधि	अभुत्साताम्	अभुत्सत

पद्.

1 अपत्सि	अपत्स्वहि	अपत्स्महि
2 अपत्थाः	अपत्साथाम्	अपध्वम्
3 अपादि	अपत्साताम्	अपत्सत

इ with अधि *

1 अध्यगीषि	अध्यगीष्वहि	अध्यगीष्महि
2 अध्यगीष्ठाः	अध्यगीषाथाम्	अध्यगीढ्वम्
3 अध्यगीष्ट	अध्यगीषाताम्	अध्यगीषत
1 अध्यैषि	अध्यैष्वहि	अध्यैष्महि
2 अध्यैष्ठाः	अध्यैषाथाम्	अध्यैढ्वम्
3 अध्यैष्ट	अध्यैषाताम्	अध्यैषत

स्था—	समस्थिषि	1 sing
दा—	अदिषि	,,
धा—	अधिषि	,,
मी—	अमासि	,,

FIFTH VARIETY OR FORM.

§ 572. Terminations:—These are obtained by prefixing the augment इ to the terminations of the Fourth Variety, dropping the स् in the case of the 2nd and 3rd per. sing.; *e. g.*

---

* Vide § 486.

Par.			Âtm.		
1 इषम्	इष्व	इष्म	1 इषि	इष्वहि	इष्महि
2 ईः	इष्टम्	इष्ट	2 इष्ठाः	इषाथाम्	इध्वम्
3 ईत्	इष्टाम्	इषुः	3 इष्ट	इषाताम्	इषत

§ 573. All roots not restricted to any of the preceding Varieties take this Variety. Consequently it is peculiar to Set roots (Vide § 565).

§ 574. (*a*) In the Parasmaipada, the final radical vowel and the penultimate अ of roots ending in र् or ल् and that of वद् and व्रज् take their Vṛddhi substitute necessarily; लू-अलाविषम्; चर्—अचारिषम् ; फल्—अफालिषम् , &c.

(*b*) The penultimate short vowel of a root takes its Guṇa substitute; बुध्—अबोधिषम् , &c.

(*c*) Vṛddhi is optionally substituted for the penultimate अ, not prosodially long, of roots having an initial consonant and not ending in र् or ल् ; पठ्—अपठिषम् , अपाठिषम गद्—अगादिषम्—अगदिषम्.

(*d*) But the vowel of roots ending in ह् , म् , य् , and of the roots क्षण् , श्वस् , जागृ, श्वि, कट् 'to cover, to surround,' चट् , 'to break, to pierce,' चत् , चद् , 'to ask, to beg,' पथ् 'to go or move,' मथ् ' to churn,' लग् 'to stick or cling to,' हस् and ह्लस् 'to sound or to be diminished,' does not take its Vṛddhi substitute.

(*e*) In the Atmanepada the radical vowel takes its Guṇa substitute; लू—अलविष्ट.

Paradigms.

स्तु—अस्ताविषम् 1 sing. अस्तावीत् 3 sing. स्तु—अस्तविषि 1 sing. अस्तविष्ट 3 sing.

सु—असाविषम् 1 sing. असावीत् 3 sing. वृ and वॄ—P. अवारिषम् 1 sing. अवारीत् 3 sing.

धू—अधाविषम्, अधविषि 1 sing.

स्तॄ—अस्तारिषम्. Par. अस्तरिषि, अस्तरीषि* Atm. 1 sing.
अस्तरिष्ठाः—रीष्ठाः 2 sing.

वृ, वॄ A.—अविरिषि-अवरीषि 1 sing. अवरिष्वहि, अवरीष्वहि, &c. अवरिष्ठाः or अवरीष्ठाः 2 sing. &c.

स्नु—अस्नाविषम् 1 sing. अस्नावीत् 3 sing

मृज्—अमार्जिषम् 1 sing. अमार्जीत् 3 sing.

हन्—अवधिषम्, अवधिषि 1 sing. Par. and Atm. (See § 569).

क्रम्—अक्रमिषम् 1 sing. अक्रमीत 3 sing.

For the optional forms of these roots see the preceding Variety.

श्वि—अश्वयिषम् 1sing. अश्वयीत् 3 sing.

जागृ—अजागरिषम् 1 sing. अजागरीत् 3 sing.

अञ्ज्—आञ्जिषम् 1 sing. आञ्जीत् 3 sing.

व्रज्—अव्राजिषम् 1 sing. अव्राजीत् 3 sing.

विज्—7. P. † अविजिषम्. 6. A. अविजिषि 1 sing.

भण्—अभाणिषम्, अभणिषम 1 sing.

वद्—अवादिषम् 1 sing. अवादीत् 3 sing.

श्वस्—अश्वासिषम् 1 sing. अश्वसीत 3 sing.

ग्रह्—अग्रहीषम्, अग्रहीषि 1 sing.

Â. P.

गुप्—‡ अगोपायिषम्, अगोपिषम् 1 sing.

तृप्—अतर्पिषम् 1 sing. अतर्पीत 3 sing.

स्यम्—अस्यमिषम् 1 sing. अस्यमीत 3 sing.

क्षम्—अक्षमिषि 1 sing. अक्षमिष्ट 3 sing.

व्यय्—अव्ययिषम्, अव्ययिषि 1 sing.

क्षर्—अक्षारिषम् 1 sing.

ह्मल्—अह्मालिषम् 1 sing.

गाह्—अगाहिषि 1 sing. अगाहिष्ट 3 sing.

गृह्—अगूहिषम् ×, अगूहिषि 1 sing.

Irregular Aorists of the Fifth Form.

§ 575. The roots दीप्, जन्, पूर्, ताय् and प्याय् optionally substitute इ for इष्ट (third person sing. Atm.).

---

* See § 475.

† Vide § 466. ‡ Vide § 461.

× Vide p. 249 foot-note †; गुह् also takes 7th Variety.

§ 576. Roots of the 8th class ending in ण् or न् drop their nasal and substitute optionally थास् and त for the terminations इष्ठाः and इष्ट of the 2nd and 3rd person sing. Atm. सन् lengthens its vowel after dropping न्.

§ 577. The vowel of ऊर्णु takes Vṛddhi optionally in the Parasm. *i. e.* optionally takes Guṇa substitute; also it optionally remains unchanged before इ (Vide § § 466, 518):

§ 578. The आ of दरिद्रा is optionally dropped in the Aorist; consequently it takes the Sixth and the Fifth Varieties.

PARADIGMS.

ऊर्णु

Parasm.

1	और्णुविषम्	और्णुविष्व	और्णुविष्म
2	और्णुवीः	और्णुविष्टम्	और्णुविष्ट
3	और्णुवीत्	और्णुविष्टाम्	और्णुविषुः

1	और्णाविषम्	और्णाविष्व	और्णाविष्म	और्णविषम्	और्णविष्व	और्णविष्म
2	और्णावीः	और्णाविष्टम्	और्णाविष्ट	और्णवीः	और्णविष्टम्	और्णविष्ट
3	और्णावीत्	और्णाविष्टाम्	और्णाविषुः	और्णवीत्	और्णविष्टाम्	और्णविषुः

Atm.

1	और्णुविषि	और्णुविष्वहि	और्णुविष्महि
2	और्णुविष्ठाः	और्णुविषाथाम्	और्णुविध्वं-ढ्वम्
3	और्णुविष्ट	और्णुविषाताम्	और्णुविषत
1	और्णविषि	और्णविष्वहि	और्णविष्महि
2	और्णविष्ठाः	और्णविषाथाम्	और्णविध्व-ढ्वम्
3	और्णविष्ट	और्णविषाताम्	और्णविषत

दरिद्रा—अदरिद्रिषम्, अदरिद्रीत्.
जन्—अजनिषि; अजनिष्ट, अजनि.
दीप्—अदीपिषि 1 sing. अदीपिष्ट-
अदीपि 3 sing.

ताय्—अतायिषि; अतायिष्ट, अताय.
प्याय्—अप्यायिषि; अप्यायिष्ट, अप्यायि.
पूर—अपूरिषि, अपूरिष्ट, अपूरि.

Roots of the 8th Class.	Roots of the 8th Class.
ऋण्—आर्णिषम् 1 sing. Par. आर्णिषि 1 sing. Atm. आर्णिष्ठाः, आर्थाः; आर्णिष्ट, आर्त 2 & 3 sing. Atm.	तन्—अतानिषम्, अतनिषम् Par. अतनिषि Atm. 1 sing. अतनिष्ठाः, अतथाः अतनिष्ट, अतत 2 & 3 sing. Atm.
क्षिण्—अक्षेणिषम् 1 sing. Par. अक्षेणिषि 1 sing Atm. अक्षेणिष्ठाः, अक्षिथाः; अक्षेणिष्ट, अक्षित 2 & 3 sing. Atm.	मन्—अमनिषि 1 sing. अमनिष्ठाः, अमथाः; अमनिष्ट, अमत 2 & 3 sing.
घृण्—अघर्णिषम्, अघर्णिषि 1 sing. Par. Atm. अघर्णिष्ठाः, अघृथाः; अघर्णिष्ट, अघृत 2 & 3 sing. Atm.	वन्—अवानिषम्, अवनिषम् 1 sing. Par. अवनिषि 1 sing. Atm. अवनिष्ठाः, अवथाः; अवनिष्ट, अवत 2 & 3 sing. Atm.
तृण्—अतर्णिषम् 1 sing. Par. अतर्णिषि 1 sing. Atm. अतर्णिष्ठाः अतृथाः; अतर्णिष्ट, अतृत 2 & 3 sing. Atm.	सन्—असानिषम्, असनिषम् 1 sing. Par. असनिषि, 1 sing. Atm. असनिष्ठाः, असाथाः; असनिष्ट, असात 2 & 3 sing. Atm.

(6) THE BENEDICTIVE (आशीर्लिङ्).

§ 579. The Parasmaipada terminations of this mood may be obtained by prefixing यास् to those of the Imperfect, dropping its final स् before the स् and त् of the 2nd and 3rd per. sings.; and the Atmanepada ones by prefixing स् to the terminations of the Atm. Potential and also to the त् and थ् occurring in them. These, therefore, are:—

	Parasm.			Âtmane.	
1 यासम्	यास्व	यास्म	1 सीय	सीवहि	सीमहि
2 याः	यास्तम्	यास्त	2 सीष्ठाः	सीयास्थाम्	सीध्वम्
3 यात्	यास्ताम्	यासुः	3 सीष्ट	सीयास्ताम्	सीरन्

(a) Parasmaipada.

§ 580 The Par. terminations are weak and therefore occasion

no Guṇa or Vṛddhi change in the root. All roots reject the augment इ.

§ 581. The final इ or उ is lengthened; final ऋ short is changed to रि, and final ॠ changed to ईर् or to ऊर् when preceded by a labial or व् before the Par. terminations of the Benedictive, and the य of the Passive; जि—जीयात्, स्तु—स्तूयात्, कृ—क्रियात्, कॄ—कीर्यात्, पॄ—पूर्यात्, &c.

§ 582. Final ऋ preceded by a conjunct consonant and the root ऋ are changed to Guṇa under the same circumstances; स्मृ—स्मर्यात्, ऋ—अर्यात्.

§ 583. Roots capable of taking Samprasâraṇa take it. शास् substitutes इ for its vowel.

§ 584. A penultimate nasal is generally dropped. Some of the roots dropping their nasal thus are:—अञ्च्, अञ्ज्, भञ्ज्, रञ्ज्, सञ्ज्, स्वञ्ज्, ग्रन्थ्, मन्थ्, उन्द्, स्कन्द्, स्यन्द्, इन्ध्, बन्ध्, दम्भ्, स्तम्भ्, दंश्, भ्रंश्, स्रंस् and तृंह्.

§ 585. दा, धा and roots assuming these forms, मा, स्था, गै, पा, 'to drink', हा, 'to abandon' and सो, change their final to ए. Final आ (original or substituted ; see § 459), if it be preceded by a conjunct consonant, is changed to ए optionally : दा—देयात्, पा—पेयात्, गै—गेयात्, ग्ला—ग्लेयात्, ग्लायात् &c.; but पा to 'protect, पायात्.

Âtmanepada.

§ 586. (*a*) इ is prefixed to the terminations after Set roots and optionally after Wet ones.

(*b*) Roots ending in ऋ preceded by a conjunct consonant, the root वृ and roots ending in ॠ admit of इ optionally.

§ 587. The Atm. terminations, are strong. Before these radical vowel takes its Guṇa substitute, but when the intermediate इ is not prefixed to the terminations, the final ऋ remains unchanged and ॠ is changed to इर्, or to उर् if a labial or व् precedes; चि—चेषीष्ट, धु—धोषीष्ट, लू—लविषीष्ट, स्तॄ—स्तरिषीष्ट, or स्तीर्षीष्ट, पॄ—परिषीष्ट or पूर्षीष्ट, &c.

Paradigms.

चि.

Par.			Âtm.		
1 चीयासम्	चीयास्व	चीयास्म	1 चेषीय	चेषीवहि	चेषीमहि
2 चीयाः	चीयास्तम्	चीयास्त	2 चेषीष्ठाः	चेषीयास्थाम्	चेषीढ्वम्
3 चीयात्	चीयास्ताम्	चीयासुः	3 चेषीष्ट	चेषीयास्ताम्	चेषीरन्

भू P. Â

1 भूयासम्	भूयास्व	भूयास्म	1 भविषीय	भविषीवहि	भविषीमहि
2 भूयाः	भूयास्तम्	भूयास्त	2 भविषीष्ठाः	भविषीयास्थाम्	भविषीध्वं-ढ्वम्
3 भूयात्	भूयास्ताम्	भूयासुः	3 भविषीष्ट	भविषीयास्ताम्	भविषीरन्

कृ. P. Â.

1 क्रियासम्	क्रियास्व	क्रियास्म	1 कृषीय	कृषीवहि	कृषीमहि
2 क्रियाः	क्रियास्तम्	क्रियास्त	2 कृषीष्ठाः	कृषीयास्थाम्	कृषीढ्वम्
3 क्रियात्	क्रियास्ताम्	क्रियासुः	3 कृषीष्ट	कृषीयास्ताम्	कृषीरन्

स्मृ Par.			ऋ Par.		
स्मर्यासम्	स्मर्यास्व	स्मर्यास्म	1 अर्यासम्	अर्यास्व	अर्यास्म
2 स्मर्याः	स्मर्यास्तम्	स्मर्यास्त	2 अर्याः	अर्यास्तम्	अर्यास्त
3 स्मर्यात्	स्मर्यास्ताम्	स्मर्यासुः	3 अर्यात्	अर्यास्ताम्	अर्यासुः

स्तृ Â.

1 स्तरिषीय	स्तरिषीवहि	स्तरिषीमहि	1 स्तृषीय	स्तृषीवहि	स्तृषीमहि

2 स्तरिषीष्ठाः	स्तरिषीयास्थाम्	स्तरिषीध्वम्-ढ्वम्
3 स्तरिषीष्ट	स्तरिषीयास्ताम्	स्तरिषीरन्

2 स्तृषीष्ठाः	स्तृषीयास्थाम्	स्तृषीध्वम्-ढ्वम्
3 स्तृषीष्ट	स्तृषीयास्ताम्	स्तृषीरन्

Conjugate स्तृ Par. like स्मृ

1 sing

स्तृ–स्तीर्यासम्, स्तरिषीय, स्तीर्षीय

वृ–वूर्यासम्, वरिषीय, वूर्षीय

दा–देयासम्, दासीय

धा–धेयासम्, धासीय

घ्रा– घ्रा-घ्रे–यासम्, घ्रासीय

वच्–उच्यासम्

स्वप्–सुप्यासम्

प्रच्छ्–पृच्छयासम्

भ्रस्ज्–भृज्ज्यासम्, भ्रक्षीय, भर्क्षीय

यज्–इज्यासम्, यक्षीय

वप्–उप्यासम्, वप्सीय

वह्–उह्यासम्, वक्षीय

वे–ऊयासम्, वासीय

व्ये–वीयासम्, व्यासीय

ह्वे–हूयासम्, ह्वासीय

ग्रह्–गृह्यासम्, ग्रहीषीय

व्रश्च्–वृश्च्यासम्

शास्–शिष्यासम्

शी–शयिषीय

हन्–वध्यात्

Irregular Benedictives.

§ 588. इ 'to go'—ईयासम्; but shortens its ई after a preposition; समियासम्; Atm. एषीय. ऊह् also, when joined with prepositions, shortens its ऊ before weak terminations beginning with य्; समुह्यासम्.

SECTION II.

THE PASSIVE.

§ 589. Every root in every one of the ten conjugational classes may take a Passive form conjugated like an Atmanepadi root of the 4th Class.*

* The only difference is in the accent; in the Passive it falls on य, whereas in the case of the primitive verbs of the 4th class, Atm., it falls on the radical syllable.

§ 590. **There are three kinds of Passive Verbs:—(1) the ve properly so called (कर्मणि प्र०), as रामेण द्रव्यं दीयते; (2) an Impersonal Passive. (भावे प्र०), as गम्यते 'it is gone;'** and (3) a Reflexive (कर्मकर्तरि प्र०), **as** ओदनः पच्यते 'rice is cooked.'

CONJUGATIONAL TENSES.

§ 591. Formation of base:—

(*a*) य is added to the root, which is weak *i. e.* no Guṇa or Vṛddhi substitute takes place before it ; नी—नीय, भिद्—भिद्य

(*b*) Before य roots undergo the same changes as they do before the Par. terminations of the Benedictive ; जि—जीय, कृ—क्रिय, स्मृ—स्मर्य, ऋ—अर्य, कॄ—कीर्य, पॄ—पूर्य, बन्ध्—बध्य, (but निन्द्-निन्द्य), वच्—उच्य, ग्रह्—गृह्य, &c.

(*c*) The final आ (original or substituted) of दा 'to give,' दे, दो, धा, धे, मा, गै, पा 'to drink,' सो and हा 'to abandon,' is changed to ई; in other cases it remains unchanged; दा and दो—दीय, गै-गीय, हा— हीय; but दा 'to cut, to purify'—दाय, ज्ञा—ज्ञाय, ध्यै—ध्याय.

§ 592. The passive base is conjugated like a root of the 4th class in the Atm.; *e. g.*

" It might even be suspected, that the occasional assumption of an Intransitive signification and a Parasmaipada inflexion by a passive verb, was the cause which gave rise to a 4th class of Primitive verbs as distinct from the Passive. Instances are certainly found of passive verbs taking Parasmaipada terminations, and some passive verbs (e. g. *jyâyate*, 'he is born,' fr. *jan* ; *pûryate*, 'he is filled,' fr. *pṛ.* ; and *tapyate* 'he is heated,' fr. *tap*) are regarded by native grammarians as Atmane. verbs of cl. 4. Again, many roots appear in class 4 as Intransitive verbs, which also appear in some one of the other nine as Transitive. For example, *yuj*, 'to join' when used in a Transitive sense, is conjugated either in cl. 7, or in the Causal; when in an Intransitive, in cl. 4. So also *push*, 'to nourish,' *kshubh*, 'to agitate;' *Klish* 'to vex'; *Sidh*, 'to accomplish.'

Monier Williams.

भू 'to be'

Present.

1 भूये	भूयावहे	भूयामहे
2 भूयसे	भूयेथे	भूयध्वे
3 भूयते	भूयेते	भूयन्ते

Imperfect.

1 अभूये	अभूयावहि	अभूयामहि
2 अभूयथाः	अभूयेथाम्	अभूयध्वम्
3 अभूयत	अभूयेताम्	अभूयन्त

Imperative.

1 भूयै	भूयावहै	भूयामहै
2 भूयस्व	भूयेथाम्	भूयध्वम्
3 भूयताम्	भूयेताम्	भूयन्ताम्

Potential.

1 भूयेय	भूयेवहि	भूयेमहि
2 भूयेथाः	भूयेयाथाम्	भूयेध्वम्
3 भूयेत	भूयेयाताम्	भूयेरन्

बुध् *Present.*

1 बुध्ये	बुध्यावहे	बुध्यामहे
2 बुध्यसे	बुध्येथे	बुध्यध्वे
3 बुध्यते	बुध्येते	बुध्यन्ते

Imperfect.

1 अबुध्ये	अबुध्यावहि	अबुध्यामहि
2 अबुध्यथाः	अबुध्येथाम्	अबुध्यध्वम्
3 अबुध्यत	अबुध्येताम्	अबुध्यन्त

Imperative.

1 बुध्यै	बुध्यावहै	बुध्यामहै
2 बुध्यस्व	बुध्येथाम्	बुध्यध्वम्
3 बुध्यताम्	बुध्येताम्	बुध्यन्ताम्

Potential.

1 बुध्येय	बुध्येवहि	बुध्येमहि
2 बुध्येथाः	बुध्येयाथाम	बुध्येध्वम्
3 बुध्येत	बुध्येयाताम्	बुध्यरन्

§ 593. (*a*) The roots खन्, जन्, तन्, and सन्, optionally drop their न् and at the same time lengthen their अ; खन्— खन्यते, खायते, &c.

(*b*) शी 'to lie down' and श्वि form their bases as शय्य and शूय.

(*c*) ऊह् shortens its ऊ when a preposition is prefixed to it.

(*d*) दरिद्रा, दीधी and वेवी drop their final vowel before य.

(*e*) ब्रू and अस् substitute वच् and भू for themselves; घस् and अज् also substitute अद् and वी respectively.

§ 594. To assist the student, the 3rd sings. pre. of some roots, regular and irregular, are given below.

Roots.	3 sing.	Roots.	3 sing.
घ्रा	घ्रायते	धे	धीयते
ज्या	जीयते	वे	ऊयते
दा I. P. 3. U.	दीयते	व्ये	वीयते
दा 2. P.	दायते	ह्वे	हूयते
धा	धीयते	गै	गीयते
पा 'to drink'	पीयते	पै	पायते
पा 'to protect'	पायते	दो	दीयते
मा	मीयते	सो	सीयते

Roots.	3 sing.	Roots.	3 sing.
हा P.	हीयते	वच्	उच्यते
हा Â.	हायते	व्रश्च्	वृश्च्यते
चि	चीयते	व्यच्	विच्यते
श्वि	शूयते	प्रच्छ्	पृच्छ्यते
मि	मीयते	विच्छ्	विच्छ्यते, विच्छाय्यते
मी	मीयते	भ्रस्ज्	भृज्ज्यते
शी	शय्यते	यज्	इज्यते
ऊर्णु	ऊर्णूयते	पण्	पणाय्यते, पण्यते
ऋ	अर्यते	ऋत्	ऋत्यते, ऋतीयते
कृ	क्रियते	अद्	अद्यते
जागृ	जागर्यते	वद्	उद्यते
स्मृ	स्मर्यते	इन्ध्	इध्यते
वॄ	वूर्यते	व्यध्	विध्यते
स्तृ	स्तर्यते	बन्ध्	बध्यते
कॄ	कीर्यते	रुध्	रुध्यते
स्तॄ	स्तीर्यते	सन्	सायते, सन्यते
दे	दीयते	जन्	जायते, जन्यते
तन्	तायते, तन्यते	वस्	उष्यते
पन्	पनाय्यते, पन्यते	वस् 'to dress'	वस्यते
गुप्	गुप्यते, गोप्यते गोपाय्यते	अस्	भूयते
वप्	उप्यते	शास्	शिष्यते
स्वप्	सुप्यते	स्रंस्	स्रस्यते
कम्	कम्यते, काम्यते	वन्द्	वन्द्यते
चुर्	चोर्यते	वह्	उह्यते
दिव्	दीव्यते	ग्रह्	गृह्यते
वश्	उश्यते	ऊह् with सम्	समुह्यते
&c.	&c.	&c.	&c.

NON-CONJUGATIONAL TENSES AND MOODS.

(1) The Perfect.

§ 595. (*a*) The Reduplicative Perfect of a root in the Passive is formed in the ordinary way, every root being considered Atmanepadi : नी—निन्ये; भू—बभूवे; निन्द्=निनिन्दे ; अश्—आनशे ; गम्—जग्मे; &c.

(*b*) The Periphrastic Perfect of the Passive does not differ from that of the Active, except in that the Auxiliary verbs take Atmanepadi terminations necessarily ; ईक्ष्—ईक्षांचक्रे, ईक्षांबभूवे, ईक्षामासे; कथयांचक्रे-बभूवे, कथयामासे &c.

(2, 3) The two Futures, (4) the Conditional and (5) the Bendedictive.

§ 596. (*a*) The forms of the two Futures, Conditional and the Benedictive of the Passive are made up in the same way as those of the Active, every root being supposed Atmanepadi ; बुध्-बोधिताहे, बोधिष्ये, अबोधिष्ये, बोधिषीय; तुद्-तोत्ताहे, तोत्स्ये, अतोत्स्ये;&c.

(*b*) Roots ending in a vowel * and the roots हन्, ग्रह्, and दृश् optionally form the two Futures, the Conditional and the Benedictive of the Passive by changing their vowel to Vṛddhi and appending the Atmanepada termination of those tenses with इ prefixed to them invariably ; in the case of roots ending in आ (and in ए, ऐ and ओ changeable to आ) य् is inserted between the root and this इ; दा–दायिताहे, दाताहे; दायिष्ये, दास्ये; अदायिष्ये, अदास्ये; दायिषीय; दासीय; and similarly ह्वे—ह्वायिताहे, ह्वाताहे; &c. नी—नायिताहे, नेताहे; नायिष्ये, नेष्ये; अनायिष्ये, अनेष्ये; नायिषीय, नेषीय; हन–घानिताहे, † हन्ताहे; घानिष्ये, हनिष्ये; अघानिष्ये, अहनिष्ये; घानिषीय, वधिषीय, 1 sing.; ग्रह्--ग्राहिताहे, ग्रहीताहे; ग्राहिष्ये, ग्रहीष्ये; अग्राहिष्ये, अग्रहीष्ये; ग्राहिषीय, ग्रहीषीय &c. दृश्—दर्शिताहे, द्रष्टाहे; दर्शिष्ये, द्रक्ष्ये; अदर्शिष्ये, अद्रक्ष्ये; दर्शिषीय, दृक्षीय, &c.

---

* नू and धू take Vṛddhi in this case though it is usually forbidden with them ; see § 463 ; दृश् takes Guṇa only

† The ह् of हन् is changed to घ् immediately before न् and before an affix containing a mute ञ् or ण्, *i. e.* य of the Passive, &c.

(6) The Aorist.

§ 597. (*a*) The Passive of the Aorist of roots belonging to the 4th, 5th and 7th Varieties, is made up similarly by appending the Atmanepada terminations to the base; भू-अभाविषि; कृ—अकारिषि; धा-अधिषि; पच्-अपक्षि; दिश्—आदिक्षि; द्विष—आद्विक्षि, &c.

(*b*) Roots belonging to the first, second, third and sixth Varieties take the fourth, fifth or seventh Variety in the Passive, in accordance with the general rules; स्था-अस्थिषि 1 sing.; ख्या-अख्यासि; जॄ—अजरिषि; श्रि—अश्रायिषि; श्रु—अश्रोषि; नम्—अनंसि, &c.

(*c*) The third per. sing. of the Aorist Passive of all roots is formed by adding इ:—

(1) Before this इ the penultimate (prosodially) short vowel takes its Guṇa substitute and penultimate अ except that of जन् and of Set roots ending in अम् except चम् with आ, कम्, and वम्, and the final vowel take their Vṛddhi substitute; भिद्—अभेदि; but निन्द्—अनिन्दि; तुद्—अतोदि; कृष्—अकर्षि; वद्—अवादि; पद—अपादि; but जन्—अजनि; गम्—अगामि; but दम्—अदमि; &c. चम् with आ—आचामि; कम्—अकामि, &c. नी—अनायि; स्तु—अस्तावि; लू—अलावि; कॄ or कृ—अकारि.

(2) Roots ending in आ original or substituted (*i. e.* of roots in ए, ऐ, ओ) insert य् before this इ; दा—अदायि; धे—अधायि; गै—अगायि; शो—अशायि, &c.

(3) रध्, जभ् and रभ् insert a nasal before their final consonant, so that their penultimate अ cannot take Guṇa or Vṛddhi substitute; अरन्धि, अजम्भि, अरम्भि.

(4) लभ् without a preposition does the same optionally and with a preposition necessarily; अलम्भि, अलाभि; but प्रालम्भि.

(5) भञ्ज् 'to break' forms अभञ्जि or अभाजि; शम्—अशमि and अशामि in the sense of 'to observe (10 A.).'

(6) मृज् takes Vṛddhi; गुह् lengthens its vowel; अमार्जि, अगूहि.

(7) इ 'to go' has अगायि; with अधि A., अध्यायि or अध्यगायि.

(*d*) The roots at § 461 will have two forms; गुप-अगोपि, अगोपायि, विच्छ्-अविच्छि, अविच्छायि &c.; ऋत्-आर्ति or आर्तायि 3 sing.

(*e*) § 596 (*b*) holds good in the Passive Aorist except in the 3rd sing.; the optional forms must be made up by appending the Atm. terminations of the 5th Variety as the roots necessarily take इ; दा—अदिषि, अदायिषि; नी—अनेषि, अनायिषि; कृ—अकृषि, अकारिषि; हन्—आहासि, अघानिषि; अवधिषि; 1 sing.; ग्रह्—अग्रहीषि, अग्राहिषि 1 sing. &c.

§ 598. Roots of the tenth Class—

(*a*) The अय् (*i. e.* अय with the final अ dropped) is optionally dropped in the General Tenses, except the Perfect. The Aorist forms, except that of the 3rd sing., are made up by adding the terminations of the Fifth Form; चुर् 1 sing. चोरयांचक्रे—बभूवे, चोरयामासे Perf ; चोरयिताहे चोरिताहे, 1st Fu. चोरयिष्ये, चोरिष्ये 2nd Fu.; अचोरयिषि, अचोरिषि, Aor. चोरयिषीय, चोरिषीय Ben.

(*b*) Roots which do not lengthen thier penultimate अ (see also § 603) lengthen it optionally in the general Tenses of the Passive, except in Perf., when अय् is dropped; कथ्—अकथयिषि, अकाथिषि; Aor. 1 sing., &c.

(*c*) The 3 per. sing. of the Pass. Aorist is formed by dropping अय् necessarily and adding इ; चोरय-अचोर्-अचोरि; पीड्-अपीडि; पृ—अपारि, &c.; रह्—अरहि, अराहि Aor. 3 sing.; रम—अरमि, अरामि Aorist, 3rd sing. &c.

PARADIGMS.

बुध् 1 P. ' to know.'

	Perfect.			*1st Future.*	
1 बुबुधे	बुबुधिवहे	बुबुधिमहे	1 बोधिताहे	बोधितास्वहे	बोधितास्महे
2 बुबुधिषे	बुबुधाथे	बुबुधिध्वे	2 बोधितासे	बोधितासाथे	बोधिताध्वे
3 बुबुधे	बुबुधाते	बुबुधिरे	3 बोधिता	बोधितारौ	बोधितारः

2nd Future.

1 बोधिष्ये	बोधिष्यावहे	बोधिष्यामहे
2 बोधिष्यसे	बोधिष्येथे	बोधिष्यध्वे
3 बोधिष्यते	बोधिष्येते	बोधिष्यन्ते

Conditoinal.

1 अबोधिष्ये	अबोधिष्यावहि	अबोधिष्यामहि
2 अबोधिष्यथाः	अबोधिष्येथाम्	अबोधिष्यध्वम्
3 अबोधिष्यत	अबोधिष्येताम्	अबोधिष्यन्त

Aorist.

1 अबोधिषि	अबोधिष्वहि	अबोधिष्महि
2 अबोधिष्ठाः	अबोधिषाथाम्	अबोधिध्वम्
3 अबोधि	अबोधिषाताम्	अबोधिषत

Benedictive.

1 बोधिषीय	बोधिषीवहि	बोधिषीमहि
2 बोधिषीष्ठाः	बोधिषीयास्थाम्	बोधिषीध्वम्
3 बोधिषीष्ट	बोधिषीयास्ताम्	बोधिषीरन्

N. B. The Passive forms of roots of the tenth class do not differ from the Passive forms of Causals for which see the forms of बुध् cau. Pass. given in the next section.

SECTION III.

DERIVATIVE VERBS (प्रत्ययान्तधातवः) and THEIR CONJUGATION.

§ 599. The Derivative Verbs are divided into four classes :—

(1) Causals or Nijantas (णिजन्ताः); (2) Desideratives or Sannantas (सन्नन्त); (3) Frequentatives or Yanantas (यङन्त);

and (4) Denominatives or Nâmadhâtus (नामधातवः). The formation and the conjugation of these will be given in the present section.

I CAUSALS.

§ 600. Any root belonging to any one of the Conjugational classes may have causal form which is conjugated like a root of the Tenth class.

§ 601. The Causal of a root implies that a person or a thing causes or makes another person or thing to perform the action, or to be in the condition, denoted by the root. It is also employed, sometimes, to convert an intransitive verb into a transitive one.

(*a*) Formation of the Causal Base.

§ 602. The Causal Base of a root is formed like that of a root of the Tenth class. In the case of roots of the Tenth class the causal form is identical with the primitive. The Causal form takes either pada. Thus from बुध comes the causal base बोधय, बोधयति-ते 'he causes to know'; क्षुभ्-क्षोभयति 'he shakes or agitates,' गण-गणयति 'he causes to count,' नी-नाययति 'he makes another lead or carry'; कृ 'to do' and कॄ to scatter—कारयति 'he causes to do or scatter' कृत—कीर्तयति, &c.

§ 603. Roots ending in अम्, except अम् 'to go' &c., कम् love,' चम् 'to eat,' शम् when it means 'to see' and यम् when it does not mean 'to eat,' and the roots* marked with an indicatory म् do not change their vowel: *i. e.* their vowel takes its Guṇa substitute; गम्-गमयति, क्रम-क्रमयति, घट्-घटयति, जन्-जनयति,

* These are:—घट्, व्यथ्, प्रथ्, प्रस्, 'to spread,' म्रद् 'to pound,' स्खद् 1 A. 'to destroy, to cut,' क्षञ्ज् 1 A. 'to go,' दक्ष्, कृप् 1 A. 'to pity,' कन्द्, क्रन्द् 1 A., त्वर्, ज्वर्, गड् 1 Par. 'to distil,' हेड् 'to surround,' वट्, भट् 'to speak,' नट् 'to dance,' स्तक् 1 P. 'to resist,' चक् 1. P. 'to shine,' कख् P. 'to laugh,' रग् P. 'to doubt,' लग् P. 'to cling to', ह्रग्, लग्, सग्, स्तग्, all meaning 'to cover,' कग, अक्, अग् 'to move in a zigzag manner,' कण्, रण् P. 'to go,' चण्, शण्, श्रण्,

व्यथ—व्यथयति; जॄ—जरयति; श्रा*—श्रपयति, ज्ञा*—ज्ञपयति, &c. but कम्—कामयते; चम्—चामयति, शम् 'to see' शामयति; but शमयति in other cases; यम्—यामयति, &c.; but यम् 'to eat'—यमयति.

(*a*) The roots वम्, नम्, वन्, ज्वल्, ह्वल्, and ह्मल्, lengthen their vowel optionally when not preceded by a preposition; नमयति, नामयति, but प्रणमयति, &c.

§ 604. Roots ending in आ (ए, ऐ or ओ changeable to आ; see § 459) and the roots ऋ 'to go,' ह्री 'to be ashamed,' री 'to go,' (9 cl.), 'to flow' (4. cl. A.) and व्ली 'to choose, to go,' insert the augment प् before अय and their vowel takes Guṇa substitute; दापयति fr. दा, दे or दो; धापयति fr. धे; गापयति fr. गै, &c. ऋ—अर्पयति; ह्री—ह्रेपयति, री—रेपयति, व्ली—व्लेपयति.

§ 605. (*a*) मि 'to throw,' मी 'to destroy,' दी 'to perish,' जि to conquer,' and क्री 'to buy,' also insert प्, but after changing their final vowel to आ; मापयति, दापयति, जापयति. क्रापयति.

(*b*) The roots क्षै, श्रा or श्रै 'to cook' and ज्ञा (*mit.*), shorten their vowel necessarily, and ग्लै and स्ना optionally, before the inserted प् when not preceded by prepositions; क्षपयति, &c. ज्ञपयति, (पशुं संज्ञपयति slays; प्रज्ञपयति शरं &c.); but ज्ञापयति, ग्लपयति, ग्लापयति; स्नपयति, स्नापयति; but प्रग्लापयति, उपस्नापयति only

§ 606. शो 'to pare, to sharpen,' छो 'to cut,' सो 'to finish,' ह्वे

P. 'to give,, श्रथ्, क्नथ्, क्रथ् क्लथ्, all P. and meaning 'to injure,' 'to kill,' चन्, 'to kill,' वन्, P. 'to honour,' ज्वल्, 'to shine,' ह्वल्, ह्मल्, 'to shake,' 'to move,' स्मृ, दॄ I P., 'to fear,' नॄ 'to guide,' श्रा 'to cook, to boil.' ज्ञा 'to kill, to gratify, to sharpen, to manifest, चल्, छद्, 'to live or to be' (छादयति in other senses), लड् 'to sport, to loll the tongue,' मद् 'to be poor, to reduce,' ध्वन्, स्वन्, अम्, जृ, कस् 'to be crooked, to shine,' रञ्, रम्, क्रम्, गम्, and फण् 1 P. 'to go.'

* See § 605 (*b*).

'to call,' व्ये 'to cover,' वे 'to weave,' सै 'to waste away,' and पा 'to drink' insert य् instead of पु्, शाययति, साययति, वाययति, पाययति, &c.

(*a*) पा 'to protect' and वे when it means 'to shake,' insert ळ् and ज् respectively before अय; पाळयति 'he protects,' वाजयति 'he shakes.'

§ 607. The roots जभ्, रध्, रभ्, and लभ् insert a nasal before their final; जम्भयति-ते, रन्धयति-ते, &c.

§ 608. The roots गुप्, विच्छ्, धूप्, पण्, पन्, and ऋत् have two forms in the causal; गोपयति-ते, गोपाययति-ते; विच्छयति-ते, विच्छाययति-ते; &c.

§ 609. दीधी, वेवी and दरिद्रा drop their final vowel before अय्; दीधयति-ते, वेवयति-ते, दरिद्रयति-ते.

§ 610 The following roots form their Causal base anomalously:—

इ 'to go'—	गमयति, with अधि 'to remember.'-अधिगमयति,-'to study' अध्यापयति. with प्रति-प्रत्याययति.
क्नू or क्नूय् 'to sound,' &c.	क्नोपयति 'he causes to sound.'
क्ष्माय् 'to tremble'	क्ष्मापयति ,, ,, ,, tremble.
गुह् 'to conceal'	गूहयति ,, ,, ,, conceal.
चि 5 cl. 'to collect'	चापयति-ते चाययति-ते,, collect.
,, 10 cl.	चपयति-ते चययति-ते ,, ,,
जागृ 'to awake	जागरयति he rouses
दुष्—'to sin, to be unchaste'	दूषयति-ते he causes to sin, but दुषयति-ते, दोषयति-ते in the sense of 'he corrupts or makes depraved.'
धू 'to shake'	धूनयति-ते he causes to shake.
प्री 'to please'	प्रीणयति ,, ,, ,, please.
भी 'to fear.'—	भाययति-ते he frightens with. भापयते, भीषयते he inspires fear.

भ्रस्ज्—'to fry'—भर्जयति-ते, भ्रज्जयति-ते he causes to fry.

मृष्—'to wipe'—मार्जयति.

रञ्ज्—to dye'—रञ्जयति he dyes or paints: also in the sense of 'he propitiates or satisfies'; *cf.* 'ब्रह्मापि नरं न रञ्जयति' Bh. Nî. Śa. 3. But रजयति only, in the sense of 'he hunts deer'; (Vide Kir. VI. 34).

रुह्—'to grow'—रोहयति-ते, रोपयति-ते he plants or causes to grow.

ला—'to take' and ली—'to embrace,' 'to adhere' } लालयति-ते, विलापयति-ते; and लीनयति, लापयति in the sense of 'melting an unctuous substance.'

वा 'to blow'—वापयति he causes to blow or move.

वाजयति he shakes.

स्मि to smile'—विस्मापयति he causes a smile by, or astonishes or frightnes by. विस्मापयते he astonishes.

वी— वापयति, वाययति he causes to conceive;

वाययति-ते in other senses.

शद् 'to fall'—शातयति he causes to fall, cuts down.

शादयति he causes to go.

सिध् 'to be accomplished' { साधयति he accomplishes or prepares. सेधयति, he makes perfect, &c. with reference to sacred rites or things only; as सेधयति तापसं तपः &c.

स्फाय्—'to swell'—स्फावयति, he causes to swell.

स्फुर्—'to tremble; to shine forth.' स्फोरयति, स्फारयति he causes to tremble or shine.

हन् 'to strike or kill'—घातयति he causes to strike, &c.

(*b*) Conjugation of the Causal Base.

§ 611. The Causal base is conjugated like the base of a root of the 10th or Churâdi class in all the ten Tenses and Moods of the Parasmaipada, the Atmanepada and the Passive. The अय with the final अ dropped is retained, as remarked before, in the General Tenses, except the Aorist and the Benedictive, and is dropped before the य of the Passive. The formation of the Aorist of causals has been fully explained along with that of the roots of the Tenth class, at § 548–556.

§ 612. Paradigms of all the Tenses and Moods in the Par. Atm. and Pass. of बुध्, Causal base बोधय्.

Special Tenses.

Present.

Par.			Atm.		
1 बोधयामि	बोधयावः	बोधयामः	1 बोधये	बोधयावहे	बोधयामहे
2 बोधयसि	बोधयथः	बोधयथ	2 बोधयसे	बोधयेथे	बोधयध्वे
3 बोधयति	बोधयतः	बोधयन्ति	3 बोधयते	बोधयेते	बोधयन्ते

Imperfect.

P.

1 अबोधयम्	अबोधयाव	अबोधयाम
2 अबोधयः	अबोधयतम्	अबोधयत
3 अबोधयत्	अबोधयताम्	अबोधयन्

A.

1 अबोधये	अबोधयावहि	अबोधयामहि
2 अबोधयथाः	अबोधयेथाम्	अबोधयध्वम्
3 अबोधयत	अबोधयेताम्	अबोधयन्त

Imperative.

P.			A.		
1 बोधयानि	बोधयाव	बोधयाम	1 बोधयै	बोधयावहै	बोधयामहै
2 बोधय	बोधयतम्	बोधयत	2 बोधयस्व	बोधयेथाम्	बोधयध्वम्
3 बोधयतु	बोधयताम्	बोधयन्तु	3 बोधयताम्	बोधयेताम्	बोधयन्ताम्

Potential.

P.			A.		
1 बोधयेयम्	बोधयेव	बोधयेम	1 बोधयेय	बोधयेवहि	बोधयेमहि
2 बोधयेः	बोधयेतम्	बोधयेत	2 बोधयेथाः	बोधयेयाथाम्	बोधयेध्वम्
3 बोधयेत्	बोधयेताम्	बोधयेयुः	3 बोधयेत	बोधयेयाताम्	बोधयेरन्

General Tenses.

Perfect.

Par.

1 बोधयांचकार—चकर *	बोधयांचकृव	बोधयांचकृम
2 बोधयांचकर्थ	बोधयांचक्रथुः	बोधयांचक्र
3 बोधयांचकार	बोधयांचक्रतुः	बोधयांचक्रुः

Atm.

1 बोधयांचक्रे *	बोधयांचकृवहे	बोधयांचकृमहे
2 बोधयांचकृषे	बोधयांचक्राथे	बोधयांचकृढ्वे
3 बोधयांचक्रे	बोधयांचक्राते	बोधयांचक्रिरे

1st Future.

Par.

1 बोधयितास्मि	बोधयितास्वः	बोधयितास्मः
2 बोधयितासि	बोधयितास्थः	बोधयितास्थ
3 बोधयिता	बोधयितारौ	बोधयितारः

Atm.

1 बोधयिताहे	बोधयितास्वहे	बोधयितास्महे
2 बोधयितासे	बोधयितासाथे	बोधयिताध्वे
3 बोधयिता	बोधयितारौ	बोधयितारः

2nd Future.

Parasm.

1 बोधयिष्यामि	बोधयिष्यावः	बोधयिष्यामः

* Also बोधयामास, बोधयांबभूव &c.

2 बोधयिष्यसि	बोधयिष्यथः	बोधयिष्यथ
3 बोधयिष्यति	बोधयिष्यतः	बोधयिष्यन्ति

Atm.

1 बोधयिष्ये	बोधयिष्यावहे	बोधयिष्यामहे
2 बोधयिष्यसे	बोधयिष्येथे	बोधयिष्यध्वे
3 बोधयिष्यते	बोधयिष्येते	बोधयिष्यन्ते

Conditional.

Par.

1 अबोधयिष्यम् अबोधयिष्याव अबोधयिष्याम, &c.

Atm.

1 अबोधयिष्ये अबोधयिष्यावहि अबोधयिष्यामहि, &c.

Par. *Aorist.* Atm.

1 अबूबुधम्	अबूबुधाव	अबूबुधाम	1 अबूबुधे	अबूबुधावहि	अबूबुधामहि
2 अबूबुधः	अबूबुधतम्	अबूबुधत	2 अबूबुधथाः	अबूबुधेथाम्	अबूबुधध्वम्
3 अबूबुधत्	अबूबुधताम्	अबूबुधन्	3 अबूबुधत	अबूबुधेताम्	अबूबुधन्त

Benedictive.

Parasm.

1 बोध्यासम्	बोध्यास्व	बोध्यास्म
2 बोध्याः	बोध्यास्तम्	बोध्यास्त
3 बोध्यात्	बोध्यास्ताम्	बोध्यासुः

Atm.

1 बोधयिषीय	बोधयिषीवहि	बोधयिषीमहि
2 बोधयिषीष्ठाः	बोधयिषीयास्थाम्	बोधयिषीध्वम्-ढ्वम्
3 बोधयिषीष्ट	बोधयिषीयास्ताम्	बोधयिषीरन्

Passive.

Present *Imperfect*

1 बोध्ये	बोध्यावहे	बोध्यामहे	1 अबोध्ये	अबोध्यावहि	अबोध्यामहि
2 बोध्यसे	बोध्येथे	बोध्यध्वे	2 अबोध्यथाः	अबोध्येथाम्	अबोध्यध्वम्
3 बोध्यते	बोध्येते	बोध्यन्ते	3 अबोध्यत	अबोध्येताम्	अबोध्यन्त

Imperative.

1 बोध्ये	बोध्यावहै	बोध्यामहै
2 बोध्यस्व	बोध्येथाम्	बोध्यध्वम्
3 बोध्यताम्	बोध्येताम्	बोध्यन्ताम्

Potential

1 बोध्येय	बोध्येवहि	बोध्येमहि
2 बोध्येथाः	बोध्येयाथाम्	बोध्येध्वम्
3 बोध्येत	बोध्येयाताम्	बोध्येरन्

Perfect.

1 बोधयांचक्रे-बभूवे	बोधयांचकृवहे-बभूविवहे	बोधयांचकृमहे-बभूविमहे
बोधयामासे	बोधयामासिवहे	बोधयामासिमहे
2 बोधयांचकृषे-बभूविषे	बोधयांचक्राथे-बभूवाथे	बोधयांचकृढ्वे-बभूविध्वे-ढ्वे
बोधयामासिषे	बोधयामासाथे	बोधयामासिध्वे
3 बोधयांचक्रे-बभूवे	बोधयांचक्राते-बभूवाते	बोधयांचक्रिरे-बभूविरे
बोधयामासे	बोधयामासाते	बोधयामासिरे

1st Future.

1 बोधयिताहे,	बोधयितास्वहे	बोधयितास्महे,
बोधिताहे	बोधितास्वहे	बोधितास्महे
2 बोधयितासे,	बोधयितासाथे,	बोधयिताध्वे,
बोधितासे	बोधितासाथे	बोधिताध्वे
3 बोधयिता,	बोधयितारौ,	बोधयितारः
बोधिता	बोधितारौ	बोधितारः

2nd Future.

1 बोधयिष्ये,	बोधयिष्यावहे,	बोधयिष्यामहे,
बोधिष्ये	बोधिष्यावहे	बोधिष्यामहे
2 बोधयिष्यसे,	बोधयिष्येथे,	बोधयिष्यध्वे,
बोधिष्यसे	बोधिष्येथे	बोधिष्यध्वे
3 बोधयिष्यते,	बोधयिष्येते,	बोधयिष्यन्ते,
बोधिष्यते	बोधिष्येते	बोधिष्यन्ते

Conditional.

1	अबोधयिष्ये	अबोधयिष्यावहि	अबोधयिष्यामहि
	अबोधिष्ये	अबोधिष्यावहि	अबोधिष्यामहि
2	अबोधयिष्यथाः	अबोधयिष्येथाम्	अबोधयिष्यध्वम्
	अबोधिष्यथाः	अबोधिष्येथाम्	अबोधिष्यध्वम्
3	अबोधयिष्यत	अबोधयिष्येताम्	अबोधयिष्यन्त
	अबोधिष्यत	अबोधिष्येताम्	अबोधिष्यन्त

Benedictive.

1	बोधयिषीय,	बोधयिषीवहि,	बोधयिषीमहि
	बोधिषीय	बोधिषीवहि	बोधिषीमहि
2	बोधयिषीष्ठाः,	बोधयिषीयास्थाम्,	बोधयिषीध्वम्-ढ्वम्
	बोधिषीष्ठाः	बोधिषीयास्थाम्	बोधिषीध्वम्
3	बोधयिषीष्ट,	बोधयिषीयास्ताम्,	बोधयिषीरन्
	बोधिषीष्ट	बोधिषीयास्ताम्	बोधिषीरन्

Aorist.

1	अबोधयिषि,	अबोधयिष्वहि,	अबोधयिष्महि,
	अबोधिषि	अबोधिष्वहि	अबोधिष्महि
2	अबोधयिष्ठाः,	अबोधयिषाथाम्,	अबोधयिध्वम्-ढ्वम्
	अबोधिष्ठाः	अबोधिषाथाम्	अबोधिध्वम्
3	अबोधि	अबोधयिषाताम्,	अबोधयिषत,
		अबोधिषाताम्	अबोधिषत

For the various irregularities, &c. see the third Variety.

---

11. DESIDERATIVES.

§ 613. Any primitive root of the ten classes, as well as any causal base, may optionally* take a Desiderative form

---

* Or the notion of desire may be conveyed by means of a sentence; *i. e.* पिपठिषति or पठितुमिच्छति 'he wishes to read,' &c.

which, like the causal base, is conjugated in all the ten Tenses and Moods of three voices.

§ 614. The Desiderative expresses the notion that a person or thing wishes (or is about) to perform the action, or to be in the condition denoted by the root or the desiderative base; पिपठिषति 'he wishes to study' from पठ्; मुमूर्षति 'he is about to die' fr. मृ; &c.

615. There are a few primitive roots, which, though they take a Desiderative form, do dot convey a desiderative sense (See § 396). As these are looked upon as primitive roots, new Desiderative bases may be derived from them according to the rules given below; as जुगुप्सिषते 'he wishes to censure' from जुगुप्स् &c.

§ 616. The Desiderative base is formed by reduplicating the root or base according to the general rules of reduplication given at § 444–449 and § 549 (*a*) (*b*), and by adding स् (which may by changed to ष् according to the rules of Sandhi) to it. The अ of the reduplicative syllable is changed to इ; *e. g.* पठ्–पपठ्–पिपठ्+स्=पिपठिष by the following rule.

N. B. The स् of a primitive root is not changed to ष् when the characteristic स् is changed to ष; सि–सिसीष्, सिच्–सिसिक्ष् (क+ष); स्मि–सिस्मयिष; सृ–सिसृष; but स्था–तिष्ठास्; सावय् cau. of सू–सुषावयिष; स्तु, however, forms तुष्टूषति.

Note:—(1) A root takes a Desiderative form only when the agent of the wish and of the action expressed by the root is the same; so शिष्याः पठन्तु इति इच्छति गुरुः and not पिपठिषति; also the sense of the root must be the object of the wish: गमनेन इच्छति cannot, therefore, be equal to जिगमिषति.

Note:—(2) Though the Desiderative form of a root is not to be found often used in classical language in its character of a verb, yet nominal and participal derivatives from it are not uncommonly to be met with.

§ 617. To this स् the augment इ is to be prefixed after Set roots, optionally after Wet ones and not after those that are Anit, subject to the following exceptions:—

(1) Roots ending in उ or ऊ, ऋ and ऌ short, and the roots ग्रह् and गुह् do not take इ; नु-नुनूष्; Vide § 618. (*d*); भू-बुभूष्, &c.

Exceptions:—ऋ 'to go,' दृ A. 'to respect,' धृ 6 A. 'to hold,' and पू A. 'to purify,' admit of इ. (see also 4 below.)

(2) स्मि, अञ्ज्, प्रच्छ्, अश् take इ necessarily.

(3) वृत्, वृध्, शृध्, स्यन्द् and क्लृप् do not admit of इ in the Par. (see § 484). In the Atm. they admit इ, the last two do so optionally; वृत्-विवृत्सति, विवर्तिषते, &c.

(4) Roots ending in long ॠ and इव् and the roots दरिद्रा, श्रि, ऊर्णु, यु, भृ, वृ, स्वृ, ऋध् 'to prosper,' दम्भ्, भ्रस्ज् ज्ञप् (*i. e.* ज्ञप् of the 10 cl. and optional Cau. Base of ज्ञा), सन् 'to give,' तन्, पत्, छ्व, मृद, छृद्, तृद्, and नृत् (Vide § 485.) take इ optionally.

Exceptions:—कॄ 'to scatter,' गॄ 'to swallow,' take इ necessarily The intermediate इ is not lengthened in the case of these roots; चिकरिष्, &c.

(5) The roots क्रम्, गम् and श्रु take इ in the Par. and reject it in the Atm.

§ 618. The radical vowels undergo the following changes before स्—

(*a*) The स् with इ is strong and without इ weak.

The usual rule as to Guṇa substitute holds good in the one case and does not in the other; वृत्-विवर्तिष, विवृत्स; दृ-दिदरिष, &c.

(*b*) The final इ and उ and the penultimate अ of हन् and गम् (substitut-d for इ 2 Par. 'to go,' and for इ with अधि 'to remember' or 'to study') are lengthened and final ऋ, short or long, changed to ईर्, or to ऊर् after labials or व when the स is unaugmented; जि-जिगीष, द्रु-दुद्रूष, कृ-चिकीर्ष, तॄ-तितीर्ष, सृ-सुसूर्ष, पृ-पुपूर्ष, &c.

(*e*) The roots रुद्, विद् and मुष् do not change their vowel to Guṇa; and the roots ग्रह्, स्वप् and प्रच्छ् take Samprasáraṇa; रुरुदिष, विविदिष, मुमुषिष, जिघृक्ष, सुषुप्स, पिपृच्छिष.

(*n*) Roots with an initial consonant, and having इ or उ short for their penultimate, and ending in any consonant, except य् or व्, change their vowel to Guṇa optionally when इ is prefixed to स; द्युत्-दिद्युतिष, दिद्योतिष; मुद्-मुमुदिष or मुमोदिष &c.

§ 619. The formation of Desiderative bases of causals and of roots of the Tenth class does not differ from that of primitive roots.

Art. § 550. should be attended to in forming Desideratives from Causals and roots of the Tenth class.

§ 620. Roots in their Desiderative forms take the same terminations, Parasm. or Atmane. that they do in the primitive. The roots ज्ञा, श्रु, स्मृ and दृश् take Atm. terminations in the Desiderative.

§ 621. The following roots form their Desiderative bases irregularly:—

Roots.	Desider. base.	Third pers sing. Pre.
अद् 'to eat'	जिघत्स	जिघत्सति
आप्	ईप्स्	ईप्सति
इ 'to go'	जिगमिष्	जिगमिषति
इ with अधि 'to study'	अधिजिगांस्	अधिजिगांसते
इ with प्रति 'to be convinced'	प्रतीषिष्	प्रतीषिषति
इ—	एषिषिष्	एषिषिषति
उ 'to sound'	ऊषिष्	ऊषिषति
ऊर्णु—	ऊर्णुनूष्	ऊर्णुनूषति-ते

Roots.	Desider. base	Third pers. sing. Pre
	ऊर्णुनुविष्	ऊर्णुनुविषति–ते
	ऊर्णुनविष्	ऊर्णुनविषति–ते
ऋ—	अरिरिष्	अरिरिषति
ऋध् 'to prosper'	ईर्त्स्	ईर्त्सति
	अर्दिधिष्	अर्दिधिषति
गम्—	जिगमिष्	जिगमिषति
„ with सम्, A	संजिगांस्	संजिगांसते
गॄ—'to swallow'	जिगरिष्	जिगरिषति
	जिगलिष्	जिगलिषति
चि 'to gather'	चिचीष्	चिचीषति
	चिकीष्	चिकीषति
जि 'to conquer'	जिगीष्	जिगीषति
ज्ञप् 10 cl. & optional	ज्ञीप्स्	ज्ञीप्सति
Cau. Base of ज्ञा—	जिज्ञपयिष्	जिज्ञपयिषति
ज्ञाप् opt. cau B. of ज्ञा	जिज्ञापयिष्	जिज्ञापयिषति
तन् 'to stretch'	तितंस् or तितांस्	तितंसति, तितांसति
	or तितनिष्	तितनिषति
तृंह् 'to kill'	तितृक्ष्	तितृक्षति
	तितृंहिष्	तितृंहिषति
दम्भ	धिप्स्, धीप्स्	धिप्सति, धीप्सति
	दिदंभिष्	दिदंभिषति
दरिद्रा	दिदरिद्रास्	दिदरिद्रासति
	दिदरिद्रिष्	दिदरिद्रिषति
दा 'to give'	दित्स्	दित्सति
दे 'to protect'	„	दित्सते
दो 'to cut'	„	दित्सति
दिव्	दुद्यूष्, दिदेविष्	दुद्यूषति, दिदेविषति
धा	धित्स्	धित्सति

Roots.	Desider. base.	3rd pers. sing Pre.
धे	धित्स्	धित्सति
नश्	निनङ्क्ष्	निनङ्क्षति
	निनशिष्	निनशिषति
पत	पित्स्	पित्सति
	पिपतिष्	पिपतिषति
पद्	पित्स्	पित्सते
पू A.	पिपविष्	पिपविषते
भ्रस्ज्	बिभर्क्ष्	बिभर्क्षति
"	बिभ्रक्ष्	बिभ्रक्षति
"	बिभर्जिष्	बिभर्जिषति
"	बिभ्रज्जिष्	बिभ्रज्जिषति
मस्ज्	मिमङ्क्ष् (also मिमज्जिष्)	मिमङ्क्षति (मिमज्जिषति)
मा 'to measure'	मित्स्	मित्सति
मि 'to throw'	"	"
मी 'to destroy'	"	"
मे 'to barter'	"	मित्सते
मुच्	मोक्ष्	मोक्षते 'he desires for liberation.'
	मुमुक्ष्	मुमुक्षते
	मुमुक्ष्	मुमुक्षति 'he wishes to be free.'
मृज्	मिमृक्ष्	मिमृक्षति
	मिमार्जिष्	मिमार्जिषति
यु	युयूष्	युयूषति
	यियविष्	यियविषति
रभ्	रिप्स्	रिप्सते
राध् 'to injure, to kill'	रित्स्	रित्सति
to propitiate'	रिरात्स्	रिरात्सति
लभ्	लिप्स्	लिप्सते
शक्	शिक्ष्	शिक्षति

Roots.	Desiderative base	Third pers. sing. Pre.
सन् 8. P. A. 'to obtain'	सिसनिष्	सिसनिषति
	सिषास्	सिषासति
सिव्	सुस्यूष्, सिसेविष्	सुस्यूषति, सिसेविषति
हन्	जिघांस	जिघांसति
हि 'to throw'	जिघीष्	जिघीषति
श्वायय् cau. of, श्वि	शिश्वाययिष्	शिश्वाययिषति
	शुशावयिष्	शुशावयिषति
स्फारय् „ „ स्फुर्	पुस्फारयिष्	पुस्फारयिषति-ते
स्वापय् „ „ स्वप्	सुष्वापयिष्	सुष्वापयिषति-ते
स्वादय् „ „ स्वद्*	सिस्वादयिष्	सिस्वादयिषति-ते
स्वेदय् „ „ स्विद्*	सिस्वेदयिष्	सिस्वेदयिषति-ते
साहय् „ „ सह्*	सिसाहयिष्	सिसाहयिषति-ते
ह्वायय् „ „ ह्वे	जुहावयिष्	जुहावयिषति-ते

(*b*) Conjugation of the Desiderative Base.

Conjugational Tenses.

§ 622. अ is added to the base in the Conjugational Tenses and then it is conjugated like the special base of the 6th class in the Active and Passive.

Non-Conjugational Tenses.

§ 623. (*a*) The Perfect is formed by adding आम् to the base and appending the Perfect forms of the auxiliary verbs अस्, भू, and कृ (see § 490, 526).

(*b*) In the Aorist the Desiderative Bases take the terminations of the 5th Variety.

(*c*) In the Benedictive the Parasm. terminations are added without इ and the Atm. ones with the intermediate इ.

(*d*) The remaining tenses have no peculiarities.

---

* These roots do not change their स् to ष्.

§ 624. In the Passive, the Aorist 3rd sing. is formed according to § 597. (*c*). The forms of the remaining tenses are made up in the usual way.

Paradigms.

बुध् desi. (3rd sing.)

Tenses.	Par.	Atm.	Passive.
Present	बुबोधिषति	बुबोधिषते	बुबोधिष्यते
Imperfect	अबुबोधिषत्	अबुबोधिषत	अबुबोधिष्यत
Imperative	बुबोधिषतु	बुबोधिषताम्	बुबोधिष्यताम्
Potential	बुबोधिषेत्	बुबोधिषेत	बुबोधिष्येत
Perfect	बुबोधिषांचकार	बुबोधिषांचक्रे	बुबोधिषांचक्रे
	बुबोधिषामास	बुबोधिषामासे	बुबोधिषामासे
	बुबोधिषांबभूव	बुबोधिषांबभूवे	बुबोधिषांबभूवे
F. Future	बुबोधिषिता	बुबोधिषिता	बुबोधिषिता
Sec. Future	बुबोधिषिष्यति	बुबोधिषिष्यते	बुबोधिषिष्यते
Conditional	अबुबोधिष्यत्	अबुबोधिष्यत	अबुबोधिष्यत
Aorist	अबुबोधिषीत्	अबुबोधिषिष्ट	अबुबोधिषि
Benedictive	बुबोधिष्यात्	बुबोधिषिषीष्ट	बुबोधिषिषीष्ट

Roots. 3 sing. Pre.	Roots. 3 sing. Pre.
रुद्—रुरुदिषति	कृत्—चिकर्तिषति, चिकृत्सति
विद्—विविदिषति	छृद्—चिच्छर्दिषति-ते, चिच्छृत्सति-ते
मुष्—मुमुषिषति	तॄ—तितरिषति, तितरीषति, तितीर्षति
स्वप्—सुषुप्सति	
प्रच्छ्—पिपृच्छिषति	वृ-P. A. विवरिषति-ते, विवरीषति-ते, वुवूर्षति-ते
कृ—चिकरिषति	
धृ—6. A. दिधरिषते	उच्छ्—उचिच्छिषति
धृ—1 P. A. दिधरिषति-ते	स्था—तिष्ठासति
गुह्—जुघुक्षति	
वृत्—विवर्तिषते, विवृत्सति	स्नु—cau सिष्णावयिषति-ते, सुष्णावयिषति-ते
द्युत्—दिद्युतिषते, दिद्योतिषते	
श्रि—शिश्रीषति, शिश्रयिषति	श्रु,, शिश्रावयिषति-ते. शुश्रावयिषति-ते
स्मृ—सुस्मूर्षति सिस्मरिषति	

Roots. 3 sing. Pre.	Roots. 3 sing. Pre.
वृध्—विवृत्सति, विवर्धिषते	प्रु,, पिप्रावयिषति-ते, पुप्रावयिषति-ते
स्यन्द्—सिस्यन्त्सति, सिस्यन्दिषते, सिस्यन्त्सते	प्लु,, पिप्लावयिषति-ते, पुप्लावयिषति-ते
कृप—चिक्लृप्सति, चिकल्पिषते, चिक्लृप्सते	च्यु,, चिच्यावयिषति ते, चुच्यावयिषति-ते
	&c. &c. &c.

III. FREQUENTATI

§ 625. A Frequentative or Intensive form may be derived from any monosyllabic root of the first nine classes, beginning with a consonant. The Frequentative or Intensive is used to signify the repetition or the intensity of the action denoted by the verb from which it is derived. *

Exceptions:—

§ 626. (*a*) † A Frequentative may be formed from अट् 'to go,' ऋ 'to go, अश् 'to eat' and ऊर्णु 'to conceal,' though these begin with a vowel; and from सूच् cl. 10 'to hint,' सूत्र् cl. 10 'to string together', and मूत्र् cl. 10. though they belong to the 10th cl.

(*b*) The Frequentative of roots signifying motion conveys the notion of tortuous motion and not of repetition. ‡ The Frequentative of roots लुप् 'to cut,' सद् 'to sink down,' चर् 'to go' जप् 'to mutter prayers,' जभ् 'to yawn,' दह् 'to burn,' दंश् 'to bite,' and गृ 'to swallow,' imply reproach on the manner of doing the act $. लोलुप्यते 'he cuts awkwardly,' सासद्यते 'falls down badly,' चञ्चूर्यते &c.

* धातोरेकाचो हलादेः क्रियासमभिहारे यङ् । Pāṇ III 1. 23 पानःपुन्यं भृशार्थश्च क्रियासमभिहारः । तस्मिन्द्योत्ये यङ् स्यात् । Sid. Kau.

† सूचिसूत्रिमूत्र्यट्यर्त्यशूर्णोतिभ्यो यङ् वाच्यः । Vart. on the above.

‡ नित्यं कौटिल्ये गतौ । Pan. III. 1. 23.

$ लुपसदचरजपजभदहदशगॄभ्यो भावगर्हायाम् । Pan. III. 1. 24.

§ 627. There are two kinds of Frequentative bases derived from roots; both are formed by a peculiar reduplication of the root; but in one the affix य (यङ्) is added to the root before reduplication takes place, and the base is conjugated in the Atm. alone; in the other the affix य is dropped (यङ्लुक्) and the base is conjugated in Parasm. only (in the Atm. also, according to some grammarians). It will be convenient to call the one of the Atm. Frequentative, and the other the Parasm. Frequentative.

ATMANEPADA-FREQUENTATIVE.

§ 628. The Atm. Frequentative base is formed by adding य to the root before which it undergoes the same changes as before the य of the Passive; दा—दीय, चि—चीय, नी—नीय, भू—भूय, स्मृ—स्मर्य, ऋ—अर्य, कॄ—कीर्य, धे—धीय &c.; भिद्—भिद्य, पॄ—पूर्य, बन्ध्—बध्य, नन्द्—नन्द्य, &c.

(*a*) घ्रा and ध्मा change their vowel to ई, and ऋ preceded by one radical consonant is changed to री, and not to रि: घ्रा—घ्रीय, ध्मा—ध्मीय, कृ—क्रीय.

(*b*) The roots व्यच्, व्यध्, स्यम्, स्वप्, ग्रह्, प्रच्छ्, भ्रस्ज् and व्रश्च् take Samprasáraṇa; ज्या and व्ये substitute ई, and ह्वे, ऊ for their final vowel; शास् becomes शिष् and प्याय् पी: व्यच्-विच्य स्वप्-सुप्य, ग्रह्-गृह्य, ह्वे-हूय, ज्या, जीय, शास्-शिष्य, प्याय्-पीय.

(*c*) § 395 should be observed.

§ 629. The form in य derived as above is reduplicated according to the general rules of reduplication.

(*a*) If a root begins with a vowel, the following syllable is reduplicated.

(*b*) The vowels इ and उ of the reduplicative syllable take their Guṇa substitute and the अ of the reduplicative syllable is lengthened; पुनः पुनरतिशयेन वा भवति बोभूयते; पचु-पापच्यते &c.

दा-दीय	by § 628	दिदीय	by reduplication	देदीय	by 629 *b*	+ ते = देदीयते
ज्ञा—ज्ञाय	,,	जज्ञाय	,,	जाज्ञाय	,,	+ ते = जाज्ञायते
धे—धीय	,,	दिधीय	,,	दधीय	,,	,, = देधीयते
भू—भूय	,,	बुभूय	,,	बोभूय	,,	,, = बोभूयते
ऋ—अर्य	,,	अर्य	by § 629 (*a*)	अरार्य	,,	,, = अरार्यते
क्री—क्रीय	,,	चिक्रीय	by reduplication	चेक्रीय	,,	,, = चेक्रीयते
पॄ—पूर्य	,,	पुपूर्य	,, ,,	पोपूर्य	,,	,, = पोपूर्यते
अट्-अट्य	,,	अटट्य	by § 629 (*c*)	अटाट्य	,,	,, = अटाट्यते
अश्-अश्य	,,	अशश्य	,, ,,	अशाश्य	,,	,, = अशाश्यते
व्रज्-व्रज्य	,,	वव्रज्य	by reduplication	वाव्रज्य	,,	,, = वाव्रज्यते

similarly ढौक्—डोढौक्यते, व्यच्—वेविच्यते, स्वप्—सोषुप्यते, शास्—शाशिष्यते, प्याय्—पेपीयते, &c.; घ्रा—घ्रीय—जिघ्रीय—जेघ्रीयते; ध्मा—देध्मीयते &c.

§ 630. When a root ends in a nasal preceded by अ and the nasal is not dropped, न् (changeable to an Anuswára or the nasal of the class to which the letter following it belongs) is inserted between the reduplicative अ and the first radical consonant; the अ of the reduplicative syllable remains unchanged (against § 629 *b.*)

यम्-यम्य, ययम्य = यंयम्यते or यय्यम्यते, जन्-जन्य-जजन्य = जंजन्यते or जञ्जन्यते, but when जन् = जाय्, the A. Freq. base is जाजाय, 3rd sing. जाजायते.

(*a*) The same rule applies to the roots चर्, फल्, जप्, जभ्, दह्, दंश्, भञ्ज् and पश्. चर् and फल् after inserting न् change the अ of the following syllable to उ; चर् = चर्य-चचर्य = चंचुर्य. or चञ्चुर्य = चंचूर्यते or चञ्चुर्यते by § 394. फल् = फल्य = पफल्य = पंफुल्यते or पम्फुल्यते; दह् = दह्य—ददह्य = दंदह्यते or दन्दह्यते जप्—जंजप्यते or जञ्जप्यते

(*b*) नी is inserted after the अ of the reduplicative syllable (which then remains unchanged) in the case of the roots वञ्च्, स्रंस्, ध्वंस्, भ्रंस्, कस्, पत, पद् and स्कन्द्; वञ्च्—वञ्च्य—ववञ्च्य—वनीवञ्च्यते; स्रंस्-स्रस्य-सनीस्रस्यते; ध्वंस्=दनीध्वस्यते, भ्रंस्=बनीभ्रस्यते. कस्=कनीकस्यते, पत्=पनीपत्यते, पद्=पनीपद्यते, स्कन्द्=कनीस्कद्यते.

§ 631. When a root contains a penultimate ऋ (ऌ) original or brought in by *samprasarana* the syllable री is inserted between the अ of the reduplicative syll. (which remains short against § 629 *b*) and the radical consonant; वृत्=वृत्य=ववृत्य=वरीवृत्यते, प्रच्छ्=पृच्छय=परीपृच्छयते, नृत्=नरीनृत्यते, ग्रह्=जरीगृह्यते

Conjugation of the Atm. Freq. Base.

§ 632. In the Conjugational Tenses the Atm. Freq. Base is conjugated like the Conjugational base of the 4th class in Atm. In the General Tenses, and in all the Tenses of the Passive, the base loses its final अ when the final य is preceded by a vowel and drops the य itself, when it is preceded by a consonant. As regards the Perfect, the Fre. Base takes the Periphrastic Perfect. In the Aorist the Atm. terminations of the 5th form are added. In the remaining Tenses the Atm. terminations with the intermediate इ prefixed to them are added as usual. The passive is also formed like the Passive of derived verbs.

§ 633. Paradigms:—The 3 sing. of बोबुध्य the Atm. Freq, Base of the root बुध् and देदीय that of the root दा.

Tenses.	Active.		Passive.	
Present.	बोबुध्यते	देदीयते	बोबुध्यते	देदीय्यते
Imperfect.	अबोबुध्यत	अदेदीयत	अबोबुध्यत	अदेदीय्यत
Imperative.	बोबुध्यताम्	देदीयताम्	बोबुध्यताम्	देदीय्यताम्
Potential.	बोबुध्येत	देदीयेत	बोबुध्येत	देदीय्येत

Tense.	Active.		Passive.	
Perfect.	बोधांचक्रे,&c.	देदीयांचक्रे&c.	Like the Active.	
Aorist.	अबोबुधिष्ट	अदेदीयिष्ट	अबोबुधि	अदेदीयि
F. Future.	बोबुधिता	देदीयिता	Like the Active.	
Sec. Future.	बोबुधिष्यते	देदीयिष्यते	"	
Conditional.	अबोबुधिष्यत	अदेदीयिष्यत	"	
Benedictive.	बोबुधिषीष्ट	देदीयिषीष्ट	"	

N. B. Irregular Atm. Fre. Bases will be given under § 639.

PARASMAIPADA FREQUENTATIVES.

The Parasm. Frequentative is peculiar to the Veda. Its forms are very rarely to be met with in Classical composition.

Formation of the Base.

§ 634. The root is reduplicated according to the general rules of reduplication; the vowels इ and उ of the reduplicative syllable take their guṇa substitute; and the अ of the reduplicative syllable is lengthened; दा-ददा-दादा; श्रि-शिश्रि-शेश्रि; भू-बुभू-बोभू; कृ-चकृ-चाकृ; विद् विविद्-वेविद्; बुध्-बुबुध्-बोबुध् &c.

§ 635. The rules § 630 (*a*) (*b*) apply likewise to the Parasm. Frequen. Base; यम्-यंयम् or यँय्यम्; दह्-ददह् or दन्दह्; वञ्च्-वनीवञ्च् &c.

§ 636. र् or the syllable रि or री is inserted between the अ of the reduplicative syllable and the radical consonant of roots ending in short ऋ or having it for their penultimate; similarly ल् or लि or ली is inserted in the case of कॢप्; वृत्=ववृत्-वर्वृत् or वरिवृत् or वरीवृत्; कृ-चकृ, or चरिकृ or चरीकृ; कॢप्-चल्कॢप्, or चलिकॢप् चलीकॢप्; दृश्-दर्दृश्, दरिदृश् or दरीदृश्.

Conjugation of the Parasm. Fre. Base.

§ 637. In the Conjugational Tenses the Parasm. Frequentatives follow the conjugation of the special base of a root of the 3rd class, ई is optionally prefixed to the terminations of the singulars of the Present, of the 2nd and 3rd singulars of the Imperf. and of the 3rd sing. of the Impera.; when ई is prefixed to these, a penultimate short vowel does not take Guṇa; दा–दादाति or दादेति; वृत्–वर्वर्ति or वरिवर्ति or वरीवर्ति or वर्वृतीति or वरिवृतीति or वरीवृतीति, कृ–चर्कर्ति or चर्करीति, चरिकर्ति or चरिकरीति, चरीकर्ति or चरीकरीति.

§ 638. As regards the formation of the Non-conjugational tenses grammarians seem to be at variance. The Perfect follows the usual rules for the polysyllabic roots. In the remaining tenses the augment इ is always prefixed except in the Benedictive.

As this form of the Freq. is mostly confined to the Veda details are not given here

Paradigms.

बोभू or बोभव् from the root भू.

Present. / *Imperfect.*

1 बोभोमि or बोभवीमि	बोभूवः	बोभूमः	अबोभवम्	अबोभूव	अबोभूम
2 बोभोषि or बोभवीषि	बोभूथः	बोभूथ	अबोभोः or अबोभवीः	अबोभूतम्	अबोभूत
3 बोभोति बोभवीति	बोभूतः	बोभुवति	अबोभोत् or अबोभवीत्	अबोभूताम्	अबोभवुः

Imperative / *Potential.*

1 बोभवानि	बोभवाव	बोभवाम	1 बोभूयाम्	बोभूयाव	बोभूयाम
2 बोभूहि	बोभूतम्	बोभूत	2 बोभूयाः	बोभूयातम्	बोभूयात
3 बोभोतु or बोभवीतु	बोभूताम्	बोभुवतु	3 बोभूयात्	बोभूयाताम्	बोभूयुः

Perfect.

1 बोभवांचकार, चकर, &c.	बोभवांचकृव, &c.	बोभवांचकृम &c.
बोभव or बोभाव or बोभूव	बोभुविव, बोभूविव	बोभुविम or बोभूविम
2 बोभवांचकर्थ, &c.	बोभवांचक्रथुः	बोभवांचक्र
बोभविथ	बोभुवथुः &c.	बोभुव
बोभूविथ	बोभूवथुः	बोभूव
3 बोभवांचकार, &c.	बोभवांचक्रतुः	बोभवांचक्रुः
बोभाव	बोभुवतुः, बोभूवतुः	बोभुवुः, बोभूवुः

Aorist.

1 अबोभूवम्	अबोभूव	अबोभूम
अबोभाविषम्	अबोभाविष्व	अबोभाविष्म
2 अबोभोः अबोभवीः	अबोभूतम्	अबोभूत
अबोभूः or अबोभूवीः		
अबोभावीः	अबोभाविष्टम्	अबोभाविष्ट
3 अबोभवीत्, अबोभोत्	अबोभूताम्	अबोभूवुः
अबोभवीत्, अबोभूत्		अबोभुवुः
अबोभावीत्	अबोभाविष्टाम्	अबोभाविषुः

1st Future.

1 बोभवितास्मि	बोभवितास्वः	बोभवितास्मः
&c.	&c.	&c.

2nd Future.

1 बोभविष्यामि	बोभविष्यावः	बोभविष्यामः
&c.	&c.	&c.

Conditional.

1 अबोभविष्यम्	अबोभविष्याव	अबोभविष्याम
&c.	&c.	&c.

Benedictive.

1 बोभूयासम्	बोभूयास्व	बोभूयास्म
&c.	&c.	&c.

Tenses.	*Atmanepada.*	Passive.
Pre.	बोभूते	बोभूयते
Imperf.	अबोभूत	अबोभूयत
Imp.	बोभूताम्	बोभूयताम्
Pot.	बोभुवीत	बोभूयेत
Perf.	बोभवांचक्रे &c.	बोभवांचक्रे
1st Fu.	बोभविता	बोभविता or बोभाविता
2nd Fu.	बोभविष्यते	बोभविष्यते or बोभाविष्यते
Con.	अबोभविष्यत	अबोभविष्यत or अबोभाविष्यत
Aor.	अबोभविष्ट	अबोभावि
Bened.	बोभविषीष्ट	बोभविषीष्ट or बोभाविषीष्ट

§ 639. The following roots form their Frequentatives irregularly.

Roots.	Atm. Fre.	Par. Freq.
ऊर्णु to cover	ऊर्णोनूयते	
कु 1 cl. to sound	कोकूयते	
खन् to dig	चङ्खन्यते or चंखन्यते or चाखायते	चंखनीति चङ्खन्ति, &c.
गृ to swallow	जेगिल्यते	जागर्ति
चर् to walk	See § 630 *a*.	चञ्चरीति or चञ्चर्ति
चाय् to worship	चेकीयते	चेकीयति or चेकेति
जन् to be born	See § 630 *a*.	जञ्जनीति or जञ्जन्ति, &c.
द्युत् to shine	देद्युत्यते	देद्युतीति or देद्योति
फल् to expand	See § 630 *a*.	पंफुलीति or पंफुल्ति

शी to lie down	शाशय्यते	शेशयीति or शेशेति
श्वि to swell	शोश्वियते or शोशूयते	शेश्वयीति or शेश्वेति
सन् to obtain	संसन्यते or सासायते	संसनीति or संसन्ति
हन् to injure	जेघीयते	जघनीति or जघन्ति
in other cases	जङ्घन्यते or जंघन्यते	

IV. NOMINAL VERBS.

§ 640. Verbs are formed from nominal bases by means of certain affixes. These are not very much in common use and are generally used in the Present Tense. They have various meanings. They sometimes convey the notion of performing, practising, or using, or treating like the thing or quality expressed by the noun and are used transitively; sometimes they express the idea of acting, behaving or becoming like the person or thing expressed by the noun; and at others they yield the sense of desiring or wishing for the thing expressed by the noun. These will be arranged here under four heads, according to the affixes by which they are derived.

(a) By means of the affix य (क्यच्) and Conjugated in Parasm.

§ 641. When the sense of 'wish' is to expressed, a nominal verb may be derived from any *Subanta* or nominal stem by affixing य to it. The derivative verbal base derived in this manner is conjugated in the Parasm. only.

§ 642. Before this य,

(1) final अ and आ are changed to ई; पुत्रं आत्मनः इच्छति—पुत्रीयति (पुत्र+य=पुत्री+य+ति) 'he wishes for a son.'

(2) final इ and उ are lengthened; कवि—कवीयति 'he wishes for a poet.'

(3) final ऋ is changed to री; कर्तृ-कर्त्रीयति.

(4) final ओ and औ are changed to अव् and आव्; गो-गव्यति; नौ-नाव्यति.

(5) a final nasal is dropped and the preceding vowel is changed like an original final vowel; राजन्-राजीयति 'he wishes for a king.'

(6) in other cases the final consonant remains unchanged; वाच्-वाच्यति 'he wishes for words,' दिव्-दिव्यति (दीव्यति according to some) 'he wishes for heaven, समिध्—समिध्यति ' he wishes for holy sticks,' &c.

(7) The Tad. affix expressing 'a descendant of' is dropped and then the changes mentioned above take place; गार्ग्य (the son of गर्ग) आत्मनः इच्छति गार्गीयति (गार्ग्य+य+ति=गार्ग+य+ति=गार्गी+य+ति), &c.

§ 643. The consonant स् and the syllable अस् are inserted between any nominal stem and the affix य; मधु आत्मन इच्छति मधुस्यति or मध्वस्यति 'he wishes for honey'; so दधिस्यति, दध्यस्यति, &c. Final अ is dropped before अस्; पुत्रस्यति.

(*a*) अस् is inserted after वृष and अश्व when the sense to be conveyed is that of longing for them, after क्षीर and लवण when the one is desired to be drunk and the other to be licked; वृषस्यति गौः 'the cow longs for the ox,' अश्वस्यति वडवा 'the mare longs for the horse;' क्षीरस्यति बालः 'the child desires to drink,' लवणस्यति उष्ट्रः 'the camel wishes for licking the salt.' But वृषीयति 'he desires to have a bull,' अश्वीयति 'he wishes for a horse,' क्षीरीयति, लवणीयति.

§ 644. The affix य is not added to nouns ending in म् and to indeclinables; कमिच्छति, स्वरिच्छति (he longs for heaven).

§ 645. अशन has अशनायति 'he wishes to eat,' and अशनीयति 'he wishes to possess food,' उदक has उदन्यति; 'he wishes to drink water' and उदकीयति 'he wishes to possess water,' and धन has

धनायति 'he wishes to acquire money,' and धनीयति 'he wishes to be wealthy,'

§ 646. This form of the Nominal verb has not always a desiderative meaning.

(a) The affix य is added in the sense of 'treating or considering like;' पुत्रीयति छात्रम् 'he treats the pupil as a son,' विष्णूयति द्विजम् 'he treats the Brâhmaṇa like Vishṇu,' प्रासादीयति कुट्यां भिक्षुः 'the beggar considers his hut a palace,' कुटीयति प्रासादे राजा 'the king in his palace considers himself to be in a hut.'

(b) It is added to नमस्, वरिवस् and चित्र in the senses of 'adoring,' 'serving' and 'striking with wonder' respectively, नमस्यति देवान् 'he adores the gods', वरिवस्यति गुरुम् 'he serves the preceptor', चित्रीयते लोकान् 'he strikes the people with wonder.' It is also added to तपस् in the sesse of 'practising,' तपस्यति.

§ 647. In the general tenses the affix य (क्यच् and क्यङ् to be given hereafter) is dropped when preceded by a consonant, समिधांचकार Perf. 1 sing. समिधिता, समिधिष्यति 1st. and 2nd Fu. 3 sing. from समिध्यति, but पुत्रीयांचकार from पुत्रीयति.

(b) By means of the affix काम्य (काम्यच्) and conjugated in Par.

§ 648. To express the sense of wishing for that which is denoted by the noun; the affix काम्य is also added like the above and the base so derived conjugated in the Par. as before, पुत्रकाम्यति 'he wishes for a son,' यशस्काम्यति 'he wishes for fame,' सर्पिष्काम्यति 'he wishes for *ghee*.'

§ 649. The restriction given at § 644 does not hold good in the case of this affix, किंकाम्यति, स्वःकाम्यति

(c) By means of the affix क्विप् (o) and conjugated in Par.

§ 650. Nominal bases are formed without the addition of any affix: the characteristic signs of the tenses and moods and the personal termintions being added immediately to the nominal base. The bases thus derived convey the notion of acting or behaving like that which is expressed by the noun, and are conjugated in the Parasm.

§ 651. The penultimate अ of a noun ending in a nasal is lengthened. The base is treated like a root of the 1st conjugation, its last vowel only taking Guna before this अ; अ (name of Vishṇu) इव आचरति—अति 'he acts like Vishṇu,' कृष्ण—कृष्णाति 'he acts like कृष्ण' (कृष्णामि 1st sing.), कवि—कवयामि 'I act the poet or behave like a poet,' वि—वयाति 'he behaves like a bird,' माला-मालाति 'he or it acts like a garland' (Perf. मालांच० &c.), पितृ-पितरति 'he acts like a father.' भू-भवति 'acts like the earth' (Perf. बुभाव, &c. as भू is the base), राजन्-राजानति 'he acts like a king,' पथिन्-पथीनति 'it serves as a road,' &c. So इदामति from इदम्, ऋभुक्षीणाति from ऋभुक्षिन् name of Indra.

(b) The words अवगल्भ (a bold man), होड (a child) and क्लीब take the affixes क्यङ् and क्विप् optionally and are conjugated in the Atmane अवगल्भते or अवगल्भायते, होडते or होडायते, क्लीबते or क्लीबायते.

(d) By means of the affix य (क्यङ्) and conjugated in the Atm.

§ 652. The affix य (क्यङ्) is added in the same sense as above to nominal stems and the nominal verbs so derived are conjugated in the Atm.

§ 653. Before this affix the final अ of a nominal base is lengthened, आ remains unchanged, other final letters undergo the same changes as they do before the other य (क्यच्). The final स् of a noun is changed to आ optionally and that of अप्सरस

and ओजस् necessarily. कृष्ण इव आचरति, कृष्णायते 'he acts like कृष्ण;' यशस्—यशायते, यशस्यते 'he behaves like one who is famous,' विद्वस्—विद्वायते, विद्वस्यते 'he acts like a learned man, &c.; but ओजस्-ओजायते 'acts like one who is lustrous' (powerful); अप्सरस्-अप्सरायते 'she behaves like an Apsaras.'

(*a*) A *feminine* noun not having क for its penultimate drops its *fem.* term., कुमारीव आचरति—कुमारायते 'he behaves like a girl,' हरिणीव आचरति हरिणायते 'she acts like a female deer'; गुर्वीव आचरति गुरूयते 'acts like a stout woman.' But पाचिका इव आचरति पाचिकायते 'she acts like a female cook,' and not पाचकायते.

(*b*) सपत्नी has सपत्नायते, सपत्नीयते and सपतीयते she acts like a co-wife, युवति has युवायते 'she behaves like a young woman.'

§ 654. The affix य is added to a few nouns, such as भृश 'much,' मन्द 'slow,' 'पण्डित' 'learned,' सुमनस 'generous-minded', उन्मनस् 'agitated,' &c. in the sense of 'becoming what it was not before,' or 'what it was not like to before,' भृशः भवति भृशायते 'what was not much now becomes much,' उन्मनायति 'he (who was not agitated before) becomes agitated,' similarly सुमनायते &c.

§ 655. The following are the different senses in which the affix क्यङ् is used in the particular cases given below.

(*a*) It is added to सत्र, कष्ट, कृच्छ्र and गहन in the sense of 'desirous of committing sin;' पापं चिकीर्षति—सत्रायते, कष्टायते, &c., added to कष्ट it has also the sense of 'prompt in', कष्टाय क्रमते—कष्टायते (पापं कर्तुमुत्सहते इत्यर्थः, Sid Kau.).

(*b*) to रोमन्थ used objectively, रोमन्थायते 'is ruminating.'

(*c*) to बाष्प 'tears,' ऊष्मन् 'heat,' and फेन, in the sense of 'sending forth, vomiting;' बाष्पायते 'he sheds tears,' उष्मायते 'gives out heat,' फेनायते 'sends forth foam.'

(*d*) to सुख and others in the sense of 'experiencing or enjoying;' सुखं वेदयते सुखायते 'he enjoys happiness'; but परस्य सुखं वेदयते 'he shows the happiness of another.'

(*e*) to शब्द, वैर, कलह, अभ्र, कण्व 'sin', सुदिन 'a fair day', दुर्दिन 'a cloudy day' and नीहार 'fog, heavy dew,' in the sense of 'making or doing;' शब्दं करोति शब्दायते 'he makes a sound' (also शब्दयति cau.), सुदिनायते &c.

(*e*) By means of the affix क्यष् (य) and
conjugated in Parasm. and Atm.

§ 656. The affix य is added to लोहित and some other words and to words ending in the affix आ (डाच्) and the nominal base thus formed is conjugated in the Parasm. and Atmane.; *e. g.* लोहित--लोहितायति-ते 'becomes red:' पटपटायते 'utters the sound *Patpat.*'

(*f*) By means of the affix इ (णिङ् and णिच्)
and conjugated in Parasm. and Atm.

§ 657. Verbal bases are formed from the nouns given below by the addition of the affixes इ (णिङ्), and इ (णिच्) with various senses; those derived by means of णिङ् are conjugated in the Atm. and those by णिच् in the Par.; *e. g.* पुच्छं with वि, उत and परि—उत्पुच्छयते 'raises the tail,' विपुच्छयते, परिपुच्छयते; सम्भाण्डयते 'collects together the vessels'; सञ्चीवरयते भिक्षुः 'the mendicant collects together or wears tattered garments;' मुण्ड—मुण्डयति माणवकम् 'he shaves Mánavaka'; मिश्र—मिश्रयति अन्नम् 'he mixes boiled rice with (curds, curry, &c.);' श्लक्ष्ण—श्लक्ष्णयति वस्त्रम् 'he weaves cloth of a very thin texture;' लवणयति व्यञ्जनम् 'mixes salt with condiments;' व्रतयति पयः 'he observes the vow of living upon milk only;' व्रतयतिशूद्रान्नम् 'he observes the vow of abstaining from eating food at a Shudrá's house;' वस्त्र-संवस्त्रयति 'he clothes with a garment;, हल—हलयति 'he uses a large plough;' कलि—कलयति 'he quarrels!' कृत—कृतयति (कृतं गृह्णाति Sid. Kau.); तूस्त 'sin or hait or matted hair,' (तूस्तं केशा इत्येके जटीभूताः केशा इत्यन्ये पापमित्यपरे। Sid. Kau.)—तूस्तयति 'ties into a braid the hair;' &c.

§ 658. इ is changed to आपि when added to सत्य, अर्थ and वेद. सत्यं करोति आचष्टे वा सत्यापयति; अर्थापयति, वेदापयति.

§ 659. इ is further added in the following cases;—सेनया अभियाति—अभिषेणयति; लोमानि अनुमार्ष्टि—अनुलोमयति; वीणया उपगायति—उपवीणयति; श्लोकैः उपस्तौति—उपश्लोकयति; त्वचं गृह्णाति—त्वचयति; चर्मणा संनह्यति—संचर्मयति; वर्णं गृह्णाति—वर्णयति; चूर्णैः अवध्वंसते—अवचूर्णयति; एनीमाचष्टे—एनयति (declares her variegated); &c., &c.

The various changes taking place here before the affix इ the student will easily notice as irregularities.

(*g*) By means of the affix य (यक्).

§ 660. There are several roots* which are also *Pratipadikas* and which may be regarded as Nominal verbal bases derived from those *Pratipadikas* by means of the affix य (यक्). The more important of these are given below:—

कण्डू-कण्डूयति-ते he scratches.
मंतु-मंतूयति he offends against, he becomes angry, also मंतूयते according to चन्द्र.
वल्गु—वल्गूयति he becomes handsome, mild or gentle, honours.
असु—असूयति-ते (अस्यति) he is jealous, he envies, &c.
सपर—सपर्यति he worships.
भिषज्-भिषज्यति treats medically.
इषुध—इषुध्यति it contains arrows.
गद्गद—गद्गद्यति he stammers.
केला, खेला—केलायति, खेलायति he sports or becomes merry.
हृणी—हृणीयते he is angry or feels ashamed.

---

* In the Kaumudi these roots are classed separately under the head of 'कण्ड्वादिगण' or the group of roots beginning with कण्डू.

ळेला—ळेलायति he shines.	रेखा—रेखायति he approaches.
उषस्—उषस्यति it dawns.	मही—महीयते he is adored, &c.
मेधा—मेधयति he is quick in understanding,	तिरस्—तिरस्यति he disappears.
	अगद-अगदयति he becomes healthy.
सुख—सुख्यति feels happy.	उरस्—उरस्यति he becomes powerful.
दुःख—दुःख्यति feels unhappy.	पयस्—पयस्यति it spreads.

CHAPTER XIII.

Parasmaipada and Atmanepada.

§ 661. As already remarked there are two Padas in Sanskrit, the Parasmaipada and the Atmanepada. The Parasm. denotes that the fruit of the action accrues to some one differnt from the agent, as पचति 'he cooks for another,' कारयति 'makes some one do something for another, &c.' The Atm. denotes that the fruit of the action is कर्तृगामि *i. e.* it accrues to the agent, पचते 'he cooks for himself,' कारयते 'he makes another do something for himself,* &c.

(*a*) If, however, there be a word showing the accrual of the fruit of the action to the agent, the Atm. is optionally used, as स्वं यज्ञं यजते or यजति 'he offers his own sacrifice,' स्वं कटं कुरुते or करोति 'he weaves his own mat,' स्वं यज्ञं कारयति-ते &c.

(*b*) When the causal form of a transitive verb is used reflexively, or when the object in the primitive sense becomes

* This distinction, however, seems to be very little observed in practice. Even the best Sanskrit writers are found using both the Padas promiscuously. It cannot even be supposed that this distinction is meant to be observed where a root admits of both the Padas. The Dashakumáracharita and the Kàdambari afford several instances in which the two Padas are used exactly in the same sense.

the agent in the causal, the Atm. is used except in the sense of 'remembering with eagerness, &c.,' भक्ता भवं पश्यन्ति 'devotees see Bhava;' भवो भक्तान् दर्शयते 'Bhava shows himself to his devotees,' but स्मरति वनगुल्मं कोकिलाः; स्मरयति वनगुल्मः (कोकिलं); उत्कंठापूर्वकस्मृतौ विषयो भवतीत्यर्थः (Sid. Kau.). Vide Sid Kau. on Pàn. 1. 3. 67.

(c) When the agent of the action denoted by a verb cannot be other than an animal, the causal of the verb takes the Par. even when the action refers to the agent as कृष्णः शेते 'Krishna sleeps,' गोपी कृष्णं शाययति 'the cowherdess lulls Krishna to sleep,' but फलं पतति 'the fruit falls down.' वायुः फलं पातयति 'the wind causes the fruit to fall down,' &c.

(d) In the case of verbs meaning 'to eat,' except अद्, and 'to move,' their causals take the Parasm. even when the fruit of the action refers to the agent; निगारयति, आशयति 'makes another eat,' चालयति, कम्पयति, 'he shakes' &c.

Exceptions to (c) and (d)—to (c) दम् 'to pacify,' यम् with आ 'to draw in' यस् with आ 'to endeavour,' परिमुह् 'to faint, रुच् 'to shine,' वद् 'to speak,' वस् 'to dwell', and धे 'to drink;' to (d)—पा 'to drink,' नृत् 'to dance;' in the case of these roots the usual rule holds good; दमयति, दमयते; शमयति-ते &c.

§ 662. When the notion of कर्मव्यतिहार i. e. doing what is not proper for one to do, or the exchange of duties is to be implied. the Atm. is used, ब्राह्मणः सस्यानि व्यतिलुनीते 'the Bràhmana reaps corn' (which is the work of a Śûdra and not his): धर्मः व्यतिस्ते 'the religious duty is changed' (as when a S'ûdra discharges the duties enjoined upon a Vaisya, &c. संप्रहरन्ते राजानः 'the kings exchange blows.

(a) But verbs implying motion, or meaning to kill, the roots हस् and other similar roots do not take the Atm. even when an exchange of action is implied, व्यतियच्छन्ति, व्यतिघ्नन्ति, व्यतिहसन्ति, व्यतिजल्पन्ति.

§ 663. The Causals of the roots बुध्, युध्, जन्, इ with अधि, द्रु, स्रु, and प्रु are Parasm: बोधयति पद्मम्, योधयति काष्ठानि, नाशयति दुःखम्, जनयति सुखम्, अध्यापयति, प्रावयति प्रापयतीत्यर्थः (Sid. Kau.); द्रावयति विलापयतीत्यर्थः (Sid. Kau.). स्रावयति स्यन्दयतीत्यर्थः (Sid. Kau.).

664. The following is an alphabetical list of the roots that change their proper Pada after certain prepositions under the circumstances given in each case.

अस्—when preceded by a preposition is conjugated in either Pada; बन्धं निरस्यति-ते.

इ with अधि–in the causal takes the Parasm. अध्यापयति.

ऊह्—when preceded by a preposition is conjugated in either Pada; पापं अपोहति-ते 'he destroys sin;' तदपोहति 'discards;' समूहति-ते 'he gathers together.'

ऋ with सम् is Atm.; समारन्त ममाभीष्टाः Bh. VIII. 16; 'all my desires have come to me i. e. are gratified.'

ऋच्छ् with सम्—is Par. when used transitively, and Atm. when used intransitively; समृच्छति 'he collects;' समृच्छते 'is collected.'

कृ—without a preposition admits of either Pada. It is Parasm. with अनु and परा*; अनुकरोति भगवतो नारायणस्य। (Kâd.); तां हनुमान्पराकुर्वन् &c. (Bhaṭṭi. VIII. 50.); it is Atm. with preposition in following senses:—(1) गन्धन † or 'hurting,' 'killing,' as उत्कुरुते 'informs against (with a view to injure);' (2) अवक्षेपण or 'censuring, overcoming;' श्येनो वर्तिकामुदाकुरुते 'the hawk reproves the snail;' (3) सेवन or serving, attending

---

* अनुपराभ्यां कृञः। Pân. 1. 3. 79.

† गन्धनावक्षेपणसेवनसाहसिक्यप्रतियत्नप्रकथनोपयोगेषु कृञः Pân.1,3,32.

upon;' as हरिमुकुरुते 'he serves Hari;' (4) साहसिक्य or 'acting violently,' 'outraging;' as परदारान् प्रकुरुते 'outrages another's wife;' (5) प्रतियत्न or 'imparting an additional quality' (सतो गुणान्तराधानम् Kâshikâ), as एधः उदकस्य उपकुरुते 'fuel imparts heat to water;' (6) प्रकथन or reciting;' as गाथाः प्रकुरुते 'recites stories from the Vedas;' (7) उपयोग or 'applying to use;' as शतं प्रकुरुते (धर्मार्थे शतं विनियुंक्ते इत्यर्थः) 'devotes a hundred (Rupees, &c.) to holy purposes;' *cf.* also Bhaṭṭi. VIII. 18;—with अधि* it is Atm. in the sense of 'forgiving or overpowering;' शत्रुं अधिकुरुते 'forgives or overpowers his enemy;' but मनुष्यानधिकरोति शास्त्रं 'the S'âstra authorises men.' With वि† it is Atm. when used transitively; छात्रा विकुर्वते 'pupils study;' स्वरान् विकुरुते गायकः 'the musician varies the tones;' but चित्तं विकरोति कामः 'Love affects the mind;' विकुर्वे नगरे तस्य Bh. VIII. 21. कृ with उप in the sense of 'helping or doing good to' is used in both the Padas; न हि प्रदीपौ परस्परस्य उपकुरुतः (Shár. Bhâ.) 'two strong lights do not indeed help (*i. e.* serve to intesify) each other;' सा लक्ष्मीरुपकुरुते यया परेषाम् 'that is wealth by means of which one obliges another' (Kir. VII. 28.).

The Causal of कृ is Atm. when मिथ्या is prefixed to it; पदं मिथ्याकारयते 'mispronounces the accent on the syllable.'

कॄ—'to scatter' with अप‡ is Atm. in the sense of 'turning up or scratching with joy,' or turning up with the intention of making an abode or for maintenance (by quadrupeds or birds);' in this sense स् is prefixed to कॄ; अपस्किरते वृषो हृष्टः 'the bull turns up the ground in joy;' similarly अपस्किरते कुक्कुटो भक्ष्यार्थी; अपस्किरते (digs a hole for lying in) श्वा आश्रयार्थी; *cf.* छायापस्किरमाणविष्किर &c. (Up. II. 9).

---

* अधेः प्रहसने Pân. 1. 3. 33.

† वेः शब्दकर्मणः । अकर्मकाच्च । Pân. 1. 3. 34-35.

‡ अपाच्चतुष्पाच्छकुनिष्वालेखने Pân. VI. 3. 142. अपात्किरतेः सुट् स्यात् । सुडपि हर्षादिष्वेव वक्तव्यः । Sid. Kau.

When the root has its original sense, the Par. is used and स् is not inserted: कुसुमानि अपकिरति स्त्री 'the woman scatters flowers;' अपकिरति गजो धूलिम् ।

क्रम्*—when not preceded by a preposition is conjugated in both the Padas. But it is used in Atm. by itself when the meaning is 'free movement, energy, development or increase,' &c;. ऋचि क्रमते बुद्धिः 'his intellect moves freely in (i. e. proves very powerful in mastering) the Rigveda;' क्रममाणोरिसंसदि 'moving unobstructed in the assembly of the enemy' (Bh. VIII. 22); अध्ययनाय क्रमते 'shows ability or energy for studying;' न रञ्जनाय क्रमते जडानाम् । Vikra.I.16 क्रमन्तेऽस्मिन् शास्त्राणि 'the Shástras find enlargement in him or are satisfactorily mastered by him.' In the same senses it is Atm. when preceded by उप and परा only (i.e. is Par. if preceded by any other prep.) उपक्रमते, पराक्रमते cf. इत्युक्त्वा खे पराक्रंस्त (showed his might); परीक्षितुमुपाक्रंस्त (made bold) राक्षसी तस्य विक्रमम् । Bh. VIII. 22-23; but संक्रामति (शास्त्रेषु बुद्धिः). When preceded by आ it is Atm. in the sense of 'the ascending or the rising of a heavenly body;' आक्रमते सूर्यः 'the sun rises;' but आक्रामति धूमो हर्म्यतलात् 'the smoke issues forth from the upper terrace.' Also when preceded by वि, in the sense of 'a graceful movement of the feet, or ascending,' साधु विक्रमते वाजी 'the horse moves gracefully;' but विक्रामति सन्धिः 'the joint splits;'—and by प्र and उप in the sense of 'beginning,' प्रक्रमते, as in वक्तुं मिथः प्राक्रमतैवमेनम् । Kum. III. 2. 'thus began to talk with him in private;' but प्रक्रामति 'goes,' उपक्रामति 'comes near.'

क्री†—'to buy' is Atm. when the prepositions अव, परि and वि are prefixed to it (with वि it means 'to sell'), अवक्रीणीते, परिक्रीणीते cf. Bh. VIII. 8. कृतेनोपकृतं वायोः परिक्रीणानमुत्थितम् ।

---

*वृत्तिसर्गतायनेषु क्रमः।उपपराभ्याम्। आङ उद्गमने। ज्योतिरुद्गमन इति वाच्यम्। Várt. वेः पादविहरणे। प्रोपाभ्यां समर्थाभ्याम्। अनुपसर्गाद्वा। Pán.1.2.38-43.

† परिव्यवेभ्यः क्रियः Pán. 1. 3. 18.

क्रीड्*—'to play' is Atm. after the prepositions अनु, आ, परि and सम्, अनु-आ-परि-सं-क्रीडते, but not when अनु governs a noun, as माणवकमनुक्रीडति *i. e.* 'plays with Mâṇavaka.' क्रीड् with सम् is Par. when it means 'to creak as a wheel,' as संक्रीडति चक्रम्.

क्षिप्†--'to throw' is Par. when preceded by the prepositions अभि, प्रति and अति; अभिक्षिपति 'throws up,' आतिक्षिपति 'throws out,' प्रतिक्षिपति 'throws back.'

क्ष्णु—with सम् is Atm; संक्ष्णुते शस्त्रं 'whets or sharpens his weapon;' उत्कंठां संक्ष्णुते 'dispels anxiety.'

गम्‡—with सम् is Atm. in the sense of 'to be proper, unite with, join'; वाक्यं संगच्छते, सखीभिः संगच्छते, &c., but ग्रामं संगच्छति goes to a village.' In the Causal it takes the Atm. in the sense of 'having patience or waiting,' आगमयस्व तावत् 'have patience first'.

गृध्—'to be greedy' is Atm in the Cau. when the sense is 'to deceive,' माणवकं गर्द्धयते 'he deceives Mânavaka;' but श्वानं गर्द्धयति 'he makes the dog greedy.'

गॄ§—with सम् is Atm. when the meaning is 'to pledge one's word, to promise, to proclaim;' संगिरते शब्दं 'he pledges his word; शतं संगिरते 'he promises 100 (Rupees, &c.),' संगिरते स्वामिनो गुणाम् 'proclaims the merits of his master,' but संगिराति ग्रासं 'he swallows down a mouthful.' If it (*i.* e गॄ 6 Con.) be preceded by अव, it is Atm. अवगिरते शोणितं पिशाचः 'the fiend drinks blood.'

चर्$—'to walk' with उद् is Atm. when used transitively;

---

* क्रीडोनुसंपरिभ्यश्च Pân,. 1. 3. 21. अनोः कर्मप्रवचनीयान्न। Sid.Kau.

† अभिप्रत्यतिभ्यः क्षिपः। Pân. 1. 3. 80.

‡ समो गम्यृच्छिभ्याम्। Pân. 1. 3. 29.

§ अवाद्ग्रः समः प्रतिज्ञाने। Pân. 1. 3. 51–52.

$ उदश्चरः सकर्मकात्। समस्तृतीयायुक्तात्। दाणश्च सा चेच्चतुर्थ्यर्थे। Pân. 1. 3. 53–75.

धर्ममुच्चरते 'he transgresses his duty.' पानशौण्डाः पयःक्षीबा वृन्दैरुदचरन्त च । Bhaṭṭ. VIII. 31; but बाष्पमुच्चरति 'vapour rises up.' With सम् or समुदा it is Atm. when used with the instrumental of a vehicle; रथेन संचरते 'he moves in a chariot' (See Bh. VIII. 32); क्वचित्पथा संचरते सुराणां Rag. XIII. 19. 'now passes through the path of gods;' रथेन समुदाचरते.

जन्—in the Causal takes the Parasm. जनयति.

जि*—when preceded by वि and परा in the sense of 'to conquer,' and 'to defeat' or 'to find unbearable,' respectively, is Atm. विजयते, शत्रून् पराजयते, अध्ययनात् पराजयते 'gets tired of study;' खं पराजयमानोसौ 'filling up the sky, &c.' तां पराजयमानां स प्रीतेः 'her who was getting disgusted with,' &c. Bhaṭṭ. VIII. 9. 71.

ज्ञा†—'to know' used intransitively by itself is Atm. सर्पिषो जानीते (सर्पिषा उपायेन प्रवर्तते Sid. Kau. *i. e.* 'proceeds to perform a sacrifice having obtained ghee for it); with the preposition अप it is Atm. in the sense of 'denying;' as शतं अपजानीते denies a hundred;' with प्रति in the sense of 'acknowledging or promising,' and with सम् in the sense of 'expecting,' it is also Atm.; शतं प्रतिजानीते 'acknowledges a hundred;' हरचापारोपणेन कन्यादानं प्रतिजानीते 'promises the hand of his daughter by (*i. e.* on the condition of) the drawing of Hara's bow;' शतं संजानीते 'looks for a hundred,' मातरि मातुर्वा संजानाति 'thinks of his mother.' When this is used without a preposition and when the fruit accrues to the agent it takes the Atm. गां जानीते; when a preposition is prefixed to it and it is used transitively, it takes the Par. स्वर्गलोकं न प्रजानाति मूर्खः. In the Desiderative this root takes the Atm.

तप्‡—'to heat' with वि or उद्, when used intransitively, is

---

* विपराभ्यां जेः । Pân. 1. 3. 19.

† अपह्नवे ज्ञः । अकर्मकाच्च । सम्प्रतिभ्यामनाध्याने । Pân. 1. 3. 44–46;

‡ उद्विभ्यां तपः । Pân. 1. 3. 27. स्वाङ्गकर्मकाच्चेति वक्तव्यम् । Vârt.

Atm. उत्तपते or वितपते सूर्यः; when used transitively it is Atm. if it has a limb of the body of the agent for its object; उत्तपते or वितपते पाणिं 'he warms his hand, but उत्तपति सुवर्णं सुवर्णकारः 'a goldsmith heats gold', चैत्रो मैत्रस्य पाणिमुत्तपति; when it means 'to practise penance' it is Atm. and is conjugated like a root of the fourth class.

According to some तप् with अनु is Atm; अनुतपते 'repents.'

दा—*'to give' (3 cl.) by itself takes either pada; but when preceded by आ it is Atm. in any other sense than opening (the mouth, &c.); धनं आदत्ते 'accepts money;' विद्यां आदत्ते 'acquires knowledge;' नादत्ते भवतां स्नेहेन या पल्लवं (Śâk.) 'does not pluck your foliage through affection;' but मुखं व्याददाति 'opens his mouth;' विपादिकां व्याददाति वैद्यः 'the doctor opens the tumour on the root;' नदीकूलं व्याददाति 'breaks open the bank of a river;' but if the mouth belongs to another the exception is removed; व्याददते पतङ्गस्य मुखं पिपीलिकाः 'ants break open the mouth of a moth' (Mâh. Bhâr.).

दा—'to give' (I. cl.) when preceded by the preposition सम् singly or coupled with any other preposition takes the Atm. provided it is used with the Instrumental in the sense of the Dative; दास्या संयच्छते or संप्रयच्छते 'gives (something) to the maid-servant;' but दास्या धनं संप्रयच्छति विप्राय 'gives wealth to a Brâhmaṇa through his maid-servant.'

दृश्—'to see preceded by उप and used intransitively takes the Atm.; संपश्यते 'sees (thinks) well;' this root takes the Atm. in the Desiderative; दिदृक्षते 'wishes to see.'

द्रु—'to run' is Par. in the Cau.

नह्—with सम् is Atm. in the sense of 'preparing, being ready

---

*आङो दोऽनास्यविहरणे । Pân. 1. 3. 20. आस्यग्रहणमविवक्षितम् Sid. Kau. पराङ्गकर्मकान्न निषेधः । Vârt.

for,' युद्धाय संनह्यते ' prepares for battle; *cf.* छेत्तुं वज्रमणीन् शिरीषकुसुमप्रान्तेन संनह्यते Bha.

नाथ्*—'to beg or solicit for any thing' is used in the Par. in the sense of 'to hope for', 'to wish well' or 'to give blessings to,' it is exclusively Atm. सर्पिषो नाथते सर्पिर्मे स्यादित्याशास्ते इत्यर्थः । Sid. Kau. मोक्षाय नाथते मुनिः (Bhop.)

In "नाथसे किमु पतिं न भूभृताम्" Kir. XIII. 59. the root is used in the Atmanepada. But Bhaṭṭoji Dikshit supposes that the reading here should be नाधसे and not नाथसे. Mammata also in his Kâvyaprahâsha finds fault with the Atm. use of this root when critising the verse दीनं त्वामनुनाथते कुचयुगं पत्रावृतं मा कृथाः &c. and says that नाथते should be नाथति.

नी†—' to lead or carry ' with a preposition or with the prepositions उद्, उप or वि is Atm. in the following senses:—

(1) सम्मानन or ' showing regard for; ' शास्त्रे नयते ' gives instruction in the conclusions of the Śâstra ' (तेन च शिष्यसम्माननं फलितम् Sid. Kau.), (2) उत्सञ्जन or ' raising up; ' दण्डमुन्नयते उत्क्षिपतीत्यर्थः; (3) आचार्यकरण or ' initiating into sacred rites, ' माणवकं उपनयते विधिना आत्मसमीपं प्रापयतीत्यर्थः । उपनयनपूर्वकेणाध्यापनेन हि उपनेतरि आचार्यत्वं क्रियते (Sid. Kau.); (4) ज्ञान or ' ascertaining the real nature of; ' तत्त्वं नयते निश्चिनोतीत्यर्थः; (5) भृति or ' employing on wages; ' कर्मकरानुपनयते ' employs labourers on wages; (6) विगणन or ' paying off as a debt, taxes ' &c ; करं विनयते राज्ञे देयं भागं परिशोधयतीत्यर्थः, and (7) व्यय or ' spending or applying to good use; ' शतं विनयते धर्मार्थं विनियुंक्ते इत्यर्थः (Sid.

---

* आशिषि नाथः । Vârtika.

† सम्माननोत्सञ्जनाचार्यकरणज्ञानभृतिविगणनव्ययेषु नियः । कर्तृस्थे चाशरीरे कर्मणि । Pân. I. 3. 36–37 नियः कर्तृस्थे कर्मणि यदात्मनेपदं प्राप्तं तच्छरीरावयवभिन्न एव स्यात् । सूत्रे शरीरशब्देन तदवयवो लक्ष्यते । तेनेह न गडुं विनयति । कथं तर्हि विगणय्य नयन्ति पौरुषमिति । कर्तृगामित्वाविवक्षायां भविष्यति । Sid. Kau.

Kas.). नी with वि is Atm. when the object is something other than a limb of the body but exists in the agent; as कोपं विनयते; but गुरोः क्रोधं विनयति शिष्यः; गण्डं विनयति (turns aside).

नु—with आ* is Atm. आनुते 'he praises.'

प्रच्छ्*—with आ is Atm. in the sense of 'taking leave of'—"आपृच्छस्व प्रियसखममुम्" Meg. 10. 'take leave of this thy dear friend,' also with the preposition सम् when used intransitively, संपृच्छते 'he ascertains.'

भुज्†—is Atm. except in the sense of 'protecting,' ओदनं भुंक्ते 'eats food,' बुभुजे पृथिवीपालः पृथिवीमेव केवलाम् 'the protector of the earth enjoyed (experienced the pleasure from the possession of) the earth alone;' वृद्धो जनो दुःखशतानि भुंक्ते 'old people suffer hundreds of miseries;' महीं भुनक्ति 'protects the world.'

मृष्—with परि is Par.; परिमृष्यति 'endures;' but आमृष्यते 'he touches.'

यम्‡—with आ is Atm. either when used intransitively or has a limb of the body of the agent for its object; आयच्छते तरुः 'the tree spreads;' आयच्छते पाणिम् 'stretches forth the hand;' but आयच्छति कूपाद्रज्जुं 'draws up the rope from the well'; preceded by सम्, उद् and आ it is Atm. except when it has a literary work for its object; वस्त्रं आयच्छते 'puts on a garment;' भारमुद्यच्छते 'lifts up a load;' व्रीहीन् संयच्छते 'gathers rice;' but उद्यच्छति वेदम् 'tries hard to learn the Veda'. यम्—with उप is Atm. in the sense of 'accepting, or espousing a girl;' दारानं उपयच्छते 'accepts the

---

* आङि नुप्रच्छ्योः । Vârtika.

† भुजोऽनवने । Pân. 1. 3. 65. अदन इति वक्तव्येऽनवन इति पर्युदासग्रहणादवनभिन्न उपभोगादावर्थेपि आत्मनेपदविधानार्थमिदम् ।

‡ आङो यमहनः । Pân. 1. 3. 28. समुदाङ्भ्यो यमो ग्रन्थे । Pân. 1. 3. 75. उपाद्यमः स्वीकरणे Pân. 1. 3. 2. 56. विभाषोपयमने । Pân. 1. 2. 16.

gift given;' उपयच्छते कन्यां 'marries a girl'; in the Aorist this drops its nasal optionally; रामः सितां उपायत (See Uttar. III. 112). उपायंस्त; but परस्य भार्यां उपयच्छति 'makes another's wife his own.'

युज्*—preceded by प्र or उप, or generally by a prep. beginning or ending with a vowel, and does not refer to sacrificial vessels, is Atm. प्रयुंक्ते, उपयुंक्ते, प्रयुञ्जानः प्रिया वाचः (Bh. VIII. 39): but यज्ञपात्राणि प्रयुनक्ति 'arranges the sacrificial vessels;' य इमां आश्रमधर्मे नियुंक्ते (S'âk.) 'who appoints her to the duties of the hermitage'; अन्वयुंक्त गुरुमीश्वरः क्षितेः Rag. XI 62. 'the lord of the earth asked his preceptor;' पणबन्धमुखान्गुणानजः षडुपायुंक्त 'Aja employed the six expedients beginning with peace.' Rag. VIII. 21.

युध्—in the Cau. takes the Par.

रम्†—'to sport' changes its Pada when preceded by the prepositions वि, आ and परि; वत्सैतस्माद्विरम 'cease, oh child, from this' (Uttar. I. 33.). रात्रिरेव व्यरंसीत् Ibid. I. 27. आरमति, विरामोऽस्त्विति चारमेत् Manu. II 79. परिरमति; क्षणं पर्यरमत्तस्य दर्शनात् 'was for a moment delighted with his sight.' With उप it is Par.; यज्ञदत्तं उपरमति रमयतीत्यर्थः (Sid. Kau.) When intransitively used it takes either Pada; उपरमति-ते. 'sports'; cf. उपारंसीच्च सम्पश्यन्; नात्र सीतेत्युपारंस्त, &c. Bhaṭṭ. VIII. 54. 55.

ली—'to melt. to embrace' is Atm. in the cau. in the sense of 'adoring, defeating or deceiving;' जटाभिर्लापयते 'is adorable on account of his matted hair;' दण्डेन लापयते श्वा 'the dog is defeated by means of a stick;' श्येनो वर्तिकामुल्लापयते वञ्चयतीत्यर्थः (overpowers); मौर्ख्येण लापयते ब्राह्मणः 'the Brâhmaṇa is deceived by reason of his folly.' बालमुल्लापयते वञ्चयतीत्यर्थः।

वञ्च्‡—in the cau. is Atm. in the sense of 'deceiving;' माणवकं वञ्चयते 'deceives Mâṇavaka;' but अहिं वञ्चयति 'avoids a serpent.'

---

* प्रोपाभ्यां युजेरयज्ञपात्रेषु। Pân. I. 3. 64. स्वरान्तोपसर्गादिति वक्तव्यम्। Vârtika.

† व्याङ्परिभ्यो रमः। उपाच्च। विभाषाऽकर्मकात्। Pân. I. 3. 83–85.

‡ गृधिवञ्च्योः प्रलम्भने Pân. I. 3. 69.

वद्—†'to speak' is Atm. in the following senses:—(1) भासन or 'showing brightness (proficiency in);' शास्त्रे वदते 'is adept in the Sâstra;' (2) उपसंभाषा or 'conciliating or coaxing' (generally preceded by उप); भृत्यानुपवदते सांत्वयतीत्यर्थः; (3) ज्ञान or 'knowledge' शास्त्रे वदते 'knows the Śâstra;' (4) यत्न or 'effort, toil;' क्षेत्रे वदते 'labours in the field;' (5) विमति or 'disagreement, quarrel,' (generally preceded by वि in this sense); विवदन्ते; परस्परं विवदमानानां शास्त्राणाम् 'of mutually conflicting Śâstras;' and (6) उपमन्त्रण or 'coaxing, requesting;' दातारं उपवदते 'praises the donour,' &c; with संप्र it is Atm. in the sense of 'distinct and loud speech (as that of men gathered together);' संप्रवदन्ते ब्राह्मणाः 'the Brâhmaṇas are speaking aloud together;' but संप्रवदन्ति पक्षिणः; वरतनु संप्रवदन्ति कुक्कुटाः 'oh beautiful one, the cocks are crowing;' with अनु it is Atm. when used intrasitively; अनुवदते कठः कलापस्य 'the Katha Brâhmaṇa imitates (speaks on the side of or recites like) the Kalâpa Brâhmaṇa;' but उक्तं अनुवदति 'reproduces what is said;' अनुवदति वीणा 'the lute imitates the notes (indistinctly);' with विप्र it is optionally Atm. in the sense of 'disagreeing or disputing;' विप्रवदन्ति-न्ते वैद्याः the physicians disagree; with अप it is Atm. in the sense of 'reviling, reproaching, refusing,' when the fruit of the action refers to the agent; अपवदते धनकामो अन्यायं 'greedy of wealth reviles others unjustly;' १० न्यायमपवदते 'refuses justice;' but अपवदति 'reproaches' (when the result does not refer to the agent); *cf.* नार्तोऽप्यपवदेद्विप्रान् Manu. IV. 236; when the fruit of the action is indicated as referring to the agent the Atm. is optional; स्वपुत्रं अपवदति-ते वा (Sid. Kau. on Pan. 1. 3. 77); वद् with उप in the sense of 'advising or speaking stealthily,' when used transitively, is Atm. शिष्यं उपवदते 'gives advice to his pupil;' परदारान् उपवदते 'speaks stealthily with another's wife.

---

† भासनोपसंभाषाज्ञानयत्नविमत्युपमन्त्रणेषु वदः । व्यक्तवाचां समुच्चारणे । अनोरकर्मकात् । विभाषा विप्रलापे । अपाद्वदः । Pâṇ. 1. 3. 47–50, 73.

वह्—is both Par. and Atm. but with प्र is restricted to the Par.; प्रवहति.

विद्*—'to know' (2nd cl.) with सम् is Atm. when used intransitively in the sense of 'knowing of, being aware of,' and adds र् to इ optionally in the 3rd per. plural; संविदते or संविद्रते 'they know well;' *cf.* के न संविद्रते वायोर्मैनाकाद्रिर्यथा सखा Bh. VIII. 17.; 'who do not know that the mountain Mainâka is the friend of Vâyu?;' but संवित्तः सहयुध्वानौ तच्छक्तिं खरदूषणौ Bhatt. V. 37, as it is used transitively. It is also Atm. with सम् in the sense of 'recognising;' as संवित्ते.

विश्†—with नि is Atm. निविशते; किष्किन्धाद्रिं न्यविशत &c. Bhatt VI. 143. Also when अभि is prefixed to नि, अभिनिविशते सन्मार्गं (Sid. Kau.) 'takes to a good path;' see Bh. VIII. 80.

शप्‡—meaning 'to reproach or to abuse' takes the Atm. even when the fruit of the action does not accrue to the agent; कृष्णाय शपते।

शिक्ष्§—takes the Atm. in the sense of 'wishing to study;' धनुषि शिक्षते 'wishes to study archery.'

श्रु—†† 'to hear' with सम् is Atm. when used intransitively; संशृणुते 'hears well;' संशृणुष्व कपे (Bhat. VII. 16.) 'Listen with heed, oh monkey;' *cf.* हितान्न यः संशृणुते स किं प्रभुः Kir. 1. 5; but शब्दं संशृणोति 'he hears the sound.' This root takes the Atm. in the Desiderative, except when आ or प्रति precedes it, शुश्रूषते; but आ—प्रति—शुश्रूषति.

स्था$—with सम्, अव, प्र and वि is Atm., संतिष्ठते; सृदौ परिभवत्रासान्न

---

* विदिप्रच्छिस्वरतीनामुपसंख्यानम्। Vârtika. वेत्तेर्विभाषा Pân. VII.1.7

† नेर्विशः Pân. I. 3. 17. ‡ शप उपालम्भे। Vártika.

§ शिक्षेर्जिज्ञासायाम् Vârtika. †† अतिश्रुदृशिभ्यश्चेति वक्तव्यम्। Vártika.

$ समवप्रविभ्यः स्थः। Pân. 1.3.22 आङः प्रतिज्ञायामुपसंख्यानम् Vârtika प्रकाशनस्थेयाख्ययोश्च। उदोऽनूर्ध्वकर्मणि। Pân. 1, 323. 24 ईहायामेव। Vàrtikas. उपान्मन्त्रकरणे। Pân. 1. 3. 25. उपाद्देवपूजासङ्गतिकरणमित्रकरणपथिष्विति वाच्यम्। वा लिप्सायाम्। Vârtikas. अकर्मकाच्च। Pân. 1. 3. 26.

संतिष्ठते (Mud. 1. 36.) 'fearing an outrage does not abide by one who is mild,' see Mṛch. 1. 36. (In the sense of standing still, &c. it is used in the Par. क्षणं न संतिष्ठति जीवलोकः क्षयोदयाभ्यां परिवर्तमानः । Hariv.); क्षणमप्यवतिष्ठते श्वसन् (जन्तुः) 'if a being remains breathing though only for a moment;' अनीत्वा पङ्कतां धूलिमुदकं नावतिष्ठते । Sis. 11. 34. प्रतिष्ठते See Ragh. IV. 6; Kum. III. 22. वितिष्ठते; पदैर्भुवं व्याप्य वितिष्ठमानं Sis. IV. 4; with आ it is Atm. in the sense of 'laying down a proposition, asserting solemnly;' शब्दं नित्यं आतिष्ठते 'Affirms that sound is eternal;' जलं विषं वा तव कारणादास्थास्ये (Mah. Bhâ.) 'for thy sake I will drink water or poison;' in the sense of 'observing' it takes the Par. when used transitively; विधिमातिष्ठति 'observes the vow.' स्था is Atm. by itself in the sense of 'disclosing one's intention or abiding by;' गोपी कृष्णाय तिष्ठते, आशयं प्रकाशयति इत्यर्थः । संशय्य कर्णादिषु तिष्ठते यः Kir. III. 14; 'who, when in doubt, takes recourse to Karṇa and others (as the deciders of the matter in hand).' With उद् it is Atm. except in the sense of 'getting up or getting by right;' मुक्तावुत्तिष्ठते 'earnestly thinks of (aspires to) absolution;' (See Kir. XI. 13. and Sis. XIV. 17.); but पीठादुत्तिष्ठति; ग्रामाच्छतमुत्तिष्ठति 'a hundred is yielded to him by a village (as tax, &c.).' With उप it is Atm. in the sense of:— (1) 'worshipping with the recital of holy texts,' आग्नेय्याग्नीध्रमुपतिष्ठते 'worships the Âgnidhra fire with the recital of Vedic texts,' ये सूर्यमुपतिष्ठन्ते मन्त्राः Bh. VIII. 13, but भर्तारमुपतिष्ठति यौवनेन (or पतिमुपतिष्ठति नारी Vop.) where the meaning is 'to approach for intercourse, to serve,' See Bhaṭṭ. V. 68, (2) 'waiting upon, worshipping (a divine being)' आदित्यमुपतिष्ठते; (the Atm. use of the root in 'स्तुत्यं स्तुतिभिरर्थ्याभिरुपतस्थे सरस्वती' Rag. VI. 6. is to be explained, thinks Bhattoji Dîkshita, by the fact that the king is considered to be a divine being), (3) 'uniting or joining; गङ्गा यमुनामुपतिष्ठते; (4) 'forming friendship with' रथिकानुपतिष्ठते मित्रीकरोतीत्यर्थः (Sid. Kau.); and (5) 'to lead to' पन्थाः स्रुघ्नं उपतिष्ठते 'this way leads to Srughna.' When a desire to get something is implied स्था with उप takes either Pada; भिक्षुकः प्रभुमुपतिष्ठति-ते

'a beggar waits on a lord (with desire of getting something).' When it is used intransitively it takes the Atm; भोजनकाल उपतिष्ठते 'comes at the dinner time.'

स्मृ—is Atm. in the Desiderative; सुस्मूर्षते.

श्रु—is Par. in the causal; श्रावयति.

स्वृ—with सम् and आ is Atm., संस्वरते 'roars so as to terrify;' द्रुतं संस्वरिषीष्ठास्त्वं Bhaṭṭ. IX. 28; आस्वरते 'utters a loud sound.'

हन्*—with आ when used intransitively or when it has a limb of the body of the agent for its object is Atm.; आहते 'kills or dashes down;' स्वशिर आहते 'strikes his own head;' but परस्य शिर आहन्ति (Sid. Kau.)

हृ†—with अनु is Atm. in the senses of 'following the habits of, acquiring the natural quality of;' पैतृकमश्वा अनुहरन्ते 'horses always follow the gait of their progenitors;' so मातरं गावः अनुहरन्ते; in the sense of 'acquiring a new quality by imitation' it takes the Par. पितरमनुहरति 'imitates his father.'

ह्वे‡—उप, preceded by उप, नि, वि, and सम् and used intransitively is Atm. उप—नि—वि—सं—ह्वयते; with आ it is Atm. in the sense of 'challenging;' कृष्णश्चाणूरमाह्वयते 'Krishṇa challenges Chânura to battle;' आह्वत चेदिराण्मुरारिं Sis. XXI. 1; but पुत्रमाह्वयति.

The following *Karikâs,* extracted from the A'khyâtachandrikâ are subjoined here, with some alterations here and there, as a help to the student in remembering much of what is given in the present chapter.

आत्मनेपदपरस्मैपदविवेकवर्गः ॥

भावे कर्मणि सर्वस्माद्धातोः स्यादात्मने पदम् ॥
ङिद्भ्यस्तथानुदात्तेभ्यो भूयते प्यायते तु दिक् ॥ १ ॥

---

* आङो यमहनः । Pân 1. 3. 28. कथं तर्हि आजघ्ने विषमविलोचनस्य वक्षः इति भारविः । अहध्वं मा रघूत्तममिति भट्टिश्च । प्रमाद एवायमिति भागवृत्तिः प्राप्येस्यध्याहारो वा । Sid. Kau. † हरतेर्गतिताच्छील्ये Vârtika.

‡ निसमुपविभ्यो ह्वः ; स्पर्धायामाङः Pân. 1. 3. 30, 31.

क्रियाव्यतिहृतौ तद्व्यातिस्ते व्यतिपिञ्जते ॥
शब्दार्थहस्प्रकाराहगतिहिंसार्थकान्न तत् ॥ २ ॥
व्यतिभ्यां जल्पति हसत्येवं हन्तीत्यमूर्दिशः ॥
नात्र संप्रवदन्ते संप्रहरन्ते निषेधनम् ॥ ३ ॥
द्विरुक्तान्यतरेतरोपपदान्नात्मनेपदम् ॥
अन्योन्यस्य व्यतिलुनन्त्येषा दिङ् निपराद्विशेः ॥ ४ ॥
परिव्यवेभ्यः क्रीणातेर्जयतेर्विपरापरात् ॥
आङो दोऽङ्गविकासस्वास्यप्रसारणयोर्न हि ॥ ५ ॥
गमेः क्षमायां णेराङि नुपृच्छ्योः क्रीडतेरनोः ॥
पर्याङ्भ्यां च समोऽकूजे जिज्ञासायां शकेः सनः ॥ ६ ॥
अपारिकरतेर्हरतेर्गततताच्छील्य आशिषि ॥
नाथेः शपेस्तु शपथे स्थो निर्णीतौ प्रकाशने ॥ ७ ॥
प्रतिज्ञायां चावसंविप्रादुदोऽनूर्ध्वचेष्टने ॥
देवार्चासंगकरणमैत्रीषु पथि कर्तृके ॥ ८ ॥
धात्वर्थे मन्त्रकरणेऽकर्मके चोपपूर्वकात् ॥
वा लिप्मायां समः पृच्छिगमृच्छिस्वृश्रुवेत्तितः ॥ ९ ॥
दृशोर्तेश्चाकर्मकेभ्य आङ् पूर्वाभ्यां यमेर्हनः ॥
उद्विभ्यां तपते स्माङ्गकर्मकेभ्योप्यथास्यतेः ॥ १० ॥
ऊहेर्वा सोपसर्गाभ्यां ह्वः संनिव्युपपूर्वकात् ॥
आङस्तु स्पर्धतेः सूचनावक्षेपणसेवने ॥ ११ ॥
प्रतियत्नप्रकथनोपयोगे साहसे कृञः ॥
अधेः प्रहसने वेस्तु शब्दकर्मण्यकर्मकात् ॥ १२ ॥
पूजाचार्यकृतिज्ञानोत्सञ्जने च भृतौ व्यये ॥
नियो विगणने कर्तस्थे तु चामूर्तकर्मणि ॥ १३ ॥
वृत्युत्साहस्फीततासु क्रमेस्तद्वदुपरोपयोः ॥
ज्योतिरुद्गमने त्वाङो वेः पादविहृतार्थकात् ॥ १४ ॥
आरम्भणेऽर्थे प्रोपाभ्यां विभाषानुपसर्गकात् ॥
अपह्नवेकर्मकाच्च ज्ञोऽनाध्याने समः प्रतेः ॥ १५ ॥

यत्नोपसान्त्वनज्ञानभासनेपूपमन्त्रणे ॥
विमत्तौ चापि वदतेः समनुभ्यां त्वकर्मकात् ॥ १६ ॥
व्यक्तवाचा सहोक्तौ च विप्रलापे विभाषया ॥
ग्रोऽन्यात्समः प्रतिज्ञाने चरेरुदि सकर्मकात् ॥ १७ ॥
समस्तृतीयायुक्तात्स्वीकरणे तूपयच्छतेः ॥
तृतीया चेच्चतुर्थ्यर्थे दाणः शिति शदेर्म्रङः ॥ १८ ॥
लिङ्लुङोश्च कृञ प्राग्वदामो यस्तु प्रयुज्यते ॥
सनः श्रुस्मृदृशिज्ञाभ्यो नानोर्ज्ञो नाङ् प्रतेः श्रुवः ॥ १९ ॥
अयज्ञपात्रेपु युजेरजायन्तोपसर्गतः ॥
समः क्ष्णौतेरनवने भुनक्तेरथ णेरणौ ॥ २० ॥
यत्कर्म णौ स कर्ता चेद्भवेदाध्यानवर्जितं ॥
यथा रोहयते हस्ती स्वयं दर्शयते नृपः २१ ॥
भीस्म्योः प्रयोजकाद्भीतिस्मययोर्वञ्चतेर्गृधेः ॥
प्रलम्भने लियः पूजान्यक्कृत्योर्वञ्चनेऽपि च ॥ २२ ॥
मिथ्याशब्दोपपदतः पौनःपुन्ये कृञो णिचः ॥
फले च कर्त्रभिप्राये स्वरितेतो ञितो णिचः ॥ २३ ॥
पचते कुरुते ब्रूते घटं कारयते तथा ॥
अपाद्वदः समाङ्नुद्भ्यो यमेरग्रन्थगोचरे ॥ २४ ॥
ज्ञश्चोपसर्गरहिताच्छब्दान्तरगतौ तु वा ॥

॥ इति आत्मनेपदाधिकारः ॥

॥ अथ परस्मैपदाधिकारः ॥

परस्मैपदमन्यस्मात्कृञोऽप्यनुपरापरात् ॥ २५ ॥
क्षिपोऽभिप्रत्यतिभ्यः प्राद्वहेर्मृषिवहोः परेः ॥
व्याङ्परिभ्यो रम उपाद्विभाषा चेदकर्मकः ॥ २६ ॥
आहारचलनार्थाण्णेरण्यन्ते यद्यकर्मकः ॥
चित्तवत्कर्तृको यद्वत्तोषयत्येष पार्थिवः ॥ २७ ॥
प्रद्रुस्नुजन्युधबुधेङ्नशिभ्यश्च णिचोथ न ॥
दम्यायमायसपरिमुहो न रुचिवद्वसः ॥ २८ ॥

तृतिधेट्पिबतिभ्यश्च क्यषन्ताच्च विभाषया ॥
वा द्युतादेर्लुङि वृद्भ्यः स्यसनोर्लृटि कल्पतेः ॥ २९ ॥
परस्मैपदमन्यस्मात्तथा शिष्टप्रयोगतः ॥

CHAPTER XIV.

VERBAL DERIVATIVES
or
PRIMARY NOMINAL BASES.

Derived by means of the Kṛt Affixes.

§ 665. The Kṛt affixes (Vide § 337) are added to roots or to their modified forms to form nouns, adjectives, and indeclinables; *e. g.* कृ—कार, कर्तृ, करण, कुर्वत्, करिष्यत्, चकृवस्, कृत्वा कर्तुम् &c. These are called Kṛdantas or Primary Nominal Bases as distinguished from the Secondary Derivatives formed with the Taddhita affixes.

§ 666. There is a peculiar class of Kṛt or Primary affixes technically designated by Sanskrit grammarians—*Uṇâdi* or those beginning with the affix उण् *i. e.* the affix उ with the mute or indicatory letter ण्, so called from the words कारु, वारु. &c. in the first Sûtra being derived with the affix. These Uṇâdi affixes form primary nouns, like other Kṛt affixes form verbal roots, but are classed separately because their application is limited, because the nouns derived by their means are either formed irregularly, or the connection between their senses and the meanings of roots from which they are supposed to be derived is not so clearly discernible as in the case of other primary derivatives; *e. g.* अश्नुते अध्वानं व्याप्नोतीति वा अश्वः 'a horse' which is derived either from अश् 'to pervade,' or from अध्वन् 'road;' and आप् with वि, &c. कारु 'an artisan' from कृ 'to do,' &c.

SECTION I.

PARTICIPLES (Declinable and Indeclinable).

1. Participles (Declinable)

(*a*) Participles of the Present Tense.

§ 667. **The participle of the present Parasm. is formed by the addition of the affix अत् to that form of a root. primitive or derivative, which it assumes before the third person plural termination of the Present Tense. If the base ends in अ, the अ is dropped;** *e. g.*

भू (1 cl.)—भव्+अन्ति Pre. 3rd pl. भव्+अत्=भवत् Pre. P. being.
स्था (1 cl.)—तिष्ठ्+अन्ति ,, तिष्ठ्+अत्=तिष्ठत् ,, standing.
द्विष् (2 cl.)—द्विष्+अन्ति ,, द्विष्+अत्=द्विषत् ,, hating.

similarly from

अद् (2 cl.) अदत् eating. रुध् (7 cl.) रुन्धत् preventing.
या (2 cl.) यात् going. कृ (8 cl.) कुर्वत् doing.
हु (3 cl.) जुह्वत् sacrificing तन् (8 cl.) तन्वत् stretching, &c.
दिव् (4 cl.) दीव्यत् playing. क्री (9 cl.) क्रीणत् buying.
सु (5 cl.) सुन्वत् extracting. मुष् (9 cl.) मुष्णत् stealing, &c.
तुद् (6 cl.) तुदत् giving pain. चुर् (10 cl.) चोरयत् stealing.
बोधय् cau. of बुध्, बोधयत् causing to know.
बुबोधिष् desid. of बुध्, बुबोधिषत् desiring to know.
दित्स desid. of दा, दित्सत् desiring to give.
चेक्षिप् freq. of क्षिप्, चेक्षिपत् throwing again and again.

&c. &c. &c. &c. &c.

(*a*) The term. अत् is optionally changed to वस् when added to the root विद्; विद्वत् or विद्वस् ' knowing. '

(*b*) The affix अत् when added to द्विष् and सु ' to extract Soma juice in a sacrifice' has the sense of an agent; as द्विषत् *m*. 'an enemy.' यज्ञे सर्वे सुन्वन्तः 'all are the extractors of Soma juice in a sacrifice.

(c) When affixed to अर्ह् it has the sense of 'fitness, respect;' अर्हत् 'one deserving respect, respectable.'

(d) इ 2 P. and धृ cau. take the affix अत् when the idea of difficulty is not present; अधीयत् 'stu lying without experiencing any difficulty;' धारयत् 'holding or bearing with ease;' but कृच्छ्रेण अधीते, कृच्छ्रेण धारयति.

§ 668. The declension of the Participles in अत् has been treated of in § 116.

§ 669. The participles of the Present Atm. is formed by adding आन to the root which undergoes the same changes before it, as before the termination अते or अन्ते of the 3rd pl. pre. आन is changed to मान, in the case of roots of the 1st, 4th, 6th and 10th classes, and all derived roots, or rather when the base ends in अ, before which the अ of the base remains unchanged; e. g. एध् (1. cl.) एधमान 'growing;' वन्द् (1 cl.) वन्दमान 'saluting'; शी (2. cl.) शयान 'lying down;' द्विष् (2. cl.) द्विषाण; हन् with आ (2. cl.) आघ्नान 'killing;' धा (3. cl.) दधान 'holding; हु (3. cl.) जुह्वान; दिव् (4. cl.) दीव्यमान 'playing;' सु (5. cl.) सुन्वान 'extracting;' तुद् (6. cl.) तुदमान 'giving pain;' रुध् (7. cl.) रुन्धान 'obstructing;' कृ (8. cl) कुर्वाण 'doing;' तन् (8. cl.) तन्वान 'stretching;' क्री (9. cl.) क्रीणान 'buying;' चुर् (10, cl.) चोरयमाण 'stealing;' &c. बुध् (1. cl.)—cau. बोधयति-बोधयमान 'causing to know;'—desiderative बुबोधिषति-बुबोधिषमाण 'being desirous to know,' &c.

§ 670. (a) The आ of आन is changed to ई in the case of the root आस् (2. cl.) 'to sit;' Pre. P. आसीन.

(b) आन added to the roots पू and यज् forms nouns; e. g. पवमानः 'that which purifies, hence, the wind' (cf. Rag. VIII. 9.) also, 'one of the sacred fires;' यजमानः 'one who sacrifices.

§ 671. * The termination आन may be added to any root

* ताच्छील्यवयोवचनशक्तिषु चानश् । Pân. III. 2. 126.

in the sense of 'in the habit of' or 'to show a particular standard of age, or capacity to do a thing; *e. g.* भोगं भुंजान: 'one habituated to enjoy pleasures:' कवचं बिभ्राण: 'of a sufficient age *i. e.* young enough to bear armour;' शत्रुं निघ्नान: 'able to kill the enemy,' &c.

§ 672. The participle of the Pre. Passive is formed by adding मान to the Passive base in य; *e. g.* बुध्यमान 'who or what is known,' अद्यमान 'what is eaten,' दीयमान who or what is given, चीयमान 'who or what is gathered,' क्रियमाण 'what is done,' कॄ—कीर्यमाण 'what is scattered,' चोर्यमाण 'who or what is stolen' बुध्—cau. Pass. बोध्यमान 'who or what is caused to know,' Des. Pass. बुबोधिष्यमाण 'who or what is desired to know,' &c.

§ 673. The participles formed according to § 669 are declined like nouns ending in अ *m. f.* and *n.*

(*b*) Participles of the Perfect.

§ 674 The terminations of the Perf. and the Past participles are weak, and therefore the radical vowel does not take its Guṇa substitute before these. The penultimate nasal is generally dropped (see § 584).

§ 675. The participle of the Perf. Par. and Atm. is formed by adding वस् and आन generally to that form of the root which it assumes before the termination of the 3rd per. plural. If this form consists of one syllable only or when the root ends in आ, वस् has the intermediate इ added to it. इ is optionally prefixed to वस् in the case of the roots गम्, हन्, दृश्, विश् and विद् (6 cl.); जन् and खन्, and गम् and हन् when they do not take इ, form this participle from that base which they would assume before the 2nd per. sing. termination, *e. g.*

PARASMAIPADA.

Root	Perf. Base (3rd pl.)	Pers. Ptc.
इ to go	ईय्	ईयिवस् who or what went
ऋ „	आर्	आरिवस् „ „

Roots		Perf. Base (3rd pl.)		Perf. ptc.
नी	to carry	निनी		निनीवस् who or what carried.
पच्	to cook	पेच्		पेचिवस् ,, cooked.
वच्	to speak	ऊच्		ऊचिवस् ,, spoke.
यज्	to sacrifice	ईज्		ईजिवस् ,, sacrificed.
भञ्ज्	to break	बभञ्ज्		बभञ्ज्वस् ,, broke.
अस्	to throw	आस्		आसिवस् ,, threw.
स्तु	to praise	तुष्टु		तुष्टुवस् ,, praised.
कृ	to do	चकृ		चकृवस् ,, did.
भिद्	to split	बिभिद्		बिभिद्वस् ,, split.
दा	to give	दद्		ददिवस् ,, gave &c.
घस्	to eat	जक्ष्		जक्षिवस् ,, ate.
दृश्	to see	ददृश्	ददृशिवस्	or ददृश्वस् ,, saw.
विद्	to know, &c.	विविद्	विविद्वस्	or विविदिवस् ,, knew, &c.
विश्	to enter	विविश्	विविशिवस्	or विविश्वस् ,, entered.

जन् has जज्ञन्वस्, खन्–चखन्वस्, गम्–जग्मिवस् or जगन्वस्, and हन्–जघ्निवस् or जघन्वस्.

(1) In the case of roots beginning with अ, न् is not inserted as it is in the Perfect; अञ्ज्–आजिवस्,

(a) For the declension of these participles see § 124.

ATMANEPADA.

नी	to carry	निन्य्	निन्यान
दा	to give	दद्	ददान
पच्	to cook	पेच्	पेचान
यज्	to sacrifice	ईज्	ईजान
कृ	to do	चकृ	चक्राण
वच्	to speak	ऊच्	ऊचान
स्तु	to praise	तुष्टु	तुष्टुवान
श्रु	to hear	शुश्रु	शुश्रुवाण
&c.		&c.	&c.

(*b*) These are declined like nouns ending in अ *m. f. n.*

§ 676. Roots ending in ॠ (तॄ and जॄ included) form their Perf. P. irregularly; वस् is added to the root, which then undergoes the changes mentioned in § 394, and is finally reduplicated: when a root is Atm. it is first reduplicated and आन afterwards added, the final ॠ changing as before; *e. g.* कॄ + वस् = कीर्वस्, by reduplication चिकीर्वस्; कॄ—by reduplication चकॄ + आन = चकिराण; similarly तॄ—तितीर्वस्; ततिराण; शॄ--शिशीर्वस् शशिराण; पॄ–पुपूर्वस्, पपुराण, &c.

§ 677. The Perfect participle is not frequently used. The only participles that are most commonly to be met with are those formed from the roots सद्, वस्, स्था and श्रु.

§ 678. The participles of the Periphrastic Perfect Par. and Atm. are formed by the addition of the Perf. Participal forms of the auxiliary verbs कृ, अस् or भू to the base in आम् *e. g.* दयामासिवस्, उन्दांबभूवस्, गण्—गणयामासिवस्, गणयांबभूवस् &c.

(*c*) Past Passive Participles.

§ 679. The Past Passive Participle is formed by the addition of the affix त to the root; *e. g.* स्ना-स्नात 'bathed,' जि-जित 'conquered,' नी-नीत 'carried,' श्रु-श्रुत 'heard,' भू-भूत 'become,' हृ-हृत 'taken away,' त्यज्-त्यक्त 'abandoned,' चित-चित्त,' 'thought or meditated upon,' &c.

§ 680. Roots capable of taking Samprasárana take it before the affix त.

§ 681. The affix त is weak.

Exceptions:—

(*a*) The roots शी, स्विद् 1 cl., मिद्, क्ष्विद्, धृष् and मृष् admit of the Guṇa change before त when इ is prefixed to it; पू 1 A. also does the same when it takes इ (see § 686*b*).

(*b*) Such of the roots of the 1st class as have उ for their penultimate change their vowel to Guṇa optionally, when the affix त is added with the intermediate इ, and the P. P. Participle is used impersonally, or when it conveys the sense of beginning to perform the action or undergoing the condition expressed by the root; मुद् 'to delight' मुदित, but 'to begin to delight' प्रमुदित or प्रमोदित; प्रमुदितं or प्रमोदितं साधुना; प्रमुदितः or प्रमोदितः साधुः; similarly, द्युत्–प्रद्युतित or प्रद्योतित &c.

§ 682. The Penultimate radical nasal is generally dropped. (See § 674).

§ 683. The augment इ is prefixed to this त in the case of certain roots, optionally in the case of some and not at all in the case of others.

§ 684. As a general rule, all roots ending in a vowel, and such as take the इ optionally before any termination, and Anit roots ending in consonants generally, do not take इ; the rules of Sandhi given in the foregoing chapters that are applicable in particular cases ought to be observed.—

Roots. P. P. Ptc.	Roots. P. P. Ptc.
पा—पात protected	त्यज्—त्यक्त abandoned..
श्रि—श्रित resorted to	भ्रस्ज्—भ्रष्ट fried.
नी—नीत carried.	यज्—इष्ट sacrificed.
श्रु—श्रुत heard.	बुध्—बुद्ध awakened.
भू—भूत become.	व्यध्—विद्ध pierced.
कृ—कृत done.	स्वप्—सुप्त slept.
ऊर्णु—ऊर्णुत covered.	लभ्—लब्ध obtained.
वे——उत woven.	बन्ध्—बद्ध bound.
व्ये—वीत covered.	दृश्—दृष्ट seen.
ह्वे*—हूत called &c.,	क्रुश्—क्रुष्ट cried out &c.

*ह्वे substitutes ऊ for its व.

Roots.	P. P. Ptc.	Roots.	P. P. Ptc.
वच्—उक्त	spoken	दंश्—दष्ट	bitten
गुह्—गूढ	concealed	द्विष्—द्विष्ट	hated, &c.
मृज्—मृष्ट	wiped off, &c.	शास्*—शिष्ट	governed
सिध्—सिद्ध	accomplished, &c.	दह्—दग्ध	burnt
तृप्—तृप्त	satisfied	वह्—ऊढ	borne
नश्—नष्ट	perished, &c.	सह्—सोढ	endured
वृध्—वृद्ध	grown	ध्वंस्—ध्वस्त	destroyed
वृत्—वृत्त &c.	happened, completed.	लिह्—लीढ	licked
		मुह्—मुग्ध or मूढ	fainted
शक्—शक्त	able	नह्—नद्ध	bound
सिच्—सिक्त	sprinkled	स्रंस्—स्रस्त	dropped
प्रच्छ्—पृष्ट	asked		

Exceptions:—

(*a*) शी, जागृ, स्था and दरिद्रा take इ; the final vowel of the first two takes Guṇa substitute, and the last two drop their final; शयित, जागरित; स्थित. दरिद्रित.

(*b*) पत् takes इ though it admits of इ optionally in the Desiderative; पतित.

(*c*) The Anit roots वस् and क्षुध् admit इ before त and क्त्वा; उषित, क्षुधित.

§ 685. Set roots (subject to § 684), and all derived roots admit of इ; roots of the Tenth Class and causals reject their final अय, Par. Frequentatives their final अ, and Atm. Frequentatives their य:—

Roots	P. P. Ptc.	Roots.	P. P. Ptc.
शङ्क्—शङ्कित	'suspected.'	कथ्—कथित	'told.'
वद्—उदित	'spoken.'	प्रथ्—प्रथित	'spread.'

*Vide § 437.

Roots. P. P. Ptc.	Roots. P. P. Ptc.
एध्—एधित 'increased	बोधय् cau. Base of बुध्, बोधित 'made to know.'
कम्प्—कम्पित 'shaken.'	चिकीर्ष् des. b. of कृ, चेकीर्षित 'desired to do.'
मुष्—मुषित 'stolen; deceived.'	बोबुध्य Atm. Fre. Base of बुध्, बोबुधित 'frequently known.'
ग्रह्—गृहीत 'taken.'	बोभूय—Par. Fre. Base of भू, बोभूयित.

Exceptions:—इन्ध्, ऋष्, 'to go, to kill,' &c., चित् 'to know; to observe,' &c., जुष्, त्रस्, दीप्, मद्, and यत्; इद्ध, ऋष्ट, चित्त, जुष्ट, त्रस्त, दीप्त, मत्त, यत्त.

N. B. There are many Set roots which reject the intermediate इ but as some of them form their P. P. participles in न and others irregularly, they will be given in their proper places.

§ 686. The following roots insert इ optionally:—

(*a*) दम्, शम्, पूर्, दस्, स्पश्, छद्, ज्ञप्, रुष्, अम्, घुष्, with सम्, स्वन् with आ, and हृष् 4. 1. Par. when used with लोमन् 'the hair,' or when it means 'to be surprised or disappointed;' दान्त, दमित; (see § 696 *a*.); शान्त, शमित; पूर्ण (see 688), पूरित; दस्त 'wasted, perished,' दासित; स्पष्ट, स्पशित; छन्न, छादित; ज्ञप्त, ज्ञपित; रुष्ट, रुषित; आन्त (See § 696 *a*), अमित; सङ्घुष्ट सङ्घुषित; आस्वान्त, आस्वनित; हृष्ट-हृषित-लोमन् 'horripilated with joy,' हृष्टो-हृषितो मैत्रः विस्मितः प्रतिहतो वा.

(*b*) क्लिश् and पू take इ optionally before त and त्वा; क्लिष्ट, क्लिशित; पूत, पवित.

(*c*) The following roots admit of इ optionally before त when the P. P. Participle is used impersonally or conveys the sense of beginning to perform the action or to undergo the state expressed by the root; तृष्, त्वर्, धृष्, फल्, भिद्, मूर्च्छ्, स्विद्, 1. 4. cl. स्फुर्च्छ्, स्फुर्ज्, क्ष्विड् and क्ष्विद् 1. 4. P. 1. A.; स्विन्न-प्रस्वे-

दित: or प्रस्विन्न: चैत्र: 'Chaitra has begun to perspire;' प्रस्वेदितं or प्रस्विन्नमनेन 'he has perspired,' &c.; स्विद् 4 cl. has स्विदित also.

N. B. When the participle is not used in the sense given above these roots reject इ; क्ष्विड्—क्ष्विण्ण; 'perspired, sounded inarticulately,' &c.

§ 687. (*a*) अञ्च् in the sense of 'to worship' takes इ; अञ्चित 'worshipped;' but अक्तः 'gone'; with सम्-समक्त (समक्तौ शकुने पादौ)

(*b*) धृष् and शस् reject इ when they express the idea of 'immodesty or rudeness;' धृष्ट 'rude,' विशस्तः 'ill-mannered;' but धर्षित overpowered, trifled with,' &c., विशसित 'tormented or ill-treated'

§ 688. न* is substituted for त when it immediately follows a final द् or र्; this final द् is also changed to न्: भिद्-भिन्न, शॄ-शीर्ण; तुर्व्-तूर्ण (See § 698).

Exceptions :—

(*a*) भिद् has भित्त when it means 'a part, a portion;' भिन्न in other senses.

(*b*) विद् 6 P. A. takes त in the sense of 'fit for enjoyment or famous;' वित्तं 'wealth, property,' वित्तः 'famous'; विन्न in other cases.

(*c*) मद्, पुर् and मूर्च्छ्; मत्त, पूर्त 'filled,' (also पूर्ण when it means the same as पॄ), मूर्त.

§ 689. Roots ending in आ* (ए, ऐ and ओ changeable to आ) and beginning with a conjunct consonant containing a semi-vowel also substitute न for त; द्रा 'to run, to sleep,' द्राण; ग्लै 'to fade,' ग्लान; स्त्यै-स्त्यान 'collected to a mass,' &c.

Exceptions :—ख्या 'to name,' &c. ध्यै 'to contemplate,' ध्ये and ह्वे; ख्यात, ध्यात, वीत and हूत.

§ 690. *The roots given at § 414 and ज्या substitute न for त.

---

* रदाभ्यां निष्ठातो नः पूर्वस्य च दः । संयोगादेरातो धातोर्यण्वतः । ल्वादिभ्यः । Pán VIII. 2. 42–44.

Roots.	P. P. Ptc.	Roots.	P. P. Ptc.
री to flow, to move	रीण	जॄ to grow old	जीर्ण
ली to melt, etc.	लीन	दॄ to tear	दीर्ण
व्ली to go, to hold	व्लीन	नॄ to load	नीर्ण
प्ली to go, to move	प्लीन	पॄ to fill, to gratify	पूर्ण
धू to shake	धून	भॄ to bear, to nourish	भूर्ण
पू to destroy	पून	मॄ to hurt, to kill	मूर्ण
लू to cut	लून	वॄ to choose	वूर्ण
ऋ to go	ईर्ण	शॄ to tear asunder	शीर्ण
कॄ to scatter	कीर्ण	स्तॄ to scatter	स्तीर्ण
गॄ to utter a sound, to praise, etc.	गीर्ण	ज्या to grow old	जीन

§ 691. दु and द्रु 'to sound indistinctly,' substitute न for त and lengthen their vowels; दून 'gone,' द्रून.

§ 692. The following roots substitute न for त:—

Roots.	P. P. Ptc.	Roots.	P. P. Ptc.
डी 4 A. to fly	डीन, उड्डीन	वै to dry, to be languid	वान
दू to torment	दून	व्री 4 A. to move, to cover	व्रीण
धी to hold, to accomplish	धीन	श्वि 1. P, to grow, to swell	शून
ली 4. A.	लीन	सू 4. A. to bring forth, to produce	सून
मी 4 A. to give pain	मीन	भञ्ज् to break	भग्न
		भुज् 6 P.	भुग्न
दी ,, to perish, to waste	दीन	मस्ज् 6. P.	मग्न
		रुज् ,, to break	रुग्ण
री ,, hurt	रीण	लज् 6. A.	लग्न
हा to go	हान	लस्ज् to be ashamed	,,
हा to abandon	हीन	स्कन्द्—with वि	विस्कन्न
विज्—	विग्न, उद्विग्न	with परि	परिस्कन्न-स्कण्ण
व्रश्च्—	वृक्ण	विद् 4. A.	विन्न
स्फुर्ज् 1. P.	स्फूर्ण		

§ 693. (*a*) ऋ* when it means 'to incur debt' substitutes न; ऋण 'debt; but ऋत, 'gone.'

(*b*) क्षि, when the P. P. Participle has an active sense, substitutes न and lengthens its इ; क्षीण, reduced, emaciated; but when a curse is implied, or pity expressed, the change is optional; क्षीणायुः or क्षितायुः भव *i. e.* 'die;' क्षीणः or क्षितः अयं तपस्वी 'oh, the poor ascetic has grown thin' but क्षितः कामो मया.

(*c*) † दिव् takes न when it does not mean 'to gamble;' द्यून 'a sport in which nothing is staked.' but द्यूतं 'gambling.'

(*d*) † वा with निर् takes न except when it has वात for its subject; निर्वाणोऽग्निः 'the fire is extinguished;' निर्वाणो मुनिः the sage is absolved; but निर्वातः वातः

(*e*) श्यै takes न when the notion of touch is not present; संश्यानो वृश्चिकः 'a scorpion contracted through cold;' when it means 'to be coagulated or cold' its य् takes संप्रसारण (ई); शीनं घृतं, but शीतं उदकं and not शीनं as the idea of touch is present here; also when preceded by प्रति; प्रतिशीनं घृतं, &c.; with अभि and अव the change is optional; अभिश्यानं or अभिशीनं घृतं, अवश्यानो or अवशीनो वृश्चिकः; but समवश्यातः

§ 694. The roots नुद्, विद्, 6. A., उन्द्, त्रै, घ्रा and ह्री take न or त; नुन्न or नुत्त, विन्न or वित्त, त्राण or त्रात, घ्राण or घ्रात and ह्रीण or ह्रीत.

§ 695. प्याय् has पीन when it is used with 'one's own limbs.' पीनं मुखं, and प्यान or पीन in other cases, as प्यानः or पीनः स्वेदः; when it is preceded by a preposition, ई is not substituted for its vowel; प्रप्यानः; but when it is used with अन्धु or ऊधस् with the preposition आ, ई is necessarily substituted; आपीनः अन्धुः, आपीनं ऊधः.

---

* ऋणमाधमर्ण्ये । Pân. VIII. 2. 60. † दिवोऽविजिगीषायाम् । निर्वाणोऽवाते । Pân. VIII. 2. 49–50

§ 696. (*a*) Roots ending in a nasal lengthen their penultimate vowel before a weak termination beginning with any consonant except a nasal or a semivowel, or before the affix क्विप्. शम्—शान्त्, क्रम्—क्रान्त, &c.

(*b*) Anit roots ending in a nasal, the root वन् 1. P. and the eight roots of the 8th class-तन् and others (see p. 355) drop their nasal before a weak termination beginning with any consonant except a nasal or a semivowel:—

Roots.	P. P. Ptc.	Roots	P. P. Ptc.
मन् 'to think', &c.	मत	नम् 'to bow'	नत
हन् ' to strike,'	हत	यम् 'to restrain '	यत
रम् 'to sport'	रत	वन् 1. P. 'to sound,	
गम् 'to go'	गत	to serve,' &c.	वत
तन्	तत	घृण् 'to shine'	घृत
क्षण्	क्षत	तृण् 'to graze'	तृत
ऋण्	ऋत	वन् 'to beg '	वत

§ 697. The roots खन्, जन् and सन्, drop their nasal and at the same time lengthen their vowel; खात, जात, सात.

§ 698. A radical व् preceding or following a vowel is sometimes changed to ऊ before त or न; when it is preceded by र it is dropped; वर्—ऊर्ण, त्वर्—तूर्ण, तुर्व्—तूर्ण, सिव्—स्यूत, श्रिव्—श्रूत or श्रून (See § 693, *c*.).

§ 699. The following roots (some forming their P. P. P. irregularly) reject इ in the limited sense attached to each:—

क्षुभ—क्षुब्ध 'a churning handle.'
स्वन्—स्वान्त 'the mind.'
ध्वन्—ध्वान्त 'darkness.'
लग्—लग्न 'attached.'
म्लेच्छ्—म्लिष्ट 'indistinct.'
विरेभ्—विरिब्ध 'a note.'
फण्—फाण्ट; 'a decoction easily prepared.' (अनायाससाध्यः कषायविशेषः Sid. Kau.)
बाह्—बाढ ' much.'

In their usual senses they have क्षुभित, ध्वनित, लगित, म्लेच्छित, विरेभित, फणित and वाहित.

§ 700. दा 'to give,' and दे, form their P. P. Ptc. as दत्त; the द of दत्त is dropped after a preposition ending in a vowel; प्रत्त-अवत्त &c.; in this latter case the preceding इ or उ is lengthened; नीत्त, सूत्त, &c.; द may optionally be retained also; प्रदत्त, अवदत्त, सुदत्त,* &c.

§ 701. The following roots form their P. P. Participles irregularly:—

Roots.	P. P. Ptc.	Roots.	P. P. Ptc.
अद् to eat.	जग्ध, अन्न	ज्यो to instruct.	जीत
अर्द् with सम्,	समर्ण, न्यर्ण्ण,	दो to cut.	दित
नि or वि	व्यर्ण्ण	दृंह् to be bulky or strong.	दृढ
with अभि in the sense		दृह् otherwise	दृंहित
of 'being near.'	अभ्यर्ण	धा to put.	हित
in other cases	अर्दित	धाव् to cleanse.	धौत or धावित
ऊय् 1. A. to weave.	ऊत	धे to suck	धीत
कष् to be difficult or painful.	कष्ट, as कष्टं व्याकरणम्. The study of grammar is very difficult; कष्टं वनं &c.; but कषितं सुवर्णम् 'gold rubbed on the touchstone.'	पच् to cook.	पक्व
		पा to drink.	पीत
		पूय् to stink, to putrify.	पूत
		फल् to expand.	फुल्ल
		मव् to bind.	मूत
		मा to measure.	मित
		मे to barter.	"
		मूर्च्छ् to faint.	मूर्त or मूर्च्छित
कृश् to be lean.	कृश	लाघ् with उत्	उल्लाघ 'convalescent.'
क्षीब् to be intoxicated.	क्षीब		
क्नूय् to stink.	क्नूत		
क्ष्माय् to shake	क्ष्मात	वृ (वृ) ह् or वृं (वृं) ह् with परि	परिवृढ a master, [परिवृ (वृ) हित or परिवृं(वृं)हित &c. 'grown, increased'].
क्षै to be thin	क्षाम		
गै to sing	गीत		
छा to split	छात or छित	शो 'to sharpen,'	शात or शित

* अवदत्तं विदत्तश्च प्रदत्तश्चादिकर्माणि । सुदत्तमनुदत्तश्च निदत्तमिति चष्यते ॥

Roots.	P. P. Ptc.	Roots.	P. P. Ptc.
स्रिव् 'to go, to become dry.'	स्रुत	स्त्यै with प्र	प्रस्तीत or प्रस्तीम 'sounded.
ह्लाद् 'to delight'	ह्लन्न		
श्रा to cook (also श्रप् cau. of श्रा)	शृत 'boiled' (when it qualifies क्षीर or हविः) else श्राण, श्रपित.	स्ना with नि with नदी	निष्णात 'clever.' नदीष्ण, 'skilful, experienced, clever.' (lit. one who knows the dangerous spots in a river); but निस्नात, नदीस्नात in other cases.
स्तंभ् with प्रति and नि	प्रतिस्तब्ध, निस्तब्ध (here the स् is not changed to ष्).		
स्फाय् 'to grow.'	स्फीत		

§ 702. (*a*) The roots सु and यज् take the affix वत् like त in an active sense; सुत्वन् 'one who extracted Soma juice,' यज्वन् 'one who has offered a sacrifice;' अत् is added to जृ optionally in the same sense; जीर्ण or जरत् ' one who has become old' (also जीर्णवत्).

§ 703. The participles in त or न follow the Declension of nouns in अ.

§ The P. P. participles have not always a passive force:—

§ 704.* The affix त added to roots having the sense of 'sitting or going, or eating' shows the place where the action takes place; इदं मुकुन्दस्य आसितं 'this is the place where Mukunda to sit, ' इदं यातं रमापतेः ' this is the path by which the husband of Ramâ used to pass, ' भुक्तं एतत् अनंतस्य ' this is the place where Ananta took his food, ' &c.

§ 705. The P. P. Participles of roots implying motion, of intransitive roots, and of the roots श्रिष्, शी, स्था, आस्, वस् 'to dwell,' जन्, रुह्, and जॄ 4. cl. have an active sense; गतोऽहं मद्रपुरम् 'I went to Madras;' म्लानो बालः 'the boy has become languid;' लक्ष्मीमाश्लिष्टो हरिः 'Hari embraced Lakshmî:' शेषमधिशयितः ' slept on Sesha; ' वैकुंठ-

* अधिकरणे च ध्रौव्यैगतिप्रत्यवसानार्थेभ्यः । Pân. III. 4, 48.

मधिष्ठित: 'dwelt in Vaikuntha;' शिवमुपासित: 'served Shiva,' हरिदिनमुपोषित: 'observed a fast on the day sacred to Hari,' राममनुजात: 'was born after Ráma;' गरुडमारूढ: sat on Garuda; विश्वमनुजीर्ण: 'grew old after the world.'

§ 706 P. P. Participles have sometimes the sense of neuter abstract nouns; as जल्पितं 'speech', शयितं 'sleep', हसितं 'laughing,' similarly स्थितं, गतं, etc.; See Bhaṭṭ. VII. 125.

§ 707. The P. P. Participles of roots meaning 'to think or to wish,' 'to know,' 'to adore,' and of the roots इन्ध्, भी etc. have the sense of the present Tense; राज्ञः मत; 'he is honoured by the king,' सतां पूजित: इद्ध: अग्नि: 'the fire is kindled,' so भीत: etc.

(*d*) Past Active Participles.

§ 708 Past Active participles are derived from the P. Passive Participles in त or न by adding to them the affix वत; *e.g.*

Roots.		P. P. Ptc.	P. Ac. Ptc.		
भू	to be	भूत	भूतवत्	one or that	has been
कृ	to do	कृत	कृतवत् ,,	,,	done
कॄ	to scatter	कीर्ण	कीर्णवत् ,,	,,	scattered
छिद्	to cut	छिन्न	छिन्नवत् ,,	,,	cut
etc.		etc.	etc.		etc.

(*e*) Participle of the Future Tense.

§ 709. The Participle of the Simple Future, Active as well as Passive, is formed from the third person singular form of the Second Future of a root. The Pararsm. Ptc. is formed simply by dropping the final इ, and the Atm. and the Passive one by substituting मान for the final ते; *e. g.*

Participles.

Roots.	Par.	Atm.	Passive.
दा—	दास्यत्	दास्यमान	दास्यमान or दायिष्यमाण
भू—	भविष्यत्	भविष्यमाण	भविष्यमाण or भाविष्यमाण

Roots.	Par.	Atm.	Passive.
चुर्	—चोरयिष्यत्	चोरयिष्यमाण	चोरयिष्यमाण or चोरिष्यमाण
गम्	—गमिष्यत्	संगमिष्यमाण	गमिष्यमाण
जि	—जेष्यत्	विजेष्यमाण	जेष्यमाण, जायिष्यमाण
कृ	—करिष्यत्	करिष्यमाण	करिष्यमाण, कारिष्यमाण
श्रु	—श्रोष्यत्	संश्रोष्यमाण	श्रोष्यमाण, श्राविष्यमाण
एध्	—A.	एधिष्यमाण	एधिष्यमाण
तुद्	—तोत्स्यत्	तोत्स्यमान	तोत्स्यमान

Similarly पिपठिष् Desi. Base of पठ्—पिपठिष्यत्, पिपठिष्यमाण &c.: बोभू Fre. B. of भू—बोभविष्यत्, बोभविष्यमाण, &c.

§ 710. These Participles are declined like words ending in त् and अ.

(*f*) Potential Participles (and Verbal Adjectives).

§ 711. The Potential Participle is formed by means of the affixes *तव्य, अनीय, त and rarely एलिम, added to a root or derivative verb. This is Passive when the verb is transitive and impersonal when the verb is intransitive. It is also used like an adjective when denoting fitness, &c.

(1) Participles in तव्य and अनीय.

§ 712. The affixes तव्य or अनीय are added to roots or derivative bases in the sense of 'must be fit to be,' &c. Before these the ending vowel and the penultimate short of a root take their Guṇa substitute. Before तव्य Set roots take इ, Anit roots do not, and Wet roots take it optionally. Before अनीय penultimate ऋ is always changed to अर् and not to र (as it sometimes does); *e. g.*

---

*तव्यत्तव्यानीयरः । Pán. III. 1. 96. केलिमर उपसंख्यानम् । Vártika.

Roots.	Pot. Ptc.			
दा—दातव्य, दानीय what must or ought to be given.				
चि—चेतव्य, चयनीय what must or ought to be searched into, &c.				
नी—नेतव्य, नयनीय	,,	,,	carried.
श्रु—श्रोतव्य, श्रवणीय	,,	,,	heard.
भू—भवितव्य, भवनीय	,,	,,	been.
कृ—कर्तव्य, करणीय	,,	,,	done.
बुध—बोधितव्य, बोधनीय, बोद्धव्य	,,	,,	known.
मुच्—मोक्तव्य, मोचनीय	,,	,,	released.
मृज्—*मार्ष्टव्य, मार्जनीय	,,	,,	wiped.
सृज्—स्रष्टव्य, सर्जनीय	,,	,,	created.
भ्रस्ज्—भर्ष्टव्य, भर्जनीय, भ्रष्टव्य, भ्रज्जनीय	,,	,,	fried.
भिद्—भेत्तव्य, भेदनीय	,,	,,	split.
निन्द्—निन्दितव्य, निन्दनीय	,,	,,	censured.
गुह्—गोढव्य, गूहनीय, गूहितव्य †	,,	,,	concealed.

§ 713. The final अय of roots of the tenth class and of causals, the final अ of Atm. Freq. Bases, when the य is preceded by a vowel and the whole य when it is preceded by a consonant, are dropped before अनीय. To Desiderative bases it is added without any change *e. g.*

कथ्—	कथनीय what must, or ought to be told.			
चुर्—	चोरणीय	,,	,,	stolen.
बोधय cau. of बुध्—	बोधनीय	,,	,,	made to know.
बोबुध्य Atm. Freq. Base of ,,	बोबुधनीय	,,	,,	known frequently

* The ऋ of मृज् is changed to आर् against § 712.

† The उ of गुह् is lengthened instead of being Guṇated before a strong termination beginning with a vowel.

बोभूय—Atm. freq.

Base of भू—बोभूयनीय what must or ought to be frequently.
बुबोधिष् Desi. Base
of बुध् बुबोधिषणीय „ „ desired to know.

(2) Participles in य (यत्, क्यप् and ण्यत्).

By means of यत् (य).

§ 714. The affix य (यत्)* is added on to roots ending in a vowel in the sense of 'fit for, or fit to be, or ought to be.' Before this य the radical vowel undergoes Guṇa substitute and final आ (ए, ऐ and ओ changeable to आ) is changed to ए.

दा—देय what is fit or ought to be given.			
धे—धेय	„	„	sucked.
गै—गेय	„	„	sung.
छो—छेय	„	„	cut.
चि—चेय	„	„	collected.
नी—नेय	„	„	led or carried.

§ 715. Roots having अ for their penultimate and ending in a consonant of the labial class take the affix य; शप्—शप्य; लभ्—लभ्य; रम्—रम्य, &c.

(*a*) When लभ् is preceded by आ, न् (changed to म्) is inserted between ल and भ्; आलभ्—आलंभ्य 'what ought or is fit to be killed;' न् is also inserted when लभ् is preceded by उप if the meaning be 'to prise;' उपलंभ्यः साधुः 'a Sâdhu ought to be praised;' but उपलभ्यं धनं 'wealth ought to be acquired.'

§ 716. The roots तक् 'to laugh at,' शस् 'to kill,' चत् to 'look for, to ask,' यत् 'to strive,' जन्, शक् and सह् take the affix य; तक्यं 'what is fit to be laughed at,' शस्यं 'what ought to be killed;' &c.

§ 717. The roots गद्, मद्, चर् and यम्, take the affix य when not preceded by a preposition; गद्—गद्य 'what ought to be spoken

* अचो यत् । Pân. III. 1. 97.

or told;' मद्य, चर्य, यम्य. चर् with आ may take this affix, if it does not mean 'a preceptor;' in which case it takes the affix ण्यत् (य) आचर्यो देशः 'a country fit to be gone to, but आचार्यः 'a preceptor.'

§ 718. The roots वद् implying reproach, पण् meaning 'to transact business,' and वृ 9. Atm. not denoting limit or restraint, take the suffix य; as अवद्यं पापं 'sin is reprehensible or merits condemnation;' but अनुद्यं (अन्+वद्+क्यप् *i. e.* य) गुरुनाम 'the name of a preceptor ought not to be uttered (out of respect);' पण्या गौः 'a cow is saleable;' but पाण्यः (पण्+ण्यत् *i. e.* य) ब्राह्मणः 'a Brâhmaṇa deserving praise;' वर्या 'that can be chosen or sought after;' as शतेन वर्या कन्या 'hundred men (*i. e.* any one) can seek the hand of a girl;' but वृत्या (वृ+क्यप् *i. e.* य) कन्या 'to be married by a particular man.

§ 719. The root वह् not denoting an instrument for carrying, and ऋ in the sense of 'a master or a Vaishya' take य; वह्यं 'a carriage or a vehicle;' but वाह्य (वह्+ण्यत्) 'what can be borne;' अर्यः 'a master or a Vaishya;' but आर्य (ऋ+ण्यत्) 'fit to be approached or adored.'

§ 720. सृ with उप in the sense of 'being conceived' takes the affix य; as उपसर्या गौः गर्भाधानार्थं वृषभेण उपगन्तुं योग्येत्यर्थः (Sid. Kau.) but उपसार्या (उपसृ+ण्यत्) काशी प्राप्तव्या इत्यर्थः (Sid. Kau.).

§ 721 जॄ takes this affix with the negative particle prefixed to it and forms अजर्य 'what cannot grow old' but this must qualify संगतं 'friendship;' *cf.* तेन संगतमार्येण रामाजर्यं कुरु द्रुतम् । Bhaṭṭi. VI. 53. In मृगैरजर्यं जरसोपदिष्टमदेहबन्धाय पुनर्बबन्ध । Rag. XVIII. 7, the word संगत must be considered as understood. If it does not qualify संगत, it will take the affix तृ; as अजरिता कम्बलः.

§ 722. हन् takes the affix यत् optionally, before which वध् is substituted for it; हन्+य=वध्य='what ought to be killed;' it optionally takes ण्यत्, in which case घात् is substituted for it: घात्यः.

By means of the affix क्यप् (य)

§ 723. The roots इ 1. 2. P. 'to go,' स्तु, शास्, वृ 5. P. A. दृ, जुष्, and roots having ऋ short for their penultimate, except क्लृप् and चृत्, take the affix क्यप् (य) in the same sense as यत्. When a root ends in a short vowel, त् is inserted between the final vowel and the affix य; *e. g.* इ–इत्य 'worthy of being approached;' स्तुत्य 'deserving praise;' शास–शिष्य 'fit to be instructed;' वृत–वृत्य; दृ–आदृत्य; जुष–जुष्य 'worthy of being served;' वृत्–वृत्य; वृध्–वृध्य 'fit to be increased as wealth, &c.' but कल्प्य (क्लृप+यत्) 'able;' चृत–चर्त्य (चृत्+ण्यत्) 'that ought to be teased or hurt.'

§ 724. According to Vâmana, the roots शंस्, दुह and गुह take the affix optionally; शंस्–शस्य 'praiseworthy;' दुह–दुह्य, गुह–गुह्य; optionally they take the affix ण्यत् (to be given hereafter); शंस्य, दोह्य, गोह्य.

§ 725. मृज् also takes this affix optionally; मृज्य 'what is fit or ought to be cleansed;' optionally it takes ण्यत् before which the final ज् is changed to ग्; मार्ग्य.

§ 726. (*a*) भू when it has a Subanta prefixed to it and is without a preposition takes the affix क्यप् impersonally; ब्रह्मणो भावः ब्रह्मभूयं 'identity with Brahman.' When no Subanta is used prepositionally with it, it takes the affix यत्; भव्य or प्रभव्य.

(*a*) वद् under similar circumstances takes either क्यप् or ण्यत् in a passive sense or impersonally; ब्रह्मोद्य or ब्रह्मवद्यं 'expounding the Veda' (ब्रह्म वेदः तस्य वदनं Sid. Kau.).

727. खन् takes this affix, but drops its न् and adds ई to its penultimate vowel खन्+य=ख+य=ख+ई+य=खेय 'what is fit or ought to be dug or excavated.'

728. भृ 1 cl. takes this affix when the participle so derived does not form a name, भृत्याः 'those who ought to be nourished or maintained, hence servants,' &c.; but भार्याः (भृ+ण्यत्) a class of Kshatriyas'; when सम् precedes भृ, क्यप् and ण्यत् are added optionally संभृत्याः or संभार्याः.

N. B. The word भार्या meaning 'a wife' ought to be derived from भृ of the 3rd class and affix ण्यत्.

§ 729. *The following seven words are irregularly formed with the affix क्यप् in the sense given in each case:—राजसूयः (राजन्+सू×क्यप्) राजा सोतव्यः अभिषवद्वारा निष्पादयितव्यः। यद्वा लतात्मकः सोमः राजा स सूयते कण्ड्यते अत्र इत्यादिकरणे क्यप्। निपातनाद्दीर्घः; also राजसूयम्; सूर्यः (सृ+क्यप्, or सू 6. P. 'to incite,' 'to impel'+क्यप्) सरति आकाशे। कर्तरि क्यप्, निपातनादुत्वं। यद्वा षू प्रेरणे तुदादिः; सुवति कर्माणि लोकं प्रेरयति† क्यपो रुट्। मृषोद्य 'falsehood' (from मृषा+वद्+क्यप्); रोचते इति रुच्यः; कुप्यं (any base metal) fr. गुप+क्यप्। गुपेरादेः कुत्वं च संज्ञायाम्। सुवर्णरजतभिन्नं धनं कुप्यम्। *Cf.* Kir. I. 35. Manu. VII. 96. गुप् in other cases takes the affix ण्यत्; गोप्यं 'what ought to be concealed' कृष्टे स्वयमेव पच्यन्ते कृष्टपच्याः कर्मकर्तरि। शुद्धे तु कर्मणि कृष्णपाक्याः। 'growing in cultivated ground;' न व्यथते अव्यथ्यः 'not feeling pain.'

§ 730. (*a*) The following two words which are the names of two rivers are derived by means of this affix; भिनत्ति कूलं भिद्यः from भिद्+क्यप्; उज्झत्युदकं उज्झ्यः, उज्झ्+क्यप्; see Rag XI. 8. In other cases these roots take the affix तृ; भेत्ता, उज्झिता.

(*b*) Similarly the words पुष्यः and सिध्यः; both the names of the constellation Pushya, are derived from पुष् and सिध् respectively with the affix क्यप्; पुष्यन्त्यस्मिन्नर्थाः पुष्यः, सिध्यन्त्यस्मिन् सिध्यः.

§ 731. The roots पू, नी and जि, preceded by वि, take this affix, when they are connected with the words मुंज, कल्क and हल respectively; विपूयो मुञ्जः 'The Munja grass to be prepared for weaving into a rope' (मुञ्जादिकरणाय शोधयितव्य इत्यर्थः Sid. Kau.); विनीयः कल्कः 'sin which ought to be destroyed;' विजित्यो

*राजसूयसूर्यमृषोद्यरुच्यकुप्यकृष्टपच्याव्यथ्याः। Pān. III. I. 114. Vide Sid. Kau. on the same.

† *Cf.* मित्रो जनान्यातयति ब्रुवाणो, &c. Rig. III. 59. 1.

हलिः 'The plough to be pulled with great force;' बलेन कृष्टव्यः, in other cases these take the affix यत्; विपत्य, विनेय, जेय.

§ 732. The following words are derived from the root ग्रह् with the affix क्यप्:—अवगृह्यं, प्रगृह्यं, पदं 'two technical terms in grammar;' गृह्यकाः 'birds restrained from free motion, such as parrots,, &c.; ' पञ्जरादिबन्धेन परतन्त्रीकृता इत्यर्थः । Sid Kau. ग्रामगृह्या सेना 'an army stationed outside a village'; आर्यैर्गृह्यते आर्यगृह्यः तत्पक्षाश्रित इत्यर्थः (Sid. Kau.) 'siding with the noble.' See Rag. II. 43.

§ 733. The roots कृ and वृ take both क्यप् and ण्यत्; कृत्य, कार्य; वृत्य, वर्य 'what ought to be chosen, best,' &c.

§ 734. युज् in the sense of 'to be harnessed' takes the affix क्यप् and changes its final to ग्; युग्यः गौः 'a bull to be harnessed to the yoke;' in other senses it takes the affix ण्यत्-योज्य.

By means of the affix ण्यत्.

§ 735. Roots ending in ऋ, and those ending in a consonant take the affix ण्यत् (य) in the same sense as यत्. Before this affix the ending च् and ज् of a root are changed to क् and ग् respectively and the final vowel and the penultimate अ take Vriddhi substitute;; any other penultimate vowel generally takes Guṇa.

कृ—कार्यं 'what ought to be done,' धृ—धार्यं 'what ought to be worn,' &c.; ग्रह्—ग्राह्यं, दम्भ्—दाम्भ्यं 'what ought to be impelled,' &c.; वच्-वाक्यं 'what is arranged, a sentence,' पच्—पाक्यं 'what is to be cooked,' मृज्—मार्ग्यं 'what is to be purified,' &c.

§ 736. The root वस् when preceded by अमा 'with' takes the affix ण्यत् before which the penultimate अ is optionlly changed to Vṛiddhi; अमा सह वसतोऽस्यां चन्द्रार्कौ अमावस्या or वास्या 'the day on which the sun and the moon are with each other *i. e.* are in conjunction.'

(*a*) मृज् when preceded by पाणि or the preposition समव takes the affix ण्यत्; as पाणिभ्यां मृज्यते पाणिमर्ग्या रज्जुः; similarly समवमर्ग्या-

§ 737. (*a*) The roots यज्, याच्, रुच्, प्रवच्, त्यज्, and पच् do not change their च् or ज् to क् or ग् before ण्यत्; याज्यम् याच्यम्; रोच्यम्, प्रवाच्यम् (ग्रन्थविशेषः), अर्च्य, त्याज्य, पाच्य.

(*b*) वच् does not change its च् to क् before ण्यत् when the meaning is 'what ought to be spoken out, speech,' वाच्यं; but वाक्यं: 'a sentence.'

(*c*) वञ्च् when it means 'to go' does not change च् its to क्; वञ्च्यम्; when it means 'to bend' the च् is changed to क्; वङ्क्यं काष्ठम्.

(*d*) युज् when it is preceded by प्र and नि, takes the affix ण्यत् in the sense of 'what is possible or capable of;' and does not change its ज् to ग्; प्रयोक्तुं शक्यः प्रयोज्यः, नियोक्तुं शक्यः नियोज्यः भृत्यः।

(*e*) भुज् has भोज्यं meaning 'food,' and भोग्यं 'what is fit to be enjoyed.'

§ 738. Roots ending in उ, short or long, take the affix ण्यत् in the sense of 'what ought or must necessarily be done;' लू—लाव्यं 'what must necessarily be cut off;' पाव्यं 'what must necessarily be purified; सू with आ—आसाव्यं, यु 'to mix,' याव्य, &c.

(*a*) The roots वप्, रप्, लप्, भप् and चप also do the same; वाप्यं 'what must necessarily be sown;' राप्यम्, 'what must be spoken of distinctly;' लाप्यम्, भाप्यम्, चाप्यम्.

§ 739. The following words are irregularly derived by means of the affix ण्यत्; आनाय्यः 'what ought to be brought from the Gârhapatya *i. e.* the Dakshinâgni;' (fr. नी with आ) दक्षिणाग्निविशेष एवेदम्। स हि गार्हपत्यादानीयतेऽनित्यश्च सततमज्वलनात्। (Sid. Kau.;) but आनेय in other cases; as 'a jar;' प्रणाय्यः (fr. नी with प्र) चोरः प्रीत्यनर्ह इत्यर्थः (Sid. Kau.); 'disgusted with worldly pleasures;' as प्रणाय्योन्तेवासी विरक्त इत्यर्थः। but प्रणेय in other cases.

740 मीयते अनेन इति माय्यं 'a measure' (fr. मा); सम्यङ् नीयते होमार्थमग्निं प्रति इति सान्नाय्यं (from. नी with सम्) हविर्विशेषः 'a kind of offering (See Śis XI. 41.)'; निचीयतेऽस्मिन्धान्यादिकं

निकाय्यः निवासः (fr. चि with नि); धीयते अनया समिदिति धाय्या (fr. धा) ऋक्; कुण्डेन पीयते (अस्मिन् सोमः) कुण्डपाय्यः क्रतुः; संचीयतेऽसौ संचाय्यः (a sacrifice); परिचाय्यः, उपचाय्यः, समूह्यः (particular places for depositing the sacrificial fire); परिचेयम्, उपचेयम्, संवाह्यम् in other cases; चीयते असौ चित्यः अग्निः; अग्नेः चयनं अग्निचित्या.

§ 741. The roots भू and गै take the affix यत्; वच् and स्था take अनीय; and जन्, प्लु and पत् take ण्यत्, in an active sense; भवतीति भव्यः (also भव्यमनेन); गायतीति गेयः 'one who sings' (also गेयं साम अनेन); प्रवचनीयः 'one who speaks' उपस्थानीयः 'one who stands by'. जन्यः, प्लाव्यः, पात्यः.

(3) By means of केलिमर् (एलिम).

§ 742. A few transitive roots take the affix एलिम having the same force as the affix य; पचेलिम fr. पच्, 'fit to ripen or to be cooked; as पचेलिमा माषाः; भिदेलिमाः (fr. भिद्) सरलाः 'the pine trees ought to be felled;' &c.

§ 743. The declension of these Participles follows that of nouns ending in अ.

II. INDECLINABLE PARTICIPLES.

(a) Indeclinable Past Participles.

§ 744. The Indeclinable Past Participles are of the nature of gerunds. They fall under two heads:—(1) Those derived by affixing त्वा to the simple root; and (2) Those derived by means of य affixed to the root compounded with prepositions or words used prepositionally; गम्—गत्वा 'having gone;' भू with अनु—अनुभूय 'having experienced;' &c.

I. Indeclinable Participles formed with त्वा.

§ 745. The indeclinable Past Participle or gerund in त्वा is formed of all roots or derivative verbal bases to which no preposition (nor a prepositional word) is prefixed. The affix त्वा is of the same nature as the त of the Past Passive Participle, so that all the changes that take place before त generally also take place before त्वा. In other words from the P. P. Ptc. of a root, separate the त or न from it, add त्वा instead, and this will be the form of the gerund in त्वा *e. g.*

Roots.	P. P. Ptc.	Ind. P. Ptc.
ज्ञा to know	ज्ञात	ज्ञात्वा
दा to give	दत्त	दत्त्वा
स्था to stand	स्थित	स्थित्वा
हा to go	हान	हात्वा
हा to abandon	हीन	हीत्वा
धा to place	हित	हित्वा
जि to conquer	जित	जित्वा
पू to purify	पवित or पूत	पवित्वा or पूत्वा
भू to be	भूत	भूत्वा
कृ to do	कृत	कृत्वा
तॄ to cross	तीर्ण	तीर्त्वा
पॄ to fill	पूर्ण	पूर्त्वा
त्रै to protect	त्रात	त्रात्वा
मुच् to release	मुक्त	मुक्त्वा
अद् to eat	जग्ध	जग्ध्वा
छो to cut	छात, छित	छात्वा, छित्वा
दृश् to see	दृष्ट	दृष्ट्वा
क्षुध्* to be hungry	क्षुधित	क्षुधित्वा, क्षोधित्वा
वस्* to dwell	उषित	उषित्वा
वच् to speak	उक्त	उक्त्वा
वह् to carry	ऊढ	ऊढ्वा
यज् to sacrifice	इष्ट	इष्ट्वा
वप् to sow	उप्त	उप्त्वा
बन्ध् to bind	बद्ध	बद्ध्वा
बुध् to know	बुद्ध	बुद्ध्वा
शास् to rule	शिष्ट	शिष्ट्वा

* See § 684 (*c*); § 750

§ 746. When the intermediate इ is inserted, the preceding vowel takes its Guṇa substitute; शि—शयित्वा, कु—कवित्वा, जागृ—जागरित्वा, &c.

(*a*) The roots तृष्, मृष्, कृष् and ऋत् take Guṇa optionally; तृषित्वा or तर्षित्वा, मृषित्वा or मर्षित्वा, कृषित्वा or कर्षित्वा, ऋत्—ऋतित्वा or अर्तित्वा.

(*b*) But the roots मृड्, मृद्, गुध्, कुष्, मुष्, and क्लिश्, the roots mentioned at § 463 and विज्, 7 cl. do not take Guṇa; मृड्-मृडित्वा 'having rejoiced;' मृद्—मृदित्वा, गुध्—गुधित्वा 'having covered;' कुषित्वा, मुषित्वा, क्लिश्—क्लिशित्वा or क्लिष्ट्वा; कुट्-कुटित्वा, विज्-विजित्वा, &c.

§ 747. Wet roots, except व्रश्च् which takes इ necessarily, and स्वृ, सू and धू which reject इ, the five roots given under § 472 and the roots marked with an indicatory उ* admit of इ optionally before त्वा *e. g.*

Roots.	Ind. P. Ptc. or Ger.
मृज् to cleanse	मार्जित्वा, मृष्ट्वा
गाह् to enter	गाहित्वा, गाढ्वा

---

* The following are the more important of the roots marked with उ; अच् 1. P. A. अञ्च् 1. 10. P. A. असु 4 P. ऋण्, कम् 5. P. 1. A. कुज्, क्रम् 1. P. क्लम् 4. P. क्षण् 8. P. A. क्षिण् 8. P. A. क्षिव् 1. 4. P. क्षीव् 1. P. क्षेद् 1. P. खन् 1. P. A. गृध् 4. P. ग्रस् 1. A. ग्रुच् 1. P. ग्लुच् 1. P. ग्लुञ्च् 1. P. घृण् 8. P. A. घृष् 1. P. चञ्च् 1. P. चम् 1. 5. P. छृद् 7. 5. A. जभ् 1. P. जस् 4. P. 10. P. A. तञ्च् 1. P. तन् 8. P. A. 1. P. A. 10. P. तृण् 8. P. A दम्भ् 5. P. दम् 4. P. दिव् 4. P. 10. A. धाव् 1. P. A. ध्वंस् 1. A. धृष् 1. P. भुष् 1. P. वस् 4. P. भृश् 4. P. भ्रम् 1. 4. P. भ्रंश् 1. A. 4. P. भ्रंस् 1. A. मन् 8. A. मृष् 1. P. मुच्, मुञ्च्, म्लुच्, म्लुञ्च्, 1. P. यस्, युप्, रुप्, लुप्, all of the 4th cl. P. वञ्च्, 1. P. A. वन् 8. P. वस्. 4. P. विष् 1. P. वृत् 1. 4. A. 10. P. A. वृध् 1. A. 10. P. A. वृष् 1. P. शम् 4. P. A. शस् 1. P. शंस् 1. P. शास् 1. P. 2. P. A. शृध् 1. P. A. श्रम्भ् 1. P. श्रम् 4. P. श्रिव् 1. 4. P. श्लिष् 1. P. सन् 1. P. 8. P. A. षिव् 1. 4. P. सिध् 1. 4. P. स्कम्भ्, स्तम्भ्, 4. 9. P. स्यम् 1. P. स्रंस् 1. A. स्रिव् 4. P. and हृष् 1. P.

Roots.	Ind. P. Ptc. or Ger.
गुह् to conceal	गुहित्वा, गूहित्वा, गूढ्वा
गुप् to protect	गोपायित्वा, गोपित्वा, गुपित्वा, गुप्त्वा
इष् to desire	एषित्वा or इष्ट्वा
सह् to endure	सहित्वा or सोढ्वा
लुभ् to covet	लोभित्वा or लुब्ध्वा
अञ्च् to go, to worship	अक्त्वा having gone, अञ्चित्वा having worshipped
क्षण् to kill	क्षत्वा, क्षणित्वा
खन् to dig	खनित्वा, खात्वा
तन् to stretch	तनित्वा, तत्वा
दम् to tame	दमित्वा, दान्त्वा
शम् to pacify	शमित्वा, शान्त्वा
क्रम् to go &c.	क्रमित्वा, क्रन्त्वा, क्रान्त्वा*
वस् 4 P. to be straight, &c.	वसित्वा, वस्त्वा
वृत् 1 A. to be	वर्तित्वा or वृत्त्वा &c. &c.

But व्रश्च्—व्रश्चित्वा, स्तृ–स्तृत्वा, सू–सूत्वा, धू–धूत्वा.

§ 748. The roots श्वि, डी, शी, पू and जॄ, Set roots ending in consonants, roots of the 10th class and all derivative verbs, admit इ before त्वा; roots of the 10th cl. preserve their अय् before त्वा; श्वि–श्वयित्वा, डी–डयित्वा, जॄ–जरीत्वा or जरित्वा, नृत्–नर्तित्वा, व्यच्–विचित्वा, लज्ज्—लजित्वा, जीव्—जीवित्वा, &c., चुर्—चोरयित्वा; कथ्–कथयित्वा, बुध्–cau. बोधयित्वा; desi. बुबोधिषित्वा; Atm. fre. बोबुधित्वा, &c.

§ 749. (*a*) The roots स्कन्द् and स्यन्द् do not drop their nasal; स्कन्द्–स्कन्त्वा; स्यन्द्–स्यन्त्वा, स्यन्दित्वा.

(*b*) The penultimate nasal of roots ending in थ् or फ् and that of वञ्च् 'to roam abroad,' 'to deceive' and लुञ्च् 'to tear out,' are optionally dropped; ग्रन्थ्–ग्रन्थित्वा, ग्रथित्वा; गुम्फ्–गुम्फित्वा, गुफित्वा; वञ्च्–वञ्चित्वा, वचित्वा, वक्त्वा; लुञ्च्–लुञ्चित्वा, लुचित्वा.

---

* The अ is lengthened optionally before त्वा.

(c) Roots ending in ञ् such as भञ्ज्, रञ्ज्, सञ्ज्, स्वञ्ज् &c. and the root तञ्च् optionally drop their nasal before त्वा; भञ्ज्—भंक्त्वा or भक्त्वा, रञ्ज्—रंक्त्वा or रक्त्वा; अञ्ज्—अञ्जित्वा, अङ्क्त्वा or अक्त्वा.

(b) मस्ज् and नश् insert a nasal optionally; मक्त्वा or मंक्त्वा; नशित्वा, नंष्ट्वा or नष्ट्वा.

§ 750. Guṇa is optionally substituted for the penultimate इ and उ, roots beginning with any consonant and ending in any except य् or व् when त्वा has इ prefixed to it; लिख्—लिखित्वा or लेखित्वा; क्लिद्-क्लिदित्वा or क्लेदित्वा (also क्लित्त्वा); लुभ्—6. P. लुभित्वा or लोभित्वा; द्युत्—द्युतित्वा, द्योतित्वा; रिष्-रिषित्वा, रेषित्वा and रिष्ट्वा; so रुष्, &c., but दिव्-देवित्वा, द्युत्वा.

2. Indeclinable Participles formed with य.

§ 751. When a root is compounded with one or more prepositions or words prefixed to verbs like prepositions, the indeclinable participle is formed by affixing य immediately to it; the य is changed to त्य after a short radical vowel (even when it combines with the final vowel of a preposition to a long vowel); e. g.

दा with आ—आदाय	इ with प्र—प्रेत्य
चि with निस्—निश्चित्य	कृ with सम्—संस्कृत्य
जि with परा—पराजित्य	कृ with द्विधा—द्विधाकृत्य
नी with वि—विनीय	भिद् with निस्—निर्भिद्य
भू with अनु—अनुभूय	प्लुत् with उत्—उत्प्लुत्य
इ with अधि—अधीत्य	&c. &c. &c.

§ 752. The rules given at §§ 394, 395, 459, 502 and 587 apply to the roots also in the gerund in य:—

दिव् with प्र—प्रदीव्य	वच् with प्र—प्रोच्य
कॄ with अव—अवकीर्य	वस् with प्र—प्रोष्य
पॄ with आ—आपूर्य	ग्रह् with वि—विगृह्य

बन्ध् with नि—निबध्य	ह्वे with आ–आहूय
मि, मी, मा and	दी with उप—उपदाय
मे* with अनु—अनुमाय	ली with वि–विलीय or विलाय
त्रै with परि—परित्राय	&c. &c. &c.
दे with आ—आदाय	

§ 753. Roots of the 8th class ending in a nasal, except सन् and the roots मन्, वन् and हन्, drop their nasal necessarily; गम्, नम्, यम and रम् do it optionally; तन् with वि-वितत्य; मन् with अव–अवमत्य; यम with नि—नियम्य or नियत्य; रम् with वि—विरम्य or विरत्य; नम् with प्र—प्रणम्य or प्रणत्य, &c.

§ 754. The roots खन्, जन् and सन् have respectively निखन्य-निखाय; प्रजन्य-प्रजाय; and प्रसन्य-प्रसाय.

§ 755. क्षि lengthens its इ before the affix य and जागृ changes its final vowel to Guṇa; प्रक्षीय; प्रजागर्य.

§ 756. वे, ज्या and व्ये do not take Samprasâraṇa; प्रवाय; प्रज्याय 'having become old;' उपव्याय 'having covered;' but व्ये with परि or सम्, takes Samprasâraṇa optionally; परिव्याय or परिवीय; संव्याय or संवीय.

§ 757. The roots mentioned under § 486 do not change their आ to ई; प्रयाय, प्रधाय, प्रमाय, &c.

§ 758. Roots of the Tenth class and Causals preserve their अय् before य, if it be preceded by a short penultimate vowel; if not, it is dropped; चोरय-प्रचोर्य; बोधय-प्रबोध्य; कृ—cau. विकार्य; नी cau. with आ—आनाय्य, &c ; but गण्-विगणय्य, प्रणमय्य, प्रकथय्य; प्रबेभिदय्य 'having again and again caused to be broken.'

§ 759. (*a*) आप् cau. may retain its अय् optionally-प्राप्य or प्रापय्य.

§ 760. Desiderative bases add य immediately and Freq. bases add it after dropping their य, when it is preceded by a consonant and dropping the final अ when it is preceded by a vowel; बुध-प्रबुबोधिष्य: Fre. प्रबोबुध्य; भू Fre. प्रबोभूय्य &c.

---

* मे changes its final to इ optionally; so अनुमित्य also.

(*b*) THE ADVERBIAL INDECLINABLE PARTICIPLE

OR

The Gerund in अम्.

§ 761. There is another Indeclinable Participle having the same sense as that in त्वा, formed with the affix अम्. Before this the root or the derivative verbal base generally undergoes the same changes as it does before the इ of the Pass. Aorist 3rd sing.; नी-नायम 'having carried or led'; दा-दायम् 'having given'; भू-भावम, भिद्-भेदम्, मह-माहम्, गम्-गमम्, &c.

§ 762. This Participle is generally used at the end of compounds; स लोष्टघातं हतः 'he was pelted to death;' बन्दिग्राहं गृहीता (Vik. I.) 'She was taken a captive;' स मूलघातं न्यवधीदरींश्च (Bhaṭṭi. I. 2.) 'He totally exterminated his enemies, &c.'

§ 763. The participles in त्वा and अम् * when repeated yield the sense of repetition of the action or condition expressed by the verb; स्मृत्वा स्मृत्वा or स्मारं स्मारम् 'having repeatedly remembered; पीत्वा पीत्वा or पायं पायम् 'having drunk again and again;' similarly भुज्—भुक्त्वा भुक्त्वा or भोजं भोजम्; श्रु-श्रुत्वा श्रुत्वा or श्रावं श्रावम्, गम्-गत्वा गत्वा or गामं गामम् or गमं गमम्, लभ्—लब्ध्वा लब्ध्वा or लम्भं लम्भम or लाभं लाभम्, प्रलम्भं प्रलम्भम्, जागृ-जागरं जागरम्, † &c.

---

* आभीक्ष्ण्ये णमुल् । Pân III. 4. 22.

† At the end of compounds this may not be repeated and yet have the sense of repetition; as in

'लतानुपातं कुसुमान्यगृह्णात्स नद्यवस्कन्दमुपास्पृशच्च ।
कुतूहलाच्चारुशिलोपवेशं काकुत्स्थ ईषत्स्मयमान आस्त ॥' Bhaṭṭi. II. 11

The descendant of Kakutstha, smiling gently, repeatedly bending down the creepers would pluck their flowers, wading through every stream (that he came across), would sip the waters, and seating himself on every charming slab would remain there (in admiration of the scenery).

§ 764 The Gerund अम् does not, in many instances, express the notion of repetition.

§ 765. This gerund or the one in त्वा is used with the words अग्रे, प्रथमं and पूर्वं, used as prepositions, although the notion of repetition is not present in these compounds; अग्रेभोजं-भुक्त्वा वा व्रजति 'having first eaten he goes out.' so प्रथमंभोजं or भुक्त्वा पूर्वं-भोजं or भुक्त्वा व्रजति.

§ 766. The gerund in अम् of the root कृ is used *

(*a*) with the noun governed by it, if it be compounded with it prepositionally when censure is implied; चौरकारं आक्रोशति (चौरशब्दं उच्चारयतीत्यर्थः) 'cries out (he is) a thief, a thief.' In this case म् is added to the noun governed.

(*b*) with the words स्वादु, लवण, and संपन्न, म् being added to these as before; अस्वादुं स्वादुं कृत्वा भुंक्ते स्वादुं-लवणं-सम्पन्नं—कारं भुंक्ते 'he eats having sweetened or seasoned his food.'

(*c*) with the words अन्यथा, एवं, इत्थं, and कथं, provided the root कृ loses its sense; अन्यथाकारं ब्रूते 'he speaks in a different manner;' एवंकारं भुंक्ते 'he eats thus:' similarly इत्थंकारं, कथंकारम्, but शिरोन्यथा कृत्वा भुंक्ते.

(*d*) with the particles यथा and तथा when an angry reply is given; यथाकारं भोक्ष्ये तथाकारं भोक्ष्ये किं तवानेन (Sid. Kau.); 'I will eat in this mnnner, I will eat in that manner, what have you do with that ?'

§ 767. The Gerund of the roots दृश् and विद् † is compounded with their objects and expresse totality; कन्यादर्शं वरयति 'chooses as many girls as he sees, *i. e.* all of them;' ब्राह्मणवेदं

---

* कर्मण्याक्रोशे कृञः खमुञ् । स्वादुमि णमुल् । अन्यथैवंकथमित्थंसुसिद्धाप्रयोगश्चेत् । यथातथयोरसूयाप्रतिवचने । Pân. III. 4. 25—28.

† कर्मणि दृशिविदोः साकल्ये । Pân. III. 6. 29.

भोजयति, यं यं ब्राह्मणं जानाति लभते विचारयति वा तं सर्वं भोजयतीत्यर्थः (Sid. Kau.) 'he feeds every Brâhmaṇa that he knows or comes across or remembers *i. e.* all of them.'

(*a*) *The gerunds of विद् 'to get' and जीव् 'to live' are joined with यावत् in the same sense; यावद्वेदं भुंक्ते 'eats what he gets.'

(*b*) † With the words चर्मन् and उदर the gerund of पूर् is used; चर्मपूरं स्तृणाति; उदरपूरं भुंक्ते 'eats so as to fill his belly'

§ 768. This gerund of पिष् is used with शुष्क, चूर्ण and रूक्ष; ‡ शुष्कपेषं पिनष्टि शुष्कं पिनष्टीत्यर्थः (Sid. Kau.); so चूर्णपेषं पिनष्टि 'he grinds to powder;' रूक्षपेषम्.

§ 769. ¶ With the words समूल, अकृत and जीव are used respectively the gerunds in अम् of the roots हन्, कृ and ग्रह् in a cognate sense; समूलघातं हन्ति 'kills destroying the roots *i. e* totally'; अकृतकारं करोति 'does what ought not to have been done;' जीवग्राहं गृह्णाति 'captures him so as to preserve him *i. e.* alive.'

(*a*) The gerund of हन् and पिष् is used with words signifying instruments (of action); पादघातं हन्ति=पादेन हन्ति 'strikes (kicking) with foot;' उदपेषं पिनष्टि=उदकेन पिनष्टि 'grinds with (using) the water.

(*b*) Similarly the gerund of वृत् and ग्रह् is used with हस्त and its synonyms, and that of पुष् with स्व; हस्तवर्तं वर्तयति; so करवर्तम्, हस्तेन गुलिकां करोतीत्यर्थः। Sid. Kau.; हस्तग्राहं गृह्णाति; similarly पाणिग्राहम्, करग्राहम्, &c.

---

* यावति विन्दजीवोः। Pân. III. 4. 30.

† चर्मोदरयोः पूरेः। Pân. III. 4. 31.

‡ शुष्कचूर्णरूक्षेषु पिषः। Pân. III. 4. 35.

¶ समूलाकृतजीवेषु हन्कृञ्ग्रहः। करणे हनः। स्नेहने पिषः। हस्ते वर्तिग्रहोः। स्वे पुषः। Pân III. 4. 36—40.

§ 770. * The gerund of बन्ध् is used with words denoting peculiar arrangements of stanzas, &c., चक्रबन्धं बध्नाति, क्रौञ्चबन्धं बद्धः, मुरजबन्धं बद्धः, मयूरिकाबन्धम्, अट्टालिकाबन्धम्, &c.

§ 771. † With the words जीव and पुरुष used subjectively the gerunds of नश् and वह् are used; जीवनाशं नश्यति जीवो नश्यतीत्यर्थः, पुरुषवाहं वहति पुरुषो वहतीत्यर्थः

(*a*) ‡ The gerunds of शुष् and पूर् are used with ऊर्ध्व similarly; ऊर्ध्वशोषं शुष्यति, वृक्षादिरूर्ध्व एव तिष्ठन् शुष्यतीत्यर्थः। ऊर्ध्वपूरं पूर्यते, ऊर्ध्वमुख एव घटादिर्वर्षोदकादिना पूर्णो भवतीत्यर्थः। Sid. Kau.

(*b*) †† Sometimes the Gerund in अम् is used with words denoting a standard of comparison; घृतनिधायं निहितं जलं 'the water was kept with as much care as ghee;' अजकनाशं नष्टः अजक इव नष्ट इत्यर्थः।

§ 772. § The gerund in अम् of roots having the sense of हिंस् 'to strike,' &c. are used with words denoting the instrument when the object of the gerund and of the principal verb is the same; दण्डोपघातं गाः कालयति *i. e.* दण्डेनोपघातं 'he collects together cows beating (them) with a stick;' दण्डताडम्; but दण्डेन चोरमाहत्य गाः कालयति.

(*a*) The gerunds of पीड्, रुध् and कर्ष्, with उप, are used with nouns having the sense of the Loc. or the Inst,; पार्श्वोपपीडं शेते *i. e.* पार्श्वाभ्यां उपपीडम्; व्रजोपरोधं गाः स्थापयति *i. e.* व्रजेन व्रजे उपरोधं वा; पाण्युपकर्षं धानाः संगृह्णाति *i. e.* पाणावुपकर्षं पाणिनोपकर्षं वा। Sid. Kau.

(*b*) Similarly केशग्राहं युध्यन्ते *i. e.* केशेषु गृहीत्वा; हस्तग्राहं *i. e.*

---

*अधिकरणे बन्धः। संज्ञायाम् Pân. III. 4. 41. 42.

† कर्त्रोर्जीवपुरुषयोर्नशिवहोः। Pân. III. 4. 43.

‡ ऊर्ध्वे शुषिपूरोः। Pân. III. 4. 44.

†† उपमाने कर्मणि च। Pân. III. 4. 45.

§ हिंसार्थानां च समानकर्मकाणाम्। सप्तम्यां चोपपीडरुधकर्षः। समासत्तौ। प्रमाणे च। अपादाने परीप्सायाम्। द्वितीयायां च। Pân. III. 4. 48–53.

हस्तेन गृहीत्वा; द्व्यङ्गुलोत्कर्षं खण्डिकां छिनत्ति i. e. द्व्यङ्गुलेन द्व्यङ्गुले वा उत्कर्षम् ।

(c) Nouns having the sense of the Ablative and the Accusative are used with this gerund of a root when haste or hurry is intended; शय्योत्थायं धावति 'runs having quickly got up from the bed;' यष्टिग्राहं युध्यन्ते; लोष्टग्राहम्, &c.

§ 773. *A root may be used in its gerundive form in अम् with its object prefixed to it if that object be a part of the body which can be severed without fatal effects; भ्रूविक्षेपं कथयति 'narrates contracting the eyebrows; but शिर उत्क्षिप्य (not शिरउत्क्षेपम्) as the severance of the head would cause death

(a) Similarly when a part of the body is completely hurt or pressed in the action, the gerund in अम् is used with that part; उरःप्रतिपेषं युध्यन्ते i. e. कृत्स्नमुरः पीडयन्तः 'afflicting the whole bosom;' उरोविदारं प्रतिचस्करे नखैः ।

§ 774. †The roots विश्, पत्, पद्, and स्कन्द् are used in their gerundive forms in अम् in the sense of 'complete occupation or pervasion or repetition' with nouns which if not compounded would have stood in the Acc.; गेहानुप्रवेशमास्ते गेहं गेहमनुप्रवेशम् । गेहमनुप्रवेशमनुप्रवेशम् । so गेहानुप्रपातम्, गेहानुप्रपादम्, गेहानुस्कन्दम्, &c.

§ 775. (a) ‡ The gerunds of अस् and तृष् are used with nouns denoting a period of time intervening between the repetition or performance of the action; द्व्यहात्यासं or द्व्यहमत्यासं गाः पाययति 'he makes the cows drink water allowing two days to intervene, i. e. every third day' अद्य पाययित्वा द्व्यहमतिक्रम्य पुनः पाययतीत्यर्थः । (Sid. Kau.); similarly द्व्यहतर्षम् or द्व्यहंतर्षम्.

---

* स्वाङ्गेऽध्रुवे । (येन विना न जीवनं तदध्रुवम् । Sid Kau.) परिक्लिश्यमाने च । Pân. III. 4. 54, 55.

† विशिपतिपदिस्कन्दां व्याप्यमानासेव्यमानयोः Pân. III. 4. 56. गेहादिद्रव्याणां विश्यादिक्रियाभिः साकल्येन संबन्धो व्याप्तिः । क्रियायाः पौनःपुन्यमासेवनम् । Sid. Kau.

‡ अस्यतितृषोः क्रियान्तरे कालेषु ।

(*b*)* Similarly the gerunds of दिश् with आ, and ग्रह् are used with नामन् and in the sense of the Acc.; नामदेशमाचष्टे; नामग्राहं मामाह्वयति, &c.

(*c*) The gerund of भू may optionally be used after तूष्णीं and अन्वच्; तूष्णींभूय-भूत्वा-भावं; अन्वग्भूय, अन्वग्भूत्वा, अन्वग्भावम्.

(*c*) The Infinitive.

§ 776. The Infinitive is formed by the affix तुम् with the same effect as the ता of the Future; *e. g.*

Roots.	Infinitive	Roots.	Infinitive.
इ to go	एतुम्	ग्रन्थ् to compose	ग्रन्थितुम्
एध् to grow	एधितुम्	पच् to cook	पक्तुम्
दा to give	दातुम्	व्रश्च् to cut	व्रश्चितुम् or व्रष्टुम्
नी to carry	नेतुम्	गुह् to cover	गूहितुम् or गोढुम्
कृ to do	कर्तुम्	सह् to bear	सहितुम् or सोढुम्
भू to be	भवितुम्	चुर् to steal	चोरयितुम्
धू to shake	धवितुम् or धोतुम्	बुध् Cau.	बोधयितुम्
वृ to choose	वरितुम् or वरीतुम्	Desi.	बुबोधिषितुम्
गै to sing	गातुम्	Atm. Freq.	बोबुधितुम्
गम् to go	गन्तुम्	&c. &c.	&c.

SECTION II.

VERBAL NOUNS FORMED BY MEANS of Various Kṛt Affixes.

§ 777. In the following list are alphabetically arranged almost all the common Kṛt affixes forming nouns (substantive and adjective) with various significations from roots or derivative bases. अ—(अच्, अण्, अप्, कञ्, खच्, खश्, खल्, घ, घञ्, ट, टक्, ड, ण, and श):—

*नाम्न्यादिशिग्रहोः । Pán III. 4. 57. 58.

अच्—denoting 'the agent' is added to—पच् and other roots; पचतीति पचः 'one who cooks;' चर्—चरः, चुर्—चोरः भू—भवः, नद्—नदः (नदी);—to भृ and पच्, when the words जार and श्वन् are prefixed to them respectively; जारभरा 'an adulteress;' श्वपचः 'a Chândâla'—to हृ when the noun governed by it is used prepositionally and when the idea of difficulty is not present or when the whole compound denotes 'age;' अंशं हरतीति अंशहरः 'one entitled to a share, a heir'; but भारहारः 'a load-bearer' (भार+हृ+अण्); कवलहरः 'a young child;' also when आ is prefixed to it in the sense of 'in the habit of.' पुष्पाणि हर्तुं शीलमस्य असौ पुष्पहरः;—to the root ग्रह् when the words शक्ति 'a missile,' लांगल 'a plough,' अंकुश 'an iron hook,' तोमर 'a javelin,' यष्टि 'a stick,' घट, घटी and धनुस् are prefixed to it; शक्तिं गृह्णातीति शक्तिग्रहः 'one armed with a spear,' &c; लांगलग्रहः &c.; also when सूत्र is prefixed to it and the root is used in the sense of 'wearing'; सूत्रग्रहः 'wearing a sacred thread;' but सूत्रग्राहः (सूत्र+ग्रह्+अण्) 'one who takes in his hand a sacred thread;'—to अर्ह् when a noun used objectively is prefixed to it; पूजामर्हतीति पूजार्हो ब्राह्मणः 'a Brâhmaṇa deserving worship;'—to रम् and जप् when the words स्तम्ब and कर्ण in the Loc. are prefixed to them respectively; स्तम्बेरमः 'an elephant,' कर्णेजपः 'one who whispers into the ear, a spy;'—to any root when the word शं is prefixed, शंकरः, शंभवः, शंवदः &c.,–to शी when a word showing the place of action precedes, खे शेते ख-(खे)शयः 'dwelling in the sky,' so हृच्छयः 'dwelling in the heart, i. e Madana'; also when words like पार्श्व उदर, पृष्ठ, &c. and उत्तान, &c. precede, पार्श्व—उदर—पृष्ठ—शयः 'sleeping on the sides,' &c., उत्तानशयः 'lying on the back with the face upwards.' so अवमूर्धशयः (अवनतो मूर्धा अस्य तथा शेते) i. e. 'with the face downwards.' When added to roots ending in इ and to some others it forms abstract nouns, चि—चयः 'a collection,' जि—जयः, भी—भयं, वृष—वर्षः 'a shower of rain.' &c.

अण्—is added to roots when the words forming their objects are prefixed to them, कुंभकारः 'a potter,' भारहारः—When a suhanta is prefixed to हन् with सम्, the न् of this root is changed to ट् optionally; वर्णसंघातः or-टः 'a collection of words.'

अप्—is added to roots ending in उ and ऋ short or long; it sometimes forms abstract nouns, sometimes shows the place or the instrument of action denoted by the root; स्तु—स्तवः praise, यु—यवः barley, पू—पवः, भू—भवः, कृ—करः the instrument of doing anything *i. e.* the hand, गृ—गरः poison, दृ—दरः fear, वृ—वरः a boon &c., स्तृ with वि—विष्टरः a tree or a seat, विस्तरः otherwise; हन् with सम् takes this affix; संघः a collection; गम् also takes it, गमः; अद् preceded by a preposition takes this affix and is changed to घस्; निघसः, प्रघसः, विघसः &c.; food or eating; (when no preposition precedes, it takes घञ्—घासः); the roots जप् and व्यध् not preceded by a preposition take अप्; जपः muttering prayers, व्यधः the act of piercing; (but when a preposition precedes, they take घञ्; as उपजापः secret whispering into the ear, separation, &c.); the roots स्वन् and हस् by themselves take अप् or घञ्; स्वन्-स्वनः or स्वानः sound; हस्-हसः or हासः; with a preposition they take the latter only; प्रस्वानः; प्रहासः &c.; यम् without any preposition or with the preposition उप, नि, वि and सम् takes either अप् or घञ्; यमः or यामः restraint, control, &c, उपयमः or यामः marriage; similarly नियमः or नियामः &c.; the roots गद्, नद्, पद् and स्वन्, with नि take अप् or घञ्; निगदः or निगादः speech, निनदः or निनादः sound, &c. क्वण् with or without नि takes अप् or घञ्; क्वणः or क्वाणः, निक्वणः or-क्वाणः the sound of a lute; the root मद् when a word other than a preposition is prefixed to it takes अप्; with a preposition it takes घञ्; धनमदः the pride of wealth, उन्मादः madness, insanity; but when preceded by प्र or सम् it takes अप् when the meaning is joy; प्रमदः or संमदः; in other cases it takes घञ्; प्रमादः, संमादः carelessness, oversight, a blunder. The affixes अप् and घञ् are added to several other roots too numerous to note here; the difference between these is that घञ् occasions Vriddhi of the preceding vowel, अप् does not.

क—is added to roots having इ, उ, ऋ, or लृ for their penultimate, and to the roots प्री and कॄ and denotes the agent; लिख्-लिख: one who writes, क्षिप्-क्षिप:; one who throws, बुध्-बुध: &c. प्री-प्रिय: one who pleases; कॄ—किर: one who scatters; it is also added to roots ending in आ with or without any preposition, the final आ being dropped; ज्ञा- ज्ञ: or प्रज्ञ: one who knows, wise; ह्वे—ह्व: or आह्व: one who calls; also when a subanta is used prepositionally with it; दा-गोद: one who gives cows or cuts the hair; पा-द्विप: (द्वाभ्यां पिबतीति) an elephant; when added to स्था it has various meanings; समस्थ: happy; विषमस्थ: placed in difficulties; प्रस्थ: a measure of corn, &c. This is also added to ग्रह्—गृहं a house, गृहा: a wife, a house.

कञ्—is added to दृश् not meaning 'to see' when a pronoun precedes it; तत्+दृश्=अ=तादृश: like that; also when the words समान and अन्य precede; सदृश: like to, अन्यादृश: like another स is added similarly; सदृक्ष:, तादृक्ष: &c.

खच् and खश्—Before these the अ of the noun forming the object of the root with which it is used prepositionally inserts the syllable म after it. खच् is added to the root वद् after प्रिय and वश; प्रियं वदतीति प्रियंवद: ' one who speaks sweetly; वशंवद: ' subject to the influence of, obedient to the will of;—कृ after the words क्षेम, प्रिय, मद्र, and भय; क्षेमं—प्रियं-मद्रं-कर: doing good, &c.; भयंकर: causing fear, dreadful, अभयंकर:;—to the root गम् after a subanta; विहङ्गम: passing through the sky, a bird; —to the roots भृ, तृ, वृ, जि, धृ, सह्, तप् and दम् when the whole is a name; विश्वंभर: God; रथंतरं a portion of the Sāma Veda; पतिंवरा a birde who chooses her husband; शत्रुंजय: an elephant, युगंधर: name of a mountain; परंतप: name of a king; अरिंदम: name of a king;—to यम् after वाच्, वाचंयम: one who restrains his speech for the observation of a vow; —to the roots सह् and दृ after the words सर्व and पुर respectively; सर्वंसहा the earth; पुरंदर: Indra;—to कष् after the words सर्व, कूल, अभ्र and करीष; सर्वंकष: all destroying, all powerful;

also a rogue; कूलंकषा (a river) sweeping away its banks; अभ्रंकष: dashing against, coming in collision with the clouds as the wind; करीषंकषा blowing away dry cowdung, as a strong wind or gale. खश् is added to एज् cau. as in जनमेजयः making the people tremble with fear; name of a king;—to अज्, धे, तुद् and हा 'to go' after the words वात, शुनी, तिला and शर्द्ध flatulence; वातमजः facing the wind, a kind of deer; शुनिंधयः a kitten; तिलंतुदः an oilman; and शर्द्धंजहाः causing flatulence (माषाः) a kind of bean;—to धे and ध्मा after the words स्तन and नाडी, respectively. स्तनंधयः a baby sucking breast; नाडिं-(डीं)धमः a goldsmith;—to तुद् after विधु and अरुष; विधुंतुदः the afflictor of the moon *i. e.* Ráhu; अरुंतुदः (अरूंषि मर्माणि तुदतीति) wounding the vital parts, painful;—to पच् after words showing measure as प्रस्थंपचा स्थाली, खारिंपचः कटाहः and after मित and नख-मितंपचः one who cooks measured corn, a miser; नखंपचा nail-scorching (as यवागूः);—to दृश् and तप् after the words असूर्य and ललाट; असूर्यंपश्याः those who do not see the sun *i. e.* the queens of a king who are shut up in the harem; ललाटंतपः scorching the forehead;—to दृश्, मद् and ध्मा afer उग्र, इरम् and पाणि respectively; उग्रंपश्य of a fierce aspect, इरंमदः lightning; पाणिंधमः a road (shrouded in such darkness that one has to clap one's hands for driving away serpents &c. that may be in the way); to मन् meaning 'to consider oneself' as, पण्डितंमन्य, a pedant, who considers himself a Pandita; गांमन्यः one who considers himself a cow i. e. who is very humble; &c.

खल—is added to any root with ईषत्, दुर् or सु prefixed to it when the idea of ease or difficulty is present, ईषत्करः done easily; दुष्कर done with difficulty; सुकर done easily; so दुःशासन, दुर्योधन, &c. &c.

घ—is added in the sense of the place or the instrument of the action or forms abstract nouns; कृ with आ-आकरः a mine; खन् with आ, आखनः a spade; पण with आ, आपणः a place of traffic; कष—निकषः a touch-stone; चर—गोचरः a pasture-ground; संचरः a path; वह—वहः a shoulder, निगमः that by which the people are guided, the Veda; अजः and व्यजः a fan. Before this छाद् not preceded by more than one preposition becomes छद्; दन्तच्छदः the lip, प्रच्छदः; but समुपच्छादः.

घञ्—added to roots ending in consonants has almost a universal application and a variety of senses; before this the final च् or ज् are changed to क् or ग्; पच्—पाकः food; कम्—कामः desire; श्रम—विश्रामः rest; सृ—सारः strength, substance, with अति-अति- or अतिसारः dysentery; हृ—हारः a necklace, पद्—पादः a foot; भू—भावः being, a thing &c.; विश्—वेशः a house; रुज्—रोगः a disease; स्पृश्—स्पर्शः touch; इन्ध्—एधः fuel; श्रन्थ्—प्रश्रन्थः laxity; चि—चायः (चीयतेऽस्मिन्नस्थ्यादिकं) the body, with नि—निकायः a house, &c.;—to रु when preceded by a preposition, विरावः the warbling of birds (otherwise रवः). The roots स्फुर् and स्फुल् change their vowel to आ before this; स्फारः or स्फालः the throbbing of the hand, &c. रु and प्लु preceded by आ take both घञ् and अप्; आरावः or—रवः a loud sound; आप्लावः—प्लवः a deluge. Sometimes the affixes घञ् and अप् are used in different senses; नी—नायः chief, प्रणयः friendship, kindness; परिणायः the act of moving a piece at chess, draughts, &c. परिणयः marriage: इ with नि—न्यायः justice, न्ययः ruin; ग्रह् with अव or नि—अवग्राहः or निग्राहः impediment, separation; अवग्रहः a grammatical mark; चोरस्य निग्रहः the confinement of a thief; but अवग्राहः—ग्रहः draught, want of rain; चि after पुष्प take the affix घञ् when the whole means 'gathering flowers with the hands' पुष्पचायः, but पुष्पचयः 'collecting flowers with a stick' &c.; it is also added to भुज् and उब्ज् with नि; भुजः the hand; न्युब्जः hump-backed, the Nyagrodha tree.

ट—is added—to the root कृ preceded by दिवा, भास्, यत्, तत्, किम्, a numeral, and nouns governed by it; दिवा करोतीति दिवाकरः, भास्करः the sun, यत्करः &c.:—to सृ preceded by पुरः, अग्रतः, अग्रे, and पूर्वः, पुरःसरः, अग्रतःसरः a leader, &c.; and to चर् preceded by भिक्षा, सेना, दाय and words showing the place of action; भिक्षाचरः a beggar, सेनाचरः a soldier, &c.

टक्—is affixed to हन् preceded by जाया or पति, हन् changing to घ्न the whole meaning 'bearing an inauspicious mark'; a husband causing the death of his wife-जायाघ्नः bearing a mark on his body indicative of the death of his wife; similarly पतिघ्नी;—this is also added to हन् when the agent of the action is not a man; पित्तघ्नं checking bile, such as ghee; पतिघ्नी (पाणिरेखा), &c.;—to हन् preceded by हस्तिन् and कपाट in the sense of 'having the power to do what is denoted by the root;' हस्तिघ्न 'one able to kill an elephant,' &c.;—and preceded by पाणि and ताड in the sense of 'one having the skill;' पाणिघः 'one who beats time with the hand, also a drummer (beating a drum with the hand);'—to पा 'to drink' and गै if not preceded by a preposition; सोमपः 'one who drinks the Soma juice'; साम गायतीति सामगः 'one who chants the Sâma Veda', but सामसंगायः (when a prep. precedes it); पा 'to protect' takes अ; क्षीरपा ब्राह्मणी, &c.

ड—is affixed to गम् preceded by अन्त, अत्यन्त, अध्वन्, दूर, पार, सर्व, अनंत, सर्वत्र, पन्न creeping on the ground,' उरस् and विहायस् and denotes the agent; to गम् preceded by दुर् and सु and shows the place of action; before this the final consonant with the preceding vowel or the final vowel of a root is dropped; अन्तं गच्छतीति अन्तगः 'one who goes to the end;' अध्वगः 'a traveller;' पन्नगः, उरोगः 'a serpent;' विहायस् is changed to विह—विहगः 'a bird,' दुर्गः 'a fortress,'&c.;—to हन् when a blessing is implied' तव पुत्रः शत्रुहः भवेत् 'may thy son be the destroyer of his enemies;' -also to हन् with अप after the words क्लेश and तमस्; क्लेशापहः 'removing pain, consoling, a son;' तमोपहः 'the dispeller of darkness, the sun;'-to जन् preceded by a word having the sense of the Loc. or of the Ab. and not denoting a class, or when it is preceded by a preposition and the whole is a name; मंदुरजः 'born in a stable;' सरसिजं 'a lotus;' संस्कारजः 'produced after some operation;' अदृष्टजः &c.; प्रजाः, अनुजः 'a younger brother;' the words द्विजः, अजः, ब्राह्मणजः &c. are also formed by means of this affix: this is also added to खन् with परि; परिखा 'a ditch'

ण—is added to roots ending in आ which insert य before it; दा-दाय: 'one who receives a share,' धा—धाय: 'one who holds,' &c—to श्ये when preceded by अव and प्रति, अवश्याय: 'mist, frost,' प्रतिश्याय: 'a catarrh or cold;—to इ, स्रु, सो and हृ preceded by a preposition; अत्याय: 'violation,' संस्राव: 'oozing, trickling;' अवसाय: 'end', अवहार: 'a thief, a seamonster';—to लिह्, श्लिष्, ग्रह्, व्यध्, श्वस् and भू; लेह: 'a lambative, an electuary;' श्लेष: 'an embrace,' ग्राह: 'an alligator,' व्याध: 'a hunter,' श्वास: 'respiration,' भाव: 'a thing;—to नी and ह्र not preceded by a preposition; नाय: 'a leader', दाव: 'a forest-fire;'—to ज्वल्, चल्, जल्, टल् 'to be confused', तल् 'to smell,' हल्, पल्, बल्, पुल्, कुल्, शल्, हुल्, पत्, कथ्, पथ्, मथ्, वम्, भ्रम्, क्षर्, सह्, शद्, क्रुश्, बुध्, and कस्, (these may also take अच्); ज्वाल: (or ज्वल:), flame or blaze,' &c:—to शील्, कम and भक्ष्, when their objects are prefixed to them; मांसशिल: 'one who keeps flesh;' मांसकम: 'one who wishes for flesh;' मांसभक्ष: 'one who eats flesh';—to ईक्ष्, क्षम and चर् with आ; सुखप्रतीक्ष: 'one desiring happiness,' बहुक्षम: 'forgiving much.' कल्याणाचार: 'good-conducted;'—to ह्वे, वे and मा after their objects; स्वर्गं ह्वयते स्वर्गह्वाय:, तंतुवाय: 'a weaver, धान्यमाय: 'measure of corn;'-to अद् with नि, न्याद: 'food.'

श—is added to पा, घ्रा, ध्मा, धे, and दृश्; पा-पिब: 'one who drinks;' घ्रा—जिघ्र: 'one who smells; दृश्—पश्य: 'one who sees;—to दा and धा 3 cl.; दा-दद: 'one who gives,' धा—दध: 'one who holds;—to लिंप् and विद्; लिंप: 'one who plasters;' विन्द:'one who knows;' also when the former is preceded by नि and the latter by गो and other words; निलिम्प: 'a god;' गोविन्द: 'name of Vishṇu;' अरविन्द: 'a lotus;'—to the Cau. of चित्, पॄ, एज् with उत्, and धृ; चेतय: 'one who thinks or knows;' पारय: 'one who fills'; उदेजय: 'one who makes another tremble,' *cf.* Bhatti. 1. 25. धारय: 'one who holds'; added to all roots it forms abstract *fem.* nouns; कृ-क्रिया 'an act;' इष्-इच्छा a 'wish;' परिचर्-परिचर्या 'service;' मृग-मृगया 'hunting;' अट अटाट्या rambling;' जागृ—जागर्या 'wakefulness, &c.'

अ-forms abstract nouns from derivative bases; कृ-चिकीर्षा a desire to do; पुत्रकाम्या a desire to have a son, &c. Also from roots ending in a consonant having a long vowel for their penultimate; ईह्-ईहा desire, ऊह्—ऊहा a guess; reasoning, &c.

अङ्—similarly forms abstract nouns; it is added to roots marked with an indicatory ष् and to भिद् and others; जॄ—जरा old age; त्रप्-त्रपा shame, &c.; भिद्-भिदा distinction; separation; चित्-चिन्ता contemplation, anxiety; मृज्-मृजा cleansing &c.—to कृप् which changes its ऋ to ऋ-कृपा mercy; to roots ending in आ if a preposition or the words श्रत् and अन्तर् precede, दा-प्रदा giving gift, भा-प्रभा lustre, &c. धा with श्रत्—श्रद्धा faith; with अन्तर्-अन्तर्धा disappearance.

वुक—(क्वुन्, ण्वुल्, वुञ्, वुन्, ष्वुन्)—

क्वुन्—is added to रञ्ज्; रजकः 'a washerman.'

ण्वुल्—is affixed to all roots and denotes the agent of the action; कृ—कारकः one who makes, acting, &c.; पच्—पाचकः one who cooks; हन्-घातकः दा—दायकः, धा—धायकः, &c; it is added to शम् and other roots of that group; but in this case the preceding vowel is not lengthened. शम्-शमकः, दम्-दमकः, वधकः a killer, जनकः a father, &c. Added to some roots it forms the name of diseases; छृद्-प्रच्छर्दिका vomiting; वह्-प्रवाहिका dysentery; diarrhœa; चर्च्-विचर्चिका itch, scab, &c; sometimes it is added to denote the meanings of roots आस्-आसिका sitting, शी-शायिका sleeping, &c.; sometimes it has the sense of futurity,. कृष्णं दर्शको याति he goes desirous of seeing Krishṇa; सतां पालकः &c.

वुञ्—is added to निन्द्, हिंस्, क्लिश्, खाद्; नश् with वि, क्षिप् with परि रट्, वद्, ध्ये, भाष् and सृ in the sense of the 'agent,' or 'in the habit of;' निन्द्—निन्दकः 'one who blames or is in the habit of blaming or censuring others,' हिंस्—हिंसकः, क्लिश्-क्लेशकः &c.; —to दिव् and क्रुश् preceded by आ; आदेवकः 'a gambler,' आक्रोशकः 'one who calls out or vociferates, reviler.'

वुन्—is added to प्रु, सृ and लु in the sense 'skilul in,' प्रु—प्रवकः सृ—सरकः, 'skilful in walking;' लवकः 'skilful in cutting:' this may by added to any root when the idea of a blessing is to be conveyed; जीवकस्त्वं भूयाः 'mayest thou live for many years,' नन्दकस्त्वं भूयाः 'mayest thou be the giver of delight.'

ष्वुन्—is added to नृत्, खन् and रञ् in the sense of 'one who knows the art of,' नर्तकः 'one who knows the art of dancing;' खनकः 'a digger,' 'a miner,' रजकः 'a dyer.'

अथु—(अथुच्)—वेप्-वेपथुः 'tremor;' श्वि—श्वयथुः 'swelling, a tumour,' 'दु—दवथुः 'pain, anxiety,' &c.

अन्—(ण्युट्, युच्, ल्यु, ल्युट्)—

ण्युट्—is affixed to गै and हा; गायनः 'a singer,' हायनः 'a year,' 'a kind of rice.'

युच्—is affixed to verbs meaning 'to go or to sound,' चल्—चलनः 'one who moves.' रु-रवणः 'one who makes a sound,' so शब्दनः &c. It is also affixed to verbs meaning 'to ornament, to deck, and to be angry,'—भूष्-भूषणः serving as an ornament: मण्ड्-मण्डनः, क्रुध्-क्रोधनः, रुष्-रोषणः angry, irascible.'--to जु, सृ, गृध्, ज्वल्, शुच्, लष्, पत्, पद्; जु-जवनः 'a swift walker:' सृ-सरणः 'one who goes' गृध—गर्धनः 'a glutton;' ज्वलनः 'that which blazes, fire;'—to some other roots ending in a consonaut, वृत्-वर्तनः, वृध्-वर्धनः &c.:-to the freq. of क्रम् and द्रम्, चंक्रमणः, दंद्रमणः 'one who goes again and again', it also forms *fem.* abstract nouns with the causals of roots and the verbs श्रन्थ्, घट्, वन्द् and इष् not meaning 'to wish,' कृ-कारणा 'doing action,' हृ-हारणा, आस्—आसना, श्रन्थ्—श्रन्थना, घट्-घटना, वन्द् वन्दना, विद्-वेदना. इष् with अनु-अन्वेषणा 'searching.'

ल्यु—is affixed to नन्द् and other roots; नंदनः 'one who delights, a son,' मद्—मदनः 'he who exhilarates, the god of love,', साध्-साधनः 'one who accomplishes,' सह्—सहनः 'one who bears,' सूद्—मधुसूदनः 'the killer of Madhu,' अर्द्—जनार्दनः 'the chastiser of the sinful,' भी—बिभीषणः 'terrifier, name of Rávana's brother.'

ल्युट्—is added to all nouns to form neu. abstract nouns; सह्—सहनं endurance, हस्—हसनं laughing, शी—शयनं sleeping, पा—पानं drinking, भुज्—भोजनं, साध्—साधनं, &c. This is also added in the sense of 'the instrument of an action'; व्रश्च्—व्रश्चनः an instrument for cutting; an axe, &c; दुह्—गोदोहनी a milk vessel (here it shows the place of action of Adhikaraṇa).

आक—(षाकन्)—is affixed to जल्प्, भिक्ष्, कुट्ट् लुंट् and वृ in the sense of 'in the habit of;' जल्पाकः (जल्पितुं शीलमस्य) 'a prattler; भिक्ष्—भिक्षाकः 'a beggar;' कुट्टाकः 'he who divides or cuts;' लुंठाकः 'a robber;' वराकः 'a poor man.'

आरु—शृ-शरारु destructive, hurtful; वंद्—वंदारु praising, a panegyrist.

आलु—is added to the cau. of स्पृह्, गृह् and पत्, to दय् and to the words निद्रा, तन्द्रा and श्रद्धा; स्पृहयालु longing for, desirous of; दयालु compassionate; निद्रालु disposed to sleep; तन्द्रालुः, श्रद्धालुः 'full of faith.'

इ—(इक्, इञ्, इण्, कि)—

इक्—कृष्—कृषिः 'one who tills the ground'; गॄ-गिरिः a mountain.

इञ्—is added to वप् and other roots; वापिः a well; वासिः a dwelling.

इण्—is added to अज् and other roots of the group; आजिः a battle, आतिः &c.

कि—is added to the roots दा and धा and others assuming these forms; धा—उपाधिः fraud, condition, &c.; निधिः a treasure, संधिः a joint, peace, &c.; जलधिः the sea (here it is used in the sense of अधिकरण).

इत्र—(इत्रच्) is added to ऋ, लू, धू, सू, खन्, सह्, and चर्; ऋ—अरित्रं a rudder, helm; an oar; लवित्रं a sickle; धवित्रं a fan made of the deer's skin; सवित्रं cause of generation; खनित्रं a spade; सहित्रं patience, forbearance; चरित्रं.

इन्—(इनि, घिनुण्, णिनि)—

इनि—is affixed to जु with प्र, जि, दृ, क्षि, श्रि with वि, वम्, व्यथ् with आ, अम् with अभि, सृ with परि and सू with प्र; प्रजविन् swift-going; जयिन् a conqueror; दरिन् timid. &c., क्षयिन् wasting away; it is also added to क्री with वि when the noun governed by it is prefixed to it and when the idea of censure or reproach is to be conveyed; तैलविक्रयी, सोमविक्रयी, &c.

घिनुण्—is affixed to त्यज्, रञ्ज्, भज्, दुष्, द्विष्, द्रुह् दुह्, युज्, यम् with आ, यस्, क्रीड् and मुष् with आ; सृ, दिव्, क्षिप्, रट्, वद्, दह्, मुह्, all with परि; सृज्, पच्, ज्वर्, all with सम्; विच् and चर् with वि; लप्, सृ, मन्थ्, वद्, वस् all with प्र; चर् with अति and अप; हन् with अभि, रुध् with अनु; and denotes the agent; त्यज्—त्यागिन् one who abandons, रागिन् full of passion, impassioned, a lover; भागिन् one who takes a share, दोषिन् one who blames; similarly द्वेषिन्, द्रोहिन्, &c.; this is also added to शम् and the other roots of that group but without occasioning any change in the roots; शम्—शमिन् tranquil; मद्—मदिन्; but मद् with उत् or प्र—उन्मादिन्, प्रमादिन्.

णिनि—is added to the roots of the ग्रह् group in the sense of 'the agent;' गृह्णातीति ग्राहिन् 'one who takes;' स्था-स्थायिन्, सि with वि—विषयिन् 'a sensualist;' राध् with अप—अपराधिन् 'one who is guilty;' भू with परि-परिभाविन् 'one who defeats;' &c.;—to हन् when preceded by कुमार and शीर्ष; कुमारं हन्तीति कुमारघातिन् 'one who murders a child,' शीर्षघातिन् 'one who cuts off the head.' This is added to any root, when the subanta other than one denoting a class, precedes it, in the sense of 'in the habit of,' 'disposed to'; उष्णभोजिन् (उष्णं भोक्तुं शीलमस्य) 'one who eats hot things;' साधुकारिन् 'one who acts well;' ब्रह्मवादिन् 'one who expounds the Vedas or the nature of Brahman;'—to मन् after any subanta. पण्डितमानिन् 'one who considers himsalf a Pandita.' दर्शनीयमानिन् 'one who considers himself handsome,' &c.; this is added in the sense of the Past Tense to यज् preceded by the name of a sacrifice; सोमयाजिन्, 'one who has performed the Soma sacrifice;' so

अग्निष्टोमयाजिन्; and to इन् when the noun governed by it is prefixed to it; पितृव्यघातिन् 'one who has killed his uncle.' This is also added to a root when a noun signifying a standard of comparison is prefixed to it; उष्ट्रक्रोशिन् 'one who utters a sound like that of a camel'; ध्वांक्षराविन् 'one who cries like a crow;' this is also added when the observance of a vow is to be indicated; स्थंडिलशायिन् 'one who observes the vow of sleeping on the alter;' also in the sense of 'necessity' or the payment of a debt; अवश्यंभाविन् 'what takes place of necessity;' शतंदायिन् 'one who pays off a debt of Rs. 100.'

इष्णु—(इष्णुच्, खिष्णुच्) is added to कृ with अलं and निरा, जन् with प्र, पच्, पत् and मद् all with उत्, रुच्, त्रप with अप, वृध्, सह्, and चर् in the sense of 'in the habit of, possessed of the properties of,' or 'expert in' 'acting well;' अलंकरिष्णु 'decorating, skilled in decorations; निराकर्तुं शीलमस्य निराकरिष्णुः (see Bhatti. V. 1.) 'repudiating, turning aside;' उत्पतिष्णु 'clever in flying up;' वर्तिष्णु, वर्धिष्णु, सहिष्णु, रोचिष्णु, &c.; it is found added to some other roots also by poets; *e. g.* प्रभविष्णु 'powerful,' भ्राजिष्णु 'resplendent,' क्षयिष्णु, &c.

इष्णु and उक–(खिष्णुच्, खुकञ्) are added to भू with the words आढ्य, सुभग, स्थूल, पलित, नग्न, अंध and प्रिय prefixed to it in the sense of अभूततद्भाव 'being what a thing or person was not before;' अनाढ्यः आढ्यः संजातः आढ्यंभविष्णुः or—भावुकः becoming rich not being rich at first, (see Bhaṭṭi. III. 1.) so आढ्यं, करणम् &c.

उ (उ, and डु)

उ—is added to Desiderative bases to form nouns; चिकीर्षु, desirous of doing; विजिगीषु: desirous of conquering, &c.; and to शंस् with आ, भिक्ष्, विद्, and इष्; आशंसुः desirous, hopeful. भिक्षुः a beggar; विदुः one who knows, knowing; इच्छुः wishing.

डु—is added to भू with वि, प्र, and सम्; विभुः all pervading, mighty, प्रभुः able, संभुः creating; also to द्रु—मितद्रुः that which moves to a measured distance; शतद्रुः which runs in a hundred streams, Name of a river.

उक—(उकञ्)-is affixed to लष्, पत्, पद्, स्था, भू, वृष्, हन्, कम्, गम्, and शॄ and denotes the agent; लष्—लाषुकः sporting, glittering पातुकः falling भू—भावुकः happening, living; हन्—घातुकः कम्-कामुकः amorous.

उर—(कुरच्)-is affixed to विद्, भिद्, and छिद्; विदुरः 'who knows, knowing;' भिदुरः 'breaking, brittle;' छिदुरः 'cutting.'

ऊक—(ऊक) is added to जागृ and the Fre. Bases of यज्, जप् and दंश; जागरूक 'watchful,' &c. (vide Bhatti. II. 22. Rag. XIV. 85. Sis. XX 36); पुनः पुनः अतिशयेन वा यजनशीलः; यायजूकः 'one who performs sacrifices frequently' (see Bhaṭṭi. II. 20.); पुनः पुनः अतिशयेन वा जपतीति जंजपूकः 'one who mutters prayers repeatedly, an ascetic;' पुनः पुनः अतिशयेन वा दशतीति दंदशूकः 'biting frequently, a serpent, demon' (vide Bhaṭṭi I. 26).

क्विन्, क्विप्, and ण्वि—Derivatives are formed with these affixes which are added to roots and then dropped; the difference between the first two is that in the case of the latter त् is inserted between it and the root, if it ends in a short vowel.

क्विन्—is affixed to स्पृश् preceded by a *subanta*; घृतस्पृश् 'one who touches ghee; मन्त्रस्पृश् 'one who touches anything after reciting a holy verse,' &c. except when the *subanta* means water; उदकस्पर्शः 'one who touches water' and not उदकस्पृश्. The following words are to be accepted as they are; यज्-ऋत्विज् (ऋतौ ऋतौ यजते) sacrificing regularly at every season; a priest who officiates at a sacrifice; धृष्—दधृष्—proud, haughty; सृज्—स्रज् a garland; दिश्—दिश् a direction; स्निह्—उष्णिह् name of a metre, words like प्राचीन derived from the roots अञ्च् and the words युज् and क्रुञ्च् ought to be considered as derived by means of this affix.

क्विप्—this is added to a root with or without any preposition prefixed to it; सूते असौ सूः or प्रसूः one who brings forth, a mother; सद्—द्युसदः those who sit in heaven, the gods, द्विष्—प्रद्विष् a powerful enemy; युज्—अश्वयुज् the constellation of stars called 'Aswini,' नी—सेनानी the leader of an army; राज्—विराज् the creator; चि—अग्निचित् one who consecrates the sacred fire, a householder; जि—इन्द्रजित् the conqueror of Indra, name of Râvaṇa's son; स्तु—देवस्तुत् he who praises the gods; सु—सोमसुत् the extractor of Soma juice; कृ—कर्मकृत्, भाषाकृत्, टीकाकृत्, &c. This is also added to दृश्, स्पृश्, and सृज् when the object governed by them is prefixed to them; सर्वदृश् seeing all; मर्मस्पृश् touching the vitals; विश्वसृज् the creator of the universe;—to अद् and हन्; क्रव्याद् a flesh-eater, a demon; ब्रह्महन् the Killer of a Bráhmaṇa;—to छाद् changed to छद्; तनुच्छद् a garment. Before this affix roots ending in a nasal lengthen their penultimate; as शम्-प्रशाम् tranquil; तन्-प्रतान् one who stretches, &c., except in the case of roots गम्, नम्, यम्, and तन्, which drop their nasal and then obey the general rule; अध्वानं गच्छतीति अध्वगत् a traveller; परि तनोतीति—परितत् stretching on all sides; सुनत् yielding, poor; संयत् well restrained, &c.; the आ of शास् is changed to इ before this; मित्रं शास्तीति—मित्रशिष् one who gives advice to his friend; आशिष् a blessing; गॄ forms गिर् speech; the roots भ्रंस्, स्रंस्, and ध्वंस् drop their nasal and insert त् before their final; वाहभ्रत् dropping down from a vehicle, उखास्रत् dropping down from a vessel; पर्णध्वत् falling down from a leaf; before this affix दिव् changes its व् to उ and other roots change their व् to ऊ; अक्षद्युत् (अक्षैर्दीव्यति) a gambler; वे-ऊः a weaver; अव्—ऊः a protector; this forms Vṛiddhi with a preceding अ; जन+ऊ=जनौः the protector of the people, ज्वर्—जूर् feverish, त्वर्—तूर् swift-going; before this affix च् or छ् following र् is dropped; मूर्च्छ्-मूर् swooned; धुर्व्-धूर् hurting, injuring; अक्षधूर् what troubles, *i. e.* presses heavily on the axle of a carriage, hence the cart-load: the following words are irregularly derived; वच्—वाच् speech, प्रच्छ्—प्राच्छ् one who asks; घु-कटप्रुः acting by will; name of Shiva, a kind of worm, a gambler; &c.; श्रि—श्रीः wealth; व्रज्—परिव्राज् an ascetic; दिव्—विद्युत् lightning; गम्—जगत् the world; ध्यै—धी the intellect.

ण्वि—is affixed to भज् which lengthens its अ before it; अंशभाज् one who takes a share; प्रभाज् devoted to, worshipping, &c.

ति—(क्तिन्) forms *fem.* abstract nouns; कृ—कृति an act, &c.; स्तु-स्तुति praise; गम्-गति gait, &c.; रम्-रति sport; नम्-नति a bow; स्था—स्थिति state; गै—गीति a song, &c; पा-पीतिः drinking; पच्—पक्तिः cooking; यज्—इष्टिः a sacrifice, &c.. It is added to the roots श्रु, त्यज्, स्तु and इष् in the sense of 'the instrument of'; श्रुतिः the instrument of hearing *i. e.* the ear, &c. To the root पद् with सम् or वि, क्तिन् or क्विप् is added; सम्पत्तिः or सम्पत्, prosperity; विपत्तिः or विपद् adversity; नि instead of ति is added to roots ending in ॠ and to लू and others; कॄ-कीर्णिः scattering. The following words are to be taken as they are:—सो—साति end; हन्—हेति a weapon; कृत्—कीर्ति fame.

तृ—(तृच्, तृन्)—तृच्—is affixed to all roots and denotes the agent; कृ-कर्तृ a doer; गम्-गन्तृ, पच-पक्तृ, सह्-सोढृ or सहितृ, इष्-एष्टृ or एषितृ &c.; क्रम्-क्रन्तृ or क्रान्तृ or क्रमितृ one who goes, &c., होतृ 'one habitually sacrificing' (तृन्) &c.

त्र—ष्ट्रन् is added to दा or दो, नी, शास्, यु, युज्, स्तु, तुद्, सिच्, मिह्, पत्, पद्, नह् and दंश् and shows the instrument of the action denoted by the root; दा or दो-दात्रं an instrument for cutting, a sickle, नेत्रं the instrument of guidance *i. e.* the eye, शस्—शस्त्रं a weapon, शास्—शास्त्रं, यु-योत्रं, युज्-योक्त्रं the rope by which an animal is tied to the pole of a carriage, स्तु-स्तोत्रं a hymn of praise, तु-तोत्रं a whip, सिच्—सेक्त्रं a watering pot, मिह्—मेढ्रं, पद्—पत्रं a vehicle, the wing of a bird, &c. नह्—नध्री a leather-strap, दंश्—दंष्ट्रा the jaw; it is also added to—पू in the sense given—पोत्रं the snout of a hog, a ploughshare, the thunderbolt, a garment;—पवित्रं an instrument for purifying, a sort of ring of *kusha* grass worn on the fourth finger on religious occasions, and to धे and धा; धात्री: a mother, a foster mother, the earth, name of a tree, Emblic myrobalan.

त्रिम—(क्त्रिम) is added to a few roots; पच्—पक्त्रिमः (पाकेन निर्वृत्तः) ripened, matured; कृत्रिम artificial from कृ, दात्रिमः produced by gift (see Bhaṭṭi. I. 10, 13).

थक—गै—गाथकः a singer.

न—(नङ्, नन्)—

नङ्—is added to यज्, याच्, यत्, विच्छ्, प्रच्छ्, and रक्ष्; यज्ञः a sacrifice, याच्ञा beggary, यत्नः an effort, विश्नः going, lustre, प्रश्न a question, रक्ष्णः protector.

नन्—स्वप्नः sleep, a dream.

नज्—(नजिङ्)—is added to स्वप्, तृष्, and धृष्, in the sense of 'in the habit of;' स्वप्नज् sleepy, तृष्णज् thirsty, धृष्णज् bold, confident.

नु—(क्नु)—is added to त्रस्, गृध्, धृष् and क्षिप् in the sense of 'in the habit of;' त्रस्नु timid, गृध्नु covetous, greedy, धृष्णु bold, क्षिप्नु throwing, casting.

मर—(क्मरच्)—सृ-सृमर going, a kind of deer, घस्—घस्मर and अद्—अद्मर voracious, gluttonous, glutton.

य—(क्यप्)—is added to व्रज्, यज् and कृ and forms *fem.* abstract nouns; व्रज्या asceticism, an attack, इज्या a sacrifice, कृत्या doing; it also takes श and क्तिन्; क्रिया, कृतिः; it is affixed to अज्, (not changed to वी in this case) with सम्, सद् and पत् with नि, मन्, विद्, सु, शी, भृ and इ in the sense of either the place or the instrument of the action denoted by the roots; समज्या assembly, निषद्या a couch, a market place, the hall where an assembly meets, निपत्या slippery ground, मन्या the nape of the neck, विद्या, सुत्या a sprinkling with the Soma juice, शय्या a bed, भृत्या wages, इत्या a vehicle.

र—is affixed to नम्, कम्प्, स्मि, कम्, हिंस्, and दीप्; नम्र bowing down, yielding, कम्प्र shaking, tremulous, स्मेर smiling, कम्र desirous, beautiful, हिंस्र injurious, murderous, दीप्र shining. The word अजस्रं *adv.* is also derived from जस् with न (changed to अ) and र.

रु—is added to दा, धे सि, शद् and सद्; दा—दारु: 'one who gives or eats;' धे—धारु: 'one who drinks;' सेरु: 'one who binds;' शद्रु: 'one who goes or destroys;' सद्रु: 'one who goes or takes rest.'

वन्—(क्वनिप्)—पारदृश्वन् from दृश् 'one who has seen the other side, hence, adept in,' राजयुध्वन्, 'one who has fought with a king'; similarly राजकृत्वन्, सहयुध्वन्, and सहकृत्वन्.

वर—(क्वरप्) is affixed to the roots इ, जि, नश् and सृ; इत्वर going, cruel, जित्वर victorious, नश्वर perishable, fleeting; it is also added to गम्; गत्वर transient, going.

CHAPTER XV.

SYNTAX.

§ 778. Syntax deals with the mode of arranging words in sentences. Of the three divisions of Syntax—Concord, Government and Order, the Syntax of Sanskṛit is mainly concerned with the first two. Syntax in English depends principally upon the last. In Sanskṛit and other cognate Languages which are rich in inflection, the relation, which one word bears to another in a sentence is determined by its grammatical form, and no change occurs in the meaning of the sentences, how-so-ever the order of words be changed. But in English and other languages, deficient in inflection, 'order' is everything. Change the order of words and there is a corresponding change in the meaning. In Sanskṛit, therefore, the mere order of words is not of material importance, though a perfect arbitrariness in that respect is not allowable. Sanskṛit Syntax also takes further into account the meaning and use of participles, the various tenses and moods, and participles. * These will be treated of in their proper order.

THE ARTICLE.

§ 779. There are no articles in Sanskrit corresponding to the English Definite and Indefinite articles. The words कश्चित् and एक, however, are often used in the sense of 'a certain' and the pron. तद् *m. f. n.* as equivalent to 'the;' कश्चित् नरः a certain man; एकः पान्थः a traveller; स राजा the king, &c.

§ 780. As already remarked (See § 54) there are three numbers in Sanskṛit: a singular number, denoting a single individual, a dual number denoting two, and a plural number denoting more than two. Besides these general senses—

---

* As the great bulk of Sanskṛit literature is thrown in the form of verse, the laws of Syntax will be found not to be always observed by the poets. In ordinary prose writings the usual order of words in a sentence is, first the subject with its adjuncts, then the object with its adjuncts, then the adverbs and other indeclinables (extensions of the predicate) and lastly the predicate. The chief characteristics of Sanskṛit style are in the words of Prof. Max Múller, 'the predominance of coordination, the use of the Locative Absolute, a fondness for compounds and indeclinable participles supplying the place of subordinate clauses, the frequent employment of the Past Participle instead of the finite verb, a predilection for passive forms, and the absence of the indirect construction and of the subjunctive mood. For the latter reason the use of the tenses and moods is comparatively simple; on the other hand, the use of the cases, being much less definite than in Latin and Greek presents some difficulties.'

M. Williams' Grammar for Beginners.

(*a*) The singular may be used to denote a class; सिंहः श्वापदराजः the lion is the king of beasts; बुद्धिमत्सु नरः श्रेष्ठः &c.

(*b*) The dual sometimes denotes a male and a female of the same class; पितरौ parents; चटकौ a male and a female of sparrow.

(1) Note:—Words like द्वय, द्वितिय, युग, द्वंद्व, &c. meaning 'a pair,' &c. which are dual in sense but singular in form ought to be always used in the singular, except when several pairs are meant.

(2) Note:—Words like हस्तौ, नेत्रे, पादौ, &c. should always be used in the dual in Sanskrit.

(*c*) The plural, like the singular, may represent a class, ब्राह्मणाः पूज्याः (or ब्राह्मणः पूज्यः) Brâhmaṇas (*i. e.* the Brâhmaṇa class) are adorable.

(1) The plural is not unfrequently used as a mark of respect or reverence. इति श्रीशंकराचार्याः; so (says) the venerable Shankarâchârya; इति आचार्यपादाः this is the opinion of the revered preceptor, &c.

(2) In the first person, great personages and writers sometimes use the plural instead of the singular; वयमपि भवत्यौ किमपि पृच्छामः we (*i. e.* I,) too ask you something; इति तु वयं but we (*i. e.* I, the writer) hold this opinion; वयमपि च गिरामीश्महे we rule over speech (*i. e.* language).

(3) Words like दाराः, गृहाः, अक्षताः, सिकताः, आपः, प्राणाः, लाजाः, &c. are always used in the plural, though some of them are singular in sense.

(4) Names of countries which are really the names of the people inhabiting them, must be used in the plural; स विदेहान् उपाययौ he went to Videha, &c.

But in the case of compounds ending in words denoting a country, such as देश, विषय, &c. the sing. must be used; अस्ति मगधदेशे पाटलिपुत्रं नाम नगरम् there is a town called Pâtaliputra in the country of Magadha.

(5) The plural of proper nouns denotes a family or race as in English; जनकानां रघूणां च यत्कृत्स्नं गोत्रमङ्गलम् Utta.

SECTION I.

CONCORD.

§ 781. Concord is the agreement of words in a sentence as regards gender, number, person or tense.

The concords deserving notice in Sanskrit are three:—(1) Concord of the verb with the Subject; (2) Concord of the Adjective with the Substantive; and (3) Concord of the Relative with its Antecedent.

CONCORD OF THE VERB WITH THE SUBJECT.

§ 782. The verb must agree with its subject in number and person; आसीत् राजा नलो नाम there was a king, Nala by name; अहं गच्छामि I go; ब्राह्मणौ गच्छतः two Brâhmaṇas go, &c.

§ 783. (*a*) When two or more subjects differing in number are connected by 'and' the verb must be plural; ततः कुन्ती च राजा च भीष्मश्च सह बन्धुभिः । ददुः श्राद्धं तदा पाण्डोः &c. Mah. Bhâ. Sometimes the verb agrees with the nearest subject in number, सा च सत्यवती देवी गान्धारी च यशस्विनी । राजदारैः परिवृता गान्धारी चापि निर्ययौ ॥ Mah. Bhâ. अहश्च रात्रिश्च उभे च सन्ध्ये धर्मोपि जानाति नरस्य वृत्तम् ॥

(*b*) But when they are connected by 'or' and are all sing. the verb will be singular, and when the subject differ in number the verb will agree with the one nearest to it; रामः गोविंदो वा व्रजतु 'Let Râma or Govinda go,' स वा इमे बालका वा आम्रं गृह्णन्तु 'let him or these boys take the mango fruit.'

§ 784. (*a*) When a verb agrees with two or more subjects of different persons connected by 'and,' the first person has preference over the second or third, and the second over the third; त्वमहं रामश्चैतत्करिष्यामः Râma, you and I shall do this; त्वं रामश्च पाठशालां गच्छतम्.

(*b*) But when the subjects are connected by 'or', the verb agrees with the one nearest to it · स वा वयं वा तत्संपादयामः he or we accomplish that; अहं रामोऽथवा राजा लक्ष्मणो वा मरिष्यति either I or King Râma or Lakshmaṇa will perish.

§ 785. The predicate may not always be a finite verb; but a participle, or an adjective or a noun may take its place.

(*a*) When a participle is used as the predicate it must agree with the subject in number and gender; स तदुक्तवान् he said that, स तदुक्तवती she said that, तेषां बन्धनानि छिन्नानि their bonds were cut off, कार्यं कृतं the work is done, लता छिन्ना the creeper is cut; &c.

(*b*) When an adjective or a noun is used as the predicate, a form of the roots अस् or भू may be used with it or may be omitted; the adjective used predicatively agrees with the subject in number and gender; words like आस्पद, पात्र, भाजन, स्थान, पद &c. retain their gender and number; सुभृत्यः दुर्लभः a good servant is difficult to be obtained, सुपुत्रः पितुः गर्वास्पदम् a good son is the object of his father's pride, सम्पदः पदमापदां riches are the abode of miseries, स तु तस्या अभिमानभूमिः &c.; in these cases the verb agrees with the subject in number and not with the noun used predicatively; सम्पदः आपदां पदं सन्ति and not अस्ति, &c.

§ 786. When a substantive or an adjective is used predicatively with verbs of incomplete predication such as 'to grow, to seem, to be, to appear,' &c. the substantive or adjective so used must agree with the subject in case; एष मे निश्चयः this is my resolve; स भूपतिः प्रजागरकृशः लक्ष्यते that king seems emaciated through wakefulness; प्रभुर्बुभूषुर्भुवनत्रयस्य desirous of being the lord of the three worlds.

(*a*) The same applies to transitive roots of incomplete predication used passively; तेन मुनिना स मूषकः बिडालः कृतः by that sage the mouse was made (transformed into) a cat, &c.: नृपो हि विष्णुः मन्यते a king is thought to be Vishṇu.

§ 787. When an indeclinable used with an adjectival force takes the place of the verb, the object governed by it is put in the Nominative case. * विषवृक्षोपि संवर्ध्य स्वयं च्छेत्तुमसांप्रतम् (Kum. II. 55.) it is not fit to cut down even a poisonous tree having first reared it up; here the indeclinable असांप्रतं is equivalent to न युज्यते and the whole sentence to वृक्षं संवर्ध्य तं च्छेत्तुं असाम्प्रतं (न युज्यते) योपि विषवृक्षः स्यात् ।

Concord of the Adjective with the Substantive.

§ 788. An adjective, particpial or qualitative, must agree with the substantive it qualifies in gender, number and case; रूपवान् पुरुषः a handsome man; रूपवती स्त्री a beautiful woman; महत्संकटम् a great calamity; एते मयूराः, तानि पुस्तकानि; गच्छन्ती नारी, &c.

But numeral adjectives of fixed gender and number remain unchanged:—शतं ब्राह्मणाः a hundred Brâhmaṇas; शतं स्त्रियः a hundred women, विंशतिः बालकानि twenty children.

§ 789. When an adjectives qualifie two or more substantives it agrees with them in their combined number; when the substantives differ in gender, the adjective will be *masculine* when the substantives are *masculine* and *feminine*; and *neuter* when they are *masculine, feminine* and *neuter* राजा राज्ञी च स्तुत्यचरितौ स्तः the king and his queen are of laudable conduct; धर्मः कामश्च दर्पश्च हर्षः क्रोधः सुखं वयः । अर्थादेतानि सर्वाणि प्रवर्तन्ते न संशयः fulfilment of duty, satisfaction of desires, pride, anger, happiness and long life; all these proceed undoubtedly from wealth.

(*a*) Sometimes the adjective takes the gender of the majority of the substantives; वृद्धौ च मातापितरौ साध्वी भार्या सुतः शिशुः । अप्यकार्यशतं कृत्वा भर्तव्या मनुरब्रवीत ॥ aged parents, a good wife and a young son should be maintained even by doing a hundred foul deeds; so has Manu spoken (laid down).

---

* निपातेनाभिहिते कर्मणि न विभक्तिपरिगणनस्य प्रायिकत्वात् । Vâman.

(*b*) And sometimes it takes the gender and number of the substantive nearest to it when the particle च is used; उद्वेगः कलहः कण्डूः सेव्यमाना च वर्धते dejection, quarrel and an itching sensation prevail all the more they are attended to; यस्य वीर्येण कृतिनो वयं च भुवनानि च (कृतानि) by whose valour we have become happy and so have the three worlds.

§ 790. When a past or potential passive participle is used as predicate with a noun in apposition to the subject, the participle agrees with the subject; कृताः शरव्यं हरिणा तवासुराः (S'ak. VI.) the demons are made the marks of your arrows by Hari.

CONCORD OF RELATIVE WITH ITS ANTECEDENT.

§ 791. The relative agrees with its antecedent in gender, number and person, the cases of the relative and its antecedent being determined by their relation to their respective clauses; यस्यास्ति वित्तं स नरः कुलीनः he who has wealth has a noble family; यस्य बुद्धिर्बलं तस्य; यद्येन युज्यते लोके बुधस्तत्तेन योजयेत् what, which is fit to be united with anything, a wise man should unite with it &c.

§ 792. When the relative has for its predicate a noun differing in gender from the antecedent the relative generally takes the gender of the antecedent noun, the demonstrative pronoun following that of the noun it qualifies; परगुणासहिष्णुत्वं हि यत्स दुर्जनानां स्वभावः–non-endurance of the merits of another is but the nature of the wicked; शैत्यं हि यत्सा प्रकृतिर्जलस्य.

§ 793. The relative pronoun यत् *neu.* sing. is used like the English 'that' to introduce a clause, the gender of the demonstrative pronoun being the same as that of the antecedent noun; यद्विद्वान् अपि नरः अन्यान् विगणयति स धनमद एव it is the pride of wealth that even a learned man slights another; सत्योयं जनप्रवादः यत्संपत्संपदमनुबध्नातीति it is a true saying that one good fortune follows another.

Obs:—Sometimes the antecedent noun or pronoun is omitted and has to be inferred from the gender and number of the relative; *e. g.* धनेन किं यो न ददाति याचके *i. e.* तस्य धनेन, &c. what is the use of wealth to him who does not bestow it on mendicants, &c.

SECTION II.

GOVERNMENT.

§ 794. The only portion of Syntax treated separately in Sanskrit grammars is the Kârakaprakaraṇa or the chapter on Government. Kâraka is the name given to the relation subsisting between a noun and a verb in a sentence. There are six Kârakas in Sanskrit belonging to the first seven cases, except the Genitive, which is, therefore, not a Kâraka case. These are कर्ता, कर्म, करण, संप्रदान, अपादान and अधिकरण.

§ 795. There are several indeclinables in Sanskrit which also govern cases. Cases governed by indeclinables are called Upapadavibhaktis, as distinguished from those governed by verbs which are called Kârakavibhaktis. In cases where both are possible the latter predominates over the former (उपपदविभक्तेः कारकविभक्तिर्बलीयसी); as in मुनित्रयं नमस्कृत्य although नमस् alone would govern the Dative.

§ 796. The Nominative, as in English and other languages is simply the naming case; its office, when used by itself, is to express the crude form of a word, gender, measure and number and nothing more.* When used with a verb it forms its subject.

THE ACCUSATIVE CASE.

§ 797. The Accusative denotes the object *i. e.* the person or thing upon whom or which the effect of an action takes place;

---

* प्रातिपदिकार्थलिङ्गपरिमाणवचनमात्रे प्रथमा Pân. II. 3. 46.

हरिं सेवते he worships Hari; ग्रामं गच्छन् तृणं स्पृशति going to a village he touches grass. *

§ 798. All transitive verbs govern an Accusative; पुष्पाण्यव-चिनोति collects flowers; अप एव ससर्जादौ (the creator) created water first, &c. Several transitive verbs govern what is called in English a factitive object besides a direct object; त्वामामनन्ति प्रकृतिं त्वामेव पुरुषं विदुः Kum. II. 13. they consider thee to be Prakriti, they know thee to be Purusha; कुमारं नेतारं कृत्वा having made Kumâra the leader (of the forces); नाम्ना तमात्मजन्मानं अजं चकार made his son Aja by name.

§ 799. † Intransitive roots govern the Accusative nouns denoting space or country, or duration of time and distance; कुरून् स्वपिति he sleeps in the country of the Kurus; तत्र कति-पयान् दिवसान् अवसत् there he dwelt for some days; गोदोहमास्ते he sits down till a cow is milked; क्रोशं प्रतिष्ठते he walks for a Kośa; क्रोशं कुटिला नदी the course of the river is winding for a Kośa; but मासस्य द्विरधीते studies twice a month; क्रोशस्यैकदेशे पर्वतः the hill is situated in a part of a Kośa.

§ 800. Roots having the sense of motion, real or metaphorical govern the Accusative of the place to which it is directed. ग्रामं गच्छति goes to a village; अधिज्यधन्वा विचचार दावम् with his bow strung he roamed all over the forest; आनन्दस्य परां कोटिमभ्य-गच्छन् they reached the highest point of joy; मनसा कृष्णमेति goes to Krishṇa (thinks of him) mentally; इति चिन्तयन्नेव स निद्रां ययौ while thus pondering he sank into sleep.

(*a*) When the motion is real, the Dative may also be used; ग्रामाय ग्रामं वा गच्छति; but not of words denoting 'a road;'

* But when the relation of object and verb is expressed by the passive termination the noun forming the object is put in the nominative case; हरिः सेव्यते.

† कालाध्वनोरत्यन्तसंयोगे । Pân. II. 3. 5.

पन्थानं गच्छति only; but उत्पथेन पथे गच्छति he reaches the main road by taking a by-path.

§ 801. The roots* शी, स्था and आस्, with अधि, govern the Accusative of the place where the action takes place; अधिशेते अधितिष्ठति अध्यास्ते वा वैकुण्ठं हरिः; शिलापट्टमधिशयाना reclining on a stone-slab; अर्धासनं गोत्रभिदोधितस्थौ occupied half of Indra's seat; अध्यास्त सर्वर्तुसुखामयोध्याम् lived in Ayodhyâ delightful in all seasons.

§ 802. † विश् with अभिनि governs the Accusative; अभिनिविशते सन्मार्गम् he pursues the path of goodness; धन्या सा गणिकादारिका यामेव भवन्मनोऽभिनिविशते happy is that harlot girl on whom you have fixed your mind (see Bhaṭṭi. VIII. 80.). Rarely this governs the Loc. अभिनिविशते पापे fondly resorts to sin. विश् with a preposition governs the Acc. but with उप meaning 'to sit' takes the Loc. आसनेऽस्मिन्नुपविश sit on this seat.

§ 803. ‡ The root वस् preceded by the prepositions उप, अनु, अधि and आ governs the Accusative case; उप-अनु-अधि-आ-वसति वैकुंठं हरिः Hari dwells in Vaikuntha; शून्यमन्ववसद्वनं he dwelt in a dreary forest; but वस् with उप meaning 'to abstain from food' is used with the Loc.; उपवसति वने रामः Râma observes a fast in the forest.

§ 804. ¶ The particles उभयतः, सर्वतः, उपर्युपरि, अधोधः, अध्यधि and धिक्; अभितः, परितः, समया, निकषा, हा and प्रति meaning 'to, and अन्तरा 'between,' and अन्तरेण 'without,' 'regarding to,' govern the Accusative; उभयतः कृष्णं गोपाः the cowherds are on both

---

* अधिशीङ्स्थासां कर्म । Pân. I. 4. 46. † अभिनिविशश्च Pân. I. 4. 47.

‡ उपान्वध्याङ्वसः । Pân. I. 4. 48.

¶ उभसर्वतसोः कार्या धिगुपर्यादिषु त्रिषु। द्वितीयाम्रेडितान्तेषु ततोन्यत्रापि दृश्यते। अभितः परितः समया निकषा हा प्रतियोगेपि। Vârtikas on Pân. I 4 48. अन्तरान्तरेण युक्ते Pân. II. 3. 4.

sides of Krishṇa—सर्वतः प्रासादं जाग्रति दंडधारिणः guards keep vigil on all sides of the palace. उपर्युपरि लोकं हरिः Hari is over all the worlds; अधोधो लोकं पातालः Pâtâla is below the world. अध्यधि लोकम्; धिग्वो जाल्मान् fie upon you rogues; धिक्सानुजं कुरुपतिं fie upon the lord of the Kurus, with all his brothers; (धिक्) is used sometimes with the Nom. and sometimes with the Voc. धिगर्थाः कष्टसंश्रयाः fie upon wealth which is attended with troubles; धिङ् मूर्ख fie upon thee fool; रक्षांसि वेदिं परितो निरास्थ-दङ्गान्ययाक्षीदभितः प्रधानम् (Bhaṭṭi I. 12) he dispelled the demons from around the altar and offered sacrifices to the minor deities arranged round the principal one. अभितस्तं पृथासूनुः स्नेहेन परितस्तरे Kir. XI. 8; ग्रामं समया-निकषा व्रजति goes near to the village. Vide Siś. I. 68, VI. 73. हा कृष्णाभक्तं woe to him who is not a devotee of Krishṇa; मन्दौत्सुक्योस्मि नगरगमनं प्रति I have but a faint desire to go to the town; अन्तरा त्वां मां हरिः हरिमन्तरेण न सुखं happiness is not possible without Hari; देवीं वसुमतीमन्तरेण with reference to queen Vasumati.

Some of the indeclinables given above are used with the Genitive; *e. g.* उपर्युपरि सर्वेषामादित्य इव तेजसा (he stood) very high above all by his lustre, like the sun, &c.

§ 805. * The following prepositions are used with the Accusative.

(*a*) अति 'superior to, higher than,' अनु 'just after, after, by the side of, inferior to,' अभि 'close to' and उप 'near, inferior to;' *e. g.* अति देवान् कृष्णः Krishṇa excels gods in might; अतिरामं गोविन्दः Govinda is superior to Râma; जपमनु प्रावर्षत् it rained just after the muttering of prayers; सर्वं मामनु ते every thing

---

* कर्मप्रवचनीययुक्ते द्वितीया Pân. II. 3. 8. Prepositions used by themselves and governing nouns are called Karmapravachanîya.

तृतीयार्थे । हीने । उपोधिके च । लक्षणेत्थंभूताख्यानभागवीप्सासु प्रतिपर्यनवः । अभिरभागे । Pân. 1. 4. 85-87. 90. 91.

of thee is after mine; अनु पितरं गच्छति सुतः the son imitates his father; न भवान् अनु रामं चेत् if you are not inferior to Râma; so अनु हरिं सुराः, भक्तो हरिं अभि the devotee is close to Hari; उपशूरं न ते वृत्तं your act is not like that of a hero (*lit.* is inferor to his); उपहरिं सुराः &c.

(*b*) The prepositions अभि, अनु, परि and प्रति are used with the Accusative when they refer to particular things; गिरिं—अभि—अनु—परि—प्रति—विद्योतते विद्युत the lightning flashes towards the mountain; also when they mean 'to every one,' &c. वृक्षं वृक्षमभि-अनु—परि—प्रति—सिंचति waters each and every tree; so अभि—अनु—परि—प्रति स्त्रीं स्त्रीं जातमन्मथः।

(*c*) अनु, परि and प्रति also govern the Accusative when they imply 'one's own share;' लक्ष्मीः हरिमनु-परि-प्रति Lakshmi is the proper share (property) of Hari.

§ 806. The roots given in the following Kârikâ govern a double Accusative—

दुह्याच्पच्दण्ड्रुधिप्रच्छिचिब्रूशासुजिमथ्मुषाम् ।
कर्मयुक्स्यादकथितं तथा स्यान्नीहृकृष्वहाम् ॥

i. e. the roots दुह् to milk, पच् to cook, दण्ड् to punish, रुध् to obstruct, प्रच्छ् to ask, चि to collect, ब्रू to speak, शास् to instruct, जि to win (as a wager), मन्थ् to churn, and मुष् to steal; as also नी, हृ, and कृष् and वह्; and the synonyms of these; गां दोग्धि पयः he milks (draws milk from) the cow; बलिं याचते वसुधां he begs the earth of Bali; तण्डुलानोदनं पचति he cooks rice (into food); similarly गर्गान् शतं दण्डयति, व्रजमवरुणद्धि गां. माणवकं पन्थानं पृच्छति, वृक्षं अवचिनोति फलानि, माणवकं धर्मं ब्रूते—शास्ति, शतं जयति देवदत्तं, सुधां क्षीरनिधिं मथ्नाति, देवदत्तं शतं मुष्णाति, मामजां नयति—हरति—कर्षति—वहति वा; So माणवकं धर्मं भाषते—वक्ति वा, बलिं वसुधां भिक्षते, &c. Vide Bhaṭṭi. VI. 8–10.

§ 807. * When these verbs are used in the passive, the secondary object in the case of the first twelve roots and the principal one in that of the last four is put in the Nominative case, the other Accusative remaining as before; धेनुः पयो दुह्यते, दशरथः रामं ययाचे कौशिकेन, उदधिः सुधां ममन्थे देवैः &c., तेन गावः ग्रामं नीयन्ते ह्रियन्ते कृष्यन्ते उह्यन्ते वा, &c.

§ 808. † In the case of the causals of roots implying 'motion,' 'knowledge,' 'eating,' roots having some literary work for their object, intransitive roots and the roots दृश् and जल्प्, भाष् with आ; लप् with वि, मृह् and श्रु, their subject in the primitive sense is put in the Accusative case.

शत्रूनगमयत्स्वर्गं वेदार्थं स्वानवेदयत् ।
आशयच्चामृतं देवान्वेदमध्यापयद्विधिम् ।
आसयत्सलिले पृथ्वीं यः स मे श्रीहरिर्गतिः ॥ Sid. Kau.

That venerable Hari is my refuge who despatched the enemies (of gods) to the next world, explained the meaning of the Vedas to his (followers), made the gods drink nectar, taught Veda to the Creator and seated the earth (made it rest) on waters.

दर्शयति हरिं भक्तान् he makes the devotees see Hari; जल्पयति भाषयति विलापयति धर्मपुत्रं देवदत्तः; पुत्रं विद्यामग्राहयत् (*cf.* Kum. I. 52); अश्रावयत्परिषदान्कथाम्. But when the double causal is used the subject ceases to be the subject of the root in the primitive sense and therefore takes the Instrumental; गमयति देवदत्तः यज्ञदत्तं, गमयति देवदत्तेन यज्ञदत्तं विष्णुमित्रः

Obs:—दृश् is sometimes found used with the Dative; प्रत्यभिज्ञानरत्नं च रामायादर्शयत्कृती Rag. XII. 64.

(*a*) The causals of नी, and वह् when it has for its subject a

---

* गौणे कर्मणि दुह्यादे नीहृकृष्वहाम् * * * लादयो मताः Sid. Kau. on Pân. VII. 1. 69.

† गतिबुद्धिप्रत्यवसानार्थशब्दकर्माकर्मकाणामणि कर्ता स णौ । Pân. 1. 4. 52. जल्पतिप्रभृतीनामुपसंख्यानम् । दृशेश्च Vártikas.

noun other than one denoting a driver, govern the Instrumental of the primitive subject;* नाययति वाहयति वा भारं भृत्येन he makes his servant carry a load; but वाहयति रथं वाहान् सूतः the charioteer makes the horses draw the chariot.

(1) † The same holds good in the case of the causal of अद् and खाद्; आदयति खादयति वा अन्नं बटुना he makes the boy eat his food.

(2) ‡ भक्ष् when it has not the sense of हिंसा 'pain or injury to a sentient thing' does the same; भक्षयत्यन्नं बटुना; but भक्षयति बलीवर्दान् सस्यम् (when the loss of corn causes pain to the mind).

(*b*) स्मृ and घ्रा which denote a kind of knowledge are construed with the Instrumental, though the former when meaning 'to remember with pain' is sometimes found used with the Accusative also; स्मारयति घ्रापयति वा देवदत्तेन; अयि चंद्रगुप्तदोषा अतिक्रान्तपार्थिवगुणान् स्मारयन्ति प्रकृतीः । Vide also Śis. VI. 56.

(*c*) § The causal of the denominative शब्दाय also is construed with the Instrumental; शब्दाययति देवदत्तेन he causes Devadatta to make a sound.

Note:—¶ By intransitive roots are meant such roots as are not capable of governing an object other than one denoting space, time, &c. and not such as, though transitive, may be used without their object being actually expressed; मासं आसयति देवदत्तं; but देवदत्तेन पाचयति and not देवदत्तं though the object of पच् is not actually expressed.

§ 809. $ The primitive subject of the verbs हृ and कृ, of

---

* नीवह्योर्न । नियन्तृकर्तृकस्य वहेरनिषेधः । Vârtikas.

† आदिखाद्योर्न । Vârtika. ‡ भक्षेरहिंसार्थस्य न । Vârt § शब्दायतेर्न Vârt.

¶ येषां देशकालादिभिन्नं कर्म न संभवति तेऽत्राकर्मकाः । न त्वविवक्षितकर्मणोऽपि Sid. Kau.

$ हृक्रोरन्यतरस्याम् Pân. I. 4. 43. अभिवादिदृशोरात्मनेपदं वेति वाच्यम् । Vârt.

अभिवद्, and दृश् when used in the Atm. is either put in the Accusative or the Instrumental; हारयति कारयति वा भृत्यं भृत्येन वा कटम् he causes the servant to take or weave a mat; अभिवादयते दर्शयते देवं भक्तं भक्तेन वा he makes the devotee bow down to, or see, God.

§ 810. *When the causal forms are used in the passive, the principal object (*i. e.* the primitive subject) is put in the Nominative case; but in the case of roots implying 'knowledge or eating' and roots having a literary work for their object the principal object is put in the Nominative case and the secondary object in the Accusative or *vice versa*; देवदत्तः कटं करोति Devadatta prepares a mat—देवदत्तं देवदत्तेन वा कटं कारयति; देवदत्तः कटं कार्यते he makes Devadatta prepare a mat, देवदत्तः ग्रामं गच्छति Dev. goes to a village; देवदत्तं ग्रामं गमयति causes Dev. to go to a village; देवदत्तः ग्रामं गम्यते; Devadatta is made to go, &c.; माणवकं धर्मं बोधयति he makes Mâṇavaka know his duty; बोध्यते माणवकं धर्मः, माणवको धर्मं इति वा. Mâṇavaka is made to know, &c., बटुमोदनं भोजयति he makes the child eat food; बटुरोदनं भोज्यते or बटुमोदनो भोज्यते the boy is made, &c.

§ 811. As regards the causal of roots governing two Accusatives the general rules given at § 808 hold good; कौशिकः दशरथं रामं अयाचत; (देवाः) कौशिकेन दशरथं राममयाचयन्; गोपोऽजां ग्रामं हरति, (ी) गोपेन अजां ग्रामं हारयति, &c.

THE INSTRUMENTAL CASE.

§ 812. † The Instrumental case primarily expresses either the agent (when the construction is passive) or the instrument or means by which an action is done; तव महिमानं अजानता मया असत्कृतोऽसि thou wast disrespected by me, not knowing thy greatness;

---

* बुद्धिभक्षार्थयोः शब्दकर्मणां च निजेच्छया । प्रयोज्यकर्मण्यन्येषां ण्यन्तानां लादयो मताः ॥ Sid. Kau. on Pân. VII. 1. 69.

† कर्तृकरणयोस्तृतीया । Pân. II. 3. 18.

रामेण बाणेन हतो वाली Vâli was killed by Râma with an arrow (here रामेण is the agent; बाणेन the instrument).

(*a*) * The Instrumental is also used in the following senses. प्रकृत्या दर्शनीयः lovely *by nature*; प्रायेण याज्ञिकः he is *almost* a ritualist; गोत्रेण गार्ग्यः Gârgya *by family name*; सुखेन याति goes with *ease*; so समेनैति, विषमेणैति, &c. द्विद्रोणेन धान्यं क्रीणाति he buys two *dronas* of corn at a time; साहस्रेण पशून् क्रीणाति he buys one *thousand* beasts at a time, &c.

(1) In the case of numerals and words expressive of measure the Acc. may also be used; द्विद्रोणं क्रीणाति धान्यं, शतेन शतेन शतं शतं वत्सान् पाययति पयः; &c.

(*b*) *Obs*:—† The root दिव् 'to play,' however, governs the Accusative or the Instrumental of the instrument used; अक्षैः अक्षान् वा दीव्यति he plays at dice.

(c) † The root ज्ञा with सम् also governs the Accusative or the Instrumental; पित्रा पितरं वा संजानीते he recognises or lives in peace with his father; but विष्णुं संजानीथ remember Vishṇu.

§ 813 ‡ When the accomplishment of an object is to be expressed, the Instrumental of words expressing the length of time or space is used; अह्ना क्रोशेन वाऽनुवाकोऽधीतः the section (of the Veda) was studied by him in a day, or a Kosa (*i. e.* by going over it); but मासमधीतो नायातः as the accomplishment does not take place.

§ 814. § Words expressing some defect in a limb of the body govern the Instrumental of the defective limb; अक्ष्णा काणः blind of one eye; so पादेन खञ्जः &c.

---

* प्रकृत्यादिभ्य उपसंख्यानम् । Vârt.

† दिवः कर्म च । संज्ञोऽन्यतरस्यां कर्मणि । Pân. I. 4. 43, II. 3. 22.

‡ अपवर्गे तृतीया । Pân. II. 3. 6. अपवर्गः फलप्राप्तिः । तस्यां द्योत्यायां कालाध्वनोरत्यन्तसंयोगे तृतीया स्यात् ।

§ येनाङ्गविकारः । Pân. II. 3. 20.

§ 815. * A characteristic attribute indicative of the existence of a particular state or condition is put in the Instrumental; जटाभिः तापसः he is an ascetic (which is apparent) from his matted hair (जटाज्ञाप्यतापसत्वविशिष्ट इत्यर्थः Sid. Kau.).

§ 816. † The Instrumental is also used to express the cause or motive or the object of purpose of an action as distinguished from the mere instrument of it; पुण्येन दृष्टो हरिः Hari was seen by (virtue of) merit; तेनापराधेन दण्ड्योऽसि thou art to be punished for that fault; अध्ययनेन वसति dwells for the purpose of studying; also when the object to be accomplished is simply implied; अलं श्रमेण away with your efforts *i. e.* they will not succeed; श्रमेण साध्यं नास्ति इत्यर्थः (Sid. Kau.)

§ 817 The Instrumental is used with words expressing the idea of—

(*a*) excelling; पूर्वान् महाभाग तयातिशेषे Oh fortunate one, you excel your ancestors in that (devotion); धाम्नातिशाययति धाम सहस्रधाम्नः (Mu. 3. 17.) he surpasses, by his lustre, the lustre of the sun; दूरीकृता खलु गुणैरुद्यानलता वनलताभिः । S'ak. I.

(*b*) resemblance, likeness, equality; स्वरेण पितरमनुहरति resembles his father in voice; देहबन्धने स्वरेण च रामभद्रमनुहरति (Utta. 4.); अस्य मुखं मातुः मुखेन संवदति his face resembles that of his mother; विष्णुना सदृशो वीर्ये equal to Vishṇu in valour.

(*c*) swearing; भरतेनात्मना चाहं शपे I swear by Bharata and myself; शापितासि मम जीवितेन I conjure thee by my life.

(*d*) rejoicing, being pleased; भक्त्या गुरौ मय्यनुकम्पया च प्रीतास्मि I am pleased with thee by thy devotion to your preceptor and compassion upon me; कापुरुषः स्वल्पकेनापि तुष्यति a low person is satisfied with little.

---

* इत्थंभूतलक्षणे । Pân. II. 3. 21.

† हेतौ । Pân. II. 3. फलमपि इह हेतुः । द्रव्यादिसाधारणं निर्व्यापारसाधारणं च हेतुत्वम् । करणत्वं तु क्रियामात्रविषयं व्यापारनियतं च । Sid. Kau.

(*e*) motion (the conveyance or the part of the body on which a thing is carried being put in the Instrumental case): रथेन संचरते 'he moves about in a chariot.'

(*f*) price (real or metaphorical) at which a thing is bought; शतेन क्रीतः bought for a hundred (rupees, etc.); स्वप्राणव्ययेनापि रक्षणीयाः सुहृदसवः 'the life of a friend ought to be saved even at the cost of one's life.'

§ 818. The following words also govern the Instrumental case:—

(*a*) Words expressing the idea of use or need, such as किं, कार्यं, अर्थः, प्रयोजनं and the like, and the root कृ with किं used in the same sense; धनेन किं यः &c. what is the use of his wealth who &c.; तृणेन कार्यं भवतीश्वराणाम्—'even the rich sometimes stand in need of grass,' similarly कोर्थः पुत्रेण जातेन यो न विद्वान्न धार्मिकः, न स्वामिपादानां मया किमपि प्रयोजनम्, &c.

(*b*) The particles अलं and कृतं meaning 'enough;' अलं रुदितेन 'enough of your weeping (do not weep):' कृतं अत्यादरेण 'away with overpressing'; अलं is also used with a gerund अलं अन्यथा संभाव्य 'away with misunderstanding.'

(*c*) Particles expressing 'accompaniment' such as साकं सार्धं, समं, सह, &c.; आस्व साकं मया सौधे (Bh. VIII. 70.); वनं मया सार्धमसि प्रपन्नः Rag. XIV. 63: आद्रो निवर्त्स्यति समं हरिणांगनाभिः। Śak I. 27. &c.

(*d*) Words meaning 'having or destitute of;' समायुक्तोप्यर्थैः (परिभवपदं याति कृपणः) 'though possessed of wealth,' &c.; अर्थेन हीनः 'destitute of wealth.'

N. B. For the optional use of the Instrumental see the Abl., the Gen. and the Loc. cases.

THE DATIVE CASE.

§ 819. * The primary sense of the Dative case is Sampra-

---

* चतुर्थी संप्रदाने Pân. II. 3. 13. कर्मणा यमभिप्रैति स संप्रदानम् Pân. I. 4. 32. क्रियया यमभिप्रैति सोपि संप्रदानम् Vârt

dâna (संप्रदानं). The indirect object of the root दा is called Sampradâna; also the person or thing with reference to whom or which an action is done; विप्राय गां ददाति 'he gives a cow to a Brâhmaṇa;' युद्धाय संनह्यते 'prepares for battle;' न शूद्राय मतिं दद्यात् 'The Sudra should not be instructed in the Veda, &c.'

*But in the case of the root यज् the proper object is put in the Instrumental case and the indirect object in the Accusative; पशुना रुद्रं यजते 'he sacrifices a bull to Rudra.'

Note:—Though the root दा ought to govern the Dat. of the indirect object, it is sometimes found used with the Gen. or the Loc. राज्यं शिबीनां वृद्धं वै ददामि तव खेचर 'Oh sky-wanderer, I will give you the prosperous kingdom of the Sibis;' यस्त्वं रामे पृथिवीं दातुमिच्छसि 'thou who art thinking of bestowing the earth upon Râma,' &c.

§ 820. † The roots रुच् and others having the same sense govern the Dative of the person or thing pleased or satisfied; हरये रोचते भक्तिः 'Hari likes devotion;' अपां हि तृप्ताय न वारिधारा स्वादुः सुगन्धिः स्वदते तुषारा 'a stream of sweet water, cool and perfumed, is not liked by one who has already drunk enough of water.'

§ 821. ‡The roots श्लाघ् 'to praise,' ह्नु 'to hide,' स्था 'to stand,' and शप् 'to swear,' govern the Dative of the person to whom some object or feeling is to be conveyed; गोपी स्मरात् कृष्णाय श्लाघते-ह्नुते—तिष्ठते-शपते वा 'a cowherdess being incited by love flatters Kṛshṇa or apparently conceals her feeling from him or waits for him or swears before him;' (Vide Bhatti. VII. 73. 74.); but राजानं श्लाघते मन्त्री 'a minister praises his king.'

§ 822. § The creditor (or the person to whom something is

---

* यजेः कर्मणः करणसंज्ञा संप्रदानस्य च कर्मसंज्ञा । Vârt.

† रुच्यर्थानां प्रीयमाणः Pân. I. 4. 33.

‡ श्लाघह्नुङ्स्थाशपां ज्ञीप्स्यमानः । Pân. I. 4. 34.

§ धारेरुत्तमर्णः । स्पृहेरीप्सितः । Pân. I. 4. 35, 36.

due) in the case of the root धृ 'to owe;' and the person or the thing desired in the case of स्पृह्, are put in the Dative case; वृक्षसेचने द्वे धारयसि मे 'you owe me two sprinklings of trees' (Sa'k.); भक्ताय धारयति मोक्षं हरिः; (Sid. Kau.) तस्यै स्पृहयमाणोसौ 'he longing for her (Bhatti VIII. 15.);' पुष्पेभ्यः स्पृहयति 'he longs for flowers;' but पुष्पाणि स्पृहयति where no longing is implied.

§ 823. * The roots क्रुध्, द्रुह्, ईर्ष्य्, and असूय्, and others having the same sense govern the Dative of the person against whom the feeling of anger, hatred, &c. is directed; हरये क्रुध्यति द्रुह्यति-ईर्ष्यति-असूयति वा (Sid. Kau.) 'he is angry with Hari, or bears hatred towards him, or is jealous of him or finds fault with him;' सीतायै नाक्रुध्यन्नाप्यसूयत (Bhatt. VIII. 75.) 'he did neither get angry with Sîtâ nor find fault with her;' but भार्यामीर्ष्यति 'he keeps a jealous watch over his wife' (that others may not see her मैनामन्योऽद्राक्षीदिति Sid. Kau.)

(*a*) † But क्रुध् and द्रुह् preceded by a preposition govern the Accusative case; किं मां संक्रुध्यसि 'why do you get angry with me?' नित्यमस्मच्छरीरमाभिद्रोग्धुं यतते (Mud. I.) 'he always endeavours to do harm to my body.'

Obs:—द्रुह् with अभि is also found used with the Dat.; मयि पुनरेभ्य एवाभिद्रुग्धमज्ञेन (Utta. VII.).

§ 824. ‡ The roots राध् and ईक्ष् both meaning 'to detemine the good or bad fortune of' govern the Dative of the person with reference to whom the inquiry is made; कृष्णाय राध्यति ईक्षते वा । पृष्टो गर्गः शुभाशुभं पर्यालोचयतीत्यर्थः । Sid. Kau.

---

* क्रुधद्रुहेर्ष्यासूयार्थानां यं प्रति कोपः । Pân. I. 4. 37. क्रोधोऽमर्षः द्रोहोऽपकारः ईर्ष्याऽक्षमा असूया गुणेषु दोषाविष्करणं । द्रुहादयोपि कोपप्रभवा एव गृह्यन्ते । अतो विशेषणं सामान्येन । Sid. Kau.

† क्रुधद्रुहोरुपसृष्टयोः कर्म । Pân. I. 4. 38.

‡ राधीक्ष्योर्यस्य विप्रश्नः । Pân. I. 4. 39.

§ 825. * श्रु with प्रति and आ meaning 'to promise,' governs the Dative of the person to whom a promise is made after solicitation विप्राय गां प्रतिशृणोति आशृणोति वा। विप्रेण मह्यं देहीति प्रवर्तितः प्रतिजानीते इत्यर्थः। Sid. Kau.

§ 826. † The root क्री with परि 'to hire, as a servent,' &c., optionally governs the Dative (and optionally the Inst.) of the price at which he is hired शतेन शताय वा परिक्रीतः। Sid. Kau.

§827. ‡ (*a*) A noun expressive of the purpose for which anything is done, or the result to which anything leads or the effect for which anything exists, is put in the Dative case; मुक्तये हरिं भजति 'worships Hari for final beatitude;' भक्तिर्ज्ञानाय कल्पते सम्पद्यते जायते वा 'devotion leads to knowledge;' मूत्राय कल्पते जायते सम्पद्यते यवागूः (Mb.) 'water gruel tends to (produce) urine,' कुण्डलाय हिरण्यं (Mah. Bhâs.) 'gold for Kundala (a kind of ornament);' यूपाय दारु 'wood for a sacrificial post,' &c.

N. B. The roots भू or अस् are often omitted after a Dative used in this sense काव्यं यशसे (भवति), poetry is for fame.'

(*d*) § An evil foreboded by a portentous phenomenon is also put in the Dative case; वाताय कपिला विद्युत 'the tawny lightning forebodes a storm.'

(*c*) $ The word हित is used with the Dative; ब्राह्मणाय हितं 'good for a Brahmana.'

---

* प्रत्याङ्भ्यां श्रुवः पूर्वस्य कर्ता। Pân. 4. 40.

† परिक्रयणे संप्रदानमन्यतरस्याम्। Pân. 4. 44. नियतकालभृत्यास्वीकरणं परिक्रयणं। Sid. Kau.

‡ तादर्थ्ये चतुर्थी वाच्या। क्लृपि संपद्यमाने च। Vârtika.

§ उत्पातेन ज्ञापिते च। Vârt. वाताय कपिलाविद्युदातपायातिलोहिनी। पीता वर्षाय विज्ञेया दुर्भिक्षाय सिता भवेत्। Mah. Bhâs.

$ हितयोगे च। Vârt.

§ 828. * The object governed by an infinitive mood not actually used but implied, is put in the Dative; फलेभ्यो याति *i. e.* (फलानि आहर्तुं) 'goes for (in order to bring) fruits;' नृसिंहाय नमस्कुर्मः (*i. e.* नृसिंहमनुकूलयितुं) 'We bow down to Nrisimha (to propitiate him).'

(*a*) The Dative of an abstract noun formed from a root may be usd to express the sense of the infinitive of the same root; यागाय याति 'goes to perform a sacrifice;' त्यागाय संभृतार्थानां (Rag. 1. 7.) 'who had amassed wealth in order to give it away,' &c.

§ 829. † The particles नमः, स्वस्ति, स्वाहा and स्वधा (exclamations used in offering oblations to gods and manes respectively), अलं meaning 'equal to, a match for' and वषट् (an exclamation accompanying an oblation to a deity) govern the Dative case; तस्मै नमः शंभवे 'bow to that Śambhu;' प्रजाभ्यः स्वस्ति 'may it be well with the subjects;' स्वस्त्यस्तु ते (Rag. V. 17.) 'Farewell to thee;' अग्नये स्वाहा 'this offering to Agni;' similarly पितृभ्यः स्वधा; दैत्येभ्यो हरिः अलं 'Hari is a match for the demons;' so अलं मल्लो मल्लाय (Mah. Bhâs.) 'one wrestler is a match for another; (see Rag. II. 39. Bhatti. VIII. 98.); इंद्राय वषट् 'this oblation to Indra.'

(*a*) But when कृ is used with नमः, it becomes the principal verb ‡ and therefore governs the Accusative case;' नमस्करोति देवान् 'bows down to gods' (when the sense of an infinitive is suppressed, of course the Dative will be used; see § 828).

(*b*) Words having the sense of अलं, such as प्रभुः, समर्थः, शक्तः, &c. and also the verb प्रभू, are used with the Dative (Sid. Kau.) दैत्येभ्यो हरिः प्रभुः समर्थः शक्तो वा; प्रभुः—समर्थः—शक्तः मल्लो मल्लाय; प्रभवति मल्लो मल्लाय; विधिरपि न येभ्यः प्रभवति (Bhar. II. 94.); प्रभु and the other words may also be used with the Genitive (Sid. Kau.)

---

* क्रियार्थोपपदस्य च कर्मणि स्थानिनः । तुमर्थाच्च भाववचनात् । Pâṇ. II. 3. 14, 15.

† नमः स्वस्तिस्वाहास्वधालंवषड्योगाच्च । Pâṇ. II. 3. 16.

‡ उपपदविभक्तेः कारकविभक्तिर्बलीयसी । Vârt.

प्रभवति निजस्य कन्यकाजनस्य महाराजः (Mâl. Mâd. IV.) the great king has power over his daughter.

(*c*) Verbs meaning 'to salute' such as प्रणम्, प्रणपत्, &c. may govern the Dative or the Accusative; न प्रणमन्ति देवताभ्यः (Kâd.) they do not bow down to deities; तां भक्तिप्रवणेन चेतसा प्रणनाम saluted her with a mind bowed down with devotion; प्रणिपत्य सुरास्तस्मै शमयित्रे सुरद्विषां (Rag. X. 15.) the gods bowed respectfully to him, the annihilator of the enemies of the immortals: वागीशं (वाग्भिरर्थ्याभिः) प्रणिपत्य (Kum. II. 3.) having bowed to the lord of speech &c.

§ 830. With verbs of telling such as कथ्, ख्या, शंस्, चक्ष्, निविद् cau. &c. and of sending such as हि with प्र, सृज् with वि, &c. the Dative of the indirect object is used; रामाभिष्वसनदर्शनोत्सुकं मैथिलाय कथयांबभूव सः । (Rag. XI. 37.); He told the king of Mithilâ that Râma was eager to see the bow; आख्याहि मे को भवानुग्ररूपः (Bhag. XI. 31.) Tell me, who thou art in this fierce form, &c., उपस्थितां होमवेलां गुरवे निवेदयामि (S'ak. IV.) I will tell my preceptor that it is time to offer the morning oblations; हरिरस्मै सुरांगनां प्रजिघाय (Rag. VIII. 79.) Indra sent a heavenly damsel against him (*i. e.* to disturb his contemplations); रक्षस्तस्मै महोपलं प्राजिघाय (Rag. XV. 21.).

§ 831. *The indirect object of the root मन् cl. 4. 'to think' if not an animal, may be put in the Accusative or the Dative case when contempt is to be shown; न त्वां तृणं मन्ये तृणाय वा I do not consider thee a straw; but न त्वां तृणं मन्वे (मन् cl.; 8) when mere comparison is meant, the Accusative is used; त्वां तृणं मन्ये (Mb.)

---

* मन्यकर्मण्यनादरे विभाषाऽप्राणिषु । Pâṇ. II. 3. 17. On अप्राणिषु Kâtyâyana remarks 'अप्राणिषु इत्यपनीय नौकाकान्नशुकशृगालवर्ज्येष्विति वाच्यम्' *i. e.* "Instead of 'If not an animal' it should be said, 'If not one of a ship, or food or a crow or a parrot or a jackal," न त्वां मन्ये नावं अन्नं वा, न त्वां शुने श्वानं वा मन्ये; in the former case though neither नौ nor अन्न is an animal, the Accusative ought to be used, in the latter though श्वन् is an animal the Dative may be optionally used.

§ 832. * The object of roots implying motion (*i. e.* the place to which the motion is directed), if it be not a road, is put in the Accusative or the Dative, when actual motion is meant; ग्रामं ग्रामाय वा गच्छति 'goes to a village;' but मनसा हरिं व्रजति, पन्थानं गच्छति.

THE ABLATIVE CASE.

§ 833. The principal sense of the Ablative case is अपादान or 'motion away from †;' hence the noun from which the motion, real or conceived, takes place is put in the Ablative case; ग्रामादायाति 'comes from a village;' धावतोऽश्वात्पतति 'falls down from a running horse'; सदाचारात् भ्रंशते.

(*a*) ‡ Words having the sense of जुगुप्सा, विराम or 'cessation,' 'pause,' and प्रमाद 'swerving from,' also govern the Ablative case; पापात् जुगुप्सते 'he hates sin;' न नवः प्रभुराफलोदयात्स्थिरकर्मा विरराम कर्मणः (Rag. VIII. 22.) the new monarch, steady in action, did not desist from efforts until they bore their fruit'; धर्मात्प्रमाद्यति 'swerves from duty'; स्वाधिकारात्प्रमत्तः (Meg. I.) 'careless, failing in the discharge of the duties (of his office)'; so धर्मान्मुह्यति; प्रसमीक्ष्य निवर्तेत सर्वमांसस्य भक्षणात् (Manu Smr. V. 49.), &c.

मद् with प्र in the sense of 'to be careless about' is used with the Loc. also; अतोऽर्थान्न प्रमाद्यन्ति प्रमदासु विपश्चितः । (Manu Smr. II. 213) on this account wise men are not careless about their wives.

§ 834. § In the case of words expressing fear or protection from fear, that from which or whom the fear proceeds is put in the Ablative case; चोराद्बिभेति is afraid of a thief; भीतो रणे श्वेतवाहात् I was afraid of the white-horsed one *i. e.* Arjuna; स्वल्पमप्यस्य धर्मस्य त्रायते महतो भयात् (Bhag. II. 40) even a little

---

* गत्यर्थकर्मणि द्वितीयाचतुर्थ्यौ चेष्टायामनध्वनि । Pân. II. 3. 12.

† अपादाने पञ्चमी । Pân II. 3. 28 ध्रुवमपायेऽपादानम् Pân. I. 4. 24.

‡ जुगुप्साविरामप्रमादार्थानामुपसंख्यानम् । Vârt.

§ भीत्रार्थानां भयहेतुः Pân. I. 4. 25.

of this (kind of) piety saves one from great fear; कपेरत्रासिषुर्नादात् (Bhaṭṭ IX. 11.) were afraid of the roar of the monkey.

(*a*) * That from which one is kept off is also put in the Ablative; पापान्निवारयति wards off from sin; यवेभ्यो गां वारयति keeps off the cow from barley.

§ 835. † In the case of जि with परा the thing unbearable is put in the Ablative case; अध्ययनात्पराजयते finds study unbearable or difficult; तां पराजयमानां स प्रीतेः (Bhaṭṭi. VIII. 71.) who got disgusted with the love (of Râvaṇa); but शत्रून् पराजयते ।

§ 836. ‡ When concealment is to be had recourse to, that whose sight one desires to avoid is put in the Ablative case; मातुर्निलीयते कृष्णः 'Kṛishṇa conceals himself from his mother; but चोरान्न दिदृक्षते.

§ 837. (*a*) § The teacher from whom something is learnt regularly is put in the Ablative case; उपाध्यायादधीते learns from the preceptor; but नटस्य गाथां शृणोति.

(*b*) Similarly the prime or original cause in the case of जन् to be born, and the source in the case of भू are put in the Ablative; ब्रह्मणः प्रजाः प्रजायन्ते the creation proceeds from Brahman; गोमयाद्वृश्चिको जायते the scorpion is born from cowdung; हिमवतो गङ्गा प्रभवति The Ganges rises from the Himalayas; कामात्क्रोधोऽभिजायते from desire anger is produced.

Note:—Verbs meaning 'to be born' or 'to be begotten upon' are often used with the Loc.; तस्यां शतानन्द आङ्गिरसोऽजायत from her was born Śatananda Âṅgirasa; मेनकायामुत्पन्नां begotten upon Menakâ; See Manu Smṛ. 154. I. 9.

---

* वारणार्थानामीप्सितः । Pân. I. 4. 27.

† पराजेरसोढः । Pân. I. 4. 26.

‡ अन्तर्धौ येनादर्शनमिच्छति । Pân. I. 4. 28.

§ आख्यातोपयोगे । Pân. I. 4. 29 जनिकर्तुः प्रकृतिः । भुवः प्रभवः । Pân. I. 4. 30. 31.

§ 838. *When the sense of an indeclinable participle is suppressed in a sentence the object governed by that ptc. or the place at or on which the action takes place is put in the Ablative case; प्रासादात् प्रेक्षते sees from a palace (प्रासादमारुह्य प्रेक्षते Sid. Kau.); similarly आसनात् प्रेक्षते=आसने उपविश्य प्रेक्षते; श्वशुराज्जिह्रेति=श्वशुरं वीक्ष्य जिह्रेति, Sid. Kau.

§ 839. (*a*) † The place or time from which the distance of another place or point of time is to be expressed is put in the Ablative case; the distance in space being put in the Nominative or the Locative and that in time in the Locative; वनात् ग्रामो योजनं योजने वा (Sid. Kau.) the village is a *yojana* from the forest; गवीधुमतः सांकाश्यं चत्वारि योजनानि चतुर्षु योजनेषु वा (Mb.); कार्त्तिक्या आग्रहायणी मासे (Sid. Kau.) the full moonday of Mârgaśîrsha is a month (at the interval of a month) from that of Kârtika समुद्रात्परी क्रोशौ.

(*b*) The Ablative is also used in questions and answers; कस्मात् त्वं । नद्याः whence art thou ? from the river; कुतो भवान् । पाटलिपुत्रात् where do you come from ? Pâtaliputra.

§ 840. ‡The words अन्य, इतर and others having a similar sense, the particles आरात् 'near or distant,' ऋते 'without,' words expressive of direction used with reference to time or space (except when they refer to the limbs of the boby) and those derived from the root अञ्च् at the end of compounds, and indeclinables ending in ओ and आहि are constructed with the Ablative; अन्यो भिन्न इतरो वा कृष्णात् different from Krishna; इतरो रावणादेष राघवानुचरो यदि Bhṭṭi. VII. 106. If he be one other than Râvaṇa and a follower of Râma; आराद्वनात् near or away from the forest; ऋते क्रौर्यात्समायातः (Bhaṭṭi. VII. 105) come without (setting aside) his cruelty; ग्रामात्पूर्वा उत्तरो वा to the

---

* ल्यब्लोपे कर्मण्यधिकरणे च । Vârt.

† यतश्चाध्वकालनिर्माणं तत्र पञ्चमी । तद्युक्तादध्वनः प्रथमासप्तम्यौ । कालात्सप्तमी च वक्तव्या । प्रश्नाख्यानयोश्च । Vârtikas.

‡ अन्यारादितरर्तेदिक्शब्दाञ्चूत्तरपदाजाहियुक्ते । Pân. II. 3. 29.

east or the north of the village; चैत्रात्पूर्वः फाल्गुनः the month of Fâlguna is prior to that of Chaitra; but पूर्वं कायस्य the (forepart) of the body; प्राक् प्रत्यग् वा ग्रामात् to the east or to the west of the village; प्राक्प्रभातात् (Bhaṭṭi. VII. 106) before the day dawned; दक्षिणा दक्षिणाहि वा ग्रामम् to the south or in the southern direction of the village; उत्तरा समुद्रात् (Bhaṭṭi.) in the north of the sea.

Obs:—ऋते is sometimes used with the Accusative; ऋतेपि त्वां न भविष्यन्ति सर्वे (Bhag. XI. 32) even without thee all will die.

(*a*) Words like प्रभृति, आरभ्य, बहिः, अनन्तरं, ऊर्ध्वं, परं &c. are used with the Ablative; the first word may also be used with adverbs of time; तस्माद्दिनात्प्रभृति from that day; ततः-तदा-प्रभृति since then; अद्यप्रभृत्यवनताङ्गि तवास्मि दासः (Kum. V. 86); ततः, तस्मा; द्दिनादारभ्य, मालत्याः प्रथमावलोकदिवसादारभ्य; ग्रामाद्बहिः outside the village; पुरगारुत्मतगोपुराद्बहिः (निरगात्) went out of the emerald gate of the town; ऊर्ध्वं संवत्सरात् (M. S. IX. 77) after a year. अत ऊर्ध्वं hence forward; वर्त्मनः परं (Rag. I. 17) beyond the path; भाग्यायत्तमतः परं; पुराणपत्रापगमादनन्तरं (Rag. III. 70.) after the dropping of old leaves; see Bhag. XII. 12.

§ 841. * The ablative is used with—

(*a*) The prepositions अप and परि meaning 'away from, without' and आ meaning 'as far as' or 'including, comprehending'; यत्संप्रत्यप लोकेभ्यो लंकायां वसतिर्भयात् (Râm.) now that he dwelt in Lankâ, in terror, away from the worlds; अप हरेः संसारः *Samsâra* exists outside Hari; अप त्रिगर्तेभ्यो वृष्टो देवः it rained everywhere, except in the country of Trigarta. Similarly परि हरेः संसारः परि त्रिगर्तेभ्यो वृष्टो देवः (Vop.) &c. आमुक्तेः संसार, आसकलाद् ब्रह्म Brahman pervades every thing; आ परितोषाद् विदुषां; until the learned are satisfied.

---

* अपपरी वर्जने । आङ्मर्यादावचने । Pân. I. 4. 88-89. पञ्चम्यपाङ्परिभिः Pân. II. 3. 10 प्रतिः प्रतिनिधिप्रतिदानयोः । Pân I. 4. 92. प्रतिनिधिप्रतिदाने च यस्मात् । Pân. II. 3. 11.

(*b*) प्रति meaning 'the representative of, in exchange for or giving in return for;' प्रद्युम्नः कृष्णात्प्रति (Sid. Kau.) Pradyumna is the representative of Krishṇa; तिलेभ्यः प्रतियच्छति माषान् gives mâshas in return for sesamum.

§ 842. * When a word expressive of 'a debt,' is merely intended to be stated as a cause, it is put in the Ablative case; शताद्बद्धं द्रव्यं a thing mortgaged for a hundred rupees; ऋणाद्बद्धं इव tied down as it were by the debt he owes.

§ 843. (*a*) The Ablative often denotes the cause of an action or condition and may be translated by 'on account of, by reason of,' &c.; मौनान्मूर्खः गण्यते one is considered a fool by reason of his silence (if he keeps silence); गोमानुषाणां वधात् (H.) on account of my killing cows and men.

(*b*) The Ablative is used to make a causative assertion or to advance an argument; पर्वतो वह्निमान् धूमात् । The mountain is fiery (has fire on it), because there is smoke; स्मृत्यनवकाशदोषप्रसङ्ग इति चेन्नान्यस्मृत्यनवकाशदोषप्रसंगात् (Ved. Su. II. 1. 1) A disputant says—if you say that our argument is liable to the fault of giving no scope to your smṛitis then we reply: this your argument will not hold; for in that case other smṛitis will have no scope given to them.

(*c*) The Ablative is used with comparatives or words having a comparative sense; भक्तिमार्गात् ज्ञानमार्गः श्रेयान् the way of knowledge is more efficient than that of devotion; अणोरप्यणीयान् smaller than an atom; अश्वमेधसहस्रेभ्यः सत्यमेवातिरिच्यते truth alone is superior to a thousand horse-sacrifices; चैत्ररथादनूने not inferior to Chaitraratha.

§ 844. † The indeclinables पृथक्, विना and नाना govern the Ablative, the Accusative and the Instrumental cases; पृथक् रामात्-रामं-रामेण वा different from or without Râma; so नाना रामं,

---

* अकर्तर्यृणे पञ्चमी । Pân. II. 4. 25.

† पृथग्विनानानाभिस्तृतीयान्यतरस्याम् । Pân. II. 3. 32.

&c. नाना नारीं निष्फला लोकयात्रा (Vop.) worldly life is vain without a woman (wife)

§ 845. * The words स्तोक 'a little.' अल्प 'a little,' कृच्छ्र 'difficulty,' and कतिपय 'some' when used in an adverbial sense with verbs, are used in the Ablative or the Instrumental; स्तोकेन स्तोकाद्वा मुक्तः let off with little; similarly अल्पेन अल्पान्मुक्तः, कृच्छ्रेण कृच्छ्राद्वा कृतः done with difficulty; कतिपयेन कतिपयाद्वा प्राप्तः, but स्तोकेन विषेण हतः killed with a little poison; when used adverbially they take the Accusative also; स्तोकं गच्छति goes a little.

(*n*) दूर and अन्तिक and others having the same sense, are used in the Ablative, the Accusative and the Instrumental cases; ग्रामस्य दूरात् दूरं दूरेण वा away from the village; so अन्तिकात् अन्तिकं अन्तिकेन वा near the village.

THE GENITIVE CASE.

§ 846. † The Genitive, as already remarked, is not a Kâraka case. It, therefore, expresses simply the relation of one noun to another in a sentence, such as that of a servant and his master (a relation which is other than that expressed by a Kâraka case); राज्ञः पुरुषः, पुत्रस्य माता, द्रव्यस्य गुणः &c.; and even in those cases where the genitive is used in the sense of other cases it expresses simple relation or सम्बन्ध only, as in सतां गतम्; सर्पिषो जानीते; मातुः स्मरति; एध उदकस्य उपकुरुते; भजे शंभोश्चरणयोः; फलानां तृप्तः, &c.

§ 847. ‡ When the word हेतु (cause, object) is used in a sentence, that which is the object and the word हेतु are put in the

---

* करणे च स्तोकाल्पकृच्छ्रकतिपयस्यासत्ववचनस्य । दूरान्तिकार्थेभ्यो द्वितीया च । Pân. II. 3. 33. 35.

† षष्ठी शेषे Pân. II. 3. 50. कारकप्रातिपदिकार्थ (the sense of the Nominative)—व्यतिरिक्तः स्वस्वामिभावादिसम्बन्धः शेषः तत्र षष्ठी स्यात् । कर्मादीनामपि सम्बन्धविवक्षायां षष्ठ्येव । Sid. Kau.

‡ षष्ठी हेतुप्रयोगे । Pân. II. 3. 27.

Genitive case; अन्नस्य हेतोर्वसति dwells for the sake of (with the object of getting) food; रोदिषि कस्य हेतोः Mark P. 23. 12. हेतोर्बोधस्य मैथिल्याः प्रास्तावीद्रामसंकथाम् (Bhaṭṭi. VIII. 103.) he began to give her an account of Râma in order to show her that he (Hanumat) was Râma's messenger.

(*a*) * When a pronoun is used with the word हेतु, the Instrumental and the Genitive may both be used; कस्य हेतोः, केन हेतुना, with what object? Why? The Ablative may also be used; तेन हेतुना, तस्माद्धेतोः, तस्य हेतोः; when a word having the same sense as हेतु, such as निमित्त, कारण, &c., is used with a pronoun it may be used in any case in agreement with the pronoun; कस्य निमित्तस्य, कस्य प्रयोजनस्य; केन निमित्तेन, कस्मै निमित्ताय &c.; but they are generally used in the Accusative used like an adverb; किं-निमित्तं-कारणं-प्रयोजनं-अर्थं, &c. when a pronoun is not used, any case except the Nominative and the Accusative may be used; ज्ञानेन निमित्तेन (हरिः सेव्यः), ज्ञानाय निमित्ताय with the object of acquiring knowledge.

§ 848. † Words ending in the termination तस् and showing direction and others having the same sense, such as उपरि, उपरिष्टात्, अधः, अधस्तात्, पुरः, पुरस्तात्, पश्चात्, अग्रे, &c. are used with the Genitive; ग्रामस्य दक्षिणतः उत्तरतः &c. to the south or to the north of the village, &c.; अर्कस्योपरि (S'ak. II. 8.) on the Arka plant; तरूणामधः (S'ak. I.) under the trees; तस्य स्थित्वा कथमपि पुरः (Meg.) standing before him with great difficulty, &c.

(*a*) ‡ Words ending in एन such as दक्षिणेन, उत्तरेण, &c. are used with the Genitive or the Accusative; दक्षिणेन ग्रामं ग्रामस्य वा to the south of the village; उत्तरेण स्रवन्तीं (Mâl. Mâd. IX. 24.) to the north of the river; दण्डकान्दक्षिणेनाहं (Bhaṭṭi. VIII.108.); धनपतिगृहादुत्तरेण (Meg. 80) to the north of Kubera's palace.

§ 849. + The words दूर and अन्तिक and their synonyms

---

* सर्वनाम्नस्तृतीया च । निमित्तपर्यायप्रयोगे सर्वासां प्रायदर्शनम् । Vârt.

† षष्ठ्यतसर्थप्रत्ययेन Pân. II. 3. 30.

‡ एनपा द्वितीया । Pân. II.3.31. एनपेति योगविभागात्षष्ठ्यपि । Sid. Kau.

\+ दूरान्तिकार्थैः षष्ठ्यन्यतरस्याम् । Pân. II. 3. 34.

govern either the Genitive or the Ablative; ग्रामात् ग्रामस्य वा वनं दूरं—निकटं-समीपं वा the forest is distant form or near the village; रामाद्दूरस्य यो दूरं पापाद्दुःखस्य सोन्तिकं he who is away from Râma or S'iva is near sin; प्रत्यासन्नो माधवीमण्डपस्य close to the bower of the Mâdhavi creeper; तस्य सकाशं, &c.

§ 850. * The root ज्ञा meaning 'to have an incorrect knowledge of' governs the Genitive; तैलं सर्पिषो जानीते supposes oil to be ghee; but सर्पिर्जानीते.

(*a*) Verbs implying 'to think of, to remember,' such as स्मृ, इ with अधि, 'to be master of,' such as ईश्, भू with प्र, &c. and to have compassion on such as दय् &c., govern the genitive of their object; कच्चिद्भर्तुः स्मरसि (Meg. 90) dost thou remember the lord? स्मरन् राघवबाणानां विव्यथे राक्षसेश्वरः Râm. VI. 60. 3 अध्येति तव लक्ष्मणः (Bhaṭṭi VIII. 119.) Lakshmaṇa remembers thee; प्रभवति निजस्य कन्यकाजनस्य महाराजः (Mâl. Mâd. 4.) the great king has mastery over his daughter; यदि तं प्रेक्षमाणा आत्मनः प्रभविष्यामि (Uttar.) if after I see him I shall have control overmyself; गात्राणां अनीशोऽस्मि संवृत्तः (S'ak. II.) I have lost all power over my limbs; कथंचिदीशा मनसां बभूवुः (Kum. III. 34.) with great difficulty they could control their minds; शौवस्तिकत्वं विभवा न येषां व्रजन्ति तेषां दयसे न कस्मात् (Bhaṭṭ. II. 33.) why dost thou feel no compassion for those whose wealth does not see the morrow? रामस्य दयमानः (Ibid. VIII 119) taking pity on Râmâ.

(*b*) कृ meaning 'to impart additional properties' governs the Genitive; एधोदकस्य उपस्कुरुते 'fuel imparts heat to water.' मा कस्यचिदुपस्कृथाः Bhaṭṭi. VIII. 119.

§ 851. † Verbs meaning 'to be afflicted with a disease'

---

* ज्ञोऽविदर्थस्य करणे। अधिगर्थदयेशां कर्मणि। कृञः प्रतियत्ने। Pân. II. 3. 51-53.

† रुजार्थानां भाववचनानामज्वरेः। Pân. II. 3. 54. अज्वरिसंताप्योरिति वाच्यम्; Vârt.

govern the Genitive of their object when used impersonally or when they have for their subject names of diseases; चौरस्य ज्वरस्य रुजा the thief is afflicted with the pain of fever; पुरुषस्य रुजयत्यतिसारः dysentery inflicts pain on the man; except when ज्वर and संताप are used as subjects; (vide Bhaṭṭi. VIII. 120;) तं रुजयति ज्वरः or संतापः fever or affliction pains him.

§ 852. * नाथ् meaning 'to wish' governs the Genitive when the idea of a benediction is implied; धृत्या नाथस्व wish to have patience; धनस्य नाथते desires to have wealth. So सर्पिषः नाथनम्.

§ 853. † The roots जस्, हन् with नि or प्र or with both, नट्, क्रथ् and पिष् govern the Genitive when meaning to injure, to punish, &c.; चौरस्योज्जासयति राजा a king punishes a thief; निजौजसोज्जासयितुं जगद्द्रुहां (Sis. I. 37.) to kill the enemies of the world (the demons) by his own power; मन्योरुज्जासयात्मनः kill (drive away) your anger; राक्षसानां निहनिष्यति or प्रहणिष्यति or निप्रहणिष्यति or प्रणिहनिष्यति रामः Râma will kill the R'akshasas; वृषलस्य—उन्नाटयति—क्राथयति does injury to a Vṛishala; साहसिकस्य पिनष्टि गजः &c; in other senses they govern the Accusative; धानाः पिनष्टि he grinds fried rice.

§ 854. ‡ The roots व्यवहृ (*i. e.* हृ with वि and अव), पण् and दिव् when they all mean to transact business, or to stake in gambling, govern the Genitive of their object; शतस्य व्यवहरति invests a hundred rupees in business; प्राणानामपणिष्टासौ he staked his life; अदेवीत् बंधुभोगानां lost his brothers and pleasures in gambling, &c.; but when दिव् is preceded by a preposition, the Accusative may also be used; शतस्य शतं वा प्रतिदीव्यति (Sid. Kau.)

§ 855. ¶ Words having the senses of कृत्वः *i. e.* denoting fre-

* आशिषि नाथः Pân. II. 3. 55.

† जासिनिप्रहणनाटक्राथपिषां हिंसायाम् । Pân II. 3. 56.

‡ व्यवहृपणोः समर्थयोः । दिवस्तदर्थस्य । विभाषोपसर्गे । Pân. II.3.57-59.

¶ कृत्वोर्थप्रयोगे कालेऽधिकरणे । Pân. II. 3. 64.

quency of time, such as द्विः, त्रिः, पञ्चकृत्वः &c. govern the Genitive of the time in the sense of the Locative; पञ्चकृत्वोऽह्नो भोजनम् taking food five times a day; द्विरह्नो भुक्तिः, &c.

§ 856. * The Genitive is used subjectively and objectively with Kṛidantas or Primary Nominal Bases derived by means of the Kṛit affixes (*i. e.* is used in the sense of the subject or the object of the action denoted by the Kridantas); कृष्णस्य कृतिः an act of Krishṇa *i. e.* of which Kṛishṇa is the agent; जगतः कर्ता the Creator of the world, which is the object of the action denoted by the noun कर्तृ; similarly सतां पालकः the protector of the good; पयसः पानं the drinking of milk; तस्य कवेः क्रिया a work of that poet; साधारणी सृष्टिरियं न धातुः (Rāmacharita XII. 117.). This is not a common creation of Brahman.

(*a*) † In the case of verbs governing two Accusatives the secondary object of the Kṛidanta may be put in the Genitive or in the Accusative; नेताश्वस्य स्रुघ्नं स्रुघ्नस्य वा (Sid. Kau.) the taker of the horse to Srughna.

(*b*) ‡ When the agent and the object of the bases derived by means of Kṛit affixes are used in a sentence, the object is put in the Genitive case and not the agent; आश्चर्यो गवां दोहोऽगोपेन the milking of cows by one who is not a cowherd is a wonder.

Exceptions.—This rule does not apply to Kṛit nouns ending in the affixes अक and अ when *feminine*; बिभित्सा भेदिका वा रुद्रस्य जगतः (Siḍ. Kau.) the desire of Rudra to split the universe or the splitting of the universe by Rudra. According to some when the Kṛit affixes are of *feminine* gender, and according to others

---

* कर्तृकर्मणोः कृति । Pân. II. 3. 65.

† गुणकर्मणि वेष्यते । Vârt.

‡ उभयप्राप्तौ कर्मणि । Pân. II. 3. 66. स्त्रीप्रत्यययोरकाकारयोर्नायं नियमः । शेषे विभाषा । Vârt. स्त्रीप्रत्यय इत्येके । केचिदविशेषेण विभाषामिच्छन्ति । Sid. Kau.

when they are of any gender, and the agent and the object are both used, the agent is put in the Instrumental or Genitive case; विचित्रा जगतः कृतिः हरेर्हरिणा वा wonderful is the creation of the world by Hari; शब्दानामनुशासनमाचार्येणाचार्यस्य वा (Sid. Kau.); शोभना खलु पाणिनेः (पाणिनिना वा) सूत्रस्य कृतिः। (Mb.).

§ 857. * When past passive participles are used in the sense of the present tense the Genitive is used; राज्ञां मतो बुद्धः पूजितो वा respected, known or honoured by kings; यो धर्मः स सतां मतः; रामस्य संमतं Bhaṭṭi. VIII. 124.

(a) Past participles showing the place of an action, as well as those used as abstract nouns are used with the Genitive मुकुन्दस्यासितमिदमिदं यातं रमापतेः। भुक्तमेतदनंतस्येत्यूचुर्गोप्यो दिदृक्षवः॥ मयूरस्य नृत्तं, कोकिलस्य व्याहृतं, नटस्य भुक्तं, छात्रस्य हसितं, &c. (Mb.) See. Bhaṭṭ. VIII. 125.

§ 858. † The Genitive is not used with present participles except that of द्विष्, verbal derivatives ending in उ and उक except that derived from कम्, verbal indeclinables, past participles, passive and active, nouns formed with the affix खल् (see p. 456) and with such as mean 'in the habit of, or having the properties of or doing any thing well'; कर्म कुर्वन् or कुर्वाणः; but मुरं मुरस्य वा द्विषन् हरिः Hari, the enemy of Mura; हरिं दिदृक्षुः desirous of seeing Hari; हरिं अलङ्करिष्णुः, दैत्यान् घातुको हरिः Hari is the killer of demons; लक्ष्म्याः कामुकः, जगत्सृष्ट्वा, सुखं कर्तुं &c. विष्णुना हता दैत्याः, दैत्यान् हतवान्; ईषत्करः प्रपंचो हरिणा worldly life goes easy with Hari; आत्मानं अलङ्करिष्णुः in habit of decorating oneself; अन्नं भिक्षुः a habitual beggar; कर्ता कटं one who prepares a mat; ‡ also in the case of nouns derived by means of the terminations

---

* क्तस्य च वर्तमाने। अधिकरणवाचिनश्च। Pân. II. 67–68.

† न लोकाव्ययनिष्ठाखलर्थतृनाम्। Pân. II. 3. 69. कमेरनिषेधः Vârt.

‡ अकेनोर्भविष्यदाधमर्ण्ययोः। Pân. II. 3. 70.

अक showing futurity and इन् showing necessary payment; हरिं दर्शको याति he goes desiring to see Hari; शतं दायी one who has to pay a hundred (rupees.).

§ 859. * In the case of Potential passive participles the agent of the action is put in the Genitive or in the Instrumental case; मया मम वा सेव्यो हरिः Hari ought to be served by me; राक्षसेन्द्रस्य संरक्ष्यं मया लव्यमिदं वनं (Bhaṭṭi. VIII. 129.) this forest which the lord of the demons ought to preserve must be destroyed by me; गन्तव्या ते वसतिरलका &c. (Meg.) Thou should go to Alakâ

§ 860. † In the case of words denoting equality or likeness, such as तुल्य, सदृश, &c., the person or thing with whom or which any object is compared is put in the Genitive case, except in the case of तुला and उपमा; तुल्यः सदृशः समो वा कृष्णस्य कृष्णेन वा equal to or like Krishṇa; कोन्योस्ति सदृशो मम who else is equal to me? but कृष्णस्य तुला उपमा वा नास्ति (Sid. Kau.).

Obs.—The words तुला and उपमा, however, are found used by good anthers with the Insrtumental against Pâṇini's rule; तुलां यदारोहति दन्तवाससा (Kum. V. 34.) which rises to the high position of being compared with your lip; स्फुटोपमं भूतिसितेन शंभुना (Sis. I. 4.) clearly deserving to be compared with S'ambhu white with ashes; see Rag. VIII. 15.

§ 861. ‡ The words आयुष्यं, मद्रं, भद्रं, कुशलं, सुखं, अर्थः and हितं and words having the same sense, when used in a sentence containing a benediction, govern the Dative or the Genitive case; आयुष्यं चिरंजीवितं कृष्णाय कृष्णस्य वा भूयात् (Sid. Kau.); may Krishṇa live long; similarly मद्रं, भद्रं, कुशलं, निरामयं, सुखं, शं, अर्थः, प्रयोजनं, हितं, पथ्यं वा भूयात् (Sid. Kau.).

* कृत्यानां कर्तरि वा । Pân. II. 3. 71.

† तुल्यार्थैरतुलोपमाभ्यां तृतीयान्यतरस्याम् । Pân. II. 3. 72.

‡ चतुर्थी चाशिष्यायुष्यमद्रभद्रकुशलसुखार्थहितैः । Pân. II. 3. 73.

§ 862. The Genitive is used with indeclinables like मध्ये, पारे, कृते, &c.; गङ्गाया मध्ये पारे वा in the middle or on the other side of the Ganges; अमीषां प्राणानां कृते for the sake of this life.

§ 863. With superlatives, and words having the sense of the superlative, the Genitive is used; नृणां ब्राह्मणः श्रेष्ठः; अग्रणीर्मन्त्रकृतामृषीणाम् (Rag. V. 4.) the chief of sages, the authors to the *Mantras*.

Note:—Words having the sense of comparatives are used with the Ablative and sometimes with the Instrumental; अयमस्माद् बलेन हीनः or अधिकः this person is superior or inferior to him in strength; similarly देवदत्तो यज्ञदत्तात्पटु: मूर्खो वा; को नु स्वन्ततरो मया who will have a happier end than I? The word अधिक is used with the Genitive, the Locative or the Instrumental; सुतेर्हि तासामधिकोऽपि सोऽभवत् he was more (*i. e.* dearer) to them than their sons; तेषामभ्यधिका मासाः पञ्च च द्वादश क्षपाः they passed five months and twelve nights more than (those years); कुडवेऽधिकः प्रस्थः *A Prastha* is larger than a *Kudavá*.

THE LOCATIVE CASE.

§ 864. * The place where an action takes place with reference to the subject or object is called Adhikaraṇa (अधिकरण) and is put in the Locative case; † स्वपिति गिरिगर्भे (Bham. 1. 60); वासो नन्दनकानने (*Ibid* 64); स्थाल्यां ओदनं पचति cooks food in a cooking utensil; कर्णे कथयति tells (something) into the ear; मोक्षे इच्छा अस्ति, &c. The Locative also denotes the time when an action takes place; तस्मिन् विप्रकृताः काले दिवौकसः (Kum. II. 1.) the gods being harassed at that time; दिनान्ते निलयाय गन्तुं (Rag. II. 15.)

(*a*) ‡ Verbal derivatives in इन् and having the sense of the p. p. participle govern the Locative of their object; अधीती

* आधारोऽधिकरणम् । † सप्तम्यधिकरणे च । Pan. 1. 4. 45, II. 3. 36.
‡ क्तस्येन्विषयस्य कर्मण्युपसंख्यानम् । साध्वसाधुप्रयोगे च । Vartikas.

व्याकरणे one by whom grammar is studied; गृहीती षट्स्वङ्गेषु by whom the six *Angas* were mastered, &c.

The words साधु and असाधु govern the Locative of that with reference to which they are used; साधुः कृष्णो मातरि well behaved towards his mother; असाधुर्मातुले ill-behaved towards his maternal uncle.

(*b*) * The object or purpose for which any thing is done is put in the Locative case when the thing desired is intimately connected with that on which the action takes place; चर्मणि द्वीपिनं हन्ति दन्तयोर्हन्ति कुञ्जरम् । केशेषु चमरीं हन्ति सीम्नि पुष्कलको हतः ॥ (Mb). (Man) kills the tiger for his skin, the elephant for his tusks, the *Chamary* deer for her hair and the musk-deer for his musk. If there is no intimate union the Dative is used.

Obs.—Sometimes the Instrumental is used to denote the object for which any thing is done; वेतनेन (for wages) धान्यं लुनाति. Sometimes the Loc. is used to denote the object in general; यथा सृष्टोसि धात्रा कर्मसु तत्कुरु since you are created by the creator to do duty, fulfil it.

§ 865. † The Locative or the Genitive is used with the words स्वामी a master, ईश्वर, अधिपति a lord, दायाद a heir, साक्षिन्, प्रतिभू a bail, and प्रसूत born for; गवां गोषु वा स्वामी the master of kine; पृथिव्याः or पृथिव्यां ईश्वरः the lord of the earth; ग्रामाणां or ग्रामेषु आधिपतिः the lord of villages, similarly पित्रंशस्य पित्रंशे वा दायादः, व्यवहारे व्यवहारस्य वा साक्षी, दर्शने दर्शनस्य वा प्रतिभूः (surety for appearance in a court); गोषु गवां वा प्रसूतः गोपः a cowherd is born for cows.

§ 866. ‡ The words आयुक्त and कुशल meaning 'appointed

---

* निमित्तात्कर्मयोगे । Vârt. निमित्तमिह फलम् । योगः संयोगः समवायात्मकः । Sid. Kau. समवायः नित्यसंबन्धः (constant, inseparable union). Tark. Kau.

† स्वामीश्वराधिपतिदायादसाक्षिप्रतिभूप्रसूतैश्च । Pan. II. 3. 39.

‡ आयुक्तकुशलाभ्यां चासेवायाम् । Pan. II. 3. 40.

or devoted to ' are construed with the Locative or the Genitive आयुक्तः कुशलो वा हरिपूजने हरिपूजनस्य वा appointed to worship Hari; कुशलोन्वेषणस्याहमायुक्तो दूतकर्मणि । (Bhatti. VIII. 115.) In other senses they are construed with the Locative; आयुक्तो गौः शकटे a bull harnessed to the yoke of a carriage; कर्मणि कुशलः expert in the performance of an act.

§ 867. *When an object or an individual is to be distinguished from a whole class, the Locative or the Genitive is used; नृणां नृषु वा ब्राह्मणः श्रेष्ठः (see Manu S. I. 96.), गोषु गवां वा कृष्णा बहुक्षीरा; गच्छतां गच्छत्सु वा धावन् शीघ्रः, छात्राणां छात्रेषु वा मैत्रः पटुः। (Sid. Kau.)

§ 868. † The words साधु and निपुण, not preceded by the prepositions अनु, परि and प्रति, are used with the Loc. when the sense of adoration is to be conveyed; मातरि साधुर्निपुणो वा reverentially disposed towards his mother; but निपुणः राज्ञः भृत्यः a clever servant of the king. When preceded by the prepositions अनु, परि and प्रति these are used with the Accusative; साधुर्निपुणो वा मातरं प्रति पर्यनु वा.

§ 869. ‡ With the words प्रसित and उत्सुक, the Locative or the Instrumental is used; प्रसित उत्सुको वा हरिणा हरौ वा intent upon Hari; पत्या प्रस्थितेन पत्यौ प्रस्थिते वा योषिदुत्सुका, a woman gets anxious (or restless) when her husband goes out; तेजस्विभिरुत्सुकानाम् Kir. XVI. 7

§ 870. § When the names of *Nakshatras* are used as showing a particular time the Locative or the Instrumental is used; मूलेनावाहयेद्देवीं श्रवणेन विसर्जयेत् । मूले श्रवणे इति वा । (Sid. Kau.)

---

* यतश्च निर्धारणम् । Pân. II. 3. 41. जातिगुणक्रियासंज्ञाभिः समुदायादेकदेशस्य पृथक्करणं निर्धारणम् । Sid. Kau.

† साधुनिपुणाभ्यामर्चायां सप्तम्यप्रतेः । Pân. II. 3. 43. अप्रत्यादिभिरिति वक्तव्यम् । Vart.

‡ प्रसितोत्सुकाभ्यां तृतीया च । Pan. II. 3. 44. विषयविवक्षया सप्तमी । करणत्वविवक्षया तृतीया । Bharata on Bhatti. VIII. 117.

§ नक्षत्रे च लुपि । Pân. II 3. 45.

§ 871. * Words expressive of the interval of time or space are used with the Ablative or the Locative; अद्य भुक्त्वायं द्व्यहे द्व्यहाद्वा भोक्ता having dined to-day he will dine again after two days; इहस्थोयं क्रोशात् क्रोशे वा लक्ष्यं विध्येत् standing here he will hit a mark two miles distant.

§ 872. † The prepositions उप in the sense of 'exceeding' and अधि in that of 'the master of' govern the Locative; उपपरार्धे हरेर्गुणाः the merits of Hari exceed a parârdha; अधि भुवि रामः or अधि रामे भूः Râma is the lord of the earth; in other senses these prepositions are used with the Accusative, for which see § 805.

§ 873. The words दूर and अन्तिक and others having the same sense are used in the Locative also; ग्रामस्य दूरे—दूरं—दूरेण—दूरात् वा: तस्याः समीपे—समीपेन— समीपात् गत्वा.

§ 874. Verbs having the sense of 'love, regard for, attachment to' such as स्निह्, अनुरञ्ज्, अभिलष्, रम्, &c. and their derivatives generally govern the Locative; पिता पुत्रे स्निह्यति a father loves his son; आति मे सोदरस्नेहोपि एतेषु (S'ak. I) I have a sisterly affection for them also; न खलु तापसकन्यकायां ममाभिलाषः I do not, indeed, love the ascetic's daughter, अशुद्धप्रकृतौ राज्ञि जनता नानुरज्यते people do not love a king whose ministers are corrupt; भ्रातुर्मृतस्य भार्यायां योनुरज्येत कामतः (Manu. S. III. 179). रहसि रमते (Mal. Mad. III. 2.) takes pleasure in solitude; रतः श्रेयसि (Bhaṭṭ. I.) devoted to his welfare.

Note:—अनुरञ्ज् and अभिलष् are sometimes used with the Accusative also; समस्थमनुरज्यन्ति (Râma.); मानुषानभिलषन्ती (Bhaṭṭ. IV. 22.)

§ 875. Verbs of acting, behaving towards, &c. such as वृत्, व्यवहृ, &c. and of throwing, such as अस्, मुच्, क्षिप्, &c. govern the Locative; गुरुषु विनयेन वृत्तिः कार्या one should act modestly towards respectable persons; कुरु प्रियसखीवृत्तिं सपत्नीजने (S'ak.

---

* सप्तमीपञ्चम्यौ कारकमध्ये। Pan. II. 3. 5.

† यस्मादधिकं यस्य चेश्वरवचनं तत्र सप्तमी। Pan. II 3. 9.

IV.); ते तस्मिन्प्रशरान् मुमुचुः चिक्षिपुर्वा; न खलु न खलु बाणः संनिपात्यो-यमस्मिन् मृदुनि मृगशरीरे । (S'ak. I.); तस्मिन्नास्थदिषीकास्त्रम् (Rag. VII. 23.).

§ 876. The root राध् with अप 'to offend' is generally construed with the Locative and sometimes with the Genitive; कस्मिन्नपि पूजार्हे अपराद्धा शकुन्तला S'akuntalâ has offended some one deserving respect; न तु ग्रीष्मस्यैवं सुभगमपराद्धं युवतिषु (S'ak. III. 9.), किंपुनर-सुरावलेपेन भवतीनामपराद्धं । Vik. I.

THE GENITIVE AND THE LOCATIVE ABSOLUTES.

§ 877. "When the participle agrees with a subject different from the subject of the verb, the phrase is said to be in the absolute construction." Bain.

In English, the Nominative is used as an Absolute case; in Sanskrit the Genitive and the Locative are so used. The English Nominative Absolute ought, therefore, to be translated by the Sanskrit Locative Absolute. When the Absolute Construction is to be used, the subject of the participle must be put in the Genitive or the Locative case and the participle made to agree with it in gender, number and case.

N. B. When the subject or object of the principal sentence is the same as that of the participal phrase, the absolute contruction should not be used; as अयोध्यां निवृत्तो रामो राज्यमकरोत् and not अयोध्यां निवृत्ते रामे स &c.; आगतेभ्यो विप्रेभ्यो दक्षिणामयच्छत and not आगतेषु विप्रेषु तेभ्यः &c.

§ 878. * When the action done or suffered by a person or thing indicates another action *i. e.* when the time of the happening of the one action which is known indicates that of the second action, the Locative Absolute be used; गोषु दुह्यमानासु गतः he went away while the cows were being milked; अवसन्नायां

---

* यस्य च भावेन भावलक्षणम् । Pan. II. 3. 37. यस्य क्रियया क्रियान्तरं लक्ष्यते ततः सप्तमी स्यात् । Sid. Kau.

रात्रौ the night being ended; कुतो धर्मक्रियाविघ्नः सतां रक्षितरि त्वयि whence can there be obstacles to our religious rites when thou art the protector of the good.

879. The locative or Genitive Absolute may be used to express the sense of the English particles 'when, while, since, although,' &c. (and may thus supply the place of a pluperfect tense); एवं तयोः परस्परं वदतोः; while they two were thus talking; दृष्टे सूर्ये पुनरपि भवान्वाहयेदध्वशेषम् (Meg. 40); Thou wilt accomplish the rest of thy journey when the sun rises again.

§ 880. * When 'contempt or disregard' is to be shown, the Genitive or the Locative Absolute is used; रुदति रुदतो वा पुत्रे पुत्रस्य वा प्राव्राजीत् he turned out a recluse disregarding his weeping son *i. e.* in spite of the weeping of his son. In this sense the Genitive Absolute is used more often. The Locative or the Genitive absolute may thus have the sense of 'in spite of,' 'notwithstanding,' &c. in English.

(*a*) The Locative Absolute be made to express the idea of 'as soon as,' 'no sooner than,' 'the moment that' &c. by compounding it with the word एव or मात्र; तस्मिन्...संहितमात्र एव (Rag. XVI. 78.) no sooner was the arrow fixed, &c. अनवसितवचन एव मयि scarcely had I finished my speech when.

Section III.

PRONOUNS.

§ 881. The chief peculiarities in the Syntax of pronouns have been already noticed in chapter IV.

§ 882. The pronouns of the first and second person *viz.* अस्मद् and युष्मद् have no gender. The other pronouns follow the

* षष्ठी चानादरे । Pan. II. 3. 38.

gender of the nouns they refer to. For the uses of the shorter forms of अस्मत् and युष्मत् see chapter IV.

§ 883. भवत् is used in the second person like 'you' in English as a courteous form of address though it is to be regarded as a pronoun of the third person and ought to be treated as such: भवान् अत्र प्रष्टव्यः you ought to be asked here, भवान् अपि तत्र गच्छतु you may also go there.

(*a*) When respect is to be shown, अत्र and तत्र are prefixed to भवत् according as the person with reference to whom it is used is near, or at a distance or absent; अत्रभवान् काश्यपः the venerable Kâshyapa (who is near); इदमासनं अलङ्करोत्वत्रभवान् may you occupy (*lit.* ornament) this seat; तत्रभवती इरावती lady Iravati (who is not present). Sometimes तद् is used with भवत् to show respect; as यन्मां विधेयविषये स भवान् नियुङ्क्ते । Mal. Mad. I.

§ 884. The pronoun तद् has often the sense of 'well known, renowned,' &c. तौ पार्वतीपरमेश्वरौ those (well-known) Pârvatî and Parameśwara; तान्येव वनस्थलानि those well-known forest sites.

(*a*) When repeated, this pronoun has the sense of 'various, several;' तेषु तेषु रम्यतरेषु स्थानेषु in those various highly delightful spots; कृतैरपि तैस्तैः प्रयत्नैः notwithstanding several efforts—कामैस्तैस्तैर्हृतज्ञानाः &c. (Bhag. VII. 20).

§ 885. The pronouns एक and अपर or अन्य are used in the plural in the sense of 'some—others;' विधवायाः पुनरुद्वाहः सशास्त्र इत्येके शास्त्रप्रतिषिद्ध इत्यन्ये कलौ निषिद्ध इत्यपरे some think that widow-remarriage is sanctioned by the S'astras, some say that it is prohibited by them, while others hold that it is not allowed in the Kali age. केचित् may take the place of एके.

§ 886. The pronouns अस्मत्, युष्मत्, यत् and किम् are often used in combination with other pronouns; सोहं—रघूणामन्वयं वक्ष्ये that I will describe the race of the Raghus; सोहं सर्वाधमो लोके

that I am the most degraded of all the people; स त्वं प्रशस्ते महिते मदीये—अग्न्यगारे—वसन् that thou dwelling in my fire-sanctuary; &c.; ते वयं दमयन्त्यर्थे चरामः पृथिवीमिमाम् we, of this description, roam over the earth for (in search of) Damayantî; sometimes अस्मत् and युष्मत् may be understood; सा क्षिप्रमातिष्ठ रथं गजं वा *i. e.* सा त्वं that thou quickly sit in a chariot or mount an elephant. सोयं पुत्रस्तव मदमुचां वारणानां विजेता this is that son of thine, the subduer of elephants shedding ichor; तथा विनाकृतः पुत्रैर्योहमिच्छामि जीवितुम् I, who wish to live still, even though deprived of my sons in that manner, &c. &c.

COMPARATIVE AND SUPERLATIVE DEGREES.

§ 887. Adjectives in the Comparative degree are used with the Ablative; वर्धनाद्रक्षणं श्रेयः protection (of one's subjects) is better than aggrandizement. अर्जुनाद्युधिष्ठिरो ज्यायान् Udhisthira was older than Arjuna.

(*a*) Sometimes the comparative is used with the Instrumental; प्राणै प्रियतरः dearer than life. See also § 863 *Note*.

§ 888. The superlative may either be construed with the Genitive or Locative; अयमेतेषां एतेषु वा गरिष्ठः गुरुतमो वा.

§ 889. The sense of the comparative and the superlative may also be expressed by the particular case used; अस्य हृदयं पाषाणात्कठिनं his heart is harder than stone; छात्राणां छात्रेषु वा चैत्रः पटुः Chaitra is the cleverest of all students.

§ 890. The words वर and प्रवर when used in the sense of the superlative govern the Genitive or the Locative; पुत्र स्पर्शवतां वरः 'a son is the best of things possessed of touch;' चतुष्पदां गौः प्रवरा लोहानां काञ्चनं वरं 'the cow is the best of quadrupeds and gold of metals'; the neu. sing of वर is used (with a word expressive of negation) in the sense of 'better and not, or but not;' अकरणान्मन्दकरणं वरं doing any thing slowly is better than not doing it at all; अजातमृतमूर्खाणां वरमाद्यौ न चान्तिमः of (the three kinds of) sons—not born, born and dead, and foolish, the first two are better, but not the last. याच्ञा मोघा वरमधिगुणे नाधमे लब्धकामा। Meg. I. 6. वरं प्राणैः वियोगः न तु मानहानिः better death than disgrace.

Section IV.

PARTICIPLES.

§ 891. All declinable participles in Sanskṛit partake of the nature of adjectives *i. e.* they agree with the nouns they qualify in gender, number, and case. The participles often discharge the functions of verbs. They are largely empolyed to take the place of the Past and Future tenses and more especially of passive verbs. When so employed they follow the same rules of syntax as are laid down for the roots from which they are derived.

PRESENT PARTICIPLES.

§ 892. The present particple is to be used when contemporaneity of action is to be indicated. It is often idiomatically used to express the sense of 'while' or 'whilst' in English; अरण्ये चरन् while wandering in the forest; विवाहकौतुकं बिभ्रत एव while he yet wore the marriage string.

Vide 670. (*b*).

§ 893. *The present participle is used to denote the manner in which an action is done or the cause or object of an action; शयाना भुञ्जते यवनाः the Yavanas dine by lying down; हरिं पश्यन् मुच्यते a man is absolved by (reason of his) seeing Hari; similarly तिष्ठन् मूत्रयति, गच्छन् भक्षयति (Mb.).

§ 894. The roots आस् and स्था are generally used with present participles to show the continuity of the action denoted by them; पशूनां वधं कुर्वन् आस्ते used to kill (always kept on killing) animals; तं प्रतिपालयन् तस्थौ remained waiting for him.

---

*लक्षणहेत्वोः क्रियायाः Pan. III. 2. 126. हेतुः फलं कारणं च। Sid. Kau.

THE PERFECT PARTICIPLES.

§ 895. The use of the perfect participles is very limited; it is used in the sense of 'who or what has done &c.'; तं तस्थिवांसं नगरोपकण्ठे (Rag. V. 61.) him who had halted in the vicinity of the city; श्रेयांसि सर्वाण्यधिजग्मुषस्ते (Rag. V. 34.) of thee who hast obtained all good things, स शुश्रुवांस्तद्वचनं (Bhaṭṭi. I. 20) when he heard his words; &c.

THE PAST PASSIVE PARTICIPLES.

§ 896. The past passive participle is very frequently used to supply the place of a verb; sometimes in conjunction with the auxiliary verbs अस् and भू. The past passive participle agrees adjectively with the object in gender, number and case, the agent being put in the Instrumental, while the past active participle is treated exactly like the verb in the past tense; तेन कार्यं कृतं by him the work was done; तेन बन्धनानि छिन्नानि by him the bonds were cut; आदिष्टास्मि देव्या धारिण्या I am commanded by queen Dhâriṇî; स कार्यं कृतवान् he did the work; रामः दैत्यान् हतवान् Râma killed the Râkshasas; कृतवत्यसि नावधीरणां thou didst never despise me, &c.

§ 897. In the case of past passive participles of intransitive roots the agent is put in the Nominative case; तदा प्ररुदितो राजा रक्षसां then the king of demons wept; सत्यं सुप्तोयं पापः &c.

§ 898. The past passive participles are often used impersonally, the agent being put in the Intrumental case; प्रद्युतितं or प्रद्योतितं सूर्येण it is shone by the sun; जितं पुत्रप्रेम्णा victorious (all powerful) is the affection for sons; पण्डितायितं तत्रभवता he showed his learning; प्रमुदितं or प्रमोदितं साधुना, &c.

§ 899. The past passive participles of the roots मन्, बुध and पूज् and their synonyms are used in the sense of the Present tense and are construed with the Genitive. (See § 857.)

For further particulars vide §§ 705—707.

§ 900. Many past passive participles are used actively in

which case they may govern the Accusative case, like a Perfect tense active; आरूढवदद्रीन् (Rag. VI. 77.) which had ascended the mountains; similarly गगनमध्यमारूढः सविता; आपादमुत्तीर्णः crossed i. e. got over the calamity; यमुनाकच्छमवतीर्णः descended to the bank of the Yamunâ, &c.

§ 901. The past passive participle is used as a *neuter* substantive; गतं departure; दत्तं a gift, खातं an excavation, भुक्तं, सुप्तं, &c.

§ 902 The past passive participle active and passive, may be used with the auxiliaries अस् and भू in any tense, the meaning of the participle changing accordingly; गतोस्मि or गतवानस्मि I have or am gone; so गतवानभवं or गतवानासं or गतोभवं I had or was gone; so कृतवानस्मि: गतो वनं श्वो भवितेति रामः that Râma is to go to the forest to-morrow; संप्राप्तः कीर्तिमतुलां भविष्यसि thou wilt obtain great glory, &c.

THE FUTURE PARTICIPLES.

§ 903 The future participle denotes that a person or thing is doing, or is about to do the action or to undergo the condition, expressed by the root; करिष्यन् going or about to do; करिष्यमाण about to do or what is about to be done.

§ 904. Besides showing simple futurity participle expresses intention or purpose; अनुयास्यन् मुनितनयाम् wishing to follow the daughter of the sage; दास्यन् wishing to give, वन्यान् विनेष्यन्निव दुष्टसत्त्वान् wishing, as it were, to tame the wild beasts.

POTENTIAL PASSIVE PARTICIPLES.

§ 905. The Potential passive participle is used in the sense of 'what should or ought to be done;' besides this, this participle yields the sense of 'fitness, obligation, necessity, capacity,' &c., the agent being put in the Instrumental case; विमर्शमकरोच्चित्ते किं कर्तव्यं मयाधुना (Devi Bhâg. IV. 7. 1.) he considered in his mind what he ought to do; धर्मः अनुसरणीयः religious duty ought to be followed; त्वया भारो वहनीयः thou art able to bear this burden; हन्तव्योऽयं शठः this rogue deserves to be killed; गन्तव्या ते वसतिरलका नाम यक्षेश्वराणां thou will have to go to Alakâ, the habitation of the lords of Yakshas, &c.

Obs.—Sometimes the agent is put in the Genitive case; मम सेव्यो हरिः Hari is to be served by me; द्विजातीनां भक्ष्यं अन्नं boiled rice to be eaten by Brâhmanas.

§ 906. Occasionally this participle is used impersonally in the *neuter* gender and singular number; तत्रभवता तपोवनं गन्तव्यं his honour should go to the penance grove; मया चाण्डालैः सह स्थातव्यं I should have to dwell in the company of *Chândalas* &c.

§ 907. The *neuter* forms भवितव्यं and भाव्यं are used impersonally in the sense of 'being,' or 'what must be or in all probability is,' the noun denoting the agent being put in the Instrumental case; अत्र केनापि कारणेन भवितव्यं there must be some cause; अस्य शब्दानुरूपेण पराक्रमेण भवितव्यं or भाव्यम् in all probability his strength must be corresponding to his sound; आर्यया प्रवाहणमारूढया भवितव्यम् the lady must (in all likelihood) be seated in the carriage, &c.

§ 908. This participle is sometimes used as a noun; प्रष्टव्यं पृच्छतस्तस्य to him who asked what was to be asked; भवितव्यं भवत्वेव let that, which is to happen, happen.

INDECLINABLE PAST PARTICIPLES OR GERUNDS.

§ 909. The past indeclinable participle in Sanskrit denotes the prior of two actions done by the same agent and corresponds to the perfect participle in English; इति उक्त्वा विरराम having said this he stopped; तान् पृष्ठमारोप्य जलाशयं नीत्वा भक्षयति having seated them on his back, he carried them to the lake and ate them up.

As the past indeclinable participles or gerunds serve the purpose of carrying on the action of the verb and act as connecting links between sentences, they account for the sparing use made in Sanskṛit composition of relative pronouns, conjunctions and connecting particles. When several gerunds are used in a sentence they should be translated by verbal tenses and copulative conjunctions; प्रवृत्ते प्रदोषसमये चन्द्रापीडः चरणाभ्यामेव राजकुलं गत्वा पितुः समीपे मुहूर्तं स्थित्वा दृष्ट्वा च विलासवतीं आगत्य स्वभवनं शयनतलमधिशिश्ये when the evening time approached, Chandrâpîda went to the royal palace on foot, remained in the presence of his father for an hour, saw Vilâsavatî, &c.

§ 910. A few gerunds are used prepositionally in Sanskṛit; विहाय, मुक्त्वा except, आदाय with, उद्दिश्य, अधिकृत्य, अनुरुध्य with reference to, &c.

THE INFINITIVE MOOD.

§ 911. The infinitive in Sanskṛit generally expresses the purpose or that for which an action is done and thus corresponds to the infinitive of purpose or gerund in English. The infinitive in Sanskṛit thus involves the sense of the Dative and may, if desired, be replaced by the Dative of the verbal noun derived from the root; पानीयं पातुं यमुनाकच्छं अवततार descended to the bank of the Yamunâ to drink water; here पातुं may be replaced by पानाय (पानीयस्य पानाय); शब्दादीन्विषयान् भोक्तुं (Rag. X. 25.) where भोक्तुं = भोगाय.

"The infinitive (formed with तुम् *tum*) in Sanskṛit" remarks Prof. Monier Williams, "cannot be employed with the same latitude as in other languages. Its use is very limited corresponding to that of the Latin supines, as its termination *tum* indicates"

(*a*) "Let the student, therefore, distinguish between the infinitive of Sanskṛit and that of Latin and Greek. In these latter languages we have the infinitive made the subject of a proposition; or, in other words, standing in the place of a Nominative and an Accusative case often admissible before it. We have it also assuming different forms, to express present, past, or future time, and completeness or incompleteness in the progress of the action. The Sanskṛit infinitive, on the other hand, can never be made the subject of a verb, admits of no Accusative before it, and can only express indeterminate time and incomplete action. Wherever it occurs, it must be considered as the object, and never the subject of some verb expressed or understood. As the object of the verb, it may be regarded as equivalent to a verbal substantive, in which the force of two cases, an Accusative and Dative, is inherent and which differs from other substantives in its power of governing a case. Its use as a substantive, with the force of the *Accusative* case, corresponds to our use of the Latin infinitive; thus तद् सर्वं श्रोतुं इच्छामि 'I desire to hear all that,' '*id audire oapio*,' where श्रोतुम् and *audire* are both equivalent to Accusative. Similarly, रोदितुं प्रवृत्ता 'she began to weep,' and महीं जेतुं आरभे, he began to conquer the earth, where महीजयं आरभे, he began the conquest of the earth, would be equally correct."

(*b*) "Bopp considers the termination of the infinitive to be the Accusative of the suffix *tu* (§ 458. *Obs.*), and it is certain that in the veda other cases of nouns formed with this suffix in the sense of infinitives occur; *e. g.* a Dative in *tave* or *tavai*, as from *han* comes *hantave* 'to kill;' fr. *anu-i anvetave*, 'to follow;' fr. *man*, *mantavai*, 'to think;' there is also a form in *tos* generally in the sense of an Ablative; *e. g.* fr. *i*. comes *etos* ' from going;' fr. *han*, *hantos*, as in *pura hantos*, ' before killing;' and a form in *tvi* corresponding to the indeclinable participle in *tvâ* of the classical language; *e. g.* fr. *han*, *hatvi* ' killing,' fr. *bhû bhûtvi* 'being,' &c. &c." Sanskṛit Grammar.

§ 912. The infinitive cannot be used as the subject or object of a verb, abstract nouns supplying its place in this case. Where, therefore, the infinitive occurs in English as the subject or the object in a sentence, the abstract noun derived from the root must be used in Sanskrit; स्वधर्माचारणं हितावहं to do one's duty is beneficial and not स्वधर्ममाचरितुं.

§ 913. * The infinitive is used with verbs and verbal nouns meaning 'to wish or desire' provided the agent of it is the same as that of the verb; को हर्तुमिच्छति हरेः दंष्ट्राम् (Mud. I.) who wishes to snatch away the jaws of the lion; माधुर्यं मधुबिन्दुना रचयितुं क्षाराम्बुधेरीहते; Bhartṛ. II. 6. But तमेतत्कर्तुमहमिच्छामि I wish him to do this, is wrong.

§ 914. † The infinitive is also used with:—

(*a*) verbs meaning to be able, to make bold, to know, to be wearied, to strive, to begin, to set about, to bear, to be pleased and to be; न शक्नोति शिरोधरां धारयितुं (Kâd.) is not able to support his neck; जानासि कोपं निग्रहीतुं you know how to restrain anger; अङ्गदेन समं योद्धुमघटिष्ट (Bhaṭṭi. XV. 77) he strove to fight with Angada; गन्तुं व्यवस्येद्भवान् (Meg. 22.) thou wilt try to go; वक्तुं प्रक्रमेथाः (Meg. 103.) begin to speak; अस्ति-भवति-विद्यते वा भोक्तुमन्नं (Sid. Kau.) there is food to eat, &c.

(*b*) ‡ words like अलं and others meaning sufficient or able, proficient or skilled in, &c.; पर्याप्तोऽसि प्रजाः पातुं (Rag. X. 25) thou art able to protect the creation; कः समर्थो दैवमन्यथा कर्तुं who is able to change destiny; प्रासादास्त्वां तुलयितुमलं (Meg. 66) the palaces are able to stand comparison with thee; भोक्तुं प्रवीणः कुशलः पटुर्वा (Sid. Kau.) skilled in eating.

(*c*) § words having the sense of 'it is time to do anything;' कालः समयो वेला अनेहा वा भोक्तुम् (Sid. Kau.) it is time to take food.

§ 915. The infinitive in Sanskrit has no passive form. In

---

* समानकर्तृकेषु तुमुन् Pân. III. 3. 158.

† शकधृषज्ञाग्लाघटरभलभक्रमसहार्हास्त्यर्थेषु तुमुन् । Pân. III. 4. 65. Vide Apte's Guide § 176 and note thereon.

‡ पर्याप्तिवचनेष्वलमर्थेषु । Pân. III. 4. 66.

§ कालसमयवेलासु तुमुन् । Pân. III. 3. 167.

turning, therefore, an active construction involving an infinitive into a passive one, the verb should be changed into the passive, the infinitive and the words governed by it remaining unaffected— स ग्रामं गन्तुं इच्छति, तेन ग्रामं गन्तुं इष्यते-except where the object of the infinitive and the verb is the same, स भारं वोढुमिच्छति, तेन भारो वोढुमिष्यते.

§ 916. The root अर्ह् 'to deserve' when used (in the second person) in combination with the infinitive expresses 'a request, a respectful entreaty,' and is generally, equivalent to the English 'I pray, be pleased, &c.;' अग्निं शमयितुमर्हसि (Meg. 55) please put out the fire; न चेद्रहस्यं प्रतिवक्तुमर्हसि (Kum. V. 40) if you have nothing to conceal from me, please answer me; द्वित्राण्यहान्यर्हसि सोढुमर्हन् (Rag. V. 25) pray wait for two or three days, O respectable one! &c. Sometimes it is equivalent to a gentle command; इमां प्रसादयितुमर्हसि (Rag. I. 89) you ought to please her; न तं शोचितुमर्हसि you ought not to bewail him. In the third person and under the same circumstances it expresses power or ability and can be translated by 'can;' द्रोणं हि समरे कोऽन्यो योद्धुमर्हति फाल्गुनात् Mah. Bhar. IV. 58. 27. दैवं प्रज्ञाविशेषेण को निवर्तितुमर्हति Ibid I. 1. 246.

§ 917. * The infinitive with the final म् dropped is joined with the nouns काम and मनस् to form an adjectival compound meaning 'wishing or having a mind to do any thing;' एतावदुक्त्वा प्रतियातुकामं शिष्यं महर्षेः &c. (Rag. V. 18) the disciple of the great sage was desirous of returning &c.; अयं जनः प्रष्टुमनास्तपोधने (Kum. V. 40) this person has a mind to ask you a question.

TENSES AND MOODS.

THE PRESENT TENSE.

§ 918. The Present tense shows that an action is taking place at the present time; अयमागच्छति तव पुत्रः here comes (is

---

* तुङ्कामनसोरपि ।

coming) thy son. * It is the Present progressive, which expresses the continuance of an action which is begun over sometime and is, remarks Prof. Bain, a true or strict Present tense. It is only by means of a special adverb or the context that the sense of the present tense can be limited to that of a present act solely; अधुना स इमां पुरीं अधिवसति now he dwells in this city.

§ 919. Besides the general sense given above the Present tense in Sanskṛit has the following senses:—

(*a*) † It is sometimes used in the sense of 'immediate futurity,' कदा गमिष्यासि when wilt thou go? एष गच्छामि Here I go (*i. e.* shall go); ऊर्ध्वं म्रिये मुहूर्तादि I shall die an hour after.

(*b*) It may also be used to denote an action which is recently completed; कदा त्वं नगरादागतोसि—अयमागच्छामि when didst thou come from the city ? Here I come (have come just now).

(*c*) In narrations it is used for the Past tense; गृध्रो ब्रूते कस्त्वं the vulture says, 'who art thou'?

(*d*) Sometimes it is used to denote a habitual or repeated action; पशुवधेनासौ जीवति.

§ 920. ‡ When a question is asked and an answer is given to it, the Present is used in the sense of the Past tense when the particle ननु is used; कटं अकार्षीः किम्—ननु करोमि भोः where करोमि

---

* "The principal use of the Present Indefinite is to express what is true at all times; 'the sun gives light; twice two is four * * *.' Hence a more suitable name would be the Universal tense. It expresses present time only as representing all time. The permanent arrangements and laws of nature, the peculiarities, habits and propensities of living beings and whatever is constant, regular and uniform, have to be represented by the Present Indefinite. * * It is only by a special adverb or by the context that we can confine this tense to mean a present act solely." Bain, Higher English Grammar.

† Pân. III. 3. 131. See p. 525.

‡ ननौ पृष्टप्रतिवचने । नन्वोर्विभाषा । Pân. III. 2. 120, 121.

is equivalent to अकार्षम् ; when the particles न and नु are used the Present may be optionally used; कटमकार्षीः किम्—न करोमि or नाकार्षम्—नु करोमि or न्वकार्षम्.

§ 921. * With interrogatives the Present is often used in the sense of the Future when thought or desire is implied; किं करोमि *i. e.* (करिष्यामि), क्व गच्छामि *i. e.* (गमिष्यामि) What shall I do ? Whither shall I go ? एतयोः कतरं or एतेषां कतमं भोजयसि (*i. e.* भोजयिष्यसि or भोजयितासि) which of these persons will you feed ? so कं नु पृच्छामि दुःखार्ता, &c.; but कः ग्रामं गमिष्यति ।

(*a*) It is also used in the sense of the Future in conditional sentences as implying a condition and the fulfilment of the desired object; योऽन्नं ददाति (दाता दास्यति वा) स स्वर्गं याति (याता यास्यति वा) he, who offers (or will offer) food, goes (or will go) to heaven *i. e.* if one offers &c.

§ 922. With the words यावत्, तावत् and others having a similar sense, the Present is sometimes used in the sense of the Future perfect; यावत्स त्वां न पश्यति तावद्दूरमपसर before he sees you, move away (before he shall have seen you, &c.).

(*b*) † With the particles पुरा and यावत् the Present has the sense of the Future when certainty is indicated; यावद्यते साधयितुं त्वदर्थम् । (Rag.V. 25.) I will endeavour to accomplish your object. पुरा सप्तद्वीपां जयति वसुधाम् (S'ak. VII. 33) he will conquer the earth consisting of seven continents. पुरानुशेते तव चञ्चलं मनः । Kir. VIII. 8.

§ 923. ‡ The particle स्म when used with the Present converts it into a Past tense; कस्मिंश्चिदधिष्ठाने मित्रशर्मा नाम ब्राह्मणः प्रतिवसति स्म in a certain village there dwelt a Brâhmaṇa Mitraśarmâ by name; पौराः शतशोऽभिधावन्ति स्म the citizens ran in hundreds. The particle

---

* किंवृत्ते लिप्सायाम् । लिप्स्यमानसिद्धौ च । Pân. III. 3. 6. 7.

† यावत्पुरा निपातयोर्लट् Pân. III. 3. 4. निपातावेतौ निश्चयं द्योतयतः । Sid. Kau.

‡ लट् स्मे । Pân. III. 2. 118.

स्म may not necessarily be joined with it; त्वं स्म वेत्थ महाराज यत्माह न बिभीषणः, मन्त्रे स्म हितमाचष्टे, &c.

§ 924. * When जातु or अपि is used in a sentence and condemnation or censure is implied, the Present may be used in the sense of the three tenses; अपि जायां त्यजसि जातु गणिकामादत्से where त्यजसि and आदत्से may have also the sense of the Past or the Future tense; जातु तत्रभवान् वृषलान् याजयति (you will even make a S'udra perform a sacrifice).

IMPERFECT, PERFECT AND AORIST.

§ 925. In Sanskrit there are three tenses denoting a past action, *viz.* the Imperfect, the Perfect, and the Aorst. Originally each of these three tenses had a signfication of its own and was used in its proper sense in ancient writings. † After Sanskrit ceased to be a spoken language the exact senses of these tenses were lost sight of and writers began to use them promiscuously, so that now any of these may be used to denote past time with certain limitations. The original senses of these as well as their other peculiarities are noticed below.

IMPERFECT.

§ 926. ‡ The Imperfect according to Pâṇini denotes past action not done to-day *i. e.* done at some time prior to the current day, तानभाषत पौलस्त्यः (Bhaṭṭi.) Bibhíshaṇa spoke to them.

§ 927. The Imperfect is optionally used for the Perfect when the particles ह and शश्वत् are used in a sentence; इति ह अकरोत् or चकार; शश्वदकरोत् or चकार.

(*a*) ¶ It may also be optionally used in asking questions refer-

---

* गर्हायां लडपिजात्वोः । Pân III. 3. 142.

† For a further explanation of the difference between these three tenses the student is referred to Dr. Bhândârkar's preface to the 1st Edition of his 2nd Book of Sanskrit.

‡ अनद्यतने लङ् । Pân. III. 2. 111.

§ हशश्वतोर्लङ् च । ¶ प्रश्ने चासन्ने काले । Pân III. 2. 116, 117.

ring to a very recent time; अगच्छत् किं (*Qu.*) (*Ans*) अगच्छत्; or जगाम किं? जगाम; but when the question refers to a very remote time the Perfect alone ought to be used; कृष्णः कंसं जघान किं? जघान.

§ 928. When the particle मा in combination with स्म is used with the Imperfect in the sense of the Imperative, the augment अ is dropped; मा स्म भवः, मा स्म करोत्, मा स्म प्ररुदितं युवाम.

PERFECT.

§ 929. *The Perfect denotes an action done before the current day and not witnessed by the speaker. It has reference to a very remote time and should, therefore, be used in narrating events of the remote past; तां ताटकाख्यां निजघान रामः। Ráma killed her whose name was Tâtakâ. प्रययाविन्द्रजित्प्रत्यक् (Bhaṭṭi. XIV.16.).

(*a*) In the 1st person the Perfect shows that the speaker was in a distracted state of mind or was unconscious when the event took place, or that he wants utterly to deny something that he has done; बहु जगद पुरस्तात्तस्य मत्ताकिलाहम् (S'is XI. 39) being frenzied I prattled much, I am told, before him; कलिङ्गेष्ववात्सीः किं? didst thou dwell in the country of the Kalingas? नाहं कलिङ्गाञ्जगाम I never went to Kalingas. With these exceptions the Perfect should not be used in the Ist person.

AORIST.

§ 930. †The Aorist simply expresses past action indefinitely *i. e.* without reference to any particular time (भूतसामान्ये लुङ्); सोऽध्येष्ट वेदांस्त्रिदशानयष्ट पितॄनपारीत्सममंस्त बन्धून्। व्यजेष्ट षड्वर्गमरंस्त नीतौ समूलघातं न्यवधीदरींश्च (Bhaṭt. I. 2.) 'He studied the Vedas, offered sacrifices to the gods, satisfied his departed ancestors, honoured

---

* परोक्षे लिट् Pân. III. 2. 115. उत्तमपुरुषे चित्तविक्षेपादिना पारोक्ष्यम्। (Sid. Kau.); अत्यन्तापह्नवे लिट् वक्तव्यः। Vârt.

† लुङ् Pân. III. 2. 110.

his relatives, subdued the collection of six (*i. e.* the six passions), took delight in politics and totally annihilated his enemies. The Aorist, however, properly denotes a recent action or one done during the course of the present day. "It is similar to the English present Perfect," remarks Dr. Bhândârkar*, "which the student will remember defines an action as having happened in a portion of time which is not yet expired; it brings past action in connection with the present time," अद्य वृष्टिरय it rained to-day.

§ 931. † The Aorist ought to be used when the idea of the continuousness or nearness of an action is to be implied; यावज्जीवमन्नमदात् (Sid. Kau.) gave food throughout his life; येयं पौर्णमासिक्रान्ता तस्यामग्नीनाधीत सोमेनायष्ट (Sid. Kâu.) he consecrated the fire on the last Purnimâ day (the full-moon day) and offered Soma, &c.

§ 932. ‡ With the particle पुरा not joined with स्म, the Aorist, the Imperfect, the Perfect or the Present may be used. वसन्तीह पुरा छात्रा अवात्सुरवसन्नूषुर्वा । (Sid. Kau.) here formerly dwelt pupils. But when स्म is used with पुरा the present alone can be used; यजति स्म पुरा he formerly sacrificed.

§ 933. The Aorist is used with the prohibitive particle मा (माङ्) or मा स्म, with the temporal augment अ cut off, and has then the sense of the Imperative; इति ते संशयो मा भूत् Ma. Bhâ. V. 132. 16. have no doubt &c. मा स्म प्रतीपं गमः do not go against. Rarely in ancient works the augment is retained मा निषाद प्रतिष्ठां त्वमगमः शाश्वतीः समाः may you not live, oh Nishâda for many years. When a root is preceded by a preposition, the अ is sometimes not dropped; मा मन्युवशमन्वगाः do not submit to

---

* Second Book of Sanskrit, P. 154.

† Pân. III. 3. 135. See next Page.

‡ पुरि लुङ् चास्मे । Pân III. 2. 122. पुराशब्दयोगे भूतानद्यतने विभाषया लुङ् चाल्लट् न तु स्मयोगे । Sid. Kau.

sorrow or anger (here the अ is not dropped); sometimes it is dropped; as in मावमंस्थाः स्वमात्मानं do not despise your soul (conscience). Some explain these anomalies by considering the particle to be मा and not माङ्.

THE TWO FUTURES.

§ 934. The difference between the Two Futures is the same as that between the Imperfect and the Aorist, the only difference being that the former refers to a future time and the latter to a past one. The First or Periphrastic expresses futurity definitely but not of this day; the Second or Simple Future expresses futurity indefinitely as also that of to-day; it is also employed to denote recent and future continuous time; as अयोध्यां श्वः प्रयातासि कपे भरतपालिताम् (Bhaṭṭi XXII,) oh monkey, to-morrow you will go to Ayodhyâ governed by Bharata; आनन्दितारस्त्वां दृष्ट्वा प्रष्टारश्चावयोः शिवम् । मातरः सह मैथिल्या तोष्टा च भरतः परम् (Bhaṭṭi. XXII. 14.) they will be delighted on seeing you and will ask you questions about the welfare of us two and Sîtâ; and Bharata also will be greatly pleased; एते...उन्मूलितारः कपिकेतनेन (Kir. III. 22) they will be extirpated by the monkey-bannered one (Arjuna); यास्यत्यद्य शकुन्तला S'ak. IV.) Śakuntalâ will go (goes) to-day; मरिष्यामि विजेष्ये वा हताश्चेत्तनया मम (Bhaṭṭi XVI. 13) if my sons are killed I will die or kill the enemy, &c.

THE FIRST FUTURE OR PERIPHRASTIC FUTURE.

§ 935. *Obs.* * When the continuousness of an action or nearness of time (*i. e.* the non-intervention of the same period between the two points of time referred to) is to be expressed the First Future must not be used; यावज्जीवमन्नं दास्यति he will give food throughout his life; and not दाता, या इयं अमावास्या आगामिनी

* नानद्यतनवत्क्रियाप्रबन्धसामीप्ययोः । भविष्यति मर्यादावचनेऽवरस्मिन् । कालविभागे चानहोरात्राणाम् । परस्मिन्विभाषा । Pân. III. 3. 135-138.

तस्यां अग्नीनाधास्यते सोमेन च यक्ष्यते he will consecrate the fires and offer a Soma sacrifice on the coming Amâvâsyâ day; and not आधाता and यष्टा; also when limit of time or place is expressed and the word अवर is used in a sentence; यः अयमध्वा गन्तव्यः आपाटलिपुत्रात् तस्य यदवरं कौशाम्ब्याः तत्र सक्तून् पास्यामः and not पातास्मः; यः अयं संवत्सरः आगामी तस्य यदवरं आग्रहायण्याः तत्र युक्ता अध्येष्यामहे and not अध्येतास्महे; but when the word रात्र is used the First Future may be used; योयं मासः आगामी तस्य यः अवरः पञ्चदशरात्रः तत्र अध्येतास्महे we will study in the earlier fortnight of the coming month. When the period of time meant lies beyond a certain point of time, the First or the Second Future may be used; योऽयं संवत्सरः आगामी तस्य यत्परमाग्रहायण्यास्तत्राध्येष्यामहे or अध्येतास्महे, &c.

THE SECOND OR SIMPLE FUTURE.

§ 936. * When the close proximity of a future action is intended, the Second Future or the Present may be used; कदा गमिष्यासि when will you go? एष गच्छामि or गमिष्यामि I shall just go,

§ 937. † When there is the idea of hope implied in a conditional form, the Aorist, the Present or the Simple Future may be used in both the clauses to denote a future time; देवश्चेदवर्षीत् वर्षति वर्षिष्यति वा धान्यमवाप्स्म वपामः वप्स्यामः वा। (Sid. Kau). if it were to rain we would sow corn.

§ 938. The Simple Future is sometimes used as a courteous way of command; पश्चात्सरं प्रति गमिष्यसि (Vik. IV.) then you will go (*i. e.* please then go) to the lake, &c,

§ 939. ‡ The Simple Future is alone used when the idea of hope is conveyed by क्षिप्र and words having the sense of क्षिप्र; वृष्टि-

---

* वर्तमानसामीप्ये वर्तमानवद्वा । Pân. III. 3. 131.

† आशंसायां भूतवच्च । Pân. III. 3. 132.

‡ क्षिप्रवचने लृट् । Pân. III. 3. 133.

श्चेत्क्षिप्रं आशु त्वरितं वा यास्यति शीघ्रं वप्स्यामः if a shower were to come quickly we would at once sow corn.

§ 940. When the word यत् is not used with roots meaning 'to remember,' such as स्मृ, &c. the Second Future is used in the sense of the Imperfect; स्मरसि कृष्ण गोकुले वत्स्यामः Krishṇa, do you remember that we dwelt in Gokula ?

§ 941. * When disbelief in or intolerance of an action is intended to be expressed, and especially in the form of a question, the Simple Future is used optionally in the sense of the Potential; न संभावयामि or न मर्षये भवान् हरिं निन्देत् or निन्दिष्यति I never believe, or cannot tolerate it, that you would or should speak ill of Hari; कः or कतरः कतमः हरिं निन्देत् or निन्दिष्यति who will speak ill of Hari (I do not believe that any body will, &c.); कं वृषलं भवान् याजयेत् or याजयिष्यति, &c.; when the word किङ्किल † (a particle, showing great anger) and roots having the sense of 'to be' precede, the Simple Future only should be used; न संभवामि or मर्षये भवान् किङ्किल वृषलं याजयिष्यति I do not believe or like that you should make a Śudra perform a sacrifice; so अस्ति भवति विद्यते वा भवान् वृषलं याजयिष्यति.

§ 942. When the idea of wonder is to be expressed and the words यच्च, यत्र and यदि do not occur in a sentence, the Simple Future should be used; आश्चर्यमन्धो नाम कृष्णं द्रक्ष्यति it is a wonder that a blind man sees Hari.

(*a*) The Simple Future is also used when the particles उत and अपि expressing a doubt are used; उत दण्डः पतिष्यति will the stick fall ? अपि धास्यति द्वारं will he close the door ?

(*b*) This Future is also used when the particle अलं meaning sure or able is used; अलं कृष्णो हस्तिनं हनिष्यति Krishṇa is sure or able to kill the elephant.

---

* किंवृत्ते लिङ्लृटौ। अनवक्लृप्त्यमर्षयोरकिंवृत्तेऽपि। Pân. III. 3.144,145.

† किंकिलास्त्यर्थेषु लृट्। Pân. III. 3. 146.

THE MOODS.

THE IMPERATIVE MOOD.

§ 943. * The Imperative Mood does not express merely command, but also entreaty, benediction, courteous enquiry, gentle advice, ability, &c.

(*a*) In the second person this Mood is used to express command, entreaty, gentle advice and benedictions or blessings; गच्छ (त्वं) कुसुमपुरं go to Kusumapura; परित्रायस्व परित्रायस्व help! help! क्षमस्वापराधं O God! forgive my faults, &c.; शुश्रूषस्व गुरून् कुरु प्रियसखीवृत्तिं सपत्नीजने (Śak. IV.) serve your elders and treat your co-wives as if they were your friends; एधि कार्यकरस्त्वं मे गत्वा प्रवद राघवं be thou my messenger, go to Râghava, and say to him; अनन्यभाजं पतिमाप्नुहीति सा तथ्यमेवाभिहता हरेण she was addressed the truth by Hara when he said 'do thou obtain a husband not devoted to any other lady.'

(*b*) In the third person it is often used to express a blessing and sometimes gentle command; विधत्तां सिद्धिं नो···प्रकीर्णः पुष्पाणां हरिचरणयोरञ्जलिरयम् may this handful of flowers scattered on the feet of Hari give us success; पर्जन्यः कालवर्षी भवतु may rain pour down in time; पश्चात्तिष्ठन्तु वीराः शकनरपतयः (Mud. V. II.).

(*c*) In the first person it expresses a question, necessity, ability, &c; किं करवाणि ते what should I do for you? अधुनाहं गच्छानि I must go now; करवामैतद्वयं देवि प्रियं तव we will (are able to) do this thing, oh queen, which is agreeable to you; नहि प्रेष्यवधं घोरं करवाण्यस्तु ते मतिः (Bhaṭṭi XX. 6.) let your thought be 'I must not commit the horrible murder of an ambassador.'

§ 944. The third person singular of the Imperative in the passive voice is often used and sometimes as a courteous form

---

* लोट् च । Pân. III. 3. 162. Vide Pân. III. 3. 161. quoted on the next page.

of expression; आनीयतां राजपुत्रः the prince should be brought श्रूयतां भो पण्डिताः may you hear, ye Pandits; एतदासनमास्यतां take this seat.

§ 945. When time after a मुहूर्त (nearly equal to an hour) is expressed, the Imperative is used; मुहूर्तायजतां स्म offer the sacrifice after an hour.

§ 946. The Imperative with the particle स्म is used when a request is courteously expressed; बालमध्यापय स्म please teach the child.

§ 947. The Imperative has sometimes the force of the present when used in combination with the particle मा; मा भवतु no, it is not so; मा च ते निघ्नतः शत्रून्मन्युर्भवतु पार्थिव ।

§ 948. इच्छामि भवान्भुञ्जीत or भुंक्ताम् I wish you should dine. See § 958.

§ 949. *There is a peculiar use of the Imperative which ought to be noticed. The Imperative second person signular is repeated when frequency of an act is indicated and the whole used with the root in any tense; याहि याहि इति याति (Sid. Kau.) he goes every now and then; so यात यातेति यूयं याथ; याहि याहीत्ययासीत्; अधीष्वाधीष्वेत्यधीते he studies steadily. The Imperative second person is also used when several acts are described as done by the same person; सक्तून् पिब, धानाः खादेत्यभ्यवहरति (Sid. Kau.) he takes his food, now eating barley, now eating fried rice; similarly अन्नं भुंक्ष्व दाधिकमास्वादयस्वेत्यभ्यवहरते (Sid. Kau.).

THE POTENTIAL MOOD.

§ 950. † The Potential Mood expresses the sense of विधि (command,, directing a subordinate, &c.), निमन्त्रण (pressing invita-

---

* क्रियासमभिहारे लोट् लोटो हिस्वौ वा च तध्वमोः । समुच्चयेऽन्यतरस्याम् । यथाविध्यनुप्रयोगः पूर्वस्मिन् । समुच्चये सामान्यवचनस्य । Pân III. 4. 1–5. क्रियासमभिहारे द्वे वाच्ये । Vârt.

† विधिनिमन्त्रणामन्त्रणाधीष्टसंप्रश्नप्रार्थनेषु लिङ् । Pân. III. 3. 16

tion), आमन्त्रण (giving permission), अधीष्ट (telling one to attend to an honorary office or duty), संप्रश्न (courteously asking a person a question), and प्रार्थना prayer. यजेत one should perform a sacrifice; त्वं ग्रामं गच्छेः go to the village; इह भवान् भुञ्जीत your honour should take food here; इहासीत भवान् you may sit here; पुत्रमध्यापयेद्भवान् you may teach my son (as an honorary duty); किं भो वेदमधीयीय उत तर्कम् what, oh ! shall I learn the Veda or logic? भो भोजनं लभेय good Sir, can I get food here? *i. e.* will you kindly give me food? (All these senses are optionally expressed by the Imperative also).

(*a*) * In the case of the first two senses *viz.* विधि and निमन्त्रण and in that of 'proper time', the potential participle may also be used for the Potential; भवता यष्टव्यम्, &c.

§ 951. † When the words 'after an hour' are used the Potential (also Imperative) or the Potential participle may be used; मुहूर्तादूर्ध्वं यजेत, यजतां, यष्टव्यं वा (Sid. Kau.).

§ 952. ‡ The Potential is used with the words काल, समय and वेला, when the word यत् is used; कालः समयः वेला वा यद्भुञ्जीत भवान् it is time now that you should dine.

§ 953. § When the idea of fitness is to be expressed the Potential or the Potential participle may be used; and sometimes the noun in तृ also; त्वं कन्यां वहेः, त्वं कन्यायाः वोढा or त्वया कन्या वोढव्या you are fit to marry the girl.

(*a*) The Potential or the Potential participle may be used when the sense of capability is implied; भारं त्वं वहेः or भारस्त्वया वोढव्यः thou canst (art able to) carry the load.

---

* प्रैषातिसर्गप्राप्तकालेषु कृत्याश्च ॥ Pân. III. 3. 163.

† लिङ् चोर्ध्वमौहूर्तिके । Pân. III. 3. 164.

‡ लिङ् यदि । Pân. III. 3. 168.

§ अर्हे कृत्यतृचश्च । शकि लिङ् च । Pân. III. 3. 169, 172.

§ 954. *With interrogative words such as किं, कतर, कतम, &c. the Potential or the Simple Future may be used when censure is implied (see § 937); कः कतरो वा हरिं निन्देत् निन्दिष्यति वा ।

(*a*) When wonder is implied the simple Future is used in preference to the Potential if the word यदि be not used; आश्चर्यं अन्धो नाम कृष्णं द्रक्ष्यति it is a wonder that a blind man should see Hari; but आश्चर्यं यदि साऽधीयीत it is wonder if he study.

§ 955. † When hope is expressed without the use of the word कच्चित् the potential is generally used; कामो मे भुञ्जीत भवान् it is my desire (I hope) that you will eat; but कच्चिज्जीवति I hope he lives.

§ 956. ‡ When the sense of 'I expect' is implied, the Potential or the 2nd Future may be used provided the word यद् used; संभावयामि भुञ्जीत भोक्षते वा भवान् I expect you will eat; but संभावयामि यद्भुञ्जीथास्त्वम् (Sid. Kau.).

§ 957. ¶ When in a conditional sentence one thing is expressed as depending upon another as effect upon a cause, the Potential or the Simple Future may be used; कृष्णं नमेच्चेत्सुखं यायात् if he will bow to Kṛishṇa he will attain happiness: so कृष्णं नंस्यति चेत्सुखं यास्यति.

§ 958. $ When words having the sense of 'to wish,' such as इष्, कम्, &c. are used, the Potential or Imperative is used; इच्छामि भवान्भुञ्जीत or भुंक्ताम् I wish you should dine; इच्छामि सोमं

---

* किंवृत्ते (गर्हायां) लिङ्लृटौ । Pân. III. 3. 144. (चित्रीकरणे) शेषे लृडयदौ । Pân. III. 3. 151.

† कामप्रवेदने कच्चिति । Pân. III. 3. 153.

‡ विभाषा धातौ संभावनवचनेऽयदि । Pán. III. 3. 155.

¶ हेतुहेतुमतोर्लिङ् । Pân. III. 3. 156.

$ इच्छार्थेषु लिङ्लोटौ । लिङ् च । Pân III. 3. 157. 159.

पिबेत्पिबतु वा भवान् (Sid. Kau.) I wish Your Honour will drink Soma.

(*a*) But when the agents of both the actions are the same, the Potential alone is used in the sense of the Infinitive; भुञ्जीयेतीच्छति (Sid. Kau.) *i. e.* भोक्तुमिच्छति wishes that he will eat (wishes to eat).

§ 959. Sometimes the Potential is used without a subject when it is used in the sense of 'a precept or advice'; आपदर्थे धनं रक्षेद्दारान् रक्षेद्धनैरपि । आत्मानं सततं रक्षेद्दारैरपि धनैरपि ॥ (a man) should save money for adversity; he should save his wife at the cost of his wealth and himself even at the expense of his wife and wealth; यद्यद्रोचेत विप्रेभ्यस्तत्तद्दद्यादमत्सरः (one) should serve Brâhmaṇas with all that they like, without being jealous.

THE BENEDICTIVE MOOD.

§ 960. The Benedictive Mood is used to confer a blessing or to express the speaker's wish; चिरं जीव्यात् भवान् may you live long! वर्धिषीष्ठाः स्वजातेषु वध्यास्त्वं रिपुसंहतीः । भूयास्त्वं गुणिनां मान्यस्तेषां स्थेया व्यवस्थितो ॥ (Bhaṭṭi. XIX. 26); कृतार्थः भूयासम् may I be successful!

THE CONDITIONAL.

§ 961. * The Conditional is used in those conditional sentences in which the Potential may be used when the nonperformance of the action is implied or in which the falsity of the antecedent is involved as a matter of fact. It expresses both future and past time. It must be used in both the antecedent and the consequent clauses; सुवृष्टिश्चेदभविष्यत्तदा सुभिक्षमभविष्यत् if there would be plentiful rain there would be an abundance of

---

* लिङ्निमित्ते लृङ् क्रियातिपत्तौ । Pâṇ. III. 3. 139. हेतुहेतुमद्भावादि लिङ्निमित्तं तत्र भविष्यत्यर्थे लृङ् स्यात् क्रियायाः अनिष्पत्तौ गम्यमानायाम् । Sid. Kau.

corn; यदि सुरभिमवाप्स्यस्तन्मुखोच्छ्वासगन्धं तव रतिरभविष्यत्पुंडरीके किमस्मिन् hadst thou obtained (which thou hast not) the sweet fragrance of her breath, wouldst thou have had any liking for this lotus ?

Obs. § 962. * When a past action is to be indicated the Conditional may be optionally used in the sense of the Potential; कथं नाम तत्रभवान्धर्ममत्यक्ष्यत् or त्यजेः how could you give up your religion ?

(*a*) Also where the Potential is used in conjunction with the particles उत, अपि, जातु &c.; अपि तत्र रिपुः सीतां नार्थयिष्यत दुर्मतिः । क्रूरं जात्ववदिष्यच्च जात्वस्तोष्यच्छ्रियं स्वकाम् ॥ संकल्पं नाकरिष्यच्च तत्रेयं शुद्धमानसा । (मृषा) सत्यामर्षमवाप्स्यस्त्वं राम सीतानिबन्धनम् ॥ (Bhaṭṭi. XXI. 3. 4.)

(*b*) When wonder is to be expressed the Conditional is optionally used where the Potential is used in combination with the particles यच्च, यत्र or यदि when the action does not take place; आश्चर्यं यत्र यच्च स्त्री कृच्छ्रेऽवर्त्स्यन्मते तव । त्रासादस्यां विनष्टायां किं किमालप्स्यथाः फलम् ॥ (Bhaṭṭi. XXI. 8).

SECTION V.

Indeclinables.

ADVERBS.

§ 963. The *neu.* singulars of the Nominative and other cases of several nouns are used as adverbs; चिरं or चिरेण or चिराय ध्यात्वा having contemplated for a long time; दुःखं or दुःखेन तिष्ठति he is in distress; so सुखं or सुखेन &c.

(*a*) The word विधा is used adverbially in combination with

* भूते च Pân. III. 3. 140.

several words such as बहु, नाना, &c.; बहुविधं, नानाविधं in various ways. The word पूर्व is also used adverbially as the latter member of a compound when some action is to be expressed as having happened before; सांत्वपूर्वं having said something by way of consolation; बुद्धिपूर्वम् thoughtfully, (*i. e.* thought preceding a certain action); अबुद्धिपूर्वं भगवन्धेनुरेषा हता मया O venerable Sir, I killed this cow unwittingly; शपथपूर्वं अकथयत् &c.

PREPOSITIONS.

§ 964. The use of Prepositions has already been explained at § 365-371. The Prepositions governing cases are already noticed under the various cases.

CONJUNCTIONS.

§ 965. The use of Conjunctions has not many syntactical Peculiarities and needs no special notice here. They are used in their proper senses in sentences.

§ 966. The most important of these conjunctions and the one very frequently used is च. It can never stand first in a sentence; nor can it be used like 'and' in English. It is used with such of the words or assertions it connects or is placed after the last of the words or assertions it joins together; रामश्च लक्ष्मणश्च or रामः लक्ष्मणश्च; कामश्च जृम्भितगुणो नवयौवनं च love with its excellences expanded, and fresh youth; कुलेन कान्त्या वयसा नवेन गुणैश्च तैस्तैर्विनयप्रधानैः ।

(*a*) Sometimes this particle has a disjunctive force; शान्तमिदमाश्रमपदं स्फुरति च बाहुः—the hermitage is tranquil yet my arm throbs.

(*b*) Rarely this particle is used in the sense of 'if'; जीवितुं चेच्छसि मूढ हेतुं मे गदतः शृणु oh fool, if you wish to live, &c.

(*c*) Sometimes it is used as an expletive; भीमः पार्थस्तथैव च.

(*d*) Sometimes it is used to connect a subordinate fact with a main one भिक्षामट गां चानय wander for alms and bring a cow; कुट्टिनी च शासिता गोपी च निःसारिता कंदर्पकेतुश्च पुरस्कृतः the procuress was chastised, the cowherdess was expelled and Kandarpaketu was honoured.

(*e*) When the particle is repeated it has sometimes the sense of 'on the one hand,' 'on the other hand,' 'and yet;' क्व च हरिणकानां जीवितं चातिलोलं क्व च निशितनिपाता वज्रसाराः शरास्ते where, on the one hand, is the extremely frail life of fawns, and where, on the other, are thy arrows hard like adamant and falling sharply; न सुलभा सकलेन्दुमुखी च सा किमपि चेदमनङ्गविचेष्टितम् । on the one hand the full moon-faced lady is not easy to obtain and yet there is this unaccountable sport of love.

(*f*) Sometimes the repetition of च shows the simultaneous or undelayed occurrence of two events; ते च प्रापुरुदन्वन्तं बुबुधे चादिपूरुषः they reached the ocean and at the same time the primeval Being also awoke.

§ 967. तथा 'likewise' often supplies the place of च; रामस्तथा लक्ष्मणश्च Râma and Lakshmaṇa; अनागतविधाता च प्रत्युत्पन्नमतिस्तथा both Anâgatavidhâta and Pratyutpannamati; तथा हि means 'for instance, to be more plain;' तथा च 'likewise;' both are often used introducing quotations.

§ 968. तु but, हि for, because, and वा are also excluded from the first place in a sentence. आत्मा पुत्रः सखा भार्या कृच्छ्रं तु दुहिता किल the son is one's own self, the wife one's friend, but the daughter a source of anxiety; अप्याज्ञया शासितुरात्मना वा प्राप्तोसि संभावयितुं वनान्माम् । कालो ह्ययं संक्रमितुं द्वितीयं सर्वोपकारक्षममाश्रमं ते ।

(V. 10.); अस्त्राणि वा शरीरं वा वरय choose either the missiles or your person.

§ 969. यदि and चेत् 'if' are usually used with the Potential or the Conditional; as यदि सोत्र सन्निहितो भवेत् तर्हि मम साहाय्यं कुर्यात् if he were here he would assist me; यदि देवदत्तोत्राभविष्यन्नूनमेतदकरिष्यत् had Devadatta been here, he would have undoubtedly done this; but they are also construed with the Present Indicative; यदि जीवति भद्राणि पश्यति if he lives he will see prosperity; यदि मया देवपादानां प्रयोजनमस्ति if Your Majesty has any thing to do with me, &c.; शापितासि मम जीवितेन यदि वाचा न कथयसि I conjure you by my life if you will not tell it in words. चेत् is never used at the beginning of a sentence; तं चेत्सहस्रकिरणो धुरि नाकरिष्यत् (S'ak. VII. 4) if the thousand-rayed one (sun) did not place him at the yoke of his car; अयि रोषमुरीकरोषि (have recourse to) नो चेत् &c.. Bha. V. I. 44.

The Particles अथ and इति.

§ 970. *अथ is used in the following senses:—(1) as a sign of auspiciousness †; अथातो ब्रह्मजिज्ञासा now begins the inquiry about Brahma; *cf.* the Bhâsya on this sûtra. (2) marks the beginning or commencement of a work; अथेदमारभ्यते प्रथमं तन्त्रम् now is begun the Ist Tantra; so अथ योगानुशासनम्, &c ; (3) 'then' after that,' &c.; अथ प्रजानामधिपः &c. (Rag. II. 1.) After that i. e. passing of the night) the lord of the earth, &c. (4.) asks a question अथ भगवान् लोकानुग्रहाय कुशली काश्यपः is the venerable Kasyapa all right that he may oblige the world? अथ शक्नोषि भोक्तुं are you able to eat? (5) 'and, including'; भीमः अथ अर्जुनः Bhîma and also Arjuna; (6) 'if;' अथ मरणमवश्यमेव जन्तोः if death is sure to befall a creature, &c.

---

* मङ्गलानन्तरारम्भप्रश्नकार्त्स्न्येष्वथो अथ । Amara.

† Properly speaking this is not the sense of अथ. The mere utterance or hearing of this word if considered as auspicious as the word is supposed to have emanated from the throat of Brahma.

§ 971. As अथ marks the beginning, so इति marks the close of a composition. This particle is used in the following senses; (1) to quote the exact words spoken by some one, thus taking the place of the quotation marks and being used generally after the words quoted; * देव काचिच्चंडालकन्यका शुकमादाय देवं विज्ञापयति...देवपादमूलमागताहमिच्छामि देवदर्शनसुखमनुभवितुमिति । O lord a certain *Chandala* girl requests Your Majesty (saying)......" I who have come to your majesty's feet wish to enjoy the happiness of the sight of Your Majesty;' ब्राह्मणाः ऊचुः कृतकृत्याः स्म इति the Brâhmanas said " we have accomplished our objects; " (2) cause (rendered in English because, since &c.); वैदेशिकोस्मीति पृच्छामि I ask you because I am a foreigner; पुराणमित्येव न साधु सर्वं every thing is not good simply because it is old; (3) purpose or motive; मा भूदाश्रमपीडेति परिमेयपुरःसरः they two took a limited number of servants with them that there should be no disturbance, &c.; (4) so, thus; as follows; रामाभिधानो हरिरित्युवाच. (5) in the capacity of, as regards; पितेति स पूज्यः गुरुरिति निन्द्यः as a father he ought to be respected, as a teacher ought to be censured; (6) to state an opinion; इति आश्मरथ्यः this is the opinion of Aśmarathya. It is often used by commentators in the sense of ' according to the rule'; इति शक्यार्थे लिङ् &c. &c.

INTERJECTIONS.

§ 972. The following stanza from the Bhaṭṭi Kâvya illustrates the uses of some of these interjections:—

आः कष्टं बत ही चित्रं हूं मातर्दैवतानि धिक् ।
हा पितः क्वासि हे सुभ्रु बह्वेवं विललाप सः ॥

---

* In Sanskṛit there is no indirect construction, so that in translating indirect constructions the actual words of the speaker followed by इति must be used.

Appendix II.

DHÂTUKOSHA.

Abbreviations.

Pre. Present लट्. Im. Imperative लोट्. Imp. Imperfect लङ्. Pot. Potential विधिलिङ्. Perf. Perfect लिट्. P. f. Periphrastic or 1st future लुट्. Fut. simple or 2nd Future लृट्. Con. Conditional लृङ्. Aor. Aorist लुङ्. Ben. Benedictive आशीर्लिङ्. Cau. Causal णिच्. D. or Des. Desiderative सन्. Fr. Frequentative यङन्त or यङ् लुगन्त. P. Parasmaipada; A. Atmanepada; U. Ubhayapada; Pass. Passive; p. p. past Passive participle. Inf. Infinitive. Ger. Gerund. The figures 1, 2, &c. after the roots refer to the conjugations to which the roots belong. Pre. p. Present Participle (शत्रन्त when the root is Parasm; शानजन्त when Atm.) Pot. p. Potential participle.

अंश् 10 U. विभाजने to distribute; अंशयति-ते (also अंशापयति-ते) pre. अंशायांचकार—चक्रे—आस—बभूव per. अंशयिता P. fut. आंशयिष्यत् con. आंशिशत्-त Aor. अंश्यात्, अंशयिषीष्ट Ben.

अंस् 10 U. like the above with the only difference of श् for स्.

अंह् 1. A. गतौ to go; अंहते Pre. आनंहे Perf. अंहिता. P. fut. आंहिष्ट Aor. अंहिषीष्ट Ben.; Cau.–अंहयति-ते Pre. आञ्जिहत्-त Aor.

अंह् 10 U. भासने to shine; अंहयति-ते Pre. अंहयांचकार—चक्रे, &c, perf. अंहयिता p. fut. आञ्जिहत-त् Aor. अंह्यात्, अंहयिषीष्ट ben. अंहितुं inf. अंहित. p. p.

अक् 1. P. कुटिलायां गतौ to move tortuously; अकति pre. आक perf. अकिता p.f. अकिष्यति fut. आकीत् aor.; Cau.–अकयति-ते. अकित p.p.

अक्ष् 1 & 5. P. to reach, to pervade, to accumulate; अक्षति-अक्ष्णोति 3 sing. अक्षसि–अक्ष्णोषि 2 sing. अक्षामि-अक्ष्णोमि. 1 sing, pre. आक्षत्-आक्ष्णोत्, आक्षः-आक्ष्णोः; आक्षम्-आक्ष्णवम् Imperf. अक्षतु-अक्ष्णोतु, अक्ष-अक्ष्णुहि, अक्षाणि-अक्ष्णवानि Impera. अक्षेत्–अक्ष्णुयात् अक्षेः-अक्ष्णुयाः; अक्षेयम्–अक्ष्णुयाम् pot. आनक्ष perf. अक्षिता–अष्टा

p. f. अक्षिष्यति-अक्ष्यति fut. अक्ष्यात् ben. आक्षिष्यत्-आक्ष्यत् con. आक्षीत् aor. आक्षिष्टाम्-आष्टाम् 3rd dual, आक्षिषुः-आक्षुः 3rd pl. अचिक्षिषति-अचिक्षति Des. Pass.—अक्ष्यते pre. आक्षि aor. Cau.—अक्षयति-ते pre. आचिक्षत्—त aor. अष्ट p.p. अक्षित्वा-अष्ट्वा ger. अक्षितुम्, अष्टुम् inf. आनक्ष्वस् Perf. Part.

अग् 1 P. कुटिलायां गतौ to move tortuously; अगति pre. आग perf. अगिता p. fut. आगीत् aor.

अघ् 10 U. पापकरणे to go wrong, to sin; अघयति-ते pre. अघयांचकार-चक्रे &c. perf. अघयिता p. f. आजिघत्-त aor. अघ्यात्-अघयिषीष्ट ben.

अङ्क् 1 A. लक्षणे to mark; अङ्कते pre. आनङ्के perf. अङ्किता p. f. अङ्किष्यते fut. आङ्किष्यत con. अङ्किषीष्ट ben. आङ्किष्ट aor. अञ्चिकिषते des. pass—अङ्क्यते.

अङ्क् 10 U. पदे लक्षणे च to count, to mark or stain, to stigmatise; अङ्कयति-ते pre. अङ्कयांबभूव-आस-अङ्कयांचकार-चक्रे perf. अङ्कयिता P. f. अङ्कयिष्यति-ते fut. आङ्कयिष्यत्-त con. आञ्चकत्-त aor. अङ्क्यात्-अङ्कयिषीष्ट ben. अञ्चिकयिषति—ते des. Pass. -अङ्क्यते (also अङ्काप्यते).

अङ्ग् 1 P. to go; अंगति pre. आनङ्ग perf. अंगिता p. f. आङ्गीत् aor. आञ्जिगिषति des. अंगितुं inf.

अङ्ग् 10 U. same as अङ्क्.

अंघ् 1 A. गत्याक्षेपे to go, to blame; अंघते pre. आनंघे perf. अंघिता p. f. आंघिष्ट aor. अंघिषीष्ट ben. अञ्जिघिषति des.

अच् 1 U. गतौ अविस्पष्टकथने च to go, to speak indistinctly; अचति-ते pre. आच or आचे perf. अचिता p. f. आचीत—आचिष्ट aor. अचिचिषति-ते des. अक्त pp. अचित्वा, अक्त्वा ger.

अज् 1. P. गतिक्षेपणयोः to go, to run, to censure; अजति pre. विवाय, विव्यिव, आजिव, विव्यिम, आजिम 1st d. and pl. विवयिथ-विवेथ, आजिथ 2nd sing. perf. वेता or अजिता p. f. वेष्यति, अजिष्यति fut. अवेष्यत्-आजिष्यत् con. अवैषीत्-आजीत् aor. वीयात् ben. विवीषति-अजिजिषति des. वीत or अजित p.p. वीत्वा or अजित्वा, संवीय

ger. Cau.—वाययति—ते pre. अवीवयत्—त aor. Pass.—वीयते pre. विव्ये perf. वायिता, वेता, अजिता p. f. वायिष्यते—वेष्यते-आजिष्यते fut. वायिषीष्ट, वेषीष्ट—अजिषीष्ट ben. अवायिष्यत—अवेष्यत—आजिष्यत con. अवायि 3rd sing अवायिषाताम्—अवेषाताम्—आजिषाताम 3rd dual; अवायिढ्वम्-ढ्वम्—अवेढ्वम्-आजिढ्वम् 2. pl. aor.

अञ्च् 1 P. गतिपूजनयोः to go, to worship; अञ्चति pre. आनञ्च perf. अञ्चिता p. f. अञ्चिष्यति fut. अच्यात may he go. अञ्च्यात् may he worship. ben. आञ्चीत् aor. आञ्चिष्यत् con. Cau.-अञ्चयति—ते pre. अञ्चिचिषति des. अञ्चित, अक्त, with सम्, समक्त p. p. अञ्चित्वा or अक्त्वा (when it means to go) ger.

अञ्च् 1 U. गतौ याचने च to go, to beg; अञ्चति-ते pre. आनञ्च-ञ्चे perf. अञ्चिष्यति-ते fut. आञ्चीत्, आञ्चिष्ट aor. pass.—अञ्च्यते अक्त p. p. अञ्चित्वा ger. आञ्चितुम् inf.

अञ्च् 10 U. विशेषणे to individualise; अञ्चयति-ते pre. अञ्चयांचकार-चक्रे &c. perf. अञ्चयिता p. f. आञ्चकत्-त aor अञ्च्यात्, अञ्चयिषीष्ट ben.

अञ्ज् 7 P. व्यक्तिम्रक्षणकान्तिगतिषु to make clear, to anoint, to decorate, to go; अनक्ति pre. आनक्-ग् imp. अनक्तु, (अङ्ग्धि 2nd sing.) Impera. अञ्ज्यात् pot. आनञ्ज perf. अञ्जिता-अङ्क्ता p. f. अञ्जिष्यति, अङ्क्ष्यति fut. आञ्जिष्यत-आङ्क्ष्यत् con. आञ्जीत् aor. अज्यात् ben. अञ्जिजिषति des. Pass.-अज्यते pre. आञ्जि aor. Cau. अञ्जयति-अञ्जयते pre. आञ्जिजत्-त aor. अक्त p. p अञ्जितव्य,* अङ्क्तव्य, व्यङ्ग्य, pot. p. अञ्जित्वा, अङ्क्त्वा, अक्त्वा ger. with वि- व्यज्य ger. अञ्जितुम्, अङ्क्तुम् inf.

अट् 1 P. गतौ to roam, to wander; अटति pre. आट perf, अटिता p. f. अटिष्यति fut. आटीत् aor. अट्यात् ben. अटिटिषति des. Cau.-आटयति-ते pre. आटिटत् Aor. अटाट्यते Freq.

अट्ट् 1 A. अतिक्रमणहिंसयोः to transgress, to kill; अट्टते pre. आनट्टे perf. अट्टिता p. f. अट्टिष्यते fut आट्टिष्ट aor. अटिटिषते—अट्टिटिषते des. Cau.—अट्टयति-ते pre. आटट्टत्-त आट्टिटत्-त aor.

* 'नाञ्चेः पूजायाम्' Pán. VI. 4. 30, अञ्च् in the sense of 'to worship' does not drop its nasal before weak terminations.

अट्ट् 10 U. अनादरे to despise; अटिट्टत्-आट्टिटत् Aor. अट्ट्यात्, अट्टयिषीष्ट ben. अट्टयितुम् inf.

अण् 1, P. शब्दे to sound; अणति pre. आण perf. आणिता p. f. आणीत् aor. अणिणिषति des. Cau.-आणयति-ते pre. आणिणत्-त Aor.

अण् 4 A. प्राणने to breathe, to live; अण्यते pre. आणे perf. आणिता p. f. आणिष्यते fut. आणिष्ट aor. अणिषीष्ट ben. अणिणिषते des. Pass.—अण्यते Pre. आणि Aor.

अत् 1 P. सातत्यगमने to go constantly; अतति pre. आत perf. अतिता p. f. अतिष्यति fut. आतिष्यत् con. अत्यात् ben. आतीत् aor. अतितिषति des. Pass.-अत्यते pre. आति aor. Cau.-आतयति-ते pre. आतितत्-त Aor. अतित p.p.

अद् 2 P. भक्षणे to eat; अत्ति per. आदः 2nd sing. आदत्, 3rd sing. Imp. आद, जघास perf. अत्ता p. f. अत्स्यति fut. अघसत् aor. जिघत्सति des. आत्स्यत् con. अद्यात् ben. Cau.—आदयते pre (also आदयति 'अकर्त्रभिप्राये') आदिदत्-त aor. Pass.—अद्यते pre. आदे-जक्षे perf. जग्ध (and अन्न food) p. p. जग्ध्वा-प्रजग्ध्य ger. अत्तुम् inf.

अन् 2 P. प्राणने to breathe, to live; अनिति pre. आनीः-नः 2nd sing. आनीत्-आनत् 3rd sing. Imp., आन perf. अनिता p. f. आनिष्यत् con. आनीत् aor. अनिनिषति des. Cau.-आनयति-ते pre. आनिनत्-त Aor. Pass.—अन्यते pre. आनि aor. अनित्वा ger. with प्र-प्राण्य.

अन 4 A. to live; अन्यते pre. आने perf. अनिता p. f. This root is the same as अण्.

अन्त P. बन्धने to bind; अन्तति pre. अन्तिष्यति fut. आन्तीत् Aor. अन्त्यात् Ben. Cau.-अन्तयति आन्तीत्-त Aor. अन्तितिषति des.

अन्ध् 10 U. दृष्ट्युपघाते दृष्ट्युपसंहारे to be blind, to close the eyes अन्धयति-ते pre. आन्धयिष्यत् con. आन्दधत्-त Aor. अन्ध्यात्, अन्धयिषीष्ट ben. अन्दिधयिषति-ते des.

अभ्र् 1 P. गतौ to go, to wander; अभ्रति pre. आनभ्र perf. आभ्रीत् Aor.

अम् 1 P. गतिशब्दसंभक्तिषु to go, to sound, to eat; अमति pre. आम perf. अमिता p. f. अमिष्यति fut. आमीत् aor. Cau.-आमयति-ते pre.

आमिमत्-त Aor. अमिमिषति Des. Pass.—आमि. Aor. अमित-आन्त. p. p.

अम् 10 U. रोगे to afflict with pain; आमयति-ते Pre. आमिमद्-त Aor. अम्यात्-अमयिषीष्ट ben.

अय् 1 A. गतौ to go; अयते, with परा—पलायते pre. अयांचक्रे perf. अयिता p. f. आयिष्ट aor. अयिषीष्ट ben. अयियिषते des. Pass.—अय्यते pre. आयि aor. Cau.—आययति-ते pre. आयियत्-त Aor. अयित्वा, with परा,—पलाय्य. ger.

अर्क् 10 U. तपने स्तवने च to heat, to praise; अर्कयति—ते pre. अर्कयांचकार-चक्रे—आस—बभूव perf. अर्कयिता p. f. आर्चिकत्—त aor. अर्क्यात्, अर्कयिषीष्ट ben. अर्कित p. p.

अर्घ् 1 P. मूल्ये to be worth, to cost; अर्घति pre. आनर्घ perf. अर्घिता p. f. आर्घीत् aor. अर्जिघिषति des Cau.—अर्घयति-ते pre. आर्जिघत्-त Aor.

अर्च् 1 P. पूजायां to worship; अर्चति pre. आनर्च perf. अर्चिता p. f. अर्चिष्यति fut. आर्चीत् aor. अर्च्यात् Ben. अर्चिचिषति des. Cau.—अर्चयति—ते pre. आर्चिचत्—त aor. Pass.—अर्च्यते pre. आर्चि aor. अर्चित्वा ger.

अर्च् 10 U. to worship; अर्चयति—ते pre. अर्चयाम्बभूव—आस—चकार—चक्रे perf. अर्चयिता p. f. अर्चयिष्यति—ते fut. अर्च्यात्—अर्चयिषीष्ट ben. आर्चयिष्यत्—त con. आर्चिचत्—त aor. अर्चिचयिषति—ते des. Pass.—अर्च्यते pre. आर्चि (आर्चयिषाताम्-आर्चिषाताम् 3rd dual) Aor.

अर्ज् 1. P. अर्जने to procure, to take; अर्जति pre. आनर्ज perf. अर्जिता p. f. अर्जिष्यति fut. आर्जीत् aor. अर्ज्यात् ben. अर्जीजिषति des. Cau.—अर्जयति-ते pre. आर्जिजत्—त aor.

अर्ज् 10 U. (also cau. of the above) प्रतियत्ने संपादने च to procure, to acquire; अर्जयिष्यति fut. अर्जिजयिषति-ते des. Pass.—आर्जि (आर्जयिषाताम्--आर्जिषाताम् dual.) Aor.

अर्थ् 10 A. उपयाच्ञायाम् to request, to sue; अर्थयते pre. अर्थयांच-

भूव-आस-चक्रे perf. अर्थयिता p. f. आर्तथत aor. अर्थयिषीष्ट ben. अर्तिथयिषते des. Pass.—अर्थ्यते, अर्थाप्यते pre. आर्थि Aor.

अर्द् 1 P. गतौ याचने च to go, to beg; अर्दति pre. आनर्द perf. अर्दिता p. f आर्दिष्यत् con. आर्दीत् aor. अर्द्यात् ben. आर्दिदिषति des. Cau.—अर्दयति—ते pre. आर्दिदत्—त aor. Pass.—अर्द्यते pre. आर्दि aor. अर्दित, समर्ण (asked), अभ्यर्ण (near) p. p.

अर्द् 10 U. हिंसायाम् to kill; आर्दिदत्—त Aor. अर्द्यात्, अर्दयिषीष्ट ben. अर्दिदयिषति-ते des. Pass.—अर्द्यते pre. आर्दि Aor. अर्दित p. p.

अर्ह् 1 P. पूजायां योग्यत्वे च to worship, to deserve; अर्हति pre. आनर्ह perf. अर्हिता p. f. आर्हिष्यत् con. आर्हीत् aor. अर्ह्यात् ben. अर्जिहिषति des. Pass.—अर्ह्यते pre. आर्हि aor. Cau.—See below अर्ह् 10 U.

अर्ह् 10 U. to worship, to deserve; अर्हयति-ते pre. अर्हयांबभूव-आस-चकार-चक्रे perf. अर्हयिता p. f. आर्जिहत्-त Aor. अर्ह्यात्-अर्हयिषीष्ट ben. अर्जिहयिषति des. Pass.-अर्ह्यते pre. आर्हि Aor. अर्हयित्वा ger.

अल् 1 U. भूषणपर्याप्तिवारणेषु to adorn, to be competent, to prevent, अलति-ते per. आल—आले perf. अलिता p. f. आलीत्—आलिष्ट aor. Cau.—आलयति-ते pre. आलिलत्—त aor. अलिलिषति—ते des. (according to some this root is Atm.)

अव् I P. रक्षणगतिकान्तिप्रीतितृप्त्यवगमप्रवेशश्रवणस्वाम्यर्थयाचनक्रियेच्छादीप्त्यवाप्त्यालिङ्गनहिंसादानभागवृद्धिषु to defend, to protect, to do good, to please, to know (and a variety of other meanings.); अवति Pre. आव perf. अविता p. f. आवीत् aor. अव्यात् ben. Cau.—आवयति-ते pre. आविवत्—त Aor. अवित p. p. Pass.—अव्यते pre. आवि aor.

अश् 5. A. व्याप्तौ संघाते च to pervade, to accumulate; अश्नुते pre. आनशे perf. अशिता-अष्टा p. f. अशिष्यते—अक्ष्यते fut. आशिष्यत, आक्ष्यत con. आशिष्ट—आष्ट aor. अक्षीष्ट, आशिषीष्ट ben. Cau.—आशयति-ते pre. आशिशत्—त Aor. अशिशिषते des. Pass.—अश्यते pre. आशि aor. अष्ट p. p. अष्ट्वा, अशित्वा, Ger. आशितुम् अष्टुम्, inf.

अश् 9 P. भोजने to eat (with प्र, to drink); अश्नाति pre. अशान 2nd sing. Impera. आश perf. अशिता p. f. आशीत् aor. अश्यात् ben. अशिशिषति des. Cau.—आशयति pre. आशिशत् Aor. Pass. —आश्यते pre. आशि Aor. अशित p. p.

अस् 2 P. भुवि to be; अस्ति pre. एधि 2nd pers. sing. Impera. बभूव* perf. भविता p. f. भविष्यति fut. &c.

अस् 4 P. क्षेपणे to throw; अस्यति pre. आस perf. असिता p. f. आसिष्यत् con. आस्थत् aor. अस्यात् ben. असिसिषति des. Cau.—आसयति-ते pre. आसिसत्—त aor. Pass —अस्यते pre. आसि aor. अस्त: p. p. असित्वा, अस्त्वा ger. असितुम् inf.

आ—

आञ्छ् 1 P. आयामे to lengthen; आञ्छति pre. आञ्छ (according to some आनाञ्छ) perf. आञ्छिता p.f. आञ्छिष्यति fut. आञ्छिष्यत् con. आञ्छीत् Aor. आञ्चिच्छिषति des. Cau.—आञ्छयति—ते pre. आञ्चिच्छत्—त Aor.

आन्दोल् 10 U. आन्दोलने to sing, to rock; आन्दुदुलत्—त Aor. आन्दुदोलयिषति—ते des.

आप् 5 P. व्याप्तौ to prevade, to obtain; आप्नोति, आप्नोषि, आप्नोमि 1st, 2nd & 3rd sing. (आप्नुवः 1st dual. आप्नुवन्ति 3rd. plu.) pre. आप्नोत् 3rd Sing (आप्नवम् 1st sing. आप्नुव 1st dual, आप्नुवन् 3rd plu.) Imp.—आप्नोतु 3rd sing. आप्नवानि 1st sing. आप्नुहि 2nd sing. आप्नुवन्तु 3rd. plu. Impera. आप perf. आप्ता p. f. आप्स्यति fut. आप्स्यत con. आपत् aor. Cau.—आपयति—ते pre. आपिपत्—त aor. आप्त p. p. आप्त्वा ger. आप्तुम् inf.

आप् 1, 10 U. लम्भने to get; आपिपत्—त Aor. (10 conj.)

आस् 2 A. to sit; आस्ते pre. आसांचक्रे—बभूव—आस perf. आसिता p. f. आसिष्यते fut. आसिष्यत con. आसिष्ट aor. आसिषीष्ट ben. Pass.—आस्यते pre. Cau.—आसयति.

---

* अस्तेर्भूः । भू is substituted for अस् in the non-conjugational tenses.

इ—

इ 1 P. गतौ to go; अयति pre. आयत् Imperf. इयाय perf. एता p. f. एष्यति fut. ऐष्यत् con. ऐषीत् Aor. इयात् ben. Cau.—आययति-ते pre. आयियत्—त Aor. इयीषति des. Pass.—ईयते pre. आयि Aor.

इ 2 P. गतौ to go; एति pre. इयाय perf. एता p. fut. एष्यति fut. ऐष्यत् con. अगात् Aor. Pass.—ईयते pre. अगायि—aor. Cau. —गमयति—ते pre. अजीगमत्—त aor. (with प्रति, प्रत्याययति-ते) जिगमिषति des. (with प्रति—प्रतीषिषति).

इ 2 A. with अधि, अध्ययने to study; अधीते pre. अधिजगे perf. अध्येता p. fut. अध्येष्यते fut. अध्यगीष्यत-अध्यैष्यत con. अध्यगीष्ट-अध्यैष्ट aor., अध्येषीष्ट ben. Pass.—अधीयते pre. अध्यगायि-अध्यायि (3rd dual, अध्यगायिषाताम्—अध्यगीषाताम्-अध्यायिषाताम्-अध्यैषाताम्) aor. अध्यायिता—अध्येता p. fut. अध्यायिष्यते-अध्येष्यते fut. अध्यगायिष्यत—अध्यगीष्यत—अध्यायिषत—अध्यैष्यत con. अध्यायिषीष्ट, अध्येषीष्ट ben. Cau.—अध्यापयति pre. अध्यापिपत्—अध्यजीगपत aor. अधीत p.p.

इख् 1 P. गतौ to go, to move; एखति pre. इयेख perf. एखिता p. fut. ऐखात् Aor.

इङ्ग् 1 P to go, to agitate; इङ्गति pre. इङ्गांचकार-बभूव-आस perf. इङ्गिता p. fut. ऐङ्गीद् aor. इङ्गित p.p. [Also A. see Bhag. VI. 16]

इट 1 P. गतौ to go; एटति pre. इयेट perf. एटिता p. fut ऐटीत् aor.

इन्द् 1 P. परमैश्वर्ये to have great power; इन्दति pre. ऐन्दत् Imperf. इन्दाञ्चकार—बभूव—आस perf. इन्दिता p. fut. इन्दिष्यति fut. ऐन्दिष्यत् con. ऐन्दीत् aor. इन्द्यात् ben. इन्दित p.p.

7 A. दीप्तौ to shine, to kindle; इन्धे pre. इन्धांचक्रे—आस—बभूव (ईधे in the Veda) perf. इन्धिता p. fut इन्धिष्यते fut. ऐन्धिष्यत con. ऐन्धिष्ट Aor. इंदिधिषते des. इंधिषीष्ट ben. Pass.—इध्यते pre. Cau.—इन्धयति—ते pre. इद्ध p.p.

इष् 6 P. इच्छायाम् to wish; इच्छति pre. इयेष perf. एष्टा or एषिता

p. fut. एषिष्यति fut. ऐषिष्यत् con. ऐषीत् Aor. एषिषिषति des. इष्यात् ben. Pass.—इष्यते pre. ऐषि aor. Cau.—एषयति—ते pre. ऐषिषत्—त aor. इष्ट्वा or एषित्वा ger. इष्ट p. p.

इष् 4 P. गतौ to go; इष्यति pre. एषिता p. fut. इषित p. p. एषित्वा ger. Other forms like those of the above.

इष् 9 P. *आभीक्ष्ण्ये to repeat; इष्णाति pre. इयेष &c. like those of इष् 6.

ई—

ई 1 P. गतौ to go; 2 P. to go, to pervade &c.; अयति-एति pre. अयां-चकार-बभूव-आस perf. एता p. fut. एष्यति fut. ऐष्यत् con. ऐषीत् aor.

ई 4 A. to go; ईयते pre. अयांचक्रे perf. एष्यते fut. ऐष्ट Aor. इयीषते des. Cau—आययति-ते pre.

ईक्ष् 1 A. दर्शने to look at, to see, ईक्षते pre. ईक्षां—चक्रे-बभूव—आस perf. ईक्षिता p. fut. ईक्षिष्यते fut. ऐक्षिष्यत con. ईक्षिषीष्ट ben. ऐक्षिष्ट aor. Cau—ईक्षयति-ते pre. ऐचिक्षत्-त aor. ईचिक्षिषते des. Pass—ईक्ष्यते pre. ऐक्षि aor. ईक्षित p. p. ईक्षित्वा ger ईक्षितुम् inf.

ईज् 1 A. गतिकुत्सनयोः to go, to censure; ईजते pre. ईजांचक्रे perf. ऐजिष्ट aor. ईजित p. p.

ईड् 2 A. स्तुतौ to praise; ईड्टे pre. ईडांचक्रे-बभूव—आस perf; ईडिता p. fut. ईडिष्यते fut. ऐडिष्यत con. ऐडिष्ट aor. ईडिषीष्ट ben. Pass—ईड्यते pre. Cau—ईडयति—ते pre. ऐडिडत्-त aor. ईडित्वा ger. ईडितुम् inf. ईडित p. p.

ईर् 1 P. गतौ to go, to shake; ईरति pre. ईरित p. p.

ईर् 2 A. गतौ to go &c.; ईर्ते pre. ईरांचक्रे perf. ईरिता p. fut ईरिष्यते fut. ऐरिष्यत con. ऐरिष्ट aor. ईरिषीष्ट ben. Cau—ईरयति-ते pre. ऐरिरत्-त aor. ईरित p. p.

---

* According to some, the forms of the p. fut. and the gerund in त्वा of this root are एषिता and एषित्वा only.

ईर् 10 U. क्षेपे to move, to throw; ईरयति—ते pre. ईरयांचकार or चक्रे perf. ऐरिरत्–त aor. ईरयिता p. fut. ईरयिष्यति—ते fut. ऐरयिष्यत्–त con. ईर्यात्–ईरयिषीष्ट Ben. ईरित p. p.

ईर्ष्य् 1 P. ईर्ष्यायाम् to envy; ईर्ष्यति pre. ईर्ष्यांचकार-आस-बभूव perf. ईर्ष्यिता p. fut. ईर्ष्यिष्यति fut. ऐर्ष्यिष्यत् con. ऐर्ष्यीत् aor. ईर्ष्यियिषति or ईर्ष्यिषिषति des. Cau—ईर्ष्ययति–ते pre. ऐर्ष्यियत्—त aor.

ईश् 2 A ऐश्वर्ये to command, to rule, to possess; ईष्टे pre. ईशांचक्रे-आस-बभूव; perf. ईशिता p. fut. ईशिष्यते fut. ऐशिष्यत् con. ईशिषीष्ट ben. ऐशिष्ट aor. Pass.—ईश्यते pre. ऐशि aor. Cau—ईशयति-ते pre. ऐशिशत्-त Aor. ईशित p. p.

ईष् 1 A. गतिहिंसादर्शनेषु to go, to kill, to see; ईषते pre. ईषांचक्रे perf. ईषिता p. fut. ईषिष्यते fut. ऐषिष्यत con. ऐषिष्ट aor. ईशिषीष्ट ben. ईषित p. p.

ईह् 1 A चेष्टायाम् to aim at; ईहते pre. ईहांचक्रे-आस-बभूव perf. ईहिता p. fut. ईहिष्यते fut. ऐहिष्यत con. ऐहिष्ट aor. ईजिहिषते des. ईहिषीष्ट ben. Cau—ईहयति–ते pre. ऐजिहत्-त aor.

उ—

उक्ष् 1. P. सेचने to sprinkle, to wet; उक्षति pre. उक्षांचकार—बभूव-आस perf. उक्षिता p. fut. उक्षिष्यति fut. औक्षिष्यत con. औक्षीत् aor. उक्ष्यात् ben. उचिक्षिषति des. उक्षित p. p.

उख् 1 P. to go, to move; ओखति pre. औखत् imperf. उवोख perf. ओखिता p. fut. ओखिष्यति fut. औखिष्यत् con. औखीत् aor. ओचिखिषति des. उख्यात् ben. Pass—उख्यते pre. Cau.—ओखयति-ते pre. ओखित or उखित p. p. (also written as उंख-उंखति pre. &c.)

उच् 4 P. समवाये to collect together; उच्यति pre. उवोच perf. ओचिता p. fut. ओचिष्यति fut. औचिष्यत् con. उच्यात् ben. औचत् aor. उचित or उग्र p. p.

उच्छ् 1 P. विवासे to finish, to abandon; उच्छति pre. उच्छामास &c. perf. उच्छिष्यति fut. औच्छित् aor. उचिच्छिषति des. Cau— उच्छयति-ते pre. औचिच्छत्-त aor. उच्छित p. p.

उज्झ् 6 P. उत्सर्गे to abandon, to avoid; उज्झति pre. उज्झांचकार-आस-बभूव perf. उज्झिता p. fut. उज्झिष्यति fut. औज्झिष्यत् con. औज्झीत् aor. Cau—उज्झयति-ते pre. औजिज्झत्-त aor. उजिज्झिषति des. उज्झित p. p.

उञ्छ् 1, 6 P. to glean; उञ्छति pre. उञ्छाञ्चकार perf. उञ्छिष्यति fut. औञ्छीत Aor. उञ्चिचिछषति des. Cau.—उञ्छयति pre. औञ्चिच्छत्-त des. उञ्छित p. p.

उठ् 1 P. उपघाते to strike, to destroy; ओठति pre उवोठ perf. ओठिता p. fut ओठिष्यति fut. औठीत् Aor. उठित p. p.

उन्द् 7 P. क्लेदने to wet, to moisten; उनत्ति pre. उन्दांचकार &c. perf. उन्दिता p. fut. उन्दिष्यति fut. औन्दिष्यत् con. औन्दीत् aor. उन्दिदिषति des. उत्त or उन्न p. p.

उभ् or उम्भ् 6 P. पूरणे to fill with, to cover over; उभति or उम्भति pre. उवोभ or उम्भाञ्चकार perf. ओभिष्यति or उम्भिष्यति fut. औभीत् or औम्भीत् aor. उभित or उम्भित p. p.

उर्द् 1 A. माने क्रीडायां च to measure, to play; ऊर्दते pre. ऊर्दाञ्चक्रे-बभूव-आस perf. ऊर्दिता p. fut. ऊर्दिष्यते fut. और्दिष्यत con. और्दिष्ट aor. ऊर्दिदिषते des Cau.—ऊर्दयति-ते pre. और्दिदत्-त aor.

उर्व् 1 P. हिंसायाम् to kill; ऊर्वति pre. ऊर्वांचकार perf. ऊर्विता p. fut और्विष्यत् con. और्वीत् aor.

उष् 1 P. दाहे to burn, to punish; ओषति pre. उवोप, ओषांचकार-आस-बभूव perf. ओषिता p. fut. ओषिष्यति fut. औषिष्यत con. उष्यात् ben. औषीत् aor. ओषित-उषित p. p.

उह् 1 P. अर्दने to hurt, to kill, to destroy; ओहति pre. उवोह perf. ओहिष्यति fut. औहत्, औहीत् Aor. उहित or ओहित p. p.

ऊ—

ऊन्—10 U. परिहाणे to lessen; ऊनयति-ते pre. ऊनयिष्यति fut. औननत् -त Aor. ऊनिनयिषति-ते des.

ऊय् 1 A. तन्तुसन्ताने to weave, to sew; ऊयते pre. ऊयांचक्रे-बभूव-आस perf. ऊयिता p. fut. ऊयिष्यते fut. औयिष्यत con. औयिष्ट aor. ऊयिषीष्ट ben. Cau—ऊययति-ते pre. ऊत p. p.

ऊर्ज 1, 10 U. बलप्राणनयोः to strengthen, to live; ऊर्जति, ऊर्जयति-ते pre. और्जीत, और्जिजत्—त aor.

ऊर्णु 2 U. आच्छादने to cover, to hide; ऊर्णोति, ऊर्णौति or ऊर्णुते pre. ऊर्णुनाव--नव or ऊर्णुनवे perf. ऊर्णविता or ऊर्णुविता p. fut. ऊर्णविष्यति-ते or ऊर्णुविष्यति-ते fut. और्णवीत्, और्णावीत, और्णु-वीत्, और्णविष्ट or और्णुविष्ट aor ऊर्णूयात्, ऊर्णविषीष्ट or ऊर्णुविषीष्ट ben. Cau—ऊर्णावयति-ते pre. और्णूनवत्-त aor. Pass. —ऊर्णूयते pre. ऊर्णुनुवे perf. और्णावि aor. ऊर्णविता, ऊर्णाविता or ऊर्णुविता p. fut. ऊर्णविषीष्ट, ऊर्णाविषीष्ट or ऊर्णुविषीष्ट ben. और्णाविष्यत, और्णविष्यत or और्णुविष्यत con,

ऊर्द् 1 A, to sport, to play; ऊर्दते pre. (same as उर्द्,)

ऊष् 1 P, रुजायाम् to be diseased or disordered; ऊषति pre. ऊषां-चकार &c. perf. औषीत् aor. ऊषित p. p.

ऊह् 1 A. (sometimes P.) वितर्के to conjecture, to reason, to infer; ऊहते pre. औहत imperf. ऊहांचक्रे &c. perf. ऊहिता p. fut. ऊहि-ष्यते fut. औहिष्यत con. औहिष्ट aor. ऊहिषीष्ट ben. Pass—ऊह्यते pre. औहि aor. Cau—ऊहयति-ते pre. औजिहत्-त aor. ऊहित p. p. ऊहित्वा ger:

ऋ—

ऋ 1 P. गतिप्रापणयोः to go, to get; ऋच्छति pre. आर्षीत् aor. } आर perf. अर्ता p. fut.

ऋ 3 P. to go; इयर्ति pre. आरत् aor. (with सम्, समारत). } आर perf. अर्ता p. fut.

अरिष्यति fut. आरिष्यत् con. अर्यात् ben. Pass.—अर्यते pre. आरि aor. आरे perf. आरिता-आर्ता p. fut. आरिष्यते-अरिष्यते fut. आरिषीष्ट-ऋषीष्ट ben. Cau.—अर्पयति-ते pre. आर्पयत्-त aor. अरिरिषति des. ऋत (also ऋण debt) p.p. ऋत्वा Ger.

ऋच् 6 P. स्तुतौ to praise, to shine; ऋचाति pre. आनर्च perf. आर्चीत् aor. ऋचित p.p.

ऋच्छ् 6 P. गतीन्द्रियप्रलयमूर्तिभावेषु to become hard, to fail in faculties, to go; ऋच्छति pre. आर्च्छत् Imperf. आनर्च्छ perf. ऋच्छिता p. fut. ऋच्छिष्यति fut. आर्च्छीत् Aor. Cau.—ऋच्छयति-ते Pre. आर्चिच्छत्-त aor. ऋचिच्छिषति des. ऋच्छित p.p.

ऋज् 1 A. गतिस्थानार्जनोपार्जनेषु to go, to acquire; अर्जते pre. आनृजे perf. अर्जिता p. fut. अर्जिष्यते fut. आर्जिष्यत con. अर्जिष्ट aor. अर्जिजिषते des. अर्जिषीष्ट ben. Pass.—ऋज्यते pre. आर्जि aor. Cau.—अर्जयति-ते pre. आर्जिजत-त aor. ऋजितं p.p.

ऋण् 8 U. to go; ऋणोति-ऋणुते, अर्णोति-अर्णुते pre. आनर्ण, आनृणे perf. अर्णिता p. fut. आर्णीत्, आर्णिष्ट-आर्त Aor. अर्णिणिषति-ते des.

ऋत्* जुगुप्सायां कृपायां च to censure, to be compassionate; ऋतीयते pre. ऋतीयांचक्रे &c. or आनर्त perf ऋतीयिता or अर्तिता p. fut. ऋतीयिष्यते, अर्तिष्यति fut. ऋतीयिषीष्ट-ऋत्यात् ben. आर्तीयिष्ट or आर्तीत aor.

ऋध् 4 p. वृद्धौ to prosper, to please; ऋध्यति pre. आनर्ध perf अर्धिता, p. fut. आर्द्धीत aor. अर्दिधिषति, ईर्त्सति des. ऋद्ध p. p. अर्धित्वा or ऋद्धा ger.

ऋधु 5 P. to increase, to prosper; ऋध्नोति pre. आर्धीत् aor. (For the remaining forms see the root ऋध् 4 P.)

ऋफ्, ऋम्फ् 6 P. to kill; ऋफति, ऋंफति pre. आनर्फ, ऋम्फाञ्चकार &c. perf.

ऋष् 6 P. approach, to injure; ऋषति pre. आनर्ष perf. अर्षिता p. fut. अर्षिष्यति fut. आर्षीत् aor. ऋष्ट p.p.

---

*This is not in the Dhátupâtha but it is given in the Sútra "ऋतेरीयङ्"

ॠ—

ॠ 9 P. to go; to move; ॠणाति pre. अराञ्चाकार &c. perf. अरिता or अरीता p. fut. अरिष्यति or अरीष्यति fut. आरीत् aor. ईर्यात् ben. ईर्ण p.p.

ए—

एज् 1 A. दीप्तौ to shine, P. कम्पने to shake; एजते—ति pre. ऐजत-त् imperf. एजांचक्रे-चकार perf. एजिता p. fut. एजिष्यते-ति fut. ऐजिष्यत-त् con. ऐजिष्ट,-ऐजीत् aor. एजित p.p.

एठ् 1 A. बाधायां to annoy, to resist; एठते pre. एठित pp.

एध्* 1 A. वृद्धौ to grow, to prosper; एधते pre. एधांचक्रे-बभूव-आस perf. एधिता p. fut. एधिष्यते fut. ऐधिष्यत con. ऐधिष्ट aor. एदिधिषते des. एधिषीष्ट Ben. Pass.—एध्यते pre. ऐधि aor. Cau.—एधयति-ते. ऐदिधत्-त Aor. एधित p.p.

एष् 1 A. to go; एषते pre. एषित p.p.

ओ—

ओखृ† 1 P. शोषणालंमर्थयोः to be dry, to adorn, to be sufficient; ओखति pre. ओखांचकार-बभूव-आस perf. ओखिता p. fut. ओखिष्यति fut. औखिष्यत् con. औखीत् aor. ओचिखिषति des. Cau.—ओखयति-ते pre. औचिखत्-त aor.

ओलंड् 10 U. उत्क्षेपणे to throw up; ओलण्डयति-ते pre. ओलण्डित p.p.

क—

कक् 1 A. लौल्ये to wish to be proud; ककते pre. चकके perf. ककिता p. fut. ककिष्यते fut. अककिष्यत con. अककिष्ट aor.

कख् 1 P. हसने to laugh; कखति pre. चकाख perf. कखिता p. fut. कखिष्यति fut. अकखिष्यत् con. अकखीत्-अकाखीत् aor.

---

* with उप=उपैधते. † With प्र=प्रोखति.

कक् 1 A. to go; कंकते pre. चकंके perf. कंकिता p. fut. अकंकिष्ट aor. कंकित p.p.

कच् 1 P. रवे to sound: कचति pre. चकाच perf. काचिता p. fut. कचिष्यति fut. अकचिष्यत् con. अक-का-चीत् aor.

कच् 1 A. बन्धने to bind; कचते pre. चकचे perf. काचिता p. fut. कचिष्यते fut. अकाचिष्यत con. अकाचिष्ट aor.

कट् or कण्ट् 1 P. to go; कटति or कंटति pre. चकाट or चकंट perf. कटिता or कंटिता p. fut. कटिष्यति or कंटिष्यति fut. अकटिष्यत् or अकंटिष्यत् con. अकटीत् or अकंटीत aor.

कठ् 1 P. कृच्छ्रजीवने to live in difficulty; कठति pre. कठिष्यति fut. अकठीत्-अकाठीत् Aor.

कण्ठ् 1 P. 10 U. आध्याने to remember with regret; कंठति-कंठयति-ते pre. चकंठ, कंठयांचकार-चक्रे &c. perf. कंठिता or कंठयिता p. fut. कंठिष्यति, कंठयिष्यति-ते fut. अकंठिष्यत् or अकंठयिष्यत्-त con. अकंठीत्, अचकंठत्-त aor.

कण्ठ् 1 A. शोके to be anxious (with उत्); कंठते pre. चकंठे perf. कंठिता p. fut. अकंठिष्ट aor.

कण्ड् 1 U. मदे to be proud; कंडति-ते pre. चकंड or चकंडे perf. कंडिता p. fut. कंडिष्यति-ते fut. अकंडिष्यत्-त con. अकंडीत्-अकंडिष्ट aor.

कण्ड् 10 U. भेदने (भेदनं वितुषीकरणं) रक्षणे च to separate the chaff, to protect; कंडयति—ते pre. कंडयांचकार-चक्रे, &c. perf. कंडयिता p. fut. कंडयिष्यति-ते fut. अचकण्डत्-त aor.

कण् 1 P. आर्तस्वरे to cry in distress; कणति pre. चकाण perf. कणिता p. fut. कणिष्यति fut. अकणिष्यत् con. अकणीत्, अकाणीत् Aor.

कण् 10 U. निमीलने to wink; काणयति-ते pre. अचीकणत-त, अचकाणत-त Aor.

कण्डूय् 1 U. गात्रविघर्षणे to rub, to scratch; कंडूयति-ते pre. अकण्डूयीत्, अकण्डूयिष्ट Aor. कण्डूय्यात्, कण्डूयिषीष्ट ben.

कत्थ् 1 A. श्लाघायाम् to praise, to boast; कत्थते pre. चकत्थे perf. कत्थिता p. fut. कत्थिष्यते fut. अकत्थिष्यत con. कत्थिषीष्ट ben. अकत्थिष्ट aor. चिकत्थिषते des. कत्थित p.p.

कथ् 10 U. वाक्यप्रबन्धे to tell; कथयति-ते Pre. कथयांचकार, &c. Perf. कथयिता p. fut. कथयिष्यति-ते fut. अकथयिष्यत्-त con. अचकथत्-त aor. चिकथयिषति-ते des. कथ्यात् or कथयिषीष्ट ben. Pass.—कथ्यते pre.

कद् 1 A. वैक्लव्ये to grieve; कदते pre. चकदे perf. कदिता p. fut. अकदिष्ट aor. कदिषीष्ट ben.

कन् 1 P. दीप्तिकान्तिगतिषु to shine &c.; कनति pre. चकान perf. कनिता p. fut. अकनीत् aor.

कनय् (denom.) कनयति pre.

कम् 1 A. कान्तौ to desire; कामयते pre. चकमे or कामयांचक्रे &c. perf. कामयिता or कमिता p. fut. कामयिष्यते or कमिष्यते fut. अकामयिष्यत or अकमिष्यत con. कामयिषीष्ट or कमिषीष्ट ben. अचीकमत or अचकमत aor. Pass. काम्यते or कम्यते pre. अकामि aor. Cau.—कामयति-ते pre. कान्त p. p. कमित्वा-कान्त्वा, कामयित्वा ger.

कम्प् 1 A. चलने to shake, to tremble; कंपते pre. चकंपे perf. कंपिता p. fut. कंपिष्यते fut. अकंपिष्यत con. कंपिषीष्ट ben. अकंपिष्ट aor. Pass.—कंप्यते pre. Cau.—कंपयति-ते pre. अचकम्पत्-त Aor. चिकम्पिषते des.

कम्ब् 1 P. to go; कम्बति pre. चकम्ब perf. कम्बिता p. fut. अकम्बीत् aor.

कर्ण् 10 U. भेदने to pierce; कर्णयति-ते pre. कर्णयांचकार-चक्रे perf. कर्णयिता p. fut. कर्णयिष्यति-ते fut. अकर्णयिष्यत्-त con. अचकर्णत्-त aor.

कर्त् 10 U. शैथिल्ये to slacken; कर्तयति-ते pre. अचकर्तत्-त Aor.

कल् 1 A. शब्दसंख्यानयोः to sound, to count; कलते pre. चकले perf. कलिता p. fut. कलिष्यते fut. अकलिष्यत con. कलिषीष्ट ben. अकलिष्ट aor. कलित p.p.

कल 10 U. गतौ संख्याने च to go, to count; कलयति-ते pre. कलयांचकार-चक्रे perf. कलयिता p. fut. कलयिष्यति-ते fut. अकलयिष्यत्-त con. अचकलत्-त aor. चिकलयिषति-ते des. कलित p.p.

कल् 10 U. क्षेपे to throw; कालयति-ते pre. कालयांचकार &c. perf. कलयिष्याति-ते fut. अचीकलत्-त Aor. चिकालयिषति-ते des. Pass. -काल्यते pre. अकालि Aor. कालित p. p.

कव् 1. A. स्तुतौ वर्णने च to praise; कवते pre. चकवे perf. कविता p. fut. कविष्यते fut. अकविष्यत् con. अकविष्ट aor. Cau.-कावयति-ते pre.

कश् 1. P. शब्दे to sound; कशति pre. अकशीत्, अकाशीत् Aor.
कश् 2 A. गतिशासनयोः to go, to punish; कष्टे pre. चकशे perf. काशिता p. fut. अकाशिष्ट aor.

कष 1 P. घर्षणे to test, to scratch; कषति pre. चकाष perf. कषिता p. fut. काषिष्यति fut. अकषिष्यत् con. अकषीत्-अकाषीत् aor. चिकषिषति des. काषित (कष्ट painful p. p.).

कस् 1 P. to go; कसति pre. चकास perf. कसिता p. fut. कसिष्यति fut. अकसिष्यत con. अकासीत्,-अकसीत् aor. चिकसिषति des. Cau. -कासयति-ते pre. अचीकसत्-त aor.

कस् 2 A. गतिनाशनयोः to go, to destroy; कस्ते pre. अकसिष्ट Aor. (Also written कंस् .)

कांक्ष् 1 P. कांक्षायां to desire, to wish; कांक्षति pre. चकांक्ष perf. कांक्षिता p. fut. कांक्षिष्यति fut. अकांक्षिष्यत् con. अकांक्षीत् aor. कांक्ष्यात् ben. चिकांक्षिषति des. कांक्षित p. p.

कांश 1, 4 A. दीप्तौ to shine; काशते or काश्यते pre. चकाशे perf. काशिता p. fut. काशिष्यते fut. अकाशिष्यत con. काशिषीष्ट ben. चिकाशिषते des. अकाशिष्ट aor. Cau. काशयति-ते pre. Pass.—काश्यते pre. काशित p.p. काशित्वा, प्रकाश्य ger.

कास् 1 A. शब्दकुत्सायाम to cough; कासते pre.-कासांचक्रे &c. perf. कासिता p. fut. कासिष्यते fut. अकासिष्यत con. अकासिष्ट aor, चिकासिषते des. कासिषीष्ट ben. Cau.-कासयति-ते अचकासत्-त aor.

कित् 1 P. संशये रोगापनये च to suspect, to cure; चिकित्सति pre. -चिकित्सांचकार &c. perf. चिकित्सिता p. fut. चिकित्सिष्यति fut. अचिकित्सिष्यत् con. अचिकित्सीत् aor. Pass.-चिकित्स्यते pre. Cau. -चिकित्सयति-ते pre. चिकित्सिषति des. (Also A. चिकित्सते pre. अचिकित्सिष्ट aor.)

कित् 1 P. इच्छायां to desire, to live; केतति pre. चिकेत perf. अकेतीत् aor.

कित् 10 P. निवासे to dwell; केतयति pre. केतयिष्यति fut. अचीकितत् aor.

किल् 1 P. श्वेतक्रीडनयोः to become white, to sport; किलति pre. चिकेल perf. केलिता p. fut. केलिष्यति fut. अकेलिष्यत् con. अकेलीत् aor.

कील् 1 P. बन्धने to bind; कीलति pre. चिकील perf. कीलिता p. fut. अकीलीत् aor. चिकीलिषति des.

कु 1 A. शब्दे to sound; कवते pre. चुकुवे perf. कोता p. fut. कोष्यते fut. अकोष्यत con. अकोष्ट aor.

कु 2 P. to sound; कौति pre. चुकाव (चुकविथ, चुकोथ 2nd sing.) perf. कोता p. fut. कोष्यति fut. अकोष्यत् con. अकौषीत् aor. चोकूयते Freq.

कु 6 A शब्दे (आर्तस्वरे) to sound, to moan; कुवते pre. चुकुवे perf. कुता p. fut. अकुत aor. कोकूयते freq.

कुच् 1 P. शब्दे तारे संपर्चनकौटिल्यप्रतिष्टम्भनविलेखनेषु च to sound loudly, to come in contact, to be crooked &c.; कोचति pre. चुकोच perf. कोचिता p. fut. कोचिष्यति fut. अकोचिष्यत् con. अकोचीत् aor.

कुच् 6 P. संकोचने (कुटादि) to contract; कुचति pre. चुकोच (चुकुचिथ 2nd sing.) perf. अकुचीत् aor. चिकुचिषति des.

कुट् 6 P. to curve, to bend; कुटति pre. चुकोट (चुकुटिथ 2nd sing.) perf. कुटिता p. fut. कुटिष्यति fut. अकुटिष्यत् con. अकुटीत् aor. Cau.-कोटयति-ते pre. कुटित p. p.

कुण् 6. P. शब्दोपकरणयोः to sound, to support; कुणति pre. चुकोण perf. कोणिता p. fut अकोणीत् aor. कुणित p. p.

कुण्ठ् 1. p. प्रतिघाते to be blunted; कुण्ठति pre. अकुण्ठीत् aor.

कुण्ठ् 10. U. वेष्टने to cover; कुण्ठयति-ते pre. अचुकुण्ठत्-त Aor.

कुत्स् 10. A. अवक्षेपणे to abuse; कुत्सयते pre. कुत्सयांचक्रे &c. perf. कुत्सयिष्यते fut. अचुकुत्सत aor. कुत्सयिषीष्ट ben.

कुन्थ् 1. P. हिंसाक्लेशनयोः to kill &c.; कुंथति pre. चुकुंथ perf. कुंथिता p. fut. कुंथिष्यति fut. अकुंथिष्यत् con. अकुंथीत् aor. चुकुंथिषति des. Cau.-कुंथयति-ते pre. Pass.-कुन्थ्यते pre. कुन्थित्वा ger. कुन्थित p.p.

कुप् 4 P. क्रोधे to be angry; कुप्यति pre. चुकोप perf. कोपिता p. fut कोपिष्यति fut. अकोपिष्यत् con. अकुपत् aor. चुकोपिषति, चुकुपिषति des. कुप्यात् ben. कुपित p.p. कोपितुम् Inf.

कुप् 10 U. भाषायां द्युतौ च to speak, to shine; कोपयति-ते pre. अचुकुपत्-त Aor.

कुर्द् 1 A. क्रीडायां to play; कूर्दते perf. चुकूर्दे perf. अकूर्दिष्ट Aor.

कुंश् 10 U. 1 P. दीप्तौ to shine; कुंशयति-ते, कुंशति pre. कुंशयांचकार-चक्रे; चुकुंश perf. कुंशयिता, कुंशिता p. fut. अचुकुंशत-त्, अकुंशीत् aor.

कुष् 9 P. निष्कर्षे to tear, to expel; कुष्णाति pre. चुकोष* perf. कोषिता p. fut कोषिष्यति fut. अकोषीत् aor. चिकोषिषति, चिकुषिषति des. Pass. कुष्यते pre. अकोषि Aor. Cau.-कोषयति-ते pre. अचूकुषत्-त Aor.

कुस् 4 P. संश्लेषणे to embrace; कुस्यति pre चुकोस perf. कोसिता p. fut. कोसिष्यति fut. अकोसिष्यत् con. कुस्यात् Ben. अकुसत् aor. चिकुसिषति, चुकोसिषति des. कुसित्वा, कोसित्वा ger.

कुंस् 10. U. 1 P. भाषायां to speak; कुंसयति-ते, कुंसति pre. अचुकुंसत्-त, अकुंसीत् Aor.

---

* With निर् this root is Wet; निश्चकोषिथ, निश्चकोष्ठ 2sing. perf. निरकोषीत्, निरकुक्षत् Aor. des. निश्चुकुक्षति also; inf. निष्कोष्टुं also.

कुह् 10 A. विस्मापने to astonish; कुहयते pre. कुहयांचक्रे, &c. perf. अचुकुहत aor. चुकुहयिषते des.

कु 6 A. शब्दे to sound, to cry in distress: कुवते pre. चुकुवे perf. कुविता p. fut. कुविष्यते fut. अकुविष्यत con. अकुविष्ट aor.

कू 9 U. शब्दे to sound; कुनाति-नीते pre. कविष्यति-ते fut. अकावीत्-अकविष्ट Aor.

कूज् 1 P. अव्यक्ते शब्दे to make an inarticulate sound, to coo; कूजति pre. चुकूज perf. कूजिता p. fut. कूजिष्यति fut. अकूजिष्यत् con. अकूजीत् aor. कूज्यात् Ben. Pass.—कूज्यते pre. अकूजि aor. Cau.-कूजयति-ते pre. कूजित्वा ger. कूजित p.p.

कूड् 6. P. दार्ढ्ये to be firm; कूडति pre. चुकूड perf. कूडिता p. fut. अकूडीत् aor.

कूण 10 U. आभाषणे to speak, to converse; कूणयति-ते pre. कूणित p.p.

कूण् 10 A. संकोचने to close; कूणयते pre. अचुकूणत Aor कूणित p. p.

कूर्द् 1 U. क्रीडायाम् to jump, to frolic; कूर्दति-ते pre. कूर्दित p.p.

कूल 1 P. आवरणे to cover; कूलति pre. चुकूल perf. कूलिता p. fut. कूलिष्यति fut. अकूलिष्यत् con. अकूलीत् aor.

कृ 5. U. हिंसायाम् to hurt, to kill; कृणोति-कृणुते pre.

कृ 8 U. करणे to do; करोति-कुरुते pre. चकार-चक्रे perf. कर्ता p. fut. करिष्यति-ते fut. अकरिष्यत् -त con. अकार्षीत्-अकृत aor. क्रियात्-कृषीष्ट Ben. Pass.-क्रियते pre. अकारि (3rd dual अकारिषाताम्, अकृषाताम्) aor. Cau.-कारिता-कर्ता p. fut. कारिष्यते-करिष्यते fut. कारिषीष्ट-कृषीष्ट, अकारिष्यत-अकरिष्यत con. Cau.-कारयति-ते pre. अचीकरत्-त aor. चिकीर्षति-ते des. कृत p.p. कृत्वा अनुकृत्य ger. कर्तुम् inf.

कृत् 6 P. छेदने to cut, to divide; कृन्तति pre. चकर्त perf. कर्तिता fut. कर्तिष्यति fut. अकर्तिष्यत् con. अकर्तीत् aor. कृत्यात् Ben. चिकर्तिषति-चिकृत्सति des. Cau.—कर्तयति-ते pre. अचकर्तत्-त &c. अचीकृतत्-त aor. Pass.—कृत्यते pre. अकर्ति Aor. कृत्त p. p. कर्तित्वा -अनुकृत्य ger. कर्तितुम् Inf.

कृत् 7. P. वेष्टने to surround; कृणत्ति pre; for perf. and other forms see the above root.

कृश् 4. P. तनूकरणे to become lean or thin; कृश्यति pre. चकर्श perf. कर्शिष्यति fut. अकर्शिष्यत् con. अकृशत् aor.

कृष् 1 P. विलेखने to draw, to pull, to plough; कर्षति pre. चकर्ष perf. कर्ष्टा or क्रष्टा p. fut. कर्क्ष्यति or क्रक्ष्यति fut. अकर्क्ष्यत्-अक्रक्ष्यत् con. अकार्क्षीत् or अक्राक्षीत् or अकृक्षत् aor. चिकृक्षति des. Cau.—कर्षयति-ते pre. अचीकृषत्-त or अचकर्षत्-त aor. कृष्ट p.p कृष्ट्वा Ger. Pass.—कृष्यते pre. अकार्षि Aor.

कृष् 6 P. A. विलेखने to make furrows, to plough; कृषति-ते pre. चकर्ष-चकृषे perf. कर्ष्टा or क्रष्टा p. fut. कर्क्ष्यति-ते or क्रक्ष्यति-ते fut. अकर्क्ष्यत्-त, अक्रक्ष्यत्-त con. अकार्क्षीत्-अक्राक्षीत्-अकृक्षत् अकृष्ट-अकृक्षत aor. कृष्यात्-कृक्षीष्ट ben. चिकृक्षति-ते des. कृष्ट p.p

कॄ 6 P. विक्षेपे to pour out, to scatter; किरति pre. चकार perf. करिता or करीता p. fut. करिष्यति-करीष्यति fut. अकरिष्यत्-अकरीष्यत् con. अकारीत् aor. कीर्यात् ben. चिकरिषति des. Pass.—कीर्यते pre. Cau.—कारयति-ते pre. कीर्ण p.p.

कॄ 9 U. हिंसायाम् to injure, to kill; कृणाति or कृणीते pre. चकार-चक्रे perf. अकारीत्, अकरि-री-त अकीर्ष्ट aor. चिकरिषति—ते, चिकरीषति-ते, चिकीर्षति-ते des.

कॄत् 10 U. संशब्दने to name, to glorify; कीर्तयति-ते pre. कीर्तयाञ्चकार-चक्रे perf. कीर्तयिता p. fut. कीर्तयिष्यति-त fut. अकीर्तयिष्यत्-त con. कीर्त्यात्-कीर्तयिषीष्ट Ben. अचीकृतत-त aor. Pass—कीर्त्यते pre. कीर्तित p.p.

क्लृप् 1 A. सामर्थ्ये to be able or fit for. कल्पते pre. चक्लृपे perf. कल्पिता, कल्प्ता p. fut. कल्पिष्यते, कल्प्स्यते-ति fut. अक्लृपत्, अकल्पिष्ट अक्लृप्त aor. कल्पिषीष्ट, क्लृप्सीष्ट ben. चिकल्पिषते, चिक्लृप्सति-des. कल्पित्वा, क्लृप्त्वा ger. कल्पितुम, कल्प्तुम् inf.

केप् 1 A. कम्पने to shake; केपते pre. चिकेपे perf. अकेपिष्ट aor.

केलृ 1 P. चलने to shake; केलति pre. अकेलीत् aor. केलित p.p.

कै 1 P. शब्दे to sound; कायति pre. चकौ perf. काता p. fut. कास्यति fut. अकास्यत् con. अकासीत् aor. कायात् Ben. चिकासति des. Pass.—कायते.

क्रथ् 1 P. 10 U. हिंसायाम् to kill; क्रथति, क्रथयति-ते pre. अक्रथीत्, अक्राथीत्, अचिक्रथत्-त aor.

क्नू 9 U. to sound; क्नूनाति-क्नूनीते pre. अक्नावीत्, अक्नविष्ट aor.

क्नूय् 1. A. शब्दे उन्दे च to make a creaking sound; क्नूयते pre. चुक्नूये perf. क्नूयिता p. fut. क्नूयिष्यते fut. अक्नूयिष्ट aor. Cau.—क्नोपयति-ते pre. अचुक्नुपत्-त aor. चुक्नूयिषते des.

क्रन्द् 1 P. रोदने, आह्वाने to cry, to weep, to call; क्रन्दति pre. चक्रन्द perf. क्रन्दिता p. fut. क्रन्दिष्यति fut. अक्रंदिष्यत् con. क्रन्द्यात् ben. अक्रन्दीत् aor. चिक्रन्दिषति des. Cau.—क्रन्दयति-ते pre. अचक्रन्दत्-त Aor. Pass.—क्रन्द्यते, क्रन्दित p.p. (Also Atm. क्रन्दते pre. अक्रन्दिष्ट aor.)

क्रन्द् 10 U. (क्रन्द्) सातत्ये to cry continually; generally with आ; क्रन्दयति-ते pre. क्रन्दयामास-बभूव &c. perf. क्रन्दयिता p. fut. क्रन्दयिष्यति-ते fut. अक्रन्दयिष्यत्-त con. अचक्रन्दत्-त aor. क्रन्दित p.p.

क्रम् 1 U. & 4 P. पादविक्षेपे to walk, to step; क्रामति, क्राम्यति, क्रमते pre. चक्राम-चक्रमे perf. क्रमिता-क्रन्ता p. fut. क्रमिष्यति-क्रंस्यते fut. अक्रमिष्यत्, अक्रंस्यत con. क्रम्यात्-क्रंसीष्ट ben. अक्रमीत्-अक्रंस्त aor. चिक्रमिषति, चिक्रंसते des. Cau.—क्रमयति-ते, अचिक्रमत्-त aor. Pass. क्रम्यते pre. क्रान्त p.p. क्रमित्वा क्रान्त्वा, क्रन्त्वा-आक्रम्य ger.

क्री 9 U. द्रव्यविनिमये to buy, to purchase; क्रीणाति or क्रीणीते pre. चिक्रीय, चिक्रिये perf. क्रेता p. fut. क्रेष्यति-ते fut. क्रीयात्, क्रेषीष्ट ben. अक्रैषीत्, अक्रेष्ट aor. चिक्रीषति-ते des. Pass.—क्रीयते. अक्रायि aor. क्रीत p.p. Caus.—क्रापयति-ते, अचिक्रपत् Aor.

क्रीड् 1 P. क्रीडायाम् to amuse oneself, to play; क्रीडति pre. चिक्रीड perf. क्रीडिता p. fut. क्रीडिष्यति fut. अक्रीडिष्यत् con. क्रीड्यात् ben. अक्रीडीत् aor. चिक्रीडिषति des. Pass.—क्रीड्यते, अक्रीडि aor. Cau.—क्रीडयति-ते, अचिक्रीडत् aor. क्रीडित p.p. क्रीडित्वा ger. क्रीडितुम् inf.

क्रुध् 4 P. क्रोधे to be angry; क्रुध्यति pre. चुक्रोध perf. क्रोद्धा p. fut. क्रोत्स्यति fut. अक्रोत्स्यत् con. क्रुध्यात् ben. अक्रुधत् aor. क्रुद्ध p.p.

Pass.—क्रुध्यते pre. अक्रोधि aor. Cau.—क्रोधयति-ते, अचुक्रुधत्-त Aor. चुक्रुत्सति des.

क्रुश् I. P. आह्वाने रोदने च to call, to cry, to lament; क्रोशति pre. चुक्रोश perf. क्रोष्टा p. fut. क्रोक्ष्यति fut. अक्रोक्ष्यत् con. क्रुश्यात् ben. अक्रुक्षत् aor. Pass.—क्रुश्यते, अक्रोशि aor. Cau. क्रोशयति-ते, अचुक्रुशत्-त aor. चुक्रुक्षति des. क्रुष्ट p.p. क्रुष्ट्वा ger. क्रोष्टुम् inf.

क्रेव् 1. A. सेवने to serve; क्रेवते pre. चिक्रेवे perf. क्रेविता p. fut. अक्रेविष्ट aor.

क्लन्द 1. P रोदने to lament, to call; क्लंदति pre. चक्लंद perf. क्लंदिता P. fut. अक्लंदीत् aor.

क्लद् 4 A. वैकल्ये to be confused: क्लद्यते pre. चक्लदे perf. क्लदिता p. fut. अक्लदिष्ट aor.

क्लप् 10 U. अव्यक्तशब्दे to whisper; क्लपयति-ते pre. क्लपयाञ्चकार—चक्रे &c. perf. क्लपयिता p. fut. अचिक्लपत्—aor.

क्लम् 1 & 4 P. ग्लानौ to be fatigued or tired; क्लामति & क्लाम्यति pre. चक्लाम perf. क्लमिता p. fut. क्लमिष्यति fut. क्लम्यात् ben. अक्लमत् aor. चिक्लमिषति des. क्लान्त p.p. क्लमित्वा, क्लान्त्वा ger.

क्लिद् 4 P. आर्द्रीभावे to become wet; क्लिद्यति pre. चिक्लेद perf. क्लेदिता, क्लेत्ता p. fut. क्लेदिष्यति, क्लेत्स्यति fut. अक्लेदिष्यत्-अक्लेत्स्यत् con. क्लिद्यात् ben. अक्लिदत् aor. क्लिन्न p.p. Pass.—क्लिद्यते, अक्लेदि aor.

क्लिन्द् (क्लिदि) 1. U. परिदेवने to lament; क्लिन्दति-ते pre. चिक्लिन्द-न्दे perf. क्लिन्दिता p. fut. क्लिन्दिष्यति-ते fut. अक्लिन्दिष्यत्-त con. अक्लिन्दीत्-अक्लिन्दिष्ट aor. Pass.—क्लिन्द्यते.

क्लिश् 4 A. उपतापे (rarely P.) to be afflicted, to suffer; क्लिश्यते pre. चिक्लिशे perf. क्लेशिता p. fut. क्लेशिष्यते fut. अक्लेशिष्यत con. क्लेशिषीष्ट ben. अक्लेशिष्ट aor. चिक्लिशिषते, चिक्लेशिषते, des. Pass. क्लिश्यते pre., अक्लेशि aor. क्लिष्ट or क्लिशित p.p.

क्लिश् 9 P. विबाधने to torment, to distress; क्लिश्नाति pre. चिक्लेश perf. क्लेशिता, क्लेष्टा p. fut. क्लेशिष्यति, क्लेक्ष्यति fut. अक्लेशिष्यत्, अक्लेक्ष्यत con. क्लिश्यात Ben. अक्लेशीत्, अक्लिक्षत् aor. चिक्लिशिषति

चिक्लीशिषति, चिक्लिक्षति des. क्लिशित or क्लिष्ट p.p. क्लिशित्वा क्लिष्ट्वा Ger.

क्लीब 1 A अधार्ष्ट्ये to be timid; क्लीबते pre. चिक्लीबे perf. क्लीबिता p. fut. अक्लिबिष्ट aor.

क्लेश् 1. A. अव्यक्तायां वाचि to speak inarticulately; क्लेशते pre. चिक्लेशे perf. क्लेशिता p. fut. क्लेशिष्यते fut. चिक्लेशिषते des.

क्वण् 1 P. अव्यक्तशब्दे to hum, to tinkle; क्वणति pre. चक्वाण perf. क्वणिता p. fut. क्वणिष्यति fut. अक्वणिष्यत् con. क्वण्यात् ben. अक्वणीत्—अक्वाणीत् aor. क्वणित p.p. Cau. क्वणयति-ते, अचिक्वणत्-त aor. चिक्वणिषति des.

क्वथ् 1 P. निष्पाके to boil, to digest; क्वथति pre. चक्वाथ perf. क्वथिता p. fut. क्वथिष्यति fut. अक्वथिष्यत् con. क्वथ्यात् Ben. अक्वथीत् aor. चिक्वथिषति des.

क्षज् 1 A. वधे to kill; क्षजते pre. क्षजिष्यते fut. अक्षजिष्ट Aor.

क्षंज् 1 A. गतौ दाने च to move, to give; क्षंजते pre. चक्षंजे perf. क्षंजिता p. fut. अक्षंजिष्ट aor. (Also 10 U. 1. P.) क्षंजयति-ते क्षंजति pre. क्षंजयिता, क्षंजिता p. fut. अचक्षंजत्-त, अक्षंजीत् aor.

क्षण् 8 U. हिंसायां to hurt, to break, to kill; क्षणोति, क्षणुते pre. क्षणु, क्षणुष्व 2nd sing. Impera. चक्षाण. चक्षणे perf. क्षणिता p. fut. क्षणिष्यति-ते fut. अक्षणिष्यत्-त con. अक्षणीत्, अक्षणिष्ट, अक्षत aor. Cau.—क्षाणयति-ते pre. चिक्षणिषति-ते des. क्षणित्वा, क्षत्वा ger.

क्षप् 10 U. क्षेपे प्रेरणे च to send, te direct; क्षपयति-ते pre. क्षपयाञ्चकार-चक्रे &c. perf. क्षपयिता p. fut. क्षपयिष्यति-ते fut. अक्षपयिष्यत्-त con.—अचक्षपत्-त aor. चिक्षपयिषति-ते des.

क्षम् 1 A. सहने to allow, to suffer. क्षमते pre. चक्षमे perf. क्षमिता, क्षन्ता p. fut. क्षमिष्यते, क्षंस्यते fut, अक्षमिष्यत्-त con. क्षमिषीष्ट, क्षंसीष्ट ben. अक्षमिष्ट, अक्षंस्त aor. चिक्षमिषते, चिक्षंसते des. Cau—क्षमयति-ते, अचिक्षमत्-त aor. क्षान्त, क्षमित p.p. क्षमित्वा; क्षान्त्वा ger. Pass.—क्षम्यते, अक्षमि aor.

क्षम् 4 P. सहने to endure; क्षाम्यति pre. चक्षाम perf. क्षमिता or क्षन्ता p. fut. क्षमिष्यति, क्षंस्यति fut. अक्षमिष्यत्, अक्षंस्यत् con. क्षम्यात् ben. अक्षमत् aor. चिक्षमिषति, चिक्षंसति des.

क्षर् 1 P. संचलने to flow. to distil; क्षरति pre. चक्षार perf. क्षरिता p. fut. क्षरिष्यति fut. अक्षरिष्यत् con. अक्षारीत् aor. चिक्षरिषति des. क्षरित p. p.

क्षल् 10 U. शौचकर्मणि to wash, to cleanse, &c.; क्षालयति-ते pre. क्षालयाञ्चकार-चक्रे perf. क्षालयिता p. fut क्षालयिष्यति-ते fut. अक्षालयिष्यत्-त con. क्षाल्यात्, क्षालयिषीष्ट Ben. अचिक्षलत्-त aor. चिक्षालयिषति-ते des. क्षालित p. p. Sometimes 1 P. also. क्षालिष्यति fut. अक्षालीत् Aor. चिक्षलिषति des.

क्षि 1 P. क्षये to decay; क्षयति pre. क्षि 5. P. हिंसायां to destroy; क्षिणोति pre. क्षि 6 P. निवासगत्योः to dwell; क्षियति pre.	चिक्षाय perf. क्षेता p. fut. क्षेष्यति fut. अक्षेष्यत् con. क्षीयात् ben. अक्षैषीत् aor. चिक्षीषति des. Cau.-क्षाययति-ते, अचिक्षयत्-त Aor. क्षित, क्षीण p. p. क्षित्वा ger. Pass.-क्षीयते.

क्षिण् 8 U. हिंसायां to kill; क्षिणोति or क्षेणोति, क्षिणुते or क्षेणुते pre. चिक्षेण or चिक्षिणे perf. क्षेणिता p. fut. क्षेणिष्यति-ते fut. अक्षेणिष्यत्-त con. अक्षेणीत् or अक्षेणिष्ट-अक्षित aor. चिक्षिणिषति-ते, चिक्षेणिषति-ते des. क्षिणित्वा, क्षेणित्वा, क्षित्वा ger.

क्षिप् 4 P. प्रेरणे to throw, to cast; क्षिप्यति pre. चिक्षेप perf. क्षेप्ता p. fut. क्षेप्स्यति fut. अक्षेप्स्यत् con. अक्षैप्सीत् aor. क्षिप्यात् ben. Pass.-क्षिप्यते-अक्षेपि aor. Cau.-क्षेपयति-ते, अचिक्षिपत्-त aor. चिक्षिप्सति des. क्षिप्त p. p.

क्षिप् 6 U. to throw; क्षिपति-ते pre. चिक्षेप, चिक्षिपे perf. क्षेप्ता p. fut. क्षेप्स्यति-ते fut. अक्षैप्सीत्, अक्षिप्त aor. चिक्षिप्सति-ते des.

क्षिव् 1, 4. P. निरसने to spit; क्षेवति, क्षीव्यति pre. चिक्षेव perf. क्षेविष्यति fut. अक्षेवीत् Aor. चिक्षेविषति, चुक्ष्यूषति des.

क्षी 4 A. हिंसायां to kill; क्षीयते pre. चिक्षिये perf. अक्षेष्ट Aor. Cau.-क्षाययति-ते, अचिक्षयत्-त Aor.

क्षि 9 P to kill; क्षिणाति pre. चिक्षाय perf. क्षेता. p. fut. क्षेष्यति fut. अक्षेष्यत् con. क्षीयात् ben. अक्षैषीत् aor.

क्षीज् 1. P. अव्यक्ते शब्दे to sound inarticulately; क्षीजति pre. चिक्षीज perf. क्षीजिता p. fut. क्षीजिष्यति fut. अक्षीजिष्यत् con. क्षीज्यात् ben. अक्षीजीत् aor. चिक्षीजिषति des. Cau. क्षीजयति-ते, अचिक्षिजत्-त aor.

क्षीब् 1. A. मदे to be intoxicated; क्षीबते pre. चिक्षीबे perf. क्षीबिता p. fut. क्षीबिष्यते fut. अक्षीबिष्ट aor. cau.-क्षीबयति-ते pre. अचिक्षीबत्-त aor. चिक्षीबिषते des.

क्षीव् 1 P. निरसने to spit; क्षीवति pre. चिक्षीव perf. क्षीविता p. fut. अक्षीवीत् aor.

क्षु 2 P. शब्दे to cough; क्षौति pre. चुक्षाव perf. क्षविता p. fut. क्षविष्यति fut. अक्षविष्यत् con. अक्षावीत् aor. क्षूयात् ben. चुक्षूषति des. Pass.-क्षूयते, अक्षावि aor. Cau.-क्षावयति-ते, अचुक्षवत्-त Aor. क्षवितुम् inf.

क्षुद् 7 U. संपेषणे to strike against, to pound; क्षुणत्ति, क्षुंत्ते pre. चुक्षोद, चुक्षुदे perf. क्षोत्ता p. fut. क्षोत्स्यति-ते fut. क्षुद्यात्, क्षुत्सीष्ट ben. अक्षुदत्, अक्षौत्सीत्, अक्षुत्त aor. चुक्षुत्सति-ते des. क्षुण्ण p.p.

क्षुध् 4 P. बुभुक्षायां to be hungry; क्षुध्यति pre. चुक्षोध perf. क्षोद्धा p. fut. क्षोत्स्यति fut. अक्षोत्स्यत् con. क्षुध्यात् Ben. अक्षुधत् aor. Cau.—क्षोधयति-ते. अचुक्षुधत्-त aor. क्षुधित p.p. क्षोधित्वा, क्षुधित्वा ger. Pass.-क्षुध्यते pre. अक्षोधि aor.

क्षुभ् 1 A संचलने to be agitated, to disturb; क्षोभते pre. चुक्षुभे perf. क्षोभिता p. fut. क्षोभिष्यते fut. अक्षोभिष्यत con. क्षोभिषीष्ट Ben. अक्षुभत, अक्षोभिष्ट aor. चुक्षुभिषते, चुक्षोभिषते des. Cau.-क्षोभयति-ते, अचुक्षुभत्-त Aor. Pass.-क्षुभ्यते, अक्षोभि aor. क्षुभित, क्षोभित p.p.

क्षुभ् 4. & 9 p. to tremble; क्षुभ्यति & क्षुभ्नाति pre. चुक्षोभ perf. क्षोभिता p. fut. क्षोभिष्यति fut. अक्षोभिष्यत् con. क्षुभ्यात् Ben. अक्षुभत् (4) अक्षोभीत् (6) aor. क्षुब्ध, क्षुभित p.p.

क्षुर् 6 P. विलेखने to scratch or draw lines; क्षुरति pre. चुक्षोर perf. क्षोरिता p. fut. अक्षोरीत् aor.

क्षै 1. P. क्षये to waste; क्षायति pre. चक्षौ perf. क्षाता p. fut. क्षास्यति fut. अक्षास्यत् con. अक्षासीत् aor. Cau.-क्षपयति—ते, अचिक्षपत्—त Aor. चिक्षासति des. क्षाम p.p.

क्ष्णु 2 P. तेजने to sharpen; क्ष्णौति pre. चुक्ष्णाव perf. क्ष्णविता p. fut. क्ष्णविष्यति fut. अक्ष्णविष्यत् con. अक्ष्णावीत् aor. चुक्ष्णूषति des. क्ष्णुत p.p.

क्ष्माय् 1 A. विधूनने to shake; क्ष्मायते pre. चक्ष्माये perf. क्ष्मायिता p. fut. क्ष्मायिष्यते fut. अक्ष्मायिष्ट aor. Cau.-क्ष्मापयति-ते, अचक्ष्मपत्-त aor. चिक्ष्मायिष्यते des. क्ष्मायित p.p.

क्ष्विड् 1 U. 4 P. स्नेहमोचनयोः to be wet, to release; क्ष्वेडति-ते, क्ष्विड्यति pre. चिक्ष्वेड, चिक्ष्विडे perf. क्ष्वेडिता p. fut. क्ष्वेडिष्यति-ते fut. अक्ष्वेडिष्यत्-त con. अक्ष्विडत्, अक्ष्वेडिष्ट; अक्ष्विडत् aor. क्ष्वेडित or क्ष्विट्ट p.p.

क्ष्विद् 1 U. 4 P. स्नेहनमोचनयोः to be unctuous, to release: क्ष्वेदति-ते, क्ष्विद्यति pre. चिक्ष्वेद, चिक्ष्विदे perf. क्ष्वेदिता p. fut. क्ष्वेदिष्यति-ते fut. अक्ष्वेदिष्यत्—त con. 4 P. अक्ष्विदत् 1 अक्ष्विदत्, अक्ष्वेदिष्ट aor. चिक्ष्विदिषति-ते, चिक्ष्वेदिषति-ते, des. क्ष्विण्ण or क्ष्वेदित p.p.

क्ष्वेल् 1 P चलने to tremble; क्ष्वेलति pre. चिक्ष्वेल perf. क्ष्वेलिता p. fut. अक्ष्वेलीत् aor. Cau.—क्ष्वेलयति-ते, अचिक्ष्वेलत्—त aor. चिक्ष्वेलिषति des.

ख.

खक्ख् 1 P. हसने to laugh; खक्खति pre. चखक्ख perf. खक्खिता p. fut. खक्खिष्यति fut. अखक्खीत् aor. खक्ख्यात् Ben.

खच् 9 P. भूतप्रादुर्भावे to be born or produced again; खच्नाति pre. चखाच perf. खचिता p. fut. खचिष्यति fut. अखचीत् or अखाचीत् aor. चिखचिषति des.

खज् 1 P. (घटादिः) मन्थे to churn, to agitate; खजति pre. खजित p. p.

खञ्ज् 1 P. गतिवैकल्ये to limp, to walk lame; खञ्जति pre. चखंज perf. खंजिता p. fut खंजिष्यति fut. अखंजिष्यत् con. अखञ्जीत् Aor. खंज्यात् Ben. खंजित p. p.

खट् 1 P. काङ्क्षायाम् to desire, to wish, to search; खटति pre. चखाट perf. खटिता p. fut खटिष्यति fut. अखटिष्यत con. अखटीत्, अखाटीत् Aor.

खट्ट् 10 U. संवरणे to cover; खट्टयति—ते pre. खट्टयाञ्चकार—चक्रे perf. अचखट्टत्—त aor.

खण्ड् 1 A. भेदने to break, to disturb; खंडते pre. खंडित p.p.

खण्ड् 10 U. also. खण्डयति—ते pre. अचखण्डत्-त Aor. चिखण्डयिषति-ते des.

खद् 1 P. स्थैर्यहिंसाभक्षणेषु to be steady, to kill, to eat; खदति pre. चखाद perf. खदिता p. fut. खदिष्यति fut. अखदिष्यत con. अखदीत् अखादीत् aor. खद्यात् ben. Pass.-खद्यते pre. अखादि aor. Cau.-खादयति-ते pre. अचीखदत्-त Aor. चिखदिषति des. खदित p.p.

खन् 1 U. अवदारणे to dig; खनति-ते pre. चखान or चख्ने perf. खनिता p. fut. खनिष्यति—ते fut. अखनिष्यत्—त con. अखनीत्, अखानीत्, अखनिष्ट aor. खन्यात्, खायात्, खनिषीष्ट Ben. Pass.—खन्यते-खायते; चखानि aor. Cau.-खानयति—ते, अचीखनत् त aor. चिखनिषति—ते des. खात p.p. खात्वा or खनित्वा ger. (with उद् उत्खाय, उत्खन्य.)

खब् 1 P. गतौ to go; खबति pre. चखाब perf. अखबीत्, अखाबीत् aor.

खर्ज् 1 P. पूजाव्यथनयो: to worship, to pain, to be uneasy; खर्जति pre. चखर्ज perf. खर्जिता p. fut. खर्जिष्यति fut. अखर्जिष्यत् con अखर्जीत् Aor. खर्जित p.p.

खर्द् 1 P. दन्दशूके to bite; खर्दति pre. चखर्द perf. खर्दिता p. fut खर्दित p.p.

खर्व् 1 P. खर्वे to be proud, to go, to move; खर्वति pre. चखर्व perf. अखर्वीत् aor. खर्वित p.p.

खल् 1 P. चलने, संचये च to move, to gather; खलति pre. चखाल perf. खलिता p. fut. खलिष्यति fut. अखालीत् aor. खलित p.p.

खव् 9 P. भूतप्रादुर्भावे to come forth, to purify; खव्नाति pre. Another reading for खच्.

खष् 1 P. हिंसायाम् to kill; खषति pre.

खाद् 1 P. भक्षणे to eat, to devour; खादति pre. चखाद perf.-खादिता p. fut. खादिष्यति fut. अखादिष्यत् con. अखादीत् aor. खाद्यात् Ben. खादित p.p.

खिद् 6 P. परिघाते परितापे च to strike, to afflict; खिन्दति pre. चिखेद perf. खेत्ता p. fut. खेत्स्यति fut. अखेत्स्यत् con. अखैत्सीत् aor. चिखित्सति des. खिन्न p.p.

खिद् 4 & 7 A. दैन्ये to be depressed, to suffer pain or misery; खिद्यते & खिन्त्ते pre. चिखिदे perf. खेत्ता p. fut. खेत्स्यते fut. अखित्त aor. खिन्न p.p.

खिल् 6 P. उञ्छे to glean; खिलति pre.

खुज् 1 P. स्तेयकरणे to steal; खोजति pre. खुग्न p.p.

खुर् 6 P. छेदने to cut; खुरति pre. अखोरीत् aor.

खूर्द् 1 A. क्रीडायाम् to sport; खूर्दते pre.

खेल् 1 P. चलने to shake, to move to and fro; खेलति pre. चिखेल perf. खेलिता p. fut. खेलिष्यति fut. अखेलिष्यत् con. अखेलीत् aor. Cau.—खेलयति pre. अचिखेलत् aor. चिखेलिषति des.

खेला—विलासे to sport; खेलायति pre. खेलायाञ्चकार &c. perf. खेला यिता p. f. अखेलायीत् aor.

खेव् 1 A. सेवने to serve; खेवते pre. चिखेवे perf. खेविष्यति fut. अखेविष्ट Ao.. Cau.—खेवयति—ते.

खै 1 P. खेदने to strike &c; खायति pre. खास्यति fut. अखासीत् Aor.

खोर् 1 P. गतिप्रतिघाते to limp; खोरति pre. अखोरीत् Aor.

ख्या 2 P. प्रकथने to relate, to tell; ख्याति pre. अख्यान्, अख्युः 3rd pl. Imperf. ख्यात p.p. This is conjugated in the Conju. tenses only, According to the Nyásakára this is not used with the prep. सम्.

ग.

गज् 1 P. शब्दे मदे च to roar, to be drunk; गजति pre. जगाज perf. गजिता p. fut. अगजीत्, अगाजीत् Aor.

गञ्ज् 1 P. to sound in a particular way; गञ्जति pre. जगञ्ज perf. गञ्जिता p. fut. अगञ्जीत् aor.

गड् 1 P. सेचने to distil, to draw; गडति pre. जगाड perf. गडिता P. fut. अगडीत् Aor.

गण 10 U. संख्याने to count, enumerate; गणयति-ते pre. गणयाञ्चकार-चक्रे &c. perf. गणयिता p. fut. गणयिष्यति—ते fut. अगणयिष्यत्-त con. अजीगणत्—त, अजगणत्—त aor. गण्यात्, गणयिषीष्ट Ben. जिगणयिषति—ते des. गणित p.p. गणयित्वा, विगणय्य ger. Pass.—गण्यते (गणाप्यते according to some) pre.

गद् 1 P. व्यक्तायां वाचि to speak; गदति pre. जगाद perf. गदिता p. fut. गदिष्यति fut. अगदिष्यत् con. अगदीत्, अगादीत् aor. गद्यात् ben. जिगदिषति des. Cau.—गादयति—ते pre. अजीगदत्—त aor. Pass.—गद्यते pre. अगादि aor. गदित्वा ger. गदितुम् inf. गदित p.p.

गन्ध् 10 A. अर्दने to injure, to ask, to go; गन्धयते pre. अजगन्धत Aor.

गम 1. P. गतौ to go; गच्छति pre. जगाम perf. गन्ता p. fut. गमिष्यति fut. अगमिष्यत् con. अगमत् aor. गम्यात् Ben. जिगमिषति des. Pass.—गम्यते, अगामि aor. Cau.—गमयति—ते, अजीगमत्-त aor. गत p.p. गत्वा ger. गन्तुम् inf.

गर्ज् 1 P. शब्दे to thunder, to roar; गर्जति pre. जगर्ज perf. गर्जिता p. fut. गर्जिष्यति fut अगर्जिष्यत् con. अगर्जीत् aor. गर्ज्यात् Ben. जिगर्जिषति des.

गर्ज् 10 U. to roar; गर्जयति—ते pre. अजगर्जत्—त Aor.

गर्द् 1 P. शब्दे to sound, to roar; गर्दति pre. जगर्द perf. गर्दिष्यति fut. अगर्दीत् Aor.

गर्द् 10 U. to sound; गर्दयति—ते pre. गर्दयाञ्चकार-चक्रे &c. perf.

गर्ध् 10 U. अभिकांक्षायां to wish; गर्धयति—ते pre. गर्धयाञ्चकार—चक्रे &c. perf. अजगर्धत्—त Aor.

गर्ब् 1 P. to go; गर्बति pre. जगर्ब perf. गर्बिता p. fut. गर्बिष्यति p. fut.

गर्व् 1 P. दर्पे to be proud; गर्वति pre. जगर्व perf. गर्विता p. fut. अगर्वीत् Aor. जिगर्विषति des.

गर्व् 10 A. माने to be proud; गर्वयते pre. अजगर्वत Aor. जिगर्वयिषते des.

गर्ह् 1 A. कुत्सायां to blame; गर्हते pre. जगर्हे perf. गर्हिता p. fut. गर्हिष्यते fut. अगर्हिष्यत con. अगर्हिष्ट aor. गर्हिषीष्ट Ben. Cau.—गर्हयति-ते pre अजगर्हत्-त Aor. जिगर्हिषते des.

गर्ह् 10 U. 1. P. विनिन्दने to censure, to reproach; गर्हयति-ते, गर्हति pre. गर्हयाञ्चकार—चक्रे &c. जगर्ह perf. गर्हयिता, गर्हिता p. fut. गर्हयिष्यति-ते; गर्हिष्यति fut. अजगर्हत्-त, अगर्हीत् aor. जिगर्हयिषति-ते; जिगर्हिषति des.

गल 1 P. भक्षणे स्रावे च to eat, to drop, to fall down; गलति pre. जगाल perf. गलिता p. fut. गलिष्यति fut. अगलिष्यत् con. अगालीत् aor. जिगलिषति des. Pass.—गल्यते pre. अगालि aor.

गल् 10 A. स्रवणे to pour out, to filter; गालयते pre. गालयाञ्चक्रे perf. अजीगलत Aor. गलित p.p.

गल्भ 1 A. धाष्टर्ये to be bold (generally with प्र); गल्भते pre. जगल्भे perf. अगल्भिष्ट Aor. जिगल्भिषते des.

गवेष् 10 U. मार्गणे to hunt for, to seek; गवेषयति—ते pre. गवेषयाञ्चकार—चक्रे &c. perf. गवेषयिता p. fut. गवेषयिष्यति—ते fut. अजगवेषत्—त aor. गवेषित p.p. गवेषयित्वा ger.

गह् 10 U. गहने to be thick, to enter deeply into; गहयति—ते pre. गहयाञ्चकार—चक्रे &c. perf. अजगहत्—त Aor.

गा 1 A. to go; गाते pre. जगे perf. गाता p. fut. गास्यते fut. अगास्यत con. अगास्त aor. गासीष्ट Ben. जिगासते des. Cau.—गापयति-ते pre. अजीगपत्—त aor. Pass.—गायते pre. अगायि aor.

गा 3 P. to praise; जिगाति pre. (Vedic.)

गाध् 1 A. प्रतिष्ठालिप्सयोर्ग्रन्थे च to stand, to seek, to compose; गाधते pre. जगाधे perf. गाधिता p. fut. गाधिष्यते fut. अगाधिष्ट aor. गाधिषीष्ट Ben. Pass.—गाध्यते pre. अगाधि aor. जिगाधिषते des.

गाह् 1 A. विलोडने to dive into, to bathe; गाहते pre. जगाहे perf. गाहिता or गाढा p. fut. गाहिष्यते, घाक्ष्यते fut. अगाहिष्यत,

अघाक्ष्यत Con. अगाहिष्ट, अगाढ aor. गाहिषीष्ट, घाक्षीष्ट Ben. Cau.— गाहयति—ते pre. अजीगहत्—त aor. गाढ, गाहित p.p. गाहित्वा, or गाढ्वा ger. गाहितुम्, गाढुम् inf.

गु 1 A. अव्यक्ते शब्दे गतौ च to sound indistinctly, to go; गवते pre. जुगुवे perf. गोता p. fut. गोष्यते fut. अगोष्यत con. अगोष्ट aor. गोषीष्ट ben. जुगूषते des. Cau.—गावयति-ते, अजगवत—त Aor.

गु 6 P. पुरीषोत्सर्गे to void by stool; गुवति pre. जुगाव perf. गुता p. fut. गुष्यति fut. अगुष्यत् con. अगुषीत् aor. गून p.p.

गुञ्, गुञ्ज् 1. P. कूजने to hum, to buzz; गोजति, गुञ्जति pre. जुगोज, जुगुञ्ज perf. अगुजीत्, अगुञ्जीत् Aor.

गुड् 6 P. रक्षणे to protect; गुडति pre. जुगोड (जुगुडिथ 2nd pers. sing.) perf. अगुडीत् Aor.

गुण् 10 U. आमन्त्रणे to invite; to advise, to multiply; गुणयति—ते pre. गुणयाञ्चकार—चक्रे perf. गुणयिता p. fut. गुणयिष्यति fut. अगुणयिष्यत् con. अजूगुणत्—त aor. जुगूणयिषति-ते des.

गुण्ठ् 10 U. वेष्टने to cover, to enclose; गुण्ठयति—ते pre. अजुगुण्ठत्-त Aor. जुगुण्ठयिषति—ते des. Also 1 P. गुण्ठति pre. जुगुण्ठ perf. गुण्ठित p.p. (Generally with अव).

गुद् 1 A. क्रीडायाम् to play, to sport; गोदते pre. जुगुदे perf अगोदिष्ट Aor. गुदित p.p.

गुध् 1 A. to sport; गोधते pre. जुगुधे perf. गोधिता p. fut. (the same as गुद्).

गुध् 4 P. परिवेष्टने to cover; गुध्यति pre. जुगोध perf. अगोधीत् Aor.

गुध् 9 P. रोषे to be angry; गुध्नाति pre. (See the above root.)

गुप् 1 P. रक्षणे to defend, to protect, to conceal; गोपायति per. जुगोप, गोपायाञ्चकार, &c. perf. गोपायिता, गोपिता, गोप्ता p. fut. गोपायिष्यति-गोपिष्यति-गोप्स्यति, fut. अगोपायीत्, अगोप्सीत् aor. जुगोपायिषति, जुगुपिषति, जुगोपिषति, जुगुप्सति des. Cau.—गोपाययति-ते, गोपयति—ते pre. अजुगोपायत्-त, अजूगुपत्-त, Aor. Pass.—गोपाय्यते, गुप्यते pre. गोपायित, गुप्त p.p. गोपायित्वा or गोपित्वा, गुप्त्वा, ger.

गुप् 1 A. निन्दायाम् to censure; जुगुप्सते pre. जुगुप्साञ्चक्रे perf. जुगुप्सिता p. fut. जुगुप्सिष्यते fut. अजुगुप्सिष्ट aor. जुगुप्सिषीष्ट Ben. Pass.—जुगुप्स्यते pre.

गुप् 4 P. व्याकुलत्वे to be confused or disturbed; गुप्यति pre. जुगोप perf. गोपिता p. fut. अगुपत् aor. Cau.–गोपयति-ते pre. अजूगुपत्-त aor. जुगुपिषति, जुगोपिषति des. गुपित p. p.

गुप् 10 U. भाषायां भासने च to speak, to shine; गोपयति–ते pre. गोपयाञ्चकार–चक्रे perf. गोपयिता p. fut. अजूगुपत्-त aor. जुगोपयिषति–ते des. गोपित p.p.

गुफ्, गुम्फ 6 P. ग्रन्थे to string together; गुफति, गुम्फति pre. जुगोफ, जुगुम्फ perf. गोफिता, गुम्फिता p. fut. अगोफीत्, अगुम्फीत् aor. गुफित, गुम्फित p.p. गुफित्वा ger.

गुर् (कुटादि) 6 A. उद्यमने to make an effort; गुरते pre. जुगुरे perf. गुरिता p. fut. गुरिष्यते fut. अगुरिष्यत con. गुरिषीष्ट Ben. अगुरिष्ट aor. Pass.—गुर्यते pre. अगोरि aor. Cau.–गोरयति—ते pre. अजूगुरत्–त aor. जुगुरिषते des. गूर्ण p. p. गुरितुम् inf.

गुर्द् 1 A. क्रीडायां to play; गूर्दते pre. गूर्दिष्यते fut. अगूर्दिष्ट aor.

गुर्द् 10 U. निकेतने to dwell; गूर्दयति-ते per. गूर्दयांचकार–चक्रे &c. perf. गूर्दयिष्यति–ते fut. अजुगूर्दत्-त aor.

गुह् 1 U. संवरणे to cover, to keep secret; गूहति-ते pre. जुगूह or जुगुहे perf. गूहिता or गोढा p. fut. गूहिष्यति-ते, घोक्ष्यति-ते fut. अगूहित् or अगूहिष्ट (V) अघुक्षत्-त or अगूढ (VII) aor. गुह्यात् गूहिषीष्ट or घुक्षीष्ट ben. जुघुक्षति-ते des. Pass.—गुह्यते pre. अगूहि aor. Cau –गूहयति–ते, अजूगुहत्–त aor. गूढ p.p.

गूर् 4 A. हिंसागत्योः to kill, to go; गूर्यते pre. जुगूरे perf. गूरिता p. fut. अगूरिष्ट aor. जुगूरिषते des. गूर्ण p.p.

गूर् 10 A. उद्यमने to make an effort; गूरयते pre. अजूगुरत् aor.

गूर्द् 10 U. स्तुतौ to praise; गूर्दयति-ते pre. अजुगूर्दत्-त Aor.

गृ 1 P. सेचने to sprinkle, to wet; गरति pre. जगार perf. गर्ता p. f. गरिष्यति fut. अगार्षीत् Aor.

गृज् 1 P. शब्दे to sound, to roar; गर्जति pre. जगर्ज perf. अगर्जीत्, Aor. Cau.-गर्जयति-ते pre. अजीगृजत्-त, अजगर्जत्-त Aor. Also गृञ्ज्, गृञ्जति pre. जगृञ्ज perf. अगृञ्जीत् Aor.

गृध् 4 P. अभिकांक्षायाम् to covet, to desire; गृध्यति pre. जगर्ध perf. गर्धिता p. fut. अगृधत् aor. Cau.-गर्धयति-ते, अजीगृधत्-त, अजगर्धत्-त Aor. जिगर्धिषति des. गृद्ध p.p. गर्धित्वा, गृद्ध्वा.

गृह् 1 A. ग्रहणे to take, to seize; गर्हते pre. जगृहे perf. गर्हिता, गर्ढा p. fut. गर्हिष्यते, घर्क्ष्यते fut. अगर्हिष्यत-अघर्क्ष्यत con. गर्हिषीष्ट, घृक्षीष्ट Ben. अगर्हिष्ट, अघृक्षत aor. जिगर्हिषते, जिघृक्षते des Cau.-गर्हयति-ते, अजीगृहत्-त, अजगर्हत्-त aor.

गृह् 10 A ग्रहणे to seize, गृहयते pre. गृहयाञ्चक्रे perf. अजगृहत aor. जिगृहयिषते des.

गॄ 6 P. निगरणे to swallow, to devour, to emit; गिरति or गिलति pre. जगार or जगाल perf. गरिता, गरीता or गलिता, गलीता p. fut. गरिष्यति, गरीष्यति or गलिष्यति, गलीष्यति, fut. अगारीत् or अगालीत् aor. गीर्यात् Ben. जिगारिषति or जिगलिषति des. Cau. -गारयति-गालयति. Pass.-गीर्यते pre. अगारि or अगालि aor. गीर्ण p. p.

गॄ 9 P. शब्दे to call out, to speak; गृणाति pre. जगार perf. गरिता. गरीता p. fut. गरिष्यति, गरीष्यति fut. अगारीत् aor. Cau.-गारयति-ते pre. अजीगरत्-त aor. जिगरिषति, जिगरीषति, जिगीर्षति des. गीर्ण p. p.

गेव् 1 A. सेवने to serve; गेवते pre. जिगेवे perf. अगेविष्ट Aor.

गेष् 1 A. अन्विच्छायाम् to seek; गेषते pre. जिगेषे perf. गेषिष्यते fut. अगेषिष्ट Aor. गेष्ण p. p.

गै 1 P. शब्दे to sing, to speak in singing manner; गायति pre. जगौ perf. गाता p. fut. गास्यति fut. अगास्यत् con. अगासीत् aor. गेयात् ben. जिगासति des. Pass.—गीयते pre. अगायि aor. Cau. —गापयति-ते pre. अजीगपत्—त aor. गीत p. p. गीत्वा (with a preposition प्रगाय.) ger.

गोष्ट् 1 A. संघाते to assemble; गोष्टते pre. जुगोष्टे perf. अगोष्टिष्ट Aor.

ग्रन्थ 1 A. कौटिल्ये to be crooked; ग्रंथते pre. जग्रन्थे perf. ग्रन्थिता p. fut. ग्रन्थिष्यते fut. अग्रन्थिष्ट aor. जिग्रन्थिषते des. Pass.-ग्रन्थ्यते pre. अग्रन्थि aor. ग्रन्थित p. p.

ग्रन्थ 9 P सन्दर्भे to put together, to fasten; ग्रथ्नाति pre. ग्रथान 2nd sing. Impera. जग्रन्थ perf. ग्रन्थिता p. fut. ग्रन्थिष्यति fut. अग्रन्थीत् aor. ग्रथ्यात् ben. Pass-ग्रथ्यते pre अग्रन्थि aor. Cau.-ग्रन्थयति-ते pre. अजग्रन्थत्-त aor. जिग्रन्थिषति des. ग्रथित p. p. ग्रथित्वा, ग्रन्थित्वा ger.

ग्रन्थ 10 U. बन्धने, सन्दर्भे च to string together, to compose; ग्रन्थयति-ते pre. ग्रन्थयाञ्चकार-चक्रे &c. perf. ग्रन्थयिता p. fut. अजग्रन्थत्-त aor. ग्रन्थ्यात्, ग्रंथयिषीष्ट ben. जिग्रन्थयिषति-ते des. Also 1. P. ग्रन्थति pre. अग्रन्थीत् Aor.

ग्रस् 1 A. अदने to swallow; ग्रसते pre. जग्रसे perf. ग्रसिता p. fut. ग्रसिष्यते fut. अग्रासिष्ट aor. ग्रसिषीष्ट ben. Cau.-ग्रासयति only pre. अजिग्रसत् Aor. जिग्रासिषते des. ग्रस्त p. p. ग्रसित्वा or ग्रस्त्वा ger.

ग्रस् 10 U. ग्रहण to take; ग्रासयति-ते pre. अजिग्रसत्—त Aor.

ग्रह् 9 U. उपादाने to take hold of, to seize; गृह्णाति, गृह्णीते pre. गृहाण 2nd sing. Impera. जग्राह, जगृहे perf. ग्रहीता p. fut. ग्रहीष्यति—ते fut. अग्रहीत्, अग्रहीष्ट aor. गृह्यात्, ग्रहीषीष्ट ben. जिघृक्षति—ते des. Pass.—गृह्यते pre. अग्राहि aor. Cau.-ग्राहयति—ते pre. अजिग्रहत्-त aor. गृहीत p. p. ग्रहीतुम् inf.

ग्राम् 10 U. आमन्त्रणे to invite; ग्रामयति—ते Pre. अजग्रामत्—त Aor.

ग्रुच् 1 P. स्तेयकरणे गतौ च to rob, to go; ग्रोचति pre. जुग्रोच perf. ग्रोचिता p. fut. अग्रोचत्, अग्रोचीत् aor. ग्रुच्यात् ben. जुग्रुचिषति जुग्रोचिषति des. Cau. ग्रोचयति—ते pre. अजुग्रुचत्—त Aor.

ग्लस् 1 A. अदने to take; ग्लसते pre. जग्लसे perf. ग्लसिष्यते fut. अग्लसिष्ट Aor. ग्लस्त p.p.

ग्लह् 1 A. उपादाने to take; ग्लहते pre. जग्लहे perf. अग्लहिष्ट Aor.

ग्लुच् 1. P. स्तेयकरणे गतौ च to steal, to go; ग्लोचति pre. जुग्लोच perf. ग्लोचिता p. fut. ग्लुक्त p. p. This root is the same as ग्रुच्.

ग्लुञ्च् 1 P. to go; ग्लुञ्चति pre. जुग्लुञ्च perf. ग्लुंचिता p. fut. अग्लुचत्, अग्लुञ्चीत् aor.

ग्लेप् 1 A. दैन्ये कम्पने च to be poor, to tremble; ग्लेपते pre. जिग्लेपे perf. ग्लेपिष्यते fut. अग्लेपिष्ट Aor.

ग्लै 1 P. हर्षक्षये (हर्षक्षयो धातुक्षयः) to be weary; ग्लायति pre. जग्लौ perf. ग्लाता p. fut. ग्लास्यति fut. अग्लास्यत् con. ग्लेयात्. ग्लायात् Ben. अग्लासीत् aor. जिग्लासति des. Pass.–ग्लायते pre, अग्लायि aor. Cau.—ग्लपयति-ते, ग्लापयति-ते pre. ग्लान p. p. ग्लात्वा, संग्लाय ger. ग्लातुं inf.

घ—

घघ् 1 P. हसने to laugh, to mortify; घघति pre. जघाघ perf. अघघीत्-अघाघीत् Aor.

घट 1 A चेष्टायाम् to be busy with, to happen; घटते pre. जघटे perf. घटिता p. fut. घटिष्यते fut. घटिषीष्ट ben. अघटिष्ट aor. Pass:—घट्यते pre. घाटिता, घटिता p. fut घटिष्यते, घाटिष्यते fut. अघाटिष्यत, अघटिष्यत con. अघाटि, अघटि aor. Cau.–घटयति-ते pre. अजीघटत्-त aor. जिघटिषते des.

घट् 10 U. भाषायां संघाते च to speak, to collect together; घाटयति-ते pre. घाटयाञ्चकार-चक्रे, &c. perf. अजीघटत्-त Aor. जिघाटयिषति-ते des.

घट्ट् I A. चलने to shake, to touch; घट्टते pre. जघट्टे perf. घट्टिता p. fut. घट्टिष्यते fut. घट्टिषीष्ट ben. अघट्टिष्ट aor. जिघट्टिषते des. घट्टित p. p.

घट्ट् 10 U चलने to stir, to disturb; घट्टयति-ते pre. अजघट्टत्-त Aor. जिघट्टयिषति-ते des.

घण्ट् 10 U भाषायां to speak; घण्टयति-ते pre. अजघण्टत्-त Aor. Also 1 P. घण्टति pre. अघण्टीत् Aor.

घस्* 1 P. to eat; घसति pre. अघसत् Imperf. जघास aor. घस्ता p. fut. घत्स्यति fut. अघत्स्यत् con. अघसत् aor. जिघत्सति des. घस्त p.p.

घिण्ण् 1 A. ग्रहणे to take; घिण्णते pre. जिघिण्णे perf. अघिण्णिष्ट Aor.

---

*This is a defective root and is very often used for the root अद्. It is conjugated in the Perf. as an optional substitute for अद्.

घु 1 A. शब्दे to sound; घवते pre. जुघुवे perf. अघोष्ट Aor. जुघूषते des. घुत p.p.

घुट् 1 A. परिवर्तने to return, to exchange; घोटते pre. जुघुटे perf. अघुटत्, अघोटिष्ट aor. घुटित p. p.

घुट् 6 P. प्रतिघाते (कुटादि) to strike against; घुटति pre. जुघोट (जुघुटिथ 2nd sing.) perf. अघुटीत Aor.

घुड् 6 P. to strike; घुडति pre. (the same as above).

घुण् 6 P. भ्रमणे to roll, to turn ronud; घुणति pre. जुघोण perf. घोणिता p. fut. अघोणीत् Aor. घुणित p.p.

घुण् 1 A. भ्रमणे to roll, to whirl; घोणते pre. जुघुणे perf. अघोणिष्ट aor.

घुण्ण् 1 A. ग्रहणे to take, to receive; घुण्णते pre. जुघुण्णे perf. घुण्णिता p. fut. अघुण्णिष्ट aor. घुण्णित p. p.

घुर् 6 P. भीमार्थशब्दयोः to be frightful, to sound; घुरति pre. जुघोर perf. घोरिता p. fut. घोरिष्यति fut. अघोरिष्यत्, con. अघोरीत् aor.

घुष् 1 P. अविशब्दने (शब्दे इत्यन्ये) to sound, to declare; घोषति pre. जुघोष perf. घोषिता p. fut. घोषिष्यति fut घुष्यात् ben. अघुषत्, अघोषीत् aor. Cau.—घोषयति-ते pre. अजूघुषत् aor. जुघोषिषति, जुघुषिषति des. घुषित, घोषित or घुष्ट p.p.

घुष् 1 A. कान्तिकरणे to be bright; घोषते pre. जुघुषे perf. अघोषिष्ट Aor. जुघो-घु-षिषते des.

घुष् 10 U. विशब्दने to proclaim aloud; आ + घुष् = क्रन्दसातत्ये to cry continuously; घोषयति-ते pre. घोषयाञ्चकार-चक्रे &c. perf. घोषयिता p. fut. घोषयिष्यति-ते fut. अजूघुषत्-त aor. घुषित-घुष्ट p.p.

घूर् 4 A. हिंसावयोहान्योः to kill, to become old; घूरते pre. अघूरिष्ट Aor.

घूर्ण् 6 U. भ्रमणे to move to and fro, to whirl; घूर्णति, घूर्णते pre. जुघूर्ण, जुघूर्णे perf. घूर्णिता p. fut. घूर्णिष्यति-ते fut. अघूर्णिष्यत्-त

con. अघूर्णीत aor. जुघूर्णिषति-ते des. Pass.—घूर्ण्यते pre. अघूर्णि aor. Cau.—घूर्णयति-ते pre. अजूघूर्णत्-त aor. घूर्णित p. p.

घृ 1 P. सेचने & 10 U. प्रस्रवणे छादने च to sprinkle, to cover; घरति & घारयति-ते pre. जघार, घारयाञ्चकार &c. perf. घर्ता, घारयिता p. fut. अघारीत्, अजीघरत्-त aor. घृत, घारित p.p.

घृण् 8 U. दीप्तौ to shine, to burn; घृणोति, घर्णोति & घृणुते, घर्णुते pre. जघर्ण, जघृण perf. घर्णिता p. fut. घर्णिष्यति-ते fut. अघर्णीत्, अघर्णिष्ट, अघृत, aor. जिघर्णिषति-ते des. घृत p.p. घृणित्वा, घृत्वा ger.

घृष् 1 P. संघर्षे स्पर्धायां च to rub, to crush, to rival; घर्षति pre. जघर्ष perf. घर्षिता p. fut. घर्षिष्यति fut. अघर्षिष्यत् con. अघर्षीत् aor. घृष्यात् ben. जिघर्षिषति des. Pass.—घृष्यते pre. अघर्षि aor. Cau.—घर्षयति-ते pre. अजीघृषत्-त, अजघर्षत्-त aor. घृष्ट p.p. घर्षित्वा & घृष्ट्वा ger.

घ्रा 1 P. गन्धोपादाने to smell; जिघ्रति pre. जघ्रौ perf. घ्राता p. fut. घ्रास्यति fut. अघ्रास्यत् con. अघ्रात्, अघ्रासीत् aor. घ्रायात्, घ्रेयात् ben. जिघ्रासति des. Pass.—घ्रायते pre. अघ्रायि aor. Cau.—घ्रापयति-ते pre. अजिघ्रपत्-त, अजिघ्रिपत्,-त aor. घ्रात, घ्राण p.p.

ङ—

ङु 1 A शब्दे to sound; ङवते pre. ङुङुवे perf. ङोता p. fut. अङोष्ट aor. ङोषीष्ट ben. ङुङूषते des.

च—

चक् 1 A. तृप्तौ प्रतिघाते च to be satisfied, to resist; चकते pre. चेके चकिता p. fut. चकिष्यते fut. अचकिष्ट Aor. Cau.—चाकयति-ते pre. अचीचकत्-त aor. चिचकिषते des. चकित p.p.

चक् 1 P. तृप्तौ to be satisfied; चकति pre. चचाक perf. चकिता p. fut. अचकीत्, अचाकीत् aor. Cau.—चकयति-ते pre. चिचकिषति des. Pass.—चक्यते pre. अचकि, अचाकि Aor.

चकास् 2 U. दीप्तौ to shine, to be prosperous; चकास्ति-स्ते pre. चकासाञ्चकार-चक्रे &c. perf. चकासिता p. fut. चकासिष्यति fut. अचकासिष्यत् con. अचकासीत्, अचकासिष्ट aor. Cau.—चकास-

पति-ते pre. अचीचकासत्-त, अचचकासत्-त aor. चकासित p.p. चकासित्वा ger. चकासितुम् inf.

चक्ष्* 2 A. व्यक्तायां वाचि to speak, to tell, to say; चष्टे pre. चचक्षे, चख्यौ, चख्ये, चक्शौ, चक्शे perf. ख्याता, क्शाता p. fut. अख्यत्-त, अक्शासीत्, अक्शास्त aor. ख्यायात्, ख्येयात्, ख्यासीष्ट, क्शायात्, क्शेयात्, क्शासीष्ट ben. Cau.—ख्यापयति-ते, क्शापयति-ते pre. अचिख्यपत्-त. अचिक्शपत्-त aor. चिख्यासति-ते des.

चञ्चु् 1 P. to go; to jump; चञ्चति pre. चचञ्च perf. चञ्चिता p. fut अचञ्चीत् aor. चञ्चित p.p.

चट् 1 P. वर्षावरणयोः to break, to cover; चटति pre. चचाट perf. चटिता p. fut. अचटीत् aor. Cau.—चाटयति-ते, pre. चिचटिषति des.

चट् 10 U. भेदने to kill, to injure. to break; चाटयति-ते pre. चाटयाञ्चकार-चक्रे, &c. perf. चटयिता p. fut. चटयिष्यति-ते fut. अचटयिष्यत्-त con. अचीचटत्-त aor. चटित p.p.

चण् 1 P. दाने गतौ च to give; चणति pre. चचाण perf. चणिता p. fut. अचणीत्, अचाणीत् aor. Cau.—चणयति-ते, चिचाणिषति des.

चण्ड् 1 A. to be angry; चण्डते pre. चचण्डे perf. चण्डिता p. fut. अचण्डिष्ट aor. Also P. चण्डति pre. अचण्डीत् aor.

चण्ड् 10 U. चण्डयति-ते pre. अचचण्डत्-त Aor. चिचण्डयिषति-ते des.

चद् 1 U. याचने to ask; चदति-ते pre. चचाद-चेदे perf. चदिष्यति-ते fut. अचदीत्, अचदिष्ट Aor.

चन 1 P. हिंसायां to kill; चनति pre. चचान perf. चानिष्यति fut. अचनीत्, अचानीत Aor, Cau—चनयति-ते, चिचनिषति des.

चन् 10 U. श्रद्धापहनयोः to believe, to strike; चानयति-ते pre. अचीचनत्-त Aor.

चन्द् 1 P. आह्लादे दीप्तौ च to be glad, to shine; चन्दति pre. चचन्द perf. चन्दिता p. fut. अचन्दीत् aor. चिचन्दिषति des.

---

*This root is defective in the Non-conjugational tenses. When it means 'to leave' it does not substitute क्शा; समचक्षिष्ट aor.

चप् 1. P. सान्त्वने to console; चपति pre. चचाप perf. चपिता p. fut. अचपीत्-अचापीत् aor. Cau.—चापयति-ते pre. चिचपिषति des.

चप् 10 U. परिकल्पने to grind; चपयति-ते pre. चापयाञ्चकार-चक्रे perf. चपयिता p. fut. अचीचपत्-त aor.

चम्प् 10 U. to go, to move; चम्पयति-ते pre. चम्पयाञ्चकार-चक्रे perf. चम्पयिता p. fut. अचचम्पत्-aor.

चम् 1 P. अदने to eat (with आ to drink); चमति pre. चचाम perf. चमिता p. fut. चमिष्यति fut. अचमीत् aor. Cau.—चामयति pre. अचीचमत् aor. चिचमिषति des. चान्त p.p. चान्त्वा or चमित्वा ger.

चय् 1 A. to go; चयते pre. चेये perf. चयिता p. fut. चयिष्यते fut. अचयिष्ट aor.

चर् 1 P. गतौ to walk (with आ to perform); चरति pre. चचार perf. चरिता p. fut. चरिष्यति fut. अचरिष्यत् con.—चर्यात् Ben. अचारीत् aor. चिचरिषति des. Pass.—चर्यते pre. अचारि aor. चरित p.p.

चर् 10 U, संशये to doubt; (with वि, असंशये to remove a doubt); चारयति-ते pre. अचीचरत्-त aor.

चर्च् 1 P. परिभाषणहिंसातर्जनेषु to abuse, to discuss; चर्चति pre. चचर्च perf. चर्चिता p. fut. चर्चिष्यति fut. अचर्चिष्यत् con. अचर्चीत् aor. चर्चित p.p.

चर्च् 10 U. अध्ययने to read over, to study; चर्चयति-ते pre. चर्चयाञ्चकार-चक्रे &c. perf. चर्चयिता p. fut. अचचर्चत्-त aor.

चर्व् 1 P. अदने & 10 U. भक्षणे to eat, to chew; चर्वति & चर्वयति-ते pre. चचर्व & चर्वयाञ्चकार-चक्रे perf. चर्विता & चर्वयिता p. fut. अचर्वीत्, अचचर्वत्-त Aor.

चल् 1 P. कम्पने to stir, to shake; चलति pre. चचाल perf. चलिता p. fut. अचालीत् aor. Cau.—चलयति-ते (चालयति-ते) pre. अचीचलत्-त aor. चलित p.p.

चल् 6. P. विलसने to sport, to frolic; चलति pre. (see above for the other forms).

चल् 10 U. भृतौ to foster; चालयति-ते pre. चालयाञ्चकार-चक्रे &c. perf. अचीचलत् Aor.

चष् 1 U. भक्षणे to eat; चषति-ते pre. चचाष, चेषे perf अचषीत्, अचाषीत्, अचषिष्ट Aor.

चह् 1 P. & 10 U. परिकल्कने to be wicked; चहति & चहयति-ते pre. अचहीत्-अचचहत्-त; अचीचहत्-त (घटादि) Aor.

चाय् 1 U. पूजानिशामनयोः to worship, to observe; चायति-ते pre. चचाय-चचाये perf. चायिता p. fut. चायिष्यति-ते fut. अचायीत्, अचायिष्ट aor. Cau—चाययति-ते pre. अचचायत्-त aor. चिचायिषति-ते des.

चि 5 U. चयने to heap up, to collect; चिनोति, चिनुते pre. चिकाय, चिचाय, चिक्ये, चिच्ये perf. चेता p. fut. चेष्यति-ते fut. अचेष्यत्-त con. अचैषीत्, अचेष्ट aor. चीयात्, चेषीष्ट ben. चिकीषति-ते des. Pass.—चीयते pre. अचायि aor. चित p. p. चित्वा ger.

चि 10 U. to gather, चययति-ते, चपयति-ते pre. चययाञ्चकार-चक्रे, चपयाञ्चकार-चक्रे perf. अचीचपत्-त, अचीचयत्-त aor.

चिट् 1 P. & 10 U. परप्रेष्ये to send out; चेटति, चेटयति-ते pre. चिचेट, चेटयाञ्चकार-चक्रे &c. perf. चेटिता, चेटयिता p. fut. अचेटीत्, अचीचिटत्-त aor.

चित् 1 P. संज्ञाने to notice, to understand; चेतति pre. चिचेत perf. चेतिता p. fut. चेतिष्यति fut. अचेतिष्यत् con. अचेतीत् aor. चित्यात् ben. चिचितिषति, चिचेतिषति des. Cau.—चेतयति-ते pre. अचीचितत्-त aor. Pass.—चित्यते pre. अचेति aor. चित्त p. p. चितित्वा & चेतित्वा ger.

चित 10 A. संचेतने to perceive, to be anxious; चेतयते pre. अचीचितत Aor. चिचेतयिषते des.

चित्र् 10 U. चित्रकरणे अद्भुतदर्शने च to paint &c.; चित्रयति-ते pre. अचिचित्रत्-त Aor. चिचित्रयिषति-ते des.

चिंत् 1. P. think, चिंतति pre. चिचिंत perf. चिंतिता p. fut. अचिंतीत् aor. चिन्तित p. p.

चिंत् 10 U. स्मृत्यां to think, to consider; चिंतयति-ते pre. चिंतयाञ्च-

कार-चक्रे, &c. perf. चिंतयिता p. fut. अचिचिंतत्-त aor. चिंत्यात् & चिंतयिषीष्ट ben. Pass–चिन्त्यते pre. अचिन्ति aor. चिंतित p. p. चिंतयित्वा ger.

चिल् 6 P. वसने to put on clothes, to dress. चिलति pre. चिचेल perf. चेलिता p. fut. अचेलीत् aor.

चिल्ल् 1 P. शैथिल्ये to become loose; चिल्लति pre. चिचिल्ल perf. चिल्लिता p. fut. अचिल्लीत् aor. चिल्लित p. p.

चीक् 10 U. 1 P. आमर्षणे to suffer; चीकयति-ते, चीकति pre. चीकयाञ्चकार-चक्रे, चिचीक perf. अचीचिकत्-त, अचीकीत् aor.

चीभ् 1 A. कत्थने to boast; चीभते pre. चिचीभे perf. चीभिता p. fut. अचीभिष्ट aor.

चीव् 1 U. आदानसंवरणयोः to take, to cover; चीवति-ते pre. चिचीवे perf. चीविता p. fut. अचीवीत् & अचीविष्ट aor.

चीव् 10 U. भाषायां दीप्तौ च to speak, to shine; चीवयति-ते pre.

चुच्य् 1 P. अभिषवे to bathe; चुच्यति pre. चुचुच्य perf. चुच्यिष्यति fut. अचुच्यीत् Aor.

चुट 6 P. छेदने (कुटादि) to cut; चुटति pre. चुचोट perf. चुटिता p. fut. अचुटीत् aor.

चुड् 6 P. संवरणे (कुटादि) to conceal; चुडति pre. चुचोड perf. चुडिता p. fut. अचुडीत् aor.

चुण्ट् 10 U. 1 P. छेदने to cut; चुण्टयति-ते, चुण्टति pre. अचुचुण्टत्-त, अचुण्टीत् Aor.

चुद् 10 U. संचोदने to direct, to throw; चोदयति-ते pre. चोदयाञ्चकार-चक्रे &c. perf. चोदयिता p. fut. चोदयिष्यति-ते fut. अचोदयिष्यत्-त con. अचूचुदत्-त aor. चुचोदयिषति-ते des चोदित p. p.

चुप 1 P. मन्दायां गतौ to move slowly; चोपति pre. चुचोप perf. चोपिता P. fut. अचोपीत् aor. चुचु-चो-पिषति des.

चुम्ब 1 P. वक्त्रसंयोगे to kiss; चुम्बति pre. चुचुम्ब perf. चुम्बिता p. fut. अचुम्बीत् aor. चुचुम्बिषति des. चुम्बित p. p.

चुम्ब् 10 U. हिंसायाम् to kill; चुम्बयति-ते pre. चुम्बयाञ्चकार-चक्रे, &c. perf. चुम्बयिता p. fut. अचुचुम्बत् aor. चुम्बित p. p.

चुर् 10 U. स्तेये to steal or rob, to take; चोरयति-ते pre. चोरयाञ्चकार-चक्रे, &c. perf. चोरयिता p. fut. चोरयिष्यति-ते fut. अचूचुरत्-त aor. चोर्यात्, चोरयिषीष्ट ben. चुचोरयिषति-ते des. Pass.—चोर्यते. अचोरि aor. चोरित p. p. चोरयित्वा ger.

चुल् 10 U. समुच्छ्राये to raise; चोलयति-ते pre. अचूचुलत्-त Aor.

चूर् 4 A. दाहे to burn; चूर्यते pre. चुचूरे perf. अचूरिष्ट Aor. चूर्ण p. p.

चूर्ण् 10 U. प्रेरणे, संकोचने to reduce to powder, to contract; चूर्णयति-ते pre. चूर्णयाञ्चकार-चक्रे &c. perf. चूर्णयिता p. fut. चूर्णयिष्यति-ते fut. अचूर्णयिष्यत्-त con. अचुचूर्णत्-त aor. चूर्णित p. p.

चूष् 1 P. पाने to drink, to suck; चूषति pre. चुचूष perf चूषिता p. fut, अचूषीत् aor. चुचूषिषति des. चूषित p. p.

चृत् 6 P. हिंसाग्रन्थनयोः to hurt, to kill, to connect; चृन्तति pre. चचर्त perf. चर्तिता p. fut. अचर्तीत् aor. चिचर्तिषति, चिचृत्सति des.

चृप् 10 U. संदीपने to kindle; चर्पयति-ते pre. चर्पयाञ्चकार-चक्रे &c. perf. चर्पयिता p. fut. अचीचृपत्-त, अचचर्पत्-त aor. Also 1 P. चर्पति pre. अचर्पीत् aor.

चेल् 1 P. चलने to move, to go; चेलति pre. चिचेल perf. चेलिता p. fut. अचेलीत् aor.

चेष्ट् 1 A. चेष्टायां to stir, to make efforts; चेष्टते pre. चिचेष्टे perf. चेष्टिता p. fut. चेष्टिष्यते fut. अचेष्टिष्ट aor. चेष्टिषीष्ट Ben. चिचेष्टिषते des. Cau.-चेष्टयति pre. अचिचेष्टत्, अचचेष्टत् Aor. Pass.-चेष्ट्यते pre. चेष्टित p. p.

च्यु 1 A गतौ to go, to drop down; च्यवते pre. चुच्युवे perf. च्योता p. fut. च्योष्यते fut. अच्योष्ट aor. च्योषीष्ट ben. Cau.-च्यावयति-ते • चुच्यूषते des. च्युत p. p.

च्युत् 1 P. आसेचने to flow, to drop down; च्योतति pre. चुच्योत perf. च्योतिता p. fut. च्योतिष्यति fut. अच्युतत्, अच्योतीत् aor. च्युत्यात् ben. Cau-च्योतयति-ते pre. अचुच्युतत्-त aor. चिच्युतिषति, चिच्योतिषति des. च्युतित, च्योतित p. p.

छ—

छद् 1 U. आच्छादने to cover; छदति-ते pre. चच्छाद, चच्छदे perf. छदिता p. fut. अच्छदीत्, अच्छादीत्, अच्छादिष्ट aor. चिच्छदिषति-ते des. छन्न p. p. Pass. छद्यते, pər. अच्छादि aor. Cau.– छादयति-ते.

छद् 10 U. to conceal; छादयति-ते pre. छादयाञ्चकार-चक्रे, &c. perf. छादयिता p. fut. अचिच्छदत्-त Aor. चिच्छादयिषति-ते des. छन्न, छादित p. p.

छम् 1 P. अदने to eat; छमति pre. चच्छाम perf. छमिता p. fut. अच्छमीत्, अच्छामीत् aor. छान्त p. p. छमित्वा, छान्त्वा ger.

छर्द् 10 U. वमने to vomit; छर्दयति-ते pre. छर्दयाञ्चकार-चक्रे perf. छर्दयिता .pfut. अचिच्छर्दत्-त aor. चिच्छर्दयिषति-ते des. छर्दित p.p.

छिद् 7 U. द्वैधीकरणे to cut, to mow; छिनत्ति & छिन्ते pre. चिच्छेद, चिच्छिदे perf. छेत्ता p. fut. छेत्स्यति-ते fut. अछेत्स्यत्-त con. छिद्यात्, छित्सीष्ट Ben. अच्छिदत्, अच्छैत्सीत् & अच्छित्त aor. चिच्छित्सति-ते des. छिन्न p. p.

छिद्र् 10 U. भेदने to bore; छिद्रयति-ते pre. अचिच्छिद्रत्–त Aor. चिच्छिद्रयिषति-ते des.

छुट् 6 P. भेदने (कुटादि) to put; छुटति pre. चुच्छोट perf. छुटिता p. fut. अच्छुटीत् aor.

छुप् 6 P. स्पर्शे to touch; छुपति pre. चुच्छोप perf. छोप्ता p. fut. छोप्स्यति fut. अच्छोप्स्यत् con. अच्छौप्सीत् aor.

छुर् 6 P. भेदने (कुटादि) to intermix, to cut; छुरति pre. चुच्छोर perf. छुरिष्यति fut. अच्छुरीत् Aor. चुच्छुरिषति des.

छृद् 1 P. & 10 U. संदीपने to kindle; छर्दति, छर्दयति-ते pre. चच्छर्द, छर्दयाञ्चकार-चक्रे &c. perf. छर्दिता, छर्दयिता p. fut. छर्दिष्यति, छर्दयिष्यति-ते fut. अच्छर्दिष्यत्, अच्छर्दयिष्यत्-त con. अच्छर्दीत्, अचिछृदत्–त, अचच्छर्दत्-त aor.

छृद् 7 U. दीप्तिदेवनयोः to shine, to play, to vomit; छृणत्ति, छृन्ते pre. चच्छर्द–चच्छृदे perf. छर्दिता p. fut. छर्दिष्यति-ते, छर्त्स्यति-ते fut.

अच्छर्दत, अच्छर्दीत् & अच्छर्दिष्ट aor. छृद्यात्, छर्दिषीष्ट & छृत्सीष्ट ben. चिच्छर्दिषति-ते, चिच्छृत्सति-ते des.

छेद् 10 U. द्वैधीकरणे to divide, to cut; छेदयति-ते pre. छेदयिष्यति fut. अचिच्छेदत्-त Aor.

छो 4 P. छेदने to cut; छ्यति pre. चच्छौ perf. छाता p. fut, छास्यति fut. अच्छास्यत् con. अच्छात्, अच्छासीत् aor. चिच्छासति des. छात, छित p. p. छात्वा, छित्वा ger. Pass.–छायते pre. अच्छायि aor.

ज—

जक्ष् 2 P. भक्ष्यहसनयोः to eat, to consume, to laugh; जक्षिति pre. अजक्षत्, अजक्षीत्, imperf. जजक्ष perf. जक्षिता p. fut. जक्षिष्यति fut. अजक्षिष्यत् con. अजक्षीत् aor. जक्ष्यात् ben. Cau.—जक्षयति pre. अजजक्षत् aor. जिजक्षिषति des. जक्षित p. p.

जज्-जञ्ज् 1 P. युद्धे to fight; जजति, जञ्जति pre. जजाज, जजञ्ज perf. जजिता, जञ्जिता p. fut. अजजीत, अजाजीत्, अजञ्जीत् aor.

जट् 1 P. संघाते to clot, to become twisted; जटति pre. जजाट perf. जटिता p. fut. अजटीत्, अजाटीत् aor.

जड् The same as above.

जन् 4 A. प्रादुर्भावे to be born; जायते pre. जज्ञे perf. जनिता p. fut. जनिष्यते fut. अजनिष्यत con. अजनि–अजनिष्ट aor. जनिषीष्ट ben. जिजनिषति des. Pass.—जन्यते or जायते pre. अजनि Aor. Cau.—जनयति pre. अजीजनत् aor. जिजनिषते des. संजाय, संजन्य, जनित्वा ger. जात p. p.

जप् 1 P. व्यक्तायां वाचि मानसे च to mutter; जपति pre. जजाप perf. जपिता p. fut. जपिष्यति fut. अजपिष्यत् con. अजपीत्, अजापीत् aor. जप्यात् ben. जिजपिषति des. Pass.—जप्यते pre. अजापि aor. Cau.—जापयति-ते pre. अजीजपत्-त aor. जपित p. p.

जभ् 1 A. गात्रविनामे to yawn; जम्भते pre. जजम्भे perf. जम्भिता p. fut. अजम्भिष्ट aor. जम्भिषीष्ट ben. जिजम्भिषते des. Cau.—जम्भयति pre. अजजम्भत् aor. Pass.–जम्भते, अजम्भि aor.

जम् 1 P. अदने to eat; जमति pre. जजाम perf. जमिता p. fut. अजमीत् aor. जान्त p. p.

जम्भ् 1 P. 10 U. नाशने to destroy; जम्भति, जम्भयति-ते pre. जजम्भ, जम्भयाञ्चकार &c. perf. अजम्भीत्, अजजम्भत् Aor.

जल् 1 P. घातने to be sharp; जलति pre. अजालीत् Aor.

जल 10 U. अपवारणे to cover; जालयति-ते pre. अजीजलत् Aor.

जल्प् 1 P. व्यक्तायां वाचि to murmur, to prattle; जल्पति pre. जजल्प perf. जल्पिता p. fut. जल्पिष्यति fut. अजल्पिष्यत् con. अजल्पीत् aor. जिजल्पिषति des. Pass.–जल्प्यते pre. अजल्पि aor. जल्पित p.p.

जष् 1 P. हिंसायां to hurt, to kill; जषति pre. जजाष perf. जषिता p. fut. अजषीत्, अजाषीत् aor.

जस् 4 P. मोक्षणे to set free· जस्यति pre. जजास perf. जसिता p. fut. अजसत् aor. जस्त p. p.

जस् 10 U. 1 P. हिंसायां ताडने च to hurt; जासयति-ते, जसति pre. जासयाञ्चकार-चक्रे &c. जजास perf. जासयिता, जसिता p. fut. अजीजसत्-त, अजसीत्, अजासीत् aor. जिजासयति-ते, जिजासिषति des.

जंस् 10 U. 1 P. रक्षणे मोक्षणे च to protect; to release; जंसयति-ते, जंसति pre. अजजंसत्–त, अजसीत् Aor.

जागृ 2 P. निद्राक्षये to awake; जागर्ति pre. जजागार-गर & जागराञ्चकार perf. जागरिता p. fut. जागरिष्यति fut. अजागरिष्यत् con. अजागरीत् aor. जागर्यात् ben. जिजागरिषति des. Pass.—जागर्यते pre. अजागारि aor. Cau.–जागरयति–ते pre. जागरित p. p.

*जि 1 P. जये अभिभवे च to conquer; जयति pre. जिगाय perf. जेता p. fut. जेष्यति fut. अजेष्यत् con. अजैषीत् aor. जीयात् ben. जिगीषति des. Cau.—जापयति-ते pre. अजीजयत्-त aor. जजीयते, जेजयीति, जेजेति freq. जित p. p. जित्वा ger. जेतुम् inf.

जिन्व् 1 P. प्रीणने to please; जिन्वति pre. जिजिन्व perf. अजिन्वीत् Aor.

जिन्व् 1 P. 10 U. भाषायां to speak; जिन्वति, जिन्वयति pre. जिजिन्व, जिन्वयाञ्चकार &c. perf. जिन्विता, जिन्वयिता p. fut. अजिन्वीत्, अजिजिन्वत्–त aor.

---

* It is Atmanepadi when preceded by the prepositions वि & परा.

जिम् 1 P. भक्षणे to eat; जेमति pre. जिजेम perf. अजेमीत् Aor. जिन्त p. p.

जिरि 5 P. to kill; जिरिणोति pre. (Vedic).

जिष् 1 P. सेचने सेवने च to sprinkle, to serve; जेषति pre. जिजेष perf. जेषिता p. fut. जेषिष्यति fut. अजेषीत् aor. जेषित्वा, जिष्ट्वा ger.

जीव् 1 P. प्राणधारणे to live; जीवति pre. जिजीव perf. जीविता p. fut. जीविष्यति fut. अजीविष्यत् con. अजीवीत् aor. Pass.-जीव्यते pre. अजीवि aor. Cau.-जीवयति-ते pre. जीवित्वा ger. जीवितुम् inf. जीवित p.p.

जुट् 6 P. (कुटादि) बन्धने to tie up or bind; जुटति pre. जुजोट perf. अजुटीत् Aor.

जुड् 6 P. गतौ to go; जुडति pre. अजोडीत् Aor.

जुत 1 A. भासने to shine; जोतते pre. जोतिष्यते fut. अजोतिष्ट Aor.

जुष 6 A. प्रीतिसेवनयोः to like, to enjoy; जुषते pre. जुजुषे perf. जोषिता p. fut. अजोषिष्ट aor. Pass.-जुष्यते pre. अजोषि aor. Cau.-जोषयति-ते pre. अजूजुषत-त aor. जुजोषिषते, जुजुषिषते des. जुष्ट p.p.

जुष् 1 P. & 10 U. परितर्कणे परितर्पणे च to think, to examine, to be satisfied; जोषति & जोषयति-ते pre. जुजोष & जोषयाञ्चकार-चक्रे perf. जोषिता, जोषयिता p. fut. अजोषीत् & अजूजुषत्-त aor. जुजुषिषति, जुजोषिषति, जुजोषयिषति-ते des. जुष्ट p. p.

जूर् 4 A. हिंसावयोहान्योः to kill, to grow old; जूर्यते pre. जुजूरे perf. अजूरिष्ट aor.

जूष् 1 P. हिंसायां to kill; जूषति pre. अजूषीत् Aor.

जृम्भ् 1 A. गात्रविनामे, to yawn; जृम्भते pre. जजृम्भे perf. जृम्भिता p. fut. जृम्भिष्यते fut. अजृम्भिष्ट aor. जिजृम्भिषते des. जृम्भित p. p.

जॄ 4 P. वयोहानौ to grow old; जीर्यति pre. जजार perf. जरिता or जरीता p. fut. जरिष्यति, जरीष्यति, fut. अजरिष्यत्, अजरीष्यत् con. अजारीत्, अजरत् aor. जीर्यात् ben. जिजरिषति, जिजरीषति, जिजीर्षति des. Cau.—जरयति-ते pre. Pass.-जीर्यते pre. जीर्ण p. p.

जॄ I & 9 P. to wear out; जरति. जॄणाति, pre. जजार perf. जरिता-जरीता p. fut. अजारीत् aor. Cau.—जारयति-ते pre.

जॄ 10 U. to grow old; जारयति—ते pre. जारयाञ्चकार—चक्रे &c. perf. जारयिता p. fut अजीजरत्—त aor. जिजारयिषति—ते des.

जेष् 1 A. to go; जेषते pre. जिजेषे perf. जेषिता p. fut. अजेषिष्ट aor.

जेहृ 1 A. प्रयत्ने गतौ च to try, to go; जेहते pre. जिजेहे perf. जेहिता p. fut. अजेहिष्ट aor.

जै 1 P. क्षये to decay; जायति pre. जजौ perf. जाता p. fut. अजासीत् aor. जायात् ben. जिजासति des.

ज्ञप् 10 U. ज्ञाने ज्ञापने च to know, to cause to know, to see, to please; ज्ञापयति-ते pre. ज्ञपयाञ्चकार-चक्रे, &c. perf. ज्ञपयिता p. fut. ज्ञपयिष्यति-ते fut. अज्ञपयिष्यत्-त con. अजिज्ञपत्-त aor. ज्ञीप्सति—ते des. Pass.—ज्ञप्यते pre. अज्ञपि, अज्ञापि aor. ज्ञप्त, ज्ञपित p. p.

ज्ञा 9 U. अवबोधने to know; जानाति, जानीते pre. जज्ञौ, जज्ञे perf. ज्ञाता p. fut. ज्ञास्यति-ते fut. अज्ञास्यत्-त con. अज्ञासीत्, अज्ञास्त aor. ज्ञायात्, ज्ञेयात्, ज्ञासीष्ट ben. जिज्ञासति-ते des. Cau.—ज्ञापयति—ते & ज्ञपयति—ते (in the sense of 'to gratify, 'to slay or to cause to see,) pre. अजिज्ञपत्-त aor. Pass.—ज्ञायते pre. अज्ञायि aor. ज्ञातुम् inf. ज्ञात्वा ger. ज्ञात p.p.

ज्ञा 10 U. नियोगे to direct; ज्ञापयति-ते pre. ज्ञापयाञ्चकार—चक्रे perf ज्ञापयिता p fut. ज्ञापयिष्यति-ते fut. Pass—ज्ञाप्यते. ज्ञापित p.p

ज्या 9 P. वयोहानौ to become old; जिनाति pre. जिज्यौ perf. ज्याता p. fut. ज्यास्यति fut. अज्यास्यत् con. अज्यासीत् aor. जीयात् ben. जिज्यासति des. Pass.—जीयते, अज्यायि aor. Cau.—ज्यापयति-ते pre. जीन p.p. जीत्वा ger.

ज्यु 1 A. to go; ज्यवते pre. जुज्युवे perf. ज्योता p. fut. अज्योष्ट aor.

ज्रि 1 P. जये अभिभवे च to conquer, to defeat. ज्रयति pre. जिज्राय perf. ज्रेता p. fut. अज्रैषीत् aor.

ज्रि 10 U. वयोहानौ to become old; ज्राययति-ते pre. ज्राययाञ्चकार—चक्रे &c. perf. ज्राययिता p. fut. अजिज्रयत्-त aor.

ज्वर् 1 P. रोगे to be hot with fever or passion; ज्वरति pre. जज्वार perf. ज्वरिता p. fut. ज्वरिष्यति fut. अज्वारीत्. aor. Cau - ज्वरयति-ते, अजिज्वरत्-त aor. जिज्वरिषति des. जूर्ण p. p.

ज्वल् 1 P. दीप्तौ to burn, to glow; ज्वलति pre. जज्वाल perf. ज्वलिता p. fut. ज्वलिष्यति fut. अज्वालीत् aor. Cau.-ज्वलयति-ते, ज्वालयति-ते (with प्र-प्रज्वलयति-ते) pre. जिज्वलिषति des. ज्वलित p. p.

झ—

झट् 1 P. संघाते to be collected or matted together; झटति pre. अझटीत्, अझाटीत् Aor.

झम् 1 P. अदने to eat; झमति pre. झमिता p. fut. अझमीत् Aor.

झष् 1 P. हिंसायाम् to kill; झषति pre. जझाष perf. झषिता p. fut. अझषीत्, अझाषीत् aor.

झष 1 U. आदानसंवरणयोः to take, to put on, to conceal; झषति-ते pre. जझाष, जझषे perf. झषिता p. fut. अझषीत्, अझाषीत, अझषिष्ट aor.

झॄ 4. 9. P. वयोहानौ to become old; झीर्यति, झॄणाति pre. जझार perf. झरिता, झरीता p. fut. अझारीत् Aor.

ट—

टङ्क् 1 P. 10 U. to bind, to tie; टङ्कति, टङ्कयति-ते pre. टटङ्क, टङ्कयाञ्चकार-चक्रे &c. perf. टङ्किता, टङ्कयिता p. fut. अटङ्कीत् अटटङ्कत्-त aor. टङ्कित p. p.

टल् 1. P. वैक्लव्ये to be confused; टलति pre. टटाल perf. टलिता fut. अटालीत् aor.

टिक् 1 A. to go, to move; टेकते pre. टिटिके perf. टेकिता p. fut. अटेकिष्ट aor. Cau.-टेकयति-ते pre. अटिटेकत्-त aor.

टिप् 10 U. क्षेपे to throw, to send; टेपयति-ते pre. टेपयाञ्चकार-चक्रे perf. टेपयिता p. fut. अटिटेपत्-त aor.

टीकृ 1 A. to go, to move; टीकते pre. टिटीके perf. टीकिता p. fut. अटीकिष्ट aor. टिटीकिषते des.

टीकृ 1. A. to go, टीकते pre. अटीकिष्ट Aor.

ड—

डप् 10 A. संघाते to gather, to heap; डापयते pre. डापयाञ्चक्रे perf. डापयिता p. fut. अडीडपते aor.

डम्ब् 10 A. क्षेपे to throw, to send; डम्बयति-ते pre. डम्बयाञ्चकार-चक्रे, perf. डम्बयिता p. fut. डम्बयिष्यति-ते fut. अडडम्बत्-त Aor..

डिप् 4 P. क्षेपे to throw; डिप्यति pre. डिडेप perf. डेपिता p. fut. अडिपत् aor.

डिप् 10 A. संघाते to gather; डेपयते pre. डेपयाञ्चक्रे perf. डेपयिता p. fut. अडीडिपत aor.

डी 1 A. विहायसा गतौ to fly, to go; डयते pre. डिड्ये perf. डयिता p. fut. डयिष्यते fut. अडयिष्ट aor. डयिषीष्ट Ben. Cau.–डाययति-ते, अडीडयत्-त Aor. डिडयिषते des. डयित, डान (with उत्) p. p..

डी 4 A. to fly, to go; डीयते pre. डिड्ये perf. डीन p. p. For other forms see 1 A.

डुल् 10 U. to throw up; डोलयति-ते pre. डोलयाञ्चकार-चक्रे perf.. डोलयिता p. fut. अडूडुलत्-त aor.

ढ—

ढौकृ 1 A. गतौ to go, to approach; ढौकते pre. डुढौके perf. ढौकिता p. fut. ढौकिष्यते fut. अढौकिष्ट aor. ढौकिषीष्ट Ben. Cau.–ढौकयति -ते pre. अडुढौकत्-त aor. डुढौकिषते des. Pass.–ढौक्यते. ढौकित p. p.

त—

तकृ 1 P. हसने सहने च to laugh, to bear; तकति pre. तताक perf. तकिता p. fut. अतकीत्, अताकीत् aor. तकित p. p.

तक्ष् 1 P. त्वचने (त्वचनं संवरणं त्वचोमर्दणं च) to conceal, to pare. तक्षति pre. ततक्ष perf. तक्षिता p. fut. अतक्षीत् Aor.

तक्ष् 1 P. तनूकरणे to pare, to cut; तक्षति, तक्ष्णोति pre. (belongs to 5th conj. optionally in the Conj. Tenses) ततक्ष perf. तक्षिता p. fut. तक्षिष्यति, तक्ष्यति fut. अतक्षीत् aor. तक्ष्यात् ben. तष्ट p. p. तक्षित्वा, तष्ट्वा ger.

तङ्क् 1 P. गतौ स्खलने कम्पने च to go, to stumble, to shake; तङ्कति pre. ततङ्क perf. तङ्किता p. fut. अतङ्कीत् aor. तङ्कित p. p.

तञ्च् 1 P. to go; तञ्चति pre. ततञ्च perf. तञ्चिता p. fut. अतञ्चीत् aor. तक्त p. p. तञ्चित्वा, तक्त्वा ger.

तञ्च् 7 P. संकोचने to contract, to shrink; तनक्ति pre. ततञ्च perf. तंक्ता, तञ्चिता p. fut. तङ्क्ष्यति, तञ्चिष्यति fut; अतञ्चीत्, अताङ्क्षीत् Aor. Cau.-तञ्चयति-ते, तितञ्चिषति, तितङ्क्षति des.

तञ्ज् same as तञ्च्.

तट् 1 P. उच्छ्राये to grow; तटति pre. ततट perf. तटिता p. fut. अतटीत्, अताटीत् aor.

तड् 10 U. आघाते भाषायां च to beat; ताडयति-ते pre. ताडयाञ्चकार-चक्रे &c. perf. ताडयिता p. fut. ताडयिष्यति-ते fut. अतीतडत्-त aor. Pass.—ताड्यते pre. ताडित p. p.

तण्ड् 1 A. ताडने to beat; तण्डते pre. ततण्डे perf. तण्डिता p. fut. अतण्डिष्ट aor.

तन् 8 U. विस्तारे to spread, to go; तनोति, तनुते pre. ततान, तेने perf. तनिता p. fut. तनिष्यति-ते fut. अतनीत्, अतानीत् & अतनिष्ट, अतत aor. तन्यात् & तनिषीष्ट ben. तितांसति-ते, तितंसति-ते, तितनिषति-ते des. Pass.—तन्यते & तायते pre. अतानि aor. Cau.—तानयति-ते pre. अतीतनत्-त aor. तत p. p. तनित्वा, तत्वा ger.

तन् 1 P. 10. U. श्रद्धोपकरणयोः to believe, to subserve; तनति, तानयति-ते pre. अतनीत्, अतानीत्, अतीतनत्-त Aor.

तन्त्र् 10 A. कुटुम्बधारणे to support, to govern; तन्त्रयते pre तन्त्रयाञ्चक्रे perf. अततन्त्रत Aor. तितन्त्रयिषते des. Pass—तन्त्र्यते.

तप् 1 P. सन्तापे to shine, to heat; तपति pre. तताप, perf. तप्ता

p. fut. अताप्सीत् aor. तप्यात् ben. तितप्सति des. Pass.—तप्यते pre. अतप्त aor. Cau.—तापयति-ते pre. अतीतपत्-त aor. तप्त p. p.

तप् 4 A. ऐश्वर्ये to rule, to be powerful; तप्यते pre. तेपे perf. तप्ता p. fut. तप्स्यते fut. अतप्स्यत con. अतप्त aor. तप्सीष्ट ben. तप्त p. p.

तप् 10 U. to heat; तापयति-ते pre. तापयाञ्चकार-चक्रे &c. perf. तापयिता p. fut. अतीतपत्-त aor.

तम् 4 P. कांक्षायां खेदे च to be anxious, to be fatigued; ताम्यति pre. तताम perf. तमिता p. fut. तमिष्यति fut. अतमिष्यत् con. अतमत् aor. तान्त p. p. तमित्वा & तन्त्वा ger.

तय् 1 A. to go तयते pre. तेये perf. तयिता p. fut. अतयिष्ट aor.

तर्क् 10 U. वितर्के to guess, to suppose. तर्कयति-ते fut. तर्कयाञ्चकार-चक्रे, &c. perf. तर्कयिता p. fut. तर्कयिष्यति-ते fut. अतर्कयिष्यत्-त con. अततर्कत्-त aor. तर्कित p. p तर्कयित्वा ger.

तर्ज् 1 P. भर्त्सने to threaten, to menace; तर्जति pre. ततर्ज perf. तर्जिता p. fut. तर्जिष्यति fut. अतर्जिष्यत् con. अतर्जीत् aor. तितर्जिषति des. तर्जित p. p.

तर्ज् 10 A. भर्त्सने to blame; तर्जयते pre. तर्जयाञ्चक्रे perf. तर्जयिता p. fut. अततर्जत aor. तर्जित p. p.

तर्द् 1 P. हिंसायां to kill, to hurt; तर्दति pre. ततर्द perf. तर्दिता p. fut. अतर्दीत् aor.

तल् 10 U. प्रतिष्ठायां to establish; तालयति-ते.

तस् 4 P. उपक्षये to be decreased; तस्यति pre. अतसत् Aor.

तंस् 1 P &. 10 U. अलंकरणे to decorate, to assume; तंसति & तंसयति-ते pre. ततंस, तंसयाञ्चकार-चक्रे perf. तंसिता, तंसयिता p. fut. अतंसीत् & अततंसत्-त aor.

ताय् 1 A. संतानपालनयोः to spread, to protect; तायते pre. तताये perf. तायिता p. fut. अतायिष्ट, अतायि aor. Cau.—तायवति-ते pre. अततायत्-त aor. तितायिषते des.

तिक् 1 A. to go; तेकते pre. तेकिता p. fut. अतेकिष्ट aor.

तिक् 5 P. आस्कन्दने वधे च to attack; तिक्नोति pre. तितेक perf, तेकिता p. fut. अतेकीत् aor.

तिग 5 P. to attack; तिग्नोति pre. तितेग perf. तेगिता p. fut. अतेगीत aor.

तिघ् 5 P. हिंसायां to hurt; तिघ्नोति pre. तितेघ perf. तेघिता p. fut. अतेघीत् aor.

तिज् 1 A. क्षमायां च to endure, to suffer with courage; तितिक्षते pre. तितिक्षाञ्चक्रे perf. तितिक्षिता p. fut. तितिक्षिष्यते fut. अतितिक्षिष्ट aor. तितिक्षिषीष्ट ben. तितिक्षिषते des. Cau.-तितिक्षयति-ते. When it means to sharpen (निशाने) तेजते pre. तेजिष्यते fut. अतेजिष्ट aor.

तिज् 10 U. निशाने to whet; तेजयति-ते pre. तेजयाञ्चकार-चक्रे perf. तेजयिता p. fut. अतीतिजत्-त aor.

तिप 1 A. क्षरणे to drop down, to sprinkle; तेपते pre. तितिपे perf. तेप्ता p. fut. तेप्स्यते fut. अतेप्स्यत con. तिप्सीष्ट ben. अतिप्त aor.

तिम् 4 P. आर्द्रीभावे to be wet; तिम्यति pre. तितेम perf. तेमिता p. fut. अतेमीत् aor. तितिमिषति, तितेमिषति des. तिमित p. p.

तिल् 1 P. गतौ to go; तेलति pre. तितेल perf. तेलिता p. fut. अतेलीत् aor.

तिल् 6 P. & 10 U. to be oily or unctuous; तिलति, तेलयति-ते pre. तितेल, तेलयाञ्चकार-चक्रे &c. perf. तेलिता, तेलयिता p. fut. अतेलीत्, अतीतिलत -त aor.

तिल्ल् 1 P. to go; तिल्लति pre. अतिल्लीत् Aor.

तीक् I A. to go; तीकते pre. तितीके perf. तीकिता p. fut. अतीकिष्ट aor.

तीम् 4 P. क्लेदने to be wet; तीम्यति pre. अतीमीत् Aor.

तीव् 1 P. स्थौल्ये to be fat. तीवति pre. तितीव perf. तीविता p. fut.. अतीवीत् Aor

तु 2 P. गतिवृद्धिहिंसासु to go, to grow, to kill; तौति, तवीति pre. तुताव perf. तोता p. fut. तोष्यति fut. अतोष्यत् con. अतौषीत् aor.

तुज् 1 P. हिंसायाम् to kill, to hurt; तोजति pre. तुतोज perf. तोजिता p. fut. अतोजीत् aor.

तुञ्ज् 1 P. प्रापणे हिंसायां बले च to reach, to kill, to be powerful; तुञ्जति pre. तुतुञ्ज perf. तुञ्जिता p. fut. अतुञ्जीत् aor.

तुज्, तुञ्ज् 10 U. हिंसाबलादाननिकेतनेषु to kill, to be strong, to live; तोजयति-ते, तुञ्जयति-ते pre. तोजयाञ्चकार-चक्रे. &c. तुञ्जयाञ्चकार-चक्रे, &c. perf. तोजयिता, तुञ्जयिता p. fut. अतूतुजत्-त, अतुतुञ्जत्-त aor.

तुट् 6 P. कलहकर्मणि (कुटादि) to quarrel, to cut; तुटति pre. तुतोट perf. तुटिता p. fut. अतुटीत् aor.

तुड् 1, 6 (कुटादि) P. तोडने to tear, to kill; तोडति, तुडति pre. तोडिता, तुडिता fut. अतोडीत्, अतुडीत् Aor.

तुड्ड् 1 P. अनादरे to mortify; तुड्डति pre. अतुड्डीत् Aor.

तुण् 6 P. कौटिल्ये to curve; तुणति pre. तुतोण perf. तोणिता p. fut. अतोणीत् aor.

तुत्थ् 10 U. आवरणे to cover; तुत्थयति-ते pre. अतुतुत्थत्-त Aor.

तुद् 6 U. व्यथने to strike, to wound; तुदति-ते pre. तुतोद, तुतुदे perf. तोत्ता p. fut. तोत्स्यति-ते fut. अतोत्स्यत्-त con. अतौत्सीत् & अतुत्त aor. तुद्यात्-तोत्सीष्ट ben. तुतुत्सति-ते des. Pass.-तुद्यते pre. अतोदि aor. Cau.-तोदयति-ते pre. अतूतुदत्-त aor. तुन्न p. p. तुत्त्वा ger.

तुन्द् 1 P. to search; तुन्दन्ति pre. तुतुन्द perf. तुन्दिता p. fut. अतुन्दीत् aor.

तुप् 1 & 6 P. हिंसायां to kill; तोपति, तुपति pre. तुतोप perf. तोपिता p. fut. अतोपीत् aor.

तुफ् 1, 6 P. हिंसायां to kill, see the above root; तोफते &c.

तुभ् 1 A. हिंसायां to kill; तोभते pre. अतुभत्, अतोभिष्ट Aor.

तुभ् 4 & 9 P. to hurt, to kill; तुभ्यति, तुभ्नाति pre. तुतोभ perf. तोभिता p. fut. अतुभत् (4) अतोभीत् (9) aor.

तुम्प्, तुम्फ्, 1, 6. (See तुप्, तुफ् above); तुम्पति, तुम्फति pre.

तुम्ब् 1 P. अर्दने to hurt, to give pain; तुम्बति pre. अतुम्बीत् Aor. Also 10 U. अदर्शने च.

तुर् 3 P. त्वरणे to make haste; तुतोर्ति pre. तुतोर perf. तोरिता p. fut. अतोरीत् aor. (Vedic)

तुर्व् 1 P. हिंसायाम् to kill, to hurt; तुर्वति pre. तुतूर्व perf. तूर्विता p. fut. अतूर्वीत् aor.

तुल् 10 U. उन्माने to weigh, to examine; तोलयति-ते pre. तोलयाञ्चकार-चक्रे perf. तोलयिता p. fut. तोलयिष्यति-ते fut. तोल्यात्, तोलयिषीष्ट Ben. अतूतुलत्-त aor. Pass.—तोल्यते pre. अतोलि Aor. तोलित p. p.

तुष् 4 P. तुष्टौ to be pleased or satisfied; तुष्यति pre. तुतोष perf. तोष्टा p. fut. तोक्ष्यति fut. अतोक्ष्यत् con. तुष्यात् ben. अतुषत् aor. Cau.—तोषयति-ते pre. अतूतुषत्-त aor. तुतुक्षति des. Pass.—तुष्यते pre. अतोषि aor. तुष्ट p. p. तुष्ट्वा ger. तोष्टुम् inf.

तुस् 1 P. to sound; तोसति pre. तुतोस perf. तोसिता p. fut अतोसीत् aor.

तुह् 1 P. अर्दने वधे च to torment, to kill; तोहति pre. अतुहत्, अतोहीत् Aor. तुतु-तो-हिषति des.

तूण् 10 A. पूरणे to fill up; तूणयते pre. अतुतूणत Aor.

तूर् 4 A. गतित्वरणहिंसयो: to go hastily, to kill; तूर्यते pre. तुतूरे perf. तूरिता p. fut. अतूरिष्ट aor. तुतूरिषते des.

तूल् 1 P. निष्कर्षे to determine the quantity or weight of; तूलति pre. तूलिष्यति fut. अतूलीत् aor.

तृक्ष् 1 P. to go; तृक्षति pre. ततृक्ष perf. तृक्षिता p. fut. अतृक्षीत् aor. तृक्ष्यात् ben.

तृण् 8 U. अदने to eat; तर्णोति, तर्णुते, तृणोति-तृणुते pre. ततर्ण, ततृणे perf. तर्णिता p. fut. तर्णिष्यति-ते fut. अतर्णीत् अतर्णिष्ट, अतृत aor. तितर्णिषति-ते des. तृत p. p. तृणित्वा, तृत्वा ger.

तृद् 7 U. हिंसानादरयोः to destroy, to disregard; तृणत्ति, तृन्ते pre. ततर्द, ततृदे perf. तर्दिता p. fut. तर्दिष्यति-ते, तर्त्स्यति-ते fut. अतर्दिष्यत्-त con. अतृदत्, अतर्दीत्, अतर्दिष्ट aor. तृद्यात्, तर्दिषीष्ट, तृत्सीष्ट ben. तितर्दिषति, तितृत्सति des. तृण्ण p. p. तर्दित्वा, तृत्त्वा ger.

तृप् 4 P. तृप्तौ to become satisfied; तृप्यति pre. ततर्प perf. तर्पिता, तर्प्ता, त्रप्ता p. fut. तर्पिष्यति, तर्प्स्यति, त्रप्स्यति fut. अतर्पिष्यत्, अतर्प्स्यत्, अत्रप्स्यत् con. अतृपत्, अतर्पीत्, अत्राप्सीत्, अतार्प्सीत् aor. तृप्यात् ben. तितर्पिषति, तितृप्सति des. Cau.-तर्पयति-ते, अततर्पत्-त, अतीतृपत्-त aor. तृप्त p. p. तर्पितुम्, तर्प्तुम् त्रप्तुम् inf.

तृप् 5 P. प्रीणने to be pleased, to please; तृप्नोति pre. ततर्प perf. तर्पिता p. fut. अतर्पीत् aor. तृप्यात् ben. तितर्पिषति, तितृप्सति des. तर्पित p. p. तर्पित्वा ger.

तृप् 6 P. to be pleased, to please; तृपति pre. (for other forms see above).

तृप् 1 P. &. 10 U. तृप्तौ संदीपने च to be satisfied, to light, to kindle; तर्पति, तर्पयति-ते pre. ततर्प, तर्पयाञ्चकार-चक्रे, &c. perf. तर्पिता, तर्पयिता p. fut. अतर्पीत्, अततर्पत्-त अतीतृपत-त aor. तृपित, तर्पित p. p.

तृफ्, तृम्फ् 6 P. प्रीणने, to please; तृफति, तृम्फति pre. अतर्फीत्-अतृम्फीत् aor.

तृम्प् 9 P. प्रीणने to please; तृम्पति pre. तृम्पिष्यति fut. अतृम्पीत् aor.

तृष् 4 P. पिपासायाम् to be thirsty; तृष्यति pre. ततर्ष perf. तर्षिता p fut. तर्षिष्यति fut. अतर्षिष्यत् con. अतृषत् aor. तृष्यात् ben. Cau.—तर्षयति-ते pre. अतीतृषत्-त अततर्षत्-त aor. तितर्षिषति des. तृष्ट p. p. तृषित्वा, तर्षित्वा ger.

तृह् 6 P. हिंसायां to kill, to hurt; तृहति pre. ततर्ह perf. तर्हिता; तर्ढा, p. fut. तर्हिष्यति, तर्क्ष्यति fut. अतर्हीत्, अतृक्षत् aor. तितर्हिषति, तितृक्षति des. Cau. (see the next root). तृढ p. p. तर्हित्वा तृढ्वा ger.

तृह् 7 P. to injure, to kill; तृणेढि pre. ततर्ह perf. तर्हिता p. fut. तर्हिष्यति fut. अतर्हिष्यत् con. अतर्हीत् aor. तृह्यात् ben. तितृक्षति des.

Cau.—तर्हयति-ते pre. अततर्हत्-त अतीतृहत्-त aor. Pass.—तृह्यते pre. अतर्हि aor. तृहित p. p. तर्हित्वा ger. तर्हितुम् inf.

तृंह् 6 P. to kill; तृंहति pre. ततृंह perf. तृंहिता, तृंढा p. fut. तृंहिष्यति तृंक्ष्यति fut. अतृंहीत्, अतार्ङ्क्षीत् aor. तृंह्यात् ben. तितृक्षति, तितृंहिषति des. तृंहितुम्, तृण्ढुम् inf.

तॄ 1 P. प्लवनतरणयोः to cross over, to swim; तरति pre.ततार perf. तरिता, तरीता p. fut. तरिष्यति, तरीष्यति fut. अतारीत् aor. तीर्यात् ben. तितीर्षति, तितरिषति, तितरीषति des. तीर्ण p.p. तीर्त्वा ger. Pass.—तीर्यते pre. तेरे perf. तारिता, तरिता & तरीता p. fut. अतारि aor. तारिषीष्ट, तरिषीष्ट, & तीर्षीष्ट ben. Cau.—तारयति-ते pre. अतीतरत्-त Aor.

तेज् 1 P. निशाने पालने च to whet, to protect! तेजति pre. तितेज perf. तेजिता p. fut. अतेजीत् aor.

तेप् 1 A. क्षरणे कम्पे च्युतौ च to drop down, to shake; तेपते pre. तितेपे perf. तेपिता p. fut. अतेपिष्ट Aor.

तेव् 1 A. देवने to play; तेवते pre. अतेविष्ट Aor.

त्यज् 1 P. हानौ to abandon; त्यजति pre. तत्याज perf. त्यक्ता p. fut. त्यक्ष्यति fut. अत्यक्ष्यत् con. अत्याक्षीत् aor. त्यज्यात् ben. Cau.—त्याजयति-ते pre. अतित्यजत्-त aor. तित्यक्षति des. Pass.—त्यज्यते pre. अत्याजि aor. त्यक्त p. p. त्यक्त्वा ger. त्यक्तुम् inf.

त्रङ्क् 1 A. to go; त्रङ्कते pre. तत्रङ्के perf. त्रङ्किता p. fut. अत्रङ्किष्ट aor.

त्रख्, त्रंख् 1 P. to go; त्रखति, त्रङ्खति pre. तत्राख, तत्रङ्ख perf. त्रखिता-त्रङ्खिता p. fut. अत्रखीत्, अत्राखीत् & अत्रङ्खीत् aor.

त्रङ्ग् 1 P. to move; त्रङ्गति pre. तत्रङ्ग pref. त्रङ्गिता p. fut. अत्रङ्गीत् aor.

त्रप् 1 A. लज्जायां to be ashamed; त्रपते pre. त्रेपे perf. त्रपिता, त्रप्ता p. fut. त्रपिष्यते, त्रप्स्यते fut. अत्रपिष्यत, अत्रप्स्यत con. अत्रपिष्ट, अत्रप्त aor. त्रपिषीष्ट, त्रप्सीष्ट ben. Cau.—त्रपयति-ते pre. अतित्रपत्-त aor. तित्रपिषते des. त्रप्त p. p. त्रपित्वा, त्रप्त्वा ger. त्रपितुम्, त्रप्तुम् inf.

त्रस् 1 & 4 P. उद्वेगे to tremble, to fear; त्रसति, त्रस्यति pre. तत्रास perf. त्रसिता p. fut. त्रसिष्यति fut. अत्रसिष्यत् con. अत्रासीत्, अत्रसीत् aor त्रस्यात् ben. Pass.—त्रस्यते pre. अत्रासि aor. Cau.—त्रासयति-ते pre. अतित्रसत्-त aor. तित्रासिषति des. त्रस्त p. p. त्रसित्वा ger. त्रसितुम् inf.

त्रस् 10 U. ग्रहणे धारणे वारणे च to take, to hold, to oppose; त्रासयति-ते pre. त्रासयाञ्चकार-चक्रे &c. perf. त्रासयिता p. fut. अतित्रसत् त aor.

त्रंस् 1 P. 10 U. भाषायां to speak; त्रंसति, त्रंसयति-ते pre. अत्रंसीत्, अतत्रंसत्-त Aor.

त्रिङ्ख् 1 P. to go; त्रिङ्खति pre. तित्रिङ्ख perf. त्रिङ्खिता p. fut. अत्रिङ्खीत् aor.

त्रुट् 6 P. छेदने (कुटादि) to tear, to break; त्रुट्यति pre. तुत्रोट perf. त्रुटिता p. fut. त्रुटिष्यति fut. अत्रुटीत् aor. त्रुट्यात् ben. Cau.—त्रोटयति-ते pre. अतुत्रुटत्-त aor. तुत्रुटिषति des. Pass.—त्रुट्यते pre. अत्रोटि aor. त्रुटित p.p. त्रुटित्वा ger.

त्रुट् 10 A. छेदने to tear; त्रोटयते pre. त्रोटयाञ्चक्रे perf. त्रोटयिता p. fut. अतुत्रुटत aor. त्रोटयिषीष्ट ben.

त्रुप, त्रुम्प् 1 P. हिंसायां to kill; त्रोपति, त्रुम्पति pre. अत्रोपीत्, अत्रुम्पीत् Aor.

त्रुफ् त्रुम्फ् Same as above.

त्रै 1 A. पालने to protect; त्रायते pre. तत्रे perf. त्राता p. fut. त्रास्यते fut. अत्रास्यत con. अत्रास्त aor. त्रासीष्ट ben. Cau.—त्रापयति-ते pre. अतित्रपत्-त aor. तित्रासते des. Pass.—त्रायते pre. अत्रायि aor. त्रात (त्राण) p.p. त्रातुम् inf.

त्रौक् 1 A. to go; त्रौकते pre. तुत्रौके perf. त्रौकिता p. fut. त्रौकिष्यते fut. अत्रौकिष्ट aor.

त्वक्ष् 1 P. तनूकरणे to pare; त्वक्षति pre. तत्वक्ष perf. त्वक्षिता, त्वष्टा p. fut त्वक्षिष्यति, त्वक्ष्यति fut. अत्वक्षीत्-अत्वाक्षीत् aor. त्वक्ष्यात् ben. तित्वक्षिषति, तित्वक्षति des. त्वष्ट p.p. त्वक्षित्वा, त्वष्ट्वा ger.

त्वङ्ग् 1 P. गतौ कम्पने च to go, to shake; त्वङ्गति pre. तत्वङ्ग perf. त्वङ्गिता p. fut. अत्वङ्गीत् aor.

त्वच् 6 P. संवरणे to cover; त्वचति pre. तत्वाच perf. त्वचिता p. fut. अत्वचीत्, अत्वाचीत् aor.

त्वञ्च् 1 P. to go, to move; त्वञ्चति pre. तत्वञ्च perf. त्वञ्चिता p. fut. अत्वञ्चीत aor. त्वच्यात् ben. तित्वञ्चिषति des. Pass.—त्वच्यते.

त्वर् 1 A. संभ्रमे to hurry, to move with speed; त्वरते pre. तत्वरे perf. त्वरिता p. fut. अत्वरिष्ट aor. त्वरिषीष्ट ben. तित्वरिषते des. त्वरित or तूर्ण p. p. Cau.—त्वरयति-ते pre. अतत्वरत्-त aor.

त्विष् 1 U. दीप्तौ to shine, to glitter; त्वेषति-ते pre. तित्वेष, तित्विषे perf. त्वेष्टा p. fut. त्वेक्ष्यति-ते fut. अत्वेक्ष्यत्-त con. अत्विक्षत्-त aor. तित्विक्षति-ते des.

त्सर् 1 P. छद्मगतौ to proceed with fraud; त्सरति pre. तत्सार perf. त्सरिता p. fut. अत्सारीत् aor.

थ—

थुड् 6 P. संवरणे (कुटादि) to cover, to hide; थुडति pre. तुथोड perf. थुडिता p. fut. अथुडीत् aor.

थुर्व् 1 P. हिंसायां to injure, to hurt; थूर्वति pre. तुथूर्व perf. थूर्विता p. fut. अथूर्वीत् aor.

द—

दश 1 P. दंशने to bite, to sting; to speak; (भाषायां च) दंशति pre. ददंश perf. दंष्टा p. fut. दंक्ष्यति fut. अदांक्षीत् (अदांष्टाम् dual) aor. दश्यात् ben. दिदंक्षति des. Pass.—दश्यते, अदंशि aor. दष्ट p. p. दंष्टुम् inf. दंष्ट्वा ger.

दंश् 10 A. दंशने to bite; दंशयते pre. अददंशत Aor. दिदंशयिषते des Pass.—दंश्यते pre. दंशित p. p.

दंश् 10 U. भाषायां to speak; दंशयति-ते pre. अददंशत्-त Aor.

दक्ष् 1 A. वृद्धौ शीघ्रार्थे (गतिहिंसनयोश्च) to grow, to go in speed, to go, to hurt; दक्षते pre. ददक्षे perf. दक्षिष्यते fut. अदक्षिष्ट Aor.

दघ् 5 P. घातने पालने च to kill, to protect; दघ्नोति pro. ददाघ perf. दघिता p. fut. अदघीत, अदाघीत, aor. (Vedic).

दण्ड् 10 U. दण्डनिपातने दमने च to fine, to punish; दण्डयति-ते, दण्डयाञ्चकार-चक्रे. &c. perf. दण्डयिता p. fut. दण्डयिष्यति-ते fut. अददण्डत्-त aor. दण्डयिषीष्ट des. दण्डित p.p.

दद् 1 A. दाने to give; ददते pre. दददे perf. ददिता p. fut. ददिष्यते fut. अददिष्ट aor. ददिषीष्ट ben. दिददिषते des. Cau.—दादयति-ते. pre. अदीददत्-त aor.

दध 1 A. धारणे to hold, to present; दधते pre. देधे perf. दधिता p. fut. अदधिष्ट aor. दधिषीष्ट ben. दिदधिषते des. Cau.—दाधयति-ते pre. Pass.—दध्यते pre.

दम्भ् 5 P. दम्भने to hurt, to deceive; दभ्नोति pre. ददम्भ perf. दम्भिता p. fut. दम्भिष्यति fut. अदम्भीत् aor. धिप्सति, धीप्सति, दिदम्भिषति des. Pass.—दभ्यते pre. अदम्भि aor. दब्ध p.p. दम्भित्वा-दब्ध्वा ger.

दम्भ् 10 U. प्रेरणे to send; दम्भयति-ते pre. दम्भयाञ्चकार-चक्रे, &c. perf. अददम्भत्-त Aor. दम्भ्यात् दम्भयिषीष्ट ben. Pass.—दम्भ्यते.

दम् 4 P. उपशमे to be tamed: दाम्यति pre. ददाम perf. दमिता p. fut. दमिष्यति fut. अदमिष्यत con. अदमत aor. Cau.—दमयते only अदीदमत् aor. Pass.—दम्यते; अदमि, अदामि aor. दमित, दान्त p. p. दमित्वा, दान्त्वा ger.

दय् 1 A. दानगतिरक्षणहिंसादानेषु to give, to be pity, to protect, to injure, to take; दयते pre. दयाञ्चक्रे. &c. perf. दयिता p. fut, दयिष्यते fut. अदयिष्ट aor. दयिषीष्ट ben. दिदयिषते des. दयित p.p.

दरिद्रा 2 P. दुर्गतौ to be poor or needy; दरिद्राति pre. दरिद्राञ्चकार. ददरिद्रौ perf. दरिद्रिता p. fut. अदरिद्रीत, अदरिद्रासीत् aor. दरिद्र्यात् ben. दिदरिद्रासति, दिदरिद्रिषति des. दरिद्रित p.p.

दल् 1 P. विशरणे to burst open, to expand; दलति pre. ददाल perf. दलिता p. fut. अदालीत् aor. दलित p.p. Cau.—to cut, to tear दलयति, दालयति pre. दिदालिषति des.

दल् 10 U. विदारणे to tear; दालयति pre. अदीदलत्-त Aor.

दस् 4 P. उपक्षये to perish; दस्यति pre. ददास perf. दसिता p. fut. अदसत् aor.

दस् 1 P. 10 A. दर्शनदंशनयोः to see, to bite; दंसति, दंसयते pre. ददंस, दंसयाञ्चक्रे &c. perf. अदंसीत्, अददंसत Aor.

दंस् 1 P. 10 U. भाषायां to speak; दंसति, दंसयति-ते pre.

दह् 1 P. भस्मीकरणे to burn, to pain; दहति pre. ददाह perf. दग्धा p. fut. धक्ष्यति fut. अधाक्षीत् (अदाग्धाम dual) aor. दह्यात् ben. दिधक्षति des. Cau.-दाहयति-ते pre. अदीदहत्-त aor. Pass.-दह्यते pre. अदाहि aor. दग्ध p.p. दग्ध्वा ger. दग्धुम् inf.

द. 1 P. दाने to give; यच्छति pre. ददौ perf. दाता p. fut. दास्यति fut. अदास्यत con. अदात् aor. देयात् ben. दित्सति des. Pass.-दीयते pre. अदायि aor. Cau-दापयति-ते pre. अदीदपत्-त aor. दत्त p. p. दत्त्वा ger. दातुम् inf.

दा 2 P. लवने to cut; दाति pre. (for perf. and fut. see above, अदासीत् aor दायात् ben. दिदासति des. Pass.—दायते. दात p. p.

दा 3 U. दाने to give, to put. ददाति, दत्ते pre. ददौ, ददे perf. दाता p. fut. दास्यति-ते fut. अदास्यत्-त con. अदात्, अदित aor. देयात्, दासीष्ट ben. दित्सति-ते des. दत्त p. p. दत्त्वा ger. दातुम् inf. Pass.-दीयते pre. अदायि aor.

दान् 1 U. खण्डने आर्जवे च to cut, to make straight; दीदांसति-ते pre. दीदांसाञ्चकार-चक्रे &c. perf. अदीदांसीत्, अदीदांसिष्ट Aor. दीदांसिषति-ते des.

दान् 10 U. छेदने to cut. दानयति-ते pre. अदीदनत्-त Aor.

दाय् 1 A. दाने to give; दायते pre. ददाये porf. दायिष्यते fut. अदायिष्ट aor.

दाश् 1 U. दाने to give; दाशति-ते pre. ददाश, ददाशे, perf. अदाशीत्, अदाशिष्ट. aor.

दाश् 5 P. हिंसायां to kill, to injure; दाश्नोति pre. (Vedic).

दास् 1 U. दाने to give; दासति-ते pre. अदासीत्, अदासिष्ट aor.

दिव् 4 P. क्रीडाविजिगीषाव्यवहारद्युतिस्तुतिमोदमदस्वप्नकान्तिगतिषु to play, to sell, to shine, to wish; to conquer, to trifle with, to rejoice, to be sleepy, &c; दिव्यति pre. दिदेव perf. देविता p. fut. अदेवीत् aor. दीव्यात् ben. दुद्यूषति, दिदेविषति des. Pass.—दीव्यते pre. Cau.-देवयति-ते pre. अदीदिवत्-त aor. द्युत or द्यून p. p.

दिव् 1 P. & 10 U. मर्दने to rub; देवति, देवयति-ते pre. दिदेव, देवयाञ्चकार-चक्रे &c. perf. अदेवीत्, अदीदिवत्-त aor.

दिव् 10 A. परिकूजने to cause, to lament; देवयते pre. अदीदिवत Aor.

दिश् 6 U. अतिसर्जने to grant, to allow; दिशति-ते pre. दिदेश, दिदिशे perf. देष्टा p. fut. देक्ष्यति-ते fut. अदेक्ष्यत्-त con. अदिक्षत्-त aor. दिश्यात्, दिक्षीष्ट ben. दिदिक्षति-ते des. Pass.-दिश्यते pre. अदेशि aor. Cau.-देशयति-ते pre. अदीदिशत्-त aor. दिष्ट p. p. देष्टुम् inf. दिष्ट्वा ger.

दिह् 2 U. उपचये to augment, to anoint; देग्धि, दिग्धे pre. दिदेह, दिदिहे perf. देग्धा p. fut. धेक्ष्यति-ते fut. अधेक्ष्यत्-त con. अधिक्षत्, अधिक्षत, अदिग्ध aor. दिह्यात्, धिक्षीष्ट ben. दिधिक्षति-ते des. Pass.-दिह्यते pre. अदेहि aor. Cau.-देहयति-ते pre. अदीदिहत्-त aor. दिग्ध p. p. दिग्ध्वा ger. देग्धुम् inf.

दी 4 A. क्षये to perish; दीयते pre. दिदीये perf. दाता p. fut. दास्यते fut. अदास्यत con. अदास्त aor. दासीष्ट ben. दिदीषते des. दीन p. p.

दीक्ष् 1 A. मौण्ड्येज्योपनयननियमव्रतादेशेषु to invest with a sacred thread, to dedicate oneself to, to sacrifice, &c.; दीक्षते pre. दिदीक्षे perf. दीक्षिता p. fut. अदीक्षिष्ट aor. Pass.-दीक्ष्यते pre. अदीक्षि aor. Cau.—दीक्षयति-ते pre. अदिदीक्षत्-त aor. दिदीक्षते des. दीक्षित p. p. दीक्षित्वा ger.

दीधी 2 A. दीप्तिदेवनयोः to shine, to appear; दीधीते pre. दीध्याञ्चक्रे perf. दीधिता p. fut. दीधिष्यते fut. अदीधिष्ट Aor. (Vedic.)

दीप् 4 A. दीप्तौ to shine, to burn; दीप्यते pre. दिदीपे perf. दीपिता p. fut. अदीपिष्ट, अदीपि aor. दीपिषीष्ट ben. दिदीपिषते des. Cau.-दीपयति-ते pre. अदीदिपत्-त & अदिदीपत्-त aor. Pass.-दीप्यते pre. अदीपि aor. दीप्त p. p.

दु 1 P. to go; दवति pre. (for other forms see the following root.) दून p.p.

दु 5 P. उपतापे to burn, to distress, to give pain; दुनोति pre. दुदाव perf. दोता p. fut. दोष्यति fut. अदोष्यत् con. अदौषीत् aor. दूयात् ben. दुदूषति des. Pass.—दूयते pre. अदावि aor. दूत p. p.

दुःख 10 U. दुःखक्रियाम् to give pain; दुःखयति pre. अदुदुःखत्-त Aor

दुर्व् 1 P. हिंसायाम् to kill; दूर्वति pre. दुदूर्व perf. दूर्विष्यति fut. अदूर्वीत् aor.

दुल् 10 U. उत्क्षेपे to shake to and fro; दोलयति-ते pre. दोलयाञ्चकार-चक्रे perf. दोलयिता p. fut. अदूदुलत्-त aor. दुदोलयिषति-ते des.

दुष 4 P. वैकृत्ये to be wrong, to be impure; दुष्यति pre. दुदोष perf. दोष्टा p. fut. अदोक्ष्यत् con. दोक्ष्यति fut. अदुषत् aor. दुष्यात् ben. Cau.-दूषयति-ते, also दोषयति-ते (to make depraved) pre. अदूदुषत्-त aor. दुदुक्षति des. Pass.-दुष्यते pre. अदोषि aor. दुष्ट p. p.

दुह् 1 P. अर्दने to hurt, to give pain; दोहति pre. दुदोह perf. दोहिष्यति fut. अदुहत, अदोहीत् aor. दुहित p. p.

दुह् 2 U. प्रपूरणे to milk, to make profit; दोग्धि, दुग्धे pre. दुदोह, दुदुहे perf. दोग्धा p. fut. धोक्ष्यति-ते fut. अधुक्षत्, अधुक्षत & अदुग्ध aor. दुह्यात , धुक्षिष्ट ben. दुधुक्षति-ते des. Pass.—दुह्यते (also दुग्धे see Pán. III. 1. 89) pre. अदोहि (also अदुग्ध, अधुक्षत) aor. Cau.-दोहयति-ते pre. अदूदुहत्-त aor. दुग्ध p. p. दुग्ध्वा ger. दोग्धुम् inf.

दू 4 A. परितापे to suffer pain, to be sorry; दूयते pre. दुदुवे perf. दविता p. fut. दविष्यते fut. अदविष्यत con. अदविष्ट aor. दिविषीष्ट ben. दुदूषते des. Cau.—दावयति-ते pre. अदूदवत्-त aor. Pass.-दूयते pre. अदावि aor. दून p. p.

दृ 6 A. आदरे to worship, to regard (with आ); द्रियते pre. दद्रे perf. दर्ता p. fut. अदृत aor. दृषीष्ट ben. दिदरिषते des. Pass.—द्रियते pre. अदारि aor. Cau.—दारयति-ते pre. अदीदरत्-त aor. दृत p. p. दृत्वा ger. दर्तुम् inf.

दृप् 4 P. हर्षमोहनयोः to be glad, to be proud; दृप्यति pre. ददर्प perf. दर्पिता, दर्प्ता, द्रप्ता p. fut. दर्पिष्यति, दर्प्स्यति, द्रप्स्यति fut.

अदर्पिष्यत्, अदर्प्स्यत्, अद्रप्स्यत् con. अदृपत्, अदर्पीत्, अदार्प्सीत् अद्राप्सीत्, aor. दृप्यात् ben. दिदर्पिषति or दिदृप्सति des. Cau.—दर्पयति-ते pre. अदीदृपत्-त, अददर्पत्-त aor. दृप्त p.p. दर्पित्वा, दृप्त्वा ger. दर्पितुं, दर्प्तुं, द्रप्तुम् inf.

दृप् 1 P. & 10 U. संदीपने to excite, to kindle; दर्पति, दर्पयति-ते pre. दर्पिता, दर्पयिता p. fut. अदर्पीत्, अदीदर्पत्-त, अददर्पत्-त aor. दृप्यात्, दर्प्यात्, दर्पयिषीष्ट ben. दिदर्पिषति, दिदर्पयिषति-ते des. Pass.-दृप्यते, दर्प्यते pre. अदर्पि aor. दृपित, दर्पित p. p.

दृभ् 6 P. ग्रन्थे to string, to put together; दृभति pre. दर्भिष्यति fut. अदर्भीत् aor. Cau.—दर्भयति-ते pre. अदीदृभत्-त, अददर्भत्-त aor. दिदर्भिषति des. दृब्ध p. p. दर्भित्वा ger.

दृभ् 1 P. 10 U. भये संदर्भे च to fear, to string together; दर्भति दर्भयति-ते pre.

दृश् 1 P. प्रेक्षणे to see, to visit, to know; पश्यति pre. ददर्श perf. द्रष्टा p. fut. द्रक्ष्यति fut. अद्रक्ष्यत् con. अदर्शत्, अद्राक्षीत् aor. दृश्यात् ben. दिदृक्षते des. Cau.—दर्शयति-ते pre. अदीदृशत्-त अददर्शत्-त aor. दरीदृश्यते, दर्दर्शीति, दर्दर्ष्टि freq. Pass.-दृश्यते pre. अदर्शि aor. दृष्ट p.p. दृष्ट्वा ger. द्रष्टुम् inf.

दृह्, दृंह् 1 P. वृद्धौ to be fixed or firm, to grow; दर्हति or दृंहति pre. ददर्ह or ददृंह perf. दर्हिता or दृंहिता p. fut. अदर्हीत् or अदृंहीत् aor. दृढ (strong) or दृहित, दृंहित p. p.

दॄ 1 P. भये to fear; दरति pre. ददार perf. दरि-री-ता p. fut. अदारीत् aor.

दॄ 9 P. विदारणे to tear, to divide; दृणाति pre. ददार perf. दरिता, दरीता p. fut. दरिष्यति, दरीष्यति fut. अदरिष्यत्, अदरीष्यत् con. अदारीत् aor. दीर्यात् ben. दिदरिषति, दिदरीषति. दिदीर्षति des. Cau.—दारयति-ते, (दरयति-ते in the sense of 'to fear'). Pass.-दीर्यते pre. अदारि aor. दीर्ण p. p. दीर्त्वा, विदीर्य ger. दरितुम्, दरीतुम् inf.

दे 1 A. पालने to protect, to cherish, दयते pre. दिग्ये perf. दाता p. fut अदित aor. दासीष्ट ben. दित्सते des. Pass—दीयते pre. Cau.—दापयति-ते pre. अदीदपत्-त aor. दात p. p.

देव् 1 A. देवने to sport, to lament; देवते pre. दिदेव perf. देविता p. fut. देविष्यते fut. अदेविष्यत con. अदेविष्ट aor. दिदेविषते des. Pass.–देव्यते pre

दै 1 P. शोधने to purify, to be purified; दायति pre. ददौ perf. दाता p. fut. दास्यति fut. अदास्यत् con. अदासीत् aor. दायात् ben. दिदासति des. Pass.—दायते pre. Cau.—दापयति-ते pre. अदीदपत्-त aor. दात p. p.

दो 4 P. अवखण्डने to cut, to divide, to move; द्यति pre. ददौ perf. दाता p. fut. अदात् or देयात् ben. दित्सति des. Cau.—दापयति-ते pre. दित p. p. दित्वा, अवदाय ger.

द्यु 2 P. अभिगमने to advance towards, to attack; द्यौति pre. दुद्याव perf. द्योता p. fut. द्योष्यति fut. अद्योष्यत् con. अद्यौषीत् aor. दुद्यूषति des. Pass.—द्यूयते pre. अद्यावि aor. Cau.—द्यावयति-ते pre. अदुद्यवत्-त aor. द्युत p. p.

द्युत् 1 A. दीप्तौ to shine; द्योतते pre. दिद्युते perf. द्योतिता p. fut. द्योतिष्यते fut. अद्योतिष्यत con. अद्योतिष्ट, अद्युतत् aor. द्योतिषीष्ट ben. दिद्युतिषते दिद्योतिषते des. Cau.—द्योतयति-ते pre. अदुद्युतत्-त aor. देद्युत्यते, देद्योत्ति freq. द्युतित-द्योतित p. p.

द्यै 1 P. न्यक्करणे to despise; द्यायति pre. द्याता p. fut. अद्यासीत् aor. द्यायात्, द्येयात् Ben.

द्रम् 1 P. गतौ to run; द्रमति pre. दद्राम perf. अद्रमीत् aor.

द्रा 2 P. कुत्सायां गतौ स्वप्ने च to run, to sleep (generally with नि); द्राति pre. दद्रौ perf. द्राता p. fut. द्रास्यति fut. अद्रास्यत् con. अद्रासीत् aor. द्रायात्, द्रेयात् ben. दिद्रासति des. द्राण p. p.

द्राघ् 1 A. सामर्थ्ये, आयामे to be able, to lengthen; द्राघते pre दद्राघे perf. अद्राघिष्ट aor. द्राघिषीष्ट ben.

द्राक्ष् 1 P. घोरवाशिते to make a discordant sound; द्राक्षति pre. दद्राक्ष perf. अद्राक्षीत् aor.

द्रु 1 P. गतौ to run, to rush, to melt; द्रवति pre. दुद्राव perf. द्रोता p. fut. द्रोष्यति fut. अद्रोष्यत् con. अदुद्रुवत् aor. दुद्रूषति des.

Pass.—द्रूयते pre. अद्रावि aor. Cau.—द्रावयति pre. अदिद्रवत् or अदुद्रवत् aor. दोद्रूयते, दोद्रवीति, दोद्रोति freq. द्रुत p. p.

द्रुण् 6 P. गतिहिंसाकौटिल्येषु to kill; to go &c.; द्रुणति pre. दुद्रोण perf. द्रोणिष्यति fut. अद्रोणीत् aor.

द्रुह् 4 p. जिघांसायाम् to bear malice or hatred; द्रुह्यति pre. दुद्रोह (दुद्रोहिथ, दुद्रोढ, दुद्रोग्ध 2nd sing.) perf. द्रोहिता, द्रोग्धा, द्रोढा p. fut. द्रोहिष्यति, ध्रोक्ष्यति fut. अद्रोहिष्यत्, अध्रोक्ष्यत् con. अद्रुहत् aor. दुद्रोहिषति, दुद्रुहिषति; दुध्रुक्षति des. Cau.—द्रोहयति-ते pre. अदुद्रुहत्-त aor. द्रुग्ध or द्रूढ p. p. द्रोहितुं-द्रोग्धुं, द्रोढुं inf. द्रुहित्वा, द्रोहित्वा, द्रुग्ध्वा, द्रूढ्वा ger.

द्रू 9 U. हिंसायाम् to kill, to hurt; द्रूणाति, द्रूणीते pre. दुद्राव, दुद्रुवे perf. द्रविष्यति-ते fut. अद्रावीत्, अद्रविष्ट aor.

द्रेक् 1 A. शब्दोत्साहयोः to sound, to show energy; द्रेकते pre. दिद्रेके perf. द्रेकिष्यते fut. अद्रेकिष्ट aor.

द्रै 1 P. स्वप्ने to sleep (generally with नि); द्रायति pre. दद्रौ perf. अद्रासीत् aor. द्रायात्, द्रेयात् ben.

द्विष् 2 U. अप्रीतौ to hate; द्वेष्टि or द्विष्टे pre. अद्वेट्-ड् (अद्विषन्-षुः 3rd pl.) Imp. दिद्वेष, दिद्विषे perf. द्वेष्टा p. fut. द्वेक्ष्यति-ते fut. अद्वेक्ष्यत्-त con. अद्विक्षत्-त aor. द्विष्यात्, द्विक्षीष्ट ben. दिद्विक्षति-ते des. Cau.—द्वेषयति-ते pre. अदिद्विषत्-त aor. देद्विष्यते, देद्वेष्टि, देद्विषीति freq. Pass.-द्विष्यते pre. अद्वेषि aor. द्विष्ट p. p. द्वेष्टुम् inf.

द्वृ 1 P. संवरणे अङ्गीकृतौ च to cover, to accept; द्वरति pre. दद्वार perf. अद्वार्षीत् aor.

ध—

धक्क् 10 U. नाशने to destroy; धक्कयति-ते pre. धक्कयाञ्चकार—चक्रे perf. अदधक्कत्-त aor.

धण् 1 P. शब्दे to sound. धणति pre. अधणीत्, अधाणीत् aor.

धन् 1 P. to sound; धनति pre.

धन् (Vedic) 3 P. धान्ये to produce fruit; दधन्ति, दधन्तः, दधनति pre. दधान Perf. धनिष्यति fut

धन्व् 1 P. गतौ to go; धन्वति pre. दधन्व perf. अधन्वीत् aor.

धा 3 U. धारणपोषणयोर्दाने च to put, to grant, to produce, to bear; दधाति, धत्ते pre. दधौ & दधे perf, धाता p. fut. धास्यति-ते fut. अधास्यत्-त con. अधात्, अधित aor. धेयात्, धासीष्ट ben. धित्सति-ते des. Pass.—धीयते pre. अधायि aor. Cau.—धापयति-ते pre. अदीधपत्-त aor. देधीयते, दाधाति, दाधेति freq. हित p. p. हित्वा, संधाय ger.

धाव् 1 U. गतिशुद्ध्योः to rub, to wash, to cleanse; धावति-ते pre. दधाव & दधावे perf धाविता p. fut. धाविष्यति-ते fut. अधाविष्यत्-त con. अधावीत् & अधाविष्ट aor. धाव्यात्, धाविषीष्ट ben. दिधाविषति-ते des. Cau.—धावयति-ते pre. अदीधवत्-त aor. धावीत-धौत p. p. धावित्वा, धौत्वा, प्रधाव्य ger.

धि 6 P. धारणे to have, to hold; धियति pre. दिधाय perf. अधेषीत् aor. दिधिषति des.

धिक्ष् 6 A. संदीपनक्लेशनजीवनेषु to kirdle, to be fatigued, to live; धिक्षते pre. दिधिक्षे perf. धिक्षिष्यते fut. अधिक्षिष्ट aor.

धिन्व् 1 P. प्रीणने to delight, to please; धिनोति pre. दिधिन्व perf. धिन्विता p. fut. अधिन्वीत् aor. धिन्व्यात् ben. धिन्वित p. p.

धिष् 3 P. to sound; दिधेष्टि pre. (used in the Vedas).

धी 4 A. आधारे to hold; धीयते pre. दिध्ये perf. धेष्यते fut. अधेष्ट aor. Cau.-धाययति-ते pre. अदीधयत्-त aor. दिधीषते des. धीन p.p.

धु 5 U. कम्पने to shake to excite; धुनोति & धुनुते pre. दुधाव, दुधुवे perf. धोता p. fut. धोष्यति-ते fut. अधोष्यत्-त con. धूयात्, धूषीष्ट ben. अधौषीत् & अधोष्ट aor. दुधूषति-ते des. धुत p. p.

धुक्ष् 1 A. संदीपनक्लेशनजीवनेषु to be kindled, to be weary, to live; धुक्षते pre. दुधुक्षे perf. धुक्षिता p. fut. अधुक्षिष्ट aor. दुधुक्षिषते des. धुक्षित p. p.

धू 1 U. कम्पने & 6 P. विधूनने to shake; धवति-ते, धुवति pre. दुधाव, दुधुवे (दुधुविथ 2nd singular of 6 which is कुटादि) perf.

धविता, धुविता p. fut. धविष्यति-ते, धुविष्यति fut. अधविष्यत्-त, अधुविष्यत् con. अधावीत्, अधविष्ट, अधुवीत्, aor. धूयात्, धविषीष्ट ben. धूत p. p. धवितुं (1) धुवितुम् (6) inf.

धू 5 & 9 U. कम्पने to shake; धूनोति, धनुते, धुनाति, धुनीते pre. दुधाव, दुधुवे perf. धोता, धविता p. fut. धोष्यति-ते, धाविष्यति-ते fut. अधोष्यत्-त अधविष्यत्-त con. अधावीत्, अधविष्ट; अधोष्ट aor. धूयात्; धविषीष्ट, धोषीष्ट ben. दुधूषति-ते des. Cau.—धूनयति; अदूधुनत् aor. Pass.-धूयते pre. अधावि aor. धूत (5) धून (9) p.p.

धू 10. U to shake; धूनयति-ते pre. धूनयाञ्चकार-चक्रे perf. धूनयिष्यति-ते fut. अदूधुनत् aor. धून्यात्, धूनयिषीष्ट ben. Cau.-धूनयति pre. दुधूनयिषति-ते des.

धूप् 1 P. संतापे to heat, to be heated; धूपायति pre. दुधूप, धूपायाञ्चकार perf. धूपिता & धूपायिता p. fut. धूपिष्यति, धूपायिष्यति fut. अधूपिष्यत्, अधूपायिष्यत् con. अधूपीत्, & अधूपायीत् aor. धूप्यात् & धूपाय्यात् ben. Cau—धूपयति-ते, धूपाययति-ते pre. अदुधूपत्-त अदुधूपायत्-त aor. दुधूपिषति; दुधूपायिषति des. Pass—धूप्यते, धूपाय्यते pre. अधूपि, अधूपायि aor. धूपित, धूपायित p. p.

धूप् 10 U. भाषायां-दीप्तौ-च to speak, to shine; धूपयति-ते pre. धूपयाञ्चकार-चक्रे &c. perf. धूपयिता p. fut. अदूधुपत्-त aor.

धूर् 4 A. हिंसागत्योः to kill, to go; धूर्यते pre. दुधूरे perf. अधूरिष्ट aor धूर्त p. p.

धृ 1 U. धारणे to hold; धरति-ते pre. दधार, दध्रे (दधर्थ, दध्रिषे 2 sing.) perf. धर्ता p. fut. धरिष्यति-ते fut. अधरिष्यत्-त con. अधार्षीत्-अधृत aor. ध्रियात् & धृषीष्ट ben. दिधीर्षति-ते des. Cau.- धारयति-ते pre. अदीधरत्-त aor. ध्रियते Pass. धृत p.p.

धृ 1 A. अवध्वंसने to destroy; धरते pre. See the above root.

धृ 6 A. अवस्थाने to be, to exist; ध्रियते pre. दिधारिषते des. For other forms see Atm. forms of धृ 1 U. above.

धृ 10 U. धारणे to hold, to bear, to support; धारयति-ते pre. धारयाञ्चकार-चक्रे. &c. perf, धारयिता p. fut. अदीधरत्-त aor. धार्यात्, धारयिषीष्ट ben. दिधारयिषति-ते des. Pass.-धार्यते. अधारि aor.

धृज्, धृञ्ज् 1 P. गतौ to go, to move; धर्जति, धृञ्जति pre. दधर्ज-दधृञ्ज perf. अधर्जीत्-अधृञ्जीत् aor.

धृष् 1 P. to come together, to hurt; धर्षति pre. दधर्ष perf. धर्षित p.p.

धृष् 5 P. प्रागल्भ्ये to be bold, to be confident, to be proud or brave; धृष्णोति pre. दधर्ष perf. धर्षिता p. fut. धर्षिष्यति fut. अधर्षिष्यत् con. अधर्षीत् aor. Cau.—धर्षयति-ते pre. अदीधृषत्-त, अददधर्षत्-त aor. दिधर्षिषति des. धर्षित, धृष्ट (immodest) p. p.

धृष् 1 P. & 10 U. प्रहसने to offend, to insult, to conquer; धर्षति & धर्षयति-ते pre. दधर्ष, धर्षयाञ्चकार-चक्रे perf. अधर्षीत्, अदीधृषत्-त, अददधर्षत्-त aor. धृष्यात्, धर्ष्यात्, धर्षयिषीष्ट ben. दिधर्षिषति, दिधर्षयिषति-ते des.

धॄ 9 P. to become old धृणाति pre. धरि-री-ष्यति fut. अधारीत् aor.

धे 1 P. पाने to suck, to draw away; धयति pre. दधौ perf. धाता p. fut. अधात्, अधासीत्, अदधत् aor. धेयात् ben. धित्सति des. Pass.—धीयते pre. अधायि aor. Cau.—धापयते (Parasm. also, if it does not convey a reflective sense; वत्सान्धापयति पयः) pre. अदीधपत aor. धीत p.p.

धोर् 1 P. गतिचातुर्ये to tread skilfully, to be skilful; धोरति pre. दुधोर perf. अधोरीत् aor.

ध्मा 1 P. शब्दाग्निसंयोगयोः to exhale, to blow, to throw away; धमति pre. दध्मौ perf. ध्माता p. fut. ध्मास्यति fut. अध्मास्यत् con. अध्मासीत् aor. ध्मायात् or ध्मेयात् ben. दिध्मासति des. Pass.—ध्मायते pre. अध्मायि aor. Cau.—ध्मापयति-ते pre. अदिध्मपत्-त aor. ध्मात p.p.

ध्यै 1 P. चिन्तायाम् to think of, to ponder over; ध्यायति pre. दध्यौ perf. ध्याता p. fut. ध्यास्यति fut. अध्यास्यत् con. अध्यासीत् aor. ध्येयात् or ध्यायात् ben. दिध्यासति des. Pass.—ध्यायते pre. अध्यायि aor. Cau.—ध्यापयति-ते pre. अदिध्यपत्-त aor दाध्यायते, दाध्याति, दाध्येति freq. ध्यात p.p. ध्यात्वा ger. ध्यातुम् inf.

ध्रज् (also ध्रञ्ज्) 1 P. गतौ to go; ध्रजति or ध्रञ्जति pre. दध्राज, दध्रञ्ज perf. अध्रजीत्, अध्राजीत्, अध्राञ्जीत् aor.

ध्रण् 1 P. शब्दे to sound, to beat a drum; ध्रणति pre. दध्राण perf. ध्रणिष्यति fut.; अध्रणीत्, अध्राणीत् aor.

ध्रस् 9 P. उञ्छे to glean; ध्रस्नाति pre. दध्रास perf. ध्रसिष्यति fut. अध्रसीत्, अध्रासीत् aor. ध्रस्त p.p.

ध्रस् 10 U. 1 P. to glean ध्रासयति-ते, ध्रसति pre. ध्रासयाञ्चकार-चक्रे, दध्रास perf. ध्रासयिता, ध्रसिता p. fut. अदिध्रसत्-त, अध्रसीत्, अध्रासीत् aor.

ध्राक्ष् 1 P. to wish, to sound; ध्राक्षति pre.

ध्राघ् 1 A. सामर्थ्ये to be able; ध्राघते pre. दध्राघे perf. अध्राघिष्ट aor.

ध्राड् 1 A. विशरणे to cut, to tear; ध्राडते pre. अध्राडिष्ट Aor.

ध्रिज् 1 P. to go; ध्रेजति pre. ध्रेजिष्यति fut. अध्रेजीत् Aor.

ध्रु 1 P. स्थैर्ये to be firm; ध्रवति pre. दुध्राव perf. ध्रोता p. fut. अध्रौषीत्, aor. दुध्रुषति des.

ध्रु 6 P. (कुटादि) गतिस्थैर्ययोः to go, to be steady; ध्रुवति pre. दुध्राव (दुध्रुविथ, दुध्रुथ 2nd. sing.) perf. ध्रुष्यति fut. अध्रुवीत् Aor.

ध्रुव् (another reading for the above); ध्रुवति pre. दुध्राव (दुध्रुविथ sing.) perf. ध्रुविष्यति fut. अध्रुवीत् Aor.

ध्रै 1 P. तृप्तौ to be pleased or satisfied, ध्रायति pre. दध्रौ perf. अध्रासीत् aor. ध्रा-ध्रे-यात् ben.

ध्वंस् 1 A. अवस्रंसने गतौ च to fall down, to perish; ध्वंसते pre. दध्वंसे perf. ध्वंसिता p. fut. ध्वंसिष्यते fut. अध्वंसिष्यत con. अध्वसत् or अध्वंसिष्ट aor. ध्वंसिषीष्ट ben. दिध्वंसिषते des. Pass.—ध्वस्यते pre. अध्वंसि aor. Cau.—ध्वंसयति-ते pre. ध्वस्त p.p. ध्वंसित्वा, ध्वस्त्वा ger.

ध्वज्, ध्वञ्ज् 1 P. to go. ध्वजति, ध्वञ्जति pre.

ध्वन् 1 P. शब्दे to sound, to echo, to thunder; ध्वनति pre. दध्वान perf. ध्वनिता p. fut. ध्वनिष्यति fut. अध्वनिष्यत् con. अध्वनीत् or अध्वानीत् aor. Cau.—to sound as a bell, ध्वनयति-ते; to utter indistinctly, ध्वानयति-ते; pre. दिध्वनिषति des. ध्वनित, ध्वान्त (darkness) p.p.

ध्वन् 10 U. अव्यक्ते शब्दे to sound indistinctly; ध्वनयति-ते pre. अद-ध्वनत्-त aor. दिध्वनयिषति-ते des. Pass.—ध्वन्यते pre. अध्वनि aor.

ध्वृ 1 P. मूर्च्छने to kill, to praise, to describe; ध्वरति pre. दध्वार perf. अध्वार्षीत् aor.

न—

नक्क् 10 U. नाशने to perish; नक्कयति-ते pre. अननक्कत्-त aor.

नक्ष् 1 P. to go, to move; नक्षति pre. ननक्ष perf. अनक्षीत् aor.

नख् 1 P. to go; नखति pre. अनखीत्-अनाखीत् aor.

नट् 1 P. नाट्ये to dance, to act; नटति pre. ननाट perf. नटिता p. fut. नटिष्यति fut. अनटिष्यत् con. अनटीत् or अनाटीत् aor. Cau.-नाटयति-ते (प्रनाट०) pre. अनीनटत्-त aor. निनटिषति des. Pass.—नट्यते pre. अनाटि, अनटि aor. नटित p.p.

नट् 10 U. भाषायाम् to speak, to shine; नाटयति-ते pre.

नद् 1 P. अव्यक्ते शब्दे to sound, to thunder; नदति pre. ननाद perf. नदिता p. fut. अनादीत् or अनदीत् aor. Cau.—नादयति-ते pre. अनीनदत्-त aor. निनदिषति des. नदित p.p.

नद् 10 U. to speak, to shine; नादयति-ते pre.

नन्द् 1 P. समृद्धौ to be pleased; to thrive; नन्दति pre. ननन्द perf. नन्दिता p. fut. अनन्दीत् aor. नन्द्यात् ben. निनन्दिषति des. नन्दित p.p. Cau.—नन्दयति-ते pre. Pass.—नन्द्यते pre.

नभ् 1 A. हिंसायामभावेऽपि to kill, to hurt; नभते pre. नेभे perf. अनभत्, अनभिष्ट aor.

नम् 1 P. प्रह्वत्वे शब्दे च to salute, to bend, to sound; नमति pre. ननाम perf. नन्ता p. fut. नंस्यति fut. अनंस्यत् con. अनंसीत् aor. नम्यात् ben. निनंसति des. Cau.—नमयति or नामयति pre. अनी-नमत्-त aor. Pass.—नम्यते pre. अनामि aor. नत p.p. नत्वा ger. नन्तुम् inf.

नय् 1 A. to go, to protect; नयते pre. नेये perf. अनयिष्ट aor.

नर्द् 1 P. शब्दे to bellow, to roar, to sound; (प्र) नर्दति pre. ननर्द perf. नर्दिता p. fut. नर्दिष्यति fut. अनर्दिष्यत् con. अनर्दीत् aor. निनर्दिषति des. नर्दित p.p.

नल् 1 P. गन्धे बन्धने च to smell, to bind; नलति pre. ननाल per. नलिष्यति fut. अनालीत् aor.

नल् 10 U. भाषायाम् to speak; नालयति-ते pre. नालयिष्यति-ते fut. अनीनलत्-त aor.

नश् 4 P. अदर्शने to be lost, to perish; नश्यति pre. ननाश perf. नशिता or नंष्टा p. fut. नशिष्यति, नंक्ष्यति fut. अनशिष्यत्-अनंक्ष्यत् con. अनशत् aor. नश्यात् ben. निनंक्षति or निनशिषति des. Cau.—नाशयति-ते pre. अनीनशत्-त aor. नष्ट p.p. नष्ट्वा, नंष्ट्वा or नशित्वा ger. नशितुम्, नंष्टुम् inf.

नह् 4 U. बंधने to tie, to bind; नह्यति-ते pre. ननाह, नेहे perf. नद्धा p. fut. नत्स्यति-ते fut. अनत्स्यत्-त con. अनात्सीत्, अनद्ध aor. नह्यात्, नत्सीष्ट ben. निनत्सति-ते des. Pass.—नह्यते pre. अनाहि aor. Cau.—नाहयति-ते pre. अनीनहत्-त aor. नानह्यते, नानहीति, नानाद्धि freq. नद्ध p.p. नद्ध्वा ger. नद्धुम् inf.

नाथ् 1 P. याच्ञोपतापैश्वर्याशीःषु to ask, to be master, to harass; नाथति pre. ननाथ perf. नाथिता p. fut. अनाथीत् aor. 1 A. to bless; नाथते pre. ननाथे perf. नाथिता p. fut. अनाथिष्ट aor. नाथित p.p.

नाध् 1 A. the same as नाथ् A.

निज् 3 U. शौचपोषणयोः to wash, to be purified, to nourish; नेनेक्ति, नेनिक्ते pre. निनेज, निनिजे perf. नेक्ता p. fut. नेक्ष्यति-ते fut. अनेक्ष्यत्-त con. अनिजत्, अनैक्षीत्, अनिक्त aor. निज्यात्, निक्षीष्ट ben. निनिक्षति-ते des. Pass.—निज्यते pre. अनेजि aor. Cau.—नेजयति-ते pre. अनीनिजत्-त aor. निक्त p.p. निक्त्वा ger.

निक्ष् 2 A. शुद्धौ to wash, to purify; निङ्क्ते (प्रणिङ्क्ते) pre. निनिक्षे perf. निक्षिष्यते fut अनिक्षिष्ट Aor. निक्षिषीष्ट ben. निनिक्षिषते des. Cau —निक्षयति-ते pre. Pass.—निक्ष्यते pre. अनिक्षि Aor. निक्षित p.p.

निन्द् 1 P. कुत्सायाम् to blame, to find fault with, to condemn; निन्दति pre. निनिन्द perf. निन्दिता p. fut. अनिन्दीत् aor. निन्द्यात् ben. निनिन्दिषति des. Cau.—निन्दयति-ते pre. अनिनिन्दत्-त aor. Pass.—निन्द्यते pre. निन्दित p.p.

निद् 1 U. कुत्सासन्निकर्षयोः to blame, to reach; नेदति-ते pre. निनेद, निनिदे perf. अनेदीत्, अनेदिष्ट aor.

निन्व् 1 P. सेचने सेवने च to sprinkle, to eat; निन्वति pre. निनिन्व perf. अनिन्वीत् Aor.

निल् 6 P. (गहने) to become thick; निलति pre. निनेल perf नेलिष्यति fut. अनेलीत् aor.

निश् 1 P. समाधौ to think, to meditate; नेशति pre. नेशिष्यति fut. अनेशीत् aor.

निष् 1 P. सेचने to sprinkle; नेषति pre. निनेष perf. अनेषीत् Aor.

निष्क् 10 A. परिमाणे to weigh, to measure; निष्कयते pre. निष्कयाञ्चक्रे perf निष्कयिष्यते fut. अनिनिष्कत Aor.

निंस् 2 A. चुम्बने to kiss; निंस्ते pre. निनिंसे perf. निंसिष्यते fut. अनिंसिष्ट aor.

नी 1 U. प्रापणे to lead, to carry off, to marry, to settle; नयति-ते pre. निनाय-निन्ये perf. नेता p. fut. नेष्यति-ते fut. अनेष्यत्-त con. अनैषीत्, अनेष्ट aor. नीयात्, नेषीष्ट ben. निनीषति-ते des. Pass.—नीयते pre. अनायि aor. Cau.—नाययति-ते pre. अनीनयत्-त aor. नेनीयते, नेनयीति, नेनेति freq. नीत p.p. नीत्वा ger. नेतुम् inf.

नील् 1 P. वर्णे to colour; नीलति pre. अनीलीत् Aor.

नीव् 1 P. स्थौल्ये to become fat, to grow; नीवति pre. निनीव perf. अनीवीत् Aor.

नु 2 P. स्तुतौ to praise, to commend; नौति pre. नुनाव perf. नविता p. fut. नविष्यति fut. अनाविष्यत् con. अनावीत् aor. नुनूषति des. Cau.—नावयति-ते pre. अनूनवत्-त Aor. नुनावयिषति-ते des. नुत p.p.

नुद् 6 U. प्रेरणे to push, to incite, to remove, to throw; नुदति-ते pre. नुनोद, नुनुदे perf. नोत्ता p. fut. नोत्स्यति-ते fut. अनोत्स्यत्-त con. अनौत्सीत्, अनुत्त aor. नुद्यात्, नुत्सीष्ट ben. नुनुत्सति-ते des. Cau.—नोदयति-ते pre. अनूनुदत्-त aor. Pass.—नुद्यते pre. अनोदि aor. नुत्त or नुन्न p.p.

नू 6 P. स्तुतौ (कुटादिः) to praise; नुवति pre. नुनाव (नुनुविथ 2nd.

sing.) perf. नुविता p. fut. नुविष्यति fut. अनुवीत् Aor. नुनूषति des. Cau.—नावयति-ते pre. अनूनवत्-त Aor. नूत p.p. नुवितुम् inf.

नृत् 4 P. गात्रविक्षेपे to dance, to represent on the stage; नृत्यति pre. ननर्त perf. नर्तिता p. fut. अनर्तीत् aor. नृत्यात् ben. निनर्तिषति—निनृत्सति des. Pass.—नृत्यते pre. अनर्ति aor. Cau.—नर्तयते only pre. अनीनृतत, अननर्तत aor. नृत्त p.p.

नॄ 1 & 9 P. नये to carry, to lead; नरति, नृणाति pre. नरिता-नरीता p. fut. नरिष्यति, नरीष्यति fut. अनारीत् Aor. Cau.—नरयति-ते (नये), नारयति-ते (अन्यत्र).

नेष् 1 A. to go, to reach; नेषते pre. निनेषे perf. अनेषिष्ट Aor.

प—

पक्ष् 1 P. & 10 U. परिग्रहे to take, to accept; पक्षति, पक्षयति-ते pre. पक्षिष्यति, पक्षयिष्यति-ते fut. अपक्षीत्, अपपक्षत्-त Aor. पिपक्षिषति, पिपक्षयिषति-ते des. Cau.—पक्षयति-ते pre.

पच् 1 U. to cook, to digest; पचति-ते pre. पपाच, पेचे perf. पक्ता p. fut. पक्ष्यति-ते fut. अपक्ष्यत्-त con. अपाक्षीत्, अपक्त aor. पच्यात्, पक्षीष्ट ben. पिपक्षति-ते des. Pass.—पच्यते pre. अपाचि aor. Cau.—पाचयति-ते pre. अपीपचत्-त aor. पक्व p.p.

पञ्च् 1 A. व्यक्तीकरणे to make clear; पञ्चते pre. पपञ्चे perf. पञ्चिष्यते fut. अपञ्चिष्ट Aor.

पञ्च् 10 U. 1 P. विस्तारवचने to spread; पञ्चयति-ते, पञ्चति pre. अपपञ्चत्-त, अपञ्चीत् Aor.

पट् 1 P. to go, to move; पटति pre. पपाट perf. पटिता p. fut. पटिष्यति fut. अपटिष्यत् con. अपटीत् or अपाटीत् aor. Cau.—पाटयति-ते pre. अपीपटत्-त aor. पिपटिषति des.

पट् 10 U. ग्रन्थे to clothe, to envelop; पटयति-ते per. पटयाञ्चकार-चक्रे &c. perf. पटयिता p. fut. अपपटत्-त aor. पिपटयिषति-ते des.

पट 10 U. भाषायां वेष्टने च to speak, to cover; पाटयति-ते pre. पाटयिष्यति-ते fut. अपीपटत्-त aor.

पठ् 1 P. व्यक्तायां वाचि लिखिताक्षरवाचने च to read, to study, to describe; पठति pre. पपाठ perf. पठिता p. fut. पठिष्यति fut. अपठिष्यत् con. अपठीत् or अपाठीत् aor. पिपठिषति des. Pass.—पठ्यते pre. अपाठि aor. Cau.—पाठयति-ते pre. अपीपठत्-त aor. पठित p.p. पठित्वा ger. पठितुम् inf.

पण्ड् 1 A. गतौ to go; पण्डते pre. पपण्डे perf. अपण्डिष्ट aor. पण्डित p.p.

पण्ड् 10 U. नाशने to destroy; 1 P. संहतौ च to heap together, to collect; पण्डयति-ते, पण्डति pre.

पण् 1 A. व्यवहारे to bargain, to bet or stake at play; पणते pre. पेणे perf. पणिता p. fut. अपणिष्ट aor. पणिषीष्ट ben. पिपणिषते des. Cau.—पाणयति-ते pre. अपीपणत्-त aor. पणित p.p

पण् 1 A. (Parasm. with आय्) स्तुतौ to praise; पणायति-पणते pre. पणायांचकार &c. पेणे perf. पणायिता-पणिता. p. fut. पणायिष्यति-पणिष्यते fut. अपणायीत्-अपणिष्ट aor. पणाय्यात, पणिषीष्ट ben. Cau.— पणाययति-ते, पाणयति-ते pre. अपपणायत्-त, अपीपणत्-त aor. पिपणायिषति, पिपणिषते des. पणायित p.p.

पत् 1 P. to fly, to alight, to fall; पतति pre. पपात perf. पतिता p. fut. पतिष्यति, fut. अपतिष्यत् con. अपप्तत् aor. पत्यात् ben. पित्सति, पिपतिषति des. Pass.—पत्यते pre. अपाति aor. Cau.—पातयति-ते pre. अपीपतत्-त aor. पतीपत्यते, पतीपतीति, पतीपत्ति freq. पतित p.p. पतित्वा ger. पतितुम् inf.

पत् 4 A. ऐश्वर्ये to be master of, to rule; पत्यते pre. पेते perf. अपतिष्ट aor.

पथ् 1 P. to go; पथति pre. पपाथ perf. अपथीत् aor.

पथ 10 U. प्रक्षेपे to throw, to send; पाथयति-ते pre. अपीपथत्-त aor.

पद् 4 A. गतौ to go; to attain; पद्यते pre. पेदे perf. पत्ता p. fut. पत्स्यते fut. अपत्स्यत con. अपादि aor. पत्सीष्ट ben. पित्सते des. Pass.—पद्यते pre. अपादि aor. Cau.—पादयति-ते pre. अपीपदत् aor. पन्न p.p. पत्त्वा ger. पत्तुम् inf.

पद् 10 A. गतौ to go; पदयते pre. पदयाञ्चक्रे perf. पदयिष्यति fut. अपपदत aor. पिपदयिषते des. Pass.—पद्यते pre. अपादि aor.

पन् 1 A. to praise; पनते, पनायति pre. पेने, पनायाञ्चकार, &c. perf. पनिता, पनायिता p. fut. पनिष्यते, पनायिष्यति fut. अपनिष्ट, अपनायीत् aor. पनिषीष्ट, पनाय्यात् ben. पनित, पनायित p.p.

पन्थ् 10 U. & 1 P. to go; पन्थयति-ते, पन्थति pre. अपपन्थत्-त अपन्थीत् aor.

पय् 1 A. to go, to move; पयते pre. पेये perf. अपयिष्ट aor.

पर्ण् 10 U. हरितभावे to make green; पर्णयति-ते pre. पर्णयाञ्चकार-चक्रे perf. पर्णयिता p. fut; अपपर्णत्-त aor.

पर्द् 1 A. to break wind; पर्दते pre. पपर्दे perf. अपर्दिष्ट aor.

पर्प् 1 P. to go; पर्पति pre. पपर्प perf. अपर्पीत् aor.

पर्व् 1 P. to go; पर्वति pre. पपर्व perf.

पर्व् 1 P. पूरणे to fill; पर्वति per. पपर्व perf. अपर्वीत् aor.

पल् 1 P. to go, to move पलति pre. पपाल perf. अपालीत् aor.

पश् 10 U. बन्धने to bind; पाशयति-ते pre. अपीपशत्-त aor. पाश्यात्-पाशयिषीष्ट ben. पिपाशयिषति-ते des.

पष् 10 U. to go; पषयति-ते pre.

पंस् 10 U. & 1 P. नाशने to perish; पंसयति-ते, पंसति pre. पंसयिता; पंसिता fut. अपपंसत्-त, अपंसीत् aor.

पा 1 P. पाने to drink, to absorb; पिबति pre. पपौ perf. पाता p. fut. पास्यति fut. अपास्यत् con. अपात् aor. पेयात् ben. पिपासति des. Pass.—पीयते pre. अपायि aor. Cau.—पाययति-ते pre अपीप्यत्-त aor. पेपीयते, पापाति, पापेति freq. पीत p.p. पीत्वा ger पातुम् inf.

पा 2 P. रक्षणे to protect, to rule. पाति pre. पपौ perf. पास्यति fut. अपास्यत् con. अपासीत् aor. पायात् ben. पिपासति des. Pass.—पायते pre. Cau.—पालयति-ते pre. अपीपलत्-त aor. पीत p.p.

पार् 10 U. कर्मसमाप्तौ to finish, to get through or over; पारयति-ते pre. पारयाञ्चकार-चक्रे perf. पारयिता p. fut. पारयिष्यति-ते fut.

अपारयिष्यत्-त con. अपपारत्-त aor. Pass.—पार्यते pre. पारित p. p.

पाल् 10 U. रक्षणे to protect; पालयति-ते pre. पालयाञ्चकार-चक्रे &c. perf. पालयिता p. fut. अपीपलत्-त aor. Pass.-पाल्यते pre. पालित p. p. पालयित्वा ger.

पि 6 P. to go, to shake; पियति pre. अपेषीत् aor.

पिञ्ज् 2 A वर्णे संपर्चने to colour, to touch; &c. पिंक्ते pre. अपिञ्जिष्ट aor.

पिञ्ज् 10 U. & 1 P. भाषायां दीप्तौ च to shine, to live, to give, to kill; पिञ्जयति-ते, पिञ्जति pre. पिञ्जयाञ्चकार-चक्रे, &c. पिपिञ्ज perf. अपिपिञ्जत्-त, अपिञ्जीत् aor.

पिट् 1 P. शब्दसंघातयोः to sound, to collect, to heap together; पेटति pre. पिपेट perf. अपेटीत् aor.

पिट् 1 P. हिंसासंक्लेशनयोः to kill, to injure; पेटति pre.

पिण्ड् 1 A., 10 U. & 1 P संघाते to heap; to roll into a lump; पिंडते, पिंडयति-ते, पिण्डति pre. पिपिंडे, पिंडयाञ्चकार-चक्रे, पिपिंड perf. अपिण्डिष्ट, अपिपिंडत्-त, अपिण्डीत् aor. पिण्डित p. p.

पिल् 10 U. to throw, to incite; पेलयति-ते pre. पेलयाञ्चकार-चक्रे, &c. perf. पेलयिता p. fut.

पिन्व् 1 P. सेचने सेवने च to sprinkle, to serve; पिन्वति pre. पिपिन्व perf. पिन्विता p. fut. पिन्विष्यति fut. अपिन्विष्यत् con. अपिन्वीत् aor. पिन्व्यात् ben. Pass.-पिन्व्यते pre.

पिश् 6 P. अवयवे दीपनायां च to form, to kindle, to light; पिशति pre. पिपेश perf. पेशिता p. fut. अपेशीत् aor. Cau.-पेशयति-ते pre. अपीपिशत्-त aor. पिपिशिषति, पिपेशिषति des. पिशित p. p. पिशित्वा ger.

पिष् 7 P. संचूर्णने to grind, to hurt; पिनष्टि pre. पिपेष perf. पेष्टा p. fut. पेक्ष्यति fut. अपेक्ष्यत् con. अपिषत् aor. पिष्यात् ben. Pass. पिष्यते pre. अपेषि aor. Cau.—पेषयति-ते pre. अपीपिषत्-त Aor. पिपिक्षति des. पिष्ट p. p. पिष्ट्वा ger. पेष्टुम् inf.

पिस् 1 P. to go; पेसति pre. पिपेस perf. पेसिता P. fut. अपेसीत् Aor.

पिस् 10 U. to go; पेसयति–ते pre. पेसयाञ्चकार–चक्रे &c. perf.

पी 4 A. पाने to drink; पीयते pre. पिप्ये perf. पेष्यते fut. अपेष्ट Aor. Cau.–पाययति–ते pre. अपीप्यत्–त, Aor. पिपीषते des.

पीड् 10 U. to press, to hurt, to oppose; पीडयति-ते pre. पीडयाञ्चकार-चक्रे perf. पीडयिता p. fut. पीडयिष्यति-ते fut. अपीडयिष्यत्-त con. अपीपिडत्-त, अपिपीडत्-त, aor. पिपीडयिषति-ते des. पीडित p. p.

पीव् 1 P. स्थौल्ये to become fat or strong; पीवति pre. पीविष्यति fut. अपीवीत् Aor.

पुंस् 10 U. अभिवर्धने to increase, to crush; पुंसयति-ते pre. अपुपुंसत्-त aor.

पुट् 6 U. संश्लेषणे (कुटादि) to embrace; पुटति pre. पुपोट (पुपुटिथ 2nd sing.) perf. पुटिष्यति fut. अपुटीत् aor.

पुट् 10 U. संसर्गे to bind together; पुटयति–ते pre. पुटयिता p. fut. अपुपुटत्-त Aor.

पुट् 10 U. भाषायां दीप्तौ च to speak, to shine, to reduce to powder, पोटयति-ते pre. पोटयाञ्चकार-चक्रे &c. perf. पोटयिष्यति-ते fut. अपुपुटत्–त aor.

पुड् 1 P. मर्दने to grind; पोडति pre. पुपोड perf. पोडिष्यति fut. अपोडीत् Aor.

पुड् 6 P. उत्सर्गे (कुटादि) to leave, to discover; पुडति pre. पुडिष्यति fut. अपुडीत् Aor. पुपुडिषति des.

पुण् 6 P. शुभकर्मणि to be pious; पुणति pre. पोणिष्यति fut. अपोणीत् Aor पुपु–पो–णिषति des.

पुथ् 4 P. हिंसायाम् to kill, to injure; पुथ्यति pre. पुपोथ perf. अपोथीत Aor.

पुथ् 10 U. भाषायां दीप्तौ च to speak, to shine; पोथयति-ते pre. अपुपुथत्-त Aor.

पुन्थ् 1 P. हिंसासंक्लेशनयोः to kill, to torment; पुन्थति pre. पुन्थिष्यति fut. अपुन्थीत् Aor.

पुर् 6 P. अग्रगमन to go ahead; पुरति pre. पुपोर perf. पोरिष्यति fut. अपोरित् Aor.

पुर्व् 1 P. पूरणे to fill; पूर्वति pre. पुपूर्व perf. पूर्विष्यति fut. अपूर्वीत् Aor. Pass.—पूर्व्यते pre. अपूर्वि aor.

पुर्व् 10 U. निकेतने to dwell; पूर्वयति-ते pre. पूर्वयिता p. fut. अपुपूर्वत्-त Aor.

पुल् 1 & 6 P. महत्त्वे & 10 U. (संघाते च) to grow, to become tall; पोलति, पुलति, पोलयति-ते pre. अपोलीत्, अपूपुलत्-त Aor.

पुष् 4 P. पुष्टौ to nourish, to develop, to bear, to show; पुष्यति pre. पुपोष perf. पोष्टा p. fut पोक्ष्यति fut. अपोक्ष्यत् con. अपुषत् aor. पुष्यात् ben. पुपुक्षति des. पुष्ट p. p.

पुष् 1 & 9 P. to nourish. &c; पोषति, पुष्णाति pre. पुपोष perf. पोषिता. p. fut. पोषिष्यति fut. अपोषीत् aor. Pass.—पुष्यते pre. अपोषि aor. Cau.—पोषयति-ते pre. अपूपुषत्-त aor. पुषित (पोषित also) p. p. पुषित्वा, पोषित्वा ger.

पुष् 10 U. धारणे to maintain, to promote; पोषयति-ते pre. पोषयाञ्चकार-चक्रे &c. perf. पोषयिता p. fut. अपूपुषत्-त Aor. पुपोषयिषति-ते des.

पुष्प् 4. P. विकसने to open, to blow; पुष्प्यति pre. पुपुष्प perf. पुष्पिता p. fut. पुष्पिष्यति fut. अपुष्पिष्यत् con. अपुष्पीत् aor. Cau.-पुष्पयति-ते pre. पुष्पित p. p.

पुस्त् 10 U. आदरानादरयोः to regard, to mortify, to tie; पुस्तयति-ते pre. अपुपुस्तत्-त aor.

पू 1 A. पवने to purify, to winnow, to invent; पवते pre. पुपुवे perf. पविता p. fut. अपविष्ट aor. पविषीष्ट ben. पिपविषते des. Cau.—पावयति-ते pre. अपीपवत्-त Aor. पोपूयते, पोपवीति, पोपोति freq. पूत p. p.

पू 9 U. to purify &c; पुनाति, पुनीते pre. पुपाव, पुपुवे perf. पविता p. fut. पविष्यति-ते fut. अपविष्यत्-त con. अपावीत, अपविष्ट aor. पूयात्, पविषीष्ट ben. पुपूषति-ते des. पूत p. p.

पूज् 10 U. पूजायाम् to adore, to receive with honour, to present with, पूजयति-ते pre. पूजयाञ्चकार-चक्रे &c. perf. पूजयिता p.

fut. पूजयिष्यति-ते fut. अपूजयिष्यत्-त con. अपूपुजत्-त aor. पुपूजयिषति-ते des. पूजित p. p. पूजयित्वा ger. पूजयितुम् inf.

पूण् 10 U. to heap together; पूणयति-ते pre. पूणयाञ्चकार-चक्रे, &c. perf.

पूय् 1 A. विशरणे दुर्गन्धे च to split, to putrify; पूयते pre. पुपूये perf. पूयिता p. fut. अपूयिष्ट aor. Cau.—पूययति-ते pre. अपूपुयत्-त aor. पुपूयिषते des. पूत p. p.

पूर् 4 A. आप्यायने to fill, to satisfy; पूर्यते pre. पुपूरे perf. पूरिता. p. fut. अपूरिष्ट, अपूरि aor. Cau.-पूरयति-ते pre. अपूपुरत्-त aor. पुपूरिषते des. पूर्त p. p.

पुर् 10 U. & 1 P. to fill, to blow, to cover; पूरयति-ते, पूराति pre. पूरयाञ्चकार-चक्रे, पुपूर perf. पूरयिता, पूरिता p. fut. पूरयिष्यति-ते, पूरिष्यति fut. अपूरयिष्यत-त, अपूरिष्यत् con. अपूपुरत्-त, अपूरीत् aor. पूरित p. p. Pass.-पूर्यते Pre.

पूर्ण् 10 U. संघाते to heap, to gather; पूर्णयति-ते, pre. अपुपूर्णत्-त Aor.

पूल् 1 P. & 10. U. to gather; to collect; पूलति, पूलयति-ते pre. पूलिता, पूलयिता p. fut. अपूलीत् , अपूपुलत्-त Aor.

पूष् 1 P. वृद्धौ to grow; पूषति pre. पुपूष perf. पूषिष्यति fut. अपूषीत् Aor.

पृ 3 P. पालनपूरणयोः to protect, to fill, to bring out; पिपर्ति pre. अपिपः imperf. पपार perf. पारिष्यति fut. अपार्षीत् Aor. प्रियात ben. Cau.-पारयति-ते pre. अपीपरत्-त aor. पुपूर्षति des.

पृ 6 A. व्यायामे व्यापारे च to be busy, to be active, (mostly used with व्या), प्रियते pre. पप्रे perf. पर्ता p. fut. परिष्यते fut. अपरिष्यत con. पृषीष्ट ben. अपृत aor. Pass.-प्रियते pre. Cau.—पारयति-ते pre. अपीपरत्-त aor. पुपूर्षते des. पृत p. p. पर्तुम् inf.

पृच् 2 A. संपर्चने to come in contact with; पृक्ते pre. पपृचे perf. पर्चिता p. fut. अपर्चिष्ट aor. पिपर्चिषते des. पृक्त p. p.

पृच् 7 P. to unite, to join; पृणक्ति pre. पपर्च perf. पर्चिष्यति fut. अपर्चीत् aor. पिपर्चिषति des. पृक्त p. p. पर्चित्वा ger. पर्चितुम् inf.

पृच् 1 P. & 10 U. to hinder, to join; पर्चति, पर्चयति-ते pre. अपर्चीत्, अपपर्चत्-त, अपीपृचत्-त aor. पिपर्चिषति, पिपर्चयिषति-ते des.

पृञ्ज् 2 A. to come in contact with; पृङ्क्ते pre. पपृञ्जे perf.

पृड् 6 P. सुखने to please, to delight. पृडति pre. पर्डिष्यति fut. अपर्डीत् aor.

पृण् 6 P. प्रीणने to please, to satisfy; पृणति pre. अपर्णीत् aor.

पृथ् 10 U. प्रक्षेपे to throw, to send; पर्थयति-ते pre. पर्थयिष्यति-ते fut अपपर्थत-त, अपीपृथत्-त Aor.

पृष् 1 P. सेचनहिंसासंक्लेशनेषु to sprinkle, to kill, to give pain to; पर्षति pre. पपर्ष perf. अपर्षीत् aor. Cau.–पर्षयति-ते pre. अपपर्षत्-त अपीपृषत्-त Aor. पिपर्षिषति des. पर्षित, पृष्ट p.p.

पॄ 3 P. पालनपूरणयोः to fill, to blow; to refresh; पिपर्ति pre. पपार perf. परिता, परीता p. fut. परिष्यति, परीष्यति, fut. अपारीत् aor. पूर्यात् ben. पुपूर्षति or पिपरिषति, पिपरीषति des. Pass.—पूर्यते pre. Cau.–पारयति-ते pre. अपीपरत्-त aor. पूर्ण, पूरित p. p. पूर्त्वा ger.

पॄ 9 P. to fill. पृणाति pre. पपार perf. &c.; see the above root. पृणत् pre. p.

पॄ 10 U. & 1 P. पारयति-ते, परति pre. पारयिष्यति-ते, परिष्यति, परीष्यति fut. अपीपरत्-त, अपारीत् aor.

पेल् 1 P. & 10 U. to go, to shake; पेलति, पेलयति-ते pre.

पेव् 1 A. सेवने to serve; पेवते pre. अपेविष्ट aor.

पेष् 1 A. सेवने निश्चये प्रयत्ने च to serve, to resolve; पेषते pre. अपेषिष्ट aor.

पेस् 1 P. to go; पेसति pre.

पै 1 P. to dry, to wither; पायति pre. अपासीत् aor.

पैण् 1 P. गतिप्रेरणश्लेषणेषु to go, to tell, to embrace; पैणति pre.

प्याय् 1 A. वृद्धौ to grow, to swell, to increase; प्यायते pre. पिप्ये perf. प्यायिता p. fut. प्यायिष्यते fut. अप्यायिष्यत con. अप्यायि; अप्यायिष्ट aor. पिप्यायिषते des. प्यान, पीन p.p.

प्यै 1 A वृद्धौ to grow, &c.; प्यायते pre. पप्ये perf. प्याता p. fut. प्यास्यते fut. अप्यास्यत con. अप्यास्त aor. पीन p.p.

प्रच्छ् 6 P. ज्ञीप्सायाम् to ask, to seek for; पृच्छति pre. पप्रच्छ perf.

प्रष्टा p. fut प्रक्ष्यति fut. अप्रक्ष्यत् con. अप्राक्षीत् (अप्राष्टाम् dual) aor. पृच्छयात् ben. पिपृच्छिषति-ते des. Pass.—पृच्छयते pre. Cau.—प्रच्छयति-ते pre. पृष्ट p.p. पृष्ट्वा ger. प्रष्टुम् inf.

प्रथ् 1 A. प्रख्याने to become famous, to increase, to rise; प्रथते pre. पप्रथे perf. प्रथिता p. fut. प्रथिष्यते fut. अप्रथिष्यत con. अप्रथिष्ट aor. Cau.—प्रथयति-ते pre. अपप्रथत-त aor. पिप्रथिषते des. प्रथित p.p.

प्रथ् 10 U. to become famous; प्रथयति-ते pre. प्रथयाञ्चकार-चक्रे &c. perf. प्रथयिता p. fut. अपप्रथत्-त aor. पिप्रथयिषति-ते des.

प्रा 1 P. पूरणे to fill; प्राति pre. पप्रौ perf. प्राता p. fut. अप्रासीत् aor. प्रायात्, प्रेयात् ben. Pass.-प्रायते.

प्री 4 A. प्रीतौ to feel affection for, to be satisfied; प्रीयते pre. पिप्रिये perf. प्रेता p. fut. अप्रेष्ट aor. प्रेषीष्ट ben. पिप्रीषते des. प्रीत p.p. प्रीत्वा ger. प्रेतुम् inf.

प्री 9 U. तर्पणे & to please, to take delight in; प्रीणाति, प्रीणीते pre. पिप्राय, पिप्रिये perf. प्रेता p. fut. प्रेष्यति-ते fut. अप्रैषीत्, अप्रेष्ट aor. प्रीयात्, प्रेषीष्ट ben. पिप्रीषति-ते des. प्रीत p.p.

प्री 10 U. & 1 U. तर्पणे to please; प्रीणयति-ते, प्रयति-ते pre. प्रीणयिष्यति-ते, प्रेष्यति-ते fut. अपिप्रीणत्-त, अप्रैषीत्, अप्रेष्ट aor.

प्रु 1 A. गतौ to go, to jump. प्रवते pre, पुप्रुवे perf. प्रोता p. fut अप्रोष्ट aor. Pass—प्रूयते pre. Cau.—प्रावयति-ते pre.

प्रुट् 1 P. मर्दने to rub; प्रोटति pre. पुप्रोट perf. अप्रोटीत aor.

प्रुष 1 P. दाहे to burn; प्रोषति pre. पुप्रोष perf. प्रोषिष्यति fut. अप्रोषीत् aor. पुप्रुषिषति, पुप्रोषिषति. des. प्रुष्ट p.p. प्रुष्ट्वा, प्रोषित्वा, प्रुषित्वा ger.

प्रुष् 9 P. स्नेहनसेवनपूरणेषु to become wet, to sprinkle, to fill; प्रुष्णाति pre. प्रुषित p.p. प्रोषित्वा ger.

प्रेङ्खोल् 10 U. आन्दोलने to swing, to shake; प्रेङ्खोलयति-ते pre. अपप्रेङ्खोलत्-त aor. Pass.—प्रेङ्खोल्यते pre.

प्रेष् 1 A. to go; प्रेषते pre. अप्रेषिष्ट Aor.

प्रोथ् 1 U. पर्याप्तौ to be full, to be equal to; प्रोथति-त pre. अप्रोथत्, अप्रोथिष्ट aor.

प्रुष् 1 U. अदने to eat; प्रुष्णाति-ते pre. अप्रुषीत्, अप्रोक्षिष्ट aor.

प्रेह् 1 P. to go; प्रेहति-ते pre. अप्रेहिष्ट aor.

प्री 9 P. to go; प्रीणाति pre. प्रेष्यति fut. अप्रैषीत् Aor.

प्लु 1 A. गतौ to float, to fly, to jump; प्लवते pre. पुप्लुवे perf. प्लोता p. fut. प्लोष्यते fut. अप्लोष्यत con. अप्लोष्ट aor. Cau.–प्लावयति-ते pre. अपुप्लवत्-त, अपिप्लवत्-त Aor. प्लुत p.p.

प्लुष् 1 & 4 P. दाहे to burn; प्लोषति, प्लुष्यति pre. पुप्लोष perf. प्लोषिता p. fut. प्लोषिष्यति fut. अप्लोषिष्यत् con. अप्लोषीत् (1) अप्लुषत् (4) aor. प्लुष्ट (1) प्लुषित (4) p.p. प्लुष्ट्वा (1) प्लुषित्वा, प्लोषित्वा (1, 4) ger.

प्लुष् 9 P. स्नेहनसेवनपूरणेषु to sprinkle, to fill, to be wet; प्लुष्णाति pre. अप्लोषीत् Aor. Other forms like (4 above).

प्सा 2 P. भक्षणे to devour, to eat; प्साति pre. पप्सौ perf. प्साता p. fut. प्सास्यति fut. अप्सास्यत् con. अप्सासीत् aor. प्सायात्, प्सेयात् ben. पिप्सासति des. Pass.—प्सायते pre. Cau.—प्सापयति pre. अपिप्सत् aor. प्सात p.p.

फ—

फक्क् 1 P. नीचैर्गतौ to behave ill, to go softly; फक्कति pre. पफक्क perf. अफक्कीत् Aor. फक्कित p.p.

फण् 1 P. गतिदीप्त्योः to go, to produce easily; फणति pre. पफाण perf. फणिता p. fut. अफणीत्, अफाणीत् aor. फण्यात् ben. पिफणिषति des. Cau.—फणयति-ते pre. अपीफणत्-त aor. फणित p.p.

फल् 1 P. विशरणे to burst, to open, to split; फलति pre. पफाल perf. फलिता p. fut. फलिष्यति fut. अफलिष्यत् con. अफालीत् aor. पिफलिषति des. फुल्ल (प्रफुल्ल) p.p.

फल् 1 P. निष्पत्तौ to go, to bear fruit, to result, to be successful; फलति pre. &c. फलित p.p. Other forms like those of the above.

फुल्ल् 1 P. विकसने to open, to blow (as a flower); फुल्लति pre. पुफुल्ल perf. फुल्लिता p. fut. फुल्लिष्यति fut. अफुल्लिष्यत् con. अफुल्लीत् aor. पुफुल्लिषति des. फुल्लित p.p.

फेल् 1 P. to go; फेलति pre. फेलिष्यति fut. अफेलीत् aor.

ब—

बंह् 1 A. वृद्धौ to grow, to increase; बंहते pre. बंहिष्यते fut. अबंहिष्ट aor. बंहित p.p.

बट् 1 P. to grow; बठति pre.

बण् 1 P. शब्दे to sound; बणति pre. बबाण perf, अब-बा-णीत् aor.

बद् 1 P. to be steady; बदति pre. बबाद perf. अब-बा-दीत् aor.

बध् 1 A. चित्तविकारे to loathe, to be disgusted with; बीभत्सते pre. बीभत्सांबभूव-आस-चक्रे perf. बीभत्सिता p. fut. बीभत्सिष्यते fut. अबीभत्सिष्यत con. बीभत्सिषीष्ट ben. अबीभत्सिष्ट aor. बीभत्सिषते des. Pass.–बीभत्स्यते pre. अबीभत्सि aor. बीभत्सित p.p.

बध् 10 U. संयमने to bind, to restrain; बाधयति, बाधयते pre. अबीबधत्-त Aor. बाध्यात्, बाधयिषीष्ट ben. बिबाधयिषति-ते des.

बन्ध् 9 P. बन्धने to bind, to attract, to form; बध्नाति pre. बबन्ध perf. बन्द्धा p. fut. भन्त्स्यति fut. अभन्त्स्यत् con. अभान्त्सीत् aor. बध्यात् ben. बिभन्त्सति des. Pass.—बध्यते pre. Cau.—बन्धयति-ते pre. अबबन्धत्-त aor. बद्ध p.p. बद्ध्वा ger.

बन्ध् 10 U. to bind; बन्धयति-ते pre. बन्धयाञ्चकार-चक्रे &c. perf. अबबन्धत्-त Aor. बिबन्धयिषति-ते des. Pass.–बन्ध्यते pre.

बर्ब् 1 P. to go; बर्बति pre. बबर्ब perf. बर्बिता p. fut.

बर्ह् 1 A. परिभाषणहिंसाप्रदानेषु to speak, to give, to hurt; बर्हते pre. बबर्ह perf. अबर्हिष्ट Aor.

बर्ह् 10 U. हिंसायां भाषायां दीप्तौ च kill; to speak, &c.; बर्हयति-ते pre. अबबर्हत्-त Aor.

बल् 1 P. प्राणने धान्यावरोधने च to live; to hoard grain; बलति pre. बबाल perf. बलिता p. fut. अबालीत् aor.

बल् 10 U. प्राणने to breathe; बलयति-ते pre.

बस् 4 P. स्तंभे to stop; बस्यति pre. बबास perf. बसिता p. fut. अबसत् aor.

बाड् 1 A. आप्लाव्ये to bathe, to dive; बाडते pre. बबाडे perf. अबाडिष्ट Aor.

बाध् 1 A. लोडने to oppress, to torment; बाधते pre. बबाधे perf. बाधिता p. fut. बाधिष्यते fut. अबाधिष्यत con. अबाधिष्ट aor. Cau.—बाधयति-ते pre. अबबाधत्-त aor. Pass.—बाध्यते pre. अबाधि aor. बाधित p. p. बाधित्वा ger. बाधितुम् inf.

बिट् 1 P. आक्रोशे to swear, to curse, to shout; बेटति pre. बिबेट perf. बेटिता p. fut. अबेटीत् aor.

बिन्द् 1 P. अवयवे to split, to divide; बिन्दति pre. बिबिन्द perf. बिन्दिता p. fut.

बिल् 6 P. भेदने to break; बिलति pre. बिबेल perf. बेलिता p. fut. अबेलीत् aor. 10 U. बेलयति-ते pre. &c.

बिस् 4 P. क्षेपे प्रेरणे च to throw, to instigate, to go; बिस्यति pre. बिबेस perf. बेसिष्यति fut. अबिसत् Aor.

बुक्क् 1 P. & 10 U. भाषणे to bark, to speak; बुक्कति, बुक्कयति-ते pre. अबुक्कीत्, अबुबुक्कत्-त aor.

बुध् 1 U. बोधने to know, to mark, to esteem; बोधति-ते pre. बुबोध, बुबुधे perf. बोधिता p. fut. बोधिष्यति-ते fut. अबोधिष्यत्-त con. अबुधत्, अबोधीत्, अबोधिष्ट aor. Cau.—बोधयति-ते pre. अबूबुधत्-त aor. बुबुधिषति-ते, बुबोधिषति-ते des. Pass.—बुध्यते pre. अबोधि aor. बुधित p. p. बुधित्वा, बोधित्वा ger.

बुध् 4 A. to know, to understand; बुध्यते pre. बुबुधे perf. बोद्धा p. fut. भोत्स्यते fut. अभोत्स्यत con. अबुद्ध, अबोधि aor. भुत्सीष्ट ben. बुभुत्सते des. Pass.–बुध्यते pre. Cau.-बोधयति-ते pre. बुद्ध p. p. बुद्ध्वा ger. बोद्धुम् inf.

बुल् 10 U. to sink, to plunge; बोलयति-ते pre. बोलयाञ्चकार-चक्रे perf. बोलयिता p. fut.

बुस् 4 P. to discharge, to emit; बुस्यति pre. बुबोस perf.

बुस्त् 10 U. to honour, to treat honourably; बुस्तयति-ते pre. बुस्तयाञ्चकार-चक्रे perf. बुस्तयिता p. fut.

बृह् 1 P. वृद्धौ to grow, to increase; बर्हति pre. बबर्ह perf. बर्हिता p. fut. बर्हिष्यति fut. अबर्हिष्यत् con. अबर्हीत् aor.

बृह् 6 P. उद्यमने to work; बृहति pre. बबर्ह (बबर्हिथ, बबर्ढ 2nd sing.) perf. बर्हिष्यति, भर्क्ष्यति fut. अबर्हीत्, अभृक्षत् aor. Cau.—बर्हयति-ते pre. अबबर्हत्-त, अबीबृहत्-त aor. बिबर्हिषति, बिभृक्षति des. बृढ p. p. बर्हित्वा, बृढ्वा ger.

बृंह् 1 P. वृद्धौ शब्दे च to grow, to roar; बृंहति pre. बबृंह perf. बृंहिष्यति fut. अबृंहीत् aor.

बेह् 1 A. प्रयत्ने to strive; बेहते pre. अबेहिष्ट aor.

ब्रू 2 U. व्यक्तायां वाचि to speak; ब्रवीति, ब्रूते-आह pre. उवाच, ऊचे perf. वक्ता p. fut. वक्ष्यति-ते fut. अवक्ष्यत्-त con. अवोचत्-त aor. उच्यात्, वक्षीष्ट ben. Pass.—उच्यते pre. Cau.—वाचयति-ते pre. अवीवचत्-त aor. उक्त p. p. उक्त्वा ger. वक्तुम् inf.

ब्रूस् 10 U. हिंसायाम् to kill, to hurt; ब्रूसयति-ते pre. ब्रूसयाञ्चकार-चक्रे perf. ब्रूसयिता p. fut. अबुब्रूसत्-त aor.

भ—

भक्ष् 1 U. see भ्रक्ष्.

भक्ष् 10 U. अदने to use, to eat, to bite; भक्षयति-ते pre. भक्षयाञ्चकार-चक्रे-आस-बभूव perf. भक्षयिता p. fut. भक्षयिष्यति-ते fut. अबभक्षत्-त aor. भक्ष्यात्, भक्षयिषीष्ट ben. बिभक्षयिषति-ते des. Pass.-भक्ष्यते pre. भक्षित p. p. भक्षयित्वा ger. भक्षयितुम् inf.

भज् 1 U. सेवायाम् to serve, to take possession of, to choose, to honour; भजति-ते pre. बभाज, भेजे perf. भक्ता p. fut. भक्ष्यति-ते fut. अभक्ष्यत्-त con. अभाक्षीत्, अभक्त aor. भज्यात्, भक्षीष्ट ben. बिभक्षति-ते ben. Pass.—भज्यते pre. अभाजि aor. Cau.—भाजयति-ते pre. अबीभजत्-त aor. भक्त p. p. भक्त्वा ges. भक्तुम् inf.

भज् 10 U. विश्राणने to cook, to give; भाजयति-ते pre. भाजयाञ्चकार-चक्रे &c. perf. भाजयिता p. fut. अबीभजत्-त aor. बिभाजयिषति-ते des.

भञ्ज् 10 U. भाषायां दीप्तौ च to speak, to illumine; भञ्जयति-ते pre. अबभञ्जत्-त aor.

भञ्ज् 7 P आमर्दने to spilt, to disappoint; भनक्ति pre. बभञ्ज perf. भङ्क्ता p. fut. भङ्क्ष्यति fut. अभङ्क्ष्यत् con. अभांक्षीत् aor. भज्यात् ben. बिभङ्क्षति des. Pass.—भज्यते pre. अभञ्जि, अभाजि aor. Cau.-भञ्जयति-ते pre. अबभञ्जत्-त aor. भग्न p.p. भक्त्वा, भङ्क्त्वा ger. भङ्क्तुम् inf.

भट् 1 P. भृतौ to receive wages, to nourish; भटति pre. बभाट perf. भटिता p. fut. अभटीत्, अभाटीत् aor.

भण्ड् 1 A. परिभाषणे to upbraid, to jest; भण्डते pre. बभण्डे perf. भण्डिता p. fut. अभण्डिष्ट aor.

भण्ड् 10 U. कल्याणे सुखे प्रतारणे च to make fortunate, to cheat; भण्डयति-ते pre. भण्डयाञ्चकार-चक्रे &c. perf. भण्डयिता p. fut. अबभण्डत्-त aor. Also 1 P. भण्डति pre. अभण्डीत् aor.

भण् 1 P. शब्दे to speak, to call; भणति pre. बभाण perf. भणिता p. fut. भणिष्यति fut. अभणीत्, अभाणीत् aor. बिभणिषति des. Pass.—भण्यते pre. अभाणि aor. भणित p.p. भणित्वा ger.

भर्त्स् 10 A. (rarely P.) to menace, to threaten, to abuse, to deride; भर्त्सयते pre. भर्त्सयाञ्चक्रे perf. भर्त्सयिता p. fut. अबभर्त्सत aor. बिभर्त्सयिषते des.

भल् 1 A. परिभाषणहिंसादानेषु to speak, to kill, to give; भलते pre. अभलिष्ट aor.

भल् 10 A. आभण्डने to see; भालयते pre. भालयाञ्चक्रे &c. perf. भालयिता p. fut. अबीभलत aor.

भल्ल् 1 A. परिभाषणहिंसादानेषु to describe, to wound, to give; भल्लते pre. बभल्ले perf. भल्लिता p. fut. अभल्लिष्ट aor. भल्लित p.p.

भष् 1 P. to bark, to rail against; भषति pre. बभाष perf. भषिता p. fut. अभषीत् aor. बिभषिषति des.

भस् 3 P. भर्त्सनदीप्त्योः to censure, to blame, to shine; बभस्ति pre. बभास perf. (used in the Vedas only).

भा 2 P. दीप्तौ to shine, to appear, to be; भाति pre. अभान्-भुः 3rd pl. Imperf. बभौ perf. भाता p. fut. अभासीत् aor. Pass.—भायते pre. अभायि aor. Cau.—भापयति-ते pre. अबीभपत्-त aor.

भाज् 10 U. पृथक्करणे to divide; भाजयति-ते pre. भाजयाञ्चकार-चक्रे perf. भाजयिता p. fut. अबभाजत्-त aor. बिभाजयिषति-ते des. भाजित p. p.

भाम् 1 A. क्रोधे to be angry; भामते pre. बभामे perf. भामिष्यते fut. अभामिष्ट aor.

भाष् 1 A. to speak, to call; भाषते pre. बभाषे perf. भाषिता p. fut. अभाषिष्ट aor. 10 U. also अबभाषत्-त aor.

भिक्ष् 1 A. भिक्षायां लाभेऽलाभे च to beg, to obtain; भिक्षते pre. बिभिक्षे perf. भिक्षिता p. fut. भिक्षिष्यते fut. अभिक्षिष्ट aor. Cau–भिक्षयति-ते pre. अबिभिक्षत्-त Aor.

भिद् 7 U. विदारणे to separate, to break down; भिनत्ति, भिन्ते pre. बिभेद, बिभिदे perf. भेत्ता p. fut. भेत्स्यति-ते fut. अभेत्स्यत्-त con. अभिदत, अभैत्सीत् (अभैत्ताम् dual), अभित्त aor. Cau.-अबीभिदत्-त Aor. बिभित्सति des. बेभिद्यते, बेभिदीति, बेभेत्ति freq. Pass.-अभेदि Aor. भिन्न (also भित्त). p.p.

भिन्द् 1 P. to divide, to cut; भिन्दति pre. बिभिन्द perf. अभिन्दीत् Aor. Pass.—भिन्द्यते pre.

भी 3 P. भये to fear, to be anxious about; बिभेति pre. बिभाय or बिभयाञ्चकार &c. perf. भेत्ता p. fut. भेष्यति fut. अभेष्यत con. अभैषीत् aor. भीयात् ben. बिभीषति des. Pass.-भीयते pre. अभायि aor. Cau.—भाययति, भापयते, भीषयते Pre. अबीभयत्, अबीभिषत्, अबीभिषत Aor. बेभियते, बेभयीति; बेभेति freq. भीत p.p.

भुज् 6 P. कौटिल्ये to bend, to curve; भुजति pre. बुभोज perf. भोक्ता p. fut. अभोक्षित् aor. भुग्न p. p.

भुज् 7 U. पालनाभ्यवहारयोः to protect; अनवने (A.) to eat, to consume, to enjoy, (P.) to rule, to govern; भुनक्ति. भुङ्क्ते pre. बुभोज, बुभुजे perf. भोक्ता p. fut. भोक्ष्यति-ते fut. अभोक्ष्यत्-त con. अभौक्षीत्, अभुक्त aor. भुज्यात्, भुक्षीष्ट ben. बुभुक्षति des. Pass.—भुज्यते pre. अभोजि aor. Cau.-भोजयति-ते pre. अबूभुजत्-त aor. बोभुज्यते, बोभुजीति, बोभोक्ति freq. भुक्त p. p.

भू (सत्तायाम्) 1 P. (rarely Atm.) to be, to live, to be born; भवति-ते pre. बभूव, बभूवे perf. भविता p. fut. भविष्यति-ते fut. अभविष्यत्-त con. अभूत्, अभविष्ट aor. भूयात्, भविषीष्ट ben. बुभूषति ते des. Pass.-भूयते pre. भाविता, भविता p. fut. भविष्ये-भाविष्ये fut. अभावि aor. भाविषीष्ट, भविषीष्ट ben. Cau.-भावयति-ते pre. अबीभवत्-त aor. बोभूयते, बोभोति, बोभवीति freq. भूत p.p.

भू 10 A. प्राप्तौ to attain, to obtain; भावयते pre. भावयाञ्चक्रे perf. भावयिता p. fut. अबीभवत aor. भावयिषीष्ट ben. Pass.-भाव्यते.

भू 10 U. (अवकल्कने) to be purified, to consider, to mix; भावयति-ते pre. भावयाञ्चकार-चक्रे perf. भावयिता p. fut. अबीभवत्-त aor. भाव्यात्, भावयिषीष्ट ben.

भूष् 1 P. (अलङ्कारे) to adorn; भूषति pre. बुभूष perf. भूषिता p. fut. अभूषीत् Aor. बुभूषिषति des.

भूष् 10 U. to adorn; भूषयति-ते pre. भूषयाञ्चकार-चक्रे &c. perf. भूषयिता p. fut. अबुभूषत्-त Aor. भूष्यात्, भूषयिषीष्ट ben. बुभूषयिषति-ते des. Pass.–भूष्यते, अभूषि Aor. भूषित p. p.

भृ 1 U. भरणे to nourish, to fill; भरति-ते pre. बभार-बभ्रे perf. भर्ता p. fut. भरिष्यति-ते fut. अभार्षीत्, अभृत aor. भ्रियात्, भृषीष्ट ben. बुभूर्षति-ते, बिभरिषति-ते des. बेभ्रीयते, बर्भति, बर्भरीति &c. freq. Pass.-भ्रियते. भृत p. p.

भृ 3 U. धारणपोषणयोः to hold, to support; बिभर्ति, बिभृते pre. बभार, बभ्रे. बिभराञ्चकार-चक्रे &c. perf. भर्ता p. fut. भरिष्यति-ते fut. अभार्षीत. अभृत aor. बिभरिषति, बुभूर्षति des. Pass.-भ्रियते pre. अभारि aor. Cau.-भारयति-ते pre. अबीभरत्-त aor.

भृज् 1 A. भर्जने to parch, to fry; भर्जते pre. बभर्जे perf. भर्जिता p. fut. अभर्जिष्ट aor. भर्जिषीष्ट ben. Cau.-भर्जयति-ते; अबभर्जत्-त aor. बिभर्जिषते des. Pass.-भृज्यते pre. अभर्जि aor. भृक्त p. p. भर्जित्वा ger

भृश् 4 P. अधःपतने to fall down; भृश्यति pre. बभर्श perf. भर्शिता p. fut. अभृशत् Aor. भृष्ट p. p. भर्शित्वा, भृष्ट्वा.

भॄ 9 P. to fry, to reproach, to support; भृणाति pre. बभार perf. भरिता, भरीता p. fut. अभारीत् Aor. भूर्ण p. p.

भेष् 1 U. भये गतौ च to be afraid, to go; भेषति-ते pre. भेषिष्यति-ते fut. अभेषीत्, अभेषिष्ट Aor. भेष्यात्, भेषिषीष्ट ben.

भ्रंश् 1 A. अवस्रंसने & 4 P. अधःपतने to fall, to decline, to escape; भ्रंशते, भ्रश्यति pre. बभ्रंशे, बभ्रंश perf. भ्रंशिता p. fut. भ्रंशिष्यति-ते fut. अभ्रंशत, अभ्रंशिष्ट; अभ्रशत् aor. भ्रंशयति-ते Cau.-अबभ्रंशत्-त aor. बिभ्रंशिषति-ते des. बाभ्रश्यते, बाभ्रशीति, बाभ्रंष्टि freq. भ्रष्ट p. p. भ्रंशित्वा, भ्रष्ट्वा ger

भ्रंस् 1 A. &. 4 P. to fall down; भ्रंसते, भ्रस्यति pre. (same as भ्रंश् with the change of स् for श्)

भ्रक्ष् 1 U. अदने to eat; भ्रक्षति-ते pre. बभ्रक्ष-क्षे perf भ्रक्षिता p. fut. अभ्रक्षीत्, अभ्रक्षिष्ट aor. भ्रक्ष्यात्, भ्रक्षिषीष्ट ben.

भ्रण् 1 P शब्दे to sound; भ्रणति pre. बभ्राण perf. भ्रणिता p. fut. अभ्रणीत्, अभ्राणीत् aor.

भ्रम् 1 चलने & 4 अनवस्थाने P. to roam about, to totter; भ्रमति, भ्रम्यति, भ्राम्यति pre. बभ्राम, (बभ्रमिथ, भ्रेमिथ 2nd sing.) perf. भ्रमिता p. fut. भ्रमिष्यति fut. (1 P.) अभ्रमीत् (4 P.) अभ्रमत् aor. Cau.-भ्रमयति pre. अबिभ्रमत् Aor. बिभ्रमिषति des. बम्भ्रम्यते, बम्भ्रमीति, बम्भ्रन्ति freq. Pass.-भ्रम्यते pre. अभ्रमि aor. भ्रान्त p. p. भ्रमित्वा, भ्रान्त्वा ger.

भ्रश् 1 A. अवस्रंसने to fall; भ्रशते pre. बभ्रशे pref. भ्रशिष्यते fut. अभ्रशात् अभ्राशिष्ट aor.

भ्रस्ज् 6 U. पाके to fry, to parch; भृज्जाति-ते pre. बभज्ज, बभर्ज, बभज्जे बभर्जे perf. भ्रष्टा, भर्ष्टा p. fut. भ्रक्ष्याति-ते, भर्क्ष्यति-ते fut. अभ्राक्षीत्, अभार्क्षीत्, अभ्रष्ट, अभर्ष्ट aor. भृज्यात्, भ्रक्षीष्ट, भर्क्षीष्ट ben बिभ्रक्षति-ते, बिभर्क्षति-ते, बिभ्रज्जिषति-ते बिभर्जिषति-ते des. Pass.—भृज्यते pre. अभर्जि, अभ्रज्जि aor. Cau.—भ्रज्जयति-ते, भर्जयति-ते pre. अबभ्रज्जत्-त, अबभर्जत्-त aor. भृष्ट p. p. भ्रष्टुं, भर्ष्टुम् inf.

भ्राज् 1 A. दीप्तौ to shine, to beam; भ्राजते pre. बभ्राजे, भ्रेजे perf. भ्राजिता p. fut. भ्राजिष्यते fut. अभ्राजिष्ट aor. भ्राजिषीष्ट ben. Cau.–भ्राजयति-ते pre. अबिभ्रजत्-त, अबभ्राजत्-त aor. बिभ्राजिषते des. Pass.–भ्राज्यते pre. अभ्राजि aor. भ्राजित p.p.

भ्राश् (भ्लाश्) 1 & 4 A. दीप्तौ to shine; भ्राशते, भ्राश्यते, pre. बभ्राशे-भ्रेशे perf. भ्राशिता p. fut. अभ्राशिष्ट aor. भ्राशिषीष्ट ben. Cau.–भ्राशयति-ते pre. अबभ्राशत्-त aor. बिभ्राशिषते des. भ्राशित p p. भ्राशितुम् inf.

भ्रास—same as above.

भ्री 9 P. भये भरण इत्येके to tear, to protect; भ्रिणाति, भ्रीणाति, pre. बिभ्राय perf. भ्रेष्यति fut. अभ्रैषीत् Aor.

भ्रुड् 6 P. आच्छादने सञ्चये to cover, to collect; भ्रुडति pre. बुभ्रोड बुभ्रुडिथ (as this is कुटादि,), perf. भ्रुडिता p. fut. अभ्रुडीत् Aor.

भ्रूण् 10 A. आशाविशङ्कनयोः to wish, to put confidence in; भ्रूणयते pre. भ्रूणयाञ्चक्रे perf. भ्रूणयिता p. fut. अबुभ्रूणत Aor. भ्रूणयिषीष्ट. ben. बुभ्रूणयिषते des.

भ्रेज् 1 A. दीप्तौ to shine, to glitter; भ्रेजते pre. बिभ्रेजे perf. भ्रेजिष्यते fut. अभ्रेजिष्ट Aor.

भ्रेष् 1 U. भये गतौ च to go, to be afraid; भ्रेषति-ते pre. बिभ्रेष, बिभ्रेषे perf. अभ्रेषिष्ट Aor.

भ्लक्ष् 1 U. to eat; भ्लक्षति-ते pre. बभ्लक्ष-बभ्लक्षे perf. अभ्लक्षीत्, अभ्लक्षिष्ट Aor.

म्लाश् (see ,, भ्राश्).
म्लास् (see ,, भ्रास्). } changing र् to ल्.
म्लेष् (see ,, भ्रेष्).

म—

मंह् 1 A. वृद्धौ to grow; P. भाषायां दीप्तौ च to speak, to shine; मंहते-ति pre. ममंहे-ह perf. मंहिता p. fut. अमंहिष्ट अमंहीत् Aor. मंहिषीष्ट, मंह्यात् ben. Pass.-मंह्यते मिमंहिषते-ति des. मंहित p. p.

मंह् 10 U. to speak, to shine; मंहयिष्यति-ते fut. अममंहत्-त Aor.

मक्क् 1 A. to go, to move; मक्कते pre. ममक्के perf. अमक्किष्ट aor.

मक्ष 1 P. संघाते to accumulate, to be angry; मक्षति pre. ममक्ष perf. अमक्षीत् aor.

मख् 1 P. गतौ to go, to creep; मखति pre. ममाख perf. मखिता p. fut. अमखीत्, अमाखीत् aor.

मङ्क् 1 A. मण्डने to adorn; मङ्कते pre. ममङ्के perf. मङ्किता p. fut. अमङ्किष्ट aor.

मङ्ख् 1 P. गतौ to go; मङ्खति pre. ममङ्ख perf. मङ्खिता p. fut. अमङ्खीत् aor. Pass.-मङ्ख्यते pre. अमङ्खि aor.

मङ्ग् 1 P. to go, to move; (same as above).

मङ्घ् 1 P. मण्डने to adorn, to decorate; मङ्घति pre. ममङ्घ perf. मंघिता p. fut. अमंघीत् aor. Pass.-मंघ्यते

मंघ् 1 A. गत्याक्षेपे आरम्भे कैतवे च to move quickly, to start; to begin, to cheat; मंघते pre. ममंघे perf. मंघिता p. fut अमंघिष्ट aor. मंघिषीष्ट ben.

मंच् 1 A. दम्भे कत्थने कल्कने च to cheat, to be wicked, to boast, to pound; मचते pre. मेचे perf. मचिता p. fut. अमचिष्ट aor.

मञ्च् 1 A. धारणोच्छ्रायपूजनेषु to hold, to grow high, to go, to adore, to shine; मञ्चते pre. ममञ्चे perf. मञ्चिता p. fut. अमञ्चिष्ट aor.

मञ्ज् 10 U. शब्दे to sound; मञ्जयति-ते pre. मञ्जयाञ्चकार-चक्रे, &c. perf. मञ्जयिता p. fut. अमिमञ्जत्-त aor.

मठ् 1 P. मर्दननिवासनयोः to grind, to dwell, to go; मठति pre ममाठ perf. मठिता p. fut. अमठीत् aor.

मण्ठ् 1 A. शोके to remember with regret, to long for; मण्ठते perf. ममण्ठे perf. मण्ठिता p. fut. अमण्ठिष्ट aor.

मण् 1 P. शब्दे to sound, to murmur; मणति pre. ममाण perf. मणिता p. fut. अमणीत् aor.

मण्ड् 1 P. भूषायाम् to decorate oneself; मण्डति pre. ममण्ड perf. मण्डिता p. fut. मण्डिष्यति fut. अमण्डीत् aor. मण्ड्यात् ben. Cau. -मण्डयति-ते pre. अममण्डत्-त aor. मिमण्डिषति des.

मण्ड् 1 A. विभाजने to distribute; मण्डते pre. ममण्डे perf. मण्डिता p. fut. मण्डिष्यते fut. अमण्डिष्ट aor. मण्डिषीष्ट ben. मिमण्डिषते des. Pass.—मण्ड्यते pre. अमण्डि Aor.

मण्ड् 10 U. to adorn; मण्डयति-ते pre. मण्डयाञ्चकार-चक्रे &c. perf. मण्डयिता p. fut. अममण्डत्-त aor. मण्ड्यात्, मण्डयिषीष्ट ben. मिमण्डयिषति-ते des.

मथ् 1 P. विलोडने to stir, to churn; मथिष्यति fut. अमथीत् Aor. Cau.—माथयति-ते pre. अमीमथत्-त aor. मिमथिषते des.

मद् 4 P. हर्षग्लेपनयोः to be glad, to be in a pitiable condition; माद्यति pre. ममाद perf. मदिता p. fut. मदिष्यति fut. अमदीत्-अमादीत् aor. Cau.—मदयति-ते (मादयति-ते to madden, to inebriate) pre. अमीमिदत्-त aor. मिमदिषति des. मामद्यते, मामदीति, मामत्ति freq. Pass. मद्यते pre. अमादि, अमदि aor. मत्त p.p.

मद् 10 A. तृप्तियोगे to please; मादयते pre. मादयाञ्चक्रे perf. मादयिता p. fut. मादयिष्यते fut. अमीमदत aor. मादयिषीष्ट ben. मिमादयिषते des. Pass.-माद्यते pre. अमादि aor. मादित p.p.

मन् 4 A. ज्ञाने to know, to think; मन्यते pre. मेने perf. मन्ता p. fut. मंस्यते fut. अमंस्यत con. अमंस्त aor. मंसीष्ट ben. मिमंसते des. Cau.—मानयति-ते pre. अमीमनत्-त aor. मम्मन्यते, मम्मनीति, मम्मन्ति, & freq. मत p.p. मत्वा ger. मन्तुम् inf.

मन् 8 A. अवबोधने to consider, to esteem; मनुते pre. मेने perf. मनिता p. fut. मनिष्यते fut. अमनिष्ट, अमत (अमनिष्ठाः, अमथाः,

2nd sing. अमनिषि 1. sing.) aor, मिमनिषते des. मनितुम् inf. Cau. &c.,—see the above root.

मन् 10 A. स्तम्भे to be proud; मानयते pre. मानयाञ्चक्रे perf. मानयिता p. fut. अमीमनत aor. मानयिषीष्ट ben. मिमानयिषते des. Pass.—मान्यते pre. मानित p.p.

मन्त्र् 10 A. गुप्तपरिभाषणे to consult, to advise, to speak; मन्त्रयते (sometimes, मन्त्रयति also) pre. मन्त्रयाञ्चक्रे perf. मन्त्रयिता p. fut. मन्त्रयिष्यते fut. अममन्त्रत aor. मिमन्त्रयिषते des. मन्त्रित p.p. मन्त्रयित्वा ger.

मन्थ् 1 & 9 (विलोडने) P. to churn, to agitate: मन्थति, मथ्नाति pre. (मथान Impera. 2nd sing. 9 conj.) ममन्थ perf. मन्थिता p. fut. मन्थिष्यति fut. अमन्थीत् aor. मथ्यात् ben. मिमन्थिषति des. Pass.— मथ्यते pre. अमन्थि aor. Cau.—मन्थयति-ते pre. अममन्थत्-त aor. मामन्थ्यते, मामन्थीति, मामन्ति freq. मथित p. p. मन्थित्वा ger. मन्थत् (1) मथ्नत् (9) pre. p.

मन्थ् 1 P. हिंसासंक्लेशनयो: to kill. to torment; मन्थति pre. ममन्थ perf. मन्थिता p. fut. मन्थिष्यति fut. अमन्थीत् aor. Pass.-मन्थ्यते pre. अमन्थि aor. मन्थित p.p. मन्थित्वा ger.

मन्द् 1 A. स्तुतिमोदमदस्वप्नकान्तिगतिषु to praise or be praised, to be glad, to languish, to sleep, to shine, to loiter; मन्दते pre. ममन्दे perf. मन्दिता p. fut. मन्दिष्यते fut. अमन्दिष्ट aor. मन्दिषीष्ट ben. Pass.-मन्द्यते pre.

मभ्र् 1 P. गतौ to go, to move; मभ्रति pre. ममभ्र perf. मभ्रिता p. fut. अमभ्रीत् aor.

मय 1 A. to go, to move; मयते pre. ममये perf. मयिता p. fut. अमयिष्ट aor. मयिषीष्ट ben.

मर्च् 10 U. शब्दे ग्रहणे च to take, to sound, to go, to injure; मर्चयति-ते pre. मर्चयाञ्चकार-चक्रे &c. perf. मर्चयिता p. fut. अममर्चत्-त aor. मर्च्यात्, मर्चयिषीष्ट ben.

मर्ब् 1 P. to go, to move; मर्बति pre. ममर्ब perf. मर्बिता p. fut. अमर्बीत् aor.

मर्व् 1 P. पूरणे to fill; मर्वति pre ममर्व perf. मर्विता p. fut. अमर्वीत् aor. Cau.—to sound; मर्वयति-ते pre.

मल् 1 A. & 10 U. धारणे to hold, to possess; मलते, मलयति-ते pre. मेले, मलयाञ्चकार-चक्रे &c. perf. मलिता, मलयिता p. fut. अमलिष्ट, अमीमलत्-त aor.

मल्ल् 1 A. to hold, to possess; मल्लते pre. same as above.

मव् 1 P. बन्धने हिंसायां च to fasten, to bind, to kill; मवति pre. ममाव perf. मविता p. fut. अमवीत्, अमावीत् aor.

मश् 1 P. शब्दे कोपे च to buzz, to be angry; मशति pre. ममाश perf. मशिता p. fut. अमशीत, अमाशीत् aor.

मष् 1 P. हिंसायां शब्दे च to hurt, to destroy; मषति pre. ममाष perf. माषिता p. fut. अम-मा-षीत् aor.

मस् 4 P. परिमाणे to weigh, to change from; मस्यति pre. ममास perf. मसिता p. fut. अमसत् aor. मस्त p.p. मसितुम् inf.

मस्क् 1 A. to go, to move; मस्कते pre. ममस्के perf. मस्किता p. fut. मस्किष्यते fut. अमस्किष्ट aor.

मस्ज् 6 P. शुद्धौ to bathe, to sink, to purify; मज्जति pre. ममज्ज (ममज्जिथ, ममङ्क्थ 2nd sing.) perf. मङ्क्ता p. fut. मङ्क्ष्यति fut. अमांक्षीत् (3rd dual अमाङ्क्ताम्) aor. मज्ज्यात् ben. मिमंक्षति des. Cau.-मज्जयति pre. अममज्जत् त aor. Pass.-मज्जते, मग्न p.p.

मह् 1 P. & 10 U. पूजायाम्, to honour, to delight, to increase; महति, महयति-ते pre. ममाह, महयाञ्चकार-चक्रे &c. perf. महिता महयिता p. fut. अमहीत्, अममहत्-त aor. मिमाहिषति, मिमहयिषति-ते des. Cau. (conj. 1)-माहयति-ते, अमीमहत्-त aor. Pass.-मह्यते pre. महित p.p. महितुम्, महयितुम् inf.

मह् 10 A. पूजायाम् to honour; महीयते pre. महीयाञ्चक्रे &c. perf. महीयिष्यते fut. अमहीयिष्ट Aor.

मा 2 P. माने to measure, to limit, to compare with, to form, to show, &c; माति pre. ममौ perf. माता p. fut. मास्यति fut. अमास्यत् con. अमासीत् aor. मेयात् ben. मित्सति des. मेमियते,

मामाति, मामेति freq. Pass.—मीयते pre. अमायि aor. Cau.—मापयति-ते pre. अमीमपत्-त aor. मित p.p. मित्वा ger.

मा 3 & 4 A. to measure, &c; मिमीते, मायते pre. ममे perf. माता p. fut. मास्यते fut. अमास्त aor. मासीष्ट ben. मित्सते des; for other forms see the above मा.

मांक्ष् 1 P. कांक्षायाम् to wish, to desire; मांक्षति pre. अमांक्षीत् aor.

मान् 1 A. जिज्ञासायाम् to seek knowledge; मीमांसते pre. मीमांसांबभूव-आस-चक्रे perf. मीमांसता p. fut. अमीमांसिष्ट aor. मीमांसिसीष्ट ben. मीमांसिषते des. Cau.-अमीमांसत्-त aor. Pass.—मीमांस्यते pre. अमीमांसि aor. मीमांसित p. p.

मान् 10 A. स्तंभे to stop, to be proud; मानयते pre. मानयिष्यते fut. अमीमनत, Aor मानयिषीष्ट ben.

मान् 10 & 1 P. पूजायाम् to honour, to worship; मानयति, मानति pre. अमीमनत्, अमानीत् Aor. मिमानयिषति, मिमानिषति des.

मार्ग् 1 P. अन्वेषणे to seek, to chase; मार्गति pre. ममार्ग perf. मार्गिता p fut. अमार्गीत् aor. मिमार्गिषति des. Pass.—मार्ग्यते pre. अमार्गि aor.

मार्ग् 10. U. to seek for, to go, to decorate; मार्गयति-ते pre. मार्गयाञ्चकार-चक्रे, &c. perf. मार्गयिता p. fut. मार्गयिष्यति-ते fut. अममार्गत्-त aor. मार्ग्यात्, मार्गयिषीष्ट des. मार्गित p. p. मार्गयितुम् inf.

मार्ज् 10 U. शब्दे शुद्धौ च to sound, to purify, to wipe; मार्जयति-ते pre. मार्जयांचकार-चक्रे, &c. perf. मार्जयिता p. fut. अममार्जत्-त aor. मार्ज्यात्, मार्जयिषीष्ट ben. मिमार्जयिषति-ते des.

मि 5 U. प्रक्षेपणे to throw, to scatter, to measure; मिनोति, मिनुते pre. ममौ, मिम्ये perf. माता p. fut. मास्यति-ते fut. अमासीत्, अमास्त aor. मीयात्, मासीष्ट ben. मित्सति-ते des. Pass.—मीयते pre. Cau.—मापयति ते pre. अमीमपत्-त aor. मित p. p.

मिथ् 1 U. मेधाहिंसयो: to unite, to understand, to hurt, to seize; मेथति-ते pre. मिमेथ, मिमिथे perf. मेथिता p. fut. अमेथीत्, अमेथिष्ट aor. मिथ्यात्, मेथिषीष्ट ben.

मिद् 1 A. स्नेहने to be unctuous, to melt, to love; मेदते pre. मिमिदे perf. मेदिता p. fut. अमिदत्, अमेदिष्ट aor. मेदिषीष्ट ben. मिमिदिषते, मिमेदिषते des. Cau.–मेदयति-ते pre. अमीमिदत्-त aor. मिन्न, मेदित p. p. मिदित्वा, मेदित्वा ger.

मिद् 4 P. to melt, &c., मेद्यति pre. मिमेद perf. मेदिता p. fut. अमिदत् aor. मिमि-मे-दिषति des.

मिद् 1 U. (see मिथ्) मेदति-ते pre. &c.

मिन्द् 1 P. & 10 U. (see मिद् 1 A.); मिन्दति, मिन्दयति-ते pre मिन्दिता, मिन्दयिता p. fut. अमिन्दीत्, अमिमिन्दत्-त aor. मिन्द्यात्, मिन्दयिषीष्ट ben.

मिन्व् 1 P. स्नेहने सेचने च to honour. to sprinkle; मिन्वति pre. मिमिन्व perf. मिन्विष्यति fut. अमिन्वीत् aor. Pass.–मिन्व्यते

मिल् 6 U. संगमे to join, to be united; मिलति-ते pre. मिमेल, मिमिले perf. मेलिता p. fut. मेलिष्यति-ते fut. अमेलिष्यत्-त con. अमेलीत् or अमेलिष्ट aor. मिमिलिषति-ते. मिमेलिषति–ते des. Pass.—मिल्यते pre. अमेलि aor. Cau.–मेलयति-ते pre. अमीमिलत्-त aor. मिलित p. p. मिलित्वा, मेलित्वा ger.

मिश् 1 P. शब्दे रोषकृते च to make a sound or noise, to be angry; मेशति pre. मिमेश perf. मेशिता p. fut. अमेशीत् aor.

मिश्र् 10 U. संपर्के to mix, to mingle; मिश्रयति-ते pre. मिश्रयाञ्चकार-चक्रे &c. perf. मिश्रयिता p. fut. अमिमिश्रत्-त aor. मिश्र्यात्, मिश्रयिषीष्ट ben. मिमिश्रयिषति-ते des. मिश्रित p.p. मिश्रयित्वा ger.

मिष् 6 P. to open the eyes, to look at; मिषति pre. मिमेष perf मेषिता p. fut. अमेषीत् aor. मिमिषिषति, मिमेषिषति des. मिषित्वा, मेषित्वा ger.

मिष् 1 P. सेचने to wet, to sprinkle; मेषति pre. &c. see the above root. मिषित्वा, मेषित्वा, मिष्ट्वा ger.

मिह् 1 P. सेचने to make water, to wet; मेहति pre. मिमेह perf. मेढा p. fut. मेक्ष्यति fut. अमिक्षत् aor. मिमिक्षति des. Cau.–मेहयति–ते pre. अमीमिहत्-त aor. मीढ p.p. मीढ्वा ger. मेढुम् inf.

मी 4 A. हिंसायां (हिंसात्र प्राणवियोगः) to die, perish; मीयते pre.

मिम्ये perf. मेष्यते fut. अमेष्ट aor. मिमीषते des. Cau.–मापयति–ते pre. अमीमपत्–त aor.

मी 9 U. हिंसायाम् to kill, to lessen, to change, to be lost मीनाति, मीनीते pre. ममौ, मिम्ये perf. माता p. fut. अमासीत् अमास्त aor. मीयात्, मासीष्ट ben. मित्सति–ते des. Pass.—मीयते pre. Cau.—मापयति–ते pre. अमीमपत्–त aor. मीत p.p. मीत्वा ger.

मी 1 P. & 10 U. गतौ to go, to understand; मयति, माययति–ते pre. मिमाय, माययाञ्चकार–चक्रे, &c. perf. मेता, माययिता p. fut. अमैषीत्, अमीमयत्–त aor.

मील् 1 P. निमेषणे to close (as the eyes); to twinkle, to be closed or shut (as the eyes of flowers), to meet, to cause to shut; मीलति pre. मिमील perf. मीलिता p. fut. अमीलीत् aor. Cau.–मीलयति–ते pre. अमीमिलत्–त, अमिमीलत्–त aor. मिमीलिषति des.

मीव् 1 P. स्थौल्ये to grow fat; to move मीवति pre. मिमीव perf. मीविता p. fut. अमीमिवत् aor.

मुच् 1 A. कल्कने to deceive, to cheat; मुञ्चते pre. मुमुञ्चे perf. अमुञ्चिष्ट aor.

मुच् 6 U. मोक्षणे to loose, to set free, to leave, to abandon; मुञ्चति–ते pre. मुमोच, मुमुचे perf. मोक्ता p. fut. मोक्ष्यति–ते fut. अमुचत्, अमुक्त aor. मुच्यात्, मुक्षीष्ट ben. मुमुक्षति (मुमुक्षते, मोक्षते intran.) des. Cau.–मोचयति–ते pre. अमूमुचत्–त aor. मुक्त p.p. मुक्त्वा ger.

मुज् or मुञ्ज् 1 P. & 10 U. शब्दे to cleanse, to purify, to sound; मोजति, मुञ्जति, मोजयति–ते, मुञ्जयति–ते pre. मुमोज, मुमुञ्ज, मोजयाञ्चकार–चक्रे, मुञ्जयाञ्चकार–चक्रे perf.

मुट् 1 P. to मर्दने to crush, to grind, to kill; मोटति pre. मुमोट perf मोटिता p. fut. अमोटीत् aor.

मुड् 6 P आक्षेपमर्दनबन्धनेषु to blame, to crush, to bind; मुटति pre See the above root.

10 U. संचूर्णने to pound, to break; मोटयति-ते pre. अमूमुटत्-त aor.

मुण्ट् 1 P मर्दने to crush, to grind; मुण्टति pre. मुमुण्ट perf. मुण्टिता p. fut. अमुण्टीत् aor.

मुण्ठ् 1 A. पालने पलायने वा to protect, to run away; मुण्ठते pre. मुमुण्ठे perf. मुण्ठिता p. fut. अमुण्ठिष्ट aor. मुण्ठिषीष्ट ben. Pass. मुण्ठ्यते pre.

मुण्ड् 1 P. खण्डने to shave, to grind; मुण्डति pre. मुमुण्ड perf. मुण्डिता p. fut. अमुण्डीत् aor. मुमुण्डिषति des. Cau.-मुण्डयति-ते pre. अमुमुण्डत्-त aor.

मुण्ड् 1 A. मार्जने मज्जने वा to sink; मुण्डते pre. मुमुण्डे perf. मुण्डिता p. fut. अमुण्डिष्ट aor.

मुण् 6 P. प्रतिज्ञाने to promise; मुणति pre. मुमोण perf. मोणिता p. fut. अमोणीत् aor.

मुद् 1 A. हर्षे to rejoice, to be glad; मोदते pre. मुमुदे perf. मोदिता p. fut. मोदिष्यते fut. अमोदिष्ट aor. मोदिषीष्ट ben. मुमुदिषते, मुमोदिषते des. मुदित, मोदित p. p.

मुद् 10 U. संसर्गे to mix, to blend, to purify; मोदयति-ते pre. मोदयाञ्चकार-चक्रे perf. मोदयिता p. fut. अमूमुदत्-त aor.

मुर 6 P. संवेष्टने to cover; मुरति pre. मुमोर perf. अमोरीत् aor.

मुर्च्छ् 1 P. मोहसमुच्छ्राययोः to faint, to become senseless, to grow, to prevail, to be match for; मूर्च्छति pre. मुमूर्च्छ perf. मूर्च्छिता p. fut. अमूर्च्छीत् aor. मूर्च्छ्यात् ben. Cau.-मूर्च्छयति-ते pre. अमुमूर्च्छत्-त aor. मुमूर्च्छिषति des. मूर्च्छित, मूर्त p.p.

मुर्व् 1 P. बन्धने to bind, to tie; मुर्वति pre. मुमुर्व perf. मुर्विता p. fut. अमुर्वीत् aor.

मुल् See मूल्.

मुष् 9 P. स्तेये to steal, to carry off; मुष्णाति pre. मुषाण 2nd sing. Impera. मुमोष perf. मोषिता p. fut. मोषिष्यति fut. अमोषीत्

aor. मुष्यात् ben. मुमुषिषति des. मुषित p.p. मुषित्वा, सम्मुष्य ger. मोषितुम् inf.

मुस् 4 P. खण्डने to cleave, to divide; मुस्यति pre. मुमोस perf.

मुस्त् 10 U. संघाते to heap up, to gather; मुस्तयति-ते pre. मुस्तयाञ्चकार-चक्रे perf. मुस्तयिता p. fut. अमुमुस्तत्-त aor. मुस्त्यात्, मुस्तयिषीष्ट ben.

मुह् 4 P. वैचित्ये to faint, to swoon, to fall, to err, to be foolish. मुह्यति pre. मुमोह perf. मोहिता, मोग्धा or मोढा p. fut. मोहिष्यति or मोक्ष्यति fut. अमोहिष्यत्-अमोक्ष्यत con. अमुहत् aor. मुह्यात् ben. मुमुहिषति, मुमोहिषति or मुमुक्षति des. Pass.-मुह्यते pre. अमोहि aor. Cau.—मोहयति-ते pre. अमूमुहत्-त aor. मुग्ध or, मूढ p.p. मोहित्वा, मुग्ध्वा, मूढ्वा, सम्मुह्य ger. मोहितुम्, मोग्धुम्, मोढुम् inf.

मू 1 A. बन्धने to fasten, ts tie; मवते pre. मुमुवे perf. मविष्यते fut. अमाविष्ट aor.

मूल् 1 P. प्रतिष्ठायाम् to be firm, to stand fast; मूलति pre. मुमूल, perf; मूलिता p. fut. अमूलीत् aor. मुमूलिषते des. Cau—मूलयति-ते pre. अमूमुलत्-त aor.

मूल 10 U. रोपणे to plant, to sprout; मूलयति-ते pre. मूलयाञ्चकार-चक्रे perf. मूलयिता p. fut. अमूमुलत्-त aor. मुमूलायषति-ते des. मूलित p. p.

मूष् 1 P. स्तेये to rob, to plunder; मूषति pre. मुमूष perf. अमूषीत् aor. मुमूषिषति des. Cau.-मूषयति-ते pre. अमुमूषत्-त aor. मूषित p.p

मृ 6 A.* प्राणत्यागे to die, to perish; म्रियते pre. ममार perf. मर्ता p. fut. मरिष्यति fut. अमृत aor. मृषीष्ट ben. मुमूर्षति des. Pass — म्रियते pre. Cau.-मारयति-ते pre. अमीमरत्-त aor. मृत p. p. मर्तुम् inf. मृत्वा ger. and the Desiderative.

---

* It is Parasmaipadi in the Perfect, the two Futures, the Conditional and the Desiderative.

मृक्ष् 1 P. सङ्घाते to strike, to collect; मृक्षति pre. ममर्क्ष perf. अमृक्षीत् aor.

मृग् 4 P. अन्वेषणे to seek, to hunt, to examine, to beg; मृग्यति pre. ममर्ग perf. मर्गिता p. fut. मर्गिष्यति fut. अमर्गीत् aor. मृगित p.p.

मृग् 10 A. अन्वेषणे to seek, &c.; मृगयते pre. मृगयाञ्चक्रे perf. मृगयिता p. fut. मृगयिष्यते fut. अममृगत aor. मृगयिषीष्ट ben. मिमृगयिषते des. Pass.—मृग्यते pre. अमृगि aor.

मृज् 1 P. शौचालङ्कारयोः to wipe etc; मार्जति pre. ममार्ज perf. (See the root below).

मृज् 2 P. शुद्धौ to wipe off, to rule, to carry (as a horse), to adorn; मार्ष्टि pre. ममार्ज perf. मार्जिता or मार्ष्टा p. fut. मार्जिष्यति or मार्क्ष्यति fut. अमार्जिष्यत्-अमार्क्ष्यत् con. अमार्जीत् or अमार्क्षीत् aor. मृज्यात् ben. मिमृक्षति, मिमार्जिषति des. Pass.—मृज्यते pre. अमार्जि aor. Cau.—मार्जयति-ते pre. अममार्जत्-त अमीमृजत्-त, aor. मृष्ट, मार्जित p. p.

मृज् 10 U. शौचालङ्कारयोः to wipe off &c.; मार्जयति-ते pre. मार्जयाञ्चकार-चक्रे, perf. मार्जयिता p. fut. मार्जयिष्यति-ते fut. अममार्जत्-त, अमीमृजत्-त aor. Pass.—मार्ज्यते pre. अमार्जि aor.

मृड् 6 & 9 P. सुखने to be gracious, to pardon, to be delighted; मृडति and मृड्नाति pre. ममर्ड perf. मर्डिता p. fut. अमर्डीत् aor.

मृण् 6 P. हिंसायाम् to kill, to destroy; मृणति pre. ममर्ण perf. अमर्णीत् aor.

मृद् 9 P. क्षोदे to press, to crush, to kill, to rub off; मृद्नाति pre. ममर्द perf. मर्दिता p. fut. मर्दिष्यति fut. अमर्दिष्यत् con. अमर्दीत् aor. Pass.—मृद्यते pre. अमर्दि aor. Cau.—मर्दयति-ते pre. अमीमृदत्-त or अममर्दत्-त aor. मिमर्दिषति des. मृदित p. p.

मृध् 1 U. उन्दने (हिंसायां च) to be moist, to hurt, to kill, (in the Vedas) to disregard; मर्धति-ते pre. ममर्ध or ममृधे perf. अमर्धीत् अमर्धिष्ट aor. मर्धित्वा, मृद्ध्वा ger.

मृश् 6 P. आमर्शने to touch, to shake, to consider; मृशति pre. ममर्श perf. मर्ष्टा or म्रष्टा p. fut. मर्क्ष्यति or म्रक्ष्यति fut. अमार्क्षीत्, अम्राक्षीत्, अमृक्षत् aor. मिमृक्षति des. Pass.—मृश्यते pre. अमर्शि aor. Cau.—मर्शयति-ते pre. अमीमृशत्-त or अममर्शत्-त aor. मृष्ट p. p. मृष्ट्वा ger.

मृष् 1 P. सेचने to sprinkle, to bear; मर्षति pre. ममर्ष perf. मर्षिता p. fut. अमर्षीत् aor. Cau.—मर्षयति-ते pre. अममर्षत्-त, अमीमृषत्-त aor.

मृष् 1 U. सहने to bear, to sprinkle; मर्षति-ते pre. (See the following root for the other forms).

मृष् 4 U. तितिक्षायाम् to suffer, to allow, to pardon; मृष्यति-ते pre. ममर्ष or ममृषे perf. मर्षिता p. fut. मर्षिष्यति-ते fut. अमर्षीत् or अमर्षिष्ट aor. मिमर्षिषति des. Pass.—मृष्यते pre. Cau.—मर्षयति-ते pre. मृषित्वा मर्षित्वा, ger.

मृष 10 U. to suffer &c.; मर्षयति-ते pre. मर्षयाञ्चकार-चक्रे, perf. मर्षयिता p. fut. अमीमृषत्-त, अममर्षत्-त aor.

मॄ 9 P. हिंसायाम् to hurt, to kill; मृणाति pre. ममार perf. मरिता or मरीता p. fut. मरिष्यति or मरीष्यति fut. अमारीत् aor. मिमरिषति, मिमरीषति, मुमूर्षति des.

मे 1 A. प्रणिदाने to exchange, to barter; मयते pre. ममे perf. माता p. fut. मास्यते fut. अमास्त aor. मासीष्ट ben. मित्सते des. Cau.—मापयति-ते pre. अमीमपत्-त aor. Pass.—मीयते pre. अमायि aor.

मेट्-मेड् 1 P. to be mad; मेटति, मेडति pre.

मेथ् 1 U. मेधाहिंसनयोः to know, to hurt; मेथति-ते pre. मिमेथ-थे perf. मेथिता p. fut. अमेथिष्ट aor.

मेदृ-मेधृ 1 U. (सङ्गमे) to meet (See the above root)

मेपृ 1 A. गतौ to go, to move; मेपते pre. मिमेपे perf. अमेपिष्ट aor.

मेवृ 1 A. सेवने to worship, to attend upon; मेवते pre.

मोक्ष् 1 P. & 10 U. to release, to loose, to shed; मोक्षति, मोक्षयति-ते pre. मुमोक्ष; मोक्षयाञ्चकार-चक्रे perf.

म्ना 1 P. अभ्यासे to repeat in the mind, to learn, to remember, to praise (in the Vedas); मनति pre. मम्नौ perf. म्नाता p. fut. म्नास्यति fut. अम्नासीत् aor. म्नायात् or म्नेयात् ben. मिम्नासति des. Cau.—म्नापयति-ते pre. अमिम्नपत्-त aor. Pass.—म्नायते pre. अम्नायि aor. म्नात p.p.

म्रक्ष् 1 P. संघाते to collect, to strike; म्रक्षति pre. मम्रक्ष perf. म्रक्षिता p. fut. अम्राक्षीत् aor.

म्रक्ष् 10 U. संयोजने स्नेहने म्लेच्छने च to heap, to mix, to anoint. to speak indistinctly; म्रक्षयति-ते pre. म्रक्षयाञ्चकार-चक्रे perf, म्रक्षयिता p. fut. अमम्रक्षत्-त aor. म्रक्ष्यात्, म्रक्षयिषीष्ट ben.

म्रद् 1 A. मर्दने to pound; म्रदते pre. मम्रदे perf. म्रदिष्यते fut. अम्रदिष्ट aor. मिम्रदिषते des.

म्रुच् 1 P. to go; म्रोचति pre. मुम्रोच perf. अम्रुचत्, अम्रोचीत् aor. मुम्रुचिषति, मुम्रोचिषति des. म्रोचित्वा, म्रुचित्वा ger.

म्रुञ्च् 1 P. to go; म्रुञ्चति pre. मुम्रुञ्च perf. म्रुञ्चिष्यति fut. अम्रुञ्चीत् aor. मुम्रुञ्चिषति des. म्रुक्त p.p. म्रुञ्चित्वा, मुक्त्वा ger.

म्रेट् (म्रेड्) 1 P. to be mad; म्रेट(ड)ति pre.

म्लक्ष् 10 U. to cut, to divide; म्लक्षयति-ते pre. म्लक्षयाञ्चकार-चक्रे perf. म्लक्षयिता p. fut. अमम्लक्षत्-त aor.

म्लुच् 1 P. to go; म्लोचति pre. मुम्लोच perf. म्लोचिता p. fut. म्लोचिष्यति fut. अम्लुचत् or अम्लोचीत् aor.

म्लुञ्च् 1. P. to go; म्लुञ्चति pre. मुम्लुञ्च perf.

म्लेच्छ् 1 P. & 10 U. अव्यक्ते शब्दे (अस्फुटे अपशब्दे च) to speak indistinctly or barbarously; म्लेच्छति, म्लेच्छति-ते pre. मिम्लेच्छ, म्लेच्छयाञ्चकार-चक्रे perf. अम्लेच्छीत्, अमिम्लेच्छत्-त aor. मिम्लेच्छिषति, मिम्लेच्छयिषति-ते des. म्लिष्ट, म्लेच्छित p. p.

म्लेट् or म्लेड् 1 P. उन्मादे to be mad; म्लेटति or म्लेडति pre. अम्लेटीत्, अम्लेडीत् aor.

म्लेव् 1 A. सेवने to worship, to serve; म्लेवते pre. मिम्लेवे perf. म्लेविष्यते fut. अम्लेविष्ट aor.

म्लै 1 P. हर्षक्षये to fade, to grow weary, to be sad; म्लायति pre. मम्लौ perf. म्लाता p. fut. म्लास्यति fut. अम्लासीत् aor. म्लायात् or म्लेयात् ben. Cau.—म्लापयति-ते pre. अमिम्लपत्-त aor. मिम्लासति des. Pass.—म्लायते per. अम्लायि aor. म्लान p. p.

य—

यक्ष् 1 P. to stir, to move; यक्षति pre. ययक्ष perf. यक्षिता p. fut. अयक्षीत् aor.

यक्ष् 10 A. पूजायाम् to honour, to adore; यक्षयते pre. यक्षयाञ्चक्रे perf. यक्षयिता p. fut. अययक्षत aor. यक्षित p.p.

यज् 1 U. देवपूजासंगतिकरणयजनदानेषु to sacrifice, to make an oblation to, to give, to associate with; यजति-ते pre. इयाज, ईजे perf. यष्टा p. fut. यक्ष्यति-ते fut. अयक्ष्यत्-त con. अयाक्षीत् (अयाष्टाम् du.), अयष्ट aor. इज्यात्, यक्षीष्ट ben. यियक्षति-ते des. Pass—इज्यते pre. अयाजि aor. Cau.—याजयति-ते pre. अयीयजत्-त aor. इष्ट p.p. इष्ट्वा, समिज्य ger. यष्टुम् inf.

यत् 1 A. प्रयत्ने to attempt, to strive after, to labour, &c; यतते pre. येते perf. यतिता p. fut. यतिष्यते fut. अयतिष्ट aor. यतिषीष्ट ben. यियतिषते des. Pass.—यत्यते pre. अयाति aor. Cau.—यातयति-ते pre. अयीयतत्-त aor. यत p.p. यतित्वा, आयत्य ger.

यत् 10 U. निकारोपस्कारयोः to injure, to encourage; यातयति-ते pre. यातयिष्यति-ते fut. अयीयतत्-त aor. यियातयिषति-ते des.

यन्त्र् 10 U. संकोचे to restrain, &c; यन्त्रयति-ते pre. यन्त्रयाञ्चकार-चक्रे, &c. perf. यन्त्रयिता p. fut. यन्त्रयिष्यति-ते fut. अययन्त्रत्-त aor. यियन्त्रयिषति-ते des. Pass.—यन्त्र्यते pre. यन्त्रित p.p. यन्त्रयित्वा ger.

यभ् 1 P. मैथुने to cohabit; यभति pre. ययाभ perf. यब्धा fut. यप्स्यति fut. अयप्स्यत् con. अयाप्सीत् aor. Cau.—याभयति-ते pre. अयीयभत्-त aor. यियप्सति des.

यम् 1 P. उपरमे to check, to offer, to lift up, to go, to show; यच्छति pre. ययाम perf. यन्ता p. fut. यंस्यति fut. अयंस्यत् con.

अयंसीत् aor. यम्यात् ben. यियंसति des. Cau.–यामयति-ते, नियमयति-ते pre. अयीयमत्-त aor. Pass.–यम्यते pre. यत p. p. यत्वा ger.

यम 10 U. परिवेषणे to surround; यमयति-ते pre. अयीयमत्-त aor

यस् 4 P. प्रयत्ने to strive, to endeavour; यसति.* यस्यति pre. ययास perf. यसिता p. fut. यसिष्यति fut. अयसत् aor. Cau.—यासयति-ते pre. (with आ A. only) यस्त p. p. यसित्वा, यस्त्वा ger. यसितुम् inf.

या 2 P. प्रापणे (प्रापणं गतिः) to do, to invade, to pass away; याति pre. ययौ perf. याता p. fut. यास्यति fut. अयासीत् aor. यायात् ben. यियासति des. Pass.—यायते pre. Cau.—यापयति-ते pre. अयीयपत्-त aor. यात p. p. यात्वा, प्रयाय ger. यातुम् inf.

याच् 1 P. A. याच्ञायाम् to beg, to demand in marriage; याचति-ते pre. ययाच-ययाचे perf. याचिता p. fut. याचिष्यति-ते fut. अयाचीत्, अयाचिष्ट aor. याच्यात्, याचिषीष्ट ben. Cau.–याचयति-ते pre. अययाचत्-त aor. याचित p. p. याचित्वा ger. याचितुम् inf

यु 2 P. मिश्रणेऽमिश्रणे च to join, to separate, यौति pre. युयाव perf. यविता p. fut. यविष्यति fut. अयवीत् aor. यूयात् ben. युयूषति or यियविषति des. Pass.—यूयते pre. अयावि aor. Cau.–यावयति-ते pre. अयीयवत्-त aor. युत p. p.

यु 9 U. बन्धने to join, to mix; युनाति or युनीते pre. युयाव or युयुवे perf. योता p. fut. योष्यति-ते fut. अयौषीत् or अयोष्ट aor. यूयात्, योषीष्ट ben. युयूषति-ते des. युत p. p.

यु 10 A. जुगुप्सायाम् to censure; यावयते pre. यावयाञ्चक्रे perf. यावयिता p. fut. अयीयवत aor. यियावयिषते des.

युज् 1 P. संयमने to unite, &c; योजति pre. युयोज perf. योक्ता p. fut अयौक्षीत् aor. युयुक्षति des.

युज् 4 A. समाधौ to concentrate the mind; युज्यते pre. युयुजे perf. योक्ता p. fut. योक्ष्यते fut. अयोक्ष्यत con. अयुक्त aor. युक्षीष्ट ben. युयुक्षते des. Cau.–योजयति-ते pre. अयूयुजत्-त aor.

---

* यस् not preceded by a preposition except सम् optionally belongs to the 1st conj.; संयस्यति, संयसति.

युज् 7 U. योगे to unite, to put to, to appoint, to give, to prepare, &c; युनक्ति or युङ्क्ते pre. युयोज or युयुजे perf. योक्ता p. fut. योक्ष्यति-ते fut. अयुजत्, अयौक्षीत् or अयुक्त aor. युज्यात्, युक्षीष्ट ben. Pass.-युज्यते pre. Cau.-योजयति-ते pre. अयूयुजत्-त aor. युयुक्षति-ते des. युक्त p. p.

युज् 10 U. संयमने to join, &c; योजयति-ते pre. योजयाञ्चकार-चक्रे, perf. योजयिता p. fut. योजयिष्यति-ते fut. अयूयुजत्-त aor. युयोजिषति-ते des.

युज् 10 A. to censure; योजयते pre.

युत 1 A. भासने to shine; योतते pre. युयुते perf. योतिष्यते fut. अयोतिष्ट aor.

युध् 4 A. संप्रहारे to fight, to conquer in fight; युध्यते pre. युयुधे perf. योद्धा p. fut. योत्स्यते fut. अयोत्स्यत con. अयुद्ध aor. युत्सीष्ट ben. Pass.-युध्यते pre. अयोधि aor. Cau.—योधयति-ते pre. अयूयुधत्-त aor. युयुत्सते des. युद्ध p. p.

युप् 4 P. विमोहने to blot out, to trouble, to make smooth; युप्यति pre. युयोप perf. योपिता p. fut. अयुपत् aor.

यूष् 1 P. हिंसायाम् to injure, to kill; यूषति pre युयूष perf. अयूषीत् aor.

येष् 1 A. प्रयत्ने to try, to attempt; येषते pre. यियेषे perf. अयेषिष्ट aor.

यौट् (ड्) 1 P. to join, together; यौट(ड)ति pre. युयौट(ड) perf. अयौटी(डी)त् aor.

र—

रंह् 1 P. गतौ to move, to flow; रंहति pre. ररंह perf. रंहिता p. fut. अरंहीत् aor. Cau.—रंहयति-ते pre. अररंहत् त aor. रिरंहिषति des.

रक् 10 U. आस्वादने प्राप्तौ च, to taste, to get; राकयति ते pre. राकयिता p. fut. राकयाञ्चकार-चक्रे perf. अरीरकद्-त aor. Also रग्, रघ्.

रक्ष् 1 P. पालने to protect, to avoid; रक्षति pre. ररक्ष perf. रक्षिता p. fut. रक्षिष्यति fut. अरक्षीत् aor. रक्ष्यात् ben. Pass.–रक्ष्यते pre. Cau.–रक्षयति-ते pre. अररक्षत्–त aor. रिरक्षिषति des. रक्षित p. p.

रख 1 P. to go, to move; रखति pre. ररख perf. अरखीत्, अराखीत् aor.

रग् 1 P. शङ्कायाम् to doubt; रगति pre. रराग perf.

रङ्ग् 1 P. to go, to move; रङ्गति pre. ररङ्ग perf. अरङ्गीत् aor.

रङ्घ् 1 U. to go quick; रङ्घति-ते pre. ररंघ, ररङ्घे perf. रंघिता p. fut. अरंघीत्, अरंघिष्ट aor.

रंघ् 10 U. to shine, to speak; रंघयति-ते pre. रंघयाञ्चकार-चक्रे perf. अररंघत्-त, अरंघीत् aor.

रच् 10 U. प्रतियत्ने to arrange, to make, to write, to adorn, to direct; रचयति-ते pre. रचयाञ्चकार–चक्रे perf. रचयिता p. fut. रचयिष्यति-ते fut. अररचत्–त aor. रिरचयिषति-ते des. रचित p. p. रचयित्वा ger.

रञ्ज् 1 & 4 U. रागे to be coloured, to paint, to be pleased, to be devoted to, to be in love with; रजति-ते, रज्यति-ते pre. ररञ्ज or ररञ्जे perf. रङ्क्ता p. fut. रङ्क्ष्यति-ते fut. अरङ्क्ष्यत्-त con. अराङ्क्षीत or अरङ्क्त aor. रज्यात् or रङ्क्षीष्ट ben. रिरंक्षति-ते des. Cau.— to dye, &c; रञ्जयति-ते pre. अररञ्जत्-त aor.—to hunt deer, रजयति-ते pre. अरीरजत्-त aor. Pass.-रज्यते pre. रक्त p. p. रजत्, रजमान (1) रज्यत्, रज्यमान (4) pre. p. रङ्क्त्वा, रक्त्वा ger.

रट् 1 P. परिभाषणे to shout, to call out, to shout with joy; रटति pre. रराट perf. रटिता p. fut. अरटीत्, अराटीत् aor. रटित p. p.

रठ् 1 P. to speak; रठति pre. रराठ perf.

रण् 1 P. शब्दे to sound, to go, to rejoice (in the Vedas); रणति pre. रराण perf. रणिता p. fut. अरणीत्, अराणीत aor. Cau. राणयति-ते pre. अरीरणत्-त, अरराणत्-त aor. रिरणिषति des.

रद् 1 P. विलेखने to split; to gnaw, to dig; रदति pre. रराद perf. रदिता p. fut. रदिष्यति fut. अरदीत् or अरादीत् aor. रिरदिषति des.

रध् 4 P. हिंसासंराध्योः (संराद्धिर्निष्पत्तिः) to hurt, to destroy, to subdue, to finish, to accomplish, (to be completed, in the Vedas); रध्यति pre. ररन्ध perf. रधिता or रद्धा p. fut. रधिष्यति or रत्स्यति fut. अरधिष्यत्-अरत्स्यत् con. अरधत् aor. Pass.—रध्यते pre. अरन्धि aor. Cau.—रन्धयति-ते pre. अररन्धत्-त aor. रिरधिषति, रिरत्सति des. रद्ध p.p.

रप् 1 P. व्यक्तायां वाचि to speak distinctly, to praise (in the Vedas); रपति pre. रराप perf. अरपीद्, अरापीत्, aor. रिरपिषति des.

रफ् 1 P. हिंसायां गतौ च to go, to hurt; रफति pre. रराफ perf.

रभ् 1 A. राभस्ये to begin, to embrace, to long for, to act rashly; रभते pre. रेभे perf. रब्धा p. fut. रप्स्यते fut. अरप्स्यत con. अरब्ध aor. रप्सीष्ट ben. रिप्सते des. Cau.—रम्भयति-ते pre. अररम्भत्-त aor. Pass.—रभ्यते pre. अरम्भि aor. रब्ध p. p.

रम्* 1 A. to play, to rejoice at, to take rest; रमते pre. रेमे perf. रन्ता p. fut. रंस्यते fut. अरंस्यत con. अरंस्त, with वि, व्यरंसीत् aor. रंसीष्ट ben. रिरंसते des. Pass.—रम्यते pre. Cau.—रमयति-ते pre. अरीरमत्-त aor. रत p. p. रत्वा, आरम्य, आरत्य ger.

रम्भ् 1 P. शब्दे to sound; रम्भते pre. ररम्भे perf. रम्भिष्यते fut. अरम्भिष्ट aor. Pass.—रम्भ्यते

रय् 1 A. to go, to move; रयते pre. रेये perf. रयिता p. fut. अरयिष्ट aor. रयित p. p.

रस् 1 P. शब्दे to roar, to make a noise, to sing, to praise (in the Vedas); रसति pre. ररास perf. रसिता p. fut. अरसीद्, अरासीत् aor. रिरसिषति des.

---

* It is Parasm. when it is preceded by वि, आ, परि and उप.

रस् 10 U. आस्वादनस्नेहनयोः to taste, to feel; रसयति-ते pre. रसयाञ्चकार-चक्रे perf. अररसत्-त aor

रह् 1 P. त्यागे to quit, to desert; रहति pre. रराह perf. रहिता p. fut. रहिष्यति fut. अरहीत् aor. रिरहिषति des.

रह् 10 U. त्यागे to leave, to abandon; रहयति-ते pre. रहयाञ्चकार-चक्रे perf. रहयिता p. fut. रहयिष्यति-ते fut. अररहत्-त aor. रहित p.p. रहयित्वा ger.

रा 2 P. दाने to give, to bestow; राति pre. ररौ perf. राता p. fut. अरासीत् aor. Cau.-रापयति-ते pre. अरीरपत्-त aor. रिरासति des.

राख् 1 P. शोषणालमर्थयोः to be dry, to adorn, to be able, to suffice; राखति pre. रराख perf. अराखीत् aor.

राघ् 1 A. सामर्थ्ये to be able; राघते pre. रराघे perf. राघिष्यते fut. अराघिष्ट aor.

राज् 1 U. दीप्तौ to shine, to glitter, to appear, to direct, to be at the head; राजति-ते pre. रराज, रराजे, रेजे perf. राजिता p. fut. राजिष्यति-ते fut. अराजीत्, अराजिष्ट aor. राज्यात्, राजिषीष्ट ben. रिराजिषति-ते des. राजित p. p. राजित्वा, विराज्य ger.

राध् 4 P. वृद्धौ to grow, to prosper; राध्यति pre. रराध perf. राद्धा p. fut. रात्स्यति fut. अरात्स्यत् con. राध्यात् ben. अरात्सीत् (अराद्धाम् dual) aor. Cau.-अरीरधत्-त aor. रिरात्सति des.

राध् 5 P. संसिद्धौ हिंसायां च to accomplish, to kill, to propitiate; राध्नोति pre. रराध (2nd sing. with अप, अपरेधिथ) perf. रिरात्सति; (रित्सति wishes to kill) des. राद्धवत् pre. p.

रास् 1 A. शब्दे to cry, to yell, to sound; रासते pre. ररासे perf. अरासिष्ट aor. रिरासिषते des.

रि 6 P. to go, to move; रियति pre. रिराय perf. रेष्यति fut. अरैषीत् aor.

रि 5 P. to hurt; रिणोति pre. (Vedic). रिरीषति des.

रि 9 U. to drive out, to expel, to go, to hurt, to emit, to separate. (in the Vedas); रिणाति, रिणीते pre.

रिख् 1 P. गतौ to go; रेखति pre. रिरेख perf. रेखिष्यति fut. अरेखित् aor.

रिङ्ख् or रिङ्ग् 1 P. गतौ to crawl, to creep, to go slowly; रिङ्खति or रिङ्गति pre. रिरिङ्ख or रिरिङ्ग perf. अरिङ्खीत्, अरिङ्गीत् aor.

रिच् 7 U. विरेचने to empty, to clear, to deprive of, to give up; रिणक्ति or रिङ्क्ते pre. रिरेच or रिरिचे perf. रेक्ता p. fut. रेक्ष्यति-ते fut. अरेक्ष्यत्-त con. अरिचत्, अरैक्षीत्, अरिक्त aor. रिच्यात् or रिक्षीष्ट ben. Pass.—रिच्यते pre. अरेचि aor. Cau.—रेचयति-ते pre. अरीरिचत्-त aor. रिरिक्षति-ते des. रिक्त p.p. रिक्त्वा ger.

रिच् 1 & 10 P वियोजनसम्पर्चनयोः to divide, to leave, to come together; रेचति, रेचयति, pre. रिरेच, रेचयाञ्चकार perf. अरैक्षीत्, अरीरिचत्-त aor. रिरिक्षति, रिरेचयिषति-ते des. रेचित p. p.

रिफ् 6 P. कत्थनयुद्धनिन्दाहिंसादानेषु to boast, to speak, to fight, to utter a rough grafing sound, to give रिफति pre. रिरेफ perf. रेफिता p. fut. अरेफीत् aor. रिरिफिषति रिरेफिषति des. रिफित p.p. (also written as रिह्).

रिभ् 1 A. to crackle, to murmur, to chatter; रेभते pre. रिरिभे perf.

रिम्फ् 6 P. to hurt, to kill; रिम्फति pre. रिरिम्फ perf. रिम्फिता p. fut. अरिम्फीत् aor.

रिश् 6 P. हिंसायाम् to tear, to injure; रिशति pre. रिरेश perf. रेष्टा p. fut. रेक्ष्यति fut. अरेक्ष्यत् con. अरिक्षत् aor. रिरिक्षति des.

रिष् 1 & 4 P. हिंसायाम् to kill, to fail, to perish, to be injured;. रेषति, रिष्यति pre. रिरेष perf. रेषिता or रेष्टा p. fut. रेषिष्यति fut. अरेषीत् (1st cl.), अरिषत् (4th cl.) aor. रिरिषिषति, रिरेषिषति des. रिष्ट p.p.

री 4 A. स्रवणे to trickle, to ooze, to flow; रीयते pre. रिरिये perf. रेष्यते fut. अरेष्ट aor.

री 9 P. गतिरेषणयोः to go, to injure, to howl; रिणाति pre. रिराय perf. रेष्यति fut. अरैषीत् aor. रिरीषति des.

रीव् 1 U. to take, to cover; रीवति-ते pre.

रु 1 A. गतिरेषणयोः to go, to hurt, to break to pieces (in the

Vedas); रवते pre. रुरुवे perf. रविता p. fut. अराविष्ट aor. Cau.—रावयति-ते pre. अरीरवत्-त pre. रुरूषते des.

रु 2 P. शब्दे to cry, to yell, to hum as bees, to sound in general; रौति or रवीति pre. रुराव perf. रविता p. fut. रविष्यति fut. अरावीत् aor. रूयात् ben. रुरूषति des. Pass.—रूयते pre. Cau.—रावयति-ते pre. रुत p.p.

रुच् 1 A. दीप्तावभिप्रीतौ च to shine, to look beautiful, to be pleased with (a person); रोचते pre. रुरुचे perf. रोचिता p. fut. रोचिष्यते fut. अरुचत्, अरोचिष्ट aor. रुरुचिषते, रुरोचिषते des. Cau.—रोचयते pre. अरूरुचत aor. रुचित p.p.

रुज् 6 P. भङ्गे to break to pieces, to afflict, to pain; रुजति pre. रुरोज perf. रोक्ता p. fut. रोक्ष्यति fut. अरौक्षीत् (अरौक्ताम् dual). aor. Cau.—रोजयति-ते pre. अरूरुजत्-त aor. रुरुक्षति des. रुग्ण p.p. रुक्त्वा ger.

रुज् 10 U. हिंसायाम् to hurt, to kill; रोजयति-ते pre. रोजयाञ्चकार-चक्रे perf. रोजयिता p. fut. अरूरुजत्-त aor.

रुट् 1 A. प्रतिघाते to strike down; रोटते pre. रुरुटे perf. अरुटत्, अरोटिष्ट aor. रोटिषीष्ट ben.

रुट् 10 U. to obstruct, to resist, to shine, to speak; रोटयति-ते pre. रोटयाञ्चकार-चक्रे perf. अरूरुटत्-त aor.

रुठ् 1 P. उपघाते to strike; रोठति pre. रुरोठ perf. रोठिष्यति fut. अरोठीत् aor.

रुठ 10 U. भाषायां दीप्तौ च to speak, to shine; रोठयति-ते fut. रोठयाञ्चकार-चक्रे perf. अरूरुठत्-त aor.

रुठ् 1 A. to resist, to oppose, to torment, to suffer pain; रोठते pre. रुरुठे perf.

रुण्ट् 1 P. स्तेये to rob, steal; रुण्टति pre. रुरुण्ट perf. अरुण्टीत् Aor. Pass.—रुण्ट्यते pre. अरुण्टि aor.

रुण्ठ् 1 P. to go, to steal, to tame, to oppose; रुण्ठति pre. रुरुण्ठ perf. This is the same as the above root; also written as रुण्ड्.

रुद् 2 P. अश्रुविमोचने to cry, to weep, to roar; रोदिति pre. अरोदत्,

अरोदीत् Imperf. रुरोद perf. रोदिता p. fut. अरुदत् or अरोदीत् aor. रुद्यात् ben. रुरुदिषति des. Pass.—रुद्यते pre. अरोदि aor. Cau.—रोदयति-ते pre. अरूरुदत्-त aor. रुदित p.p.

रुध् 4 A. (with अनु) कामे to desire, to obey; रुध्यते pre. रुरुधे perf. रोत्स्यते fut. अरुद्ध aor. रुरुत्सते des.

रुध् 7 U. आवरणे to besiege, to oppose, to hold up, to oppress; रुणद्धि or रुन्द्धे pre. रुरोध or रुरुधे perf. रोद्धा p. fut. रोत्स्यति-ते fut. अरुधत्, अरौत्सीत्, अरुद्ध (अरौद्धाम्, अरुत्साताम् dual) aor. रुध्यात्, रुत्सीष्ट ben. रुरुत्सति-ते des. Pass.—रुध्यते pre. अरोधि aor. Cau.—रोधयति-ते pre. अरूरुधत्-त aor. रुद्ध p.p. रोद्धुम् inf.

रुप् 4 P. विमोहने to confound, to suffer, to violate, to pain (in the Vedas), to disturb; रुप्यति pre. रुरोप perf. अरुपत् aor. Cau.—रोपयति-ते pre. अरूरुपत् aor. रुरुपिषति, रुरोपिषति des.

रुश् 6 P. हिंसायाम् to hurt, to destroy; रुशति pre. रुरोश perf. अरुक्षत् aor. रुरुक्षति des.

रुंश् 10 U. 1 P. भाषायां दीप्तौ च to speak, to shine; रुंशयति-ते, रुंशति pre. रुंशयिष्यति, रुंशिष्यति fut. अरुरुंशत्-त, अरुंशीत् aor.

रुष् 1 P. हिंसायाम् to kill, to hurt, to be annoyed; रोषति pre. रुरोष perf. रोषिता or रोष्टा p. fut. रोषिष्यति fut. अरोषीत् aor. रुरुषिषति, रुरोषिषति des. रुषित्वा, रोषित्वा, रुष्ट्वा ger. रोषितुम्, रोष्टुम् inf.

रुष् 4 P. to kill, to hurt, to vex; रुष्यति pre. अरुषत् aor. (For the other forms see the above root).

रुष् 10 U. रोषे to be angry; रोषयति-ते pre. अरूरुषत्-त aor.

रुह् 1 P. बीजजन्मनि प्रादुर्भावे च to grow, to increase, to rise, to reach; रोहति pre. रुरोह perf. रोढा p. fut. रोक्ष्यति fut. रुह्यात् ben. अरुक्षत् aor. रुरुक्षति des. रूढ p.p. रूढ्वा, आरुह्य ger. रोढुम् inf.

रूक्ष् 10 U. पारुष्ये to be rough, to be unkind, to make dry, (in the Vedas); रूक्षयति-ते pre. रूक्षयाञ्चकार-चक्रे perf. रूक्षयिता p. fut. अरुरूक्षत्-त aor.

रूप् 10 U. रूपक्रियायाम् to find out, to form, to consider, to fix, to appoint; रूपयति-ते pre. रूपयाञ्चकार-चक्रे perf. रूपयिता p. fut. अरुरूपत्-त aor. रुरूपयिषति-ते des.

रूष् 1 P. भूषायाम् to adorn, to decorate, to anoint; रूषति pre. रुरूष perf. रूषिता p. fut. अरूषीत् aor. रूषित p.p.

रेक् 1 A. शङ्कायां to doubt, to suspect; रेकते pre. रिरेके perf. रेकिष्यते fut. अरेकिष्ट aor.

रेज् 1 A. to shine, to shake; रेजते pre.

रेट् 1 U. परिभाषणे to speak, to ask; रेटति pre. रिरेट perf. अरेटीत् aor.

रेप् 1 A. to go; रेपते pre. रेपिष्यते fut. अरेपिष्ट aor.

रेभ् 1 A. शब्दे to sound, to low; रेभते pre.

रेष 1 A. अव्यक्ते शब्दे to utter an indistinct sound, to neigh; रेषते pre. रिरेषे perf. रेषिता p. fut. अरेषिष्ट aor. रेषित p.p. (Also written as रेव्).

रै 1 P. to sound, to bark at; रायति pre. ररौ perf. अरासीत् aor.

रोड् 1 P. अनादरे उन्मादे च to despise; रोडति pre. रुरोड perf. अरोडीत् aor.

रौट् (रौड् also) 1 P. to despise, रौटति, रौडति pre.

ल—

लक् 10 U. आस्वादने प्राप्तौ च to taste, to obtain; लाकयति-ते pre. लाकयाञ्चकार-चक्रे perf. लाकयिता p. fut. अलीलकत्-त aor.

लक्ष् 1 A. आलोचने to perceive, to observe; लक्षते pre. ललक्षे perf. लक्षिता p. fut. अलक्षिष्ट aor. लक्षयिषीष्ट ben.

लक्ष् 10 U. दर्शनाङ्कनयोः to notice, to define, to regard; लक्षयति-ते pre. लक्षयाञ्चकार-चक्रे &c. perf. लक्षयिता p. fut. अललक्षत्-त aor लक्षित p.p. लिलक्षयिषति-ते des.

लख् or लङ्ख् 1 P. to go; लखति or लङ्खति pre.

लग 1 P. सङ्गे to attach oneself to, to touch, to meet, to follow closely; लगति pre. ललाग perf. लगिता p. fut. अलगीत् aor. लिलगिषति des. लग्न p.p.

लग 10 U. आस्वादने प्राप्तौ च to taste, to obtain; लागयति-ते pre. लागयाञ्चकार-चक्रे perf. लागयिता p. fut. अलीलगत्-त aor.

लङ्ग् 1 P. to go, to go lame; लङ्गति pre.

लंघ् 1 P. शोषणे to dry, (भाषायां दीप्तौ सीमातिक्रमे च) to speak, to shine, to transgress; A. गत्यर्थे भोजननिवृत्तौ च to go, to fast; लंघति-ते pre. ललंघ-ललङ्घे perf. लंघिता p. fut. अलंघीत् or अलंघिष्ट aor. लंघित p. p.

लंघ 10 U. to speak, to shine; लंघयति-ते pre. लंघयिष्यति-ते fut. अललंघत्-त aor. लङ्घ्यात्, लंघयिषीष्ट ben. लिलंघयिषति-ते des.

लच्छ् 1 P. लक्षणे to mark; लच्छति pre. ललच्छ perf.

लज् 1 P. भर्जने to fry; लजति per. ललाज perf. लाजिता p. fut. अलजीत्, अलाजीत् aor. (Also written as लज्ज्).

लज् 6 A. व्रीडने to be ashamed; लजते pre. लेजे perf. लजिता p. fut. अलजिष्ट aor. लिलजिषते des. लग्न p.p.

लज् 10 U. प्रकाशने to appear; लजयति-ते; अपवारणे to conceal, लाजयति ते pre. लजयाञ्चकार-चक्रे, लाजयाञ्चकार-चक्रे &c. perf. लजयिता, लाजयिता p. fut. अललजत्-त, अलीलजत्-त aor.

लञ्ज् 1 P. हिंसाबलादाननिकेतनेषु भाषायां दीप्तौ च to kill, to be powerful, to take, to dwell, to speak, to shine; लञ्जति pre. ललञ्ज perf. अलञ्जीत् aor.

लञ्ज् 10 U. (see the above root) to give also; लञ्जयति-ते pre. लञ्जयाञ्चकार-चक्रे perf. लञ्जयिता p. fut.

लट् 1 P. बाल्ये to be or act like a child, to prattle, to cry; लटति pre. ललाट perf. अलटीत् aor.

लड् 1 P. विलासे to play, to sport; लडति pre. अलडीत्, अलाडीत् aor.

लड 10 U. उपसेवायां to fondle, to caress; लाडयति-ते pre. लाडयाञ्चकार-चक्रे perf. अलीलडत्-त aor.

लप् 1 P. व्यक्तायां वाचि to talk in general, to wail, to whisper, to lament; लपति pre. ललाप perf. लपिता p. fut. अलपीत्, अलापीत् aor. Cau.—लापयति-ते pre. अलीलपत्-त aor. लिलापिषति des.

लभ् 1 A. प्राप्तौ to get, to take, to have, to be able, &c.; लभते pre.

लेभे perf. लब्धा p. fut. लप्स्यते fut. अलब्ध aor. लिप्सते des. Cau.—लम्भयति-ते pre. अललम्भत्-त aor. लब्ध p. p.

लम्ब् 1 A. शब्दे अवस्रंसने च to sound, to hang down, to sink, &c.; लम्बते pre. ललम्बे perf. लम्बिता p. fut. अलम्बिष्ट aor. Pass.—लम्ब्यते pre. अलम्बि aor. Cau.—लम्बयति-ते pre. अललम्बत्-त aor. लिलम्बिषते des. लम्बित p. p.

लय् 1 A. to go, to move; लयते pre. लेये perf. लयिता p. fut. अलयिष्ट aor.

लर्व् 1 P. to go, to move; लर्वति pre. ललर्व perf. अलर्वीत् aor.

लल् 1 P. विलासे to play, to move about; ललति pre. ललाल perf. ललिष्यति fut. अललीत् aor. लिललिषति des. Cau.—लालयति pre. अलीललत् aor. ललित p. p.

लल् 10 A. ईप्सायां to desire, to fondle; लालयते pre. लालयाञ्चक्रे perf. लालयिता p. fut. अलीललत aor. लिलालयिषते des.

लश् 10 U. शिल्पयोगे to use any art; लाशयति-ते pre. लाशयाञ्चकार-चक्रे perf. अलीलशत्-त aor. V. l. for लस्.

लष् 1 & 4 U. कान्तौ to wish, to long for; लषति-ते, लष्यति-ते pre. ललाष or लेषे perf. लषिता p. fut. अलषीत्, अलाषीत्, अलषिष्ट aor. लिलषिषति des. लषित p. p.

लस् 1 P. श्लेषणक्रीडनयोः to appear, to embrace, to play, to shine; लसति pre. ललास perf. लसिता p. fut. अलसीत्-अलासीत् aor. Cau.—लासयति-ते pre. अलीलसत्-त aor. लिलसिषति des. लसित p. p.

लस् 10 U. शिल्पयोगे See लश् above.

लस्ज् 1 A. व्रीडने to be ashamed, to blush; लज्जते pre. ललज्जे perf. लज्जिता p. fut. अलज्जिष्ट aor. Pass.—लज्ज्यते pre. अलज्जि aor. Cau.—लज्जयति-ते pre. अललज्जत्-त aor. लिलज्जिषते des. लग्न p. p.

ला 2 P. आदाने दाने च to take, to obtain; लाति pre. ललौ perf. लाता p. fut. अलासीत् aor. Cau.—लापयति-ते, लालयति-ते (to cause to melt) pre. अलीलपत्-त, अलीलयत्-त aor. लिलासति des.

लाख् 1 P. शोषणालमर्थयोः to be dry, to adorn, to suffice; लाखति pre. अलाखीत् aor. Cau.—लाखयति-ते.

लाघ् 1 A. सामर्थ्ये to be equal to or able; लाघते pre. अलाघिष्ट aor.

लाज् or लांज् 1 P. भर्जने भर्त्सने च to fry; to blame; लाजति or लांजति pre. अलाजीत, अलांजीत् Aor.

लाञ्छ् 1 P. लक्षणे to mark; लाञ्छति pre. अलांछीत् aor.

लिख् 6 P. अक्षरविन्यासे to write, to rub, to touch, to peck as a bird; लिखति pre. लिलेख perf. लेखिता p. fut. अलेखीत् aor. लिलिखिषति or लिलेखिषति des. Cau.—लेखयति-ते pre. अलीलिखत्-त aor.

लिङ्ग् 1 P. to go, to move; लिङ्गति pre.

लिङ्ग् 1 P, to go, to move; लिङ्गति pre. लिलिङ्ग perf. लिङ्गिता p. fut. अलिङ्गीत aor. लिङ्गित p. p.

लिङ्ग् 10 U. चित्रीकरणे to paint, to inflect (a noun); लिङ्गयति-ते pre. लिङ्गयाञ्चकार-चक्रे &c. perf. लिङ्गयिता p. fut. अलिलिङ्गत्-त aor.

लिप् 6 U. उपदेहे (उपदेहो वृद्धिः) to anoint, to cover, to stain; लिंपति-ते pre. लिलेप, लिलिपे perf. लेप्ता p. fut. लेप्स्यति-ते fut. अलिपत्-त, अलिप्त aor. Cau.—लेपयति-ते pre. अलीलिपत्-त aor. लिलिप्सति-ते des. लिप्त p. p.

लिश् 4 A. अल्पीभावे to be small or reduced; लिश्यते fut. लिलिशे perf. लेक्ष्यते fut. अलिक्षत aor. Cau.-लेशयति-ते pre. अलीलिशत्-त aor. लिलिक्षते des. लिष्ट p. p.

लिश 6 P. to go; लिशति pre. लिलेश perf. अलिक्षत aor. लिलिक्षति des.

लिह् 2 U. आस्वादने to lick, to taste; लेढि, लीढे pre. लिलेह, लिलिहे perf. लेढा p. fut. लेक्ष्यति-ते fut. अलिक्षत्-त, अलीढ aor. लिह्यात्, लिक्षीष्ट ben. लिलिक्षति-ते des. लीढ p. p.

ली 1 P. & 10 U. द्रवीकरणे to melt, to dissolve; लयति, लाययति-ते pre. लिलाय. लाययाञ्चकार-चक्रे &c. perf. अलैषीत्, अलीलयत्-त aor. लिलीषति, लिलाययिषति-ते des.

ली 4 A. श्लेषणे to stick, to lie on; लीयते pre. लिल्ये perf. लेता, लाता

p. fut. लेष्यते, लास्यते fut. अलेष्ट, अलास्त aor. लेषीष्ट लासीष्ट ben. Cau.—लाययति-ते pre. लिलीषते des. लीन p.p. लीत्वा, विलाय, विलीय ger.

ली 9 P. श्लेषणे to adhere, to melt; लिनाति pre. लिलाय, ललौ perf. लेता, लाता p. fut. लेष्यति, लास्यति fut. अलैषीत्, अलासीत् aor. लिलीषति des.

लुञ्च् 1 P. अपनयने to pluck, to pull, to tear off; लुञ्चति pre. लुलुञ्च perf. लुञ्चिता p. fut. अलुञ्चीत् aor. लुलुञ्चिषति des. लुञ्चित p.p.

लुञ्ज् 1 P. & 10 U. हिंसाबलादाननिकेतनेषु भाषायां दीप्तौ च to kill, to be strong &c. लुञ्जति, लुञ्जयति-ते pre. अलुञ्जीत्, अलुलुञ्जत्-त aor.

लुट् 1 A. प्रतिघाते to oppose; लोटते pre. लुलुटे perf. लोटिता p. fut. अलुटत्, अलोटिष्ट aor. लुलुटिषते des.

लुट् 1 P. विलोडने to roll, to wallow on the ground; लोटति pre. लुलोट perf. लोटिता p. fut. अलोटीत् aor. लुलुटिषति or लुलोटिषति des. Cau.—लोटयति-ते pre. अलूलुटत्-त, अलुलोटत्-त aor. लुटित, लोटित p. p.

लुट् 4 P. to roll, &c.; लुट्यति pre. लुलोट perf. लोटिता p. fut; अलुटत् aor. (See the above root for the other forms.)

लुट् 6 P. (कुटादिः) संश्लेषणे see लुट् below.

लुट् 10 U. भाषायां दीप्तौ च to speak, to shine; लोटयति-ते pre. लोटयाञ्चकार-चक्र &c. perf. लोटयिता p. fut.

लुठ् 1 P. उपघाते to strike, to knock down; लोटति pre. लुलोट perf. लोटिता p. fut. अलोटीत् aor. Cau.—अलूलटत्-त, अलुलोटत्-त aor.

लुठ् 1 A. प्रतिघाते to oppose, to roll; लोठते pre. लुलुठे perf. लोठिता p. fut. अलुठत्, अलोठिष्ट aor.

लुठ 6 P. संश्लेषणे (कुटादिः) to wallow; लुठति pre. लुलोठ perf. लुठिष्यति fut. अलुठीत् aor. लुलुठिषति des.

लुड 1 P. विलोडने to stir, to churn; लोडति pre. लुलोड perf. लोडिता p. fut. अलोडीत्-aor. Cau.—लोडयति-ते pre. लुलुडिषति des.

लुड् 6 P. (कुटादिः) to cover, to adhere; लुडति pre. (See लुट above for the other forms.)

लुण्ट् 1 P. स्तेये to rob, to be lazy; लुण्टति pre. लुलुण्ट perf. लुण्टिष्यति fut. अलुण्टीत् aor.

लुण्ट् 10 U. see लुण्ठ below.

लुण्ठ् 1 P. आलस्ये प्रतिघाते च to be idle, to agitate; लुण्ठति pre. लुण्ठिष्यति fut. अलुण्ठीत् aor. Cau. लुण्ठयति-ते pre. अलुलुण्ठत् त aor. लुलुण्ठिषति des.

लुण्ठ् 10 U. स्तेये to rob, to plunder; लुण्ठयति-ते pre. लुण्ठयिष्यति-ते fut. अलुलुण्ठत्-त aor.

लुण्ड् 10 U. to plunder; लुण्डयति-ते pre. लुण्डयाञ्चकार-चक्रे perf. (Same as लुण्ट्)

लुन्थ् 1 P. हिंसाक्लेशनयोः to strike, to kill; लुन्थति pre. लुलुन्थ perf. लुन्थिष्यति fut. अलुन्थीत् aor.

लुप् 4 P. विमोहने to confound, to be destroyed; लुप्यति pre. लुलोप perf. लोपिता p. fut. अलुपत् aor. Cau.—लोपयति-ते pre. अलूलुपत्-त, अलुलोपत्-त aor. लुलुपिषति, लुलोपिषति, des. लुप्त्वा, लुपित्वा, लोपित्वा ger. लुप्त p. p.

लुप् 6 U. छेदने to break, to take away, to seize, to suppress; लुम्पति-ते pre. लुलोप, लुलुपे perf. लोप्ता p. fut. अलुपत्, अलुप्त aor. लुप्यात्, लुप्सीष्ट ben. लुलुप्सति-ते des. Pass.—लुप्यते pre. अलोपि aor. Cau.—(See the above root); लुप्त p. p.

लुभ् 1 & 4 P. गार्ध्ये to covet, to be perplexed; लोभति, लुभ्यति pre. लुलोभ perf. लोभिता, लोब्धा p. fut. अलोभीत् (1) अलुभत् (4) aor. Cau.—लोभयति-ते pre. अलूलुभत्-त aor. लुलुभिषति, लुलोभिषति des. लुब्ध p. p.

लुभ् 6 P. विमोहने to be bewildered, to confound; लुभति pre. अलोभीत् aor. लुभित p. p.

लुम्ब् 1 P. अर्दने to torment; लुम्बति pre. अलुम्बीत् Aor.

लू 9 U. छेदने to divide, to cut off; लुनाति, लुनीते pre. लुलाव, लुलुवे

perf. लविता p. fut. अलावीत, अलविष्ट aor. लूयात्, लविषीष्ट ben. लुलूषति-ते des. Cau.—लावयति-ते pre. लून p. p.

लूष 1 P. भूषायां; लूषति pre. लुलूष perf. अलूषीत् aor.

लूष 10 U. हिंसायां to injure, to rob; लूषयति-ते pre. लूषयाञ्चकार-चक्रे perf. अलूलुषत-त aor.

लेख् 4 P. स्खलने to stumble; लेख्यति pre. अलेखीत् aor.

लेप् 1 A. to go, to worship; लेपते pre. अलेपिष्ट aor.

लैण् 1 P. to go, to send, to embrace; लैणति pre. अलैणीत् aor.

लोक् 1 A. दर्शने to see, to perceive; लोकते pre. लुलोके perf. लोकिता p. fut. अलोकिष्ट aor. लुलोकिषते des. Cau.—लोकयति-ते pre. अलुलोकत्-त aor. लोकित p. p.

लोक् 10 U. भाषायां दीप्तौ च to behold, to shine, to know, to seek; लोकयति-ते pre. लोकयाञ्चकार-चक्रे perf. लोकयिता p. fut. अलुलोकत्-त aor. लुलोकयिषति-ते des.

लोच् 1 A. दर्शने to see; लोचते pre. लुलोचे perf. लोचिता p. fut. अलोचिष्ट aor. लोचित p. p.

लोच् 10 U. to speak, to shine; लोचयति-ते pre. लोचयाञ्चकार चक्रे-आस-बभूव perf. लोचयिता p. fut. अललोचत्-त aor. (See लोक् 10 above).

लोट् 1 P. धौर्त्ये पूर्वभावे स्वप्ने च to deceive, to precede; लोटति pre. लुलोट perf. अलोटीत् aor.

लोड् 1 A. संघाते to heap up; लोटते pre. लुलोटे perf. अलोटिष्ट aor.

व—

वक्ष् 1 P. रोषे संघाते च to be angry, to grow; वक्षति pre. ववक्ष perf. वक्षिष्यति fut. अवक्षीत aor.

वख्-वङ्ख् 1 P. to go, to move; वखति, वङ्खति pre. ववाख, ववङ्ख perf.

वङ्क् 1 A. कौटिल्ये गतौ च to be crooked, to go; वङ्कते pre. अवङ्किष्ट aor.

वङ्ग् 1 P. to go; वङ्गति pre.; same as वङ्क्.

वच् 2 P. परिभाषणे to speak, to relate; वक्ति pre. उवाच perf. वक्ता p. fut. वक्ष्यति fut. अवोचत् aor. उच्यात् ben. विवक्षति des. Cau.—वाचयति-ते pre. अवीवचत्-त aor.

वच् 1 P. & 10 U. to speak, to read; वचति, वाचयति-ते pre. उवाच, वाचयाञ्चकार-चक्रे, &c. perf. वक्ता, वाचयिता p. fut. अवाक्षीत्, अवीवचत्-त aor. उक्त, वाचित p. p.

वज् 1 P. to go, to roam about; वजति pre. ववाज perf. वजिता p. fut. अवजीत्, अवाजीत् aor.

वज् 10 U. to trim, to go; वाजयति-ते pre. वाजयामास &c. perf. अवीवजत्-त aor.

वञ्च् 1 P. to go, to arrive at; वञ्चति pre. ववञ्च perf. वञ्चिता p. fut. अवञ्चीत् aor. विवञ्चिषति des. वञ्चित p. p. Pass.—वच्यते pre. अवञ्चि aor.

वञ्च् 10 A. प्रलम्भने to cheat; वञ्चयते pre. वञ्चयामास &c. perf. अववञ्चत aor. विवञ्चयिषते des.

वट् 1 P. वेष्टने to surround, to cover; वटति pre. ववाट perf. अवटीत्, अवाटीत् aor.

वट् 10 U. ग्रन्थे, विभाजने to string, to divide, to surround; वटयति-ते pre. वटयाञ्चकार-चक्रे perf. अवीवटत्-त aor. विवटयिषति-ते des.

वठ् 10 P. स्थौल्ये to be strong or fat; वठति pre. ववाठ perf. अवठीत्, अवाठीत् aor.

वण् 1 P. शब्दे to sound; वणति pre. अवणीत्, अवाणीत् aor. विवणिषति des.

वण्ट् 1 P. &. 10 U. विभाजने to divide वण्टति, वण्टयति-ते pre. वण्टिष्यति, वण्टयिष्यति fut. अवण्टीत्, अववण्टत्-त aor.

वद् 1 P. व्यक्तायां वाचि to say, to tell, to lay down; वदति pre. उवाद perf. वदिता p. fut. अवादीत् aor. विवदिषति des. Pass.—उद्यते pre. अवादि aor. उदित p. p.

वद् 1 & 10 U. संदेशवचने to inform; वदति-ते, वदयति-ते pre. ववाद, ववदे, वादयाञ्चकार &c. perf. अवादीत्, अवदिष्ट, अवीवदत्-त aor.

वन् 1 P. शब्दे सम्भक्तौ च to sound, to honour, to aid; वनति pre. ववान perf. वनिष्यति fut. अवनीत्, अवानीत् aor. Cau.—वानयति-ते pre. विवनिषति des.

वन् 8 A. (P. according to चन्द्र) to beg, to seek for; वनुते pre. वेने perf. अवनिष्ट, अवत aor. विवानिषते des.

वन् 1 P. & 10 U to favour, to injure, to sound; वनति, वानयति-ते pre.

वन्द् 1 A. अभिवादनस्तुत्योः to salute, to adore, to praise; वन्दते pre. ववन्दे perf. वन्दिता p. fut. अवन्दिष्ट aor. विवन्दिषते des. Pass.—वन्द्यते pre. वन्दित p. p.

वप् 1 U. बीजसन्ताने छेदने च to sow, to scatter, to weave, to cut, to shave; वपति-ते pre. उवाप, ऊपे perf. वप्ता p. fut. अवाप्सीत्, अवप्त aor. उप्यात्, वप्सीष्ट ben. Cau.—वापयति-ते pre. अवीवपत्-त aor. विवप्सति-ते des. Pass.—उप्यते pre. अवापि aor.

वभ्र् 1 P. to go; वभ्रति pre. अवभ्रीत् aor.

वम् 1 P. उद्गिरणे to vomit, to pour out; वमति pre. ववाम perf. वमिता p. fut. अवमीत् aor. Cau.—वमयति-ते, वामयति-ते (with a prep. वमयति-ते only) pre. अवीवमत्-त aor. वमित, (वान्त according to some) p. p.

वय् 1 A. to go; वयते pre. वयिष्यते fut. अवयिष्ट aor.

वर् 10 U ईप्सायां to ask for, to get; वरयति-ते pre. वरयाञ्चकार-चक्रे perf. वरयिता p. fut. अववरत्-त aor.

वर्च् 1 A. दीप्तौ to shine, to be bright; वर्चते pre. ववर्चे perf. अवर्चिष्ट aor.

वर्ण् 10 U. वर्णक्रियाविस्तरगुणवचनेषु प्रेरणे च to colour, to explain, to extol, to send, to grind; वर्णयति-ते pre. वर्णयाञ्चकार-चक्रे-आस-बभूव perf. वर्णयिता p. fut. अववर्णत्-त aor. विवर्णयिषति ते des. वर्णित p. p.

वर्ध् 10 U. छेदनपूरणयोः to cut, to fill; वर्धयति-ते pre. अववर्धत्-त aor. विवर्धयिषति-ते des.

वर्ष् 1 A. स्नेहने to love; वर्षते pre. अवर्षिष्ट aor.

वल् 1 A. संवरणे, सञ्चरणे च to cover, to move about; वलते per. वलिष्यते fut. अवलिष्ट aor. विवलिषति-ते des.

वल्क् 10 U. परिभाषणे to speak; वल्कयति-ते pre. वल्कयाञ्चकार-चक्रे perf. अववल्कत्-त aor.

वल्ग् 1 U. to go, to dance, to be pleased, to eat; वल्गति-ते pre. ववल्ग, ववल्गे perf. वल्गिता p. fut. अवल्गीत्, अवल्गिष्ट aor. वल्गित p. p.

वल्भ् 1 A. भोजने to eat; वल्भते pre. अवल्भिष्ट aor.

वल्ल् 1 A. संवरणे to cover or be covered; वल्लते pre. ववल्ले perf.

वल्ह् 1 A. परिभाषणहिंसाप्रदानेषु to speak, to be prominent, to kill, to give; वल्हते pre. ववल्हे perf. अवल्हिष्ट aor.

वश् 2 P. कान्तौ to wish, to shine; वष्टि pre. उवाश perf. वशिता p. fut. अवशीत्, अवाशीत् aor. उश्यात् ben. विवशिषति des. Pass.—उश्यते pre. अवाशि aor. उशित p. p.

वष् 1 P. हिंसायां to injure, to kill; वषति pre. ववाष perf. अवषीत्, अवाषीत् aor.

वस् 1 P. निवासे to dwell, to be, to spend (time); वसति pre. उवास perf. वस्ता p. fut. अवात्सीत् aor. उष्यात् ben. विवत्सति des, Pass.—उष्यते pre. अवासि aor. Cau.—वासयति-ते pre. अवीवसत्-त aor. उषित p. p. उषित्वा, प्रोष्य ger.

वस् 2 A. आच्छादने to wear, to put on; वस्ते pre. ववसे perf. वसिता p. fut. अवसिष्ट aor. Cau.—वासयति-ते pre. अवीवसत्-त aor. विवसिषते des. वसित p. p.

वस् 4 P. स्तम्भे to be straight, to be firm, to fix; वस्यति pre. वसिष्यति fut. अवसत् aor. वस्त p. p. वसित्वा, वस्त्वा ger. वसितुम् inf.

वस् 10 U. स्नेहच्छेदापहरणेषु to love, to cut, to take away; वासयति-ते pre. वासयिष्यति-ते fut. अवीवसत्-त aor. वास्यात्, वासयिषीष्ट ben.

वस् 10 U. निवासे to dwell; वसयति-ते pre. वसयिता p. fut. अववसत्-त aor.

वस्क् 1 A. to go; वस्कते pre. वास्कष्यते fut. अवस्किष्ट aor.

वस्त् 10 A. अर्दने to hurt, to kill, to ask, to go; वस्तयते pre. वस्तयाञ्चक्रे perf. अववस्तत aor. (Also written as बस्त्).

वह् 1 U. प्रापणे to bear along, to carry, to flow, to marry (with उद्) &c. वहति-ते pre. उवाह, ऊहे perf. वोढा p. fut. वक्ष्यति-ते fut. अवाक्षीत्, अवोढ aor. उह्यात, वक्षीष्ट ben. विवक्षति-ते des. Cau.-वाहयति-ते pre. अवीवहत्-त aor. ऊढ p.p.

वा 2 P. गतिगन्धनयोः to blow, to go, to strike, to kill; वाति pre. ववौ perf. वाता p. fut. अवासीत् aor. वायात् ben. Cau.—to cause to blow, वापयति-ते; to shake, वाजयति-ते pre. विवासति des. वात p.p. (with निर्-निर्वाण when वात 'wind' is not the subject; as निर्वाणो मुनिरग्निर्वा).

वांक्ष् 1 P. कांक्षायां to wish, to desire, वांक्षति pre. वांक्षिष्यति fut. अवांक्षीत् aor.

वाञ्छ् 1 P. वाञ्छायाम् to wish, to desire, to seek for; वाञ्छति pre. ववाञ्छ perf. वाञ्छिता p. fut. अवाञ्छीत् aor. विवाञ्छिषति des. Pass.—वाञ्छ्यते pre. अवाञ्छि aor.

वाड् 1 A. to bathe, to dive; वाडते pre. ववाडे perf.

वात् 10 U. सुखसेवनयोः to be happy, to serve; वातयति-ते pre. वातयिष्यति-ते fut. अववातत्-त aor. विवातयिषति-ते des.

वाश् 4 A. शब्दे to roar, to hum; वाश्यते pre. ववाशे pre. वाशिता p. fut. अवाशिष्ट aor. वाशित p.p.

वास् 10 U उपसेवायां to scent, to make fragrant; वासयति-ते pre. वासयाञ्चकार-चक्रे &c. perf. वासयिता p. fut. अववासत्-त aor. विवासयिषति-ते des.

वाह् 1 A. प्रयत्ने to try, to make an effort; वाहते pre. ववाहे perf. अवाहिष्ट aor.

विच् 7 U. पृथग्भावे to separate &c.; विनक्ति, विङ्क्ते pre. विवेच, विविचे perf. वेक्ता p. fut. अविचत्, अवैक्षीत्, अविक्त aor. विच्यात्, विक्षीष्ट ben. विविक्षति-ते des. विक्त p.p.

विच्छ् 6 P. to go; विच्छायति pre. विविच्छ, विच्छाञ्चकार &c. perf. विच्छिता, विच्छायिता p. fut अविच्छीत् अविच्छायीत aor. Cau.—विच्छयति-ते, विच्छापयति-ते pre. अविविच्छत्-त, अविविच्छायत्-त aor. विविच्छिषति, विविच्छायिषति des. Pass.-विच्छ्यते, विच्छाय्यते pre.

विच्छ् 10 U. भाषायां दीप्तौ च to speak, to shine; विच्छयति-ते pre. विच्छयाञ्चकार-चक्रे p rf. अविविच्छत्-त aor.

विज् 3 U. पृथग्भावे to spearate to distinguish; वेवेक्ति, वेविक्ते pre. विवेज, विविजे perf. वेक्ष्यति-ते fut. अविजत्, अवैक्षीत्, अविक्त aor. विविक्षति-ते des.

विज् 6 A. भयचलनयोः to fear, to tremble; विजते pre. विविजे perf. विजिता p. fut. अविजिष्ट aor. Cau.—वेजयति pre. अवीविजत् aor. विविजिषति des.

विज् 7 P. to shake, to fear: विनक्ति pre. विवेज perf. विजिता p. fut. अविजीत् aor. विविजिषति des.

विट् 1 P. आक्रोशे शब्दे च to curse, to sound, to rail at; वेटति pre. विवेट perf. अवेटीत् aor.

विड् same as विट्.

विडम्ब् 10 U. विडम्बने to mock, to deceive; विडम्बयति-ते pre. अविविडम्बत्-त aor.

विथ् 1 A. याचने to beg; वेथते pre. वेथिष्यते fut. अवेथिष्ट aor.

विद् 2 P. ज्ञाने to know, to regard; वेत्ति, वेद pre. विवेद, विदाञ्चकार perf. वेदिष्यति fut. अवेदीत् aor. विद्यात् ben. विदित p.p. Cau.—वेदयति-ते pre. अवीविदत्-त aor. विविदिषति-ते des.

विद् 4 A.. सत्तायां to happen, to be; विद्यते pre. विविदे perf. वेत्ता p. fut. वेत्स्यते fut. अवित्त aor. वित्सीष्ट ben. विवित्सते des. वित्त p.p.

विद् 6 U. लाभे to get, to find, to feel; विन्दति-ते pre. विवेद, विविदे perf. वेदिता, वेत्ता p. fut. अविदत्, आवित्त. अवेदिष्ट aor. विद्यात्, वेदिषीष्ट, वित्सीष्ट ben. विवित्सति-ते, विवि-वे-दिषति-ते des. विन्न (वित्त) p.p.

विद् 7 A. विचारणे to discuss, to consider; विन्त्ते pre. विविदे perf. वित्त or विन्न p. p. For other forms see विद् 4 A.

विद् 10 A. चेतनाख्याननिवासेषु to feel, to tell, to dwell; वेदयते pre. वेदयाञ्चक्रे perf. वेदयिता p. fut. अवीविदत aor. विवेदयिषते des. Pass.–वेद्यते pre. अवेदि aor.

विधू 6 P. विधाने to pierce: विधति pre. वेधिष्यति fut. अवेधीत् aor. Cau.—वेधयति-ते pre. अवीविधत्–त aor.

विश् 6 P. प्रवेशने to enter, to fall to the share of; विशति pre. विवेश perf. वेष्टा p. fut. अविक्षत्-त aor. विविक्षति des. विष्ट p. p.

विष 1 P. सेचने to sprinkle, to pour out; वेषति pre. विवेष perf. वेक्ष्यति fut. अविक्षत् aor. विष्ट p.p.

विष 3 U. व्याप्तौ to pervade, to surround; वेवेष्टि. वेविष्टे pre. विवेष, विविषे perf. वेष्टा p. fut. अविक्षत्, अविक्षत aor. विविक्षति-ते des.

विष 9 P. विप्रयोगे to separate; विष्णाति pre. विवेष perf. अविक्षत् aor.

विष्क् 10 A हिंसायां to kill; U. दर्शने to see; विष्कयते, विष्कयति-ते pre. अविविष्कत, अविविष्कत्-त aor.

वी 2 P. गतिव्याप्तिप्रजननकान्त्यसनखादनेषु to go, to pervade, to conceive, to be born, to shine, to botain, to throw, to be beautiful, to desire, to eat; वेति pre. विवाय perf. वेता p. fut. अवैषीत् aor. वीयात् ben. विवीषति des. Cau.—वाययति-ते, (वापयति-ते) pre. वीत p.p.

वीज् 10 U. व्यजने to fan; वीजयति-ते pre. अवीविजत्-त aor.

वीर् 10 A. विक्रान्तौ to display valour; वीरयते pre. वीरयिष्यते fut. अविवीरत aor.

वृ 1 U. आवरणे to cover. to surround: वरति-ते pre. (See the following root).

वृ 5 U. वरणे to choose, &c.; वृणोति, वृणुते pre. ववार, वव्रे perf. वरिता, वरीता p. fut. अवारीत, अवरिष्ट, अवरीष्ट, अवृत aor. व्रियात्, वरिषीष्ट, वृषीष्ट ben. Cau.-वारयति-ते pre. अवीवरत्-त aor. विवरिषति-ते, विवरीषति-ते, वुवूर्षति-ते des.

9 A. to choose &c.; वृणीते pre. वव्रे perf. (Same as the above A.).

वृक् 1 A. आदाने to take, to accept; वर्कते pre. ववृके perf. वर्किष्यते fut. अवर्किष्ट aor. विवर्किषते des.

वृक्ष् 1 A. आवरणे to cover; वृक्षते pre. ववृक्षे perf. अवृक्षिष्ट aor.

वृच् 7 P. वर्जने to choose; वृणक्ति pre. ववर्च perf. वर्चिष्यति fut. अवर्चीत् aor. वृक्त p.p.

वृज् 2 A. वर्जने to avoid, to shun; वृक्ते pre. ववृजे perf. वर्जिष्यते fut. अवर्जिष्ट aor. विवर्जिषते des.

वृज् 7 P. वर्जने to avoid, to choose, to turn away, to move, to hurt: वृणक्ति pre. ववर्ज perf. वर्जिता p. fut. अवर्जीत् aor. विवर्जिषति des.

वृज् 1 P. & 10 U. to shun, to abandon, to exclude &c.; वर्जति, वर्जयति-ते pre. ववर्ज, वर्जयाञ्चकार-चक्रे &c. perf. वर्जिता, वर्जयिता p. fut. अवर्जीत्, अवीवृजत्-त, अववर्जत्-त aor.

वृञ्ज् 2 A. वर्जने to avoid; वृङ्क्ते pre. वृञ्जिष्यते fut. अवृञ्जिष्ट aor.

वृण् 6 P. प्रीणने to give pleasure; वृणति pre. ववर्ण perf. अवर्णीत् aor.

वृत्* 1 A. वर्तने to exist, to happen, to live on, to occupy &c.; वर्तते pre. ववृते perf. वर्तिता p. fut वर्तिष्यते, वर्त्स्यति fut. अवृतत्, अवर्तिष्ट aor. वर्तिषीष्ट ben. विवर्तिषते, विवृत्सति des. Cau.—वर्तयति-ते pre. अवीवृतत्-त, अववर्तत्-त aor. वृत्त p. p.

वृत् 4 A. वरणे to choose, to divide; वृत्यते pre. (See the above root.)

वृत् 1 P. & 10 U. भाषायां दीप्तौ च to speak, to shine; वर्तति, वर्तयति-ते pre. ववर्त, वर्तयाञ्चकार-चक्रे &c. perf. अवर्तीत्, अवीवृतत्-त, अववर्तत्-त aor.

वृध्* 1 A. वृद्धौ to grow; वर्धते pre. ववृधे perf. वर्धिता p. fut. वर्धिष्यते, वर्त्स्यति fut. अवृधत्, अवर्धिष्ट aor. वर्धिषीष्ट ben. वृद्ध p.p. विवर्धिषते, विवृत्सति des.

वृध् 1 P. & 10 U. भाषायां दीप्तौ च to speak, to shine; वर्धति, वर्धयति-ते pre. (See वृत् above).

वृश् 4 P. वरणे to choose; वृश्यति pre. ववर्श perf. वर्शिष्यति fut. अवृशत् aor.

वृष् 1 P. सेचनहिंसाक्लेशनेषु to rain, to pour forth, to torment; वर्षति pre ववर्ष perf. वर्षिता p. fut. अवर्षीत् aor. विवर्षिषति des. वृष्ट p. p.

---

* It is also Parasmaipadi in the 2nd future, conditional, aorist, and desiderative.

वृष् 10 A. शक्तिबन्धने to have virile power; वर्षयते pre. वर्षयिष्यते fut. अवीवृषत, अववर्षत aor.

वृह् 6 P. उद्यमने to exist, to work; (see बृह्).

वॄ 9 U. वरणे to choose; वृणाति, वृणीते pre. ववार, ववरे perf. वरिता, वरीता p. fut. अवारीत्, अवरिष्ट, अवरीष्ट, अवूर्ष्ट aor. वूर्यात्, वरिषीष्ट, वूर्षीष्ट ben. वुवूर्षति-ते, विवरिषति-ते, विवरीषति-ते des.

वेॆ 1 U. तन्तुसन्ताने to weave, to cover; वयति-ते pre. उवाय, ऊये, ऊवे, ववौ, वव perf. वाता p. fut. अवासीत्, अवास्त aor. ऊयात्, वासीष्ट ben. विवासति-ते des. Cau.—वाययति-ते pre. Pass.—ऊयते pre. अवायि aor. उत p.p. उत्वा, प्रवाय ger.

वेण् 1 U. गतिज्ञानचिन्तानिशामनवादित्रग्रहणेषु to go, to know, to contemplate &c.; वेणति-ते pre. विवेण, विवेणे perf. वेणिष्यति-ते fut. अवेणीत्, अवेणिष्ट aor.

वेथ् 1 A. याचने to beg, to solicit; वेथते pre. अवेथिष्ट aor.

वेन् Same as वेण् which see.

वेप 1 A. कम्पने to tremble, to quake; वेपते pre. विवेपे perf. वेपिता p. fut. अवेपिष्ट aor. Cau.—वेपयति-ते pre. अविवेपत्-त aor. विवेपिषते des.

वेल् 1 P. चलने to shake, to be wanton; वेलति pre. विवेल perf. वेलिता p. fut. अवेलीत् aor.

वेल् 10 U. कालोपदेशे to count the time; वेलयति-ते pre. वेलयाञ्चकार-चक्रे perf. वेलयिता p. fut. अविवेलत्-त aor.

वेल्ल् 1 P. चलने to go, to shake; वेल्लति pre. विवेल्ल perf. अवेल्लीत् aor.

वेवी 2 A. गतिव्याप्त्यादिषु to go, to obtain, to be pregnant, to pervade, to eat, to wish, to shine; वेवीते pre. अवेविष्ट aor. (Vedic).

वेष्ट् 1 A. वेष्टने to surround, to wind round, to dress; वेष्टते pre. विवेष्टे perf. वेष्टिता p. fut. अवेष्टिष्ट aor. Cau.—वेष्टयति-ते pre. विवेष्टिषते des.

वेह् 1 A. to endeavour; वेहते pre. विवेहे perf. अवेहिष्ट aor.

वै 1 P. शोषणे to dry, to be weary; वायति pre. ववौ perf. वास्यति fut. अवासीत् aor.

व्यच् 6 P. व्याजीकरणे to cheat, to surround, to pervade; विचति pre. विव्याच perf. व्यचिता p. fut. अव्यचीत्, अव्याचीत् aor. विच्यात् ben. Pass.-विच्यते pre. विव्यचिषति des. Cau.-व्याचयति-ते pre. विचित p.p.

व्यथ् 1 A. भयचलनयोः to fear, to be vexed or afflicted, to tremble; व्यथते pre. विव्यथे perf. व्यथिता p. fut. अव्यथिष्ट aor. Cau.-व्यथयति-ते pre. विव्यथिषते des. व्यथित p.p.

व्यध् 4 P. ताडने to hurt, to pierce; विध्यति pre. विव्याध perf. व्यद्धा p. fut. अव्यात्सीत् aor. विध्यात् ben. विव्यत्सति des. Pass.-विध्यते pre. Cau.—व्याधयति-ते pre. अविव्यधत्-त aor. विद्ध p.p.

व्यय् 1 U. to go; व्ययति-ते pre. वव्याय, वव्यये perf. व्ययिष्यति-ते fut. अव्ययीत्, अव्यायिष्ट aor.

व्यय् 10 U. वित्तसमुत्सर्गे to expend, to bestow; व्यययति-ते pre. व्यययाञ्चकार-चक्रे, &c. perf. व्यययिष्यति-ते fut. अवव्ययत्-त aor. विव्यययिषति-ते des.

व्युष् 4 P. दाहे विभागे च to burn, to separate; व्युष्यति pre. वुव्योष perf. व्योषिष्यति fut. अव्योषीत्, (अव्युषत् to separate) aor.

व्ये 1 U. संवरणे to cover, to sew; व्ययति-ते pre. विव्याय, विव्ये perf. व्याता p. fut. अव्यासीत्, अव्यास्त aor. वीयात्, व्यासीष्ट ben. विव्यासति-ते des. Pass.—वीयते pre. Cau.-व्याययति-ते pre. अविव्ययत्-त aor. वीत p. p.

व्रज् 1 P. to proceed, to pass away (as time); व्रजति pre. वव्राज perf. व्रजिता p. fut. अव्राजीत् aor. विव्रजिषति des. व्रजित p.p.

व्रज् 10 U. मार्गसंस्कारगत्योः to sweep the way, to go; व्राजयति-ते pre. अविव्रजत्-त aor.

व्रड् 6 P. संवरणे (कुटादि) to cover, to be gathered, to sink; व्रडति pre. व्रडिष्यति fut. अव्रडीत् aor.

व्रण् 1 P. शब्दे to sound; व्रणयति pre. वव्राण perf. अव्रणीत्, अव्राणीत् aor.

व्रण् 10 U. गात्रविचूर्णने to wound; व्रणयति-ते pre. व्रणयाञ्चकार-चक्रे perf. अवव्रणत्-त aor.

व्रश्च् 6 P. छेदने to cut, to tear, to wound; वृश्चति pre. वव्रश्च perf. व्रश्चिता, व्रष्टा p. fut. अव्राक्षीत्, अव्रश्चीत् aor. वृश्च्यात् ben. विव्रश्चिषति, विव्रक्षति des. Pass.-वृश्च्यते pre. वृक्ण p.p. व्रश्चितुम्, व्रष्टुम् inf.

व्री 4 A. वरणे to select; व्रीयते pr. विव्रिये perf. व्रेष्यते fut. अव्रेष्ट aor. व्रीण p.p.

व्री 9 P. to choose; व्रिणाति, व्रीणाति pre. व्रेष्यति fut. अव्रेषीत् aor.

व्रीड् 4 P. चोदने लज्जायां च to throw, to be ashamed; व्रीड्यति pre. विव्रीड perf. अव्रीडीत् aor.

ब्ली 9 P. वरणे to select, to go; ब्लिनाति pre. ब्लेष्यति fut. अब्लेषीत् aor. Cau —ब्लेपयति-ते pre.

श—

शंस् 1 P. स्तुतौ दुर्गतौ च to relate, to suggest, to praise, to hurt; शंसति pre. शशंस perf. शंसिता p. fut. अशंसीत् aor. शस्यात् ben. शिशंसिषति des. Pass.-शस्यते pre. अशंसि aor. शंसित्वा, शस्त्वा ger. शस्त p.p.; with आ A. इच्छायां to hope, to bless; आशंसते pre. आशंसिष्यते fut. आशंसिष्ट aor. आशंसिषीष्ट ben. आशिशंसिषते des.

शक् 4 U. मर्षणे to endure, to be able; शक्यति-ते pre. शशाक, शेके perf. शकिता, शक्ता p. fut. शकिष्यति-ते, शक्ष्यति-ते fut. अशकत्, अशकिष्ट, अशक्त aor. शिशकिषति-ते des.

शक् 5 P. शक्तौ to be able, to endure, to be powerful; शक्नोति pre. शशाक perf. शक्ता p. fut. अशकत् aor. शक्यात् ben. शिक्षति des. Pass.-शक्यते pre. Cau.—शाकयति-ते pre. अशीशकत्-त aor. शक्त p.p.

शङ्क् 1 A. शङ्कायां to doubt, to be afraid; शङ्कते pre. शशङ्के perf. शङ्किता p. fut. अशङ्किष्ट aor. शिशङ्किषते des. शङ्कित p.p.

शच् 1 A. व्यक्तायां वाचि to speak, to tell; शचते pre. शेचे perf. अशचिष्ट aor.

शट् 1 P. कैतवे to deceive, to hurt, to kill, to suffer; to pain; शठति pre. शशाठ perf. शठिता p. fut. अशठीत्, अशाठीत् aor.

शट् 10 U. सम्यगवभाषणे to speak well or ill, to deceive; शठयति-ते pre. शठयाञ्चकार &c. perf. शठयिता p. fut. अशशठत्-त aor. शठित p.p.

शट् 10 U. असंस्कारगत्योः to leave unfinished, to go; शाठयति-ते pre. शाठयिष्यति-ते fut. अशीशठत्-त Aor. शाठित p.p.

शठ् 10 A. श्लाघायां to flatter; शाठयते pre. शाठयिष्यते fut. अशीशठत aor. शठित p.p.

शण् 1 P. दाने गतौ च to give, to go; शणति pre. शशाण perf. शणिष्यति fut. अशणीत्, अशाणित् aor.

शद् 1 P. (but Atm. in conjugational tenses.) शातने to perish, to decay; शीयते pre. शशाद perf. शत्ता p. fut. अशदत् aor. शद्यात् ben. शिशत्सति des. Cau.-शातयति-ते, (also शादयति-ते) pre. शन्न p.p.

शप् 1 & 4 U. आक्रोशे to curse, to wear, to blame; शपति-ते, शप्यति-ते pre. शशाप, शेपे perf. शप्ता p. fut. अशाप्सीत्-अशप्त aor. शप्यात्, शप्सीष्ट ben. Pass.—शप्यते pre. Cau.—शापयति-ते pre. अशीशपत्-त aor. शिशप्सति-ते des. शप्त p. p.

शब्द् 10 U. to sound, to call out, to speak; शब्दयति-ते pre. शब्दयाञ्चकार-चक्रे perf. शब्दयिता p. fut. अशशब्दत्-त aor. शब्दित p.p.

शम् 4 P. उपशमे to grow calm, to put an end to, to stop; शाम्यति pre. शशाम perf. शमिता p. fut. अशमत् aor. शम्यात् ben. Pass.-शम्यते pre. Cau-शमयति-ते, शामयति-ते pre. शान्त p. p.

शम् 10 A. आलोचने to look at, to show; शामयते pre. शामयाञ्चक्रे &c. perf. शामयिता p. fut. अशीशमत aor. शिशामयिषते des.

शम्ब् 10 U. सम्बन्धने to accumulate, to collect together; शम्बयति-ते pre. शम्बयाञ्चकार-चक्रे &c. perf. अशशम्बत्-त Aor.

शर्ब् 1 P. to go, to injure, to kill; शर्बति pre. शशर्ब perf. अशर्बीत् Aor.

शर्व् 1 P. हिंसायाम् to kill; शर्वति pre.

शल् 1 A. चलनसंवरणयोः to shake, to agitate; शलते pre. शेले perf. शलिता p. fut. अशलिष्ट Aor.

शल् 1 P. to go, to run; शलति pre. शशाल perf.

शल्भ् 1 A. कत्थने to praise, to boast; शल्भते pre. शशल्भे perf.

शव् 1 P. to go, to approach, to utter; शवति pre. शशाव perf. अशवीत्, अशावीत् Aor.

शश् 1 P. प्लुतगतौ to leap, to jump; शशति pre. शशाश perf. शशिता p. fut. अशशीत्, अशाशीत् aor.

शष 1 P. हिंसायां to hurt, to kill; शषति pre. शशाष perf. अशषीत्, अशाषीत् Aor.

शस् 1 P. हिंसायां to cut up, to destroy; शसति pre. शशास perf. शसिता p. fut. अशसीत्, अशासीत् aor. शस्त p. p.

शाख् 1 P. व्याप्तौ to pervade; शाखति pre. अशाखीत् Aor.

शान् 1 U. तेजने to sharpen, to whet; शीशांसति-ते pre. शीशांसिष्यति-ते fut. अशीशांसीत्, अशीशांसिष्ट Aor.

शाल 1 A. श्लाघायां दीप्तौ च to tell, to praise, to shine, शालते pre. शशाले perf. शालिष्यते fut. अशालिष्ट Aor. शिशालिषते des.

शास् 2 P. अनुशिष्टौ to teach, to inform, to govern, to correct, to advise; शास्ति pre. शशास perf. शासिता p. fut. अशिषत् aor. शिष्यात् ben. शिशासिषति des. Pass.--शिष्यते pre. शिष्ट p. p. शासित्वा, शिष्ट्वा ger.

शास् with आ 2 A. इच्छायां to expect, to bless; आशास्ते pre. आशशासे perf. आशासिष्ट Aor.

शि 5 U. निशाने, to whet, to sharpen, to excite; शिनोति, शिनुते pre. शिशाय, शिश्ये perf. शेष्यति-ते fut. अशैषीत्, अशेष्ट Aor. शिशीषति-ते des.

शिक्ष् 1 A. विद्योपादाने to learn; शिक्षते pre. शिशिक्षे perf. शिक्षिता p. fut. अशिक्षिष्ट aor. शिशिक्षिषते des. शिक्षित p. p.

शिङ्घ् 1 P. to go; शिङ्घति pre. शिशिङ्घ perf. शिङ्घिष्यति fut. अशिङ्घीत् aor.

शिंघ् 1 P. आघ्राणे to smell; शिंघति pre. शिशिंघ perf. शिंघिता p. fut. अशिंघीत् Aor.

शिञ्ज् 2 A. अव्यक्ते शब्दे to tinkle, to jingle; शिङ्क्ते pre. अशिञ्जिष्ट Aor.

शिट् 1 P. अनादरे to disregard; शेटति pre. शिशेट perf. अशेटीत् Aor.

शिष 1 P. हिंसायां to hurt, to kill; शेषति pre. शिशेष perf. शेक्ष्यति fut. अशिक्षत् Aor. (According to some this is Set; शेषिता, शेषिष्यति, अशेषीत् &c.)

शिष 1 P. & 10 U. to leave a residue (with वि, to excel; अतिशये.);

शेषति, शेषयति-ते pre. शिशेष, शेषयाञ्चकार-चक्रे &c. perf. आशिक्षत्, अशिशिषत्-त Aor.

शिष् 7 P. विशेषणे to leave, to distinguish from others; शिनष्टि pre. शिशेष perf. शेष्टा p. fut. अशिषत् aor. शिष्यात् ben. शिशिक्षति des. Cau.—शेषयति-ते pre. शिष्ट p. p.

शी 2 A. स्वप्ने to lie down, to sleep; शेते pre. शिश्ये perf. शयिता p. fut. अशयिष्ट aor. शयिषीष्ट ben. शिशयिषते des. Pass.—शय्यते pre. अशायि aor. Cau.-शाययति-ते pre. शयित p. p.

शीक् 1 A. सेचने to sprinkle, to move gently; शीकते pre. शिशीके perf. अशीकिष्ट Aor.

शीक् 1 P. & 10 U. आमर्षणे to be angry; (10 U. भाषायां दीप्तौ च) to speak, to shine; शीकति, शीकयति-ते pre. शिशीक, शीकयाञ्चकार-चक्रे perf.

शीभ् 1 A. कत्थने to speak, to communicate; शीभते pre. शिशीभे perf. अशीभिष्ट Aor.

शील् 1 P. समाधौ to contemplate; शीलति pre. शिशील perf. शीलिता p. fut. अशीलीत् aor.

शील् 10 U. उपधारणे to study, to exercise, to honour, to visit; शीलयति-ते pre. शीलयाञ्चकार-चक्रे perf. शीलयिता p. fut. अशिशीलत्-त aor. शिशीलयिषति-ते des.

शुक् 1 P. to go, to move; शोकति pre. शुशोक perf. शोकिता p. fut. अशोकीत् aor.

शुच् 1 P. शोके to bewail, to grieve for, to regret; शोचति pre. शुशोच perf. शोचिता p. fut. अशोचीत् aor. शुशुचिषति, शुशोचिषति des. शुचित, शोचित p. p.

शुच् 4 U. पूतीभावे (क्लेदे) to be wet, to be afflicted; शुच्यति-ते pre. शुशोच, शुशुचे perf. शोचिता p. fut. अशुचत्, अशोचीत्, अशोचिष्ट aor. शुचित p. p.

शुच्य् 1 P. स्नानपीडनसुरासंन्धानेषु to bathe, to distil, to churn to press; शुच्यति pre. शुशुच्य perf. अशुच्यात् Aor.

शुठ् 1 P. to resist, to be lame, to be impeded; शोठति pre. शुशोठ perf. शोठिता p. fut. अशोठीत् aor.

शुठ् 10 U. आलस्ये to be idle, to be lazy; शोठयति-ते pre. शोठयाञ्चकार-चक्रे perf. अशुशुठत्-त Aor.

शुण्ठ् 1 P. (see शुठ् above). अशुण्ठीत्. Aor.

शुण्ठ् 1 P.& 10 U. शोषणे to dry, to purify; शुण्ठति, शुण्ठयति-ते pre. शुशुण्ठ, शुण्ठयाञ्चकार-चक्रे perf.

शुध् 4 P. शौचे to be pure, to have the doubts removed; शुध्यति pre. शुशोध perf. शोद्धा p. fut. अशुधत् aor. Pass.—शुध्यते pre. अशोधि aor. Cau.—शोधयति-ते pre. अशूशुधत्-त aor. शुशुत्सति des. शुद्ध p. p.

शुन् 6 P. to go, to move; शुनति pre. शुशोन perf. अशोनीत् Aor.

शुन्ध् 1 P. शुद्धौ & 10 U. शौचकर्मणि to purify, to clear; शुन्धति, शुन्धयति-ते pre. शुशुन्ध, शुन्धयाञ्चकार-चक्रे perf. अशुन्धीत्, अशुशुन्धत्-त Aor. शुन्धित p. p.

शुभ् 1 A. दीप्तौ to shine, to be happy; शोभते pre. शुशुभे perf. शोभिता p. fut. अशुभत्, अशोभिष्ट aor. शुशुभिषते, शुशोभिषते des.

शुभ्, शुम्भ् 1 P. भाषणे, भासने हिंसायां च to speak, to shine, to hurt; शोभति, शुम्भति pre. शुशोभ, शुशुम्भ perf. शोभिष्यति, शुम्भिष्यति fut. अशोभीत्, अशुम्भीत् Aor. शुभित, शोभित, शुम्भित p. p.

शुभ् 6 P. शोभायां to shine, to be splendid; शुभति pre. शुभित p. p. शुभत् pre. p. (also शुम्भ्)

शुल्क् 10 U. अतिस्पर्शने to gain, to pay, to forsake; शुल्कयति-ते pre. शुल्कयाञ्चकार-चक्रे perf. अशुशुल्कत्-त aor.

शुल्ब (शुल्व्) 10 U. माने to measure, to produce; शुल्ब(ल्व)यति-ते pre.

शुष 4 P. शोषणे to dry up, to be dried, to be afflicted; शुष्यति pre. शुशोष perf. शोष्टा p. fut. अशुषत् aor. Cau.—शोषयति-ते pre. अशूशुषत्-त Aor. शुशुक्षति des. शुष्क p. p.

शूर 4 A. हिंसास्तम्भनयोः to strike, to be firm; शूर्यते pre. शुशूरे perf. अशूरिष्ट Aor. शूर्ण p. p.

शूर् 10 A. विक्रान्तौ to act as the hero, to make great exertions; शूरयते pre. शूरयाञ्चक्रे perf. अशुशूरत Aor. शुशूरयिषते des.

शूर्प् 10 U. माने to measure; शूर्पयति-ते pre. शूर्पयाञ्चकार-चक्रे perf. अशुशूर्पत्-त Aor.

शूल् 1 P. रुजायां संघाते च to be ill, to collect; शूलति pre. शुशूल perf. अशूलीत् Aor.

शूष 1 P. प्रसवे to produce, to bring forth; शूषति pre. शुशूष perf.

शृध् 1 A. शब्दकुत्सायाम् (but it is also Parasmaipadi in the 2nd future, aorist & conditional) to break wind downwards; शर्धते pre. शशृधे perf. शर्धिता p. fut. शर्धिष्यते, शर्त्स्यति fut. अशृधत्, अशर्धिष्ट aor. शिशर्धिषते, शिशृत्सति des. शृद्ध p. p

शृध् 1 U. उन्दने to be wet or moist; शर्धति-ते pre. शर्धिष्यति-ते fut. अशर्धीत्, अशर्धिष्ट Aor.

शृध 1 P. 10 U. प्रसहने to mock at, to ridicule; शर्धति, शर्धयति-ते pre. अशर्धीत्, अशशर्धत्-त, अशीशृधत्-त Aor

शॄ 9 P. हिंसायां to tear to pieces, to hurt, to kill; शृणाति pre. शशार perf. शरिता, शरीता p. fut. अशारीत् aor. शिशरिषति, शिशरीषति, शिशीर्षति des. Pass.—शीर्यते pre. शीर्ण p. p.

शेल् 1 P. to go, to tremble; शेलति pre. शिशेल perf. शेलिता p. fut. अशेलीत् Aor.

शेवृ 1 A. सेवने to serve; शेवते pre. (See सेवृ).

शै 1 P. पाके to cook; शायति pre. शास्यति fut. अशासीत् Aor.

शो 4 P. तनूकरणे to sharpen, to make thin; श्यति pre. शशौ perf. शाता p. fut. अशात्, अशासीत् aor. शिशासति des. Pass.–शायते pre. Cau.—शाययति-ते pre. शात, शित p. p.

शोण् 1 P. वर्णगत्योः to become red, to go; शोणति pre. शुशोण perf. अशोणीत् Aor.

शौट् (शौड्) 1 P. गर्वे to be proud or haughty; शौट(ड)ति pre. शौटिष्यति fut. अशौटीत् aor.

श्चुत् 1 P. क्षरणे to ooze, to trickle; श्चोतति pre. चुश्चोत perf. श्चोतिता p. fut. अश्चोतीत्, अश्चुतत् aor. श्चुतित, श्चोतित p. p.

श्चुत् 1 P. to ooze, to scatter श्च्योतति pre. (See the above root).

श्मील् 1 P. निमेषणे to wink, to contract the eyelids; श्मीलति pre. शिश्मील perf. अश्मीलीत् Aor.

श्यै 1 A. to go, to dry up, to congratulate; श्यायते pre. शिश्ये perf. श्याता p. fut. अश्यास्त aor. श्यान, शीन, शीत p. p.

श्रङ्क् 1 A. to go, to creep; श्रङ्कते pre. शश्रङ्के perf. अश्रङ्किष्ट Aor.

श्रङ्ग् 1 P. to go, to move; श्रङ्गति pre. शश्रङ्ग perf.

श्रण् 1 P. & 10 U. दाने (generally with वि) to give, to bestow; श्रणति, श्राणयति-ते pre. शश्राण, श्राणयाञ्चकार-चक्रे perf. अश्रणीत्, अश्राणीत्, अशिश्रणत्-त, अशश्राणत्-त Aor.

श्रथ् 1 P. हिंसायां to injure, to kill: श्रथति pre. शश्राथ perf. अश्रथीत्, अश्राथीत् Aor.

श्रथ् 1 P. & 10 U. मोक्षणे हिंसायां इत्येके to liberate, to release, to kill: श्रथति, श्राथयति-ते pre. शश्राथ, श्राथयाञ्चकार-चक्रे perf. अश्रथीत्, अश्राथीत्, अशिश्रथत्-त Aor.

श्रथ् 10 U. दौर्बल्ये to be weak; श्रथयति-ते pre. श्रथयाञ्चकार-चक्रे perf. श्रथयिता p. fut. अशश्रथत्-त aor.

श्रन्थ् 1 A. शैथिल्ये to be loose, श्रन्थते pre. शश्रन्थे perf. अश्रन्थिष्ट aor.

श्रन्थ् 9 P. विमोचनप्रतिहर्षयोः to loosen, to delight, to arrange; श्रथ्नाति pre. शश्रन्थ, श्रेथ perf. श्रन्थिता p. fut. अश्रन्थीत् aor. शिश्रन्थिषति des.

श्रन्थ् 1 P. & 10 U. ग्रन्थसन्दर्भे to compose a work; श्रन्थति, श्रन्थयति-ते pre.

श्रम् 4 P. तपसि खेदे च to take pains, to mortify, to be fatigued; श्राम्यति pre. शश्राम perf. श्रमिता p. fut. अश्रमत् aor. श्रान्त p. p. श्रमित्वा, श्रान्त्वा g[illegible]

श्रम्भ् 1 A. प्रमादे to be careless, to err; श्रम्भते pre. शश्रम्भे perf. श्रम्भिता p. fut. अश्रम्भिष्ट aor. श्रब्ध p. p.

श्रा 2 P. पाके to cook, to dress; श्राति pre. शश्रौ perf. श्राता p. fut. अश्रासीत् aor. Cau.—श्रापयति-ते pre. श्रात, श्राण p. p.

श्रि 1 U. सेवायां to cling to, to depend upon; श्रयति-ते pre. शिश्राय, शिश्रिये perf. श्रयिता p. fut. अशिश्रियत्-त aor. श्रीयात्, श्रयिषीष्ट ben. शिश्रीषति-ते, शिश्रयिषति-ते des. Pass.—श्रीयते pre. अश्रायि aor. Cau.—श्राययति-ते pre. अशिश्रयत्-त aor. श्रित p. p.

श्रिष् 1 P. दाहे to burn; श्रेषति pre. शिश्रेष perf. श्रेषिता p. fut. अश्रेषीत् Aor.

श्री 9 U. पाके to cook, to dress, to boil; श्रीणाति, श्रीणीते pre. शिश्राय, शिश्रिये perf. श्रेता p. fut. अश्रैषीत्, अश्रेष्ट aor. शिश्रीषति-ते des. श्रीत p. p.

श्रु 5 P. श्रवणे to hear, to obey; शृणोति pre. शुश्राव perf. श्रोता p. fut. अश्रौषीत् aor. श्रूयात् ben. शुश्रूषते des. Pass—श्रूयते pre. अश्रावि- aor. Cau.—श्रावयति-ते pre. अशुश्रवत्-त, अशिश्रवत्-त aor. श्रुत p. p.

श्रै 1 P. पाके to cook; श्रायति pre. शश्रौ perf. श्राता p. fut. अश्रासीत् aor. श्रायात्, श्रेयात्, ben.

श्रोण् 1 P. संघाते to collect, to be collected; श्रोणति pre. शुश्रोण perf.

श्लङ्क् 1 A. to go, to move; श्लङ्कते pre. शश्लङ्के perf. अश्लङ्किष्ट Aor.

श्लङ्ग् 1 A. to go, to move; श्लङ्गते pre. शश्लङ्गे perf.

श्लथ् 1 P. हिंसायां to hurt, to be loose; श्लथति pre. शश्लाथ perf. अश्लथीत्, अश्लाथीत् Aor.

श्लाख् 1 P. व्याप्तौ to pervade; श्लाखति pre. शश्लाख perf. अश्लाखीत् Aor.

श्लाघ् 1 A. कत्थने to praise, to flatter, to boast of; श्लाघते pre. शश्लाघे perf. श्लाघिता p. fut. अश्लाघिष्ट aor. शिश्लाघिषते des. श्लाघित p. p.

श्लिष् 1 P. दाहे to burn; श्लेषति pre. शिश्लेष perf. श्लेषिता p. fut. अश्लेषीत् Aor. श्लिष्ट p. p. श्लिषित्वा, श्लेषित्वा, श्लिष्ट्वा ger.

श्लिष् 4 P. आलिङ्गने to embrace, to cling to, to join; श्लिष्यति pre. शिश्लेष perf. श्लेष्टा p. fut. अश्लिक्षत् (to embrace), अश्लिषत् (in any other sense) Aor. शिश्लिक्षति des. श्लिष्ट p. p.

श्लेष् 10 U. श्लेषणे to embrace; श्लेषयति-ते pre. अशिश्लिषत्-त aor.

श्लोक् 1 A. संघाते to compose in verse, to acquire; श्लोकते pre शुश्लोके perf. अश्लोकिष्ट Aor. शुश्लोकिषते des.

श्लोण् 1 P. संघाते to heap together; श्लोणति pre. शुश्लोण perf. अश्लोणीत् Aor.

श्वङ्क् 1 A. to go, to move; श्वङ्कते pre. शश्वङ्के perf.

श्वच् 1 A. to go, to be opened; श्वचते, श्वञ्चते pre. शश्वचे, शश्वञ्चे perf. अश्वाचिष्ट, अश्वाञ्चिष्ट Aor.

श्वठ् 10 U. असंस्कारगत्योः to leave unfinished, to go; श्वाठयति-ते pre. श्वाठयाञ्चकार-क्रे &c. perf. श्वाठयिष्यति-ते fut. अशिश्वठत्-त Aor. (Also श्वण्ठ्)

श्वठ् 10 U. सम्यगवभाषणे to speak well or ill; श्वठयति-ते pre. श्वठयाञ्चकार-चक्रे &c. perf. अशश्वठत्-त Aor.

श्वभ्र् 1 U. to go, to make a hole; श्वभ्रयति-ते pre. श्वभ्रयाञ्चकार-चक्रे perf.

श्वल 1 P. आशुगमने to run; श्वलति pre. शश्वाल perf. श्वलिता p. fut. अश्वालीत् aor.

श्वल्क् 10 U. परिभाषणे to tell; श्वल्कयति-ते pre. श्वल्कयाञ्चकार-चक्रे, &c. pref. अशश्वल्कत्-त Aor.

श्वल्ल् 1 P. आशुगमने to run; श्वल्लति pre. शश्वल्ल perf. अश्वल्लीत् Aor.

श्वस् 2 P. प्राणने to breathe, to sigh, to hiss; श्वसिति pre. शश्वास perf. श्वसिता p. fut. अश्वसीत् aor. शिश्वासिषति des. श्वसित (but आश्वस्त) p. p.

श्वि 1 P. गतिवृद्ध्योः to go, to swell, to increase; श्वयति pre. शुशाव or शिश्वाय perf. श्वयिता p. fut. अश्वत्, अश्वयीत्, अशिश्वियत् aor. शूयात् ben. शिश्वयिषति des. Pass.—शूयते pre. अश्वायि aor. Cau.—श्वाययति-ते pre. अशिश्वयत्-त, अशूशवत्-त aor. शून p. p. श्वयित्वा, उच्छूय ger.

श्वित् 1 A. वर्णे to become white; श्वेतते pre. शिश्विते perf. श्वेतिता p. fut. अश्वितत्, अश्वेतिष्ट Aor.

श्विन्द् 1 A. श्वैत्ये to become white; श्विन्दते pre. शिश्विन्दे perf. अश्विन्दिष्ट Aor.

ष—

ष्ठिव् 1 & 4 P. निरसने to spit, to sputter: ष्ठीवति. ष्ठीव्यति pre. तिष्ठेव, टिष्ठेव perf. ष्ठेविता p. fut. अष्ठेवीत् aor. ष्ठीव्यात् ben. तिष्ठेविषति, तुष्ठ्यूषति, टुष्ठ्यूषति des. Cau.—ष्ठेवयति-ते pre. ष्ठ्यूत p. p.

ष्वष्क् 1 A. to go, to move; ष्वष्कते pre. षष्वष्के perf. ष्वष्किता p. fut. अष्वष्किष्ट aor.

स—

सग् 1 P. संवरणे to cover; सगति pre. सगिष्यति fut. असगीत् Aor.

सघ् 5 P. हिंसायां to kill; सघ्नोति pre. असघीत्, असाघीत् Aor.

सङ्केत 10 U. आमन्त्रणे to invite; सङ्केतयति-ते pre. अससङ्केतत्-त Aor.

संग्राम 10 A. युद्धे to fight; संग्रामयते pre. संग्रामयिष्यते fut. अससंग्रामत Aor.

सच 1 A. सेचने सेवने च to sprinkle, to serve; सचते pre. सचिष्यते असचिष्ट Aor.

सच् 1 U. समवाये to be collected; सचति-ते pre. असचीत्, असाचीत्, असचिष्ट aor.

सञ्ज् 1 P. सङ्गे to embrace, to cling to, to fasten; सजति pre ससञ्ज perf. सङ्क्ता p. fut. असाङ्क्षीत् aor. सज्यात् ben. Pass.—सज्यते pre. असञ्जि aor. सक्त p. p.

सट् 1 P. अवयवे to be a limb or part of; सटति pre. असटत्, असाटीत् Aor.

सट्ट् 10 U. हिंसायां to kill, to be strong, to dwell, to give; सट्टयति-ते pre. सट्टयाञ्चकार-चक्रे perf. सट्टयिता p. fut. अससट्टत्-त aor.

सठ् 10 U. to finish, to adorn, to go, to leave unfinished; साठयति-ते pre. साठयाञ्चकार-चक्रे perf. साठयिता p. fut. असीसठत्-त aor.

सत्र् 10 A. सन्तानक्रियायां to extend; सत्रयते pre. सत्रयिष्यते fut. अससत्रत aor.

सद् 6 P. विशरणगत्यवसादनेषु to break, to go, to sink down, to decay, to be languid; सीदति pre. ससाद perf. सत्ता p. fut. असदत् aor. सद्यात् ben. सिषत्सति des. Pass—सद्यते pre. Cau.—सादयति-ते pre. असीषदत्-त aor. सन्न p. p.

सद् 10 U. to go; सादयति-ते pre. असीषदत्-त Aor. सिषादयिषति-ते des.

सन् 1 P. सम्भक्तौ to divide & 8 U. दाने to give, to worship; सनति, सनोति, सनुते pre. ससान, सेने perf. सनिता p. fut. असानीत्, असनीत्, असनिष्ट, असात (8) aor. सिसनिषति, सिषासति, सिषानिषति-ते, सिषासति-ते des. Pass.—सन्यते, सायते pre. सनित (1) सात (8) p. p.

सप् 1 P. समवाये to connect; सपति pre. ससाप perf. सपिता p. fut. असपीत्, असापीत् aor.

सभाज् 10 U. प्रीतिदर्शनयोः to serve, to honour, to gratify; सभाजयति-ते pre. अससभाजत्-त Aor.

सम् 1 P. वैकल्ये to be confused; समति pre. ससाम perf. असामीत् Aor.

सम् 4 P. परिणामे to be transformed; सम्यति pre. ससाम perf. असमत् Aor.

सम्ब् 1 P. सम्बन्धने to be connected; सम्बति pre. ससम्ब perf. सम्बिता p. fut. असम्बीत् aor.

सम्ब् 10 U. to collect; सम्बयति-ते pre. सम्बयाञ्चकार-चक्रे perf. अससम्बत्-त Aor.

सय् 1 A. to go, to move; सयते pre. ससये perf.

सर्ज् 1 P. सर्जने to gain, to earn by labour; सर्जति pre. ससर्ज perf. सर्जिता p. fut. असर्जीत् aor.

सर्ब् 1 P. to go, to move; सर्बति pre. सर्बिष्यति fut. असर्बीत Aor.

सर्व् 1 P. गतौ हिंसायां च to go, to hurt, to kill; सर्वति pre. ससर्व perf.

सल् to go, to move; सलति pre. ससाल perf. असालीत् Aor.

सस् 2 P. स्वप्ने to sleep.; सस्ति pre. ससास perf. (Vedic).

सस्ज् 1 U. गतौ to go, to become ready; सज्जति-ते pre. ससज्जे perf. सज्जिता p. fut. असज्जीत्, असज्जिष्ट aor. सिसज्जिषति-ते des.

सह् 1 A. मर्षणे to suffer, to allow, to forbear; सहते pre. सहे perf. सहिता, सोढा p. fut. सहिष्यते fut. असहिष्ट aor. सहिषीष्ट ben. सिसहिषते des. Cau.—साहयति-ते pre. असीषहत्-त aor. सिसाहयिषति-ते des. सोढ p. p.

सह् 4 P. तृप्तौ to be pleased, to endure; सह्यति pre. ससाह perf. सहिता, सोढा p. fut. असहीत् Aor. सिसहिषति des. सहित p. p.

सह् 1 P. 10 U. मर्षणे to forbear; सहति, साहयति-ते pre. असहीत् असीषहत्-त Aor. सहित, साहित p. p.

साध् 5 P. संसिद्धौ to finish, to accomplish; साध्नोति pre. ससाध perf. साद्धा p. fut. सात्स्यति fut. असात्सीत् aor. Cau. साधयति-ते pre. सिषात्सति des.

सान्त्व् 10 U. सामप्रयोगे to appease. to comfort, to soothe; सान्त्वयति-ते pre. सान्त्वयाञ्चकार-चक्रे &c. perf. सान्त्वयिता p. fut., अससान्त्वत्-त aor. सिसान्त्वयिषति-ते des. सान्त्वित p. p.

साम् 10 U. सान्त्वप्रयोगे to conciliate; सामयति-ते pre. अससामत्-त Aor. सिसामयिषति-ते des.

सार् 10 U. दौर्बल्ये to be weak; सारयति-ते pre. अससारत्-त Aor.

सि 5 & 9 U. बन्धने to bind, to tie; सिनोति, सिनुते, सिनाति, सिनीते pre. सिषाय, सिष्ये perf. सेता p. fut. असैषीत्, असेष्ट aor. सीयात्; सेषीष्ट ben. सिषीसति-ते des. Pass—सीयते pre. सित, सिन p. p.

सिच् 6 U. क्षरणे to sprinkle, to water, to pour in, to impregnate; सिञ्चति-ते pre. सिषेच, सिषिचे perf. सेक्ता p. fut. सेक्ष्यति-ते fut.

असिचत्-त, असिक्त aor. सिच्यात्, सिक्षीष्ट ben. सिसिक्षति-ते des. Pass.—सिच्यते pre. असेचि aor. Cau.—सेचयति-ते pre. सिक्त p. p.

सिट् 1 P. अनादरे to disregard, to despise; सेटति pre. सिषेट perf. असेटीत् Aor.

सिध् 1 P. to go, to drive off; सेधति pre. सिषेध perf. सेधिता p. fut. असेधीत् aor. सिध्यात् ben. Cau.—सेधयति-ते pre. असीषिधत्-त aor. सिसिधिषति, सिसेधिषति des. सिद्ध p. p. सिधित्वा, सेधित्वा-सिद्ध्वा ger.

सिध् 1 P. शास्त्रे माङ्गल्ये च to ordain, to command, to turn out auspiciously; सिषेध (सिषेधिथ, सिषेद्ध 2nd sing.) perf. सेधिता, सेद्धा p. fut. असेधीत्, असैत्सीत् (असेधिष्टाम्, असैद्धाम् dual) aor. सिधिषति, सिसित्सति, सिसेधिषति des.

सिध् 4 P. संराद्धौ to reach, to attain one's end, to succeed, to accomplish; सिध्यति pre. सिषेध perf. सेद्धा p. fut. असिधत् aor. सिषित्सति des. Cau.—साधयति-ते (सेधयति-ते to cause one to ascertain).

सिन्व् 1 P. सेचने to wet; सिन्वति pre. सिषिन्व perf. सिन्विता p. fut. असिन्वीत् aor.

सिव् 4 P. तन्तुसन्ताने to sew, to write, to join; सीव्यति pre. सिषेव perf. सेविता p. fut. असेवीत् aor. सीव्यात् ben. Pass.—सीव्यते pre. स्यूत p. p. सेवित्वा, स्यूत्वा ger.

सीक् 1 A. सेचने to sprinkle, to go, to move; सीकते pre. सिषीके perf. सीकिता p. fut. असीकिष्ट aor.

सु 1 P. प्रसवैश्वर्ययोः to permit, to prosper; सवति pre. सुषाव perf. सोता p. fut. असावीत्, असौषीत् aor. सुसूषति-ते des.

सु 2 P. प्रसवैश्वर्ययोः to allow, to possess power or supremacy; सौति pre. सुषाव perf. सोता p. fut. असौषीत् aor.

सु 5 U. स्नपनपीडनस्नानसुरासन्धानेषु to sprinkle, to pour out, to bathe, to press out juice, to distil; सुनोति, सुनुते pre. सुषाव, सुषुवे perf. सोता p. fut. असावीत्, असोष्ट aor. सूयात्, सोषीष्ट ben.

सुसूषति-ते des. Pass.—सूयते pre. असावि aor. Cau.—सावयति-ते pre. असूषवत्-त aor.

सुख् 10 U. सुखक्रियायां to make happy; सुखयति-ते pre.

सुट्ट् 10 U. अनादरे to despise; सुट्टयति-ते pre.

सुभ् 1 & 6 P. भाषाहिंसयोः to speak, to hurt; सोभति, सुभति pre. असोभीत् Aor. Also सुम्भ् 1 & 6 P.

सू 2 & 4 A. प्राणिगर्भविमोचने to bring forth, to produce; सूते, सूयते pre. सुषुवे perf. सोता, सविता p. fut. असोष्ट, असविष्ट aor. सोषीष्ट, साविषीष्ट ben. सुसूषते des. Pass.—सूयते pre. असावि aor. Cau.—सावयति-ते pre. असूषवत्-त aor. सूत (2), सून (4) p. p.

सू 6. P. प्रेरणे to excite, to impel; सुवति pre. सविष्यति fut. असावीत् Aor.

सूच् 10 U. पैशुन्ये to point out, to betray; to indicate by gesture, to trace out; सूचयति-ते pre. सूचयाञ्चकार-चक्रे perf. सूचयिता p. fut. असुसूचत्-त aor. सुसूचयिषति-ते des. सूचित p. p.

सूत्र् 10 U. वेष्टने to string, to write in the form of a concise rule, to plan, to unbind; सूत्रयति-ते pre. सूत्रयामास perf. सूत्रयिता p. fut. असुसूत्रत्-त aor.

सूद् 1 A. क्षरणे to strike, to pour out, to deposit, to destroy; सूदते pre. सुषूदे perf. सूदिता p. fut. असूदिष्ट aor. सुसूदिषते des. Cau.—सूदयति-ते pre. असूषुदत्-त aor.

सूद् 10 U. क्षरणे to incite, to strike, to cook, to dress, to pour out, to promise; सूदयति-ते pre. सूदयाञ्चकार-चक्रे perf. सूदयिता p. fut. असूषुदत्-त aor. सूदित p. p.

सूर्क्ष् 1 P. आदरे to respect, to disregard; सूर्क्षति pre. सुषूर्क्ष perf. सूर्क्षिता p. fut. असूर्क्षीत् Aor.

सृ 3 (Vedic) & 1 P. to go, to run; ससर्ति, सरति (धावति he runs) pre. ससार perf. सर्ता p. fut. असरत् (3 P.), असार्षीत् (1 P.) aor. स्रियात् ben. सिसीर्षति des. Cau.—सारयति-ते pre.

सृज् 4 A. विसर्गे to let loose, to send forth; सृज्यते pre. स्रक्ष्यते fut. असृष्ट Aor. सिसृक्षते des

सृज् 6 P. विसर्गे to create, to let loose, to shed; सृजति pre. ससर्ज perf. स्रष्टा p. fut. स्रक्ष्यति fut. अस्राक्षीत् aor. सृज्यात् ben. सिसृक्षति des. सृष्ट p.p. स्रष्टुम् inf.

सृप् 1 P. गतौ to creep, to go; सर्पति pre. ससर्प perf. सर्प्ता, स्रप्ता p. fut. असृपत् aor. सृप्यात् ben. सिसृप्सति des. Cau.—सर्पयति-ते pre. अससर्पत्-त, असीसृपत्-त aor. सृप्त p.p.

सृभ्, सृम्भ् 1 P. हिंसायां to kill, to injure; सर्भति. सृम्भति pre. ससर्भ, ससृम्भ perf. असर्भीत्, असृम्भीत् Aor.

सेक् 1 A. to go, to move: सेकते pre. सिषेके perf. सेकिता p. fut. असेकिष्ट aor.

सेल् 1 P. to go, to move, सेलति pre. सिषेल perf. सेलिता p. fut. असेलीत् aor.

सेव् 1 A. सेवने to serve, to pursue, to enjoy; सेवते pre. सिषेवे perf. सेविष्यते fut. असेविष्ट aor. सिसेविषते des. Cau.—सेवयति-ते pre. असिषेवत्-त aor. सेवित p.p.

सै 1 P. क्षये to waste away, to decline; सायति pre. सास्यति fut. असासीत् Aor.

सो 4 P. अन्तकर्मणि to destroy, to bring to an end; स्यति pre. ससौ perf. साता p. fut. असात् असासीत् aor. सेयात् ben. सिषासति des. Pass.—सीयते pre. Cau.—साययति-ते pre. सित p. p.

स्कन्द् 1 P गतिशोषणयोः to go, to jump, to be dried, to perish; स्कन्दति pre. चस्कन्द perf. स्कन्ता p. fut. अस्कन्दत्, अस्कान्त्सीत् aor. स्कद्यात् ben. चिस्कन्त्सति des. Pass.—स्कद्यते pre. Cau.—स्कन्दयति-ते pre. अचस्कन्दत्-त aor. स्कन्न p.p.

स्कन्ध् 10 U. to collect; स्कन्धयति-ते pre. स्कन्धयाञ्चकार-चक्रे perf.

स्कम्भ् 1 A. प्रतिबन्धने to stop; स्कम्भते pre. चस्कम्भे perf. अस्कम्भिष्ट aor.

स्कम्भ् 5. 9. P. रोधनस्तम्भनयोः to create, to hinder, to restrain; स्कभ्नोति, स्कभ्नाति pre. चस्कम्भ perf. स्कम्भिता p. fut. अस्कभत्, अस्कम्भीत् aor. स्कभ्यात् ben. स्कब्ध p.p.

स्कु 5 & 9. U. आप्रवणे to go by leaps, to approach, to cover, to lift; स्कुनोति, स्कुनुते, स्कुनाति, स्कुनीते pre. चुस्काव, चुस्कुवे perf. स्कोता p. fut. अस्कौषीत्, अस्कोष्ट aor. चुस्कूषति des.

स्कुन्द् 1 A. आप्रवणे to jump, to lift up; स्कुन्दते pre. चुस्कुन्दे perf. अस्कुन्दिष्ट Aor.

स्कुम्भ् 5 & 9 P. रोधने धारणे च to stop, to hold; स्कुभ्नोति, स्कुभ्नाति pre. अस्कुम्भीत् aor.

स्खद् 1 A विद्रावणे to rout, to cut, to destroy; स्खदते pre. चस्खदे perf. स्खदिष्यते fut. अस्खदिष्ट aor.

स्खल् 1 P. सञ्चलने to move; to totter, to err; स्खलति pre. चस्खाल perf. स्खलिता p. fut. अस्खालीत् aor. चिस्खलिषति des. स्खलित p. p.

स्तक् 1 P. प्रतिघाते to resist, to strike against; स्तकति pre. तस्ताक perf. स्तकिता p. fut. अस्ताकीत् aor.

स्तग् 1 P. संवरणे to cover; स्तगति pre. स्तगिष्यति fut. अस्तगीत् Aor.

स्तन् 1 P. शब्दे to sound, to thunder, to sigh; स्तनति pre. तस्तान perf. स्तनिता p. fut. अस्तनीत्, अस्तानीत् aor. तिस्तनिषति des. Cau.—स्तनयति-ते pre.

स्तन् 10 U. देवशब्दे to thunder; स्तनयति-ते pre. स्तनयाञ्चकार-चक्रे perf. अतस्तनत्-त aor.

स्तम् 1 P. अवैक्लव्ये not to be confused or weak; स्तमति pre. तस्ताम perf. अस्तमीत् Aor.

स्तम्भ् 1. A. प्रतिबन्धने to make immovable, to support, to stop; स्तम्भते pre. तस्तम्भे perf. स्तम्भिता p. fut. अस्तम्भिष्ट aor. तिस्तम्भिषते des.

स्तम्भ् 5 & 9 P. रोधने धारणे च to stop, to fix firmly, to support; स्तभ्नोति, स्तभ्नाति pre. तस्तम्भ perf. स्तम्भिता p. fut. अस्तभत्, अस्तम्भीत् aor. स्तभ्यात् ben. तिस्तम्भिषति des. Pass.—स्तभ्यते pre. Cau.—स्तम्भयति-ते pre. स्तब्ध p.p. स्तम्भित्वा, स्तब्ध्वा ger.

स्तिप् 1 A. क्षरणे to drip, to drop; स्तेपते pre. तिष्टिपे perf. अस्तेपिष्ट aor. तिस्तिपिषते, तिस्तेपिषते des.

स्तिम् or स्तीम् 4 P. आर्द्रीभावे to become wet, to become fixed; स्तिम्यति, स्तीम्यति pre. तिष्टेम, तिष्टीम perf. स्तेमिष्यति, स्तीमिष्यति fut. अस्तेमीत्, अस्तीमीत् Aor.

स्तु 2 U. स्तुतौ to praise, to extol, to worship by hymns; स्तौति-स्तवीति, स्तुते-स्तुवीते pre. तुष्टाव, तुष्टुवे perf. स्तोता p. fut. स्तोष्यति-ते fut. अस्तावीत्, अस्तोष्ट aor. स्तूयात्, स्तोषीष्ट ben. तुष्टूषति-ते des. Pass.-स्तूयते pre. अस्तावि aor. Cau.—स्तावयति-ते pre. अतुष्टवत्-त aor. स्तुत p.p.

स्तुभ् 1 A. स्तम्भे to stop, to suppress; स्तोभते pre. तुष्टुभे perf. अस्तोभिष्ट Aor. स्तुभित्वा, स्तुब्ध्वा ger.

स्तुम्भ् 5 & 9 P. रोधने धारणे च to stop, to expel, to stupify; स्तुभ्नोति स्तुभ्नाति pre. तुष्टुम्भ perf. अस्तुम्भीत् Aor.

स्तूप 4 P. & 10 U. समुच्छ्राये to heap up, to erect; स्तूप्यति, स्तूपयति-ते pre. तुष्टूप, स्तूपयाञ्चकार-चक्रे &c. perf. अस्तूपीत्, अतुस्तुपत्-त aor.

स्तृ 5 U. आच्छादने to cover; स्तृणोति, स्तृणुते pre. तस्तार, तस्तरे perf. स्तर्ता p. fut. अस्तार्षीत्, अस्तरिष्ट, अस्तृत aor. स्तर्यात्, स्तृषीष्ट, स्तरिषीष्ट ben. तिस्तीर्षति-ते des. Pass.—स्तर्यते pre. Cau.-स्तारयति-ते pre.

स्तृक्ष् 1 P. to go, to move; स्तृक्षति pre. तस्तृक्ष perf. अस्तृक्षीत् aor.

स्तृह् 6 P. हिंसायाम् to strike, to kill; स्तृहति pre. तस्तर्ह perf. स्तर्हिता स्तर्ढा p. fut. अस्तर्हीत्, अस्तृक्षत् aor. तिस्तृहिषति, तिस्तृक्षति des. Cau.-स्तर्हयति-ते pre. अतस्तर्हत्-त, अतिस्तृहत्-त Aor.

स्तॄ 9 U. आस्तरणे to spread, to cover; स्तृणाति, स्तृणीते pre. तस्तार तस्तरे perf. स्तरिता, स्तरीता p. fut. अस्तरीत्, अस्तरिष्ट, अस्तरीष्ट, अस्तीर्ष्ट aor. स्तीर्यात्, स्तरिषीष्ट, स्तीर्षीष्ट ben. Pass.—स्तीर्यते pre. तिस्तरिषति-ते des.

स्तेन् 10 U. चौर्ये to steal; स्तेनयति-ते pre. स्तेनयाञ्चकार-चक्रे perf. अतिस्तेनत्-त aor.

स्तेप् 1 A. क्षरणे to ooze; स्तेपते pre. तिष्टेपे perf. स्तेपिता p. fut. अस्तेपिष्ट aor.

स्तै 1 P. वेष्टने to cover, to put on, to adorn; स्तायति pre. तस्तौ perf. अस्तासीत् aor.

स्त्यै 1 P. शब्दसंघातयोः to sound, to collect into a heap, to spread about; स्त्यायंति pre. तस्त्यौ perf. स्त्याता p. fut. अस्त्यासीत् aor. स्त्यायात्, स्त्येयात् ben. तिस्त्यासति des. Cau.—स्त्यापयति-ते pre.

स्थग् 1 P. संवरणे to cover; स्थगति pre. तस्थाग perf. स्थगिता p. fut. अस्थगीत् aor. तिस्थगिषति des. Cau.—स्थगयति-ते pre. अतिष्ठगत्-त Aor.

स्थल् 1 P. स्थाने to stand firm; स्थलति pre. तस्थाल perf. स्थलिष्यति fut. अस्थालीत् aor.

स्था 1 P. गतिनिवृत्तौ to stand, to wait, to be, to be at hand &c. तिष्ठति pre. तस्थौ perf. स्थाता p. fut. अस्थात् aor. स्थेयात् ben. तिष्ठासति des. Pass.—स्थीयते pre. अस्थायि aor. Cau.—स्थापयति-ते pre. अतिष्ठिपत्-त aor. स्थित p.p. स्थित्वा ger.

स्थुड् 1 P. संवरणे to cover; स्थुडति pre. तुस्थोड perf. स्थुडिष्यति fut. अस्थुडीत् aor.

स्थूल् (Denom.) P. to become big or stout; स्थूलयति pre. अतुस्थूलत् aor.

स्नस् 4 P. निरसने to object; स्नस्यति pre. सस्नास perf. अस्नसीत्, अस्नासीत् Aor.

स्ना 2 P. शौचे to bathe, to perform an ablution; स्नाति pre. सस्नौ perf. स्नाता p. fut. अस्नासीत् aor. स्नायात्, स्नेयात् ben. सिस्नासति des. Pass.—स्नायते pre. अस्नायि aor. स्नात, (but निष्णात proficient in) p.p. Cau.—स्नपयति, स्नापयति pre.

स्निह् 4 P. स्नेहे to have affection for, to be kind to; स्निह्यति pre. सिष्णेह perf. स्नेहिता, स्नेग्धा, स्नेढा p. fut. अस्निहत् aor. सिस्निक्षति, सिस्निहिषति, सिस्नेहिषति des. स्निग्ध, स्नीढ p. p. स्निहित्वा, स्नेहित्वा, स्निग्ध्वा or स्नीढ्वा ger.

स्निह् 10 U. स्नेहे to love; स्नेहयति-ते pre. असिष्णिहत्-त Aor. स्नेहित p.p.

स्नु 2 P. to flow, to distil; स्नौति pre. सुष्णाव perf. स्नविता p. fut. अस्नावीत् aor. स्नूयात् ben. Pass.—स्नूयते pre. Cau.—स्नावयति-ते pre. असुष्णवत्-त aor. स्नुत p.p.

स्नुह् 4 P. उद्गिरणे to vomit; स्नुह्यति pre. सुष्णोह perf. स्नोहिता, स्नोग्धा, स्नोढा p. fut. स्नोहिष्यति, स्नोक्ष्यति fut. अस्नुहत् aor. स्नुग्ध स्नूढ p. p.

स्ने 1 P. वेष्टने (शोभायामित्येके शौच इत्यन्ये) to dress, to envelop; स्नायति pre. सस्नौ perf. अस्नासीत् Aor.

स्पन्द् 1 A. किञ्चिच्चलने to throb, to go; स्पन्दते pre. पस्पन्दे perf. स्पन्दिता p. fut. अस्पन्दिष्ट aor. पिस्पन्दिषति des. Cau.—स्पन्दयति pre. अपस्पन्दत् aor. स्पंदित p. p.

स्पर्ध् 1 A. संघर्षे to contend with, to challenge; स्पर्धते pre. पस्पर्ध perf. स्पर्धिता p. fut. अस्पर्धिष्ट aor. पिस्पर्धिषते des.

स्पर्श् 10 A. to touch, to take, to embrace; स्पर्शयते pre. स्पर्शयाञ्चक्रे &c. perf. स्पर्शयिता p. fut. अपस्पर्शत aor.

स्पश् 1 U. बाधनस्पर्शनयोः to obstruct, to touch, to spy; स्पशति-ते pre. पस्पाश, पस्पशे perf. अस्पशीत्, अस्पाशीत्, अस्पाशिष्ट Aor.

स्पश् 10 A. ग्रहणसंश्लेषणयोः to take, to embrace; स्पाशयते pre. अपिस्पशत Aor.

स्पृ 5 U. to gratify, to protect; स्पृणोति pre. पस्पार perf. (Vedic)

स्पृश् 6 P. संस्पर्शने to touch, to come in contact with; स्पृशति pre. पस्पर्श perf. स्पर्ष्टा, स्प्रष्टा p. fut. अस्प्राक्षीत्, अस्पार्क्षीत्, अस्पृक्षत् aor. स्पृश्यात् ben. पिस्पृक्षति des. Cau.—स्पर्शयति-ते pre. स्पृष्ट p.p. स्पर्ष्टुम्, स्प्रष्टुम् inf.

स्पृह् 10 U. ईप्सायाम् to desire, to envy; स्पृहयति-ते pre. स्पृहयाञ्चकार-चक्रे &c. perf. स्पृहयिता p. fut. अपिस्पृहत्-त aor. Pass.—स्पृह्यते pre. पिस्पृहयिषति-ते des. स्पृहित p.p.

स्पॄ 9 P. to hurt, to kill; स्पृणाति pre. पस्पार per.

स्फर् 6 P. (कुटादिः) सञ्चलने to tremble, to throb; स्फरति pre पस्फार perf. अस्फारीत् Aor.

स्फाय् 1 A. वृद्धौ to increase, to grow fat; स्फायते pre. पस्फाये perf. स्फायिता p. fut. अस्फायिष्ट—aor. Cau.—स्फावयति-ते pre. अपि-स्फवत्-त aor. पिस्फायिषते des. स्फीत p.p.

स्फिट् 10 U. स्नेहने to love; स्फेटयति-ते pre. स्फेटयाञ्चकार-चक्रे &c. perf. अपिस्फिटत्-त Aor.

स्फिट्ट् 10 U. हिंसायाम् to kill; स्फिट्टयति-ते pre. अपिस्फिट्टत्-त Aor.

स्फुट् 1 A. विकसने to blow, to burst open; P. विशरणे to split open, to break; स्फोटति-ते pre. पुस्फुटे, पुस्फोट perf. अस्फुटत्, अस्फोटीद्, अस्फोटिष्ट Aor. पुस्फुटिषति, पुस्फुटिषते, पुस्फोटिषते des. Cau.—स्फोटयति-ते pre. अपुस्फुटत्-त Aor. स्फुटित, स्फोटित p. p.

स्फुट् 6 P. (कुटादिः) विकसने to split open, to blossom; स्फुटति pre. पुस्फोट, (पुस्फुटिथ 2 sing;) perf. स्फुटिता p. fut. अस्फुटीत् aor. पुस्फुटिषति des. स्फुटित p. p.

स्फुट् 10 U भेदने to break open; स्फोटयति-ते pre. स्फोटयाञ्चकार-चक्रे &c. perf. अपुस्फुटत्-त Aor. स्फोटयिषति-ते des.

स्फुड् 6 P. संवरणे (कुटादिः) to cover; स्फुडति pre. पुस्फोड (पुस्फुडिथ 2nd sing.) perf. अस्फुडीत् Aor.

स्फुण्ट् 1 P. परिहासे to joke, to jest; स्फुण्टति pre. पुस्फुण्ट perf. स्फुण्टिष्यति fut. अस्फुण्टीत् Aor.

स्फुण्ट् 10 U. to joke, to laugh at; स्फुण्टयति-ते pre. अपुस्फुण्टत्-त Aor.

स्फुण्ड् 1 P. & 10 U. same as स्फुण्ट्.

स्फुर् 6 P. स्फुरणे (कुटादिः) to tremble, to throb, to flash, to shine; स्फुरति pre. पुस्फोर perf. स्फुरिता p. fut. अस्फुरीत् aor. स्फुरित p. p. Cau.—स्फोरयति, स्फारयति pre.

स्फुर्छ् 1 P. विस्तृतौ to spread; स्फूर्च्छति pre. पुस्फूर्च्छ perf. अस्फूर्च्छीत् Aor. स्फूर्च्छित, स्फूर्ण p p.

स्फुल् 1 P. सञ्चलने (कुटादिः) to tremble, to collect, to kill स्फुलति pre. पुस्फोल (पुस्फुलिथ 2nd sing.) perf. अस्फुलीत् Aor.

स्फुर्ज् 1 P. वज्रनिर्घोषे to thunder, to glitter; स्फूर्जति pre. पुस्फूर्ज perf. स्फूर्जिता p. fut अस्फूर्जीत् aor. पुस्फूर्जिषति des. Cau.—स्फूर्जयति-ते pre. अपुस्फूर्जत्-त aor. स्फूर्जित, स्फूर्ण p. p.

स्मि 1 A. ईषद्धसने to smile, to bloom; स्मयते pre. सिष्मिये perf. स्मेता p. fut. अस्मेष्ट aor. सिस्मयिषते des. Cau.—स्माययति-ते, स्मापयते pre.

स्मिट् 10 U. अनादरे to despise, to love, to go; स्मेटयति-ते pre. स्मेटयाञ्चकार-चक्रे perf. स्मेटयिता p. fut. असिस्मिटत्-त aor.

स्मील् 1 P. निमेषणे to wink, to blink; स्मीलति. pre. सिस्मील perf.

स्मृ 1 P. चिन्तायां to remember; आध्याने to think upon or long for; स्मरति pre. सस्मार perf. स्मर्ता p. fut. अस्मार्षीत् aor. सुस्मूर्षते des. Pass.—स्मर्यति pre. Cau. स्मारयति-ते, स्मरयति-ते (आध्याने) Pass.—स्मर्यते pre. अस्मारि, अस्मरि Aor. स्मृत pp.

स्मृ 5 P. to live, to please; स्मृणोति pre. सस्मार perf. Cau.—स्मारयति-ते (Vedic).

स्यन्द् 1 A. प्रस्रवणे to ooze, to run, to trickle, to flow out; स्यन्दते pre. सस्यन्दे perf. स्यन्दिता, स्यन्ता p. fut. स्यन्दिष्यते, स्यन्त्स्यति-ते fut. अस्यन्दत्, अस्यन्दिष्ट, अस्यन्त aor. स्यन्दिषीष्ट, स्यन्त्सीष्ट ben. सिस्यन्दिषते, सिस्यन्त्सति-ते des. स्यन्न pp. स्यन्दित्वा. स्यन्त्वा ger. Cau.—स्यन्दयति-ते pre.

स्यम् 1 P. शब्दे to sound, to go, to consider; स्यमति pre. सस्याम perf. स्यमिता p. fut. अस्यमीत् aor. सिस्यमिषति des. स्यान्त pp. स्यमित्वा, स्यान्त्वा ger.

स्यम् 10 A. वितर्के to reflect; स्यामयते pre. स्यामयाञ्चक्रे &c. perf. स्यामयिता p. fut. असिस्यमत aor.

स्रंस् 1 A. अवस्रंसने to fall down, to sink, to hang down, to go. to be pleased; स्रंसते pre. सस्रंसे perf. स्रंसिता p. fut. अस्रंसिष्ट अस्रसत् aor. स्रंसिषीष्ट ben. सिस्रंसिषते des. Pass.—स्रस्यते pre. अस्रंसि aor. स्रस्त pp. स्रंसित्वा ger.

स्रंह् 1 A. to confide, to trust; स्रंहते pre. सस्रंहे perf. स्रंहिता p. fut. अस्रंहिष्ट aor.

स्रङ्क् 1 A. गतौ to go; स्रङ्कते pre. सस्रङ्के perf. अस्रङ्किष्ट Aor.

स्रम्भ् 1 A. विश्वासे to entrust, to confide; स्रम्भते pre. सस्रम्भे perf. स्रम्भिता p. fut. अस्रभत्, अस्रम्भिष्ट aor. Cau. अस्रम्भियति-ते pre. असस्रम्भत्-त Aor. सिस्रम्भिषते des. स्रब्ध pp. स्रम्भित्वा, स्रब्ध्वा ger.

स्रिव् 4 P. गतिशोषणयोः to go, to become dry; स्रीव्यति pre सिस्रेव perf. स्रेविष्यति fut. अस्रेवीत् Aor. Cau. स्रेवयति-ते pre. असिस्रिवत्-त Aor. सिस्रेविषति, सुस्रयूषति des. Pass. स्रीव्यते pre. अस्रेवि aor. स्रूत pp.

स्रु 1 P. to flow, to go, to trickle away; स्रवति pre. सुस्राव perf. स्रोता p. fut. असुस्रुवत्-त aor. स्रूयात् ben. Cau.—स्रावयति pre. असुस्रवत्, असिस्रवत् aor. सुस्रूषति des. स्रुत pp.

स्रेकृ 1 A. to go; स्रेकते pre. स्रेकिष्यते fut. अस्रेकिष्ट Aor

स्रै 1. P. to boil, to sweat; स्रायति pre. सस्रौ perf. See श्रै.

स्वञ्ज् 1 A. परिष्वंगे to embrace; स्वजते pre. सस्वञ्जे, सस्वजे perf. स्वङ्क्ता p. fut. स्वङ्क्ष्यते fut. अस्वङ्क्त aor. स्वङ्क्षीष्ट ben सिस्वङ्क्षते des. Pass.—स्वज्यते pre. अस्वञ्जि aor. Cau. स्वञ्जयति-ते pre. असस्वञ्जत्-त aor. स्वक्त pp. स्वङ्क्त्वा, स्वक्त्वा ger.

स्वद् 1 A. आस्वादने to be pleasant to the taste, to please to eat; स्वदते pre. सस्वदे perf. स्वदिता p. fut. अस्वदिष्ट aor. Cau. स्वादयति-ते pre. असिस्वदत्-त aor. सिस्वदिषते des. स्वदित pp.

स्वद् 10 U. to sweeten; स्वादयति-त pre. स्वादयाञ्चकार-चक्रे perf. स्वादयिता p. fut. असिष्वदत्-त aor.

स्वन् 1 P. शब्दे to sound, to make a noise, to sing; स्वनति pre. सस्वान perf. स्वनिता p. fut. अस्वनीत्, अस्वानीत् aor. Cau. स्वानयति-ते pre. असिस्वनत्-त aor. सिस्वनिषते des. स्वनित (स्वान्त the mind) pp.

स्वन् 1 P. अवतंसने to decorate, to adorn. (See the above root) Cau. स्वनयति-ते pre. Pass. स्वन्यते pre. अस्वानि, अस्वनि aor.

स्वप् 2 P. शयने to sleep, to repose स्वपिति pre. अस्वपत्, अस्वपीत् imperf. सुष्वाप perf. स्वप्ता p. fut. अस्वाप्सीत् aor. सुप्यात् ben. सुषुप्सति des. Cau. स्वापयति-ते pre. असिष्वपत्-aor. Pass.— सुप्यते pre. सुप्त pp.

स्वर् 10 U. आक्षेपे to find fault with, to blame; स्वरयति-ते pre. स्वरयाञ्चकार-चक्रे perf. स्वरयिता p. fut. अससस्वरत् Aor. स्वर्यात् स्वरयिषीष्ट ben. सिस्वरयिषति-ते des.

स्वर्द् 1 A. आस्वादने to taste; स्वर्दते pre. सस्वर्दे perf. स्वर्दिता p. fut अस्वर्दिष्ट aor. सिस्वर्दिषते des.

स्वल् 1 P. to go, to move; स्वलति pre. सस्वाल perf.

स्वस्क् 1 A. to go; स्वस्कते pre. सस्वस्के perf.

स्वाद् 1 A. आस्वादने (see स्वद्) to taste, to be pleasant; स्वादते pre. सस्वादे perf. स्वादिष्यते fut. अस्वादिष्ट aor. सिस्वादिषते des.

स्वाद् 10 U. आस्वादने to taste; स्वादयति-ते pre. असिस्वदत्-त Aor. सिस्वादयिषति-ते des. स्वादित pp.

स्विद् 1 A. (स्नेहनमोचनयोः स्नेहनमोचनयोरित्येके) to be annointed, to be greasy; स्वेदते pre. सिस्विदे perf. स्वेदिष्यते fut. अस्विदत्, अस्वेदि aor. Cau.—स्वेदयति-ते pre. सिष्विदिषते सिस्वेदिषते des. स्विन्न, स्विदित, स्वेदित pp.

स्विद् 4 P. गात्रप्रक्षरणे to sweat, to perspire; स्विद्यति pre. सिष्वेद perf. स्वेत्ता p. fut. अस्विदत् aor. स्विन्न pp.

स्वुर्च्छ् 1 P. to spread, to forget स्वूर्च्छति pre.

स्वृ 1 P. शब्दोपतापयोः to sound, to praise, to go, to be pained; स्वरति pre. सस्वार perf. स्वरिता, स्वर्ता p. fut. अस्वारीत्, अस्वार्षीत् aor. स्वार्यात् ben. सिस्वरिषति, सुस्वूर्षति des. Cau. स्वारयति-ते pre. असिस्वरत्-त aor. स्वृत pp.

स्वॄ 9 P. to hurt, to kill; स्वृणाति pre. सस्वार perf.

स्वेक् 1 A. to go; स्वेकते pre. सिष्वेके perf.

ह—

हट् 1 P. दीप्तौ to shine, to be bright; हटति pre. जहाट perf. हटिता p. fut. अहटीत् अहाटीत् aor. हटित pp.

हठ् 1 P. प्लुतिशठत्वयोः to leap, to jump, to bind to a post, to oppress; हठति pre. जहाठ perf. अहठीत्, अहाठीत् aor

हद् 1 A. पुरीषोत्सर्गे to void excrement, to discharge faces; हदते pre. जहदे perf. हत्ता p. fut. अहत्त aor. जिहत्सते des. हन्न pp.

हन् 2 P. to kill, to beat, to hoat, to conquer &c.; हन्ति pre. अहन् (pl. अघ्नन्) imperf. जघान perf. हन्ता p. fut. अवधीत्, आहत, अवधिष्ट aor. वध्यात् ben. जिघांसति des. Pass.—हन्यते pre. अघानि, अवधि aor. Cau.—घातयति-ते pre. अजीघनत्-त aor. जेघ्नीयते, जंघन्यते जङ्घनीति, जंघन्ति freq. हत pp. हत्वा ger.

हम्म् 1 P. गतौ to go; हम्मति pre. जहम्म perf. हम्मिष्यति fut. अहम्मीत् Aor.

हय् 1 P. to go, to worship, to sound, to be weary; हयति pre. जहाय perf. हयिता p. fut. अहयीत् aor. हयित pp.

हर्य् 1 P. गतिकान्त्योः to go, to worship, to take; हर्यति pre. जहर्य perf. अहर्यीत् Aor. जिहर्यिषति des.

हल् 1 P. विलेखने गतौ च to plough, to go; हलति pre. जहाल perf. अहालीत् Aor. जिहलिषति des.

हस् 1 P. हसने to smile, to laugh at, to excel, to bloom &c.; हसति pre. जहास perf. हसिता p. fut. अहसीत् aor. Pass.—हस्यते pre. Cau.– हासयति-ते pre. अजीहसत्-त aor. जिहसिषति des. हसित pp.

हा 3 A. to go, to attain, to get; जिहीते pre. जहे perf. हाता p. fut. हास्यते fut. हासीष्ट ben. अहास्त aor. जिहासते des. Pass.—हायते. pre. अहायि aor. हान pp.

हा 3 P. त्यागे to abandon, to resign, to let fall, to omit; जहाति pre. जहौ perf. हाता p. fut. अहासीत् aor. हेयात् ben. जिहासति des. Pass.—हीयते pre. अहायि aor. Cau.—हापयति-ते pre. अजीहपत्-त aor. हीन pp. हित्वा ger.

हि 5 P. गतौ च to go, to send, to shoot, to promote; हिनोति pre. जिघाय perf. हेता p. fut. अहैषीत् aor. हीयात् ben. जिहीषति des. Cau.—हाययति-ते pre. अजीहयत्-त aor. Pass. हीयते pre. अहायि aor. हित pp.

हिंस् 1 P. हिंसायां to kill, to injure, to torment, to hit; हिंसति pre. जिहिंस perf. हिंसिता p. fut. अहिंसीत् aor. Pass.—हिंस्यते pre. अहिंसि aor. जिहिंसिषति des. हिंसित pp.

हिंस् 7 P. to kill &c.; हिनस्ति pre. अहिनत्-द् imperf. हिन्धि 2nd sing. impera. (See the above root for the other forms).

हिंस् 10 U. to kill, &c.; हिंसयति-ते pre. हिंसयाञ्चकार-चक्रे-आस-बभूव perf. हिंसयिता p. fut. अजिहिंसत्-त aor. जिहिंसयिषति-ते des.

हिक् 1 U. अव्यक्ते शब्दे to make an indistinct sound, to hiccough हिकति-ते pre. जिहिक, जिहिके perf. हिकिता p. fut. अहिकीत्, अहिकिष्ट Aor. हिकित pp.

हिक् 10 A. हिंसायां to hurt, to kill; हिकयते pre. हिकयाञ्चक्रे &c. perf. अजिहिकत् Aor.

हिट 1 P. आक्रोशे to curse, to swear; हेटति pre. जिहेट perf. अहेटीत् Aor.

हिट्ट 9 P. भूतप्रादुर्भावे to reappear; हिट्टणाति pre. जिहेट perf. अहेटीत् Aor.

हिण्ड् 1 A. गत्यनादरयोः to go, to wander, to disregard; हिण्डते pre. जिहिण्डे perf. हिण्डिता p. fut. अहिण्डिष्ट aor. हिण्डित pp.

हिन्व् 1 P. प्रीणने to please; हिन्वति pre. जिहिन्व perf. अहिन्वीत् Aor.

हिल 6 P. भावकरणे to sport amorously, to indicate amorous desire; हिलति pre. जिहेल perf. अहेलीत् Aor.

हु 3 P. दानादनयोः to offer, to perform a sacrifice, to eat; जुहोति pre. जुहुधि impera. 2nd sing. जुहाव, जुहवाञ्चकार perf. होता p. fut. अहौषीत् aor. हुयात् ben. जुहूषति des. Cau.—हावयति-ते pre. अजूहवत्-त aor. हुत pp.

हुड् 1 P. to go; होडति pre. जुहोड perf. होडिष्यति fut. अहोडीत् Aor.

हुड 6 P. संघाते to collect; हुडति pre. जुहोड perf. Cau. होडयति-ते pre. अजूहुडत्-त aor.

हुण्ड् 1 A. संघाते वरणे (हरणे इत्येके) to collect, to choose, to take away; हुण्डते pre. जुहुण्डे perf. अहुण्डिष्ट aor.

हुर्छ् 1 P. कौटिल्ये to be crooked, to deceive; हूर्च्छति pre. जुहूर्च्छ perf. हूर्च्छिता p. fut अहूर्च्छीत् aor. हूर्च्छित, pp.

हुल् 1 P. to go, to cover, to kill; होलति pre. जुहोल perf. होलिष्यति fut. अहोलीत् Aor.

हूड् 1 P. to go; हूडति pre. जुहूड perf. अहूडीत् Aor.

ह 1 U. हरणे to take, to lead, to draw to a distance, to deprive of, to win, to obtain, &c.; हरति-ते pre. जहार, जह्रे perf. हर्ता p. fut. हरिष्यति-ते fut. अहार्षीत्, अहृत aor. ह्रियात्, हृषीष्ट ben. जिहीर्षति-ते des. Cau. हारयति-ते pre. अजीहरत्-त aor. Pass.— ह्रियते pre. अहारि aor. हृत pp.

हृणी A. रोषणे लज्जायां च to be angry, to be ashamed; हृणीयते pre. हृणीयाञ्चक्रे perf. हृणीयिष्यते fut. अहृणीयिष्ट aor.

हृष् 1 P. अलीके to tell a lie; हर्षति pre. जहर्ष perf. अहर्षीत् Aor. जिहर्षिषति des. cau. हर्षयति-ते pre. अजहर्षत्-त, अजीहृषत्-त aor. हृष्ट pp.

हृष् 4 P. तुष्टौ to be delighted, to stand erect, (as hair.) हृष्यति pre. जहर्ष perf. हर्षिता p. fut. अहृषत् aor. हृषित, हृष्ट pp.

हेठ्-ड् 1 A. विबाधायां to be wicked, to strike, to be born, to purif हेठ-डते pre. अहेटिष्ट, अहेठिष्ट, aor.

हेड् 1 P. वेष्टने to surround, to attire; हेडति pre. जिहेड perf हेडिष्यति fut. अहेडीत् Aor. जिहेडिषति des.

हेड् 1 A. अनादरे to disregard; हेडते pre. जिहेडे perf. अहेडिष्ट Aor.

हेल् 1 A. to disregard; हेलते pre, (same as हेड्).

हेष् 1 A. अव्यक्तशब्दे to neigh, to roar; हेषते pre. जिहेषे perf. हेषिता p. fut. अहेषिष्ट aor. हेषित pp.

होड् 1 P. चलने to go, to come; होडति pre. जुहोड perf. होडिष्यति fut. अहोडीत् Aor.

होड् 1-A. अनादरे to disregard; होडते pre. जुहोडे perf. होडिष्यते fut. अहोडिष्ट Aor. Cau. होडयति-ते pre. अजुहोडत्-त Aor.

होड् 1 P. to disregard, to go; होडति pre.

ह्नु 2 A. अपनयने to take away, to conceal; ह्नुते pre. जुह्नुवे perf. ह्नोता p. fut. ह्नोषीष्ट ben. अह्नोष्ट aor. जुह्नूषते des. ह्नुत pp.

ह्मल् 1 P. to go; to shake; ह्मलति pre. जह्माल perf. अह्मालीत् Aor.

हृग 1 P. संवरणे to hide, to cover; हृगति pre जह्लाग perf. हृगिष्यति fut. अहृगीत् Aor.

हृप 10 U. व्यक्तायां वाचि to speak, to sound; ह्रापयति-ते pre. ह्रापयाञ्चकार &. perf. ह्रापयिता p. fut. अजिह्रपत्-त aor.

ह्रस 1 P. शब्दे लाघवे च to sound, to disappear, to lessen; ह्रसति pre. जह्रास perf. ह्रसिता p. fut. अह्रासीत, अह्रसीत् aor. जिह्रसिषति des. ह्रसित pp.

ह्राद 1 A. अव्यक्ते शब्दे to sound, to roar; ह्रादते pre. जह्रादे perf. ह्रादिता p. fut. अह्रादिष्ट aor.

ह्री 3 P. लज्जायां to blush, to be ashamed; जिह्रेति pre. जिह्रयाञ्चकार &c., जिह्राय perf. ह्रेता p. fut. अह्रैषीत् aor. ह्रीयात् ben. जिह्रीषति des. Pass.—ह्रीयते pre. अह्रायि aor Cau.—ह्रेपयति-ते pre. अजिह्रिपत्-त aor. ह्रीत, ह्रीण pp.

ह्रीच्छ 1 P. लज्जायां to blush, to feel shame; ह्रीच्छति pre. जिह्रीच्छ perf. अह्रीच्छीत् Aor.

ह्रुड or ह्रूड 1 P. to go, to contract; ह्रोडति or ह्रूडति pre.

हेप 1 A. to go; ह्रेपते pre. जिह्रेपे perf. ह्रेपिता per. fut.

हेष 1 A. अव्यक्ते शब्दे to neigh, to go; हेषते pre. जिहेषे perf. (See हेष)

ह्रौड 1 P. to go; ह्रौडति pre.

ह्लग 1 P. संवरणे to cover; ह्लगति pre. जह्लाग perf. ह्लगिता p fut. अह्लगीत् aor.

ह्लप 10 U. व्यक्तायां वाचि to speak, to sound; ह्लापयति-ते pre. ह्लापयाञ्चकार &c. perf. ह्लापयिष्यति-ते fut. अजिह्लपत्-त Aor.

ह्लस 1 P. शब्दे to sound; ह्लसति pre. जह्लास perf. अह्लसीत, अह्लासीत aor.

ह्लाद् 1 A. सुखे, अव्यक्ते शब्दे च to be glad, to sound; ह्लादते pre. जह्ला perf. ह्लादिता p. fut. अह्लादिष्ट aor. Cau.—ह्लादयति-ते pre. जिह्लादिषते des. ह्लन्न pp.

ह्वल 1 P. वैक्लव्ये to be afflicted, to go, to shake; ह्वलति pre. जह्वा perf. ह्वलिता p. fut. अह्वालीत् aor. Cau. ह्वलयति-ते, ह्वालयति-ते (with a pre. ह्वलयति-ते only) pre. अजिह्वलत्—aor. जिह्वलिषति des. ह्वलित pp.

ह्वृ 1 P. कौटिल्ये to be crooked, to deceive, to be afflicted; ह्व pre. जह्वार perf. ह्वर्ता p. fut. ह्वरिष्यति fut. अह्वार्षीत् aor. ह्वर्यात् ben. जुहूर्षति des. Cau.— ह्वारयति-ते pre. ह्वृत pp.

ह्वे 1 U. स्पर्धायां शब्दे च to vie with, to call by name, to invoke, to call upon, to ask; ह्वयति-ते pre. जुह्वाव, जुहुवे perf. ह्वाता p. fu. अह्वत् त, अह्वास्त aor. हूयात्, ह्वासीष्ट ben. जुहूषति-ते des. Pass.- हूयते pre. अह्वायि aor. Cau.—ह्वाययति-ते pre. अजूहवत् aor. हूत pp. हूत्वा ger. ह्वातुम् inf.

FINIS.

(जय्यद प्रेस बल्लीमारान देहली)